Nonmetropolitan America in Transition

Institute for Research in Social Science Monograph Series

Published by The University of North Carolina Press in association with the Institute for Research in Social Science at The University of North Carolina at Chapel Hill

Nonmetropolitan America in Transition

Edited by Amos H. Hawley
and Sara Mills Mazie

The University of North Carolina Press
Chapel Hill

Library of Congress Cataloging in Publication Data

Main entry under title:

Nonmetropolitan America in transition.

   Includes index.
   Contents: An overview / Amos H. Hawley and Sara Mills
Mazie -- The deconcentration of population: Diversity in
post-1970 population trends / David L. Brown and Calvin L.
Beale. Residential preferences in the United States / James
J. Zuiches. Local perspectives on community growth / Mark
Baldassare -- The changing structure of economic opportunity:
Agriculture and the community / Olaf F. Larson. Manufactur-
ing industry / Thomas E. Till. The service sector / Mark
David Menchik. The availability of passenger transportation
/ Arthur Saltzman and Lawrence W. Newlin. Energy and loca-
tion /

Irving Hoch -- [etc.]
   1. Cities and towns--United States--Addresses, essays,
lectures. 2. Urban policy--United States--Addresses, essays,
lectures. 3. United States--Social conditions--1960-   --
Addresses, essays, lectures. 4. United States--Population--
Addresses, essays, lectures. 5. Migration, Internal--United
States--Addresses, essays, lectures. I. Hawley, Amos Henry.
II. Mazie, Sara Mills, 1941-   .
HT123.N65   307.7'2'0973   81-3511
ISBN 0-8078-1490-3   AACR2

Publication of this work has been made possible in part
by a grant from the Andrew W. Mellon Foundation.

Notice: The chapters in this book were prepared under contract (No. 53-3157-9-12) between the Institute for Research
in Social Science and the U.S. Department of Agriculture,
Farmers Home Administration. The statements and findings in
the book are those of the authors and do not necessarily
reflect the views of the U.S. government, the Department of
Agriculture, or the Farmers Home Administration.

Contents

Tables

Figures

Preface

Nonmetropolitan America is in a state of transition as unanticipated and dramatic changes sweep the countryside. For the first time in many decades, these areas are attracting more people than they are losing and are growing faster than metropolitan areas. The nonmetropolitan economy and the jobs it generates are growing and diversifying. And the reach of urban institutions has extended to encompass the continent and with that nonmetropolitan areas. Many policymakers and policy analysts are not fully aware of the origins and scope of these changes. Few have the time to draw together the data and the knowledge required to gain a full appreciation of these ongoing changes.

Yet, the advances in national integration indicated in these trends carry significant implications for governmental policy. With the blurring of the old urban-rural or the newer metropolitan-nonmetropolitan distinction, it would seem no longer sensible to entertain policy proposals that treat one member of the dichotomy independently of the other. It is more than likely that the needs and problems of the national society will lie on a different dimension than that recognized in the past.

To examine what is known about changes taking place and their implications for both the present and the future, and to make that knowledge generally available, the assistant secretary for rural development of the U.S. Department of Agriculture established the Future of Rural America Advisory Group within the Farmers Home Administration. This group of outstanding scholars was chaired by Amos H. Hawley, Kenan Professor Emeritus of Sociology, University of North Carolina at Chapel Hill. The members of the Group, who served without compensation, were:

Dr. William Alonso
Center for Population Studies
Harvard University

Kenneth Deavers
Director, Economic Development Division
Economics and Statistics Service
U.S. Department of Agriculture

Dr. Glenn Fuguitt
Professor, Department of Rural Sociology
University of Wisconsin

Dr. Davis McEntire
Professor Emeritus
Agricultural and Resource Economics
University of California at Berkeley

Dr. Peter Morrison
The Rand Corporation
Santa Monica, California

Dr. Facundo Valdez
Counseling and Resource Center
Santa Fe, New Mexico

Dr. Wilbur R. Thompson
Department of Economics
Wayne State University

Dr. Wilbur Zelinsky
Professor of Geography
Pennsylvania State University

At meetings during an eighteen-month period, the Group undertook several interrelated tasks. First, it identified significant dimensions of nonmetropolitan life on which the Group believed systematic knowledge ought to be available. Second, it assisted in identifying qualified scholars to prepare state-of-knowledge papers. Third, as drafts of the papers became available, it reviewed with the authors in a thorough and intensive fashion both the implications of these findings and how the papers might be strengthened. The commitment of the Group and the excitement it came to share in mapping the significant changes now occurring in nonmetropolitan areas were contagious for the authors who frequently undertook extensive revisions of their work. Nonmetropolitan American in Transition, composed of a series of original papers by individual authors, is also a result of the collective effort of the Future of Rural America Advisory Group.

What emerges is a picture of one of the most dynamic parts of American society, a diverse and changing scene, as yet sparsely investigated and inadequately understood in many of the main centers of scientific inquiry. It is certain to attract the attention of both policymakers and scholars as the magnitude of the changes occurring in non-metropolitan America is recognized.

Vincent P. Rock
Director, Policy Development Staff
Farmers Home Administration
September 1980

Acknowledgments

The editors would like to thank all those who contributed in
so many ways to this book. Whatever success it enjoys is
due in large part to their efforts. Vincent P. Rock, director of the Policy Development Staff of Farmers Home Administration, had the vision and impetus to make a promising idea
a reality. The Future of Rural America Advisory Group and
this book would never have existed without him. To others
at FmHA, who gave encouragement, support, and time to the
Group, we are also indebted.

We also owe a great deal to the members of the Group,
who devoted so much time and thought to the development of
the book. Their enthusiastic and informed discussion of the
issues and their willingness to read and carefully comment
on the draft chapters were of immeasurable value. The meetings were also enhanced by the participation of others who
added their insight into the changes occurring in nonmetropolitan America.

In both the preparation and editing of their respective
chapters, all the authors were very easy to work with,
making our job much more pleasant and manageable. For this
we are most appreciative.

The project was greatly aided by the hard work, patience, and perseverance of Elizabeth M. Fink, associate
director of the Institute for Research in Social Science,
who served as liason with FmHA, Mary Ellen Marsden, research
associate of the Institute, who coordinated the publication
process, and Ellie and Jim Ferguson who copy edited the
manuscript and prepared camera-ready copy.

Pat Coleman of FmHA provided secretarial support for the
project and with Andi Baker typed much of the manuscript.
Anna Tyndall of the University of North Carolina Department
of Sociology helped untangle the extensive bibliographies.

To all of these people we say, thank you.

Amos H. Hawley
Sara Mills Mazie

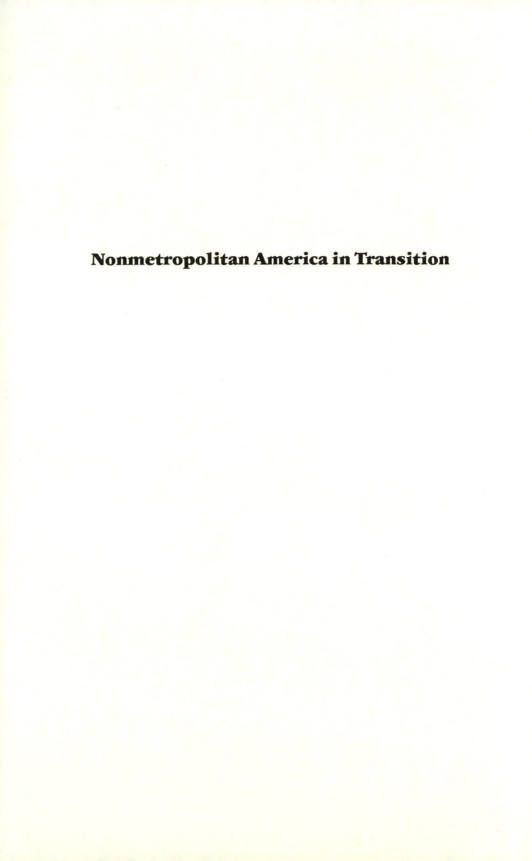

Nonmetropolitan America in Transition

Amos H. Hawley
Sarah Mills Mazie

An Overview

PATTERNS OF POPULATION REDISTRIBUTION PRIOR TO 1970

In the years since 1920, extending up to 1970, three dis-
tinguishable though interwoven trends of population distribution were in process. Each differed in respect to its
duration and its territorial scope. The oldest and broadest
of these was a continuation of the interregional movement of
population toward the West. That drift, due partly to differential natural increase and partly to a net westward
migration, is represented by the continued relocation of the
center of continental population as plotted by the U.S.
Bureau of the Census (1972). Noteworthy is the fact that the
line of movement has been toward the southwest since 1910.
The southern turn of the westward drift became more pronounced after 1960 as the southeast began to exercise a new
pull on the course of redistribution.

A second trend, also with a history beginning in the
preceding century, has operated within regions. That is the
familiar rural to urban, and more recently the nonmetropolitan to metropolitan, movement of population. The rapid
mechanization of agriculture combined with the decline of
foreign immigration after the 1920s accelerated the urban-
ward migration of the domestic population. In the fifty
years ending in 1970 the urban share of the total population increased from 51 percent to 73 percent. During that
five-decade period the rural population changed very
slightly in absolute number, from 51 million to 54 million.
The composition of the rural population, however, shifted
dramatically; the farm population declined from 30 percent
of the total to less than 5 percent, while the rural nonfarm proportion increased from 19 to 22 percent. That
shift may be regarded as a harbinger of events to come.
Most of the urban population and a substantial share of the
rural population was being absorbed in metropolitan areas
that were growing in number and geographical scope as well
as in proportion to the total population. Of the counties

comprising nonmetropolitan territory not less than 36 percent of them lost population in every decade and the proportion losing population rose to 60 percent in the 1950-
60 period. The net gains in the aggregate nonmetropolitan
population supplied by the remaining 40 percent of the
counties disappeared in the 1960-70 decade as an absolute
loss for the total was reported.

A third distribution trend, contained within the interregional and the intraregional movements, is a local deconcentration of urban agglomerations. As cities grew, their
innermost spaces were preempted by business and public uses
and population growth increments were added to their peri-
pheries. Improvements in local transportation, at first
railway commuter service but later and more significantly
the motor vehicle, accelerated the outward movement and
allowed urban residents to congregate in nearby villages
and in open spaces between scattered villages and the
advancing edge of built-up areas of major cities. Although
the centrifugal movement of urban population began with the
largest agglomerations, by 1920 the suburban territories of
all cities of 50,000 or more population were in the aggregate growing at rates three times as high as the growth
rates of the central cities (Hawley 1956). Thus while the
nation's population was continuing to be absorbed in metropolitan areas, the suburbanization process continued to
gather momentum, producing absolute declines in some central cities, while slowing the growth in others.

It is important to recognize that the local centrifugal
movement of urban populations was a response to a number of
changes in basic conditions. Of these, the improvement in
local transportation, including not only vehicles but also
local road and street networks, was doubtlessly the most
critical. This permitted a widening scatter of residences
without loss of access to destinations of interest. But
there was also an accumulation of urban services in outlying areas. These included extension of telephone lines and
toll-free zones, of power lines, of gas and water pipelines;
a reorganization of local governments enabling them to provide more effective police and fire protection, street
lighting and maintenance, schools and recreation facilities,
and numerous other amenities; and a proliferation of retail
and professional services. One of the important changes in
the formerly rural territory adjoining large urban places
has been the deconcentration of manufacturing industry.
Sometimes leading, sometimes following the local movements
of population, the relocations of industry have provided a

large part of the fiscal support for the development of urban services in outlying areas as well as supplied substantial numbers of job opportunities for suburban residents.

The net effect of these diverse but complementing
centrifugal movements has been to create the metropolitan
area as a new kind of urban unit. Whereas at the outset the
metropolitan area could be characterized as a central city
together with a subordinate tributary area, it has become a
complex economic and social unit in which territorial differentiation along functional lines has gained ascendancy
over political or administrative distinctions. So important
have metropolitan areas become in the territorial organization of society that the old urban-rural dichotomy has lost
much of its meaning. Until recently many rural settlements
within metropolitan areas have borne little similarity to
rural settlement outside of those areas. Likewise nonmetropolitan towns and cities possessed characteristics not
shared by incorporated places within metropolitan areas. As
viewed in historic perspective, the rural-urban division of
the settlement pattern is useful for the period before 1920;
thereafter the nonmetropolitan-metropolitan[1] distinction is
a more apt description of the principal territorial sectors
of the national life. Whether even this latter distinction
will prove useful in the long run is questionable.

Confusion is often associated with the use of the term
"rural," whether referring to areas or populations. Rural
is often used in a generic sense to mean those bucolic and
less settled areas outside cities and suburbs. However, the
term rural also has the more precise meaning of open country
and places of less than 2,500 as defined by the Bureau of
the Census. In this volume, in an attempt to minimize the
confusion, rural is generally used in the latter sense. The
more inclusive term "nonmetro" is used to describe not only
the villages and open spaces of rural areas but also cities
and towns of some size and significance albeit not metro
centers.

NEW DIRECTIONS IN POPULATION DISTRIBUTION: POST-1970

A shift in the distribution of population, little noticed
in the years following 1950, surged to prominence after
1970. Not only had total growth rates in metro counties
been subsiding since the earlier years, but the ability of
metro counties to attract population from nonmetro areas

diminished significantly. By the early 1970s, growth in
metro areas due to internal migration had shifted from a
net gain to a net loss (Beale and Fuguitt 1978). Meanwhile,
of course, nonmetro counties were growing at increasing
rates. Although much of that growth was supplied by natural
increase, the important and novel source of growth was a
turnaround in net migration; in the late 1950-60 decade nonmetro counties were losing population through out-migration,
while after 1970 the net loss turned into a net gain. The
reversal of the trend was most notable in the nonmetro counties that are not adjacent to metro areas, for those had the
longest histories of decline. Nine out of ten nonadjacent
nonmetro counties, or 979 counties, had been losing population through migration prior to 1970. After 1970 that declined to four of ten, or 438 counties.

Changes such as these raise a number of interesting
questions. Is it an altogether new feature of population
distribution trends; if so, in what sense is it new? How is
the apparent change in direction of movement to be explained? And, third, what are the implications of the change for
nonmetro territory?

To the first question a qualified answer must be given.
For nonmetro counties to gain population through net migration is a new development in the present century. On the
other hand, the centrifugal drift of the urban population
into relatively unurbanized territory nearby is not new.
That outward drift has been increasing for several decades.
The recent spillover into nonmetro counties, therefore,
should not be entirely surprising. As noted in an earlier
paragraph, the widening spread was heralded by the steady
growth of the rural nonfarm population.

CAUSES OF THE TURNAROUND IN POPULATION MOVEMENT

To explain the reversal of nonmetro population decline is a
more difficult task. Clearly there is no simple answer to
the problem. A starting point, however, is that the resump-
tion of nonmetro growth had been in preparation since the
turn of the century. Of prime importance in that development
has been a progressive extension of the communication and
transportation networks. The introduction of rural free
delivery of the mails and of parcel post, the all-weather
surfacing of roads and especially the development of the
interstate highway system, the rapid spread of motor vehi-

cle ownership among farm and small-town residents (Boorstin, 1973: ch. 14), the linkage of local telephone companies with the Bell system, the rural electrification program of the 1930s, the radio, and finally the television brought most nonmetro localities within daily access to metro centers. The consequent diffusion of urban influences over the countryside has been manifested in the spread of standardized consumer services, an increasing amount of nonagricultural employment, and a modernization of local governments (see Richards 1978). In short, as living conditions in nonmetro territory have become increasingly urbanized the distance restraints on the general centrifugal drift of urban population have been relaxed and the movement has accelerated.

But the reduction of rural isolation and the urbanization of nonmetro areas must be regarded as essentially a generalized necessary condition for what appears to have been a quantum leap in the deconcentration movement. What specific and possibly sufficient conditions have operated to facilitate the trend? Knowledge on this score is far from complete. Yet a number of indications are clear enough to be highly suggestive. Some of these indications are found in studies of the characteristics of the places to which people are moving and others are derived from data obtained in field surveys. There remains a realm of speculation that points at least to research needs.

Nonmetro counties gaining through net migration since 1970 possess one or another of several demographic characteristics, as the chapter in this volume by David Brown and Calvin Beale shows. They are counties with large proportions of retirees, with relatively large proportions of their residents engaged in the recreation industry, with concentrated energy resources, particularly coal deposits, or with manufacturing industry as a significant source of employment (see also McCarthy and Morrison 1979). Each of these characteristics may be regarded as presumptive evidence of the operating inducements to migration. They also call attention to regional diversity in the operating factors. Some caution is needed in this connection, however, for there are substantial differences in the sizes of the base populations against which net migration rates are computed. Coal producing and recreation industry counties, for example, typically have small populations. That is also the case with some, though not all, counties with relatively large numbers of retirees. And it is least true of manufacturing industry counties. Missing from the list of gaining

counties are those with large proportions of people employed
in farming. In fact, counties in which agricultural industry
predominates have been foremost amoung counties continuing
to lose population.

It is also to be noted that the most radical turnaround
in percentage terms in the migration experience of nonmetro
counties has occurred in counties in which the largest
village or town is less than 2,500 population (Beale and
Fuguitt 1978). Although that outcome is observed in all
such nonmetro counties, whether they are adjacent or not
adjacent to metro areas, it is more pronounced in the
latter. It would be premature, however, to conclude that
nonmetro America is being inundated by a tide of urban
refugees seeking an escape from urban conditions. Whereas
there are no data as yet available that contradict such an
inference, answers to a question asked in a national sample
concerning preferred place of residence, reported by James
Zuiches in this volume, indicate a modal preference for
residence places located within thirty miles of a city of
50,000 or more population. The meaning of this finding is
confounded somewhat by results obtained in an unpublished
National Opinion Research Center survey that show an overriding preference for present places of residence (Taylor
et al. 1979). The apparent contradiction might conceal a
distinction between survey questions which do and do not
pose a conditional intention to move.

The literature on residential preferences, which James
Zuiches reviews, tends to suggest that economically neutral
life-style considerations govern the movement to nonmetro
areas while the movement to metro areas has been a response
to stark economic determinants. Such a view, however, is
the product of a common propensity for oversimplification.
Persons moving to nonmetro territory can no more subsist on
amenities alone than can movers to metro areas be content
with wages without amenities. The centrifugal movement, as
noted earlier, is a response to a widening universe of
employment opportunity. It is also a universe with a wide
range of options in land costs and real property taxes, of
access to recreation facilities, of risks of losses from
crime, and of quality of educational and consumer service.
Moreover, transfer payments, where they are involved, follow the mover wherever he may go. A reasonable assumption
is that every move is the result of a mix of noneconomic
and economic factors. The problem for the individual considering migration is: what trade-offs is he or she willing
to make?

On the other hand, there is no convincing evidence of injurious effects on communities at the receiving end of the migration. Mark Baldassare, in examining the research literature dealing with this matter, concludes that growth in formerly stagnant communities improves their resources and physical amenities and, by providing "a critical mass of residents," enriches the cultural and other avocational opportunities. The same point of view is expressed somewhat equivocally by respondents in the NORC survey mentioned earlier. They demonstrated a high degree of consensus on beliefs that population growth in their communities promises to improve government services, public transportation, the number of jobs available, recreational service and even the extent of tolerance (Taylor et al., 1979: 31). The same survey disclosed an even more pronounced agreement that growth threatens increases in taxes and cost of living, problems of pollution, unemployment, overcrowding together with a possible loss of privacy, overloading of service, and the incidence of unfriendliness (Taylor et al., 1979: 32). Thus the influx of migrants is regarded with mixed feelings by the residents of receiving communities. But apparently that, if indeed it is anticipated, is not a sufficient deterrent to migration.

THE CHANGING STRUCTURE OF ECONOMIC OPPORTUNITY

The population redistribution trends of recent years, and particularly of the post-1970 period, are symptomatic of the increasing involvement of the nonmetro sector of the nation in the processes of change so long characteristic of metro areas. The cumulative effect of those processes is a reduction of the differences between the two sectors. The trend is at work in many aspects of the collective life. The papers in this volume document the drift toward convergence.

Conspicuous among the changes in the nonmetro sector is the decline of agriculture as a source of economic opportunity. The mechanization and increasing scale of farm production have changed the index of worker productivity from 21 in 1940 to 113 in 1970, a more than fivefold increase. Each farm worker produced enough to supply the food requirements of 10.7 individuals in the former year and 47.1 persons in the latter year (U.S. Bureau of the Census 1975a). Because the domestic demand for farm products, particularly

the food component, is relatively inelastic, the excess of
farm productivity increase over total population increase
has displaced workers and families from agriculture.
Accordingly, the farm population declined from 23 percent
in 1940 to 4.8 percent in 1970, and further to 3.9 percent
in 1976.

Behind this figure lies a trend of reorganization of
the agricultural industry. That includes a reduction in the
number of farms, an increasing size of farm, a specialization of farm production, an increasing capitalization of
farms, a shift from family-owned and operated farms to
corporate-owned and managerially operated farms, and an
absorption of many farm activites by industrial concerns.
In 1974, 6.6 percent of the farms produced more than half
the products sold in the market; in 1964 almost 10 percent
of the farms were required to produce that large a share of
the total (U.S. Bureau of the Census 1977a). By 1970 some
25,000 of the larger farms had assumed corporate form or
had passed into corporate ownership. Fully one-fourth of
those were operated as adjuncts of other businesses, such
as material processing, retailing and wholesaling, and
manufacturing (U.S. Bureau of the Census 1975b). Agricultural technology has passed into the hands of manufacturers
of farm implements and chemicals. Furthermore, representatives of corporations manufacturing farm equipment are
prominent members of research policy committees of land-
grant colleges (Hightower, 1972: ch. 6). This complex trend
has imposed an organizational structure upon a large segment
of agriculture not unlike that which prevails in the metro
sector of the economy.

Nor is the changing face of agriculture visible only in
respect to the production function. Farm population has come
to rely heavily on supplementary sources of income, largely
from off-farm employment and to a lesser extent from rents
and investments. Without such income three-fifths of the
farm families would have had income, in 1977, below the
poverty threshold, as Olaf Larson shows in his chapter in
this volume. Off-farm workers in the farm population, along
with the majority of nonfarm workers in nonmetro areas,
have found employment in the expanding manufacturing and
service industries. Manufacturing plants may be located in
open country but service establishments are generally clustered in nonmetro cities and towns. In either case commuting
distances and times are relatively long, particularly for
off-farm workers.

The increase in manufacturing employment opportunities, as Thomas Till's chapter suggests, is a result largely of plant expansions and the creation of new industries rather than relocations of older industries. Industrial growth has involved a changing composition of the manufacturing sector. Unlike the older, heavy industries that required deep-water locations, the newer and lighter industries, for example the chemical, electronic, and aircraft industries, enjoy a much greater location freedom. They have been much more responsive, therefore, to the availability of worker amenities and political considerations than was formerly possible. But it appears also to be true that some industrial relocations are guided by low costs of an indigenous labor force. Such industries commonly bring their skilled workers with them and rely on the local labor supply for unskilled and semiskilled jobs. A moot question is whether that kind of employment has an upgrading effect on a local labor force. A recent report to the Southern Growth Policies Board (Brunson 1979) expresses serious concern over the long-term benefits of the practice.

The increase in employment opportunities in nonmetro areas resulting from the deconcentration of manufacturing industry, notably to the south and west, has rivaled that in the nation as a whole. Of greater quantitative importance, however, is the growth of employment in the service industry, in both the private and the public sectors. As Mark Menchik shows in his chapter, service has been the principal growth industry in nonmetro areas. While some of that is clearly attributable to population growth, a large part is due to changes in the consumer habits of nonmetro people. The older farm segments as well as the newer non-farm segments of nonmetro population have been brought rather fully into what Boorstin (1973) calls the "consumer community."

That large structural changes should have significant effects on local service centers in nonmetro counties is to be expected. These are examined in detail by Olaf Larson in his chapter on "Agriculture and the Community." Increases in farm size and the decline in number of family-operated farms reduce service demands in local areas, thereby undermining the viability of many service centers. The consequences of changes in the organization of agriculture appear to have their major impact on small service centers. The larger centers have benefited from the changes. Another source of change, having a similar differential effect on size of communities, has been the improvements in transportation and communication. Art Gallaher's (1961) follow-up study of Plainville, U.S.A. (West 1945), fifteen years later, found that the improvement of roads, the increased prevalence of automobile ownership, and the general acquisition of television, had spread the interests and activities of the farm community residents over a much wider area at the expense of the old local associations and the patronage of village stores. Fuguitt and Beale (1976), having examined the growth experiences of nonmetro villages and towns over the years from 1950 to 1970, reported a resurgence of growth in small places, particularly in the South, a trend that is contrary to what has been the trend in village service functions. The authors offer the interesting suggestion that business functions and residential functions need not follow the same course, especially in an era of relatively wide separation of home from work and shopping places.

As noted in an earlier paragraph, the elaborate network of roads and highways is undoubtedly an important facilitator of the movement into nonmetro territory. It has also made possible a substitution of communication for residence changes—for example, an unmeasured amount of the nonfarm population increase is quite probably a result of an occupational rather than a spatial move. A consistent finding in many surveys is that nonmetro farm workers travel farther than do metro workers. The post-1970 tendency for nonmetro growth to accumulate in open country around cities and towns may be contributing to an increase in average trip distances. Thus nonmetro population is vulnerable to rising energy costs and possible shortages. Irving Hoch has developed a carefully reasoned argument in this volume for the prospect of a general shortening of work and other trips. If so, the present deconcentration trend may turn out to be a reconcentration in smaller and more numerous agglomerations scattered over nonmetro territory. A possible secondary effect of reduced energy use for transportation is a decline of road maintenance, for as gasoline sales are curtailed, so are returns from state gasoline taxes from which funds for road maintenance are drawn. But, on the other hand, regroupings of settlement in more dense units may be postponed by the efficiencies of a "wired society," about which Mark Menchik writes. The distribution of information, entertainment, banking, and other services by electronic means has already eliminated the necessity for many trips.

DIFFERENTIAL ACCESS TO OPPORTUNITY

As economic and other activities in nonmetro areas were
being caught up in the organizational hierarchies centered
in metro areas, the distribution of nonmetro residents on
various status scales has tended to approach the distribution found in metro areas. The decline of farm occupations
was an important factor in that convergence. Significant
differences remained in 1978, however, and changes between
1970 and 1977 did little to reduce those differences. In
that seven-year interval nonmetro areas closed the gap
separating them from metro areas with respect to proportions of workers engaged in professional, clerical, crafts,
machine tending, and transport occupations, but lost ground
in managerial, sales, and nonfarm labor occupations. In the
matter of education the proportion of persons twenty-five
years of age and over in nonmetro areas who had completed
high school in 1977 surpassed that for metro areas of 1970
by a significant margin, but failed to keep pace with the
1970-77 metro gains in the proportion that had completed
high school. That quite possibly was due to the continuing
migration of young adults to metro areas coupled with the
metro to nonmetro movement of persons over thirty-five
years of age (Zuiches and Brown, 1978: 66). The most substantial gains in nonmetro areas were registered in median family incomes. Measured in 1976 dollars nonmetro
incomes increased 7 percent between 1969 and 1976, while
metro median incomes were subjected to small losses. Even
so, nonmetro incomes at the end of the period were still
approximately 20 percent below metro incomes. This may or
may not reflect a difference in cost of living between the
two areas. The 20 percent increase in incomes of nonmetro
black families contrasts sharply with the 7 percent gain
experienced by nonmetro white families. Despite that gain
black incomes were still, in 1976, but little more than half
those of white families.
    The data pertaining to the status pattern in nonmetro
areas suggest that, indications of convergence with the
nonmetro pattern notwithstanding, there is still a discrepancy pointing to the continued disadvantaged position of
nonmetro areas. Or to state the matter differently, the
absorption of nonmetro area and its activities into the
corporate structure of the nation is not yet reflected in a
corresponding territorial distribution of the personnel of
that structure.
    The lingering handicap burdening nonmetro counties is

apparent in many indicators of differential access to opportunity. Official data on unemployment and underemployment
in the labor force population reveal in somewhat opaque
fashion the disadvantaged condition of nonmetro people.
Those data suggest that unemployment is masked in underemployment and that that deception is deepened where urbanization is least. But such data, as Vernon Briggs makes
abundantly clear, are far from satisfactory; they err both
on the side of understatement and their usefulness for
analytical purposes.

Although available information on poverty also lacks
incisiveness, as Stephen Seninger and Timothy Smeeding
point out, it is much less equivocal than are employment
data. There is no question that nonmetro areas, particularly
those in the southern regions, harbor disproportionate
shares of the nation's poor people, despite recent gains in
the reduction of poverty. The search for an understanding
of the persistence of poverty and its regional concentration
leads to two seemingly different perspectives, the human
resource-income maintenance approach, as represented by
Seninger and Smeeding's chapter, and the political economy
or structuralist approach, as developed in the chapter by
Candace Howes and Ann Markusen. In fact, however, the two
approaches are complementary. The one deals with the inability of workers to compete effectively in a labor market
owing to a lack of appropriate skills, inadequate education,
and immobility. These characteristics are demonstrably prevalent in poverty areas. The recent turnaround in migration
trends, in Seninger and Smeeding's view, holds no early
promise of altering those features of the nonmetro labor
force. Nor do the locations of industry in nonmetro areas
offer grounds for optimism, for industries locating there
that are not seeking a low wage labor force tend to bring
their skilled personnel with them. They may contribute
little more than to increase the number of working poor.
Most government programs addressed to the amelioration of
poverty contain a marked metro bias. On the other hand, the
political economy approach offers much by way of explanation
of the deficiencies of human capital in the nonmetro labor
force. It deals with changes in resource quality and availability, technological shifts, the emergence of substitute
products, competitive conditions within industries, and wage
policy and labor management practices in industries. Factors
such as these result in atrophied skills and pockets of
stranded workers who lack the wherewithal for mobility.

The combination of lack of appropriate "human capital"

and of institutional restraints operating on the preservation of poverty is nowhere better illustrated than in two
large minority populations, the blacks and the Chicanos.
John Moland decribes how the acquisition by nonmetro blacks
of the requisite skills and other qualifications for labor
market participation is severely hampered by inappropriate
vocational training programs and insufficiently financed
schools, by a general lack of community services, and by a
continuous loss of leadership through migration of the more
able members. But even where the appropriate qualifications
have been acquired blacks encounter discriminatory wage and
hiring practices. Apathy and alienation are thus endemic in
the impoverished black population. Chicanos, as with blacks,
suffer in part from the disadvantages of the regions in
which they are concentrated, the blacks in the southeastern
and south central regions, and the Chicanos in the Southwest
and West. In her chapter in this volume, Marta Tienda shows
that Chicanos also lack sufficient educational preparation
and are afflicted by discrimination in employment opportunity and the provision of community service. The separation
of cultural and legal status influences from other determining circumstances is not a simple matter, however. Nevertheless, Chicanos have been more successful in escaping the
depths of poverty than have blacks. They may continue to do
so as they scatter more widely over the regions of the
country.

The poor and the disadvantaged are held in that state
partly by their lack of access to suitable transportation
facilities. Many live in communities that have been bypassed
in the construction and maintenance of intercity routes.
Others lack automobiles or the wherewithal to keep them in
operating condition. And all suffer from the limitations
that low densities impose upon conventional, commercial public transportation. The disabled and the aged in nonmetro
areas are isolated in much the same fashion. A possible
solution to that lack of access, as Arthur Saltzman and
Larry Newlin point out, may be found in what are called
"paratransit" arrangements, that is, service with small
vehicles provided to particular clienteles, now being tried
in different places and circumstances. The transportation
innovation may be taken as illustrative of the "small technology" recommended elsewhere in this volume by Stephen
Coelen and William Fox. It is of interest to note, however,
that dissatisfaction with the lack of public transportation
is not restricted to the poor and the handicapped. Respondents to the NORC survey mentioned earlier were less than

pleased with the distances they had to travel to work and were hopeful that community growth would bring improvements in public transportation.

THE DISTRIBUTION OF AMENITIES

The matter of access to services and community amenities has been touched upon tangentially in preceding paragraphs. Considerations of minimum population densities for community viability, of industrial location decision, of energy costs, and of lack of purchasing power or poverty, though discussed largely with reference to economic opportunity, unavoidably raise questions of the availability and quality of supporting facilities. Services and related amenities constitute a set of externalities without which employment opportunity is somewhat barren.

Shelter is, of course, an amenity of first importance. Yet very little systematic knowledge about housing and the housing market in nonmetro areas is available. The chapter in this volume prepared by Wilbur Thompson and James Mikesell is a pioneering effort to repair that defect. A large volume of unanalyzed data on nonmetro housing is available in a recent report issued by the U.S. Bureau of the Census (1977b). From this source it is learned that, the post-1970 migration into nonmetro counties notwithstanding, vacancy rates are virtually the same in both nonmetro and metro areas and that the downward trend in one class of place has been matched by that in the other. Nor is there evidence of overcrowding in nonmetro housing. A significant difference was found in respect to median value; nonmetro housing was approximately two-thirds the value of metro housing. The quality of housing in nonmetro cities compared favorably with that in metro areas. But in the villages and open country a relatively high incidence of needed repairs and absence of modern plumbing was found, reflecting perhaps the higher average age of housing in that sector. That may in part account for the higher costs of home heating in nonmetro areas reported by Irving Hoch.

The delivery of public services in nonmetro communities is affected directly by the factor of population size or, better still, by density of population. The problem is acute in low density areas, as Coelen and Fox make clear. It is not a problem that can be successfully attacked from the urban perspective. As the authors point out, discussions

of scale economies are usually premised on a particular
technology, which commonly is a highly capitalized technology. But there are various small technologies that promise optimal service levels at lower population thresholds.
There is always the possibility, of course, that community
growth, or population reconcentration in response to energy
shortages, will obviate the service delivery problem. Unfortunately, the interactions between growth and service
installation development, including the lag effects on each
side of the equation, are so incompletely explored that
satisfactory projections cannot be made. Coelen and Fox
illustrate the direction needed research might take. An
unanswered question of a different kind is: If public services are deemed desirable, if not necessary, why do people
move into areas where they are not available? Do they wish
to avoid the costs, do they misjudge their needs, or do they
expect services to follow their movement?

Unlike many public services, health services were once
widely distributed but have become increasingly concentrated
in large urban places. Their concentration is to be understood in much the same terms that make the distribution of
other services to low density areas difficult, namely,
large capitalization costs. Specialized medical training is
a capitalization cost analogous to the costs of diagnostic
equipment and modern buildings. Such developments have led
to a near abandonment of low density areas by health services despite the prevalence of need in those areas, as
documented in Roger Rosenblatt's chapter. The dilemma thus
posed has attracted a large number of innovations that con-
form to the "small technology" principle mentioned earlier.
The most feasible solution to the health delivery problem
is an organization of an integrated hierarchy of nested
service areas in which medical services are graded from
general practice in the most localized area to increasingly
specialized in the more inclusive service area. In such a
system telephonic and computerized distribution of critical
knowledge could replace some of the transportations of
patients while the circulations of specialists could further compensate for the limitations of scale in subareas.

GROWTH, ENVIRONMENTAL IMPACT, AND PLANNING

If the extreme complexity of contemporary American society
needs further illustration, it is readily found in the

tangled issues of growth, environmental protection, and
planning processes in nonmetro territory. This is not to
say that the nonmetro area has been a stagnant backwater of
bucolic simplicity--a myth that has had some currency in
metro circles. It is rather that upon its own environmental
relationships and preoccupations recent events are imposing
conditions which have long been intrinsic to the relatively
congested life in metro areas. That becomes increasingly
apparent as one follows Marion Clawson's account of the
"urbanization" of nonmetro land uses. Invasions of public
lands by private uses, land transfers to nonproductive
uses, and inadvertent conversions of the usefulness of
spaces between nonfarm uses, though seemingly unimportant
when viewed separately, nevertheless cumulate in changes in
land-use patterns of major significance. Embedded in that
set of changes, moreover, is a strain of ambivalence in
nonmetro people toward a popular desire for land-use controls, on the one hand, and the individual's privilege to
exercise his prerogatives of private ownership, on the
other hand. Such incompatible attitudes constitute an
important obstacle to effective measures for environmental
protection.

The nonmetro resident's ambivalence is also encountered
in a larger political arena in the form of a contest between environmental protection and area development. Development can be an ambiguous term. But here it is construed
to mean bringing the nonmetro population to the same level
of opportunity, access to needed services, and political
expression as that enjoyed by metro people. Benign as this
construction of the term appears to be, its application as
a program of action entails threats to environmental maintenance. The multiplication of industrial and service employment opportunities in nonmetro areas, the facilitation
of mobility for the satisfaction of avocational and other
interests, and the raising of the consuming power of nonmetro people may not be feasible without increases in the
scale of organization. That in turn carries almost unavoidable risks of further removal from direct contact with and
concern for the physical environment. The issue posed by
Frederick Buttel in his chapter is whether the major trade-
off required for a resolution of the environment-development
dilemma might not be a lower standard of living for environmental preservation. Unless the issue is decided in favor of
environment, in Buttel's view, the costs of pollution control and the rate of energy use will hasten the day of
resource exhaustion.

Yet the marshaling of local initiative for problem
solving in nonmetro areas has long been frustrated by the
smallness of population and resources of the great majority
of local government units. Small scale has limited governmental capacity and dampened the will of local electorates
and their representatives to engage in aggressive action.
Even so the numbers of local governmental units, exclusive
of school districts, have changed very little in recent
decades. A possible explanation for that persistence in the
context of the increasing complexity of modern life and the
more recent growth experience is the development of numerous
substitutes for limited scale. These, as presented and
analyzed by Alvin Sokolow, include various information and
technical assistance services provided by professional
associations, intergovernmental councils, and state and
federal specific and general purpose programs of grants and
loans to local governments. That these have enhanced the
will as well as the capacity of local governments to exercise initiative is manifested in instances of cooperation
among local governments, of innovations in utilizing professional personnel, and in citizen participation. A factor
of unassessed importance in the changes that have occurred
in local governments is the influence of former metro
residents who brought their service expectations with them.
A consequence of the multifaceted invasion of local
autonomy, as Sokolow points out, is to attach local government processes to extralocal government systems, that of
the federal government in particular. That is reflected,
according to Thomas Stinson, in an escalating reliance of
local governments on external sources of funds. Stinson
seriously doubts that local governments will ever regain
their lost autonomy. Increased scale seems to be an inescap-
able requirement for effective solutions to environmental
and other problems, short of a return to a life-style in
which such problems do not occur.
The management of change confronts at least two major
related administrative problems--an avoidance of the undesirable effects of increasing scale, and a constructive
resolution of the many critical trade-offs that must be
made. That planning is essential to the attainment of these
ends is scarcely arguable. Accordingly the federal government has built a large and intricate structure of plans and
planning agencies. Pat Choate's comprehensive review of the
contact points of that apparatus with nonmetro needs reveals, among its many farsighted and constructive provisions, numerous duplications, conflicting objectives, and

failures of application. Planning for nonmetro areas is
also obstructed by the plethora of jurisdictions, the
incapacity of state governments to exercise their powers,
and a neglect of the training of nonmetro planners. Choate
is thus not as optimistic as Sokolow regarding the ability
of local governments to find ways of dealing with growth.
Some promise lies with the emerging multijurisdictional
agencies. But they must find ways of working within the
complex fabric of laws and programs created by federal and
state governments.

CONCLUSION

The reversal of the trends of population decline in many
nonmetro counties has been described as a resurgence of
nonmetro America, as a rediscovery of nonmetro America, and
in various other optimistic phrases. But the many state-of-
knowledge papers comprising this volume counsel a more
restrained interpretation of what is taking place. That
there has in fact been a turnaround in the movements of
population is subject to one's point of view: at the nonmetro receiving end there has indeed been a turnaround,
but at the metro origin there has only been a continuation
of a long-term trend toward deconcentration.

The implications of the renewal of growth in nonmetro
counties must be put forward with more than a few reservations. In the first place, the available data pertaining to
correlated trends are surprisingly deficient. Although they
bulk large in quantity, they contain numerous lacunae, or
they are in too aggregated a form for discriminating analysis, or they are designed to include concepts that have
logical faults. In many instances, therefore, authors have
had to rely on case materials and theoretical inferences. A
second basis for caution lies with the early stage in the
process at which present observations are made. Trends
might be projected with more confidence were it not for the
extraordinary intrusion of an acute energy shortage. The
effect of that on what were expected continuities remains in
the realm of speculation.

Given these caveats, it appears that events in industrial movements, local government changes, the shifting status
pattern, and the growing inclusiveness of the organizational
structure of the nation point toward a convergence of nonmetro and metro sectors. Institutions and life-styles

cultivated in metro areas are taking fuller possession of
nonmetro territory, and in the process are being modified
by and adapted to nonmetro conditions. Out of that ferment
a more complete integration of the national life may be
expected to arise. There is, however, much unevenness in
the processes currently at work. The immobility of disadvantaged segments of nonmetro population persists; the decon-
centrations of industries have not meant an equal sharing
of opportunities as between nonmetro and metro labor forces;
of the various community and health services only education
seems to have responded effectively to the scale requirements of modern demands for quality; and the problems of
environmental protection have yet to be resolved. But again
the process of change has not run its course. The observer
should not be diverted from long-term trends by short-term
lags and variations. In the end one might expect a disappearance of the distinction between nonmetro and metro
sectors.

NOTES

1. For reasons of simplification the terms "metropolitan" and "nonmetropolitan" are hereafter shortened to metro
and nonmetro, except for instances where they appear in
quotations from published sources. Another term that appears
occasionally in the following pages is "Standard Metropolitan Statistical Area"; its shortened form is SMSA. This
term, employed in publications of the U.S. Bureau of the
Census, refers to a county with a central city of 50,000 or
more population, or with two or three cities whose aggregate
population is 50,000 or more, together with contiguous
counties that are functionally integrated with the central
county. In 1975 the Bureau of the Census identified 276
SMSAs, comprising 573 counties.

BIBLIOGRAPHY

Beale, Calvin L., and Fuguitt, Glenn V. "The New Pattern of
    Nonmetropolitan Population Change." In Social Demogra-
    phy, edited by Karl E. Taeuber, Larry L. Bumpass, and
    James A. Sweet, chapter 8. New York: Academic Press,
    1978.

Boorstin, Daniel J. The Americans: The Democratic Experi-
ence. New York: Random House, 1973.
Brunson, E. Evan. Small Cities and Rural Communities in the
South: An Analysis of Recent Trends and Policy Needs.
Southern Growth Policies Board Research Report. Research
Triangle Park, N.C.: Southern Growth Policy Board, 1979.
Fuguitt, Glenn V., and Beale, Calvin L. Population Change in
Nonmetropolitan Cities and Towns. U.S. Department of Ag-
riculture, Economic Research Service, Report no. 323.
Washington, D.C., 1976.
Gallaher, Art, Jr. Plainville Fifteen Years Later. New York:
Columbia, 1961.
Hawley, Amos H. The Changing Shape of Metropolitan America:
Deconcentration Since 1920. Glencoe, Ill.: The Free
Press, 1956.
Hightower, Jim. Hard Tomatoes, Hard Times: The Failure of
the Land-Grant College Complex. Washington, D.C.:
Agribusiness Accountability Project, 1972.
McCarthy, Kevin M., and Morrison, Peter A. The Changing
Demographic and Economic Structure of Nonmetropolitan
Areas in the United States. Santa Monica, Calif.: Rand
Corporation, 1979.
Richards, Robert O. "Urbanization of Rural Areas." In Hand-
book of Contemporary Urban Life, by David Street and
Associates, chapter 18. San Francisco, Calif.: Jossey-
Bass, 1978.
Taylor, D. Garth; Sherman, Susan; and Rusciano, Frank. "Some
Social and Financial Aspects of Nonmetropolitan Life in
America." Unpublished report, National Opinion Research
Center. Chicago, Ill., 1979.
U.S. Bureau of the Census. Census of Agriculture, vol 1.,
pt. 51, p. 8. Washington, D.C.: U.S. Government Printing
Office, 1977a.
_____. Census of Agriculture. Special Reports, Part
5, Corporations in Agricultural Production. Washington,
D.C.: U.S. Government Printing Office, 1975b.
_____. Current Housing Reports. "Vacancy Rates and
Characteristics of Housing in the United States: Annual
Statistics, 1976." Washington, D.C.: U.S. Government
Printing Office, 1977b.
_____. Historical Statistics of the United States:
Colonial Times to 1970, vol 1., pp. 498, 500. Washing-
ton, D.C.: U.S. Government Printing Office, 1975a.
_____. 1970 Census of Population, vol. 1, pt. A, fig.
9, p. 14. Washington, D.C.: U.S. Government Printing
Office, 1972.

West, James. Plainville, U.S.A. New York: Columbia, 1945.
Zuiches, James J., and Brown, David L. "The Changing Charac-
    ter of the Nonmetropolitan Population 1950-75." In
    Rural U.S.A.: Persistence and Change, edited by Thomas
    R. Ford, chapter 4. Ames, Iowa: Iowa State University
    Press, 1978.

I.

The Deconcentration
of Population

David L. Brown
Calvin L. Beale

1
Diversity in Post-1970 Population Trends

INTRODUCTION

Diversity is a necessary key to understanding current conditions in nonmetro America. Social, economic, and demographic conditions all vary greatly among communities
outside of metro areas. As a consequence, broad generalizations about nonmetro trends and issues often conceal as
much information as they provide. For example, there is
much diversity in nonmetro areas today in their rate of
population growth, and in the extent to which the direction
of change represents a continuing trend or a reversal of
trend. Diversity is also evident in the economic structure
of nonmetro America. Dependence on agriculture as a primary
source of employment and personal income has declined to
the point where farming is the primary source of employment
in only a minority of nonmetro counties. Manufacturing and
services provide most jobs in the majority of cases. Population composition also varies widely among nonmetro counties,
as reflected in age, ethnicity, and income differences
(Hines et al. 1975).

This chapter develops a framework for describing the
diversity of sociodemographic conditions in nonmetro America. Key aspects of population change and composition and
employment structure are identified and their geographic
distribution is noted. The association between differences
in sociodemographic composition and in post-1970 patterns
of population change is analyzed. This allows for a description of the context within which nonmetro population change
is occurring. An appendix to this chapter further explores
the diversity of nonmetro America from the standpoint of
geographically based areas.

A TYPOLOGY OF POST-1970
NONMETROPOLITAN POPULATION CHANGE

The post-1970 (from 1970 to 1978) population change experi
ence of nonmetro counties can be classified in five categories, defined as follows: (1) Continuous Population
Growth: growth during both the 1960s and 1970s (1,093
counties, 44 percent of total). (2) Reverse Turnaround:
growth during the 1960s and decline during the 1970s (80
counties, 3 percent of total). (3) Continuous Population
Decline: decline during both the 1960s and 1970s (446
counties, 18 percent of total). (4) Extreme Turnaround:
21.8 percent growth or more from 1970 to 1978 (triple the
national average) and/or 16.5 percentage points or more
positive difference in the 1970-78 rate of growth compared
with the 1960s rate, a change equal to 20 percentage point
positive difference if continued until 1980 (388 counties,
16 percent of total). (5) Low to Moderate Turnaround: less
than 21.8 percent growth from 1970 to 1978 and/or less tha
16.5 percentage points of positive difference in the 1970-
78 rate of growth compared with the 1960s rate (462 counties, 19 percent of total).

The distribution of counties among these categories
provides an essential perspective for considering the nature and magnitude of the post-1970 nonmetro population
turnaround (see Table 1.1). Turnaround refers to the fact
that for the first time in the twentieth century the rate
of population growth of the nonmetro category exceeds that
of the metro category (10.5 percent in nonmetro areas versus 6.1 percent in metro areas between 1970 and 1978). It
does not mean that all nonmetro counties were previously
declining and are now growing.

The nonmetro rate of growth now exceeds that of metro
areas because many previously growing counties increased
their rates of growth, and many previously declining areas
decreased their rates of decline or reversed to population
gain. Migration is the basic dynamic of these demographic
changes because natural increase is now much reduced although still showing some regional or situational variatio
Indeed, many nonmetro counties that grew in the 1960s experienced net out-migration in that decade and their growt
was attributable to natural increase. But their continued,
and often accelerated, growth since 1970 usually is attrib
utable to net in-migration. Both increased nonmetro in-
migration and decreased nonmetro out-migration are involve
(Tucker 1976; Zuiches and Brown 1978).

Table 1.1. A Typology of Population Growth Experience in Nonmetropolitan Counties, 1960-1978

Region	All Nonmetro[a]	Growth in 1960s		Decline in 1960s		
		Growth in 1970s	Decline in 1970s	Decline in 1970s	Growth in 1970s	
		Continuous Growth	Reverse Turnaround	Continuous Decline	Extreme Turnaround	Low to Moderate Turnaround
United States						
Number of counties	2,469	1,093	80	446	388	462
Percentage of counties	100.0	44.3	3.2	18.1	15.7	18.7
Northeast-Great Lakes						
Number of counties	367	259	18	13	25	52
Percentage of counties	100.0	70.6	4.9	3.5	6.8	14.2
Great Plains-Corn Belt						
Number of counties	756	143	33	306	112	162
Percentage of counties	100.0	18.9	4.4	40.5	14.8	21.4
South						
Number of counties	984	494	15	96	160	219
Percentage of counties	100.0	50.2	1.5	9.8	16.3	22.3
West						
Number of counties	362	197	14	31	91	29
Percentage of counties	100.0	54.4	3.9	8.6	25.1	8.0

Source: U.S. Bureau of the Census, 1970 Census of Population, vol. 1, pt. A, and Current Population Reports, series P-25, no. 873.

Note: See text for definitions of growth categories and regions.

[a]Nonmetro as of 1974.

GEOGRAPHIC DISTRIBUTION OF COUNTIES
WITH DIFFERING PATTERNS OF POPULATION GROWTH

The geographic distribution of counties in these typological
categories is displayed in Table 1.2 and Figure 1.1. The
regional classification used is not that of the standard
census regions, which consists of entire states. This one
splits states in places in order to increase homogeneity.
It collects the Northeast (including Baltimore and Washington) into a region with the industrial and nonagricultural
parts of the Great Lakes. The Corn Belt and the Great Plains
(both north and south) are grouped into a region that is
basically the agricultural heartland of the country. The
rest of the country is grouped into areas of the West and
the South that are somewhat more restrictive than the Bureau
of the Census regions.
    Nonmetro counties that grew in the 1960s and 1970s are
spread throughout the nation. They are not concentrated in
popularly known growth regions such as the Florida peninsula, the Southwest, and the Pacific Coast. Northern New
England, the Upper Great Lakes, the Ozark-Ouachita Plateau,
and the Mid-South Uplands all contain large numbers of continuously growing nonmetro counties.
    Reverse turnaround counties are found disproportion-
ately in the Northeast-Great Lakes and Great Plains-Corn
Belt regions. They are often located between metro areas
in regions of comparative metro and industrial stagnation.
    Persistent nonmetro decline is much more concentrated.
The 446 counties in this category are located mainly in the
Great Plains, the western Corn Belt, and the Mississippi
Delta. Declining areas in the Great Plains and Corn Belt
are not poor economically, but are continuing to adjust to
diminished agricultural employment and insufficient occupational alternatives. In contrast, nonmetro decline in
the delta is characterized by low income, further farm adjustments, and continued out-migration of the black population.
    The reversal from population decline to population
growth is clearly delineated in Figure 1.1. Areas containing
a substantial number of turnaround counties are located in
the southern Appalachian coalfields, the coastal plain
Tobacco and Peanut Belt, the old coastal plain Cotton Belt
stretching from South Carolina to Mississippi, East Texas,
the Rio Grande Valley, and in a dispersed fashion throughout
the Great Plains, especially the western part.
    Slightly more than one-half (462) of the turnaround

Table 1.2. Regional Location of Counties by Recent Population Growth Experience

Region	All Nonmetro[a]	Growth in 1960s		Decline in 1960s		
					Growth in 1970s	
		Growth in 1970s	Decline in 1970s	Decline in 1970s	Extreme Turnaround	Low to Moderate Turnaround
		Continuous Growth	Reverse Turnaround	Continuous Decline		
	%	%	%	%	%	%
United States	100.0	100.0	100.0	100.0	100.0	100.0
Northeast–Great Lakes	14.9	23.7	22.5	2.9	6.4	11.3
Great Plains–Corn Belt	30.6	13.1	41.3	68.6	28.9	35.1
South	39.9	45.2	18.6	21.5	41.2	47.4
West	14.7	18.0	17.6	7.0	23.5	6.3

Source: U.S. Bureau of the Census, 1970 Census of Population, vol. 1, pt. A, and Current Population Reports, series P–25, no. 873.

Note: See text for definitions of growth categories and regions.

[a]Nonmetro as of 1974.

Figure 1.1 Typology of Recent Nonmetropolitan Population Change

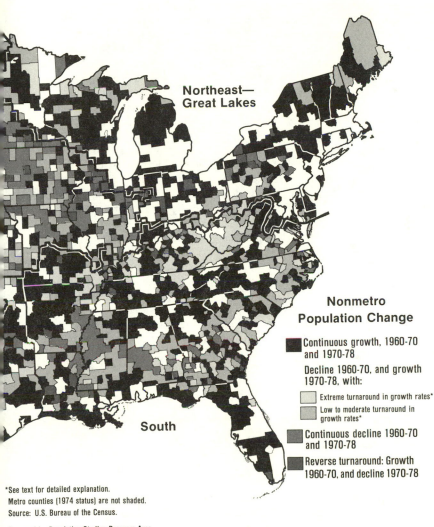

Northeast—
Great Lakes

South

**Nonmetro
Population Change**

Continuous growth, 1960-70
and 1970-78

Decline 1960-70, and growth
1970-78, with:

Extreme turnaround in growth rates*

Low to moderate turnaround in
growth rates*

Continuous decline 1960-70
and 1970-78

Reverse turnaround: Growth
1960-70, and decline 1970-78

*See text for detailed explanation.
Metro counties (1974 status) are not shaded.
Source: U.S. Bureau of the Census.

Prepared by Population Studies Program Area,
Economic Development Division, Economics and Statistics Service,
U.S. Department of Agriculture

situations are in the moderate category, whereas 388 fall
into the extreme category. These extreme turnaround counties
are mainly in the South and West, particularly in the southern Appalachian coalfields, along the front range of the
Rockies, and in the northern Great Plains. Mineral extraction appears to be involved in many of these situations,
especially coal mining in the southern Appalachians, but not
in the majority of cases. Large numbers of these counties
are areas where earlier rapid declines from agricultural
change have bottomed out.

The determinants of moderate turnaround are often difficult to specify. Employment deconcentration, retirement,
recreation, and increased governmental activity have been
shown to be involved (McCarthy and Morrison 1978).

Growth rates of the levels experienced by most of the
extreme turnaround counties are higher than can generally
be absorbed by an area without difficulty. Local governments frequently cannot make decisions, obtain money, and
put programs or laws into effect quickly enough to cope
efficiently with such growth. Thus, areas that shift from
chronic decline to rapid growth may exchange one set of
problems for another. All in all, most of them would probably rather have problems of growth rather than decline,
but their difficulties are real. This would seem especially
true in comparatively small counties with limited government personnel who have no previous experience with modern
growth.

SOCIOECONOMIC DIMENSIONS OF NONMETROPOLITAN AMERICA

POPULATION COMPOSITION

Age, race, and income are basic attributes of population
composition. These interrelated factors are important indicators of social well-being and the quality of life.
High proportions of the elderly, racial minorities, or the
poor often signal the need for public policy to deal with
social problem areas.

The concentration of elderly persons in certain areas is
now one of the most characteristic aspects of age composition in nonmetro America. In the Great Plains and Midwest,
decades of uninterrupted out-migration of young adults have
left a disproportionately high number of elderly persons in
many communities (see Figure 1.2). Numerous counties now

have one-sixth or more of their population at age sixty-five and over, with the proportion reaching one-fifth in many of them. This circumstance is clearly associated with special needs and difficulties in providing essential services for the elderly, often accompanied by local tax base problems.

Scores of other rural communities are acquiring high proportions of elderly through in-migration of retired people. These retirement areas have often been low in economic development and population size and provide a limited range of public and private services (for example, the Ozarks, Upper Great Lakes, Texas Hill Country). Only 17 percent of the net migration to nonmetro areas between 1970 and 1977 was of persons sixty-five and over, but persons of this age only make up 12 percent of the nation's total population. Consequently, recent migration to nonmetro areas is increasing the disparity between metro and nonmetro areas in the percentage of older persons.

The racial minority population of the nonmetro United States is heavily concentrated in the Southeast and Southwest (see Figure 1.3). In the Southeast, the minority population is mainly black. Blacks comprise over one-third of the population in numerous counties in the Mississippi Delta, the old Black Belt, and in the rest of the coastal plain, although their proportion tends to be declining. Hispanics are the primary minority group in most of the Southwest, especially in the Rio Grande Valley and much of Arizona and New Mexico. Inconsistency of reporting methods has made it difficult to judge accurately the trend of Hispanic rural concentrations. Birthrates are high and reinforcement through immigration continues. Thus, despite heavy urban movement, the number and proportion of nonmetro Hispanics (usually Mexican-Americans) may be growing. Indians are the dominant minority group in the Four Corners region of the Southwest, the northern Great Plains, and (along with Eskimos) Alaska. Both their absolute and relative frequency in rural areas has been increasing, given high birthrates and an apparent lessening of net out-migration.

All of these groups live under conditions of substantial poverty, poor housing, high welfare dependence, and below average education in the rural setting. Although conditions have improved, the presence of large proportions of blacks, Hispanics, and native Americans still typically indicates areas of economic and social need.

Thirty-eight percent of nonmetro blacks (more than 10 percentage points higher than for metro blacks), and 27

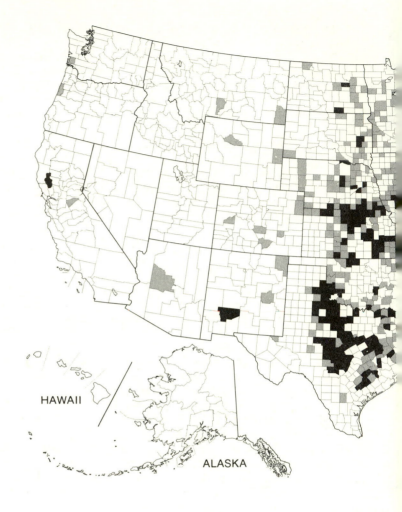

Figure 1.2 Nonmetropolitan Counties with High Percentage of Older Population, 1976

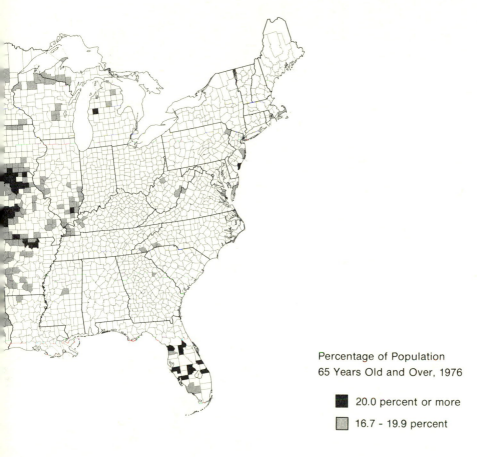

Percentage of Population
65 Years Old and Over, 1976

■ 20.0 percent or more

▨ 16.7 - 19.9 percent

Source: Administration on Aging

Prepared by Population Studies Group,
EDD, ESCS, U.S. Dept. of Agriculture

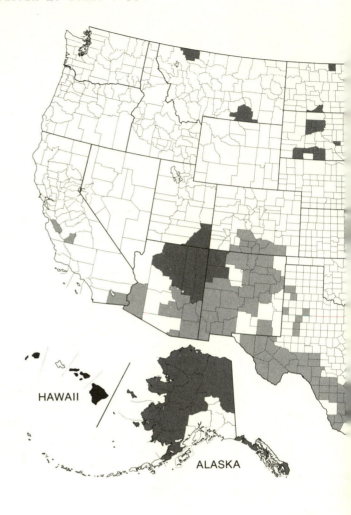

Figure 1.3 Concentration of Nonmetropolitan Racial Minorities, 1970

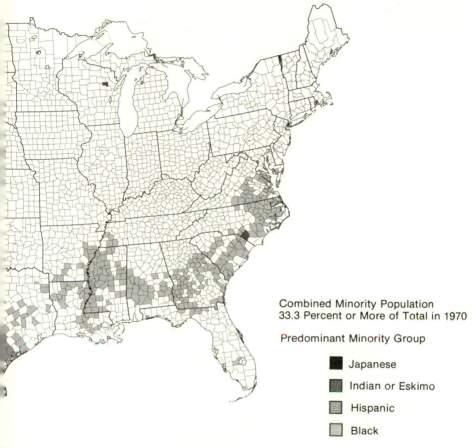

Combined Minority Population
33.3 Percent or More of Total in 1970

Predominant Minority Group

■ Japanese

▨ Indian or Eskimo

▨ Hispanic

☐ Black

Source: U.S. Census of Population, 1970

Prepared by Population Studies Group,
EDD, ESCS, U.S. Dept of Agriculture

percent of nonmetro Hispanics are poor (according to the
federal government criteria for poverty). This far exceeds
the 12 percent of nonmetro whites who are below the poverty
level (although whites, because they make up a large share
of the total nonmetro population, constitute a numerical
majority of the nonmetro poor). The incidence of poverty
among nonmetro Indians is probably even greater than that
of blacks.

The birthrate is still high in areas dominated by
Indians and Hispanics in particular. In combination with a
young age structure this produces large families and a very
high rate of natural increase. The Indian and Eskimo nonmetro areas still have nearly four times as many births
as deaths, and the Hispanic areas run close to three births
for each death. Rural black fertility has traditionally
been very high, but has fallen substantially in the last
decade, although it is still above that of nonmetro whites.

Because of residence patterns of rural minorities, and
historical patterns of economic development in the United
States, rural poverty is heavily concentrated in the South
(see Figure 1.4). More than half of the nonmetro poor live
in that region, where 18 percent of the nonmetro population
failed to receive incomes above the poverty level in 1976.
The incidence of southern nonmetro poverty is like that in
many northern cities; for example, Detroit, Chicago, and
Baltimore. (It should be noted that numerous nonmetro counties in the Northeast and North Central regions contain a
large absolute number of poor persons, but they do not
constitute a high proportion of these relatively large
populations.)

There is a close relationship between areas with a
high concentration of poverty and those with a residential
dominance of minority populations, with two notable exceptions. The exceptions occur in the southern Appalachian
Cumberland Plateau and Ozark-Ouachita Uplands that are almost exclusively white, but have a long history of physical
and cultural isolation and economic underdevelopment. The
economy of these areas has long been dominated by mining
(in the Appalachians), marginal agriculture, and low-wage
manufacturing.

EMPLOYMENT COMPOSITION

People in nonmetro America now make their living from a
wide-ranging set of activities that are increasingly like

those of metro Americans (Beale 1980). In 1977, 27.5 million nonmetro residents were employed. By major industry
group, the largest employer was manufacturing (6.7 million)
followed by 5.3 million in trade, and 5.2 million in professional services such as health and education. Only 2.2
million worked solely or primarily in agriculture, forestry,
and fishing. Thus, just 8 percent were in agriculture compared with 24 percent in manufacturing.

As with other nonmetro conditions, there are important
regional variations. For example, there are many nonmetro
counties in which agriculture continues to be the principal
economic activity, and where vitality of local communities
is determined largely by the course of farming. As of 1970,
there were 331 counties, concentrated mainly in the Great
Plains and central and western Corn Belt, in which 30 percent or more of total employment was in agriculture (see
Figure 1.5). However, these counties contained only 2.1
million people in 1978, or less than 4 percent of the
nonmetro total.

The dominance of manufacturing as the principal source
of nonmetro employment occurs primarily in the South and
East, with a scattering of manufacturing counties in Michigan, Washington, and Oregon. Some 638 nonmetro counties had
30 percent or more of their employment in manufacturing in
1970, and contained 35 percent of the nonmetro population in
1978, or 20.7 million people. Predominant in the West are
nonmetro counties with a service-based economy. Counties in
this region tend to have high employment in public administration (such as management of public lands, dams, military
bases, Indian affairs) and professional services (especially
health and education). Mining is not a major employer of
nonmetro workers nationally, but its importance in certain
locales such as Appalachia and scattered areas of the West
has grown in this decade, mostly because of intensified
production of mineral fuels.

Commuting to metro workplaces is extremely important in
many nonmetro situations. Relatively convenient and affordable commuting on good roads allows many people to combine
rural living with occupational pursuits in the more diversified metro labor market. Regional variation shows the West
to have less commuting whereas commuting is especially great
in the Northeast and east North Central regions because of
the large number of metro areas within a convenient distance.

At the national level, about 9 percent of all employed
heads of households in nonmetro counties commute to metro
employment. For all employed nonmetro residents this figure

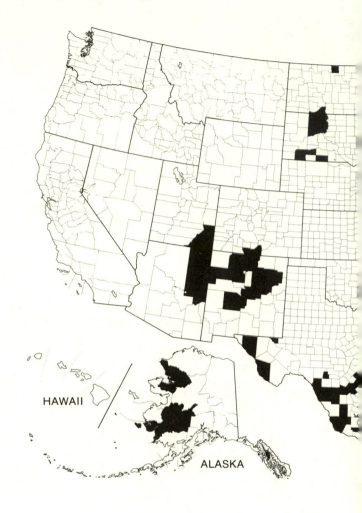

Figure 1.4 Nonmetropolitan Low-Income Counties

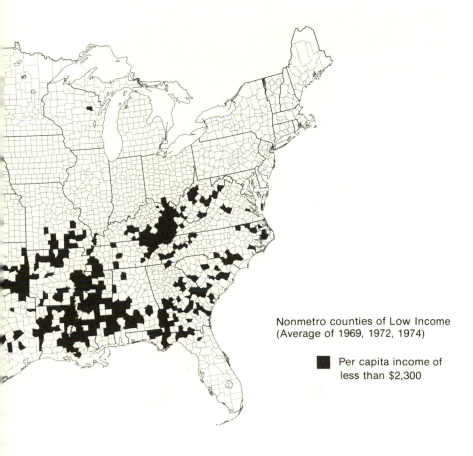

Nonmetro counties of Low Income
(Average of 1969, 1972, 1974)

◼ Per capita income of
less than $2,300

Source: U.S. Bureau of the Census

Prepared by Population Studies Group,
EDD, ESCS, U.S. Dept. of Agriculture

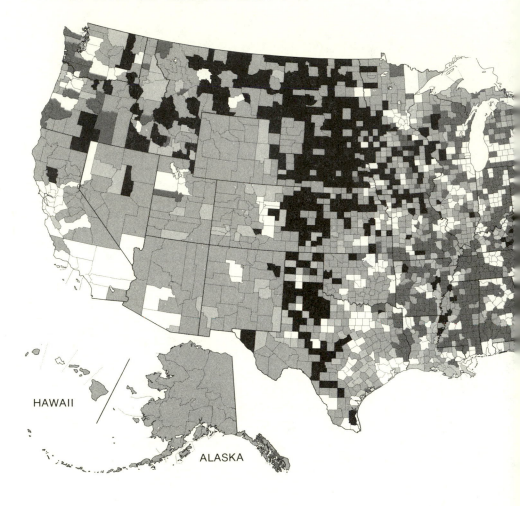

Figure 1.5 Principal Industry of Employment in Nonmetropolitan
Counties, 1970

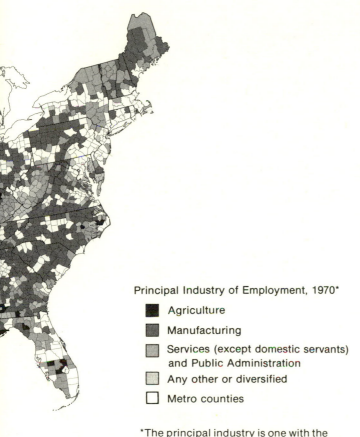

Principal Industry of Employment, 1970*

- ■ Agriculture
- ■ Manufacturing
- ▨ Services (except domestic servants) and Public Administration
- ▦ Any other or diversified
- ☐ Metro counties

*The principal industry is one with the largest employment and at least 25% of total employment. Counties with no industry employing 25% or more were coded "diversified."

Source: U.S. Census of Population, 1970

Prepared by Population Studies Group, EDD, ESCS, U.S. Dept. of Agriculture

was as high as 30 percent in a few counties in 1970. By
definition, counties with more than this percentage are
treated as metro in most cases. The greater the degree of
metro commuting, the more rapid the rate of population
growth since 1970 has been. Nonmetro counties that had at
least 20 percent of their workers commuting to a metro area
in 1970, grew in population by 15.8 percent from 1970 to
1978. By contrast, those with metro commuting rates of less
than 3 percent in 1970 grew by 9.8 percent. However, the
growth differential between the two classes of counties is
not nearly as great as it was in the 1960s. The population
turnaround has been greater in the more remote nonmetro
counties than it has in those more closely linked economically with metro areas (Beale 1976).

COMPARATIVE PROFILE OF NONMETROPOLITAN COUNTIES
WITH DIFFERING PATTERNS OF RECENT POPULATION CHANGE

Table 1.3 contains information on the size and location of
nonmetro counties with differing patterns of recent population growth and Table 1.4 compares the sociodemographic and
employment characteristics of the five growth classes.
Employment data in Table 1.4 indicate the types of jobs in
the growth category, not necessarily the industry structure
of resident workers. The data are for 1970, thus indicating
the industrial composition of employment prior to the reversal of relative growth rates between the metro and nonmetro
categories.

CONTINUOUS GROWTH COUNTIES

Continuous population growth has taken place in relatively
urbanized nonmetro settings. The data in Table 1.3 show that
the average population of continuously growing nonmetro
counties was 34,000, and that almost one-third of the counties in this category contained a city of at least 10,000
people. In comparison, the average population of all nonmetro counties was 24,000 and only one-fifth contained a
place of 10,000 or more inhabitants. In the South, where 45
percent of continuously growing counties are located, their
average population was 30,000 compared with 25,000 for all
nonmetro counties in the region.

Table 1.3. Size and Location of Counties by Recent Population Growth Experience

Item	All Nonmetro[a]	Growth in 1960s		Decline in 1960s		
		Growth in 1970s	Decline in 1970s	Decline in 1970s	Growth in 1970s	
		Continuous Growth	Reverse Turnaround	Continuous Decline	Extreme Turnaround	Low to Moderate Turnaround
Number of counties	2,469	1,093	80	446	388	462
Population, 1978 (000s)	60,120.9	37,036.3	2,479.9	5,294.0	5,446.4	9,864.3
Mean county population, 1978	24,350	33,885	30,999	11,870	14,037	21,351
Percentage totally rural, 1970	35.0	24.1	13.8	51.3	57.2	29.9
Percentage with place of 10,000+, 1970	21.5	31.7	45.1	8.5	7.0	17.8
Percentage adjacent to SMSA, 1970	39.2	50.1	36.3	22.9	29.6	37.9
Percentage with interstate highway, 1970	29.7	37.8	22.5	18.8	25.0	26.4

Source: U.S. Bureau of the Census, 1970 Census of Population, vol. 1, pt. A, and Current Population Reports, series P-25, no. 873. Interstate highway status obtained from maps of the period.

Note: See text for definition of population growth experience categories.

[a]Nonmetro as of 1974.

Table 1.4. Sociodemographic and Employment Characteristics of
Nonmetropolitan Counties by Recent Population Growth Experience

Item	All Nonmetro[a]	Growth in 1960s	
		Growth in 1970s	Decline in 1970s
		Continuous Growth	Reverse Turnaround
Number of counties	2,469	1,093	80
Sociodemographic			
Percentage retirement communities[b]	14.6	27.4	3.8
Percentage of population black, 1970	9.4	7.3	5.1
Per capita wage and salary income, 1970	$2,264	$2,363	$2,821
Employment[c]			
Percentage of labor force employed in:			
Agriculture, 1970	15.0	12.0	9.1
Mining, 1970	1.6	1.0	1.0
Manufacturing, 1970	20.8	23.2	22.9
Average percentage commuting out of county, 1970	17.4	19.1	13.4

Source: Age, race, and commuting data are from the 1970
Census of Population. Employment and income data are from
the Bureau of Economic Analysis. Retirement data are from
the Economics and Statistics Service and University of
Georgia.

Note: See text for definition of population growth
categories.

[a]Nonmetro as of 1974.

[b]Counties with at least 10 percent net in-migration at
ages 60+ during 1960-70 period.

[c]Data are for county work force, not resident employed.

	Decline in 1960s	
Decline in 1970s	Growth in 1970s	
Continuous Decline	Extreme Turnaround	Low to Moderate Turnaround
446	388	462
3.4	4.6	5.2
13.4	10.0	15.3
$2,155	$1,896	$2,023
24.8	20.8	18.9
1.5	6.2	2.0
14.2	12.0	19.8
12.9	16.8	18.8

The spatial situation of continuously growing areas also differs from other types of counties. One-half of the counties in this class are located next to a metro area and 38 percent have an interstate highway within their borders, whereas the corresponding figures for all nonmetro counties were 39 percent and 30 percent, respectively.

Counties that grew in both the 1960s and 1970s were characterized by high rates of in-migration at retirement ages, relatively high per capita income, low employment in agriculture and mining, and high employment in manufacturing (see Table 1.4). This profile is consistent across all four regions except in the South, where continuously growing counties have a lower than average percentage of blacks, and in the Northeast-Great Lakes region, where employment in agriculture and manufacturing is neither inordinately low nor high.

REVERSE TURNAROUND COUNTIES

Eighty nonmetro counties, about 3 percent of the total, experienced population decline in the 1970s after growth in the prior decade, and thus have had a reverse turnaround that contrasts with the general pattern. Some of these counties, especially in the South, have been dominated by an institution such as a military base or large college and have experienced events negatively affecting that source of population and jobs. Others, in the Northeast and Great Lakes region, have older nonmetro industrial cities that have experienced in miniature the same economic and demographic malaise common to the metro areas of those regions. This is reflected in Table 1.4, which shows that reverse turnaround counties (except in the South) had a relatively high proportion of jobs in manufacturing, relatively high per capita income, and low employment in agriculture and mining. Reverse population turnaround does not reflect the chronically depressed condition usually visualized for areas of population decline.

The reverse turnaround counties as a whole have an average population that is almost as large as that of the continuous growth class (30,999 versus 33,885). They are the least likely to be completely rural (only 14 percent) and the most likely to contain a city of 10,000 or more people (45 percent). Almost 40 percent are adjacent to a metro area. This is especially true in the Northeast-Great Lakes region. However, somewhat above average adjacency to a metro area is not associated with a high level of inter-county commuting. Rather, the reverse turnaround counties have a low proportion of workers crossing county lines and possess relatively self-contained labor markets.

CONTINUOUS DECLINE COUNTIES

Continuous population decline is largely found in very rural settings. One-half of the counties in this category have no villages or towns of 2,500 population or more. Average population size is just 12,000, only 23 percent are adjacent to metro areas, and just 19 percent have an interstate highway--values that in each case are the lowest of any category. Two-thirds of the counties of this type are located in the Great Plains-Corn Belt region.

Sociodemographic and employment characteristics in Table 1.4 further emphasize the rural nature of continuously de-clining counties. One-quarter of all jobs are in agricul-ture, the highest by far of any category, and only 14 per-cent are in manufacturing. These overall patterns are con-sistent across all four regions.

Continuously declining counties in the South have the highest proportion of black population found in any of the county types. In general, continuous decline is found among Great Plains and Corn Belt areas that lack accompanying urbanization or nonfarm job alternatives and in heavily black counties of the South from which the outflow of blacks has persisted. In-migration at retirement age is character-istically low in declining counties.

TURNAROUND COUNTIES

Turnaround counties are intermediate between continuously growing and declining areas in terms of population size and location (see Table 1.3). However, in population size, they are much closer to the declining category. Moderate turn-around counties are much more highly urbanized than extreme turnaround areas. The turnaround appears to have taken place in relatively rural settings. Indeed, it could hardly do otherwise, for many of the more urbanized nonmetro counties were already growing in earlier years.

Both classes of turnaround counties have relatively low per capita income, and a high initial proportion of employ-ment in agriculture. The extreme turnaround group shows higher than average employment in mining, and lower than average employment in manufacturing (see Table 1.4).

This characterization is applicable to all four regions, although some exceptions are notable. Extreme turnaround counties are not especially high in mining employment in the West or Plains-Corn Belt region (there is little variation in the proportion in mining among growth categories in the Plains-Corn Belt region). Also, moderate turnaround counties in the Northeast-Great Lakes region are only average in the percentage employed in agriculture. Moderate turnaround counties have a high percentage of blacks, but only in the South. Turnaround in these counties is probably due to increased in-migration of whites, decreased out-migration of both races, and continued high fertility among blacks. Increased in-migration of blacks is probably not involved.

In summary, the comparative profile that emerges from the data in Tables 1.3 and 1.4 suggests that continuous growth and reverse turnaround counties are relatively urbanized and industrialized while continuous decline and positive turnaround have taken place in relatively rural and agricultural settings. Similarly, income tends to be highest in continuous growth and reverse turnaround counties.

Previous research has shown retirement to be an important determinant of renewed nonmetro population growth, but the association is not so evident in this analysis. Although continuous growth counties were shown to have higher than average retirement, and vice versa for counties with continuous decline, no consistent association was evident for the turnaround categories. In the 1970s, retirement migration has played its role largely in increasing the rate of growth of the continuously growing counties, which frequently experienced a turnaround in the 1960s or earlier.

CONCLUSION

The period since 1970 has been marked by a striking revival of population growth in rural and small-town America (Beale 1976, 1977; Beale and Fuguitt 1978). Fully two-thirds of previously declining nonmetro counties grew between 1970 and 1978, and for the first time in this century the rate of nonmetro population growth (10.5 percent) exceeded that

of metro areas (6.1 percent). This population turnaround is
regarded as one of the most significant demographic events
of recent decades.

However, as noted earlier, broad generalizations about
the demographic situation of nonmetro America often conceal
as much as they reveal. Nonmetro counties are widely diverse in patterns of population change, sociodemographic
composition, and economic structure. Moreover, the sociodemographic context within which recent population change
has occurred varies significantly across the country.

Modern means of communication and transportation indisputably introduce trends of social and economic convergence
between metro and nonmetro areas and among nonmetro areas
themselves. However, the country is far too large and diverse in climate, physiography, history, and natural resources for homogeneity to prevail in its nonmetro areas
except at subregional levels. Furthermore, the very process
of moving away from an overwhelming dependence on agriculture and other extractive industries implies greater diversity of economy, while it also implies more similarity to
the structure of metro areas.

The vast majority of nonmetro counties (about nine-
tenths of them) have experienced increased acquisition or
retention of population in the 1970s. This is the most
common recent theme of nonmetro America but the circumstances of this change vary. For some areas it is an ac-
centuation of an older trend, and for others it is a major
(and usually unexpected) reversal of long-endured trends of
population decline. Moreover, the contexts of population
growth vary as do the rates of such growth. This research
has shown that the population turnaround has occurred in
relatively rural, agricultural, and low income settings.
This is similar to the character of counties that have
experienced continuous population decline, but opposite to
the general context of counties that have grown since 1960
or of those that have reversed from previous growth to
decline.

Although our analysis of areal contexts of recent population change does not directly evaluate the determinants
of growth, it is fair to conclude that the diversity shown
argues against a single all-inclusive explanation. In one
area renewed growth is the product of industrial employment.
In another it is a product of retirement and recreation, in
yet another it is brought about by commuters, or by people
moving for noneconomic reasons in directions that defy

conventional migration models. Frequently, several major determinants occur in concert.

When the patterns of population change, the rates of such change, the causes of change, the sources of employment, the levels of income, degree of access to urban centers, and the extent and location of disadvantaged ethnic minorities are taken into account, various combinations of sociodemographic nonmetro diversity are evident. It is essential to comprehend and to recognize this diversity in the formation of rural policy and programs.

APPENDIX

A CHARACTERIZATION OF TYPES OF NONMETROPOLITAN AREAS

Calvin L. Beale

It is easy to travel the United States and be impressed both with the commonalities of existence that all its residents share and with the diversity that is still imposed by vastness, the wide range of climate and physiography, the residue of history, differences in resources and agriculture, and variations in ethnicity and culture. The purpose of this appendix is to insure that in the necessary course of generalizing a nonexistent sameness is not assumed. Procrustean policy beds, of the one-size-fits-all variety, are all too common in public affairs. Therefore, a characterization is provided here of some of the principal sociodemographic and economic subregional situations that are found in rural America today. These areas are for the most part well recognized and reasonably distinctive. No effort is made to encompass the entire country.

Interstitial Rural Areas in the Northeastern Metro Belt

Around the belt of major metro areas that stretches from southern Maine to northern Virginia live more than 3 million nonmetropolitan people. This is the most densely settled nonmetro population in the United States, averaging about one hundred forty persons per square mile, but outnumbered 12 to 1 by the central city and suburban population. Most of the rural and small-town communities are within reasonable commuting distance of metro areas and are quasi-metro in character and orientation. All of the nonmetro counties are used to some degree for second home

and recreation purposes by the massive nearby urban population in the Boston, New York, Philadelphia, Baltimore, and
Washington areas.

Although there are some fringes of good farming country
--as in the Delmarva Peninsula--agriculture is quite subordinate to manufacturing and the large service-oriented
economy. The population of the nonmetro counties has been
growing steadily for several decades (18 percent just from
1970 to 1978) despite metro losses. In the process, some
counties are gradually changing character and becoming
added to the suburban ring. Income levels are good.

An analogous situation exists along the Hudson River-
Mohawk Valley-Lake Ontario corridor, dominated by Albany,
Syracuse, Rochester, and Buffalo. But the densities of
rural and small-town population are somewhat lower, incomes
are lower, and no net in-movement of people occurred in the
1970s, although out-movement has become negligible.

Northern New England-St. Lawrence Area

This entirely nonmetro subregion does not have a particularly large population (1.6 million), but has been
receiving a substantial amount of publicity, and has a very
self-conscious rural and small-town culture. An in-movement
of people has developed (66,000 from 1970 to 1978) into
what was widely regarded as a classically depressed area
not very long ago. There are the new gentry--people of
professional skills and good incomes--and what might be
called the new peasantry--"homesteaders" inclined to self-
sufficiency and simple living. Here, as nowhere else, is
use of wood for fuel so prominent, as well as a general
high interest in environmentalism, conservation, alternative fuel sources, rural esthetic values, home food production, and local self-government. Centers, institutes, journals, and supportive philosophies of life abound. Manufacturing is still the main strength of the economy, but
there has been an increase in tourism and other service
industries.

The megalopolitan population to the south is so large--
especially the 25 million people in the Boston to New York
axis--that further spillover into the Northern New England-
St. Lawrence area seems inevitable, so long as even a small
fraction of people become disaffected with the big cities
and attracted to the vision of a more satisfying neorural
life.

Lower Great Lakes Industrial and Agricultural Subregion

From Cleveland through southern Michigan and around to
Green Bay is the midwestern equivalent of the Northeastern
Metro Belt. Chicago, Detroit, Cleveland, Milwaukee, Indian-
apolis, and lesser cities provide large metro populations
separated by nonmetro areas. There are many small nonmetro
industrial cities, but the flat, open, rural hinterland is
uniformly committed to a highly productive agriculture.
Corn Belt and assembly line exist in close proximity. Four
million nonmetro people reside in the subregion. Agriculture
is vital, but manufacturing, which is heavily oriented toward metal products, is not primarily farm related.

Unlike the Northeastern Metro Belt, nonmetro population
here is not experiencing much growth (5 percent from 1970
to 1978) and this large subregion is unique as the only one
in the nation that does not show improved retention of
nonmetro residents in the 1970s. Some of the nonmetro
manufacturing towns are like northern metro centers in
miniature, in the sense of heavy dependence on an older
manufacturing economy that is experiencing losses to other
regions. Without resorts, retirement attractions, energy
development, or other common sources of nonmetro population
growth, the combined dominance of an older manufacturing
economy and agriculture has produced a small increase in
out-movement from rural areas and small towns. But the
level of living is good.

Upper Great Lakes Area

The territory around the Upper Great Lakes resembles
Northern New England in being a previously depressed
resource-based rural area on the periphery of a densely
settled metro belt. However, the cultural setting is different. The set-piece New England village image is replaced
by the Paul Bunyan logging and mining camp tradition. Rapid
growth has come in the 1970s after an earlier start in the
1960s. Second homes, recreation, and retirement are supplemented by some increase in manufacturing, but agriculture
is now negligible--mercifully curtailed in the last generation.

The area is an arch example of the propensity for modern
rural growth to come in open country areas and unincorporated settlements, rather than in the small cities and towns.
Some growth rates are very high--in the northern half of
the lower peninsula of Michigan, for instance--severely
testing the ability of sparsely settled counties to cope
with rapid and seemingly inexorable development. Natural

lakes abound, both small and large, and are the basis for
much of the amenity-based attraction of the area and for
the policy issues of land and water use and control that
the area faces.

Southern Coastal Plain

The Coastal Plain from eastern Virginia to the Mississippi Delta has over 7 million nonmetro people. No area has
changed more greatly in the last generation. One has only
to read the economic and social literature of the 1930s to
be aware of how impoverished in every way the rural communities of this region were, and of how dependent the mass
of people--many landless--were on unmechanized cotton and
tobacco farming. Central to any consideration of the region,
too, was the segregated and subordinate position of the
black population.

In the three decades from 1940 to 1970, a vast outpouring of people from this region took place as agriculture was
mechanized, and blacks went to the North. In the 1950s
alone, a net of 1.7 million people left the nonmetro counties, a majority of them black. Despite the disproportionate
out-movement of blacks, a majority of Southern Coastal Plain
counties still had 30 percent or more blacks in their total
population in 1970, and in eighty-seven counties better than
50 percent of the people were black.

Substantial introduction of manufacturing has taken
place, although not to the extent found in the Piedmont.
There are a number of small to middle-sized metropolitan
areas scattered around (such as Richmond, Norfolk, Raleigh,
Columbia, Macon, Montgomery, Jackson, and Memphis), but
this is still a part of the country in which the nonmetro
population outnumbers the metro, and in which the bulk of
the nonmetro people are not adjacent to a metro area. There
is still much rural and small-town poverty, partly associated with the low socioeconomic status of blacks, but also
derived from low wage scales and insufficient economic
development.

Like most parts of the South, the rural population is
widely distributed. The open country portions contain many
residences, stores, other business places, churches,
schools, and even factories, unlike the more concentrated
settlement pattern of the Corn Belt, Great Plains, and West.
Government outside of incorporated places functions almost
entirely at the county level. Township government does not
exist, nor are there generally independent school districts.
Agriculture is still important, but its occurrence is

spottier than in the Midwest, with many more wooded areas. Cotton is now of minor importance except in the Mississippi Delta. Tobacco and peanuts continue to be planted and soybeans claim much of the old cotton land. The tenant system of farming is greatly reduced, and no more than 10 percent of nonmetro blacks are any longer associated directly with agriculture. Since 1970, out-movement and in-movement in the region have been almost in balance. Few counties are growing rapidly but, except in the Mississippi Delta, few are any longer declining in population. A number of people who left in earlier decades are now moving back in retirement, but there are few retirement or resort-recreation communities as such.

Southern Piedmont

Inland from the Southern Coastal Plain and stretching from central Virginia to eastern Alabama is the Southern Piedmont, a more rolling area in topography characterized by its reddish-orange soil. The Piedmont, with its water power, became the cradle of southern industrialization in the late nineteenth century. The emphasis was and still is on textiles, but much diversification has occurred and the degree of concentration on manufacturing in the economy is often startling. Forty-six percent of the entire nonmetro working population was employed in manufacturing in 1970, a percentage rarely reached in metro areas. (Only 4 percent worked in agriculture.) Labor force participation rates for women are the highest in the United States. Factories may be in towns of every size or in the open country.

It is difficult to say that this area has any particular inherent advantage for manufacturing today because water power and locally produced cotton (for raw material) are no longer important. But the historic industrial base has been successfully added to in the modern period. In the last two decades the minority black population has finally gained access to the mills, and a variety of products beyond the staples of textiles and furniture has been introduced. Atlanta, in the southern end of the area, has emerged as the leading metropolis of the Southeast, with far-reaching influence. Piedmont wage scales tend to be somewhat higher than in the Coastal Plain and, with high labor force participation by women, family income levels are better.

The black population averaged a little more than one-fifth of the total in 1970, but reached a majority in only seven counties. Most of the farmland of fifty years ago has

either reverted to forest or been placed in pasture. Rural
settlement densities tend to be high, although not at the
level of the Northeastern Metro Belt. The visual context of
most of the area is rural and small town, but the economy
is the most exclusively dependent on production of manufactured goods of any rural area in the country.

Florida Peninsula

In both the 1960s and the 1970s, the Florida Peninsula
was the most rapidly growing subregion of the United States,
in metro and nonmetro areas alike. In that part of the
state south of St. Augustine and Gainesville, the nonmetro
population doubled from 1960 to 1978 while the metro areas
increased by about 85 percent. In the 1970s, nearly all of
this growth came from people moving in from other states.
There is very little excess of births over deaths because so
much of the in-movement consists of people of retirement
age. Better than one-fourth of the nonmetro residents of
the peninsula are now sixty years old or more.

There are about 7 million people living in the semi-
tropical part of Florida today--that part where citrus
fruits can be grown. Not more than one-eighth of them are
still officially nonmetro because rapid growth has created
six new metro areas just since 1970, in addition to the
somewhat older ones. However, the metro areas frequently
contain many rural people and much of the best agriculture.
In this sense Florida farming is analogous to that in California, with vegetables and fruits dominating a highly
specialized agriculture based on large operations and extensive use of ethnic-minority hired labor in a frequently
metro setting. There is the climatic capacity to produce
crops not generally growable elsewhere, especially in
winter. But the runaway growth of population coming into
the peninsula for retirement, recreation, or the warm
climate is putting increasing pressure on the supply and
cost of farmland.

As the southern and central parts of the peninsula have
filled, growth has moved farther north into areas that are
not frost proof and do not have idyllic palm fringed
beaches. Still, they are relatively attractive to people
from colder regions. One county, Citrus, grew by 126
percent with the addition of about twenty-five thousand
people in just the eight years from 1970 to 1978, despite
having more deaths than births. In such a situation--or
anything remotely approaching it--many problems of rapid

growth appear, although one seldom hears the alarm in
Florida that attends much smaller booms in the energy areas
of the West where communities are unaccustomed to it.

Although the retirement phenomenon exists in an unpar-
alleled way in Florida, it must not be thought that most of
the newcomers are retired. About 70 percent of the in-
movement to nonmetro parts of the peninsula consists of
people less than sixty years old (and their children) who
for the most part are in the labor force. However, the
distinctive reality for most of the area is the dominance
of recreation and retirement, and the supporting service
industries. The future of the rural and small-town areas of
the Florida Peninsula is hard to picture if growth at recent
rates continues. Although many parts were thinly settled
thirty and forty years ago, this is no longer true. Living
costs have risen greatly, but the potential population
wanting to settle in the area--especially in retirement--is
huge. The peninsula's total population has become larger
than that of all but eight states, and except for a minor
segment, all of its rural and small-town people now live in
or adjacent to metro counties.

Corn Belt and Great Plains

If there is an idealized type of the agrarian and small-
town image in America, it surely belongs to the Corn Belt
and the Great Plains--the land of the Homestead Act, the
frugal, hard-working farmer, of Garland's Son of the Middle
Border, Rolvaag's Giants in the Earth, Lewis's Main Street,
Inge's Picnic, Wilson's Music Man, and Grant Wood's American
Gothic. A land of struggle--not always rewarded--and even
occasional strife, but without the degrading legacy of
slavery, sharecropping, grinding poverty, and soil depletion
that has overlaid the rural South.

The visual reality of agriculture is overwhelming in an
area of seven hundred and fifty thousand square miles. At
least 85 percent of the land surface is in farms. The open
fields and ranges extend to the horizon with level to rolling terrain and few woods. The rural population of the
region has gone through an extended period of open country
decline, and small-town and city concentration, lasting
longer than that elsewhere. Goods and services tend to be
absent from the countryside, as compared with the South.
Many farmers have relocated into town and commute to work,
although the majority still live on their farms except in
some areas of the High Plains.

The region is indisputably the grain and meat basket of

the nation. Except for some minerals, there is little to the
economy of the plains part of the region other than agriculture, but farming is highly commercial and family operated.
The ratio of farm operators to hired farm workers is typically 2 to 1 (in contrast to the Southern Coastal Plain, for
example, where it is generally less than 1 to 1).

Because of its greater rainfall, the Corn Belt part of
the agricultural heartland has smaller farms, greater productivity per acre, with an emphasis on soybeans, corn,
pork, and fed beef. In addition there are relatively more
small towns and a moderate infusion of manufacturing
activity, some of which is related to agriculture.

In the Great Plains, the average density of people is
just eight per square mile, barely one-fourth that of the
Corn Belt. Metro centers are few and small, except for
Denver, and most of the region lies beyond convenient ac-
cessibilty to urban centers. As a result, smaller cities
often serve functions not found in places of comparable
size in the East or the South. For example, towns tend to
acquire such facilities as television stations or airline
service at a smaller size than is common in more densely
settled areas. With some exceptions, the physical size of
counties in the plains is not exceptional as it so often is
in the West. When combined with the low density, this produces an average population of only eleven thousand people per county, the lowest of any major part of the country.
Thus, local units of government are small, lack economies
of scale in furnishing services, and are confronted with
the social costs of space.

Except where irrigation prevails, most Great Plains and
Corn Belt counties have declined in population for several
decades, because of farm consolidations and lack of other
job opportunities. Considerable distortion of the age composition has resulted, with an undercutting of the young-
adult and young-child groups. Widespread introduction of
irrigated farming, spreading up from the Texas Panhandle
to western Kansas, has developed areas with high-yield
production of corn and sorghum and even new crops such as
sugar beets. However, depletion of the underground aquifer
threatens a short life for these practices and a difficult
readjustment to dry farming.

At present, the Corn Belt has about 6.25 million nonmetro population and the Great Plains subregion has a little less than 5 million. The Corn Belt as a whole is still
having some net out-migration. In the plains the degree of
turnaround in population trend in recent years is greater

than in the Corn Belt, but much of the difference is accounted for by growth around those cities now reaching metro status, such as Fort Collins, Greeley, Rapid City, and Bismark.

Parts of the northern Great Plains encompass the zone of recent and potential coal development. The affected communities are as yet few in number—not more than ten or so. However, the potential effect is larger if and when coal gasification plants become a reality and as more mines and mine-mouth generating plants are built. The coal communites lack the size, experience or confidence to deal with these developments and are now legally entitled to special impact assistance.

Southern Appalachian Coalfields

Probably no other rural region has had a more unfavorable stereotyped image in the public mind than the more isolated parts of the Southern Appalachians. The hillbilly, moonshiner-revenuer, Li'l Abner image has been accompanied by the picture of the coal-blackened underground miner and the violence of mine strikes. This was about the last area of the United States to be modernized in terms of electricity, telephones, highways, and housing. Yet, no other rural region has had a greater degree of nonmetro turnaround in population trend since 1970 than the Southern Appalachian Coalfields. The area—broadened to include the nonmining parts of the Cumberland Plateau—has about 1.7 million rural and small-town people, all but a comparative few of whom are white highlanders of colonial stock. The heart of it is characterized by the most dissected topography in America. Narrow winding creek valleys with their tributary hollows often comprise the only level land. In an intensely rural region, level land suitable for home sites, schools, industrial parks, or any purpose is actually in short supply. Only one-sixth of the population is urban, and except in West Virginia there are still no towns of even ten thousand people.

Fewer than 5 percent of the people are engaged primarily in farming, and those who do are generally in small-scale operations. Coal mining is the main single source of income. On any map of wage rates, the coal counties look very good —well above the national average. But the intermittency of work, the high frequency of work-limiting health conditions, the relative lack of employment for women, and the residual influence of long years of isolation and underemployment create conditions of social dependency and poor levels of

living that are incongruent with unionized work and miners'
pay scales. Outside the mining counties wage rates fall to
some of the lowest in the nation.

The region was an area of heavy out-movement of people
in the 1950s and 1960s as coal mining and agriculture declined. Since 1970, the population has been increasing as
quickly as it declined. Mining jobs have revived (although
not to the extent expected), a number of people who had
left in earlier years have returned (many with pensions),
and improved highways and industrial job development programs have brought some broadening of the economy. Conditions are changing, but the topography and cultural
heritage will continue to make the area distinctive. Many
problems related to mining, employment, living conditions,
and small-scale farming remain to be handled.

Lower Ohio Valley--Southern Interior Uplands

The subregion described here is not as distinctive or
popularly recognized as some others with more familiar
names. Perhaps it is best described as bounded by better-
known areas such as the Corn Belt on the north, the Southern
Appalachians to the east, and the Southern Coastal Plain on
the south and west. Basically the subregion includes the
Lower Ohio Valley and the lower courses of the Tennessee
and Cumberland rivers. It contains 3 million nonmetro people. It is all southern or border southern. Some sections
of it are reminiscent of the white highland culture of the
Appalachians; others have black minorities, but were never
characterized by the plantation system of the Coastal Plain
or a predominantly black population.

Within the Lower Ohio Valley and Southern Interior Uplands are some prosperous agriculturally well-endowed areas
such as the Kentucky Bluegrass and the Nashville Basin.
However, there are many poorer areas, such as the Highland
Rim country with its hills, poor soil, and legacy of white
poverty. A characteristic feature of all but the southern
part of the subregion is the presence of thousands of small
tobacco farms, which produce most of the country's burley,
snuff, and chewing tobaccos. Labor-saving procedures have
come slowly to this industry, yet the system of allotments
and price supports used in tobacco farming has created a
relative tenacity in the persistence of such farming despite
the often tiny alloted acreages that a family may have.

Cincinnati, Louisville, and Nashville have long provided
islands of metro activity and employment, and in one section
of Kentucky there is coal mining (the western Kentucky coal-

fields). However, a high dependence on small-scale farming led to heavy rural out-migration at midcentury. Today much of the subregion continues to be intensively rural, but the development of the Tennessee and Cumberland rivers changed the power supply, created large reservoirs, and together with general modernization, stimulated manufacturing and other activities.

So rapid has been the economic transformation of the subregion that from 1940 to 1970 employment in agriculture dropped from 50 percent to just 8 percent of all nonmetro workers, while manufacturing jobs increased from 10 percent to 30 percent of the total. This reflects consolidation of farms, some abandonment of farming, and, in part, the large-scale entry of women into manufacturing and other nonfarm work. A majority of counties now have manufacturing as the leading source of income, although not with the intensity of the Southern Piedmont. The factories are rather diverse in character, ranging from small sewing operations to large aluminum mills.

Much of the potential agricultural displacement from the Lower Ohio Valley-Southern Interior Uplands had been completed by 1970. In the 1970s, a net in-movement of 176,000 people took place through 1978, as former out-migrants returned and new in-migrants entered. This contrasts with the Southern Coastal Plain where the "rural turnaround" up to this point consists essentially of a stemming of the previous large outflow of people—especially blacks—with no net in-migration occurring.

Ozark and Ouachita Uplands

The west-of-the-Mississippi version of the southern highlands is, like its eastern counterpart, an area of distinctive conditions and notable changes. Southern Missouri, northern and western Arkansas, and eastern Oklahoma have a nonmetro population of about 1.8 million living in a rolling-to-hilly plateau (the Ozarks) and a ridge-and-valley mountain area (the Ouachitas), separated by the valley of the Arkansas River. With the exception of some mining activity in Missouri (mostly lead), the area was long one of small-scale farming and timber work, with a pattern of poor transportation, low income, and relative isolation, settled primarily by white southern highlanders.

After 1940, a period of population loss ensued, lasting until about the mid-1960s. Farming began to be abandoned or consolidated, and many people moved elsewhere. However, the area became a major locus for dam building, especially on

the White and Osage rivers, resulting in only moderate
significance for electric power, but producing a series of
reservoirs in a woodland setting. Resorts and the in-
movement of retired people developed quickly--despite a low
level of service facilities for older people. Furthermore,
a variety of manufacturing (mostly low wage) began to develop in the area. Population increased in several places
and since 1970 the growth has spread to all but one of the
eighty-five nonmetro counties (the one exception being a
military county). Some of the newcomers are returnees, some
are midwesterners of urban origin, and others are back-to-
the-land types who buy small farmsteads. And some growth
stems from less out-movement of natives. Many counties have
now returned to their former population levels, and outright
rapid growth is not uncommon.

The Ozark and Ouachita region today finds itself with a
mixture of success and problems. The isolation and stagnation of the past are largely gone and more jobs are available. Outsiders evaluate the region as attractive rather
than shunning it. Yet, the future of the region creates
concern. The population is not dense but some of the lakes
are now having pollution problems. Some resort areas have
become distinctly "touristy" with commercial attractions
that have no relation to the rural charm and natural beauty
that give character to the region. Population in small
counties is often growing more rapidly than can be readily
absorbed. (The average annual growth of rural and small-
town population has been about 2 percent in the region as a
whole--rising to 5 percent in some counties.) The region is
a conspicuous example of a rural problem area of the past
that has opened up and developed in an unexpected manner
but is faced with a variety of nagging problems created by
growth that are different from those of the past, but merit
no less attention.

Rio Grande Valley and Southwest

The Rio Grande Valley and the rest of the Southwest are
as distinctive for the composition of their rural population
as they are for their climate and landscape. The land--
defined here as Arizona, most of New Mexico, and the Rio
Grande portions of Colorado and Texas--is a mixture of arid
to semiarid plateaus and mountains, and key river valleys.
Of the 1.67 million nonmetro residents in 1970, about two-
fifths were of Mexican-American origin and one-tenth were
Indians. Only in the Southern Coastal Plain are there such
large ethnic minority rural populations. The living situa-

tion of Mexican-Americans and Indians, similar to blacks in
the rural South, is often associated with low income, poor
housing, large families, low education, limited labor-force
participation, and other social problems.

The region described here has well over three hundred
thousand square miles, but a nonmetro population density
that averages only about six persons per square mile even
with the rapid growth that many sections have experienced
since 1970. Crop agriculture is essentially impossible
without irrigation. Where water is available, there are
productive districts where cotton, vegetables, and citrus
products are raised. Cattle and sheep ranching extend over
wide areas. But much of the land was never taken up under
any settlement scheme and (except in Texas) about three-
eighths of it remains in federal ownership.

Besides farming, scattered mining activities (copper,
uranium, and oil and gas) and tourist attractions (for
example, Grand Canyon and Carlsbad Caverns) are the major
economic functions. In Arizona and southern New Mexico,
retirement areas are attracting increasing numbers of people. Many counties have none of the common rural goods-
producing activities (agriculture, mining, and manufacturing) as the leading source of income. The combined effect
of the federal presence (much of it through landownership),
ethnic minority populations with high social service needs,
plus the growing retired population, has caused transfer
payments and income from employment in public administration
and professional services to become the leading sources of
income and growth of income in a majority of counties.

Central Valley of California

In a slight arc stretching from north to southeast, the
Central Valley of California extends for four hundred miles.
There is no area of comparable size on which Americans are
as dependent for food supply, but it is quite different
from the good farm areas of the Midwest. As the Corn Belt
and the Wheat belt epitomize the domain of the independent
family farmer providing most of his labor, the Central
Valley reflects large-scale corporate farming and family
farms engaged in crops that require large amounts of
seasonal hired work.

Farming has changed over the years in the valley, but
from the first period of American settlement it has been
conducted on a large and capital-intensive scale, always
on the leading edge of innovations in machinery, techniques,
new crops, and marketing. With extensive irrigation, pro-

ductivity is high. In 1978 the Central Valley produced more
than $5 billion worth of farm goods for sale, as much as
the combined total of Alabama, Mississippi, and Tennessee.
The output is highly varied, with commodities such as cotton, rice, grapes, barley, tomatoes, sugar beets, peaches,
plums, oranges, almonds, walnuts, cattle, milk, and eggs
all being produced in major quantities. A great deal of
employment is generated in packing and processing and the
servicing of farms.

Here much of the agriculture is metropolitan. Sacramento, Stockton, Modesto, Fresno, and Bakersfield all are in
the valley and serve agricultural functions. Only in the
northern part are metropolitan centers not within accessible
distance to rural people.

About one-sixth of the nonmetro and rural metro population was Mexican-American in 1970, with an additional 4
percent of blacks and Asians. But these percentages do not
reflect the real degree of ethnic aspects of agriculture in
the daily life of the valley. Resident hired farm workers
alone outnumber farm operators by better than 2 to 1, but
among Mexican-Americans the ratio of hired workers to farm
operators is 10 to 1. Thousands of migrant seasonal workers
are also used who come into the area from other U.S. areas
or from Mexico. The Central Valley, along with other similar
California farm sections, such as the Coastal Valleys and
the Imperial Valley, is the center of farm labor unionization efforts, land-redistribution movements (160-acre irrigation limitation), and legal challenges to the thrust of
land-grant university research policies. In sum, there is a
much greater degree of social activism relating to agriculture and rural ethnic divisions than is common in most
other regions.

In addition to farming, there are oil and gas fields in
the southern part of the valley and a number of military
bases that add to rural employment.

The Mormon Country

Several subregions of the West lend themselves to characterization as distinctive rural environments other than
the Central Valley of California and the Rio Grande Valley
and Southwest already discussed. In the case of the Mormon
Country the unifying theme is not so much physiographic and
economic as cultural.

After the Latter Day Saints or Mormons made their trek
to the Salt Lake Basin in 1847, they soon began a systematic
series of settlements in other parts of Utah and in south-

eastern Idaho. Except for mining developments, most later settlers crossing the continent bypassed the Mormon areas. The result today is that in an area embracing almost all of Utah and southeastern Idaho, plus smaller neighboring portions of southwestern Wyoming and eastern Nevada, the great majority of the population is actively Mormon or of Mormon background.

This fact has secular significance in several ways, especially in regard to social conservatism and rural demography. If there is a Mormon ethic it surely includes self-reliance, hard work, education, and the importance of the family. It also manifests itself in political conservatism, a somewhat negative view of the role of federal government and of labor unions, a conservative view of the societal role of women, and abstinence from tobacco and alcoholic beverages. Some of these traits are not necessarily different from those of many other non-Mormon westerners in the Mountain States, but seem to be stronger among the Mormons.

The most striking demographic feature of the Mormon areas is the relatively high birthrate and the near immunity of this population from the substantial reductions in childbearing that almost all other segments of rural and small-town America have made since the early 1960s. The nonmetro Mormon counties (with a population of about six hundred thousand) have as many births as they did in 1961, when the national number of births peaked, and have three-and-a-half times as many births as deaths, with about 1.8 percent annual natural increase. The nonmetro U.S. population as a whole had an annual natural increase of only .6 percent in the 1970s, whereas births have decreased by one-fourth since 1960, and the ratio of births to deaths is only 1.5 to 1. The Mormon areas, therefore, have a youthful age structure with a large potential for natural growth, even without in-migration. In consequence, they have a much greater need for continued job development if they are to avoid the necessity of exporting their youth to other areas as they enter the labor force.

The economy of this subregion has been basically agricultural, with a mixture of ranching, dairying, irrigated crops, and dry farming. But there has been a surge in mining, particularly fuels--coal, oil, gas, and uranium. This industry brings in outsiders, as it did in the past at the older copper and coal mines. In addition, there is a growth of recreation business in the unique scenic areas of southern Utah (e.g., Lake Powell, Zion National Park, and Bryce Canyon National Park) that attracts many people from

other regions. Altogether, the Mormon Country had a net in-
movement of nearly fifty thousand people from 1970 to 1978,
a factor that leads to a gradual dilution of the cultural
homogeneity of the population. When combined with the high
rate of retained natural growth, the Mormon Country has had
a near explosive nonmetro growth of 25 percent in the years
from 1970 to 1978, with every part of the area affected.
Overall density is still low, for there are vast nearly
uninhabited arid areas, but the impact on the environment
and culture is high, especially when the likelihood of
further similar growth rates is considered.

North Pacific Coast

Large-scale timber industry is the most characteristic
feature of the western portions of Washington and Oregon
and northwestern California. This area containing only 3
percent of the nation's land surface has two-fifths of all
the growing stock of softwood timber and one-half of the
national volume of softwood sawtimber that is cut. The
mountains and hills of the Coast Ranges and the Cascades
are covered with fir, spruce, hemlock, and (in California)
redwood, made especially verdant by the moist and comparatively mild marine climate. The combination of topography,
location, climate, and forests has produced a distinctive
regional setting.

The Willamette River Valley and Puget Sound Lowlands
provide an axis of settlement, farming, and transportation
in an otherwise difficult terrain. Some of the subregion's
2 million nonmetro people have access to the large Seattle-
Tacoma and Portland metro areas, but about one-half are in
distinctly distant and self-contained rural and small-town
communities. The timber industry of the Northwest has suffered from periodic recessions and the closure of smaller
operations. Despite sustained-yield forestry practices,
imbalances of supply, demand, and mill capacity still occur,
producing local or more general bouts of unemployment and
underemployment. Such a trend is now officially predicted
for sizable areas of Orgeon in coming years.

Nevertheless, the nonmetro population of the subregion
has been growing rapidly—with a 22 percent increase and
260,000 in-migrants from 1970 to 1978. Some of the increase
is stimulated by economic growth but some is an excellent
example of the infusion of metro people into a rural and
small-town area for noneconomic style-of-life considerations. For example, many urban Californians have moved into
southwestern Oregon, despite their inability to avoid some

unemployment or to earn as much as they did formerly. Many
have the desire to shift from former wage and salary work
to self-employment.

Some of the rural areas are attracting retired people,
such as the islands and shore areas of Puget Sound, the
valleys and coastal areas of southwest Oregon, and even
localities on the drier eastern side of the Cascades. Probably no state has made so plain its desire not to attract
in-migration and rapid population growth as has Oregon, and
environmental concerns about growth are generally high
throughout the North Pacific Coast. But the subregion is
growing nevertheless, and with its "Cloud Belt" status it
exemplifies the fact that Sunbelt is a very imperfect
synonym for population growth.

BIBLIOGRAPHY

Beale, Calvin L. "The Changing Nature of Nonmetropolitan
    Employment." In New Directions in Urban-Rural Migration:
    The Population Turnaround in Rural America, edited by
    David L. Brown and John M. Wardwell, chapter 2. New
    York: Academic Press, 1980.
_____. "A Further Look at Nonmetropolitan Population
    Growth Since 1970." American Journal of Agricultural
    Economics 5 (1976): 953-58.
_____. "The Recent Shift of United States Population
    to Nonmetropolitan Areas 1950-75." International
    Regional Science Review 2 (Winter 1977): 113-22.
_____, and Fuguitt, Glenn V. "The New Pattern of Non-
    metropolitan Population Change." In Social Demography,
    edited by Karl E. Taueber, Larry L. Bumpass, and James
    A. Sweet, pp. 157-77. New York: Academic Press, 1978.
Hines, Fred K.; Brown, David L.; and Zimmer, John M. "Social
    and Economic Characteristics of the Population in Metro-
    politan and Nonmetropolitan Counties, 1970." Agricultur-
    al Economic Report, no. 272. Economic Research Service,
    U.S. Department of Agriculture. Washington, D.C.: 1975.
McCarthy, Kevin, and Morrison, Peter A. "The Changing Demo-
    graphic and Economic Structure of Nonmetropolitan Areas
    in the 1970s." Report P-6062. Santa Monica, Calif.:
    Rand Corporation, 1978.
Tucker, C. Jack. "Changing Patterns of Migration Between
    Metropolitan and Nonmetropolitan Areas in the United
    States: Recent Evidence." Demography 13 (1976): 435-44.

U.S. Bureau of the Census. Current Population Reports,
    series P-25, no. 873. Washington, D.C.: U.S. Government
    Printing Office, 1980.
_____. 1970 Census of Population, vol. 1, pt. A.
    Washington, D.C.: U.S. Government Printing Office, 1972.
Zuiches, James J., and Brown, David L. "The Changing Char-
    acter of the Nonmetropolitan Population, 1950-1975." In
    Rural U.S.A.: Persistence and Change, edited by Thomas
    R. Ford, chapter 4. Ames, Iowa: Iowa State University
    Press, 1978.

James J. Zuiches

2

Residential Preferences in the United States

INTRODUCTION

In the history of population redistribution in the United States, the migration reversal of the 1970s, with rural areas gaining migrants from urban areas, is comparable to the dramatic reversal in fertility trends caused by the baby boom of the 1940s and 1950s. Taeuber (1972: 72) summarized the pre-1970 history: "the dominant geographic fact in the demography of the coterminous United States in the twentieth century has been metropolitan concentration." In the 1960s 2 million people moved to metro counties; by 1970, 148 million people lived there, but the majority within metro areas lived outside the central cities in the suburban ring. Although the deconcentration around central cities continued into the 1970s and suburban areas gained 5.4 million people at the expense of central cities, the long-term trend reversed. From March 1970 to March 1978, nonmetro areas enjoyed a net in-migration of just over 3 million people (U.S. Bureau of the Census 1975, 1978).

This revival of population growth in nonmetro America has contributed to a resurgence of interest in the migration process. The decline since 1957 in fertility rates has also increased the importance of migration as a factor in community growth. Finally, alternative explanations for the migration turnaround, not easily explained by classical cost/benefit models, have postulated that personal preferences for community attributes may reinforce economic motivations. In this context, preference explanations for migration have been increasingly important and the last eight

This report is based on work supported by the Michigan Agricultural Experiment Station, Project no. 1160 (journal article no. 9734), contributing to Western Regional Project W-118, the Center for the Study of Metropolitan Problems, NIMH, and the Economic Development Division, ESCS, USDA.

to nine years have seen extensive outpouring of empirical research.

The literature on migration is filled with theoretical models of movement among regions, metro areas, and labor markets. Ritchey (1976) has classified most of these studies as labor mobility studies, dependent on ecologically aggregated statistics. As macroanalytic models they are part of the tradition of gravity studies, intervening opportunity research, and place-to-place stream analysis. Alternatively, microanalytic models of mobility depend upon individual statistics and focus on the compositional selectivities associated with migration. In his review of explanations of migration, however, Ritchey suggested a third orientation: its source of data is often a survey of individuals or families, but locational or geographic characteristics are included as critical aspects of "the decision-making process of migration and a critical determinant of migration and its direction" (Ritchey, 1976: 397). It is within this "cognitive behavioral approach" that the rapidly increasing literature on residential preferences and migration fits. Although searching for the cause and explanations of migration in attitudinal data has not been a traditional or predominant mode of analysis, as classic economic constraints to mobilty decrease (Carpenter 1977), the decision-making phase of the migration process takes on new complexion.

In a recent review of the research literature on residential preferences, mobility expectations, and actual migration, Zuiches (1980) noted that no study prior to 1971 treated the issues of migration plans and destination selection more than superficially. Why the merits of a decison model that included migration expectations, destination selection, and actual mobility were not realized may be very much the result of data-bound theoretical models. Earlier models of migration behavior were guided by a place-to-place focus, an ecological/economic theory of locational imbalances primarily with respect to sustenance needs, and based on aggregated data from census sources. Even the human capital models often failed to measure the social costs and benefits of migration in favor of more easily operationalized economic costs and benefits. Recent studies by DaVanzo (1976) and Williams and McMillen (1980), however, have introduced a social variant, location-specific capital, with noneconomic operational indicators.

PREFERENCE MODELS

Although only a handful of studies have incorporated preferences, moving plans, and migration into a research
design, the cognitive-behavioral model provides a theoretical basis for designing such a study. The decision to move
can be conceptually divided into a phase of evaluation of
one's current residence, in which a threshold of dissatisfaction may be reached bringing the household to consider
the possibility of a move. The second stage involves the
search and selection procedures and includes a comparative
evaluation of alternative sites. It is at this stage that
locational preferences play a role in the selection process,
and finally, a decision to move is made. (See Speare et al.
1974, for elaborated discussion of this model in intraurban
mobility.) The migration literature shows in every case
that expectations for mobility are associated with higher
probabilities for future mobility, in contrast to a lower
probability of a move for those not expecting one. Similarly, one might argue that a preference to live elsewhere
than one's current residence would be associated with
expectations to move and future actual mobility. In classic
syllogistic form, preferences for residential relocation
ought to be associated with future mobility.

In two recent papers (Heaton et al. 1979), such a model
has been tested and preference status, that is, a discrepancy between current and preferred size-location characteristics of residential location, plays an important role in
the migration decision-making process. This is in addition
to the effect of satisfaction with one's community and the
usual selectivities associated with migration expectations:
age, length of residence, home ownership, educational
attainment, and size of current residence (Fredrickson et
al. 1980). But the crucial issue of the role of preferences
in population redistribution remains: how do locational
preferences get translated into redistribution among city
size-classes, regions, and metro-nonmetro sectors?

Wardwell (1977) has proposed three preference-based
hypotheses to explain nonmetro growth and the turnaround.
The first suggests that preferences for rural areas are
related to age and retirement plans, so that rural growth
becomes a function of changing population composition. In
the second, preferences for urban areas are seen as de-
clining--perhaps as a result of negative conditions in
those areas and the presumably positive features of rural
areas--with a resultant shift of population outward. In

the third hypothesis, preexisting preferences for rural areas are now being satisfied as the structural constraints to living in rural communities are reduced.

Although Wardwell discounted the first hypothesis on the basis of the mixed results from recent cross-sectional surveys (Dillman and Dobash 1972; Carpenter 1975; Fuguitt and Zuiches 1975), he may have been a bit premature and his original hypothesis merits reconsideration. Wardwell also suggested that the recent structural changes mitigating the historical disadvantage of nonmetro communities in employ-ment, income, services, and facilities may have increased the importance of preexisting long-term preferences for such areas, permitting them to be satisfied under condi-tions of greater locational flexibility. In his discussion, Wardwell built upon the argument of Mazek and Laird (1974) who postulate that, under a condition of income convergence across city size-classes (or regions), long-held latent preferences for small cities and rural areas will be satis-fied. They argue that until this convergence occurs, there is an unavoidable trade-off between income and quality of life. The assumption that preferences are long-term and latent, however, has been shown to be false by Zuiches and Rieger (1978).

A more dynamic relationship between city size and pre-ferences has been suggested by Price (1978). When prefer-ences for a larger city size exist and size of current place of residence does not increase, out-migration from smaller places occurs up the size hierarchy and a momentum of large-city growth develops. As such growth occurs, those in the large city whose taste had not changed while the city grew, will begin to depart, partially attentuating the growth. If preferences are stable and population in the city increases, residents with smaller city preferences migrate down the hierarchy. This downward redistribution, likewise, aggravates the growth of smaller places until new nuclei or settlements are created. "The net effect will be for all existing settlements to grow larger and more close-ly spaced in the hierarchy, and for the bottom of the hier-archy to be regenerated by new settlement" (Price, 1978: 78).

Price notes that this model assumes free migration without the constraints and inertia associated with oppor-tunity structures, community integration, the effects on family and friends, and the social and psychological costs of a move. Yet it adds to the complexity of migration and preferences discussion by a consideration of the effect of migration and a new residential experience upon the migrant, of the effect of growth on the long-term residents, and on movement up and down the size hierarchy by primary and return migrants. It is in the decomposition of households by residential history and growth context as well as compositional characteristics that additional insights concerning future migration and distribution patterns may develop.

This chapter proposes to organize what we know about the relationship between locational preferences and migration, and will consider the role of preferences in explanations of the the urban-rural reversal in migration and the implications for future redistribution of population in the United States. The chapter is organized to show historical trends, where available, in as much geographical detail as possible, and to highlight the compositional characteristics of those preferring and moving to rural areas. After a discussion of the future redistribution anticipated by this body of research, the potential consequences for rural areas will be considered. This research will not formally test hypotheses, but by pulling together evidence from multiple studies, by a process of replication and triangulation, the general substantiation of results will unfold. A critical evaluation of each piece of research is precluded in this report, but comments and caveats will be noted where appropriate.

PREFERENCES IN THE CLASSES-OF-GROWTH TYPOLOGY

As Brown and Beale noted in the previous chapter, nonmetro counties in the United States are remarkable for their diversity of rates of growth, even in the context of the recent reversal in net migration and growth rates. Although the turnaround is apparent in almost all subregions for 1970 to 1974 (Beale and Fuguitt 1978), detailed analysis by county continues to show areas of continuing decline, of growth in the 1960s and decline in the 1970s, of reversal between the 1960s and 1970s, of modest continued growth of the two time periods, and of rapid growth. Not all of these specific contexts have had the good fortune of being included in recent social demographic research projects. Similarly, although the adjacency effect has been considered in demographic analysis, survey researchers have rarely defined the county locations so precisely, and, finally, a consideration of regional variations is often possible only by looking at statewide studies in particular regions.

In the typology of growth, a few studies have been completed and the character of areal growth will be noted in the discussion. Sofranko and Williams (1980) surveyed residents and in-migrants of rapid growth and reversal counties, and Campbell et al. (1977) have recently completed a study of Ozark counties experiencing long-term modest growth. Numerous rural sociological studies have involved surveys of residents in turnaround counties (Rieger et al. 1973; Ploch 1978); but for studies of counties continuing to decrease, one must draw on the past studies of rural sociologists (Cowhig et al. 1960; Yoesting and Bohlen 1968). No research has been found on the one hundred counties that shifted from growth in the 1960s to decline in the 1970s; but in an attempt to evaluate the consequences of rapid growth through migration, Clay and Price (1979) provide some comparisons of counties experiencing negative, low, and high migration rates.

From the perspective of most preferences studies, the typology is simply not appropriate, but it does provide a reasonable basis for comparison with other studies and will be acknowledged where possible. The crucial classification of residential location in most survey research of urban/rural or metro/nonmetro does permit extensive analysis by this category. Most of the following discussion will focus on the metro/nonmetro typology, and size-of-place as a subdivision within this dichotomy.

A problem with such political or statistical definitions of geographic units, as in metro/nonmetro, is the inability to relate census or political geography to the mental definition of space. The geographers have done extensive work on mental maps of the United Sates and the individual perception of the spatial organization of places (Gould and White 1974; Fuller and Chapman 1974), but have not incorporated into their studies the relationship of these mental images to migration. An exception is the study of White (1974) in Kentucky. White surveyed residents of twenty-five cities and asked them to rate the residential desirability of all the cities, except one's own. These microevaluations were combined into an aggregate score of preference value that was assigned to each city. In a multivariate analysis of in-migration rates during the 1960s, the aggregate preference index was the best variable predicting urban in-migration. Other variables included population size, income, employment levels and knowledge and experience in the cities. The integration of subjective, individual evaluations of a place and aggregated, demograph-

ic analysis and the demonstration of a strong relationship
strengthens the argument for use of such attitudinal
variables in other contexts.

THE MEASUREMENT OF LOCATIONAL PREFERENCES

The initial research on residential preferences developed
to explain the discrepancy between popular (Gallup, Harris,
and others) survey results on preferences and the historical
migration patterns of metro concentration, suburban deconcentration, and nonmetro population losses due to migration.
Little rigorous research had been done prior to 1971, yet
policy suggestions and recommendations were often based on
responses to questions such as the Gallup Poll asked: "If
you could live anywhere in the U.S. that you wanted to,
would you prefer a city, suburban area, small town or farm?"
From 1948 through 1978, polls using similar questions showed: (1) less than one-fourth of the respondents preferred
cities, (2) most respondents would like to live in small
towns and rural areas, and (3) the proportion preferring
rural areas exceeded that currently resident there. It is
this anomaly (see Fuguitt and Zuiches, 1975, for the detail concerning studies up to 1971) that continues in national surveys conducted in 1976 and 1978 that raised the
inital concern. Why was the growth of suburban areas within
a metro context not revealed by preference surveys? And why
were the seemingly favored rural areas not experiencing
rapid growth in the 1960s? The fact that there was in the
1970s a net migration to the nonmetro counties does not, in
itself, justify the use of such unidimensional questions. A
single, undifferentiated question on size-of-place preferred
fails to capture the complexity of locational behavior.
Such a question particularly fails to distinguish a key
relational characteristic of places people claim to prefer,
that is, the proximity to other places, especially to a
large central city, but also to smaller or medium-sized
cities as well. The introduction of a distance-qualifier
question also redefines the preference into a spatial
framework that could be comparable to political or census
definitions of geographic space, such as metro versus
nonmetro counties.
    In a statewide survey of Wisconsin (Zuiches and Fuguitt
1972) in 1971, respondents were asked a size-of-place question similar to that of Gallup and the Population Commission, and a proximity question, that is, preferences for

residence within thirty miles of a large city. The results
broadly agreed with those of Gallup, the Population Commission, and others. The distance-qualifying question, however, showed that well over one-half of the 79 percent
preferring to live in small towns and rural areas stated
that they would like their residence to be within thirty
miles of a city of more than 50,000 population. This finding sheds considerable light on the paradox noted above:
the realization of these preferences would result in a net
movement out of central cities and nonmetro areas into
metro rings, which is consistent with the overall trends
that prevailed in Wisconsin at least through 1970.

The definition of a metro ring as an area within a
thirty-mile radius from the central city provided a rough
correspondence with Wisconsin Standard Metropolitan Statistical Areas in 1970. In this way, the preference results
could then be compared with the migration and growth rates
of metro and nonmetro counties, and of size-classes within
these counties. An additional refinement, used only in the
Wisconsin study, was the attempt to define suburbs as the
census-designated Urbanized Area around a central city.

Although the complexity of metro and urbanized areas
is irrelevant to most respondents, only by providing
equivalent measures can survey data be applied usefully to
project population redistribution trends. This is the crux
of the criticism of most residential preferences surveys.
They fail to adequately operationalize the statistically,
politically, or socially defined units whose demographic
change these studies intend to discuss. The statistically
defined units, especially SMSAs, are typically very carefully defined for current residence, but large cities and
suburbs are then assumed to represent the totality of a
metro county or counties, and small towns and rural areas
assumed to be found only in nonmetro counties. This is the
inherent problem of all the popular surveys as well as that
of the Population Commission (Mazie and Rawlings 1972), the
Continuous National Survey (Morgan 1977; Taylor et al.
1979), and the HUD Survey (1978). "Suburbs" as a locational
concept, likewise, "has never been given more than an ad
hoc definition by researchers using the term" (Hadden 1969).
Finally, what is an appropriate definition of "rural"? In
these surveys, the use of terms such as "rural," "open
country," "farm," and "outside of cities and towns," implies both a locational concept and a density component
in the definition. Few studies directly address the density
of residential units, especially in the nonmetro areas,

although Dillman and Dobash (1972) include density implicitly in their questions.

Finally, the definition of size-of-place needs consideration. For large cities, medium-sized cities, and small
cities, one can specify a size range to be associated with
the question. But what are the dividing lines among a small
city, a town, and a village, or between a village and open
country? Although most of the studies have specified size
ranges for each category, occasionally categories are
merged with some unforeseen results, for example, Sofranko
and Williams (1980) categorize all areas of less than 1,000
population as villages, effectively excluding analysis of
small aggregations in contrast to open country residential
locations. Another approach, used by DeJong and Sell (1977),
is to name a city in a given size class for reference purposes. Unfortunately, such a strategy means that all the
other connotations and psychological impacts besides size
associated with a given place may affect the preference
response. For example, DeJong found an exceptionally low
preference (one-half of what might have been expected,
based on nationwide surveys) for medium-sized cities,
referenced as "about size of Harrisburg, Bethlehem, or
Johnstown." Because Johnstown had been losing population
for five decades, Harrisburg for two, and Bethlehem for
one, in addition to being identified in the public mind as
Steeltown, U.S.A., their use as reference cities may have
affected the responses for that size category.

Even the two alternative forms of questions most closely
approximating the census and political definitions are not
truly equivalent and simple extrapolation from these is
risky. In a series of studies that approached the issue of
residential location from a community perspective, Dillman
and Dobash (1972), Carpenter (1975), Ryan et al. (1974),
and Christenson (1974) specified community as a county or
region with an identifiable city of a specific size, suburbs, and a descriptor for the amount of open country in
the area. Counties were likewise defined as metro, semiur-
ban, or rural. Although this unit of analysis is perhaps
congruent within metro-nonmetro definitions of counties, it
fails to permit respondents to select locations within each
county context. For example, in the Washington study
(Dillman and Dobash 1972), choosing the largest metro area
(Seattle and King County) seems to foreclose selecting a
rural location in that county, yet in 1970, 7.5 percent of
King County was rural; similarly, in all the metro counties
of Washington state in 1970, 33 percent of the population

of Washington state in 1970, 33 percent of the population
did not live in an identifiable place (U.S. Bureau of the
Census 1971) yet the county-unit preference strategy precludes
designating such a setting as one's first preference.

Fuguitt and Zuiches (1975), on the other hand, developed the proximity-to-a-large-city question as a surrogate
for the metro county definition. In addition, respondents
were asked to define their current residence using the same
categories of size-of-place and location with respect to
a large city. In this way, comparisons of current and preferred residence were in the same metric, although there
is still a problem of equivalence with census definitions.
In an evaluation of respondent ability to identify their
current residence by size and location, only 6 percent
misreported the distance to a large city by more than ten
miles, and only 14 percent misreported the size class in
which they resided by more than one class interval. Moreover, most of these deviant responses were plausible as,
for example, some who reported being in large cities appeared to be in rural territory adjacent to a large city
(Fuguitt and Zuiches 1975).

The extrapolation of these survey results to census
categories of places, however, must be done with caution.
While respondents are able to respond with a meaningful
understanding of their current place of residence, the use
of a thirty-mile ring around a central city to indicate a
metro area may overbound or underbound the metro areas.
Individual metro areas likely to be underbounded by the
thirty-mile ring are New York, Los Angeles, or Chicago, but
the overall effect is to include within the thirty-mile
radius a large proportion of nonmetro residents. Based upon
the 1972 survey evaluation, in which coding by the National
Opinion Research Center of Survey Research Center belt
status of each county was compared to the factual location
of a respondent by the thirty-mile ring, only 3.3 percent
of the metro county residents lived outside the thirty-mile
ring. Overbounding clearly occurred insofar as 37 percent
of the respondents actually lived within thirty miles of a
metro central city. This overbounding effect may be a partial explanation for the fact that neither the Wisconsin,
Pennsylvania (Zuiches and Fuguitt 1972; DeJong and Sell
1975), nor the 1972 national surveys (Fuguitt and Zuiches
1975) served as forecasts or leading indicators of the
turnaround in migration patterns.

PREFERENCE TRENDS

Keeping in mind the issues raised concerning the measurement of locational preferences, we can consider a reasonably long series of size-of-place surveys, in which the
questions are roughly comparable, insofar as they ask for
preferences that include large cities, suburbs, small city,
towns, or villages, and rural areas or farms. The results
(see Table 2.1) of all these surveys continue to reflect
basically the same pattern over the past thirty years: (1)
less than one-fourth of the respondents prefer a large
city, (2) most respondents would like to live in small
towns and rural areas, (3) the proportion holding this
latter preference exceeds that currently residing there,
and (4) the proportion preferring suburbs is considerably
less than the 38 to 40 percent resident in the metro area
surrounding a central city. Yet, it is precisely this
sector of metro counties that is experiencing the largest
volume of in-migrants, although not the highest migration
rates. Even the HUD survey, which comes quite close to
equivalence with the metro definition, fails to permit
respondents to choose a rural area within the so-called
suburban area about a city. In sum, the clearest point in
Table 2.1 is the consistency in responses to a given set of
size-class questions over the period of time in which the
migration reversal occurred. Based on these surveys, one
would have a difficult time drawing inferences about the
future redistribution patterns.

Alternatively, a consideration of the preference surveys that include the distance relationship to larger cities provides a closer approximation to metro-nonmetro
identification of preferred areas.

Earlier research (Zuiches and Fuguitt 1972; Fuguitt
and Zuiches 1975) demonstrated that the commonly found
preference for living in rural areas and small towns
required modification to include proximity to larger
cities. In Table 2.2, both the size of place and locational preferences are included for the 1972 and 1974
national surveys. There is a substantial degree of consistency between the preferred distribution at the two
dates. In both surveys 20 percent of the respondents
lived in central cities with more than 500,000 population,
but only 9 percent preferred such a location. The medium-
sized cities contained less than 25 percent of the respondents and were preferred by about 15 percent. More than a
majority at both dates preferred living within commuting
range of a large central city, though the proportion

Table 2.1. A Comparison of Surveys of Residential Preferences in the United States from 1948 to 1978

| Preferred Residence | Roper 1948 | Gallup | | | | | Population Commission 1971 | Research Analysis Corp. 1976 | HUD[a] 1978 |
		1966	1968	1970	1972	1976			
	%	%	%	%	%	%	%	%	%
Cities	15	22	18	18	13	13	17[d]	8	24
Suburbs	20	28	25	26	31	29	18[d]	25	26
Small towns	41[b]	31	29	31	32	21	30[d]	30[e]	23
Rural areas	24	18[c]	27[c]	24[c]	23[c]	37	34[d]	36[e]	25
No opinion, other	0	1	1	1	1	0	1	1	2
Total	100	100	100	100	100	100	100	100	100

Source: 1948 Roper study cited in Lee et al., 1971, p. 33; Gallup results in American Institute of Public Opinion 1970, and National Area Development Institute 1973; Population Commission results from internal memorandum of the Population Commission 1971; Research Analysis Corp. data supplied to author; HUD 1978.

[a]Large and medium size city combined; medium size city and small city town or village in suburbs combined; small city, town or village not in suburbs, and rural area.

[b]Includes respondents preferring small cities and small towns. The Roper question was: "If you had a choice, where would you like best to live--in the country, a small town, a small city, a suburb, a large city?"

[c]Farm used instead of rural area in the Gallup question, which was: "If you could live anywhere in the U.S. that you wanted to, would you prefer a city, suburban area, small town or farm?"

[d]Large and medium cities combined; suburbs of large and medium cities combined; small cities and small towns combined; and farm and open country combined in this table. The Population Commission question was: "Where would you prefer to live? On a farm, open country (not on a farm), in a small town, in a small city, in a medium size city, in a large city, in a suburb of a medium size city, in a suburb of a large city?"

[e]"Assuming you could live anywhere you wanted, where would you prefer to live most--in a big city, in a suburb of a big city, in a small city or in a rural or farm area?"

Table 2.2. Actual and Preferred Residential Location in the United States, 1972 and 1974

Type of Location	Actual Residence		Preferred Residence	
	1972	1974	1972	1974
	%	%	%	%
City more than 500,000	20	19	9	9
City 50,000 to 500,000	24	22	16	13
Within 30 miles of a city with 50,000+ population:				
Small city	23	25	31	25
Rural	11	13	24	27
More than 30 miles from a city with 50,000+ population:				
Small city	12	15	10	13
Rural	9	6	9	14
Total	100	100	100	100
Number[a]	1,447	1,476	1,447	1,476

Source: National Opinion Research Center General Social Survey with added preference questions, conducted in March 1974; NORC Amalgam Survey conducted in November 1972, reported in Fuguitt and Zuiches 1975.

[a]Excludes 34 respondents in 1972 and 8 in 1974 with missing data on preferences.

preferring smaller cities in this location declined in 1974 and the proportion preferring rural areas increased. Similarly, the proportion preferring rural areas and small cities more remote from large urban centers is slightly larger at the later date, increasing the preference for more distant settings from 20 to 26 percent. The increase in preference for living more than thirty miles from a large city, roughly equivalent to being outside of a metro area, is very suggestive in that it parallels the new non-metro growth trend. Whether this difference between the surveys is real or a result of sampling variation or ques-

tion wording, however, is uncertain. Conceptually, both
surveys sought the same preference information. Practically, in 1972 two questions, on size and location, were asked; but in 1974 a single question with size-of-place and
proximity evaluated simultaneously was used. In 1972, preferences were sought with a separate question in which
respondents were asked to rank three major alternative
categories, and the distribution for first-ranked preferences was similar to that for the single question in 1974.
Thus, 19 percent preferred a large city; 55 percent, near
locations; and 26 percent far locations. Because the respondents in 1974 were aware of all their options for preferred location before responding, including location
near or away from a large city, this may well explain the
differences from the two-question set of 1972. Obviously,
it is difficult to discover the exact preferred geographic
distribution of the population with a single set of questions, but the consistency over time and with various
questions is evident.

The net effect of redistribution according to preferences would be a surge in suburban growth around central
cities, an associated loss within cities of more than
50,000, and a slight increase at the periphery of cities in
more rural locations. Such a shift in overall population
would be reasonably consistent with the trends actually
reported for the 1970-74 period.

In a detailed analysis in which size of current residence is controlled (Zuiches and Fuguitt 1976), a location
within thirty miles of a medium-sized city is the modal
preferred category for every residential location except
the more isolated villages and rural areas, for which a
small city and its periphery is the modal preference.

In addition to these national surveys, state surveys by
Friedman (1974) and DeJong and Sell (1977) indicated for
Wisconsin and Pennsylvania a preference for residence
within the commuting ring for large cities. Surveys in
Washington (Dillman and Dobash 1972), Arizona (Carpenter
1975), Indiana (Ryan et al. 1974), and North Carolina
(Christenson 1974) have focused on the preferred community
a respondent would like to live in or near. In Dillman
(1973) these studies are summarized: all indicate a lack of
preference for the small, remote communities and a strong
preference for rural areas within proximity to a larger
place, especially to a city with a population of less than
50,000.

REGIONAL PREFERENCES

An often overlooked but yet pertinent part of the structure
of locational preferences is the regional preferences of the
population. Only two national surveys in the last decade
have inquired about regional relocation, Morgan (1978), in
an analysis of the Continuous National Survey of 1973, and
Research Analysis Corporation in its 1976 survey "Mood of
America." Morgan's discussion of regional redistribution of
those who wanted to move showed an overwhelming increase in
the Mountain states and Pacific states. Losing regions were
the North Central and mid-Atlantic. New England and the
East and West South Central regions would remain essentially stable.

In a reanalysis of the "Mood of America" survey, based
on a 1976 telephone survey of 2,005 households, the pattern
of regional preferences is roughly similar. (As noted above,
popular surveys tend not to be congruent with census definitions of regions, size-of-place, etc., but they are in-
ternally consistent and the distribution by actual residence approximates census distribution.) In Table 2.3, preferences are greatest for the Rocky Mountain and Far West
regions, with nearly a doubling of the population, if only
preferences were taken into account. The only other region
to show net positive preference is the Southwest. The
Northeast and Midwest areas would decline dramatically. A
more constrained distributuon is presented in the last column of the table. Here only those who answered "yes" about
"plans to move in the next few years" were redistributed
according to preferences. The results are even more consistent than with those of Morgan. Whereas the redistribution
would continue toward the Mountain and Far West states, it
would be at the expense of the Northeast, Southeast, and
Midwest. This potential redistribution may be in accord
with other surveys and looks reasonable, yet it implies a
redistribution of 8 million persons "in the next few years,"
three times the net regional redistribution from 1970 to
1975. It also fails to echo the South-North migration
reversal. Does this imply a slowing of the net migration
gain in the South or is it simply a result of the regional
definitions? It may remain a problem of question wording
and definition, insofar as the South is the destination of
choice of migrants up through 1978 (Biggar 1979).

Even though this regional analysis does not seem to be
predictive of moves and redistribution in the past few
years, the introduction of regional preference questions

Table 2.3. Regional Preferences and Redistribution Using
Plan to Move, 1976

Region	Actual Residence	Preferred Residence	Preferred and Plan to Move
	%	%	%
Northeast	27	19	26
Southeast	22	20	20
Midwest	26	18	25
Southwest	9	12	9
Rocky Mountain and Far West	16	31	20
Total	100	100	100
Number[a]	1,872	1,872	1,872

Source: Calculated from data provided by Research Analysis
Corp. 1976.

[a]Seven percent with no preference were excluded.

ought to be considered in future surveys. As regional and
urban/rural redistribution will probably continue, especially in the South, additional research should focus on
the origins of in-migrants and contributions of preferences
to this migration.

COMMUNITY AND SUBSTATE REGIONAL STUDIES

The national and statewide studies provide estimates of the
parameters of preference mobility, but it is at the local
community level that these preferences are lived and at
which the effects of in- or out-migration are most likely
to be felt. A number of small-scale studies have been completed that focus on preferences of specific subgroups of
the population. For example, the out-migration of rural
youth has often been analyzed in terms of expectations for
mobility and actual migration to urban areas. That rural
youth also prefer urban destinations is a reasonable assumption and supported by numerous studies. This section
will begin with preference surveys and the consequences for
mobility and include cases in which expectations and
mobility, but not preferences, are discussed.

A major study reported by Hansen (1973) interviewed
(in 1969 to 1971) rural youth in eastern Kentucky, Mexican-
American youth in south Texas, Indians in New Mexico and
Arizona, and whites and blacks in southern Mississippi. In
all settings, the preferences for out-migration to urban
areas were quite high even though no economic advantage (in
wage rates) was expected. In the case of economic improvements, the proportion who would prefer to leave their
current residence varies from 55 to 81 percent.

Although Hansen does not provide sufficient information
to indicate the demographic changes in the areas studied,
the counties appear to have been experiencing net migration
losses. Two rural community studies in Michigan (Cowhig et
al. 1960, and Rieger et al. 1973), however, did focus on
counties experiencing heavy out-migration and the preferences of rural youth. In the mid-Michigan survey, whereas
61 percent expected to leave the community, 40 percent (or
two-thirds of those expecting to leave) were not eager to
leave; in fact 82 percent preferred a small town or open
country residence. Although no follow-up study was completed, one might anticipate even higher levels of out-migration
than were expected or preferred. In the Hamilton, Iowa
study (a demographically stable county) Bohlen and Wakeley
(1950) and Yoesting and Bohlen (1968) found that of those
intending to leave over 80 percent did so in one year, of
those not intending to leave 21 percent left, and of those
undecided 40 percent also left.

A similar result was found in the Ontonagon County
study (Rieger et al. 1973). Although nearly one-half of the
1957/58 graduating cohort preferred the local size character
of their community and likewise were not eager to leave,
seven years later only 14 percent had not left the community, and one-half lived in urban areas. This study, however, not only followed the migrants (and stayers) but
also reinterviewed them about their preferences for different size classes of community, and added new cohorts at
each reinterview date. The relationships between preferences and migration over the life cycle have been analyzed
by Zuiches and Rieger (1978). In the longitudinal panel, it
is clear that residential redistribution is associated with
preferences and that previous attitudes are often modified
by urban and rural location experience. A process of return
migration is definitely occurring while preferences for
rural areas are increasing. Also, over the life cycle, an
increased congruence between preferred and actual location

seems to be taking place. In the intercohort comparisons, it is also evident that there is an increase in preferences for rural areas on the part of younger cohorts. This may be indicative of and contribute to the retention of rural youth in their home counties.

Finally, a series of southern studies, USDA Regional Research Project S-81, "Development of Human Resource Potentials of Rural Youth in the South and Their Patterns of Mobility" (Cosby and Howard 1976; Lever 1974; Stuart and Dunkelburger 1974), merit mention. The regional project involved a series of surveys from 1966 to 1972 of high-school students in east and south Texas, Alabama, Georgia, and South Carolina. Over the six-year period, a definite shift on the part of southern rural youth occurred in aspirations and mobility expectations away from urban areas toward rural areas. These changes took place for both whites and blacks and suggest a definite increase in the desire and plans of these youth to stay in rural areas. Whether such retention occurs will depend on multiple other factors determining migration, in addition to preferences, but such an attitudinal shift does seem to have preceded the migration turnaround. One might also point out that most of these counties were low-income counties similar to those in the northern Michigan studies.

POSTMIGRATION REVERSAL STUDIES

The impact of the turnaround in migration and the subsequent explanations, both structural and preference based, have generated new studies, primarily of reversal areas, in which in-migrants are compared with the local residents on sociodemographic characteristics and all subgroups are surveyed for migration preferences, expectations, and plans. In this way, some pertinent aspects of the growth potential of study areas are highlighted. Three studies, in particular, merit detailed attention: the Sofranko and Williams (1980) survey of growth counties in the North Central region, the Campbell et al. (1977) study of the Arkansas-McClellan Kerr river system, and Ploch's (1978) study of Maine. In thinking about these studies, a simple typology is quite useful (see Table 2.4). If one categorizes all respondents on the basis of prior migration, there are three types of residents: (1) current residents (both non-movers and local movers within the community), (2) return

migrants (prior residents, migration away and return), and
(3) primary migrants (new to the community, with limited or
no prior connections).

The growth of nonmetro areas is clearly a result of
primary in-migration, but yet a large part of this growth
is a result of return migration as well. In the North Central regional study, 25 percent of the recent in-migrants
were returning to a county they had lived in previously and
32 percent to a general area of prior residence. In the
Ozark region 43 percent were return migrants, and in Maine,
20 percent. Regardless of area, this is a significant increase over the 4 to 13 percent return migration noted by
Olsen and Kuehn (1974) in four rural areas of Arizona, the
Ozarks, Mississippi, and Arkansas during the 1965 to 1970
period. What is the potential for retaining both these
returnees and primary migrants?

In the North Central region, Sofranko and Williams
found that whereas most respondents found no difficulty in
adjusting (67 percent), there was a significant proportion
who preferred to live elsewhere and were also expecting to
move out of the county in the next three years. Only 9
percent of the long-term resident population expected to
move, but 22 percent of those with former metro residential
locations, and 31 percent of nonmetro-origin migrants anticipated another move. These former metro residents also
expressed a preference for a large town or city (36 percent). In trying to interpret this high level of dissatisfaction, the authors found that potential out-migration was
associated with in-migration for employment reasons. Forty
percent of the in-migrants had been attracted by the promise
of new or better jobs and continued to assess their job
opportunities and look for better employment. This group of
potentially mobile respondents also was characterized by
higher education and incomes. Thirty-eight percent of the
job seekers expected to move and preferred a big city. This
contrasts sharply with the 16 percent of in-migrants seeking
amenities who expect to move and 14 percent who preferred a
large city. Unfortunately, similar analysis has not been
completed on the return and primary migrants. Because the
return migrants are heavily tied to the community, however,
they might be expected to be less mobile than those in-
migrating for environmental or employment reasons.

Stuart (1980) compared the elderly migrants with younger
in-migrants and noted for the elderly that 59 percent had
ties to the area but only 39 percent of the younger. Similarly, although about equal proportions of the return mi-

Table 2.4. Migrant Status Typology by Reasons for Move, Characteristics of Migrants, and Mobility Plans

Migrant Status	Percentage Distribution	Reasons for Move	Migrant Characteristics	Percentage Expecting to Move	Percentage Preferring Urban Destination
Nonmover				6-9	
Local mover	c. 40	Job-related	Younger, in labor force	18-31	
Return migrant	c. 40	Amenities family, kin-related	Elderly, retired less well educated	10-24	14-16
Primary migrant	c. 20	Job-related	Young, educated labor force active white-collar occupants	36-45	36

Source: Sofranko and Williams 1980; Ploch 1978, 1979; Campbell et al. 1977; quoted in Zuiches, 1980: 182.

grants were elderly and young, the elderly were twice as likely to own a home, had larger social networks, and greater interest in the environmentally satisfying attributes of the community. Thus, only about 10 percent of the elderly migrants expect or prefer to live elsewhere. A similar response was found by Koebernick and Beegle (1978) in Clare County, Michigan: only 10 percent preferred another destination, but 20 percent have considered moving from Clare. Across the North Central growth counties, potential out-migration by the elderly is only one-half that of other age groups. Again, this is clearly the effect of intensive ties to the community, a satisfactory environment, and a low concern for job opportunities.

A comparable analysis of recent migrants to a high-growth area is the study by Campbell et al. (1977). Forty-three percent of the recent migrants were returnees, 19 percent primary migrants, and 38 percent local movers. They report that:

> Returnees are older than the other migrants, largely because most of the retirement migrants were returnees. Associated with age are the reasons for moving, with returnees most likely to give family-related or amenities reasons. Job-related reasons were more common among local movers, and especially pronounced for the younger, higher-educated primary migrants. Very few primary migrants are not in the labor force, and the most frequent occupations for this group are in white-collar classes. The durations of current residence support the staging pattern associated with levels of development: local movers, followed by returnees, and, as greater economic diversity occurs, primary migrants. Differences on education, income, and occupation between returnees and local migrants are not significant, but the primary migrants exhibit levels that are markedly higher than the other two groups. (Campbell et al., 1977: 37.)

With respect to future mobility, only 6 percent of the long-term residents expect to move, but 45 percent of the primary migrants, 24 percent of the returnees, and 18 percent of the local movers expect to move. The crucial difference in the Ozarks, like the North Central region, seems to be the fact that primary migrants are extremely well attuned to the economic and living conditions (54 percent are staying for these reasons), whereas the return migrants

are linked into the community by family and kin ties (37
vs. 5 percent for primary movers). The authors also comment
that those who remigrate will probably come from the pool
of primary migrants and that most returnee in-migrants are
probably there to stay, especially the elderly.

Finally, in his study of Maine in-migration, Ploch
(1978, 1979) makes a number of pertinent comments about the
in-migrants. First, although only 20 percent have been born
in Maine, another 20 percent have visited, or vacationed
there regularly. Second, the return migrants are older than
primary migrants, and have lower educational attainment
than either the primary migrants or local resident population. Third, primary migrants are more likely to have moved
for job-related reasons (38 percent) than returnees (25
percent); but for both groups the major motivating factor
was a dissatisfaction with the former community and a
preference for Maine.

In all three studies, the emphasis on quality-of-life
considerations for returnees versus economic considerations
for primary migrants or local movers adds to the importance
of determining locational preferences, their meaning, and
use in projecting future migration for particular subgroups
of the population. It is evident, moreover, that areas
experiencing heavy rates of return migration are more
likely to retain those migrants in contrast to the areas
with high volumes of primary migrants. The relative trade-
offs of amenities, family ties, and economic opportunity
are different for each subgroup and the consequences for
retention or remigration are a function of the relative
proportion of each subgroup in recent streams. Similarly,
areas attracting primary and return migrants also seem
capable of attracting local migrants as well as retaining
long-term residents. Building from these results, the
concept of "chronic movers" again becomes relevant, particularly for the younger, labor-force-active, economically
motivated recent movers. Their preferences and mobility
expectations need to be further studied to determine the
efficiency of such migration for the community and the
social and economic costs and benefits for the individual
or family.

SELECTIVITY IN MIGRATION AND PREFERENCES

This section will consider further the selectivity associated with preferences for metro and nonmetro areas. First,
the associations between individual characteristics and
migration will be briefly cited and then an application of
these relations to preferences will be sketched out. This
will be followed by a comparison among five major studies of
selectivities associated with locational preferences and the
expected consequences of these relations for communities.

In a recent review of the literature, Ritchey (1976)
lists life-cycle variables, socioeconomic factors, community
and kinship ties, and minority group status as the pertinent
attributes. Zuiches (1980) reviewed these attributes in
relation to migration expectations and migration. (The
following discussion is taken from that review.)

Summarizing the demographic variables, the traditional
life-cycle effects are apparent: (1) the young, unmarried,
or small family is both associated with expecting to move
and actually moving, and (2) mobility is often induced by
changing family size in relation to housing needs.

Besides the life-cycle indicators, stayers do seem to
be differentiated from movers by three community attachment
indicators: investments in a home, long-term residency in
the community, and a degree of satisfaction with the
community. Moreover, these are not simply surrogates for
one another; each contributes an independent degree of
explanation.

PREFERENCES FOR METROPOLITAN-NONMETROPOLITAN DESTINATIONS

Based on the overview of compositional differences among
movers, expectant movers, and nonmovers, a number of
hypotheses present themselves; however, to account for the
locational preferences of movers requires more than simply
ascribing the above compositional differences to all migrant streams. Dillman and Dobash (1972) have argued that
preferences for a major change in residential location
(moving from metro to nonmetro locations or the reverse)
increase as the amount of experience in the destination
environment increases. The preference literature, furthermore, is unanimous in demonstrating that the single most
preferred location is one's current location. Additionally,
previous experience, either as a child or in prior mobility

or travel, often provides a basis for judgment about the qualities and desirability of a community.

The contribution of socioeconomic status to explaining preferred location rests on a discussion of consumption patterns, job opportunities, and an assumption that the urbane values of higher-status respondents require large city locations. Thus, people with higher socioeconomic status prefer to move to metro areas. The nonmetro migrant is often assumed to be a return migrant and, therefore, will probably be of lower status than the metro origin population, although research by Ploch and Campbell has shown this to be a faulty assumption.

The life-cycle predictions would also follow: metro preferences would be expressed by the young and nonmetro by older ages. A corollary of this age relation would be that young families and unmarried individuals would also prefer the job and social opportunities of the larger cities.

Finally, "people are less likely to want to move to another community if they have a great deal invested in their present community," for example, home ownership, long-term residency, and established social, occupational, and organizational involvement (Dillman and Dobash, 1972: 15). It is this condition of location-specific capital that could operate both to impede migration and facilitate it. In Williams and McMillen's study (1980), multiple links and ties to the rural community through prior residence, family, and friends are identified as extremely important in the selection of destination.

The patterns of relationships found in five preference surveys for those preferring but not residing in one or the other destinations are summarized in Table 2.5. These destinations are defined broadly as metro and nonmetro. Although no study is perfectly congruent with census definitions of these areas, all imply a size and proximity to a large "central city" pattern of population distribution that approximates the statistical distinction. The association between the characteristics and mobility preferences is recorded as positive (+), negative (-), no relation (0), curvilinear (U), or left blank if the association was not reported. Also, if only one study reported on a specific variable, such as occupation or density, for the sake of brevity, these single associations were ignored.

Beginning with the demographic variable of age, a consistent inverse relation held between age and preferring a metro location. In all five studies, nonmetro respondents

Table 2.5. Associations Between Preferences for Mobility and Respondent Characteristics by Preferred Destination

Respondent Characteristics	Preferred Destination — Metropolitan					Preferred Destination — Nonmetropolitan				
	Ariz. 1973	Wash. 1971	Wis. 1971	Pa. 1975	U.S. 1974	Ariz. 1973	Wash. 1971	Wis. 1971	Pa. 1975	U.S. 1974
Demographic										
Age	−	−	−	−	−	+	0	+	−	−
Family size	−	+	+	+	−	+	+	+	−	−
Socioeconomic										
Education	+	+	+	+	+	+	−	−	+	+
Income	−	+	−	−	−	+	−	+	+	+
Employed (yes)	−	−	−	−		−	+	+	−	
Home ownership		−		−			+	+	−	
Occupational status	+	+	+	+	+	−	−	−	+	+
Community										
Duration in residence		−		−	−		−		−	−
Community satisfaction		−		−	−		−		−	−
Size of prior residence	+	+	+	0	+		+	+	+	+

Source: Arizona 1973, Carpenter 1975, Table 10 recalculated; Washington 1971, Dillman and Dobash 1972, Tables 15, 16, 17; Wisconsin 1971, Zuiches and Fuguitt 1972, Tables 3, 4, 5; Pennsylvania 1975, DeJong and Sell 1975, Tables 10, 11, 12; U.S. 1974 calculated by author from NORC General Social Survey.

who prefer a metro area are younger than those who prefer their current nonmetro residence. The potential stream from metro to nonmetro areas, however, is mixed; two studies show those preferring a nonmetro destination to be older, two show them as younger and one shows no difference in comparison with those preferring not to move.

The relationship between family size and destination is likewise mixed across the three studies that incorporated this variable. When looking at socioeconomic status, an interesting pattern appears. Those preferring a metro move are better educated, have higher occupational status, but generally (four out of five) lower current income level than those preferring no move. The neatness of this result, however, is not duplicated for nonmetro destination preferences. Educational attainment and occupational status have mixed results; and in four out of five surveys, income level is positively associated with a nonmetro preference.

Perhaps the differentials in income for comparable educational and occupational attainment between the two sectors would provide an explanation for this anomaly. Another explanation might be that in none of these studies was more than a bivariate analysis performed. If it were, one or more of these variables might be dismissed as irrelevant. DeJong and Sell (1975) have performed some multivariate analyses but the comparisons and variables did not match those used here.

Employment status (employed or unemployed) was reported in three studies. Nonmetro unemployed preferred a metro move more than the employed, but the pattern seems to reverse for metro residents preferring a more distant location. With only three studies detailing this information, however, not much should be made of it. Likewise, homeownership status, a powerful variable in migration analysis, has not been commonly reported by preference researchers.

The most consistent and probably most important set of relations is found in community attachment and experience. In every study for both metro and nonmetro destinations, long-term residency and high levels of community satisfaction are inversely associated with preferences for a residential relocation. Also, in seven out of eight tests, prior residential experience in an area is positively associated with a preference for mobility to the area. The one anomaly (DeJong and Sell) is perhaps a result of comparing broad groups of city sizes; with added detail, it would probably also show a positive relationship.

An obvious criticism of all the preferences research

is that it has not subsequently reinterviewed respondents
to determine their success at achieving preferences. DeJong
and Sell's work (1977) is the exception. In a follow-up
interview one year after the preference survey, DeJong and
Sell found that 3 percent of the sample moved to a nonmetro
setting. In an analysis of the nonmetro direction movers,
compared with nonmovers, they found the nonmetro movers
were younger, better educated, of higher occupational status, and in higher income classes. Although these movers
were nuclear families, they tended to be smaller than nonmover families, as one might expect from the age structure
of the movers. With the exception of family size of movers,
the other characteristics would have been predicted from
DeJong's preference data in Pennsylvania.

Two other studies, moreover, have described in some
detail the compositional differences of both metro and
nonmetro streams. These studies by DeJong and Humphrey
(1976) and Zuiches and Brown (1978) use census sources so
not all of the variables of Table 2.5 are replicated. But
the sociodemographic characteristics of each stream can be
examined to resolve some of the ambiguities.

In their analysis of population redistribution in
Pennsylvania (1965-70), DeJong and Humphrey (1976) report
that migrants to metro areas are younger, better educated,
have a larger family size, and are more likely to be employed, white-collar workers than nonmetro nonmovers. Income differences are nonexistent. Migrants to nonmetro
areas display the same differentials except for family
size, which is not significantly different from metro nonmovers. Moreover, they note that this selectivity also
applied to the stream comparisons, with the metro to nonmetro migrant stream being younger and of a higher socioeconomic status than the metro-directed stream.

A comparable pattern has been shown nationally for
1970 to 1975 by Zuiches and Brown (1978) and Wardwell
(1977). Migrants to nonmetro areas tended to be younger,
better educated families, rather than single individuals,
and in white-collar occupations when compared to either
origin or destination nonmover populations. Income differences, again, were negligible.

Comparing these analyses with the patterns derived
from Table 2.5, it is clear that the inverse association
between age and mobility pertains for each destination and
that some of the positive relationships between age and
nonmetro preferences need to be reevaluated. Perhaps, there
are specific factors in Wisconsin and Arizona that help

explain the positive relationships. Both states have
experienced extensive retirement migration that may dominate the expected stream of nonmetro migrants. With respect
to income differences, the preference surveys were mixed
and the actual mobility showed no real differences, except
in the Pennsylvania longitudinal study. Educational and
occupational status, however, were consistently positively
associated with mobility in both directions. Again, the
preference surveys revealed this pattern for metro migration, but not for nonmetro mobility. This lack of congruency
could mean that nonmetro preferences may not be as intensive
and well formed as metro preferences.

Because these census-based replications do not include
duration-in-residence, community satisfaction, or prior residential experience, three of the more important predictors
of preferences and mobility, using them as a test for comparing stream composition of preferred and actual mobility
may be presumptuous. However, on the basis of sociodemographic attributes, using surveys to predict the composition
of metro streams at least seems justified.

RACIAL DIFFERENCES IN PREFERENCES

The preference studies, unfortunately, are based on national
samples in which the number of blacks is quite small, and
with the imposition of a control for regional location,
analysis is extremely risky. The behavior and preferences
of blacks, however, comprise a significant proportion of
nonmetro to metro migration and, therefore, their preferences ought to be evaluated. In Table 2.6, based upon the
1972 NORC survey, preferences are presented by race, controlling for size of actual residence.

Looking at the marginals, first, blacks have a much
lower preference for small towns and rural areas located
over thirty miles from a metro-sized central city. Only
8 percent prefer such a location in contrast to 21 percent
of the whites. Almost twice the percentage of blacks (45)
as whites (23), however, prefer the large (more than 50,000
population) central cities.

Controlling for present location (1972), of central
city residents, about one-half of the whites and blacks
prefer that location. Blacks have a lower preference for
the far rural locality. Of those presently residing in
small towns and rural areas within thirty miles of a central city (approximates suburbs) or farther out, about

Table 2.6. Preferred Residences by Present Location and Race of Respondent, 1972

Race and Residence	Preferences: Size of Place and Location				
	More than 50,000	Less than 50,000		Total	(N)[a]
		Less than 30 Miles to Places 50,000+	More than 30 Miles to Places 50,000+		
	%	%	%		
Black					
More than 50,000 population	50	47	3	100	(121)
Less than 50,000 population and less than 30 miles away	35	54	11	100	(26)
Less than 50,000 population and more than 30 miles away	30	35	35	100	(20)
Total	45	47	8	100	(167)
White					
More than 50,000 population	47	40	13	100	(512)
Less than 50,000 population and less than 30 miles away	5	80	15	100	(471)
Less than 50,000 population and more than 30 miles away	7	45	48	100	(282)
Total	23	56	21	100	(1,265)

Source: NORC Survey of the United States 1972; quoted in Zuiches, 1980: 177.

aOther races, don't knows, and no answers are omitted (N=49; 3 percent of 1,481).

one-third of the blacks prefer a large city, whereas less
than 7 percent of the whites prefer the large city.

The linkages via historical migration patterns and
family ties plus job, housing, and social opportunities for
blacks have primarily been found in the central city and
preferences in this case are indicative of the patterns of
mobility already existing for blacks. Whites, on the other
hand, are suburbanizing rapidly and this is evident both in
terms of suburban residents preferring their present location (80 percent) and the high percentages (40 and 45) of
nonsuburbanites preferring such a residential location.

For blacks, too, a step migration process may be un-
folding as rural residents prefer the large city, large-
city residents prefer the suburban locality, and suburban
residents prefer their present location.

This review of the literature on preferences, migration
expectations, migration, and the compositional characteristics associated with each attitude and activity can be
summarized as follows: (1) Demographic (age, family size,
and persons/room) and community attachment (satisfaction
and duration in residence) characteristics were systematically related to expected and actual mobility, but socioeconomic variables were not. Home ownership clearly lessens
the expectations for and probability of moving; and educational attainment is generally positively associated with
mobility; but income and employment status show mixed
results. (2) Demographic, in particular age, socioeconomic
indicators, and community attributes were consistently
(across all studies) associated with preferring a metro
location; but only the community attachment attributes had
a consistency for nonmetro preferences. (3) In a limited
comparison of compositional association with recent migration statistics for the U.S. and Pennsylvania, preference
surveys do seem to be able to provide some clues to who
will migrate to nonmetro areas.

This partial resolution with respect to nonmetro areas
makes prediction of future migration patterns difficult,
based solely on preferences. But linking the preference-
based explanations with the changing structural conditions
in nonmetro areas as Beale (1975), Wardwell (1977), and
Carpenter (1977) have done strengthens the argument. The
deconcentration of industry, increased transportation accessibility, rising recreational opportunities, the growth
in service jobs, increased disposable income, and improved
retirement benefits have all contributed to the realization
of locational preferences. Whenever structural changes

lessen the economic differentials between areas and permit
greater locational flexibility, the preferences of mobile
segments of the population are more likely to be achieved.
An added element in the preference model, which the geographers have extensively researched, is the role of
environmental preferences. (See Svart 1976, for a discussion of environmental preferences in migration and regional
development.)

Based on preference surveys, therefore, there seems to
be a sizable reservoir of potential migrants, but why they
fail to act on their preferences needs to be determined as
well as the compositional characteristics of these nonmovers.

The act of moving, for example, makes it easier to move
again, especially if the differences between expected conditions and reality are too great. Zuiches and Fuguitt (1976)
have shown that one-half of those who preferred nonmetro
areas would give up their preference when potential income
declines were a condition of the move. Likewise, in Arizona,
whereas a majority (52 percent) preferred living in a community of less than 50,000 people, only 3 percent were interested in moving if it involved loss of income or lengthy
commuting (Carpenter 1977). Similarly, the recent movers
to nonmetro areas may discover inadequacies of income, services, and social, recreational, and job opportunities.
Subsequent remigration to the metro areas is distinctly
possible.

In Table 2.7, based on the 1974 NORC national survey,
this expectation is borne out. When respondents are classified by mobility status (recent in-migrants and nonmovers)
and current residence, recent migrants to the large cities
and to the small cities and rural areas over thirty miles
from a large city (essentially nonmetro areas) are more
likely than nonmovers to prefer another major relocation.
Recent in-migrants to small cities and rural areas within
commuting distance of a large city are least likely to
prefer another location. These differences are even more
dramatic when we look at the percent expecting a move out
of their current community in the next three years. Recent
in-migrants to nonmetro areas are twice as likely to expect
to move again in contrast to nonmovers. Large-city in-
migrants are also expecting substantially greater mobility
then nonmovers, but those living in suburban locations show
only minor differences.

According to the Bureau of the Census, 6.7 million
people moved into nonmetro areas during 1970 to 1975. Have

Table 2.7. Preferences and Expected Mobility by Actual
Residence and Mobility Status, 1970-1974

	Actual Residence 1974		
	Large Cities 50,000+ Population	Rural Small Cities	
		Within 30 Miles of Large City	More than 30 Miles to Large City
Percentage preferring other than current residence (number)			
Mobility status			
Recent in-migrants[a]	66 (132)	13 (161)	37 (68)
Nonmovers	52 (483)	19 (393)	26 (239)
Percentage expecting to move in next 3 years			
Mobility status			
Recent in-migrants[a]	43 (132)	27 (161)	44 (68)
Nonmovers	16 (483)	21 (393)	22 (239)

Source: 1974 NORC General Social Survey, with additional
preference and mobility questions.

[a]From 1970 to 1974.

these recent movers satisfied their preferences or might we
expect additional mobility, a counterstream of metro return
migration? The implication of Table 2.7 and the postreversal
studies is that for many recent migrants there still remains
a lack of congruence between preferences and actual residence, particularly in the large cities and nonmetro areas.
This potential for further mobility does not discount the
structural changes that have made the turnaround a reality.
The point is made to demonstrate the complexity of applying
preference data to migration analysis.

Another distinction can be made between recent in-
migrants with no prior experience in the destination and
return migrants. DaVanzo (1976) has noted that families,
even those with a history of mobility, which finally move
to a place lived in before are less likely to move (again)
than families which have never moved. Because this result
occurred at the level of interdivisional migration, its
substantiation by Campbell et al. (1977) and Sofranko and

Williams (1980) for nonmetro areas suggests a high retention of return migrants. Furthermore, although all of the preferences studies show a consistent relation between prior residence and preference, such an indicator of potential return migration has not been exploited.

Finally, whereas the nonmetro areas have been able to attract in-migrants and recent surveys indicate these areas remain highly preferred, retention of current residents is also a crucial component of the turnaround. Although the preference surveys all show a desire for life in the country or small towns, the single most preferred location remains one's current location. Rural residents strongly desire to stay where they are living.

Because the structural and preference factors affecting nonmetro growth have not changed, continued slow growth might be expected in these areas, but it will be a growth accompanied by large flows of population. It is the analysis of population composition--who these movers are--that provides further insight into the causes and impacts of this mobility. This review has shown some of the continuities in empirical migration research; unfortunately, the gaps remain.

ORIENTATIONS TOWARD COMMUNITY

The emphasis on quality-of-environmental conditions in rural areas has almost made it a cliché, but such an orientation toward noneconomic amenities is so consistently held that it reinforces further the explanations for the reversal that go beyond the structural changes.

Nationally, people who preferred smaller communities gave the following reasons: less crime, better quality of air and water, better life for children, and lower cost of living. People preferring to live in a big city gave as their reasons: higher wages, better jobs, contacts with a variety of people, and recreational and cultural opportunities (Fuguitt and Zuiches 1975). People who preferred a particular size of place were also likely to desire the same kinds of things that people valued who actually lived there and intended to remain.

In a survey of Arizona residents, respondents said they felt that schools, police services, and outdoor recreational facilities were better in nonmetro areas, as were community spirit and pride, satisfaction, and friendliness. They did not judge medical services as being as good, nor availability of jobs, cultural activities, and the privacy of personal life (Blackwood and Carpenter 1978). Perhaps people are simply responding to stereotypes about privacy, environmental quality, and services. Yet the pattern of attractive characteristics and of problems tends to be consistent with the views of policymakers as to problems in health care, public services, housing quality, and jobs in the rural sector.

Beyond the preference surveys, the postreversal studies corroborate these findings. In the Ozarks, the living conditions, environment, and lake-associated features are given as the dominant reasons for mobility to the area. The rural benefits of a "simple life style--slow pace of life, peacefulness-serenity, friends, relatives in Maine, qualities of the people, general environmental quality, lack of pollution, natural beauty, and the ocean coast" are listed by Ploch (1978: 300) as the pull factors to Maine. Sofranko and Williams (1980) point out that the migrants in their study still move for employment considerations, but they suggest that quality-of-life considerations rank higher in the determination of a destination. Campbell et al. (1974) point out that black return migration to the South is, likewise, heavily influenced by social and family motivations in contrast to economic reasons.

Underlying much of this discussion is the implicit notion that individuals are trading off income for quality-of-life attributes and psychological and social benefits associated with rural and small-town residential locations. Ploch (1978) notes that over one-half of his sample reported lower income after migrating. The North Central study also reports that one-half of the migrants had lower income in the first year postmove, but in only a short period of time premove income levels were reestablished and slightly higher in 1976 than prior to the move (Fliegel and Williams 1980). Finally, at the national level, McCarthy and Morrison (1978) replicate Beale's finding that counties with lower earning levels experienced larger proportionate increases in migration rates than counties with higher earnings. The shift from a direct association between income level in a county and net migration to no relation in the 1970s is argued to indicate a shift in life-style orientation.

Most of the studies also indicate that new migrants are not experiencing difficulty adjusting to the new communities, that the features of increased safety and privacy are excellent, and that high levels of satisfaction seem to prevail postmigration.

An issue that merits further work is the effect of migration on these turnaround areas. Maintenance of rural attributes in a pristine state becomes harder and harder as more people move in. Use patterns change, costs accelerate, and environmental regulations are both a benefit and a burden to the community. As population grows, any lack of financial support for the planning and implementation of plans may lead to a deterioration of the very features originally attracting residents. Sufficient water supplies, energy services, and waste and garbage disposal cannot be taken for granted as the population expands. Many of the services required for household and commercial developments are more costly and less conveniently provided in a rural community. Planning is needed to ensure that population growth will not lead to the destruction and contamination of the rural environment.

In an innovative study, Clay and Price (1979) calculated a score for each county indicating the concern of residents in the county for various aspects of community life. This score was then correlated with the migration rate for all Michigan counties. In general, high rates of net in-migration were associated with perceived problems in municipal services, education and welfare programs, health care, and recreational and cultural facilities. In an analysis of community solidarity, they found that perceptions of concern were highest in counties rapidly growing or rapidly losing population. Rapid population change represents a disturbance to the community's social organization. The implication of such a study, however, is not to limit growth in counties or communities only recently suffering decline, but to consider the strategies of dealing with community change.

DISCUSSION

The simplicity of early analyses (1970 through 1975) of residential preferences data made them attractive as alternative or complementary explanations to structural changes for the migration turnaround in nonmetro areas. Recent research, however, in which expressed preferences are evaluated under constraints of income loss, mobility expectations, and the actual achievement of preferences

reveal the complexity inherent in such explanations.
Background characteristics of the individual, especially
prior experience in a locality and migration history,
life-cycle status and attitudes toward quality-of-life
attributes, significantly affect migration based on preferences and, likewise, stability after migration.

At a highly generalized level, if redistribution according to preferences were to occur either nationally or
in states for which we have data, a radical shift of 20 to
30 percent of the population would occur. Such a redistribution is highly unlikely. In the national surveys, only 20
percent expect to make a major move, but the great majority
of such moves will remain intra- or interurban and local in
character. A redistribution across metro/nonmetro boundaries
would occur, but the net effect would be felt very gradually. Using the 1974 NORC survey of migration history, preferences, and migration expectations for projections of
redistribution, Zuiches and Fuguitt (1976) have shown the
gradual pattern of change one might expect. From 1964 to
1974 only a 2 percent shift in distribution occurred with
percentage point losses in the central cities and rural,
nonmetro sector and a 2 percent gain in the suburban-metro
sector. To project a 20 percent shift from central cities
to suburbs and nonmetro areas, based on preferences is
unlikely. Projections of 5 percent shifts, based on migration expectations, are still quite large, but more reasonable. In such a projection, the communities within a thirty-
mile radius of central cities, including open country, small
towns, and major suburban cities, would continue to increase
in population at the expense of central cities. Additionally, the more distant areas still retain their attractiveness
to the more serious potential migrants and would have a
proportionally greater increase in population. Although
these projections are probably high, they do indicate a
continued redistribution favoring nonmetro areas.

Decomposing the population into subgroups by prior
locational history and cause of move would provide the
basis for better local area projections. For example, as
jobs in rural areas increase for rural youth, one would
expect increased retention of population in the rural areas.
Retention of the elderly would be predicted from duration-
of-residence and location-specific capital models. The
attraction of earlier out-migrants (returnees) seems to
be a consequence of returning for family and amenity
reasons and for the increased employment opportunities
available in rural areas. Retention of these recent in-

migrants is much more likely than for those primary migrants whose crucial locational decision-making criterion is employment opportunity. Nevertheless, the turnover of primary migrants is not necessarily inefficient for either the individuals concerned or the community. Such turnover indicates a vitality on the part of the community's economic base and the long-term potential for continued growth. The compositional attributes of these primary migrants are positively selective with respect to education, occupational status, and income in comparisons with local residents, and their contribution to local social organizational development may outlast their residence in the community.

Some of the problems can be anticipated. Social integration is upset by high rates of growth or decline, community solidarity is perceived to be threatened, and conflict may arise over issues such as school bond support, property taxes, and policies for community development. Fiscal problems are likely as infrastructural requirements mean higher local expenditures for medical services, police and fire protection, utility services, and larger physical facilities and personnel. Although Ploch (1978) has also raised these issues, little research has focused on such problems.

Implicit in this literature on the turnaround is an impression of momentum of growth that results from new channels of migration opening up or changes in the import of causal factors in migration. The expectation is for a continuation of the present dual process—the increased retention of population in nonmetro areas coupled with return migration of previous residents. This, along with the continued attractiveness of rural areas to potential new in-migrants, should result in their further growth. However, preferences are changeable. If the conditions of living in rural areas relative to other areas were to be significantly altered—as, for example, by the sudden rise in energy costs of transportation and services or by the rapid population growth—the effect on residential preferences could be immediate and the lag time for changes in mobility very short. Although the phenomena of growth spurts or chronic decline in nonmetro communities may be mitigated by structural changes in the larger society, the effect of such changes is partially felt through residential attitudes and preferences. The fluidity of preferences—and their rapid translation into mobility—means efforts to monitor preferences and migration behavior more closely ought to be initiated.

But the point to be emphasized is that simultaneous with the in-migration, the community itself is changing. In its growth spurt, new services, new use patterns and costs, and new demands are generated. To cope with these demands, a continuing process of adjustment at both the community and individual level must occur. In the context of nonmetro development, programs of infrastructural support ought to be continued to maintain a minimum level of services neces- sary for community health and vitality. The provision of these minimum levels of services in a variety of communities increases the potential for further growth as individuals selectively pick and choose new residential locations ac- cording to their personal desires for a rural community and the environment it implies, or the return to a family home, or the search for employment. Not only is it enough to satisfy the preferences of retirees and younger families to maintain the nonmetro environment, but to retain current residents and recent in-migrants or to attract others, further strengthening of the economic base of nonmetro areas must occur. As a consequence of this dual role of nonmetro areas, satisfying both economic and noneconomic needs of the resident and migrant populations, our models of migration must increase in complexity.

The weak link in most preferences research remains the failure to provide for a longitudinal evaluation through migration behavior. Methodologically, the study of migration at the microanalytical level requires longitudinal studies that extend the work of these early surveys. Unfortunately, without additional postmigration follow-up studies such as DeJong and Sell (1977) and Zuiches and Rieger (1978) have completed, there still remains an uncertainty about the ability of respondents to achieve a preferred destination. In the longitudinal study of rural youth in Michigan, resi- dential redistribution is associated with preferences, but attitudes were often modified in the wake of residential experiences. Similarly, in the Pennsylvania study, although 79 percent of the intercommunity movers went in the direc- tion of their preferences, so much intraurban mobility occurred that overall only 14 percent of the total sample achieved their preferences (Fredrickson et al. 1980, data provided by DeJong). The less than total success at predict- ing direction of movers and the discovery of cohort and life-cycle effects on preferences suggests a further dis- aggregation of nonmovers and movers to determine the historical as well as more proximate causes of moves. Also required is a standardization of questions and a systematic evaluation of the reliability and validity of the questions currently used. Decomposing the migration streams into return movers, new movers, and retained nonmovers means using survey questions appropriate to the conditions of the respondent.

The organization of a research program that complements the studies of the Current Population Survey and other census studies could provide the basis for integrating individual and aggregate analysis. Complementing large-scale national and state surveys with in-depth small area case studies would provide a valuable counterpoint as both national estimates of mobility trends and theoretical insight would be possible. A first step in this direction would be the incorporation of a carefully designed set of preferences questions in the Annual Housing Surveys. The continued efforts of rural sociologists to study smaller, substate, state or regional areas also need to be support-ed. As the importance of migration increases, the gaps in theoretical understanding and empirical information need attention at both national and local levels.

BIBLIOGRAPHY

American Institute of Public Opinion. Gallup Opinion Index, Report no. 57. Princeton, N.J.: The Gallup Organiza-tion, Inc., 1970.

Beale, Calvin L. The Revival of Population Growth in Non-metropolitan America. ERS-605. Washington, D.C.: U.S. Department of Agriculture, Economic Research Service, 1975.

_____, and Fuguitt, Glenn V. "The New Pattern of Non-metropolitan Population Change." In Social Demography, edited by Karl E. Taeuber, Larry L. Bumpass, and James A. Sweet, chapter 8. New York: Academic Press, 1978.

Biggar, Jeanne C. "The Sunning of America: Migration to the Sunbelt." Population Bulletin 34, no. 1. Washington, D.C.: Population Reference Bureau, 1979.

Blackwood, L. G., and Carpenter, Edwin H. "The Importance of Anti-urbanism in Determining Residential Preferences and Migration Patterns." Rural Sociology 43 (1978): 31-47.

Bohlen, Joe M., and Wakeley, Ray E. "Intentions to Migrate and Actual Migration of Rural High School Graduates." Rural Sociology 15 (1950): 328-34.

Campbell, R. R.; Johnson, D. M.; and Stangler, G. J. "Return Migration of Black People to the South." Rural Sociology 39 (1974): 514-28.

_____; Stangler, Gary J.; Dailey, George, H.; and McNamara, Robert L. Population Change, Migration, and Displacement Along the McClellen-Kerr Arkansas River Navigation System. IWR Contract Report 77-5. Fort Belvoir, Va.: Institute for Water Resources, 1977.

Carpenter, Edwin H. "The Potential for Population Dispersal: A Closer Look at Residential Locational Preferences." Rural Sociology 42 (1977): 352-70.

_____. Residential Preference and Community Size: Implications for Population Redistribution in Arizona. Department of Agricultural Economics, Research Report no. 7. Tucson, Ariz.: University of Arizona, 1975.

Christenson, James A. "Community Preference and Population Distribution." Through our Eyes, vol. 4. Miscellaneous Extension Publication no. 112, 1974.

Clay, Dan, and Price, Michael. "Structural Disturbances in Rural Communities: Some Repercussions of the Migration Turnaround in Michigan." Paper prepared for presentation at the Annual Meetings of the Rural Sociological Society, Burlington, Vt., 1979.

Commission on Population Growth and the American Future. Population and the American Future. Washington, D.C.: U.S. Government Printing Office, 1972.

Cosby, Arthur G., and Howard, William G. Residential Preferences in America: The Growing Desire for Rural Life. Rural Development Seminar Series. Washington, D.C.: USDA Extension Service, 1976.

Cowhig, James; Artis, Jay; Beegle, J. Allan; and Goldsmith, Harold. Orientations Toward Occupation and Residence: A Study of High School Seniors in Four Rural Counties of Michigan. Bulletin 428. East Lansing, Mich.: Michigan State University Agricultural Experiment Station, 1960.

DaVanzo, Julie. "Why Families Move: a Model of the Geographic Mobility of Married Couples." Santa Monica, Calif.: Rand Corporation R-1972-DOL, 1976.

DeJong, Gordon F., and Humphrey, Craig. "Selected Characteristics of Metropolitan to Nonmetropolitan Area Migrants: A Study of Population Redistribution in Pennsylvania." Rural Sociology 41 (1976): 526-38.

DeJong, Gordon F., and Sell, Ralph R. "Population Redistribution, Migration, and Residential Preferences." Annals 429 (1977): 130-44.

_____. "Residential Preferences and Migration Behavior." In Population Change and Redistribution in Nonmetropolitan Pennsylvania, 1940-1970, by Wilbur Zelinsky et al. A report submitted to NIH, HEW. University Park, Pa.: Population Issues Research Office, 1975.

Dillman, Don A. "Population Distribution Policy and People's Attitudes: Current Knowledge and Needed Research." Paper prepared for the Urban Land Institute under a grant from U.S. Department of Housing and Urban Development, authorized under Section 701(b) of the Housing Act of 1954, as amended, 1973.

_____, and Dobash, Russell P. "Preferences for Community Living and Their Implications for Population Redistribution." Washington Agricultural Experiment Station, Bulletin 764. Pullman, Wash.: Washington State University, 1972.

Fliegel, Frederick C., and Williams, James D. "Migration and Changing Household Conditions." In Rebirth of Rural America, edited by Andrew Sofranko and James Williams. Ames, Iowa: Iowa State University, North Central Rural Development Center, 1980.

Fredrickson, Carl; Heaton, T.; Fuguitt, G. V.; Zuiches, J. J. "Residential Preferences in a Model of Migration Intentions." Population and Environment 3 (1980): 280-97.

Friedman, Stephen B. People and Places: A Report on Wisconsinites' Locational Preferences. State Planning Office. Madison, Wisc.: Bureau of Planning and Budget, 1974.

Fuguitt, Glenn V., and Zuiches, James J. "Residential Preferences and Population Distribution." Demography 12 (1975): 491-504.

Fuller, Gary, and Chapman, Murray. "On the Role of Mental Images in Migration Research." International Migration Review 8 (1974): 491-505.

Gould, P. R., and White, R. Mental Maps. Baltimore: Penguin, 1974.

Hadden, Jeffrey. "Use of Ad Hoc Definitions." In Sociological Methodology, edited by Edgar F. Borgotta, pp. 276-85. San Francisco: Jossey-Bass, Inc., 1969.

Hansen, Niles M. Location Preferences, Migration and Regional Growth. New York: Praeger, 1973.

Heaton, Tim; Fredrickson, Carl; Fuguitt, Glenn V.; Zuiches, James J. "Residential Preferences, Community Satisfaction, and the Intention to Move." Demography 16 (1979): 565-73.

Koebernick, T., and Beegle, J. A. "Migration of the Elderly to Rural Areas: A Case Study in Michigan." In Patterns

of Migration and Population Change in America's Heart-
land, edited by J. A. Beegle, pp. 86-104. East Lansing,
Mich.: Michigan State University Agricultural Experiment
Station Research Report no. 344, 1978.

Lee, Everett S.; Bresee, J. C.; Nelson, K. P.; and Patter-
son, D. A. An Introduction to Urban Decentralization
Research. Department of Housing and Urban Development
ORNL-HUD-3. Oak Ridge, Tenn.: Oak Ridge National
Laboratory, 1971.

Lever, Michael F. "Place of Residence Projections of East
Texas Rural Youth: Changes Between 1966 and 1972."
College Station, Tex.: Texas Agricultural Experiment
Information Report 74-1, 1974.

McCarthy, Kevin F., and Morrison, Peter A. "The Changing
Demographic and Economic Structure of Nonmetropolitan
Areas in the 1970s." Report P-6062. Santa Monica,
Calif.: Rand Corporation, 1978.

Mazek, Warren F., and Laird, William E. "City-Size Preferences and Population Distribution: The Analytical
Context." Quarterly Review of Economics and Business 14
(1974): 113-21.

Mazie, Sara Mills, and Rawlings, Steve. "Public Attitude
Towards Population Distribution Issues." In Population
Distribution and Policy, edited by Sara Mills Mazie,
pp. 559-616. Vol. 5 of Commission Research Reports.
Washington, D.C.: U.S. Government Printing Office,
1972.

Morgan, David. "Patterns of Population Redistribution: A
Residential Preference Model and Its Dynamic." Research
Paper no. 176, Department of Geography. Chicago:
University of Chicago, 1978.

National Area Development Institute. "Public Opinion Favors
Nonmetro Areas." Area Development Interchange 3 (1973):
1, 4.

Newman, Sandra. The Residential Environment and the Desire
to Move. Ann Arbor: Institute for Social Research,
1974.

Olsen, Duane A., and Kuehn, John A. "Migrant Response to
Industrialization in Four Rural Areas, 1965-70."
Agricultural Economic Report no. 270. Washington, D.C.:
U.S. Department of Agriculture, ERS, 1974.

Ploch, Louis. "The In-migrants: Some Are Returning Home."
Update 7 (1979): 3-6. University of Maine at Orono:
Life Sciences and Agricultural Research Station.

_____. "The Reversal in Migration Patterns--Some
Rural Development Consequences." Rural Sociology 43

(1978): 293-303.
Price, Colin. "Individual Preference and Optimal City Size."
   Urban Studies 15 (1978): 75-81.
Rieger, Jon H.; Beegle, J. Allan; and Fulton, Philip N.
   Profiles of Rural Youth: A Decade of Migration and
   Social Mobility. East Lansing, Mich.: Michigan State
   University Agricultural Experiment Station, Research
   Report no. 178, 1973.
Ritchey, P. Neal. "Explanations of Migration." In Annual
   Review of Sociology, edited by Alex Inkeles, vol. 2,
   pp. 363-404. Palo Alto: Annual Reviews, Inc., 1976.
Ryan, Vern D. et al. "Community Size Preferences Patterns
   among Indiana Residents: Implications for Population
   Redistribution Policies." West Lafayette, Ind.: Purdue
   University Agricultural Experiment Station Bulletin 55,
   1974.
Sofranko, Andrew J., and Williams, James D., eds. Rebirth
   of Rural America. Ames, Iowa: Iowa State University,
   North Central Rural Development Center, 1980.
Speare, Alden, Jr.; Goldstein, Sidney; and Frey, William.
   Residential Mobility, Migration and Metropolitan
   Change. Cambridge, Mass.: Ballinger Press, 1974.
Stuart, Nina G. "The Older Metropolitan Migrant as a Factor
   in Rural Population Growth." In Rebirth of Rural America,
   edited by Andrew Sofranko and James Williams, chapter
   9. Ames, Iowa: Iowa State University, North Central
   Rural Development Center, 1980.
_____, and Dunkelburger, J. E. "Residential Projec-
   tions of Northeast Alabama Youth: A Historical Compari-
   son." Paper presented at the Southwestern Sociological
   Association Meetings, Dallas, 1974.
Svart, Larry M. "Environmental Preference Migration: A
   Review." Geographical Review 66 (1976): 314-30.
Taeuber, Irene B. "The Changing Distribution of the Popu-
   lation in the United States in the Twentieth Century."
   In Population Distribution and Policy, edited by Sara
   Mills Mazie, pp. 35-107. Vol. 2 of Commission Research
   Reports. Washington, D.C.: U.S. Government Printing
   Office, 1972.
Taylor, D. Garth; Sherman, Sue; and Rusciano, Frank. "Some
   Social and Financial Aspects of Non-Metropolitan Life
   in America." Final Report to Farmers Home Administra-
   tion. Chicago: NORC, 1979.
U.S. Bureau of the Census. "Geographical Mobility: March
   1975 to March 1976." Current Population Reports, P-20
   no. 305. Washington, D.C.: U.S. Government Printing

Office, 1977.

_____. "Mobility of the Population of the United States, March 1970 to March 1975." Current Population Reports, P-20 no. 285. Washington, D.C.: U.S. Government Printing Office, 1975.

_____. Number of Inhabitants. Final Report PC(1)-A49. Washington, D.C.: U.S. Government Printing Office, 1971.

U.S. Department of Housing and Urban Development. A Survey of Citizens Views and Concerns about Urban Life. Study no. 2795, conducted by Louis Harris and Associates, Inc. Washington, D.C., 1978.

Wardwell, John M. "Equilibrium and Change in Nonmetropolitan Growth." Rural Sociology 42 (1977): 156-79.

White, Stephen E. "Residential Preference and Urban Inmigration." Annals of the Association of American Geographers 6 (1974): 47-50.

Williams, James D., and McMillen, David B. "The Utilization of Location-Specific Capital in Migration Decision-Making." In New Directions in Urban-Rural Migration Research, edited by David L. Brown and John Wardwell. New York: Academic Press, 1980.

Yoesting, Dean R., and Bohlen, Joe M. "A Longitudinal Study of Migration Expectations and Performance of Young Adults." Journal of Human Resources 3 (1968): 482-98.

Zuiches, James J. "Residential Preferences in Migration Theory." In New Directions in Urban-Rural Migration Research, edited by David L. Brown and John Wardwell. New York: Academic Press, 1980.

_____, and Brown, David L. "The Changing Character of the Nonmetropolitan Population, 1950-1975." In Rural U.S.A: Persistence and Change, edited by Thomas R. Ford, pp. 55-72. Ames, Iowa: Iowa State University Press, 1978.

Zuiches, James J., and Fuguitt, Glenn V. "Residential Preferences and Mobility Expectations." Paper presented at the Annual Meetings of the American Sociological Association, New York, 1976.

_____. "Residential Preferences: Implications For Population Redistribution in Nonmetropolitan Areas." In Population Distribution and Policy, edited by Sara Mills Mazie. Vol. 5 of Commission Research Reports. Washington, D.C.: U.S. Government Printing Office, 1972.

Zuiches, James J., and Rieger, Jon R. "Size of Place Preferences and Life Cycle Migration: A Cohort Comparison." Rural Sociology 43 (1978): 618-33.

Mark Baldassare

3

Local Perspectives on Community Growth

INTRODUCTION

There is growing evidence of a unique trend in population redistribution in the United States. For most of the post-World War II era, interest in migration focused on a massive movement of residence and workplace from major urban centers to peripheral suburban areas (Farley 1976; Hawley 1972; Kasarda 1978; Zimmer 1975). In the more recent past, the decline of population in the urbanized regions of the United States (i.e., particularly the Northeast and North Central States) and the considerable movement of people and commerce to the South and West has been of increasing concern (Alonso 1971; Perry and Watkins 1977; Morrison 1977c). By the mid-1970s, attention shifted to an unprecedented resurgence of nonmetro population growth (Beale 1975; Berry 1976; McCarthy and Morrison 1978). The extent, meaning, and causes of this population turnaround are more fully explored elsewhere.

The purpose of this chapter is to present evidence that complements and expands knowledge about the social consequences of nonmetro growth. This topic draws upon sociological theories about the rural to urban transformation of communities in modern society, and in particular the effects of this growth upon individuals' actions and attitudes within their localities. The most common research method for determining the existence of what is described later as a more "urban way of life" is the ecological approach, which contrasts aggregate rates of community or individuals' characteristics with demographic change in the locality. Historical (or longitudinal) and comparative designs can be employed in these types of analyses. Although some information of this sort is reviewed here, as well as case-study data, major attention is devoted to the social impact as-

---

The research for this paper was supported by NIMH Grant #MH 30488 and the Center for the Social Sciences, Columbia University.

sessment. This method considers nonmetro residents' self-
reports of community conditions and personal satisfaction
from random surveys and relates these data to the local
population changes experienced by the respondents. In
general, the research findings do not offer convincing
support that rapid nonmetro growth results in severe
personal and community disorganization.

Evidence about the social impacts of nonmetro growth is
essential to understanding the present and future status of
this phenomenon. If large migrations have been under way,
it is possible that an adverse impact on the quality of
life for residents may disrupt future growth or cause out-
migrations. These predictions take on meaning when we review evidence later that suggests that seeking a better
(or at least different) life-style seems to be an important
motivation for leaving metro areas as well as remaining in
nonmetro places. Additionally, urban migrants may be demanding, in qualitative and quantitative terms, goods and
services not typically found within rural communities.
Dissatisfaction may occur when these urban expectations
remain unfulfilled, even though positive rural amenities
are present. Another general concern is the extent to which
population growth is creating a different type of nonmetro
community. It may be that areas experiencing the population
turnaround do not really reflect a return to traditional
rural ways of life, and instead present a distinct and
perhaps more urban alternative. This could be evidence of
the further blurring of the rural-urban dichotomy in a
society where the vast majority of people reside in the
metropolises or within commuting distances to them. Data
from residents are thus required in order to better understand the effects of the migration presently underway as
well as to help predict future trends.

WHY STUDY RURAL RESIDENTS'
ATTITUDES AND BEHAVIORS: EMPIRICAL TRENDS

It has been reported for some time that many Americans
favor residence in small villages and towns to living in
the suburbs or central cities. Such preferences can be
found in popular accounts (Robertson and Robertson 1978)
and one could argue that they merely represent a societal
tendency to publicly degrade urban living. However, repu-
table opinion polls and social surveys have replicated this

sentiment in the general population (Zuiches and Fuguitt
1972; Mazie and Rawlings 1972; Fuguitt and Zuiches 1975).
Using national survey data collected prior to the discovery
of the population turnaround, Morgan and Murray (1974: 100)
found that rural farm areas would grow by 31 percent and
that cities across the nation would lose 18 percent of
their population if people actually moved as they wished.
Importantly, about one-half of the rural farm residents who
desire to live elsewhere expressed a preference for another
similar area. An antiurban bias thus seems present in the
general population, which probably influences opinions
about present and preferred residential locations.

Very little is known about the specific attitudes that
are associated with a desire for nonmetro areas among potential movers. Better employment opportunities and economic
circumstances seem not to be sole concerns, although improvements in the residential environment (e.g., recreation
facilities, clean air and water, low crime, good schools)
and the social environment (e.g., proximity to family and
friends, contact with different people, better surroundings
for children) seem to be increasingly significant reasons
for these people (Fuguitt and Zuiches 1975). An important
finding has emerged that suggests that the preference for
nonmetro relocation is conditioned upon being within
commuting distance to a metro area (Zuiches and Fuguitt
1972; Fuguitt and Zuiches 1975; Carpenter 1977). However, a
panel study of movers in Pennsylvania has raised questions
about the significance of this attitude among potential
movers for predicting their actual destinations. DeJong
(1977) found that only a small percentage of moves were to
the desired nonmetro location in proximity to a metro area.
Attitudinal studies thus not only refer to possible reasons
for moving but also point to discrepancies between what is
achieved and what is desired among urbanites migrating to
rural areas. In additon, underlying their locational
preferences may be expectations that certain urban services
be reachable or available.

A definitive study that links preferred migration and
the actual movement of the population during the 1970s has
not been conducted. Still, there is evidence that a repopulation of nonmetro areas has occurred during the time in
which a preference has been expressed by the general population to leave large urban centers and settle outside
of the metropolis. Beale's research (1975) found that the
nonmetro population grew at a faster rate than the metro
population during the 1970s. Metro out-migration was more

pronounced than in the past, while nonmetro out-migration slowed considerably. Overall, nonmetro areas gained 1.6 million more people than they lost during the period of 1970 to 1975, and migrants were from a broad spectrum of age and economic groups (Tucker 1976). Though counties adjacent to Standard Metropolitan Statistical Areas (SMSAs) have for some time now grown at a more rapid rate than more distant rural areas, the population turnaround has been discovered in many kinds of nonmetro areas (Berry 1976; Morrison and Wheeler 1976; Zelinsky 1978). No doubt, many of these urban migrants have relocated with expectations of finding a new and perhaps better life-style. In the process, they have also altered community conditions at their destination.

There are apparently many reasons for the current population turnaround besides antiurban and prorural attitudes. Its multifaceted origins may in fact provide the best clue as to why it initially took demographers by surprise. Some have pointed to the role of government programs in stimulating growth in underdeveloped areas (Alonso 1971; Beaton and Cox 1977). It has also been noted that a larger proportion of retirees in the United States has freed more individuals from the need to live in metro areas (Chevan and Fischer 1978). Other changes in the national economy have brought about new energy boom towns, communities that specialize in leisure pursuits, and a deconcentration of employment (McCarthy and Morrison 1978; Wardwell and Gilchrist 1978). Of course, the ability of the society to offer the opportunity to live, work, and play with increasing frequency outside of the metropolis is very much a function of improvements in transportation and communication (a phenomenon McCarthy and Morrison, 1978: iii, call "increasing accessibility to the metropolitan economy"). These sets of circumstances have brought a diverse group of urban actors into the nonmetro sphere: highly skilled technicians, bureaucrats, blue-collar workers, retirees, oil and coalfield workers, the "me" generation in search of leisure and recreation, counter-culturalists, and rural romanticists. Each has arrived with different expectations that influence not only their adjustment but also ultimately the demands and disruptions they place on the communities and the original residents.

When we consider the research that is concerned with personal motivations for actual relocation, quality-of-life considerations seem to be of the highest priority. A recent study of Kansas migrants concluded that "life-style" and the "environment and crime" were among the most signif-

icant reasons reported by those moving to turnaround areas
and by those remaining within these same communities (Flora
and Flora 1978). Interviews with recent migrants of growing
North Central nonmetro counties also suggested the primary
importance of environmental "pull" factors (e.g., crime
safety, prorural attitudes, environmental quality) for
out-migrants of metropolises (Williams and Sofranko 1979).
An analysis of in-migrants to rural Connecticut counties
conducted by Steahr et al. (1978) found that movers during
the turnaround era (i.e., post-1970) were more likely to
cite disillusionment with urban life (e.g., traffic, crime,
poverty, slums) than those who had migrated somewhat earlier. Though metro to nonmetro migrations appear to be motivated more by personal or social preferences rather than
jobs per se, this is not to say that they are not rational
decisions. Such moves could be considered as calculated
risks because national surveys in the 1970s have reported
the highest levels of community satisfaction in nonmetro
places (Campbell et al. 1976; Morgan 1975). Of course,
whether or not small-scale areas can maintain these high
evaluations after experiencing an influx of migrants, or
whether the newcomers will be similarly impressed with
local conditions, is open to question.

Unfortunately, the often heated debate about the consequences of rapid population growth in nonmetro areas has
not been very enlightening. Some environmentalists and ecologists have prejudged the impact as being damaging to personal well-being and the community fabric (see, for example,
Watt 1970). Recent attempts by communities to "close the
door" on newcomers (Morrison 1977a, 1977b; Robertson and
Robertson 1978) or to limit their sizes through growth
management plans (Scott et al. 1975; Burrows 1978) may be
misguiding barometers. They could, for example, reflect
exclusionary and elitist strategies to maintain the status
quo without local deterioration having really occurred.
Before we turn to the methods and evidence presently available for considering the consequences of rural growth for
community and personal satisfaction, theories concerned
with the overall impacts of community growth are reviewed
in order to generate hypotheses.

THEORIES ABOUT THE SOCIAL
CONSEQUENCES OF POPULATION GROWTH

Because a considerable amount of early sociological theo-
rizing was concerned with the rural to urban transformation
of western societies in the nineteenth century, these discussions become relevant to our interest in the consequences
of rapid nonmetro growth. There is considerable agreement
that the growth of population in most communities results in
increased differentiation, specialization, and diversity in
roles, activities, and facilities. Differences among theor-
ists, however, can be found in their predictions of other
consequences of population change. On the one hand, Spencer
(1895) assumed that communities are better able to meet the
needs of their people as the division of labor increases,
resulting in greater happiness. The dominant viewpoint,
however, is that population growth has adverse consequences
for the community and the individual, because a life once
characterized by intimate personal ties and likemindedness
gives way to more formal and superficial relationships
among people who have little in common with one another
(see Durkheim 1964; Toennies 1957). This "loss of community"
and its consequences for personal life (e.g., alienation,
suicide) has been a consistent theme that influenced much
of the thinking about community growth and provided a foundation for the work that followed by students of urban life.
   The basic assumptions about the social and psychological
consequences of urbanization can be found in essays prepared
by Georg Simmel, Robert Park, and Louis Wirth. In an essay
entitled "The Metropolis and Mental Life," Simmel (1969)
reasoned that a high number of potential personal contacts,
resulting from increased size and density, threatened the
psychological state of urbanites with the possibility of
overstimulation (see also Milgram 1970). If coping mechanisms do not evolve, serious mental health problems are a
possibility. The adjustments that are made lead to new
styles of personal interaction: noninvolvement, withdrawal
from some daily encounters, and blasé attitudes towards
others. Relationships in urbanizing or urbanized places
take on a much more functional, superficial, and transient
character to the detriment of the individual and the community. Park, in "The City" (1915), suggested that the
ecological separation of human activities, which is a result of differentiation due to greater growth and density,
has important consequences. Community solidarity, the moral
regulation of individuals, and the maintenance of intimate

relationships gives way to deviance, mental health problems,
a lack of social consciousness, a wide range of diverse but
superficial associations, and more privacy and freedom.
Louis Wirth's (1938) essay "Urbanism as a Way of Life"
discussed the problems associated with greater population
size, population density, and social heterogeneity. The
consequences of social differentiation within a more dense
context seem to be heightened opportunities for conflict,
frustration, and competition for scarce resources. Social
relations tend to deteriorate from a more personal and
intimate level to an increased reliance upon brief and
superficial encounters with other community members. A
shift from informal methods to formal institutions for
social control occurs, and psychological problems (anomie,
loneliness, withdrawal) seem to be more prevalent (see reviews in Fischer 1972, 1976; Baldassare 1979; Luloff 1979).

Nowhere are specific discussions of the social impacts
of community growth more explicit and alarming than in the
writings of the Chicago School of Urban Sociology. Burgess
(1967: 57) argued that "rapid urban expansion is accompanied
by excessive increases in disease, crime, disorder, vice,
insanity, and suicide, rough indexes of social disorganization." McKenzie (1967: 70) also spoke of the "disorganization of our rural and small-town institutions" due to an
inability to cope with population growth. At the very least,
these writers believed that communities undergoing rapid
population increases would necessarily go through a difficult period of transition before they could come to grips
with the new circumstances brought about by increased size.
Importantly, "successful" adjustment meant a more urban way
of life (Wirth 1938), itself not without costs to the residents (e.g., anomie, superficial ties, deviance, alienation). Another point of relevance to the population turnaround is that the most severe consequences of growth were
purported to take place when increase in population size
was a result of in-migration (Park, 1967: 59). This is
apparently due to the need to provide special services for
newcomers to communities (e.g., housing, jobs, and institutions to integrate them into community life) and the "shaky"
psychological status of a mobile population.

There is, at present, some theoretical conflict about
the consequences of urbanization, which probably reflects a
more general uncertainty about the impacts of growth. This
is best exemplified by views given by two prominent sociologists. In a presidential address to the American Sociological Association, Philip Hauser (1969) argued that increasing

size, density, and heterogeneity have led to personal, social, and organizational difficulties in modern urban society. Some of the problems cited (in the tradition of earlier human ecologists) are social conflict, the break-down of community and primary groups (e.g., the family, friendships), institutional overload, and the depersonal-ization of human relationships. Amos Hawley (1972), in a presidential address to the Population Association of America, emphasized the benefits that accrue due to greater density of human settlement. For example, these conditions create the possibilty for diverse services and facilities at a relatively lower cost in terms of travel time and energy. Opportunities for efficient information exchange and regular social contact also improve, as urbanization decreases both the friction of space (through transporta-tion and communication) and perhaps the distances between potential contacts. Growth could therefore be viewed as producing a more desirable life-style as well as a more urban way of life. Of course, as population size increases so does the demand for more services, resulting in new op-portunites for both consumers and those seeking employment.

Recent sociological interest in growth and decline has added some new and important perspectives to the debate. Molotch (1976) has argued that community elites seek to maximize the growth rates of their localities (and thus their profits) with little concern for the social and envi-ronmental consequences for the general population. Logan (1976, 1978) has countered by arguing that residents and communities vary in their abilites to achieve desired rates of growth and to implement the necessary adjustments to cope with growth. Thus, the causes and consequences of growth may vary according to the community and personal resources at hand, and the potential to mobilize these resources to achieve the desired conditions. Thus, "growing pains" may be more severe in certain contexts, despite the fact that growth rates may be similar.

Obviously, sociological theory has proven to be a rich source of predictions about the social impacts of nonmetro growth. The following hypotheses are offered, which will be evaluated after reviewing the research evidence: (1) The greater the growth rate, the more complaints residents have about their community conditions and personal circumstances. (2) Personal and community characteristics may result in differences in adjustments and complaints in regard to rapid population growth. Exact predictions, however, are difficult to make. On the one hand, longer length of residence, lower income, less education, and nonurban experiences might lead to more actual disruptions and an inability to cope. However, more education, higher incomes, a shorter length of residence, and urban residential experiences may lead to a greater awareness of problems and higher expectations about the "quality of life." (3) Nonmetro areas undergoing rapid population growth due to migration have more serious problems than suburban or central city areas undergoing equivalent population change. The severe change in community scale creates the need for new institutions and a much more differentiated locality. The adjustments in service delivery needed to satisfy urban migrants' expectations place a strain on the community's resources; there is a high probability that the original population will be dissatisfied with these changes, and/or the new residents will not have the desired services. (4) Rapidly growing nonmetro areas are undergoing a transformation to a more urban way of life, resulting in greater similarities with metro residents in attitudes about community conditions and personal life.

METHODS FOR ASSESSING THE SOCIAL CONSEQUENCES OF GROWTH IN NONMETROPOLITAN AREAS

As was mentioned earlier, there are several approaches to measuring the social consequences of population change and social impact assessment is stressed in this chapter. These methods are briefly reviewed here in order to better understand the inherent strengths and weaknesses of the research reviewed in the next section. It should be kept in mind that all of the studies reviewed later have in common the following deficits: no standard definition of rapid growth; discussions of the effects of population growth that are not always distinct from demographic change; and a lack of attention to the intervening effects of community size upon disruptions due to population change. These unresolved methodological and substantive issues are a cause for confusion in interpreting the overall impacts of nonmetro growth.

The ecological method is used to determine aggregate social changes as a result of alterations in the demography of the community, such as population growth. The dependent variables or consequences typically reflect publicly recorded measures of social disorganization (e.g., crime

rates, mental hospital admissions, suicides, health problems) or community organization (e.g., specialized institutions, complexity of the division of labor). Communities
that vary in growth rates could be contrasted to determine
the influence of growth, or communities that have experienced migration could be studied longitudinally. The advantages include a rather straightforward determination
of the structural changes that occur on the community level.
The disadvantages include the use of highly aggregated data
that lead to unwarranted generalizations about individuals'
lives, problems of reliability and validity, and the limitations of using only data that are public records.

The case study approach can vary considerably in method
and content. At one extreme, it may involve impressionistic
and anecdotal accounts of rapid population growth based
upon limited observations of the community and informal
interviews with local residents and leaders. It can, on the
other hand, be based upon more intensive field studies that
involve systematic information (e.g., surveys, public records) collected over a lengthy period of time. Problems
of validity and reliability are the major causes for caution in interpreting the results of these types of studies.
However, when case studies can allow for comparisons with
other types of growth circumstances, or at least involve
baseline data for the locality experiencing growth, it may
be possible to generalize these findings to communities
with similar attributes.

A social impact assessment utilizes data that are systematically collected from individuals in the community
(see Christensen 1976; Finsterbush and Wolf 1977). In the
case of nonmetro growth, a contextual analysis (see Lazarsfeld et al. 1972) is employed in which differences in reported behaviors and attitudes could be attributed to the
demographic changes experienced by the individual. It is
essential to employ control variables through multivariate
techniques, as well as bivariate analyses, in order to
determine if the variations are due to growth per se. The
sample may also be partitioned in order to assess the impacts of population growth on specific population subgroups
(e.g., urban migrants versus original residents). Social
impact assessment specifically requires either baseline
data on the community in question (i.e., a longitudinal
design) or comparisons of localities with different growth
rates (e.g., no growth versus rapid growth). Christensen
(1976: xi) lists several substantive areas for social
impact studies: personal safety and privacy; recreation and

commerce; transportation facilities; perceived environmental
quality; and local amenities and disamenities. The social
scientist, examining the possibilities of social disorganization and organizational complexity in growing areas, would
want to measure other factors: general attitudes towards
the home and residence; evaluations of local facilities and
services; the quality and quantity of social experiences
both intimate and secondary in nature; and evaluations of
personal well-being, health, mental health, and happiness.
Additional data to be merged with these survey responses
involve published reports of the population and housing
characteristics of the community, including measures of
population change such as net migration over some recent
period of time (for a discussion of problems in using
county-level data, see Greenwood and Luloff 1979). The
timing of baseline and follow-up studies, as well as the
selection of study sites for comparative purposes, are of
course crucial to interpretations about the effects of
growth. A difficulty with social impact assessment is that
reports of problems by local residents may be either exaggerated or underrated when compared with objective measures
of community change. However, because these attitudes influence migration preferences and actual desires to stay
in or leave the locality, self-reports are of obvious
significance.

EMPIRICAL INFORMATION ABOUT THE
SOCIAL CONSEQUENCES OF NONMETROPOLITAN GROWTH

ECOLOGICAL RESEARCH

There are limited data concerning the aggregate effects of
nonmetro growth on social disorganization. The available
studies are dated before the turnaround and provide inconsistent results. In Ogburn's (1935) classic study of cities
and crime rates, a national sample of twenty-two nonsouthern
cities within the population range of 38,000 to 50,000 was
examined. The rate of population growth between 1920 and
1930 was not significantly associated with the rate of reported crimes for the locality in 1930. Higher growth rates
were related to two other possible measures of community
disruption: the number of police employees per 100 residents
and the rate of church membership in the locality. Of
course, the lower ratio of police to residents in growing

areas may be due to lower crime rates in these places rather than a lack of municipal resources or responsiveness. A later study by Wechsler (1961) examined growth rates between 1950 and 1960 among fifty Massachusetts communities within a twenty-five-mile radius of Boston. The fastest-growing localities, which were the smaller towns on the periphery, had the highest rates of suicide and hospitalized depression. Although the author presents a number of arguments as to why growth ought to produce mental problems, it must be remembered that the demographic characteristics of these communites were not controlled in the analysis. In addition, at least the findings on hospitalized depression are in doubt, because outpatient care may be lacking in smaller towns and Wechsler (1961: 13) admits that depression was a more commonly used diagnostic category in the communities with higher growth rates.

More recent information exists regarding the relationship between nonmetro growth and the increasing complexity or development of specialized services within communities, but the evidence here also lacks consistency. In a study of 410 Wisconsin towns with a population size of 2,500 or less, a low positive association was found between population change and the availability of retail services (Fuguitt and Deeley 1966). In a later study of Wisconsin villages, which included 1970 data, Johansen and Fuguitt (1973) found a general decline in retail service functions among both growing and declining localities. Communities near metro areas gained people and lost services, while more distant places lost both people and services. Although an overall trend of decline in service functions existed, there was a growth in leisure and tourist activities among nonmetro locales. In a nationwide study, Frisbie and Poston (1976) found that growing counties had more distinct sustenance functions and greater organizational complexity than counties that were losing population. However, as Luloff and Stokes (1977) report in their study of North Carolina communities, which found a weak relationship between population size and differentiation, the causal direction is not at all clear (i.e., does differentiation lead to growth or does growth lead to differentiation). In agreement with Luloff and Stokes (1977: 493), this author concludes that size and growth may be necessary but not sufficient causes for increased complexity and services. Other factors, such as community social and economic characteristics, are undoubtedly of importance in examining aggregate-level organization and disorganization.

CASE STUDY RESEARCH

These studies consist of discussions of particular communities that have undergone rapid and recent increases in population. They usually lack precise measurements of community disorganization, comparison or control groups, and guidelines for the selection of sites that would allow the determination of how these findings can be generalized to other circumstances. Research is divided into those studies that use nonsystematic data collection and those that involve at least some attempt to survey the local population.

Journalistic accounts usually paint a dark picture of the effects of nonmetro growth. A nationally broadcast special on the "coal boom" (American Broadcasting Company, 21 March 1979) pointed to the plight of Craig, Colorado and Gillette, Wyoming, which were ranchland areas now subject to the rapid influx of migrants seeking high-paying energy-related employment. Schools and local facilities are inadequate and overcrowded, whereas social problems of all kinds seem to be on the increase. In the Sierra Nevada mountains of California, similar cries of overcrowding and the inadequacy of the local infrastructure are heard (Los Angeles Times, 25 March 1979), though the factors causing this migration seem to be related to life-style considerations. An article in Science (Gilmore 1976) pointed to the rapid growth of "Pistol Shot," a fictitious name given to a western energy boom town. A "breakdown" in the institutions (labor, education, housing, health) and a resident population that is alienated, suspicious, and in need of high levels of mental health services is perceived by Gilmore (1976: 536). Local government seems inadequate and disorganized in its attempts to remedy the situation. The scenario for these energy boom towns is repeated in discussions by Morrison (1977a: 8) who states that "today's instant cities, like the earlier boom towns, are characterized by a transient, largely male population and the 4 D's: drunkenness, depression, delinquency, and divorce." Case studies of small cities that were conducted by the U.S. Department of Housing and Urban Development (1979: 219-57) cited severe problems of infrastructure (e.g., schools, roads, sewers, police, fire protection) in most of the places undergoing rapid growth; of course, because the study is a basis for further federal assistance, encouragement for reporting serious problems is evident. Although energy boom towns or other special growth circumstances may produce problems, though the evidence is hard to assess

because of the scarcity of data in these accounts, other
factors that are neglected (e.g., the socioeconomic status
and tax base of the locality) may also account for the
severity of disruption. Further, these accounts do not
represent a cross section of nonmetro communities experiencing growth.

Some case studies of growing nonmetro areas provide
survey data from local residents or in some cases a sample
of recent migrants. Because urban newcomers sometimes differ
in social characteristics (e.g., they are younger, better
educated, and more occupationally skilled than the original
population; for contrasting evidence see Wardwell 1977)
discussions of "cultural clashes" seem to be a common theme
in many of these reports. In a study of a growing Colorado
mountain town, Graber (1974) argues that many of the new
urban migrants tend to commute to cities for work and have
chosen a nonurban location in order to improve their social
and physical surroundings. These newcomers were more likely
than oldtimers to favor growth controls in order to protect
the amenities they moved to achieve. Ploch (1978), in a
study of rural growth in Maine, discovered the emergence of
conflict over school policies due to the better-educated
status of new residents (cited in Clay and Price 1979), and
also a greater concern with preservation and land-use controls than among long-term residents (cited in Christensen
and Garkovich forthcoming). Colfer and Colfer's (1978) study
of a western town that experienced a steady in-migration of
government employees found clashes in basic values between
the original population and middle-class families (i.e.,
the latter's strong beliefs in universalism versus parti-
cularism; the importance of education, frugality and efficiency: cited in Clay and Price 1979). Also, in a study
of black returnees to the South, Campbell et al. (1974)
cite the potential conflict between the migrants' desire
for social and economic assimilation with prevailing racial
attitudes and barriers at their destination points. There
is some limited evidence that migrants complain more about
service inadequacies than original residents, based upon
recent surveys in Kansas (Flora and Flora 1978). However, a
study of two growing agricultural communities in Colorado
found more complaints about services among the older, native, long-term residents (Mileti et al. 1979). The Colorado study also reported greater dissatisfaction with community change among older, native, better-educated, and
high-income individuals, whereas a decline in the sense
of community was also sensed more by the better-educated,

native, and long-term residents. The contrast in findings
between the Colorado and Kansas studies points to the
difficulties of generalizing from case-study information.
Obvious questions could be raised about sampling techniques,
the reliability of data, the characteristics of study sites,
and the validity of self-reports. There may also be distinctive social variation in the original population, migrant groups, and urban migrants' experiences and expectations that account for these variations in complaints among
subgroups. In conclusion, although value differences may
exist between urban migrants and the original residents,
there is no evidence to suggest that serious conflicts,
civil unrest, or any form of disorganization has emerged
due to varying viewpoints about community planning and
development. Evidence about service inadequacies seems even
more tenuous, and in fact urban migrants may be characterized as perceiving a better quality of life in nonmetro
areas rather than demanding special facilities when they
arrive (see Blackwood and Carpenter 1978).

SOCIAL IMPACT RESEARCH

These studies examine attitudes and behaviors of local
residents as a function of population change in the residential environment. Comparisons are within the nonmetro
community over time, or among nonmetro communities that vary
in growth rates (holding other factors constant), or among
nonmetro communities that differ along social dimensions
(holding growth constant). Substantive issues include attitudes towards future development, general social values,
attitudes towards the residential environment, evaluation
of services and facilities, reports concerning social life
and personal relations, and ratings of psychological well-
being and health. Some, but certainly not all, studies distinguish recent urban migrants from the original nonmetro
population.
    Several studies are limited to the realm of general
value orientations of the population and specific attitudes
about future growth, and thus they do not bear directly upon
the issues of community disorganization. Research conducted
in North Carolina and Kentucky during the 1970s indicates
considerable value consensus among potential nonmetro movers
and those individuals who wish to remain in their present
nonmetro locations (reported in Christensen 1979a; and
Christensen and Garkovich forthcoming). Only on the issue

of leisure did differences emerge, and this finding was explained by the younger age of potential movers. Several problems exist in the interpretation of these findings. New urban migrants are pooled with long-term residents, and thus possible value differences between (potential and actual) urban migrants and the original population may become diffused. Further, a study of potential metro to nonmetro movers may be misleading, because only a proportion and perhaps special subset of this population actually migrates. Finally, the actual impact upon growing nonmetro communities is only inferred, because we do not know if the destination choices of potential in-migrants will conflict with the specific values of the individuals living in high-growth-rate areas. A nonmetro study conducted in northern Michigan sought to examine the relationship between the growth rates of townships (between 1970 and 1973) and attitudes towards future development (Marans and Wellman, 1978: 140-43), while ignoring the present social impacts of population change. Growth was related only weakly to the amount of new development and increased population that residents desired. In all, the surveys reviewed here present no evidence for the negative effects of growth in nonmetro areas. Admittedly, the substantive issues examined and the methodologies employed are not precise enough to address the major social impact issues.

Some studies contrast the social consequences of population change in areas experiencing or expecting growth that vary along some important community dimensions. Jobes (1979) contrasted a western rural community with a sizable western town, using a longitudinal design that allows one to examine changes in attitudes over time. No major changes in community satisfaction, evaluations of facilities and services, or reports of personal dissatisfaction were found in the town, although the author reported growing discontent in the smaller rural community. Though "size of place" could account for these findings, it must be stated that growth in the small locality was more anticipated than actual, whereas the larger locality has experienced real rapid growth. In addition, the anticipated change was viewed as "externally caused" (i.e., coal development) in the smaller place, probably leading to more worries and discontent. This author concludes that the information from the larger locality is more useful for present purposes, because actual growth was involved, and does seem to indicate a lack of negative effects due to growth. Ongoing research in the Ozark-Ouachita Uplands (Dailey and Campbell

1979) examines rural counties with a rapid influx of urban
migrants and compares them with rural counties experiencing
similar growth rates due to a high proportion of retirees.
All areas seem to lack basic infrastructure, experience
service inadequacies, and undergo environmental degradation.
Taxation and planning do not seem to keep pace with these
problems. Communities with urban migrants who are retirees
seem to have additional burdens: inadequate health and
transportation facilities, and new residents who are un-
willing to become involved in community affairs. This
study, in contrast to the reports from the western rural
areas mentioned above, finds serious social impacts of
growth, particularly among older urban migrants. The
original economic resources of this southern region, the
responsiveness of government, and the characteristics of
recent urban migrants (i.e., social and attitudinal) may
account for these discrepancies.

We now turn to surveys conducted during the population
turnaround that can compare residents in communites varying
in growth rates. Data reported from three Pennsylvania
counties (Luloff 1978) were reanalyzed using the growth
measure of percent county net migration from 1970 to 1975
(from the U.S. Bureau of the Census 1977). One county experienced decline between 1970 and 1975 (it had also declined between 1960 and 1970), the other had in-migration
during both periods, whereas the final county was a true
case of turnaround (i.e., decline between 1960 and 1970,
and grew between 1970 and 1975). Thirty-six survey items
involved problems in service and facilities, social conflict, and community spirit. These data were ranked in
terms of which county had the highest and which had the
lowest percentage of reported problems in each domain.
The county with continued population decline had the most
complaints for twenty-two items, whereas the turnaround
county had the highest percentage of complaints for only
eleven items, and the continued growth county outscored the
others for only three items. When considering which county
reported the least problems within each domain, the turnaround county fared slightly better than the other counties
(i.e., sixteen versus eleven for the continued growth
county and nine for the declining county). These findings
appear to be in contradiction with a statewide survey of
Michigan conducted by Clay and Price (1979), who found that
county-level growth leads to dissatisfaction with services and
the residential environment. Though the conclusions differ,
there are similarities in reports of problems (i.e., in

particular dissatisfaction with infrastructure and municipal services) and no findings that suggest a significant loss of community solidarity. In fact, Clay and Price (1979) also did not find proof of overall community disorganization (e.g., no effects of growth upon recreation and cultural facilities, programs for the elderly, or local employment). Finally, a study of one hundred North Carolina communities by Christensen (1979b) adds further evidence of the limited effects of population growth. The author found increases in material well-being and the quality of services with higher county densities (usually an indicator of growth in the nonmetro sector), whereas greater community satisfaction seemed to occur with lower densities. Christensen (1979b: 398) concludes, "perhaps in small growth centers, people could have the best of both worlds, quality services, economic well-being, and community sentiment (i.e., social well-being)." This is basically in agreement with the thrust of findings reported thus far, though information from a national survey is examined next before a final assessment can be made.

EVIDENCE FROM NATIONAL SURVEY DATA:
BALDASSARE AND PENNIE (1979)

This author used a subsample of 839 nonmetro area respondents from the Quality of Life Survey (Campbell et al. 1976) to study the social impacts of growth. Residents' perceptions of "place," "social life," and "personal well-being" were examined, using "percent county net migration between 1960 and 1970" as the causal variable. Empirical indicators of residents' complaints involved survey items measuring satisfaction with local facilities, housing and neighborhood satisfaction, family and friendship ties, voluntary associations, and health and mental health. Statistical techniques included bivariate cross-tabulation analysis with the Chi-square test, correlation analysis, and stepwise multiple regression. For the analysis, the research population of nonmetro area residents was partitioned into subpopulations based upon "percent net migration." This resulted in four subgroups: (1) loss of population, -1 percent or less; (2) stagnant, 0 to 5 percent; (3) slow, 6 to 20 percent; and (4) rapid, 21 percent or more.
    Evaluations of place, social life, and well-being by growth rate yielded no evidence to support the idea that

growth leads to disorganization. In fact, satisfaction with roads and police, the availability of public transit, and satisfaction with convenience of location are positively related to growth. Residents of rapidly growing nonmetro areas also report more satisfaction with spare time than residents of equivalent areas undergoing slower growth or loss of population.

The possibility was considered that differential satisfaction with the community, social, and personal life is a partial function of the length of residence and socioeconomic status of the residents of these communities. However, when comparing subgroups based on these classifications no change in the reported evaluations was observed. That is, residents of ten or more years were not more negative in their evaluations, nor were families with annual incomes of less than ten thousand dollars. The lack of negative effects of growth was further supported in the regression analysis of each of the dependent variables on growth. Controls were used for the personal variables of respondent's age, education, and home ownership, and the contextual variable median income for the county. Some of the relationships were significant and indicated that growth is positively related to satisfaction with police, availability of public transit, and satisfaction with convenience of location. Results of regression analyses that controlled for whether or not the respondent ever lived in a different type of place, and subgroup analyses based upon this dichotomy, did not provide evidence that would suggest that past residential experiences (e.g., urban residence) affect evaluations in growing areas. Personal characteristics do not seem to result in a differential ability to adjust to demographic growth or increase the probability of dissatisfaction with the community or life in general within rapidly growing nonmetro areas.

In order to explore the possibility that rapid growth has a greater effect on nonmetro areas than upon the suburbs and central cities, the entire respondent population of 2,164 was partitioned into "nonmetropolitan," "suburban," or "central city" residence based upon the University of Michigan classifications. Then only those respondents living in areas experiencing rapid growth were selected for a repeated bivariate cross-tabulation analysis. Similarity of attitudes is particularly apparent in regard to satisfaction with local facilities and services where the negative effects of increasing urbanization are generally most significantly felt by local residents. Apparently, problems with roads, schools, and a lack of a sufficient police force are universally experienced in rapidly growing communities regardless of whether they are located in the central cities, suburbs, or nonmetro areas. It is curious to note that although nonmetro area residents show the least satisfaction with police protection, these residents are the most satisfied with safety from crime. The nonmetro area residents also indicate the most satisfaction with the community and their dwelling units and are the least likely to move. Similarity of attitudes is shown in regard to satisfaction with health, life, and fear of a nervous breakdown although nonmetro area residents show the highest satisfaction with personal well-being overall. Satisfaction with intimate ties and secondary relationships is highly evident in the nonmetro areas, discounting notions that increasing urbanization unilaterally yields a disruption of personal relationships and an increase in perceived anonymity. Comparing the reports of all metro residents with the evaluations in fast-growing nonmetro areas, we also found gross differences in evaluation of place and personal life, indicating that a transformation to an urban way of life has not occurred (in agreement with Fischer 1979).

Before discussing the interpretations and implications of these and other results, a word of caution about the limitations of this research is in order. Obviously the size of the sample, particularly the present group of one hundred respondents experiencing rapid population growth, is a factor that severely constrains the ability to make definitive statements. A partial (and not entirely satisfactory) response to this issue would be to aggregate data on all respondents experiencing considerable growth (i.e., slow and rapid), which would leave us with very similar conclusions and a sample more than twice as large. One could also argue that the selection of sites, because it was based on an attempt to draw a national sample of households, was inappropriate for addressing the social impacts of rapid growth. It would of course be preferable to choose sites that vary in growth, social, economic, and regional contexts, and to have sample sizes that would allow controlled comparisons. In defense of the present sample, over thirty nonmetro counties were involved in the study and they did vary along significant economic and geographic dimensions (e.g., one-third of the respondents were within fifty miles of an SMSA, and about one-half were within one hundred miles of an SMSA of more than 350,000; about one-half of the counties were peripheral to an SMSA and the

remainder were in more distant rural areas). The present
study could also be questioned because it involves pre-
turnaround survey and census data. However, when population
updates of the sampled counties are reviewed (U.S. Bureau
of the Census 1977), at least from the perspective of gross
categorization, the change in results would likely be minimal (e.g., two-thirds had the same rate of growth between
1970 and 1975 as between 1960 and 1970, 20 percent moved
from decline to stagnation, and only four counties experienced a significant shift towards fast or slow growth).
Perhaps the most difficult criticisms to respond to involve
the lack of longitudinal data related to attitude change in
rapidly growing communities and the global nature (in temporal and spatial terms) of the growth measure. Data limitations allowed only for a comparison of communities varying in rates of migration, using county measures as surrogates for local growth. Admittedly this study is a preliminary attempt, using secondary data sources, to address a
complex and controversial topic of national importance.

CONCLUSIONS

There is no convincing support for the contention that net
migration to nonmetro areas has adverse effects on community
residents. The research evidence is contradictory and at
times even points to higher evaluations of residential
amenities and some aspects of personal life in growing
areas. The general views about the negative consequences of
growth in rural areas thus seem narrow in perspective.
Further, there was no indication that rapid nonmetro growth
was more troublesome than growth in metro areas, and no
evidence that residents in rapidly growing nonmetro areas
report attitudes about their community and personal life
that are distinct from metropolitanites' views. Finally,
past residential experiences, length of stay in the community, and economic resources of the respondents did not
seem consistently to make adjustments to rapid growth more
troublesome.
     There appear to be two reasons for arguing that the
costs of nonmetro growth may be overrated and its benefits
understated by most rural sociologists. One is that population growth may sometimes be associated with affluence,
allowing for an investment of economic resources to improve
the institutions and physical amenities of a nonmetro lo-

cale. Another explanatory factor may be that the increase in community size and density provides more of a "critical mass" for diverse facilities and activities (see Fischer 1976). This would heighten the possibility over time for congruence (Michelson 1976) between residents' needs and environmental circumstances, and perhaps explain why residents of growing nonmetro areas are sometimes more satisfied with their leisure pursuits and more involved in voluntary groups.

At the same time, the findings could be interpreted to suggest that, despite the significance of the population turnaround, we ought not to forget the serious plight of declining and stagnant communities in nonmetro areas. Results of the national survey show, particularly in regard to accessibility, services, and facilities, that this group of respondents has deficits in levels of satisfaction. Whether these communities will continue to lag behind other places in quality-of-life terms, or whether the population turnaround will worsen their difficulties, is of course not known. This evidence should, however, serve to rekindle our interest in decline and stagnation in rural areas and is consistent with other theory and research on this topic (McKenzie 1967; Ogburn 1935).

Based on the self-reports of residents examined here, it does not seem likely that the population turnaround will be reversed because rapid population growth is not generally associated with personal and community disorganization. Undoubtedly, the controversy over the negative effects of growth in nonmetro areas will continue because of specific cases to the contrary. A definitive resolution of this issue will not occur until longitudinal studies are conducted, using systematic data collection techniques within carefully selected communities. In the future, the continued use of social impact assessments in conjunction with economic and demographic analysis will aid in the pursuit of rationally evaluating the pros and cons of growth, testing important sociological theories, and perhaps even predicting what is in store for the future.

BIBLIOGRAPHY

Alonso, William. "Problems, Purposes, and Implicit Policies for a National Strategy of Urbanization." Working Paper no. 158. Berkeley: Institute of Urban and Regional

Development, 1971.

Baldassare, M. Residential Crowding in Urban America. Berkeley: University of California Press, 1979.

_____, and Pennie, R. C. "The Effects of Nonmetropolitan Growth on the Community and the Individual." Prepared for the Population Association of America Meetings, Philadelphia, 1979.

Beale, C. The Revival of Population Growth in Nonmetropolitan America. Economic Development Division, U.S. Department of Agriculture, ERS-605. June 1975.

Beaton, W., and Cox., J. "Toward Accidental National Urbanization Policy." Journal of the American Institute of Planners 43 (1977): 54-61.

Berry, B. "The Counterurbanization Process: Urban America Since 1970." In Urbanization and Counterurbanization, edited by B. Berry, pp. 15-30. Beverly Hills: Sage, 1976.

Blackwood, L., and Carpenter, E. "The Importance of Anti-urbanism in Determining Residential Preferences and Migration Patterns." Rural Sociology 43 (1978): 31-47.

Burgess, E. W. "The Growth of the City: An Introduction to a Research Project." In The City, edited by R. E. Park and E. W. Burgess, pp. 47-62. Chicago: University of Chicago Press, 1967.

Burrows, L. B. Growth Management: Issues, Techniques and Policy Implications. New Brunswick: Center for Urban Policy Research, 1978.

Campbell, A.; Converse, F.; and Rodgers, W. The Quality of American Life. New York: Russell Sage, 1976.

Campbell, R., and Johnson, D. "Propositions on Counterstream Migration." Rural Sociology 41 (1976): 127-45.

_____; and Stangler, G. "Return Migration of Black People to the South." Rural Sociology 39 (1974): 514-28.

Carpenter, E. "Potential for Population Dispersal: A Closer Look at Residential Location Preferences." Rural Sociology 42 (1977): 357-70.

Chevan, A., and Fischer, L. "Retirement and Interstate Migration." Paper presented at the Population Association of America Meetings, Atlanta, 1978.

Christensen, J. "Urbanism and Community Sentiment: Extending Wirth's Model." Social Science Quarterly 60 (1979b): 387-400.

_____. "Value Orientations of Potential Migrants and Nonmigrants." Rural Sociology 44 (1979a): 331-44.

_____, and Garkovich, L. "A Comparison of the Value Orientations of Potential and Actual Migrants with Those of Nonmigrants." In Migration: Perception, Values, and Realities, edited by J. Steel and R. Geruson. Forthcoming.

Christensen, K. Social Impacts of Land Development. Washington, D.C.: Urban Institute, 1976.

Clay, D., and Price, M. "Structural Disturbances in Rural Communities: Some Repercussions of the Migration Turnaround in Michigan." Paper prepared for the Rural Sociological Society Meetings, Burlington, Vt., August 1979.

Colfer, C., and Colfer, M. "Inside Bushler Bay: Lifeways in Counterpoint." Rural Sociology 43 (1978): 204-20.

Dailey, G., and Campbell, R. "Consequences of Retirement Migration in the Ozark-Ouachita Uplands: An Exploratory Research." Unpublished paper, 1979.

DeJong, G. "Residential Preferences and Migration." Demography 14 (1977): 169-78.

Durkheim, E. The Division of Labor in Society. 1893. New York: Free Press, 1964.

Farley, R. "Components of Suburban Population Growth." In The Changing Face of the Suburbs, edited by B. Schwartz, pp. 3-38. Chicago: University of Chicago Press, 1976.

Finsterbusch, K., and Wolf, C. P. Methodology of Social Impact Assessment. Stroudsburg, Pa.: Dowden, Hutchinson, and Ross, 1977.

Fischer, C. S. "The Spread of Violence from the City to the Countryside: 1955-1975." Paper presented at the American Sociological Association Meetings, Boston, 1979.

_____. The Urban Experience. New York: Harcourt, Brace, Jovanovich, 1976.

_____. "Urbanism as a Way of Life: A Review and an Agenda." Sociological Methods and Research 1 (1972): 187-242.

Flora, J., and Flora, C. "Kansas on the Move." Unpublished paper. Kansas State University, 1978.

Frisbie, W., and Poston, D. "The Structure of Sustenance Organization and Population Change." Rural Sociology 41 (1976): 354-69.

Fuguitt, G., and Deeley, N. "Retail Service Patterns and Small Town Population Change: A Replication of Hassinger's Study." Rural Sociology 31 (1966): 53-63.

Fuguitt, G., and Zuiches, J. "Residential Preferences and Population Distribution." Demography 12 (1975): 491-504.

Gilmore, J. "Boom Towns May Hinder Energy Resource Development." Science 191 (1976): 535-40.

Graber, E. "Newcomers and Oldtimers: Growth and Change in a

Mountain Town." Rural Sociology 39 (1974): 504-13.

Greenwood, P., and Luloff, A. E. "Inadvertent Social Theory:
Aggregation and Its Effects on Community Research." New
England Agricultural Economics Journal 9 (1979).

Hauser, P. M. "The Chaotic Society: Product of the Social
Morphological Revolution." American Sociological Review
34 (1969): 1-19.

Hawley, A. H. "Population Density and the City." Demography
9 (1972): 521-29.

Jobes, P. C. "Changing Country, Changing Town: A Comparison
of Satisfaction and Feelings Regarding Development in
High Expansion Potential Communities." Unpublished
paper, 1979.

Johansen, M., and Fuguitt, G. "Regional Retail Activity in
Wisconsin Villages." Rural Sociology 38 (1973): 207-18.

Kasarda, J. "Urbanization, Community, and the Metropolitan
Problem." In Handbook of Contemporary Urban Life,
edited by D. Street, pp. 27-57. San Francisco: Jossey-
Bass, 1978.

Lazarsfeld, P.; Pasanella, A,; and Rosenberg, M. Continuities in the Language of Social Research. New York:
Free Press, 1972.

Logan, J. "Growth, Politics, and the Stratification of
Places." American Journal of Sociology 84 (1978):
404-16.

_____. "Notes on the Growth Machine: Toward a Compar-
ative Political Economy of Place." American Journal of
Sociology 82 (1976): 349-52.

Luloff, A. E. "The Good Community: A Research Agenda." Paper
presented at the Rural Sociological Association Meetings, Burlington, Vt., 1979.

_____. "Identifying the Locus for Action: What Local
Residents Have to Say." Small Town 9 (1978): 11-14.

_____, and Stokes, C. S. "A Note on Population Size
and Community Differentiation in Nonmetropolitan
Communities." Sociology and Social Research 61 (1977):
486-95.

McCarthy, K., and Morrison, P. "The Changing Demographic and
Economic Structure of Nonmetropolitan Areas in the
1970s." Report P-6062. Santa Monica, Calif.: Rand
Corporation, 1978.

McKenzie, R. E. "The Ecological Approach to the Study of the
Human Community." In The City, edited by R. E. Park and
E. W. Burgess, pp. 63-79. Chicago: University of
Chicago Press, 1967.

Marans, R., and Wellman, J. The Quality of Nonmetropolitan

Living. Ann Arbor: Institute for Social Research, 1978.

Mazie, S., and Rawlings, S. "Public Attitudes Towards Population Distribution Issues." In *Population Distribution and Policy*, edited by S. Mazie, pp. 599-615. Vol. 5 of Commission Research Reports. Washington, D.C.: U.S. Government Printing Office, 1972.

Michelson, W. *Man and His Urban Environment*. Reading, Mass.: Addison-Wesley, 1976.

Mileti, D.; Santopolo, F.; and Williams, G. "Resident Perceptions in Growth-Impacted Western Agricultural Communities." Paper presented at the Rural Sociological Society Meetings, Burlington, Vt., 1979.

Milgram, S. "The Experience of Living in Cities." *Science* 167 (1970): 1461-68.

Molotch, H. "The City as a Growth Machine: Toward a Political Economy of Place." *American Journal of Sociology* 82 (1976): 309-31.

Morgan, D. "Subjective Indicators of the Quality of Life in U.S. Communities." Unpublished report, National Opinion Research Center, 1975.

Morgan, D. J., and Murray, J. R. "A Potential Population Distribution and Its Dynamics: The Expressed Preference for Residential Location." Unpublished report, National Opinion Research Center, 1974.

Morrison, P. "Current Demographic Change in Regions of the United States." Series P-6000. Santa Monica, Calif.: Rand Corporation, 1977c.

_____. "Emerging Public Concern Over U.S. Population in an Era of Slowing Growth." Series P-5873. Santa Monica, Calif.: Rand Corporation, 1977b.

_____. "Migration and Rights of Access: New Public Concerns of the 1970s." Series P-5785. Santa Monica, Calif.: Rand Corporation, 1977a.

_____, and Wheeler, J. "Rural Renaissance in America?" *Population Bulletin* 31 (1976): 2-26.

Ogburn, W. F. "Factors in the Variation of Crime Among Cities." *Journal of the American Statistical Association* 30 (1935): 12-34.

Park, R. "The City: Suggestions for the Investigation of Human Behavior in the Urban Environment." *American Journal of Sociology* 20 (1915): 577-612.

_____. "The Urban Community as a Spatial Pattern and a Moral Order." In *Robert E. Park on Social Control and Collective Behavior*, 1926, edited by R. H. Turner, pp. 55-68. Chicago: University of Chicago Press, 1967.

Perry, D. C., and Watkins, A. J., eds. *The Rise of the*

Sunbelt Cities. Beverly Hills: Sage, 1977.

Ploch, L. "The Reversal in Migration Patterns: Some Rural
Development Consequences." Rural Sociology 43 (1978):
293-303.

Robertson, J., and Robertson, C. The Small Towns Book. New
York: Anchor, 1978.

Scott, R,; Brower, D.; and Miner, D. Management and Control
of Growth. Vol. 1. Washington, D.C.: Urban Land
Institute, 1975.

Simmel, G. "The Metropolis and Mental Life." In Classic
Essays on the Culture of Cities, 1905, edited by R.
Semmett, pp. 47-60. New York: Appleton, 1969.

Spencer, H. Principles of Sociology. Vol 1. New York:
Appleton and Company, 1895.

Steahr, T.; Brown, J.; and Wright, J. "An Analysis of In-
migrants to Rural Connecticut Since 1970." Paper
presented at the Population Association of America
Meetings, Atlanta, 1978.

Toennies, F. Community and Society. 1887. East Lansing,
Mich.: Michigan State University Press, 1957.

Tucker, C. "Changing Patterns of Migration Between Metropolitan and Nonmetropolitan Areas in the United States:
Recent Evidence." Demography 13 (1976): 435-43.

U.S. Bureau of the Census. County and City Data Book, 1975.
Washington, D.C.: U.S. Government Printing Office,
1977.

U.S. Department of Housing and Urban Development. Developmental Needs of Small Cities. Washington, D.C.: U.S.
Department of Housing and Urban Development, 1979.

Wardwell, J. "Equilibrium and Change In Non-metropolitan
Growth." Rural Sociology 42 (1977): 156-79.

_____, and Gilchrist, C. "Metropolitan Change and
Nonmetropolitan Growth." Paper presented at the Population Association of America Meetings, Atlanta, 1978.

Watt, K. E. "Needed: A Modern Approach to State Planning."
Cry California 5 (1970): 36-39.

Wechsler, H. "Community Growth, Depressive Disorders, and
Suicide." American Journal of Sociology 67 (1961): 9-16.

Williams, J., and Sofranko, A. "Motivations for the In-
migration Component of Population Turnaround in Nonmetropolitan Areas." Demography 16 (1979): 239-56.

Wirth, L. "Urbanism as a Way of Life." American Journal of
Sociology 44 (1938): 1-24.

Zelinsky, W. "Is Nonmetropolitan America Being Repopulated?
The Evidence from Pennsylvania's Minor Civil Divisions."
Demography 15 (1978): 13-40.

Zimmer, B. "The Urban Centrifugal Drift." In Metropolitan
    America in Contemporary Perspective, edited by A. Hawley
    and V. Rock, pp. 23-92. New York: John Wiley, 1975.
Zuiches, J., and Fuguitt, G. "Residential Preferences:
    Implications for Population Redistribution in Nonmetro-
    politan Areas." In Population Distribution and Policy,
    edited by S. M. Mazie, pp. 617-30. Vol. 5 of Commission
    Research Reports. Washington, D.C.: U.S. Government
    Printing Office, 1972.

II.

The Changing Structure of Economic Opportunity

Olaf F. Larson

4

Agriculture and the Community

INTRODUCTION

How do the characteristics of farms and farm people bear
upon the attributes and problems of small communities in
America? How do the distinctive qualities and functions of
these communities influence farms as production units and
the quality of life of farming people? What are the effects
of current changes and trends on the interrelationships of
agriculture and the rural community? The main purpose of
the present chapter is to review in a summary manner current knowledge about the answers to these questions. Some
implications for rural development policy will also be
discussed.

The reader should be aware at the outset of some important limitations faced in this review. First, there is a
dearth of timely and specific studies on the interrelationships of agriculture and the community. Second, comprehensive information about rural communities and recent social
change in American rural society does not equal that available in the 1920s, 1930s, and 1940s, aside from demographic
and similar census-type data. This is because systematic
nationwide studies that would provide this information have
not been continued.[1] Third, some of the statistical information that is available nationwide on farms and farm
people must be used with caution, especially in interpreting
trends. For example, the U.S. Census of Agriculture and the
U.S. Department of Agriculture data on the number of farms
classified by gross sales of products cannot be used as a
valid measure of recent trends in the distribution of farms
by size without adjusting for changing price levels. Thus,
the unadjusted figures show that farms with sales of $20,000
or more increased from 340,000 in 1960 to 831,000 in 1977,
giving the impression that the number of commercial farms
more than doubled. However, when an adjustment is made for
inflated prices, the number of farms equivalent to those
having sales of $20,000 or more in 1977 is found to have

been remarkably stable during this time period, that is,
837,000 in 1960 as compared with 831,000 in 1977 (Stanton
1979).[2]

First, selected guiding concepts and definitions essential in this review will be introduced and then a sketchy
perspective will be provided on farms, farm people, and
rural communities in contemporary America. From this background it should be clear, for example, that the farm population is not synonymous with the rural population and
the rural population is not commensurate with the nonmetro
population; rather, the farm population is one component of
the rural population and the rural is a component of the
nonmetro population. The failure to understand the distinction between the farm and rural categories has fostered the
myth of rural population decline. The public statements of
national policymakers have too often reflected a lack of
understanding of the distinction, thereby confusing the
public and perhaps adding to the difficulty of formulating
farm and rural development policies.

CONCEPTS AND DEFINITIONS

The primary source of information on farms comes from the
periodic complete enumerations across the nation made for
the U.S. Census of Agriculture. Currently, and for some
time in the past, in general a "farm" consists of all the
land under the day-to-day control of individual management
and on which agricultural operations are conducted during
the reference year. The land may be in one tract or several.
The criteria that qualify a place to be counted as a farm
have not been constant over the years, but the test has
usually involved a minimum number of acres or a minimum
value of products sold. In 1969 a place was counted as a
farm if it had at least ten acres of land and product sales
of $50 or more or if it had less than ten acres but the
estimated sales were put at $250 or more. In 1974 the acre-
age criterion was discarded and the sole test was whether
sales of agricultural products for the year were at least
$1,000. Each farm has only one person designated as the
operator, even in the case of partnerships, cooperatives,
and corporations. Analytically, each farm is a production
unit or, in economic terms, a business firm.

The farm population consists of all persons who reside
on a farm. Residence on a farm does not necessarily mean
that an individual is engaged full time or even part time

in work on the farm, except for the operator. Some 92
percent of the farm population, in 1975, lived in farm
operator households (Banks, 1978b: 3). The balance was most
often hired farm laborers and their families. A gradually
increasing percentage of farm operators, now roughly 10
percent, do not live on the farm they operate (U.S. Bureau
of the Census, 1978b: 7). The majority of these nonresident
operators and their families are excluded in the count of
farm population (U.S. Bureau of the Census, 1978b: 111-15).[3]
The majority of hired farm workers, even among those employed on a year-round basis, now live in a nonfarm residence (Rowe, 1979: 27) and, accordingly, are not included
as a part of the farm population.

The nonmetro population is the sum of three components:
urban, rural nonfarm, and farm populations. Urban includes
all population living within places of 2,500 or more inhabitants. That category comprised 41 percent of the nonmetro population in 1970. The rural nonfarm population
includes residents of villages and towns with less than
2,500 people together with those living in open country but
not on farms. Forty-four percent of the nonmetro population
occupied rural nonfarm residences. The remainder, or 15
percent, of the population lived on farms. Because farm
population numbers have continued to shrink since 1970
(Banks, 1978a: 3) while even entirely rural counties have
registered some gains (Beale, 1978: 51), the farm population
share of the total nonmetro population has declined to
around 12 percent.

For our present purposes we will use "rural community"
to designate what is usually referred to as the "trade-
center community" or the "service-area community."[4] Thus,
it includes a village or small town center and the surrounding farm and open country area within which the majority of the families use the social and economic services of
the center.[5] These communities vary greatly in the size
of their centers, the size of the geographic area included,
the services provided, the degree of identification the
residents have with their community, their social unity,
and in other ways.

A PERSPECTIVE ON NONMETROPOLITAN AMERICA

The boundaries of operating farms encompass over one-half,
nearly 54 percent, of the land area within the forty-eight
contiguous states.[6] An extension of farms, but outside

their fences, is the grassland, brushland, and forest used
for seasonal grazing of livestock.[7] This land, predominantly in the western states, includes an additional 15
percent of the land area (Frey 1973). The extent to which
the land is within farms varies greatly across the nation.
In the four northern Plains states and Iowa, farms occupy
over 90 percent of the land, whereas in all of the New
England states except Vermont, in New Jersey, and in the
western Mountain states of Nevada and Utah less than 25
percent of the land is in farms (Frey, 1973: 23-24).

Since the high point in farm acreage, nationally, was
recorded around 1950, about 12 percent has been shifted
from farm to nonfarm uses (U.S. Department of Agriculture,
hereafter USDA, 1978: 26). In the Northeast the acreage in
farms in 1974 was half that in 1940, continuing a trend
under way since 1880 (Stanton and Plimpton, 1979: 8).

A close association between farm and family has generally prevailed in the United States, with the farm providing a place of residence for the family and the family
doing the majority of the farm work. One result of this
close association, because of the land requirements for
most forms of farm production, has been a low density of
farm population and a dispersed settlement pattern in the
countryside. Low density and dispersed settlement, in turn,
have fostered the development of relatively small-scale
rural communities and local institutions, agencies, and
organizations.

The number of farms into which the more than 1 billion
acres of farmland are divided was reduced by 62 percent
between 1940 and 1974, to stand at 2,314,000[8] as compared
with more than 6 million at all times between 1910 and 1940
(USDA, 1978: 26). The number of farm households was similarly reduced, by 62 percent between 1940 and 1970 (U.S.
Bureau of the Census, 1975: 43). Farm population fell even
more sharply, declining by 70 percent between 1940 and 1974
(Beale and Banks, 1973: 14; Banks and De Are, 1979: 3),
while the total hours of labor used for farm work decreased
most of all, by 75 percent, during the same period (Durost
and Black, 1978: 32). The number of persons living on farms
in 1978 was estimated at 8,005,000 under the previous farm
definition and at only 6,501,000 under the new definition
adopted in 1974 (Banks and De Are, 1979: 1), both numbers
in dramatic contrast with the more than 30 million farm
residents reported for the years from 1910 through 1941.

The loss of farms and of farm population has been unevenly distributed. There have been marked shifts among the

major census regions, with the North Central and West
gaining and the South and the Northeast losing. The North
Central share of the nation's farms increased from 34 percent in 1940 to 44 percent in 1974, whereas the South's
share decreased from 49 percent to 40 percent (U.S. Bureau
of the Census, 1978a: 1-10). The regional shifts were even
larger for the farm population. The South held 54 percent
of the nation's farm people in 1940 as against 34 percent
in 1977. During the same time the North Central share rose
from 31 percent to 46 percent (Beale and Banks, 1973: 26;
Banks, 1978b: 3).[9]

The relative importance of the remaining farm population, only 3.7 percent of the nation's total population in
1978 by the old definition and 3.0 percent by the current
(Banks and De Are, 1979: 1), varies widely from state to
state and county to county, but even within local rural
communities farm people typically are becoming an ever-
smaller minority, numerically. This variation is reflected
in Figure 1.5 (see Chapter 1), which shows counties according to the percentage of employed workers in 1970 who were
employed in agriculture. Agricultural workers were compari-
tively most numerous in an area that in the North runs from
western Minnesota westward to eastern Montana, includes
much of Idaho and eastern Oregon, and then runs southward
in an inverted pyramid to include the Great Plains and
western Corn Belt. The area tapers off to include western
Oklahoma and a middle section of western Texas, including
the Panhandle. A scattering of counties with similar concentrations is found elsewhere. Only 331 counties had 30
percent or more of their workers employed in agriculture
in 1970 (Beale 1976). In comparison, in 1960 some 822
counties had at least this percentage of agricultural
workers and such workers made up at least one-half of those
employed in 117 counties.[10]

The current idea of rural community does not imply
self-containment. Rural locality group arrangements, like
farms, have been changing over time (Kolb, 1959: 1-11).
What has happened is that centers of reasonable size and
completeness of service have emerged as rural community
centers in an interdependent differentiated system that
also includes smaller and larger centers. It has been well
demonstrated that neither farmers nor other rural people
typically use a single center exclusively.[11] As a determinant of community boundaries, trade has become less
important over time, and educational, organizational,
social, and, to a lesser extent, religious relations more

important in uniting country and town (Kolb and Brunner, 1952: 218). Many thousands of rural hamlets and villages[12] do not now qualify as centers of rural communities, as defined, because they are too small and offer too few services for the people in the surrounding countryside. Frequently, however, such centers are the nucleus for a subcommunity or neighborhood within the rural community.[13]

At the community level, generally, the smaller the center, the larger the proportion of farmers in the community's total population, and vice versa (Kolb and Brunner, 1952: 231). Thus, the smaller centers, especially those in the areas in which the relative importance of farming is greatest and those remote from larger urban centers, are most vulnerable to changes in farms and farm population (Beale, 1974: 5-7; Nesmith, 1963: 178). In the process of change, centers with more than 2,500, the official dividing line between rural and urban for U.S. Census purposes, have frequently emerged as the community center for farm families within a radius of perhaps ten to twelve miles. With increased differentiation and interdependence some communities, usually the smaller ones, become "communities within communities," as in three cases in one Wisconsin county when the smaller communities each joined a larger one for high school services (Kolb, 1959: 10). Under different conditions, relative stability in small community boundaries has been found. Thus, for most of thirteen New York communities with centers of 908 to 5,037 population in 1970, the boundaries delimiting the area served were generally the same in 1974 as in 1936 (Richardson and Larson 1976).

How many rural communities, as defined, are there in the United States today? This is a question that cannot be answered precisely because the task of identifying them has been attempted on only a limited basis and the most comprehensive efforts are now obsolete. As a very rough approximation, the number of rural communities of the service area type and for which farming and agriculture have some local significance can be put at around 15,000.[14] Of these, about 12,500 have centers of less than 2,500 in population, and the remaining 2,500 communities have larger centers.

FARMS AND THE COMMUNITY

FARMS IN THE AGGREGATE AND THE COMMUNITY ECONOMY

Farms are a heterogeneous lot as indicated by acreage, value of sales, dominant type of enterprise, who controls the resources and makes the decisions, who does the work, goals for the farm and the family, or by any other major classificatory measure. Such characteristics, along with the number of farms, have a bearing on the character and the welfare of rural communities. Conversely, just as the farm situation influences the rural community, so do the services offered, the economic and social opportunities afforded, and other aspects of the community affect the welfare of farm people.

Before considering information available about specific characteristics of farms in the community context, however, selected economic aspects of farms and farm families in the aggregate will be highlighted because of their potential significance for the economic life of small communities.

The share of farm income used for purchased farm inputs has continued to increase over time (Economics, Statistics, and Cooperatives Service, hereafter ESCS, 1979: 31). For example, of the $99.0 billion cash income from farming in 1977, about 90 percent was spent for farm production purposes. This translates into an average cost outlay of $32,807 per farm (ESCS, 1979: 32). The 30 percent of the farms with value of sales of $20,000 or more, the current dividing line between small and larger farms for some federal policy purposes, accounted for nearly 87 percent of the production expenses and for 78 percent of the net farm income (ESCS, 1979: 52, 55, 56). No attempt will be made here to categorize the farm production expenditures.[15]

After the farm production expenses were paid, a net income of $19.8 billion was left from the 1977 farming operations. This Department of Agriculture net income figure includes, however, $8.5 billion of nonmoney income, that is, $7.2 billion for the rental value of the farm dwellings plus an allowance for the value of farm products consumed directly in farm households, so that the net cash income per farm averaged about $3,800 (ESCS, 1979: 1, 2, 39, 59).

If we turn from the farm to the farm operator family we find that in 1977 these families had an estimated $31.9 billion in off-farm income from wages and salaries received at off-farm work by the operator or other family members

and from other nonfarm sources.[16] Thus, the average income for farm operator families was put at $18,692, before
personal taxes and contributions to social insurance, with
$11,781 derived from nonfarm sources, $3,791 net cash
income from the farm, and $3,120 in nonmoney income (ESCS,
1979: 32, 39, 59). The gross and net farm income are much
more variable year-to-year than the off-farm income.

Another income concept relates to all people who live
on farms, thereby including farm-resident farm laborers and
their families but excluding operators who do not live on a
farm. This concept, disposable personal income of the farm
population, excludes personal tax and nontax payments to
governments but includes the nonmoney net farm income. In
1977 the per capita farm population disposable income from
all sources was $4,946, about 82 percent of that for the
nation's nonfarm population (ESCS, 1979: 36). Just as the
amount of farm production expenses and the expenditure
patterns affect numerous types of business establishments,
so do the amount available for family living purposes and
the expenditure patterns affect a wide variety of business
firms and services.

Although farm operators and members of their families
account for more than two-thirds of the average number of
persons doing farm work over the course of a year (USDA,
1978: 35), 2,730,000 persons were hired in 1977 to perform
254 million man-days of farm work (Rowe, 1979: 3, 31, 34).
These hired farm workers were predominantly drawn from the
local community; only 7 percent of the total number, an
estimated 191,000, were migrants who traveled overnight away
from their usual place of residence (Rowe, 1979: 8). Nearly
four-fifths of the hired workers lived off the farm, as
compared with 35 percent in the 1940s. Many of the workers
were school-age males and females hired during the summer
vacation and housewives who earned an income through seasonal employment. Only 30 percent of the male hired workers
and 16 percent of the females had hired farm work as their
primary employment status during the year. At the same time,
37 percent of all males who did any hired farm work during
the year had school attendance as their primary status and
70 percent of the female farm workers had attended school
or kept house as their primary status (Rowe, 1979: 21).

Not only has there been a great shrinkage in the number
of farms but also what is referred to as the structure of
agriculture has been undergoing drastic modification. This
is shown by such indicators as the steady increase in the
average number of acres per farm, the increased specializa-

tion of production, increased differentiation in who controls the factors of production, and the increase of farm
output marketed through forward contracts and integrated
production operations. This section of the review will
consider selected aspects of the structure of agriculture
as related to community, namely, size or scale of farm
as measured by acres and by value of sales, part-time
farming, and control of land, capital, and decision making.
Also considered will be the type of farm enterprise and
goals and values of farm people.

TYPE OF FARM ENTERPRISE

The type of farm classification indicates the crop or
livestock item that represents the major source of income
for a farm from the sale of farm products. The distribution
of the farm population by type of farm in 1975 (Banks,
1978a: 33) was as follows:

Type of Farm	Percentage of Total Farm Population
Livestock	39.1
Cash-grain	27.3
Dairy	11.8
Tobacco	7.3
Other field crops	4.4
Fruit and nut	2.8
Cotton	1.9
Poultry	1.6
Vegetables	1.6
Miscellaneous	2.2
Total	100.0

Farms with given types of enterprise tend to predominate within particular geographic areas for reasons of
climate and soil, so that areas are designated as the Corn
Belt, the dairy region, etc. Thus, the cash-grain farms
have their greatest concentration in the Corn Belt, with
wheat concentrated in the Plains states. Dairy farms are
concentrated in the Northeast and in the Lake states,
tobacco farms are concentrated in areas of six southern

states, and cotton farms are now concentrated in areas of
Arkansas, Mississippi, Texas, Arizona, and California.
Similarly, within a few states, areas of concentration are
found for other field crops, fruits, and vegetables. On the
whole, livestock farms, producing cattle, hogs, and sheep
for the most part, do not have the same concentration.
These type-of-farming areas are not necessarily stable
geographically, as demonstrated by the major shift of cotton
growing since the 1940s from the old Cotton Belt of the
Southeast to the Southwest and California and the replacement of cotton in the South with livestock, cash-grain, and
soybeans. Correspondingly, there have been major shifts in
the proportion of farms and farm people associated with
each type of farm. In the mid-1940s some 48 percent of the
nation's farm population was found in the 690 counties then
identified as the Cotton Belt (Raper, 1949: 346, 467). By
contrast, although not directly comparable, was the 2
percent of the farm population on cotton farms in 1975.

Several studies have used type-of-farming areas as the
focus for an analytical description of important aspects of
rural life. The most comprehensive of these has been the
work in the mid-1940s by Taylor et al. (1949: 329-491) for
the seven major type-of-farming areas into which the United
States was divided for the study purposes. It was noted,
for example, that the roles of the towns differed in response to the major types of farm, with their differing
seasonal work rhythms, tenure systems, socioeconomic groupings, and methods of marketing farm products and obtaining
farm supplies. The type of farming in a locality was a
major factor affecting town-country relationships, the
range and quality of professional and other expert services
available locally, and the likelihood of farm people and
townspeople belonging to the same civic organizations and
churches. Even the appearance of most towns took its character from the dominant type of farming. There was a biracial pattern in the communities and neighborhoods in the
Cotton Belt. The same study also noted that especially in
the wheat and range-livestock areas, comparatively recently
settled, with trading centers far apart and many smaller
ones in decline, rural community boundaries had not
stabilized (Raper, 1949: 485-87).[17]

Although there is a wide variation among farms within
each enterprise type in such respects as acreage, there are
conspicuous differences among the types in such economic
concomitants as scale of operations, marketing arrangements
such as the extent of use of forward contracts and vertical

integration (Kyle et al., 1972: 6, 8), and the employment
of hired farm workers. These are factors that do have local
community effects.

FARM NUMBERS AND FARM SIZE

One immediate effect of the shrinkage in the number of
farms has been the decreased number of opportunities to
enter farming as an owner or tenant. Another direct effect
has been a great thinning out of the farm population, a
lowered density, because the average acreage per farm rose
from 175 in 1940 to 440 in 1974. The community effects are
tempered by such factors as the availability of nonfarm
employment, within the community or by commuting, to the
displaced farm population; the level of gross farm and net
family income for the remaining farm operators; the relative
importance of farming in the community's economy and population; and net migration into or out of the community.

Net migration of the total population during 1960 to
1970 was related to the percentage of workers in the county
engaged in agriculture--the higher the proportion in agriculture, the higher the net out-migration rate (Bowles et
al., 1977: 225-39). This relationship was consistent for
all four census regions regardless of sex or color and was
most marked for young adults. To illustrate, in the North
Central region the counties with 50 percent or more of
their workers in agriculture in 1960 had a net out-migration
between 1960 and 1970 of 19 percent of their total population and 66 percent of their males aged twenty to twenty-
four years, whereas the counties with less than 10 percent
in agriculture had virtually no loss by net migration for
the total population and only about a 6 percent loss of
males aged twenty to twenty-four. In the South, counties
with one-half or more of their workers in agriculture had a
net out-migration by 1970 of 12 percent of their white and
36 percent of their nonwhite population, but the counties
with less than 20 percent in agriculture had a small gain
in their total and white population through in-migration.

The influence of the net out-migration from the areas
most dependent on farming was reflected in loss of total
population[18]--a 10.7 percent loss from 1960 to 1970 for
counties with 30 percent or more employed in agriculture
(Beale 1976)--as well as a loss in rural population. During
1940 to 1970 a 36 percent loss occurred in the Cotton Belt
sections of the southern Coastal Plain from South Carolina

to east Texas, a 32 percent loss in the northern and southern Great Plains combined, and a 23 percent loss in the part of the Corn Belt west of the Mississippi (Beale, 1978: 41-43). The smaller towns were the ones most likely to be adversely affected in the situations where the heavy out-migration resulted in population loss. In the North Central states the towns with a population of less than 500 were less likely to have a stable or growing population than were the nonmetro rural incorporated towns with more than 500 people (Beale, 1974: 5-7).

With the population reversal of the 1970s the net out-migration and population loss were greatly reduced in farming areas. The counties with 30 percent or more of the work force in agriculture had net out-migration drop to less than 1 percent from 1970 to 1974 (Beale 1976). The median age of farm operators started to go down, and the number of farm operators under the age of thirty-five increased by 35 percent from 1970 to 1975. Entry into farming by persons with nonfarm backgrounds was reported as noticeable in less advantaged farming areas such as northern New England, the Ozarks, the Upper Great Lakes, the Blue Ridge Mountains, and parts of the Far West (Beale 1976). The 500 or so counties that showed a population loss for 1970 to 1975 continued, however, to be concentrated in the areas with the heaviest dependence on agriculture and most remote from large urban centers, just as in the preceding decades (Ross and Green, 1979: 9).

Under the conditions that prevailed during the 1960s, family incomes of the farmers left behind benefited from the departure of their farmer neighbors. The higher the rate of farm population decline, the faster the growth of median farm family income according to state and county level data (Gardner 1974). This relationship was strong even when controlling for characteristics that might change as a result of the migration process, for example, education and days worked off the farm.

Farm population decline was not found to have an adverse effect on long-term (ten years) changes in rural nonfarm median family incomes during the 1960s, with the possible exception of the most rural counties (Gardner 1974). And in the West North Central states, although the counties losing population had smaller median incomes for all families than did the growing counties, the losing counties had more rapid rates of income growth, thus narrowing the relative income gap as measured by median family income (Beale, 1974: 17-18). Such income figures do not, however, deal

with the public sector and collective effects of changes in
the number of farms and farm people.

The number of farm people per square mile has a bearing
on their ease of access to economic and social services in
a community and on the cost of such services. In turn, the
availability of the services and their cost to the nonfarm
people of the community are also affected in some degree by
the farm situation because of what has been referred to as
the principle of "unit requirements" (Kolb and Brunner,
1952: 228-29). According to this principle, a minimum
volume of business, in people or dollars, is required for
the effective operation of a service, be it a grocery
store, a high school, a general practitioner, or the local
unit of a voluntary organization such as the Grange.[19]
The alternatives to a minimum volume are to maintain the
service at higher cost or lower quality, to bulge the
service area to get the volume, to consolidate, or to go
without the service.

Examination of the growth and decline of nonsuburban
incorporated villages with a population of 250 to 1,000 in
the United States from 1940 to 1950, found that in some
states considerable increases in the size of farms reduced
the number of farm homes tributary to a given center, and
thus reduced the volume of demand for goods and services
supplied by the village (Brunner 1952). This in turn reduced local employment opportunities. Village population
decline was associated with these changes.

The economic consequences of a decrease in farm numbers
and increase in average acreage may differ over time in
generally comparable situations. As one example, for Alabama counties the faster the rate of increase in the proportion of large farms (260 acres or more), the lower the
rate of growth in median family income between 1960 and
1970 and the more the tendency for inequality in the
distribution of income to increase (Wheelock 1979). The
counties that started the decade with relatively large
farms, however, tended to have slightly higher rates of
increase in median family income and a reduction in income
inequality. For a second example, in a small Nebraska community, changes in the total number of business enterprises
as of the early 1950s did not appear to be following trends
in population or in farm numbers (Anderson and Miller 1953).
The number of business establishments had not varied greatly
for half a century, although both open-country and village
population declined, while the size of farms increased pro-
gressively as the number decreased. The types of business

services in the Nebraska community increased in the face of
population decline, reflecting both new consumer shopping
trends and the demands for services generated by new technology. About ten years later, however, studies in rural
areas of Kansas and Nebraska indicated that lowered density
had a strongly adverse effect on the trade done in small
towns, that the smaller towns had a declining market radius,
and that the dominant larger towns increased their market
radius (Nesmith, 1963: 178).

The nonfarm employment multipliers provided by farm
employment have been studied using economic base and other
techniques. It was estimated in North Dakota, to cite one
example, that the annual loss at that time of 3,700 on-the-
farm workers associated with farm enlargement and reorganization decreased nonfarm employment by 5,772 persons
(Schreiner, 1972: 341).

The change in farm numbers and farm people changes the
composition of a rural community directly or indirectly.
The direction of the effect on the farm-nonfarm balance of
citizens is demonstrated by a hypothetical analysis for
counties made up entirely of farms of different sizes
(Mosher 1957). With all the farms fifty to ninety-nine
acres in size the farm operator population would be 59
percent of the county total, as compared with 0.5 percent
of the total if all farms were 580 acres or more; the
assumptions for this comparison were derived from the
results of a farm management study in northern Illinois in
1954. Because the large farms would be more dependent on
hired labor, this same analysis indicated that changes in
the occupational and class structure of the farming and
community population would be related to farm size.

Where the decrease in farm numbers has been associated
with high rates of net out-migration and population loss,
the out-migration of young adults has been accentuated,
distorting the normal age structure of the community to
give a far larger proportion of older persons than normal
and, where continued for some time, leading to a progres-
sively smaller number of families and children, and in the
more extreme instances to more deaths than births in the
community (Beale, 1974: 9-11, 15-16). The near disappearance of black farm operators and the extensive migration
of rural blacks from agricultural areas has resulted in
blacks being a smaller proportion of the population in
southern rural communities and reduced the number of such
communities that are predominantly black (Brown and Larson
1979; see also Chapter 12).

AN OUTPUT MEASURE OF FARM SIZE: GROSS FARM SALES

The size-of-farm patterns as measured by acreage--an input measure--vary widely from area to area as suggested by the range in state averages, from 102 acres (Rhode Island) to 6,539 acres (Arizona) in 1974. Farms of even the same acreage vary greatly, however, in such respects as soil, topography, rainfall, and in the production and management practices followed. And accordingly the output, labor requirements, and other aspects vary widely for farms in the same acreage group. A 160-acre irrigated farm has a production potential quite different from that of 160 acres of dry land in wheat or 160 acres of arid grazing land.

Among the other measures of farm size, the value of sales--an output measure--is most widely used. Gross farm sales as the measure of farm size not only has serious limitations for use in making comparisons over time, however (Stanton, 1979: 14), but also is an imperfect measure for identifying family farms or for developing a small farm or a large farm policy. Sales of $100,000 can be easily generated, at current price levels, by a one- or two-man farm (Stanton 1978). The value of farm sales is, nevertheless, a convenient measure to use for assessing the consequences of different farm sizes at a given point in time.

By the value of sales measure, the great majority of farms are small farms. Some 70 percent had gross sales in 1977 amounting to less than $20,000, 36 percent had gross sales of less than $2,500, whereas 6 percent, 157,000 farms, had sales of $100,000 or more (ESCS 1979: 52). There are large differences among the states as to the relative importance of large and small farms by this measure. The proportion of sales (for all farms with sales of $2,500 or more in 1974) accounted for by the farms with gross sales of $100,000 or more ranged from 22 to 94 percent (Buttel and Larson 1979).

Heady and Sonka (1974) used value-of-sales classes in projecting the effects of four different farm-size alternatives for the number of farms, farm employment, economic activity in rural areas, and other factors for the United States in 1980. The small farm alternative corresponded to farms with gross farm sales of less than $10,000; in 1969 these had an average of 232 acres. The large farm alternative was characterized by farms with sales of $40,000 or more; these, in 1969, averaged 1,603 acres. There was also a medium sized alternative and, for comparison, a mix of the three. The results, using detailed procedures, indicated

that increased farm size would reduce total farm employment
and net income to the farm sector but would be an advantage
to those who operated the larger units. A structure of
small farms, it was concluded, would lead to greater income
generation in rural communities, but the net income from
farming of the families operating these farms would be at
what is now characterized as the poverty level. The same
general pattern of relationships was displayed, with few
exceptions, for each of the ten production regions into
which the United States was divided.

A Kansas study (Nesmith, 1963: 178) found that larger-
scale farmers with increased disposable incomes were more
likely to shop away from their hometown, with an adverse
effect on the selection offered by merchants to the remaining customers. In rural Louisiana parishes, size of farm as
measured by both value of sales and acreage was reported to
be related to the incidence of rural poverty; the higher
the percentage of large farms, the higher the percentage of
poor people (Davis 1978).

The value of farm sales from the 1959 Census of Agriculture was used by Smith (1969), along with the tenure and
hired or unpaid family labor status, to indicate the patterns of social class or social stratification of farm personnel in the United States. Smith concluded from the preliminary analysis by states that an essentially one-class
system, a middle class, prevailed among farm personnel
throughout all of many states and in many sections of
others. Several kinds of two-class systems were found in
some areas in which the lower class was numerically dominant. Thus, plantation sections of the South were characterized by a small planter class and as many as 80 percent in
the lower class, whereas in areas dominated by nonfamily
corporation farms the percentage in the lower class was as
large or larger than in the plantation areas. This analysis
was carried one additional step by Goldschmidt (1978b), who
demonstrated a high correlation, on a state basis, between
the percentage of gross sales accounted for by farms with
sales of $100,000 or more in 1964 and the percentage of the
farm personnel placed by Smith in the lower class. Eleven
southern and border states tended to have a higher and
eight northwestern and Mountain states a lower proportion
of lower-class farm population in relation to large-scale
farms than was characteristic for the nation as a whole. A
replicate of Goldschmidt's analysis with 1969 data likewise
found that an increase in the predominance of large-scale
farms was associated with an increase in the percentage of

farm personnel in the lower class (Harris and Gilbert 1979).

Median farm operator family income was positively related to an increase in the predominance of large farms (again as indexed by the percentage of sales in a state by farms with sales of $100,000 or more), strongly in the 1959-60 period and moderately in 1969-70 (Harris and Gilbert 1979). Less expected was the strong positive relationship between median farm worker family income and large farms in 1959-60; this association, however, was weak, although positive, in 1969-70. At the same time there was a moderate negative relationship between large farms and a rural social welfare indicator, namely, median rural family income, in the 1959-60 period and ten years later.

TENURE OF FARM OPERATORS

Full owners operated 1,424,000, more than 62 percent, of the nation's farms in 1974 (USDA, 1978: 26).[20] Some 11 percent of the farms were operated by tenants. In between were the 27 percent operated by farmers who owned part and rented part of their farmland. Tenant-operated farms, including those run by sharecroppers, have disappeared at a much faster rate than the others. In 1930, when the number of tenant farms reached a high point, they accounted for more than 40 percent of all the farms. Part-owner farms were only 10 percent of the total as late as 1940; there has been a steady growth since in the proportion. This part-owner development in tenure arrangements represents increased flexibility on the part of farm operators in seeking the best combination of their land, labor, and capital resources. Land for rental by part owners is owned by retired farmers, by sons and daughters who left the parental farm for nonfarm employment, by those who have given up most of their farming activities but retain the land and even their residence on it, and by other nonfarming landowners.

During the years when there was a growing concern with the rise in the percentage of tenant-operated farms, numerous studies compared the economic and social characteristics and conditions associated with the major types of land tenure found in the United States. Areas of high tenancy were found to differ from areas of high ownership even when allowance was made for the tenant's usually being in an earlier stage of the family life cycle than the owner and

allowing for the complicating factor of a large number of
sharecroppers in the South. It was found, for instance,
that the adverse social consequences for the community
began to show when more than 20 percent of the farms were
tenant operated. Beyond that point the proportion of tenants
belonging to and active in church and all important forms
of voluntary organizations became smaller than for owners
(Kolb and Brunner, 1952: 90).[21] The corollary was that in
tenant-dominated communities all types of social organizations tended to be weaker and less progressive than where
owners were predominant.

The tenure categories differ markedly in the average
amount of land per farm. The part-owner units had the
largest acreage, except for the relatively few manager-
operated farms, 852 acres in 1974 (USDA, 1978: 26), followed by tenants, with an average of 467 acres. Owner-operated
farms, with 252 acres, had the smallest average size.[22]

FAMILY AND OTHER FARMS, SMALL AND LARGE--
CONTROL OF RESOURCES AND DECISIONS

Such commonly used terms as family farms, small farms, and
corporate farms are ambiguous, but they reflect society's
concern with the organization of the nation's farms--who
owns the land and provides the capital, who makes the
management decisions, and who does the labor.

Four structural types of farms were identified by
Rodefeld (1978: 159-77) by rating farms as high or low on
two factors simultaneously, namely, landownership and the
labor provided by the operator (and other family members)
of the farm. The relative importance nationally of each
type in 1964 is summarized as follows: Type A, designated
as "family-type," has the majority of both land and labor
provided by the operator. Farms with these approximate
characteristics accounted for 79 percent of all farms and
49 percent of all sales. Average sales were about $7,000
(p. 122). Type B, "tenant-type," has a low level of landownership but over one-half of the labor is provided by the
operator. Farms approximating Type B accounted for 16.5
percent of all farms and 15 percent of all sales. The sales
averaged $10,300. Type C, "larger-than-family type," has a
high level of landownership by the operator but the majority
of the labor is hired. Farms approximating these characteristics accounted for 4 percent of all farms and 25 percent
of all sales, which averaged about $73,000. Type D, "indus-

trial type," is the polar opposite, structurally, of the
family farm in that it has low levels of both landownership
and labor provided by the manager (who may be hired or be a
renter). Farms approximating this type accounted for 1 percent of all farms and 10 percent of all sales and had sales
that averaged close to $110,000 in 1964. The continued
predominance of the family-type farm is documented by
Rodefeld's analysis, but he presents evidence that points
to recent increases in the number of industrial-type farms
and in their share of product sales (pp. 174-76).

Fifteen percent of the work force on family-type farms
was hired, as compared to 85 percent on larger-than-family
and industrial-type farms in a Wisconsin sample (Rodefeld
and Lancelle 1978). The acreage of these farms averaged
583, 907, and 2,129, respectively.[23] When the work force--
family and hired--for the three types was compared, the
family-type work force had the most job and residential
stability, the highest average net family income, the
largest average net worth, the most involvement in voluntary associations, the largest financial contributions to
churches, and the highest percentage voting in school board
and in local, state, and federal elections, among other
differences. The industrial-type farm work force was lowest
on all of these characteristics and the larger-than-family
type was intermediate. The three types did not differ
significantly in the percentage of eleven personal and
eleven farm items purchased in the community when available, although the family-type work force did have the
highest percentage of purchases locally and the industrial
type the lowest percentage. The work force for the three
farm types differed little in the percentage who were
church members and in average church attendance.[24] Because
of the difference in the work-force composition, a shift
from family to larger-than-family and industrial-type farms
would suggest that a reduced level of involvement would
result for almost all community institutions and organizations. Estimates indicated that the aggregate size of the
farm work force would be cut substantially by a shift away
from family-type farms; therefore the man-land ratio would
decrease, with potentially adverse effects on the number and
variety of community businesses, and rural farm political
power would be expected to be reduced (see also Rodefeld,
1973: 4057-62 and Rodefeld, 1978: 122-23).

A comparison by Goldschmidt (1978a)[25] of a small-farm
community and a large-farm community in California's upper
San Joaquin Valley in the 1940s found major economic and

social differences between the two. Selected to be similar
in soil, climate, and size of center, both produced high-
value crops under intensive irrigation farming. The small-
farm community had farms that averaged 57 acres; 94 percent
were less than 160 acres. The large-farm community's farms
averaged 497 acres; 56 percent were less than 160 acres and
one corporation operated about 10,000 acres.[26] One important
concomitant of the scale of farming operations was the resulting occupational composition of the community (p. 218).
In the small-farm community 48 percent of the family heads
were farm operators and professionals, managers, and pro-
prietors; 32 percent were unskilled laborers. In the large-
farm community 16 percent of the heads were farm operators,
professionals, and entrepreneurs and 68 percent were unskilled laborers. A second major concomitant was the difference
in the economic and social life of the two communities (pp.
282-85). The small-farm community supported more separate
business establishments by a ratio of nearly two to one and
had a 61 percent greater volume of retail trade. Major
differences were found, to the advantage of the small-farm
community, in such respects as average family levels of
living, physical facilities for community living, school
services, local newspapers, and arrangements for making
decisions on community issues. A limited follow-up comparison of the two communities twenty-five years after the
first study indicated that the differences in educational,
social, and other facilities had persisted (La Rose, 1973:
4076-83), as did a reexamination in 1977 (Report of the
Small Farm Viability Project, 1977: 218-30). Recent studies[27] of a larger number of California communities have
found comparable relationships between farm size and the
number of essential community services. LeVeen (1979) found
in Fresno County, California that the larger-than-family
farm mode of production gave both a higher level of family
income and a more even distribution of that income than did
the industrial farm mode. The economic welfare of the
Spanish-speaking population was below that of other families, however, in both farming areas.

The more rapid the rate of increase in the proportion
of farms with 260 acres or more during the 1960s, the more
likely were Alabama counties to experience a decrease in
the relative size of their labor force in managerial positions (Wheelock 1979), consistent with Goldschmidt's observations.[28] A relationship between farm and overall
rural social welfare was found, at the state level, in both
the 1959-60 and 1969-70 periods; median family income of

farm operators and of hired farm workers was positively associated with the median rural family income (Harris and Gilbert 1979). The same state-level analysis also had results, however, that ran counter to some of the generalizations suggested by Goldschmidt's small farm and large farm community cases. Although the relationship between the percentage of the farm personnel in the lower class and farmer and farm worker median family income was negative in the 1959-60 period, as hypothesized, both relationships were moderately positive ten years later. Further, contrary to expectations, the relationship (at the state level) between the predominance of the lower farm class and median rural family income was moderately positive in both 1959-60 and 1969-70.

Farms with a corporate form of organization were counted at 28,442 in 1974, or 1.7 percent of all farms with sales of $2,500 and more. Of these, the majority--21,578--were classed as family held,[29] 5,115 were nonfamily independent corporations (neither controlling nor being controlled by another corporation), and 1,569 were parent corporations owning or controlling one or more subsidiaries (U.S. Bureau of the Census 1978c).

Studies of the community integration and related characteristics of the hired workers on nonfamily corporate farms are generally consistent with the conclusions reported above for the Wisconsin sample (Heffernan 1972, for poultry farms in one county; Martinson et al. 1976, for large-scale farm personnel in Wisconsin; and Heffernan and Lasley 1978, for grape producers in Missouri).

Case evidence has been used to support the contention that the independent and parent types of farm corporations have an adverse effect on the local community not only because of the compositional effects of their labor force but also because they purchase fewer inputs from local sources, are more likely to buy directly from suppliers, and are less likely to rely on local financial institutions (Bible 1972 in Rodefeld, 1978: 205-16). Also, such corporations are likely to bypass the regular market system. In addition, it is asserted that these large firms have been able to externalize some of their costs to the disadvantage of the community (Raup, 1973: 3962-71).

MULTIPLE WORK ROLES--OFF-FARM WORK AND PART-TIME FARMING

The percentage of the farm-resident labor force employed in
nonagricultural industries has risen to the point where it
about equals the percentage employed in agriculture (USDA,
1978: 35). The proposal has been made that to better understand the structure of agriculture and for developing information for policy and program purposes a basic two-way
classification of farms would be a useful starting point,
namely: (1) those where the principal occupation of the
operator is farming and (2) part-time units of all types
(Stanton, 1979: 8).

As measured by the percentage of operators reporting
work off their own farm, the relative importance of part-
time farming, of having dual work roles, has been maintained
at a high level and has even increased over the past thirty
years or so (Cavazzani, 1979: 6). Over one-half, 55 percent,
of the farmers who reported on the question in 1974 (and
nearly one-fifth did not report) did some work off their
farm during the year (U.S. Bureau of the Census, 1977:
1-2). More than one-third, 36 percent, of the operators
worked 200 days or more away from their farm, and 37 percent considered their principal occupation (on the basis
of the division of their work time) to be other than
farming (U.S. Bureau of the Census, 1977: 1-2). Farmers
primarily engaged in an off-farm job can be found in all
value-of-sales categories, but the principal occupation was
other than farming for 52 percent of the operators with
sales less than $20,000, as against 9 percent of those with
sales of $20,000 or more (Larson and Lewis, 1979: 22).
Reliance on off-farm work was least prevalent in the West
North Central states. Among farms with sales of $20,000 or
more, the farm operators in the South and in the Pacific
census division had the highest percentage with a nonfarm
principal occupation (Larson and Lewis, 1979: 21-22).

Wives and members of the farm family other than the
operator also contribute to the family income from work off
their own farm, and their contributions do not show up in
classifications based solely on the farm operator. Nearly
one-third, 32 percent, of all farm women aged sixteen and
over were in the labor force as of 1970 (U.S. Bureau of the
Census, 1972: 504), largely--88 percent--in nonfarm occupations (Flora and Johnson, 1978: 177).[30]

Off-farm income exceeded net farm income as a contributor to total family income for all gross farm sales classes
less than $20,000, that is, for 70 percent of all farms, in

Table 4.1. Sources of Farm Household Income by Amount of
Gross Farm Sales, 1977

Gross Farm Sales Class	Percentage of All Farms	Average Net Farm Income[a]	Average Off-Farm Income	Average Total Farm Family Income
Less than $2,500	35.6	$1,492	$15,401	$16,893
2,500-4,999	11.4	1,432	14,549	15,981
5,000-9,999	11.3	2,567	12,220	14,787
10,000-19,999	11.6	4,769	9,479	14,248
20,000-39,999	11.8	9,590	7,016	16,606
40,000-99,999	12.5	17,672	6,135	23,807
100,000 or more	5.8	34,840	9,822	44,662
All farms	100.0	6,911	11,781	18,692

Source: Economics, Statistics, and Cooperatives Service,
USDA, 1979.

[a]Including nonmoney income.

1977 according to Department of Agriculture estimates (ESCS,
1979: 59). Wages and salaries account for the majority of
the income from nonfarm sources received by farm families
(Reinsel, 1972: 13; U.S. Bureau of the Census, 1977: 1-14).
    The value-of-sales class of a farm is a poor indicator
of the income level of the family running the farm, because
of the importance of off-farm work and the income some have
from other sources, as shown in Table 4.1 (ESCS, 1979: 52,
59).[31]
    We do not know the variations around the averages shown
above, but the farmers with gross sales of less than $2,500
had family incomes larger, on the average, than those of
farmers with $2,500 to $20,000 in sales and about the same
as farmers with sales of $20,000 to $40,000.
    The rather limited amount of recent research on part-
time farmers[32] indicates that they are a heterogeneous
group, thereby giving support to alternative views that
have been advanced (Cavazzani 1979) about the role of
part-time farming in agriculture and for the individuals
and families involved. They vary, for example, in the time

commitment to off-farm work--that is, full time, regular
part time, seasonal, or sporadic--and in the place of
part-time farming in their career pattern (Bertrand 1967;
Fuguitt 1961; Wardle and Boisvert, 1974: 35-41). They vary
in the reasons for being part-time farmers, for example,
economic necessity to support the family or to finance the
farm operations, preference for rural living, seeking to
enter full-time farming, or to pursue a hobby.

The linkage of the farm and the nonfarm sectors that
results from multiple work roles for farm family members
has community effects that have been little studied. The
effect on involvement in local community activities and on
use of local economic services might be expected to be
influenced by such factors as whether the off-farm work
requires long-distance commuting and the type and time
requirements of the job. Average distance to the nonfarm
job was 6.6 miles among dairy farmers with below average
herd size in a New York county, and the maximum commuting
distance was 50 miles (Wardle and Boisvert, 1974: 37).
Part-time farmers are high in ownership of their land, and
their work force, with limited use of hired labor, does not
have the kind of compositional effect on the local community
associated with larger-than-family or industrial-type farms.

GOALS AND VALUES OF FARM PEOPLE

A recent exhaustive review of the research literature published since 1960 and of national surveys dating from 1965
concluded that rural society in America has maintained
a distinctiveness in prevailing major value orientations
and related beliefs, in the face of increased linkage and
interdependence with the larger society, that cannot be
shrugged off as inconsequential or disregarded (Larson,
1978: 109-12). Rural America was found to differ substantially from urban, especially large-city, America on 79
percent of a set of forty-three questions taken as indicators of values and closely related beliefs. Differences
were greatest in matters moral and religious. Although farm
men and women generally took a value position corresponding
with that prevailing among rural people as a whole, they
were the more distant from the position taken by the majority or plurality of large-city dwellers.

Values have consequences for human behavior, including
the governance of people and the solution of community and
societal problems. For social systems, values are a factor

in the determination of goals and the selection of means to
achieve goals. Primacy given to goal attainment and adaptive
values such as efficiency, rationality, and progress clearly
have guided the drastic changes made in the farming sector
during recent decades. The results are well-known, for example, high productivity per worker, larger scale, increased
differentiation of functions, reduced independence in
decision-making by operators, fewer farms, and fewer farm
people. Quite aside from the self-interest of individuals
in specific situations, deeply embedded values are involved
in such issues as larger-than-family versus family-type and
small-farm scale of organization, relations of man and
nature as exemplified by land use and environmental quality,
and economic growth.

The review of the studies of values mentioned above did
not find complete unanimity among farmers or other rural
people on any statement from which values were inferred.
Rather, there was a degree of diversity, or cultural pluralism. Some of this diversity is as highly visible as the
cultural island groups such as the Amish and others whose
religious precepts guide their style of farming (Olshan
1979), or the nuclear family homesteaders most commonly
found in areas marginal for conventional farming, and
occasional rural group communes who are among the diverse
strands of a rural revivalist movement that has gathered
momentum during the last decade (Larson, 1978: 108-9). The
value-based diversity[33] among farmers is reflected in the
limits on farming practices acceptable among the Amish, in
the practices emphasized by the organic farmers, and in the
contrasts between German and Irish farming communities in
Illinois in farm inheritance practices over half a century
(Salamon 1979).

The interrelationship of farm and family is typically
important in goal setting, with the expressed goals strongly
correlated with the stage of the family cycle (Larson, 1961:
155-56). The statement of goals elicited also varies with
the technique used to discover them, and the distinction
is not always clear as to means and ends. Security, self-
respect, and, frequently, farm ownership and the occupation
of farming seem most commonly to show up, directly or indirectly, as goals; beyond these generalized conclusions,
diversity appears (Larson, 1961: 155). Thus, 30 percent of
the full-time farmers in a sample of Michigan farmers with
sales in 1969 of less than $20,000 did not aim to expand
farming operations in the next two years (Thompson and Hepp
1976). Noneconomic factors rank high among smaller-scale

farmers as a reason for farming; a strong identification
with farming as a life-style and a preference for a farm
environment to raise children came through again and again
in a sample of New York dairy farmers with below-average
size herds (Wardle and Boisvert, 1974: 43). In a statewide
New Mexico sample of farmers with gross sales less than
$40,000, quality of life was clearly the top-ranked goal
for the family and for the farm operation (Eastman et al.
1979). A high-level concern of these farmers was reflected
in their second-ranked goal for the farm--to avoid being
forced out of agriculture.

TYPES OF COMMUNITY SITUATIONS
AND COMMUNITY-FARM RELATIONSHIPS

The emphasis in this review to this point has been on the
farm side of community-farm relationships, on how the
characteristics and trends of farms not only affect the
people engaged in farming but also have demographic, economic, and social consequences for communities. The relative importance of farming and farm people varies a great
deal from region to region, as do farm characteristics and
trends; the smaller the community the greater the influence
of the farming component.

   This section of the review will give a brief consideration to some aspects of how the farming component is influenced by the characteristics and trends of communities.
Although farm people have a special interest in the types
of business firms and professional services directly related
to the farm business, they also share with other community
residents a common interest in essential economic, educational, health, and social services. From the trend for a
decreased number of opportunities in farming and the increase in off-farm work roles by family farm members, it
follows that farm people also have a stake in the number
and type of nonfarm employment opportunities available in
the community or nearby. Further, the farm sector is affected by the community population trends, not only in
rapidly growing but also in stable communities.

   The same general forces that have resulted in fewer,
larger, and more specialized farms have a counterpart in
what has been happening with respect to economic, educational, health, medical, and similar services in small
rural communities. Larger scale and specialization have

been the trend. For example, 76 percent of a national
sample of incorporated villages with a population of less
than 2,500 in 1960 had fewer retail and service business
activities and fewer functions in 1970 than in 1960; the
average number of establishments decreased from twenty-
three to eighteen (Johansen and Fuguitt 1979). The study of
thirteen small New York communities that, on the whole,
evidenced growth or stability over a fifty-year period concluded that the evidence of vitality was generally stronger
for noneconomic than for economic activities (Richardson
and Larson 1976). Studies have repeatedly demonstrated a
strong positive relationship between size of center and
number of business establishments. However, the national
sample of incorporated villages showed a decline between
1950 and 1970 in the number of business firms or functions
corresponding to a given population size (Johansen and
Fuguitt 1979), suggesting that a shift of retail firms to
larger centers has been under way. The change in establishments and also, but in a less sensitive way, the change in
functions within the national sample of villages was related
in a complex way to their population trends and to their
distance from the nearest urban center of at least 10,000
population. Village growth favored an increase in business
establishments, but nearness to the business competition of
a larger urban center was associated with a decrease in
such firms. Overall, up to the start of the 1970s, this
national study indicated a trend toward the decreasing
importance of rural villages as retail service centers.
    Community population growth trends and location in
relation to larger urban centers, especially the central
cities and urbanized areas of standard metropolitan statistical areas (SMSAs), impact on farmers in other ways than
the availability of the services listed in Dun and Bradstreet. In the areas of population decline represented by
the Great Plains and western Corn Belt, where farming has a
high relative importance, the contention is that the nonfarm sector of rural communities has borne the major costs
of structural changes in the farm sector (Heady and Sonka
1974). Attention is directed to the economic and social
problems and the adjustments faced by the "communities left
behind" (Whiting 1974). In contrast, in high-growth and
urban expansion areas, where farmers already are or are
rapidly becoming very much a minority,[34] attention is
directed at the costs borne by farmers (Conklin 1979) along
with the adjustment problems unique to expanding communities
(Larson and Lutz, 1961: 293-95).

The institutional overload on tax-supported services, the culture clash between newcomers and old-timers, and the scattering of nonfarm people into rural areas combine in their impact on farmers. The actual physical displacement of farming is limited to a relatively small part of the total area under the influence of urban pressure and high growth (Zeimetz et al., 1976: 8-14). More significant than direct loss of farmland is held to be the dehabilitation of farming that occurs long before the land is needed for non-farm purposes (Conklin 1979). As farm assessments are driven up due to tax assessments based on speculative values and the price of nonfarm rural properties in order to pay for expanded and new public services, and as farming activities are hampered by the demands and activities of the nonfarm neighbors, a critical point is reached. Investment ceases for farm improvements. Cropland shifts into idle open land as it passes into the hands of speculators. Essential agricultural services in the area are adversely affected in the process, thus further discouraging remaining farmers.

A number of institutional innovations are being tried as a result of the farm-related problems encountered in high-growth areas. They include: zoning to separate farmers and nonfarmers or to regulate farming practices; transfer of the rights to develop farmland; purchase of farmland development rights by governments at various levels; assessment of farmland at the value for farming purposes; tax exemptions for new farm improvements; and agricultural districts to keep good farmland in farming until needed for other purposes (Conklin 1979).

In comparatively stable communities, as nonfarmers replace farmers the remaining farmers encounter in some degree the same type of problems found in growing communities.

SOME IMPLICATIONS OF OUR STATE OF KNOWLEDGE ABOUT FARMING AND THE COMMUNITY

One of the major consequences of the reorganization that has taken place in the farm structure of the United States and of the choice of about 55 million people to live in rural areas has been to drastically change the population mix in rural communities toward the nonfarm side. At the same time an unprecedented settlement pattern has developed, with large numbers of nonfarm families living in the countryside rather than in the village centers. Heterogeneity prevails

in the characteristics of the remaining farms and farm
families as well as in the communities to which farmers
relate. This heterogeneity increases the difficulty of
formulating public policies and designing programs that
will be effective and well accepted.

Farm and other country families share in common, however, the costs of overcoming space to gain access to essential and specialized services. The rural communities
share in common the characteristic that their local governments, their agencies, and their services are typically
relatively small in scale as compared with those that prevail in larger urban areas. To illustrate, the average size
of incorporated villages of less than 2,500 population in
1970 was 745 (Johansen and Fuguitt 1979). And, especially
around larger centers, numerous subcommunities exist that
are cohesive units for voluntary action on manageable
problems of local concern.

Typically the rural community comprised of center and
country has no agency, public or private, that has a legitimate right to represent and act for the community as a
whole in a wide range of concerns. In one specialized area,
education, the centralized or consolidated public school
district may approximate in its boundaries the community
embracing both village and country residents. Otherwise,
local government is segmented within the community between
an incorporated center and one or more towns (townships) or
the equivalent or has only county-level government. Thus,
rural communities, as such, are handicapped in decision
making and taking action on problems of communitywide
concern.

FARMS

Insofar as national and state policies affect the number and
characteristics of farms and the income of farmers, the
policies have a direct or indirect influence, in varying
degrees, on rural communities. The available evidence points
on the whole to a negative impact on the rural community of
larger-than-family and of industrial-type farms. The policies that have been proposed to restrain the increase of
larger farms and to encourage family-type farms include,
without regard to their political acceptability: differential taxation; a land trust or land settlement authority to
foster adequate family farms; divorcing from equity considerations the capital supplied by public agencies for smaller-

scale farming operations; revising income tax laws that
favor tax-loss farming and absentee ownership; restricting
corporate or foreign ownership of farmland; modifying federal farm price support payments to limit or remove the
advantage of large-scale operations; and assisting farmers
on smaller farms to take advantage of scale economies
through cooperatives (Heady and Ball, 1972: 373-98).

Although family-type farms continue to predominate
numerically, the concern expressed for "the disappearing
middle" (Madden and Tischbein 1979) is substantiated by
recent trends in farm acreage. Between 1969 and 1974 the
percentage of farms in the middle (from 50 to 999 acres) was
reduced by about 3 percent in all census regions, with the
reduction more for farms of 50 to 179 acres, except in the
West, than for those 180 to 999 acres (Nichols et al. 1979).
These smaller farms very likely include many of the limited-
resource farmers seeking to remain in farming full time, but
a better identification of this group is needed.

Part-time farmers have persisted in large numbers, although they seem not to have much consideration as an issue
in national farm and food policy. Further, it has been noted
(Fuguitt, 1975: 61) that the rural development literature
gives little attention to designing programs to support
viable part-time farming. It would seem that part-time
farming and part-time farmers (not to be confused, as we
have seen, with low-income farm families) deserve much more
searching study from the perspective of rural communities
and rural development.

COMMUNITIES

As noted, rural communities are poorly equipped by their
structure to make decisions and take action on problems of
common concern. Local government boundaries seldom coincide
with the boundaries of the "natural" community (Richardson
and Larson 1976). Where there has been incorporation of
villages and towns, this has set up a legal barrier to joint
action by town and country. The alternatives to neglect or
segmented or uncoordinated decision making and action in
rural communities include: (1) voluntary cooperation among
local governments (where they exist below the county level),
(2) the organization of a communitywide nonprofit corporation, and (3) the formation of a special district similar to
the rural municipality idea once authorized but never used

in North Carolina. Cooperative extension could assist in
overcoming this handicap.

In addition, the small-scale local governments in rural
areas do not have the personnel resources to take full advantage of federal and state assistance, which requires that
action be initiated locally, in contrast to formula grants
(Larson and Richardson 1977). The cooperative employment of
personnel or assistance from existing public agencies such
as county or regional planning bodies could help overcome
this disadvantage.

In the view of small community representatives, federal
agencies supposed to provide rural development help through
grants, loans, or technical assistance often do not have the
capacity to work effectively with small communities (Larson
and Richardson 1977). The most satisfactory relations, from
the community point of view, appear to be where the agency
representative is most readily accessible. Any agency move
toward centralization of its staff reduces the access that
community representatives value.

ADDITIONAL IMPLICATIONS

In discussion of rural development policy it is essential
that the distinction between farm and rural population and
the relationship between the two be kept in mind. Similarly,
understanding of the conceptual distinction between the farm
and farm family and the relationship between them is important, and when one is considering income data, clarity here
is essential.

Studies that focus directly on farm-community relationships in the context of specific communities and different
types of communities are few and cannot claim to be representative in any customary statistical sense. Much of what
is projected as the community consequences of given farm
characteristics or trends comes from studies of aggregate
county- or state-level data or from samples drawn from the
population on farms of specified categories. Much of our
information about rural communities is outdated. In this
review we found little evidence of studies of the economic
and social aspects of the most rapidly growing form of farm
tenure, the part owner. Although farm tenancy has diminished
greatly, there seem to be few studies of contemporary farm
tenancy.

Finally, what assessment may be made of the assorted

implications for the farming part of rural communities of
the population reversal, of the return or in-migration of
people who have a decided preference for a small-scale
life-style and the rural environment and who give heavy
weight to noneconomic considerations in choosing the place
to live? The implications are not solely those of the costs
of institutional overload, of conflict, and value clash.
The in-migrants may provide professional services, such as
medical and dental care, often in short supply in rural
communities, as was found in Maine (Ploch 1978). They acquire and rebuild small businesses, especially retail establishments. The newcomers by their volunteer efforts may
take the leadership in strengthening such facilities as
libraries or starting new cultural activities. Case illustrations of in-migrants with organizational skills adaptable
for rural development activity may readily be found. Is it
possible that the population reversal may find the in-
migrants frequently making common cause with family-type
and part-time farm families in their goals for the development of their rural community?

NOTES

1. Studies were made in a national sample of 140
village-centered communities in agricultural areas in 1924,
1930, and 1936 (Brunner et al. 1927, 1933, 1937). In the
early 1940s a series of studies of rural life and rural
social organization was initiated by the former Division of
Farm Population, Bureau of Agricultural Economics, USDA, in
seventy-one counties selected to be representative of the
major type-of-farming areas in the United States. The prohibition placed on such studies by Congress in the Agricultural Appropriation Act of 1947, a prohibition that continued in annual appropriation acts until the Bureau of
Agricultural Economics was dismantled, brought an end to
leadership in the federal government for comprehensive
studies of rural life (see Hardin 1946). Unpublished material from the seventy-one county studies was drawn upon for
nine chapters on rural regions in Rural Life in the United
States (1949) by Carl C. Taylor and associates; the seven
major type-farming areas included were the Cotton Belt, the
Corn Belt, the wheat areas, the range-livestock areas, the
dairy areas, the western specialty-crop areas, and the
general and self-sufficing areas.

2. Two further illustrations of the need to be aware of
the limitations of available data are offered. First, small
farms are much more frequently missed in census enumerations
than larger farms. The U.S. Bureau of the Census estimated
95.3 percent of all farms with sales of $2,500 or more were
included in the 1974 Census of Agriculture enumeration, as
compared with 74.1 percent of those with sales less than
$2,500 (U.S. Bureau of the Census, 1978b: 9-10). In the 1964
Census of Agriculture, it was estimated that 24.1 percent of
the farms with less than 10 acres were missed, as compared
with 6.9 percent of those with 220 acres or more (Foote,
1970: 20). Second, changes in definition influence the count
of farms and farm people. Thus, the estimate of farm population for 1978 was 1,504,000 less under the new definition
of farm adopted for the 1974 Census of Agriculture than it
was using the previous definition of farm (Banks and De Are,
1979: 1).

3. Place of residence was not reported in the 1974
Census of Agriculture by 17.8 percent of the respondents
for individual and partnership-operated farms. An enumer-
ative survey in 1974 by the USDA Statistical Reporting
Service indicated about 11 percent of the farm operators
did not live on their farm. The 1940 Census of Agriculture,
which had a low nonresponse rate, reported about 5 percent
of the operators lived off their farm. Of the nonresident
operators in 1974, 57 percent lived in an urban area, 18
percent lived in a rural area but not on a farm, and 25
percent lived on a farm other than the one operated. The
practice of a farm operator residing in a village or town
is most prevalent in the West, for example, in the northern
Great Plains wheat areas where open-country population
density is very low, in the Mormon irrigated communities,
and in the Spanish-speaking villages in the southern Rocky
Mountain area.

4. Despite the fact that the rural community is commonly
held to be one of the most important social units in rural
society, the concept is used in a far less precise way in
research investigations than the terms farm, farm population, and rural population. For a discussion of alternative
ways of delineating rural communities in the United States
and for summaries of rural locality group characteristics
and relationships, see, for example, Douglas Ensminger
(1949) in Rural Life in the United States (pp. 55-57) or
John H. Kolb and Edmund de S. Brunner's A Study of Rural
Society (1952: 209-36).

5. We are excluding from review communities that may

qualify as rural by census definition but that do not have,
or have not had, a farming component within their service
area. Thus, for example, outside our purview are industrial
and mining places that can be characterized as "closed"
centers because they are largely dependent upon their own
people for support, and suburban villages described as
"attached" centers because they are chiefly places of
residence for those employed in nearby urban centers (Kolb
and Brunner, 1952: 195).

6. The total land area in the forty-eight coterminous
states was put at approximately 1,896,959,000 acres in
conjunction with the 1970 Census of Population (Frey, 1973:
24).

7. Much of the public grazing land is treated as an
extension of privately held lands that control water, winter
range, and access (Wunderlich, 1974: 11). Access to nonfarm
grazing land is of greatest importance to beef cattle and
sheep producers in the eleven western states.

8. This number of farms is based on the more restrictive
definition introduced in the 1974 Census of Agriculture. Under the old definition the number would have been 2,446,123.
The USDA, however, estimated the number of farms at
2,795,000 in 1974 (ESCS, 1979: 32).

9. The Northeast's share of farms was 8 percent in 1940
and 5.5 percent in 1974; the region's share of farm population was 8 percent in 1940 and 7 percent in 1977. The
corresponding percentages for the West were: for farms, 8
and 10; for farm people, 8 and 12.

10. Data provided by Gladys K. Bowles, ESCS, USDA.

11. For example, the average number of centers used for
services by Walworth County, Wisconsin, country families was
4.3 in a 1947-48 study (Kolb, 1959: 113).

12. The number of centers with less than 2,500 population in 1940 numbered 78,177, of which 58,818 were hamlets
with less than 250 population and 19,359 were villages of
250 to 2,499 population (Marshall 1946). Although centers
grow or decline in population, some disappear and new ones
appear, the total number of centers this size appears to be
quite stable. Not all of the small centers are in farming
areas.

13. Numerous illustrations of community arrangements
for rural people could be drawn from research such as that
for Chilton County, Alabama (Sanders and Ensminger 1940);
Adams community in Nebraska (Anderson and Miller 1953);
Oneida County, New York (Hay and Polson 1951); and Walworth
County, Wisconsin (Kolb and Day 1950). This type of detailed

attention to locality groups, however, was generally before
the drastic reduction in farms and farm population.

14. This estimate is arrived at by: (a) including the
4,191 places of 1,000 to 2,500 enumerated in rural territory
in 1970 by the U.S. Census of Population; (b) assuming the
same number of incorporated rural places of 500 to 1,000 as
enumerated in 1960, i.e., 3,127; (c) assuming that an equal
number of unincorporated places of 500 to 1,000 serve as
rural community centers; (d) assuming that 1,000 of the
incorporated places with population less than 500 and an
equal number of unincorporated places serve as community
centers; and (e) of the urban centers outside of urbanized
areas in 1970, including 75 percent of those 2,500 to
10,000, 50 percent of those 10,000 to 20,000, and one-third
of those 20,000 or more. The present estimate of 15,000
rural communities appears more likely to be low than high.
The number was estimated at approximately 35,000 in the late
1940s by Ensminger (1949: 60), but to arrive at this figure
he had to consider as community centers a far larger proportion of those with less than 500 population.

15. A percentage breakdown of farm production expenditures in 1977 by categories may be found in the USDA 1978
Handbook of Agricultural Charts, p. 11. The annual data on
farm production expenses and capital expenditures in Farm
Income Statistics, also a USDA publication, gives a somewhat
different classification.

16. Income from nonfarm sources consists of income
received from nonfarm wages and salaries, business and
professional income, interest, and transfer payments such as
unemployment compensation, social security, and veterans
benefits, and rental income from nonfarm sources (ESCS,
1979: vi).

17. It was recognized that the major regions varied not
only in predominant farming enterprises but also in such
factors as relative importance of the farm population,
presence of nonagricultural resources, transportation and
communication facilities, distance to larger urban centers,
and recency of settlement.

18. An index of general agriculture that included the
percentage of the population employed in agriculture and the
percentage of the population rural farm in 1960 was found to
explain more of the rate of population change from 1960 to
1970 for the nonmetro counties in the forty-eight states
than the seven alternative measures of sustenance organization and seven alternative predictors such as proximity to
the nearest SMSA, explaining over one-half of the total

variation (Frisbie and Poston 1975). There was a strong
relationship between this agricultural index and population
decrease.

19. Numerous studies have been made to show the population base required for a variety of economic and social
services or to identify the smallest size of center that can
ordinarily support a type of service.

20. The 61.5 percent who were full owners in 1974
included the small percentage of manager-operated farms, as
managers were not reported separately. In 1964 manager-
operated farms accounted for less than 1 percent (0.6) of
all farms but for 10.2 percent of all land in farms, up from
the 6.3 percent in 1940 (Timmons, 1972: 236).

21. The studies of the social and economic characteristics associated with different forms of tenure are too
numerous to attempt to cite in this papar.

22. The 252-acre average reported by the 1974 Census of
Agriculture for full owners also includes manager-operated
farms, small in number but large in size. In 1964 the
manager-operated farms averaged 4,146 acres, as against the
246-acre average for full owners (Timmons, 1972: 237). At
that time part-owner farms averaged 761 acres and tenant
farms 302 acres, so both types were substantially smaller
than in 1974.

23. The study sample was intended to represent farm
types that were increasing at a rapid rate, and therefore
smaller family farms were excluded. The averages for the
three types of farms in the sample may be compared with the
179-acre Wisconsin average at the time.

24. When only the operators (and their wives and children) of the combined family-type and larger-than-family
farms were compared with the industrial-type hired managers
(and their wives and children) as to their integration into
local community social systems, most of the expected differences were not found. However, the expected differences
between the hired full-time workers (and their families on
the combined larger-than-family and industrial-type farms)
and both owner-operators and hired managers were found. The
owner-operators were combined by Rodefeld and Lancelle
(1978) because the family-farm and larger-than-family types
differed significantly on only 25 of 203 comparisons; they
differed mostly in income, wealth, levels of living, and
voluntary organization membership. The hired full-time
workers on larger-than-family and industrial-type farms were
combined because they differed significantly on only 6 of
181 comparisons.

25. The first edition of Walter Goldschmidt's As You Sow
appeared in 1947. The 1978 edition is used here, however,
because it also includes Goldschmidt's report "Small Business and the Community," made in 1946 to the U.S. Senate
Special Committee to Study Problems of American Small
Business, along with two new sections.

26. When converted to "standard" acres to account for
differences in income-producing capacity, the size difference was reduced, with the farms in the small-farm community
averaging 84 acres and in the large-farm community averaging
247 acres (Goldschmidt, 1978a: 218). There were also tenure
differences in the two communities; 78 percent of the
operators in the small-farm community were full owners as
compared with 35 percent in the large-farm community (p.
314), which also had a larger proportion of absentee owners
(p. 402).

27. Goldschmidt (1978a) cites Fujimoto's (1977) study of
social and economic facilities in 130 towns in an eight-
county San Joaquin Valley area, a study also summarized in
Report of the Small Farm Viability Project (1977: 230-43).
Goldschmidt, using the data on community facilities for
twenty-one of the towns in the upper San Joaquin Valley,
found a significant negative correlation between average
farm size in 1940 and the number of facilities in the
community over thirty years later (p. xlii). LeVeen (1979)
cautions against uncritically accepting the conclusions of
these studies, suggesting that there are plausible alternative hypotheses.

28. Wheelock also found that the more rapidly farm size
increased, the slower the rate of population increase. In
addition, Alabama counties with a large proportion of
smaller farms were more likely during the 1960s to have
increased the proportion of the labor force employed in
manufacturing.

29. The U.S. Census classed a corporation as family
held if 51 percent or more of the stock was owned by persons
related by blood or marriage and the corporation neither
controlled nor was controlled by another corporation. A
comprehensive review of family corporations in farming may
be found in Harl (1972: 270-89); a comparable review of
nonfamily corporations may be found in Ottoson and Vollmar
(1972: 290-313). A comprehensive guide to recent literature
on corporate farming may be found in Goss and Rodefeld
(1978).

30. Because of space limitations, the present review
does not include recent research on the changing role of

women in farming. On this topic see, for example, Lodwick
and Fassinger (1979), Pearson (1979), and Wilkening and
Ahrens (1979). Trends in the labor force activity of women
in nonmetro areas and in farming and other occupations are
given in Brown and O'Leary (1979).

31. The average off-farm income figures reported by the
1974 Census of Agriculture for comparable classes are much
lower than shown here (Larson and Lewis, 1979: 23-24). The
census figures for average realized net farm income also
differ substantially, especially for the lower value of
sales classes, in part because ESCS includes and the census
excludes the nonmoney income from the farm.

32. The literature cited in Cavazzani's (1979) bulletin
provides the most up-to-date identification of part-time
farming studies seen in preparing the present work.

33. Among the topics excluded from this review for
reasons of space are the recent studies pertaining to the
extent to which farmers and others and different categories
of farmers adhere to the tenets of what has been given such
labels as the "agrarian ideology," the "Jeffersonian creed,"
and the like. For examples of such studies see Flinn and
Johnson (1974) and Buttel and Flinn (1975).

34. Some 84 percent of all farmers and 75 percent of
all employed farm laborers resided outside of SMSAs in 1974
(Littman, 1975: 13). Within the suburban rings that surround
the SMSA central cities, farmers and farm laborers each made
up less than 1 percent of the employed work force.

BIBLIOGRAPHY

Anderson, A. H., and Miller, C. J. The Changing Role of the
    Small Town in Farm Areas. Bulletin 419. Lincoln, Nebr.:
    Experiment Station, University of Nebraska, 1953.
Banks, Vera J. Farm Population Estimates for 1977. Econom-
    ics, Statistics, and Cooperatives Service, U.S. Depart-
    ment of Agriculture, Rural Development Research Report
    no. 4. Washington, D.C., 1978b.
    _____. Farm Population Trends and Farm Character-
    istics. Economics, Statistics, and Cooperatives Service,
    U.S. Department of Agriculture, Rural Development
    Research Report no. 3. Washington, D.C., 1978a.
    _____, and De Are, Diana. Farm Population of the
    United States: 1978. Current Population Reports, Farm
    Population Series P-27, no. 52, U.S. Bureau of the

Census and U.S. Department of Agriculture. Washington,
D.C., 1979.
Beale, Calvin L. "A Further Look at Non-metropolitan Popula-
tion Growth Since 1970." American Journal of Agricul-
tural Economics 58 (1976): 953-58.
_____. "People on the Land." In Rural U.S.A.:
Persistence and Change, edited by Thomas R. Ford. Ames,
Iowa: Iowa State University Press, 1978.
_____. "Quantitative Dimensions of Decline and
Stability Among Rural Communities." In Communities Left
Behind: Alternatives for Development, edited by Larry R.
Whiting. Ames, Iowa.: Iowa State University Press,
1974.
_____, and Banks, Vera J. Farm Population Estimates,
1910-70. Rural Development Service, U.S. Department of
Agriculture, Statistical Bulletin no. 523. Washington,
D.C., 1973.
Bertrand, Alvin L. "Research on Part-Time Farming in the
United States." Sociologia Ruralis 7 (1967): 295-304.
Bible, Alan. "Impact of Corporation Farming on Small Busi-
ness." In Change in Rural America: Causes, Consequences,
and Alternatives, edited by Richard D. Rodefeld et al.
St. Louis, Mo.: C. V. Mosby Company, 1978.
Bowles, Gladys K.; Beale, Calvin L.; and Lee, Everett S. Net
Migration of the Population, 1960-70 by Age, Sex, and
Color. Part 7, Analytical Groupings of Counties. Eco-
nomic Research Service, U.S. Department of Agriculture;
Institute for Behavioral Science, University of Georgia;
and Research Applied to National Needs, National Science
Foundation. Athens, Ga., 1977.
Brown, David L., and O'Leary, Jeanne M. Labor Force Activity
of Women in Metropolitan and Nonmetropolitan America.
Economics, Statistics, and Cooperatives Service, U.S.
Department of Agriculture, Rural Development Research
Report no. 15. Washington, D.C., 1979.
Brown, Minnie M., and Larson, Olaf F. "Successful Black
Farmers: Factors in Their Achievement." Rural Sociology
44 (1979): 153-75.
Brunner, Edmund de S. "The Small Village: 1940-1950." Rural
Sociology 17 (1952): 127-31.
_____; Hughes, Gwendolyn S.; and Patten, Marjorie.
American Agricultural Villages. New York: George H.
Doran Co., 1927.
Brunner, Edmund de S., and Kolb, John H. Rural Social
Trends. New York: McGraw-Hill Book Co., 1933.
Brunner, Edmund de S., and Lorge, Irving. Rural Trends in

Depression Years. New York: Columbia University Press, 1937.

Buttel, Frederick H., and Flinn, William L. "Sources and Consequences of Agrarian Values in American Society." Rural Sociology 40 (1975): 134-51.

Buttel, Frederick H., and Larson, Oscar W., III. "Farm Size, Structure, and Energy Intensity: An Ecological Analysis of U.S. Agriculture." Rural Sociology 44 (1979): 471-88.

Cavazzani, Ada. Part-time Farming in Advanced Industrial Societies: Role and Characteristics in the United States. Bulletin no. 106. Ithaca, N.Y.: Department of Rural Sociology, Cornell University, 1979.

Clay, Daniel C., and Price, Michael L. "Structural Disturbances in Rural Communities: Some Repercussions of the Migration Turnaround in Michigan." Paper delivered at the Annual Meeting of the Rural Sociological Society, Burlington, Vt., August 1979.

Conklin, Howard E. "The Urban/Agriculture Interface and Farmland Preservation." Unpublished paper. Ithaca, N.Y.: Department of Agricultural Economics, Cornell University, 1979.

Davis, LeRoy. "The Relationship of Farm Size on Rural Poverty." Journal of Social and Behavioral Sciences 24 (1978): 6-16.

Durost, Donald D., and Black, Evelyn T. Changes in Farm Production and Efficiency, 1977. Economics, Statistics, and Cooperatives Service, U.S. Department of Agriculture, Statistical Bulletin Bulletin no. 612. Washington, D.C., 1978.

Eastman, Clyde: Harper, Wilmer; and Gomez, Bealquin. "New Mexico Small Farms and Ranches: Challenges for Research and Extension." Paper delivered at the Annual Meeting of the Rural Sociological Society, Burlington, Vt., August 1979.

Economics, Statistics, and Cooperatives Service, U.S. Department of Agriculture. Farm Income Statistics. Statistical Bulletin no. 627, 1979.

Ensminger, Douglas. "Rural Neighborhoods and Communities." In Rural Life in the United States, by Carl C. Taylor et al. New York: Alfred A. Knopf, 1949.

Flinn, William L., and Johnson, Donald E. "Agrarianism Among Wisconsin Farmers." Rural Sociology 39 (1974): 187-204.

Flora, Cornelia B., and Johnson, Sue. "Discarding the Distaff: New Roles for Rural Women." In Rural U.S.A.: Persistence and Change, edited by Thomas R. Ford. Ames, Iowa: Iowa State University Press, 1978.

Foote, Richard J. Concepts Involved in Defining and Identi-
    fying Farms. Economic Research Service, U.S. Department
    of Agriculture, ERS 448. Washington, D.C., 1970.
Frey, H. Thomas. Major Uses of Land in the United States:
    Summary for 1969. Economic Research Service, U.S.
    Department of Agriculture, Agricultural Economic Report
    no. 247. Washington, D.C., 1973.
Frisbie, W. Parker, and Poston, Dudley L., Jr. "Components
    of Sustenance Organization and Nonmetropolitan Change: A
    Human Ecological Investigation." American Sociological
    Review 40 (1975): 773-84.
Fuguitt, Glenn V. "Critique: 'A Typology of Part-time Farm-
    ing' and 'The Problems of Part-time Farming Conceptual-
    ized.'" In Part-time Farming: Problem or Resource in
    Rural Development, edited by Anthony M. Fuller and
    Julius A. Mage. Proceedings of the First Rural Geography
    Symposium, University of Guelph. Norwich, England: Geo
    Abstracts Ltd., 1975.
_____. "A Typology of the Part-time Farmer." Rural
    Sociology 26 (1961): 39-48.
Fujimoto, Isao. The Communities of the San Joaquin Valley:
    The Relation Between Scale of Farming, Water Use, and
    the Quality of Life. Testimony before the Federal Task
    Force on Wetlands, California. Sacramento, 4 August
    1977.
Gardner, Bruce L. "Farm Population Decline and the Income of
    Rural Families." American Journal of Agricultural
    Economics 56 (1974): 600-606.
Goldschmidt, Walter. As You Sow. New York: Harcourt, Brace
    and Co., 1947.
_____. As You Sow: Three Studies in the Social
    Consequences of Agribusiness. Montclair, N.J.: Allan-
    held, Osmun and Co., 1978a
_____. "Large-scale Farming and the Rural Social
    Structure." Rural Sociology 43 (1978b): 362-66.
Goss, Kelvin F., and Rodefeld, Richard D. Corporate Farming
    in the United States: A Guide to Current Literature,
    1967-1977. AE & RS 136. University Park, Pa.: Department
    of Agricultural Economics and Rural Sociology, Pennsyl-
    vania State University, 1978.
Hardin, Charles M. "The Bureau of Agricultural Economics
    Under Fire: A Study in Valuation Conflicts." Journal of
    Farm Economics 28 (1946): 635-68.
Harl, Neil E. "The Family Corporation." In Size, Structure,
    and Future of Farms, edited by A. Gordon Ball and Earl
    O. Heady. Ames, Iowa: Iowa State University Press, 1972.

Harris, Craig K., and Gilbert, Jess C. "Large-scale Farming,
    Rural Social Welfare, and the Agrarian Thesis: A
    Re-examination." Paper delivered at the Annual Meeting
    of the Rural Sociological Society, Burlington, Vt.,
    August 1979.
Hay, Donald G., and Polson, Robert A. Rural Organizations
    in Oneida County, New York. Bulletin 871. Ithaca, N.Y.:
    Cornell University Agricultural Experiment Station,
    1951.
Heady, Earl O., and Ball, A. Gordon. "Public Policy Means
    and Alternatives." In Size, Structure, and Future of
    Farms, edited by A. Gordon Ball and Earl O. Heady. Ames,
    Iowa: Iowa State University Press, 1972.
Heady, Earl O., and Sonka, Steven T. "Farm Size, Rural Com-
    munity Income, and Consumer Welfare." American Journal
    of Agricultural Economics 56 (1974): 534-42.
Heffernan, William D. "Sociological Dimensions of Agricul-
    tural Structures in the United States." Sociologia
    Ruralis 12 (1972): 481-99.
_____, and Lasley, Paul. "Agricultural Structure and
    Interaction in the Local Community: A Case Study." Rural
    Sociology 43 (1978): 348-61.
Johansen, Harley E., and Fuguitt, Glenn V. "Population
    Growth and Retail Decline: Conflicting Effects of Urban
    Accessibility in American Villages." Rural Sociology 44
    (1979): 24-38.
Kolb, John H. Emerging Rural Communities; Group Relations
    in Rural Society. A Review of Wisconsin Research in
    Action. Madison, Wis.: University of Wisconsin Press,
    1959.
_____, and Brunner, Edmund de S. A Study of Rural
    Society. 4th ed. Boston: Houghton Mifflin Co., 1952.
Kolb, John H., and Day, LeRoy J. Interdependence in Town and
    Country Relations in Rural Society. Research Bulletin
    172. Madison, Wis.: University of Wisconsin Agricultural
    Experiment Station, 1950.
Kyle, Leonard R.; Sundquist, W. B.; and Guither, Harold D.
    "Who Controls Agriculture Now?--The Trends Underway."
    In Who Will Control U.S. Agriculture?--Policies Affect-
    ing the Organizational Structure of U.S. Agriculture,
    edited by Harold D. Guither. Cooperative Extension
    Service Special Publication 27, North Central Regional
    Extension Publication 32. Urbana-Champaign: University
    of Illinois, 1972.
LaRose, Bruce L. "Arvin and Dinuba Revisited: A New Look at
    Community Structure and the Effects of Scale of Farm

Operations." In The Role of Giant Corporations in the American and World Economies. Part 3, Corporate Secrecy: Agribusiness. Hearings before the Subcommittee on Monopoly of the Select Committee on Small Business, U.S. Senate, 92nd Congress. Washington, D.C.: U.S. Government Printing Office, 1973.

Larson, Donald K., and Lewis, James A. "Small Farm Profile." In Small-Farm Issues: Proceedings of the ESCS Small-Farm Workshop, May 1978. Economics, Statistics, and Cooperatives Service, U.S. Department of Agriculture, ESCS-60. Washington, D.C., 1979.

Larson, Olaf F. "Basic Goals and Values of Farm People." In Goals and Values in Agricultural Policy. Assembled and published under the sponsorship of the Iowa State University Center for Agricultural and Economic Adjustment. Ames, Iowa: Iowa State University Press, 1961.

_____. "Values and Beliefs of Rural People." In Rural U.S.A.: Persistence and Change, edited by Thomas R. Ford. Ames, Iowa: Iowa State University Press, 1978.

_____, and Lutz, E. A. "Adjustments in Community Facilities Taking Place and Needed." In Adjustments in Agriculture--A National Basebook, edited by Carlton F. Christian. Ames, Iowa: Iowa State University Press, 1961.

Larson, Olaf F., and Richardson, Joseph L. "Small Community Use of Special Purpose Federal Programs." Paper delivered at the Annual Meeting of the Rural Sociological Society, Madison, Wis., September 1977.

LeVeen, E. Phillip. "Enforcing the Reclamation Act and Rural Development in California." Rural Sociology 44 (1979): 667-90.

Littman, Mark S. Social and Economic Characteristics of the Metropolitan and Nonmetropolitan Population: 1974 and 1970. Current Population Reports, series P-23, no. 25, U.S. Bureau of the Census. Washington, D.C., 1975.

Lodwick, Dora G., and Fassinger, Polly A. "Variations in Agricultural Production Activities of Women on Family Farms." Paper delivered at the Annual Meeting of the Rural Sociological Society, Burlington, Vt., August 1979.

Madden, J. Patrick, and Tischbein, Heather. "Toward an Agenda for Small Farm Research." Paper delivered at the Annual Meeting of the American Agricultural Economics Association, Pullman, Wash., July 1979.

Marshall, D. G. "Hamlets and Villages in the United States:

Their Place in the American Way of Life." American Sociological Review 11 (1946): 159-65.

Martinson, Oscar B.; Wilkening, Eugene A.; and Rodefeld, Richard D. "Feelings of Powerlessness and Social Isolation Among 'Large Scale' Farm Personnel." Rural Sociology 41 (1976): 452-72.

Mosher, M. L. Farms Are Growing Larger. Bulletin 613. Urbana, Ill.: University of Illinois Agricultural Experiment Station, 1957.

Nesmith, Dwight A. "The Small Rural Town." In A Place to Live: The Yearbook of Agriculture 1963. Washington, D.C.: U.S. Government Printing Office, 1963.

Nichols, E. H.; Fliegel, F. C.; and VanEs, J. C. "An Emerging Pattern of Small Farms in the North Central Region." Paper delivered at the Annual Meeting of the Rural Sociological Society, Burlington, Vt., August 1979.

Olshan, Marc A. The Old Order Amish in New York State. Bulletin no. 94. Ithaca, N.Y.: Department of Rural Sociology, Cornell University, 1979.

Ottoson, Howard W., and Vollmar, Glen J. "The Nonfamily Corporation in Farming." In Size, Structure, and Future of Farms, edited by A. Gordon Ball and Earl O. Heady. Ames, Iowa: Iowa State University Press, 1972.

Pearson, Jessica. "Note on Female Farmers." Rural Sociology 44 (1979): 189-200.

Ploch, Louis A. "The Reversal in Migration Patterns--Some Rural Development Consequences." Rural Sociology 43 (1978): 292-303.

Raper, Arthur F. "The Cotton Belt" and "Comparisons and Contrasts of Major Type-Farming Areas." In Rural Life in the United States by Carl C. Taylor et al. New York: Alfred A. Knopf, 1949.

Raup, Phillip M. "The Impact of Trends in the Farm Firm on Community and Human Welfare." In Emerging and Projected Trends Likely to Influence the Structure of Midwest Agriculture, 1970-1985, edited by John R. Brake. Monograph no. 11. Iowa City: University of Iowa, Agricultural Law Center, 1970.

_____. "Needed Research into the Effects of Large-Scale Farms and Business Firms on Rural America." In The Role of Giant Corporations in the American and World Economies. Part 3, Corporate Secrecy: Agribusiness. Hearings before the Subcommittee on Monopoly of the Select Committee on Small Business, U.S. Senate, 92nd Congress. Washington, D.C.: U.S. Government Printing Office, 1973.

Reinsel, Edward L. People With Farm Earnings...Sources and
    Distribution of Income. Economic Research Service, U.S.
    Department of Agriculture, ERS-498. Washington, D.C.,
    1972.
Report of the Small Farm Viability Project. The Family Farm
    in California. Final report submitted to the state of
    California, November 1977, available from the Office of
    Economic Development, Community Services Administration,
    Washington, D.C.
Richardson, Joseph L., and Larson, Olaf F. "Small Community
    Trends: A 50-Year Perspective on Social-Economic Change
    in 13 New York Communities." Rural Sociology 41 (1976):
    45-59.
Rodefeld, Richard D. "The Current Status of U.S. 'Corporate'
    Farm Research." In The Role of Giant Corporations in
    the American and World Economies. Part 3, Corporate
    Secrecy: Agribusiness. Hearings before the Subcommittee
    on Monopoly of the Select Committee on Small Business,
    U.S. Senate, 92nd Congress. Washington, D.C.: U.S.
    Government Printing Office, 1973.
_____. "Trends in U.S. Farm Organizational Structure
    and Type." In Change in Rural America: Causes, Conse-
    quences, and Alternatives, edited by Richard D. Rodefeld
    et al. St. Louis, Mo.: C. V. Mosby Company, 1978.
_____, and Lancelle, Mark. "Resident Owners, Hired
    Managers and Hired Full-time Workers of Large Wisconsin
    Farms: Background-SES, Family Structure and Behavioral
    Integration Characteristics." Paper delivered at the
    Annual Meeting of the Rural Sociological Society, San
    Francisco, Calif., 1978.
Ross, Peggy J., and Green, Bernal L. Impacts of the Rural
    Turnaround on Rural Education. Las Cruces, N.Mex.:
    Educational Resources Information Center, Clearinghouse
    on Rural Education and Small Schools, New Mexico State
    University, 1979.
Rowe, Gene. The Hired Farm Working Force of 1977. Economics,
    Statistics, and Cooperatives Service, U.S. Department of
    Agriculture, Agricultural Economic Report no. 437.
    Washington, D.C., 1979.
Salamon, Sonya. "Ethnic Differences in Farm Family Land
    Transfers." Paper delivered at the Annual Meeting of the
    Rural Sociological Society, Burlington, Vt., August
    1979.
Sanders, Irwin T., and Ensminger, Douglas. Alabama Rural
    Communities: A Study of Chilton County. Bulletin 136.
    Montevallo, Ala.: Alabama College, 1940.

Schreiner, Dean F. "Rural Community Services in a Dynamic
    Rural Economy." In Size, Structure, and Future of Farms,
    edited by A. Gordon Ball and Earl O. Heady. Ames, Iowa:
    Iowa State University Press, 1972.
Smith, T. Lynn. "A Study of Social Stratification in the
    Agricultural Areas of the U.S.: Nature, Data, Proce-
    dures, and Preliminary Results." Rural Sociology 34
    (1969): 496-509.
Stanton, B. F. "Perspective on Farm Size." American Journal
    of Agricultural Economics 60 (1978): 727-37.
_____. Some Political Arithmetic of Large and Small.
    Staff Paper no. 79-19. Ithaca, N.Y.: Department of
    Agricultural Economics, Cornell University, 1979.
_____, and Plimpton, L. M. People, Land, and Farms:
    125 Years of Change in the Northeast. Ithaca, N.Y.:
    Department of Agricultural Economics, Cornell Univer-
    sity, 1979.
Taylor, Carl C. et al. Rural Life in the United States. New
    York: Alfred A. Knopf, 1949.
Thompson, Ronald, and Hepp, Ralph. Description and Analysis
    of Michigan Small Farms. Research Report 296. East
    Lansing, Mich.: Michigan Cooperative Extension, Michigan
    State University, 1976.
Timmons, John F. "Tenure and Size." In Size, Structure, and
    Future of Farms, edited by A. Gordon Ball and Earl O.
    Heady. Ames, Iowa: Iowa State University Press, 1972.
U.S. Bureau of the Census. Historical Statistics of the
    United States, Colonial Times to 1970, Bicentennial
    Edition, Part 1. Washington, D.C.: U.S. Government
    Printing Office, 1975.
_____. 1970 Census of Population. General Social and
    Economic Characteristics. Final Report PC(1)C1 United
    States Summary. Washington, D.C.: U.S. Government
    Printing Office, 1972.
_____. 1974 Census of Agriculture. Vol. 1, pt. 51,
    United States Summary and State Data. Washington, D.C.:
    U.S. Government Printing Office, 1977.
_____. 1974 Census of Agriculture. Vol. 2, Statistics
    by Subject, Pt. 3, Tenure, Type of Organization, Con-
    tracts, Operator Characteristics, Principal Occupation.
    Washington, D.C.: U.S. Government Printing Office,
    1978a.
_____. 1974 Census of Agriculture. Vol. 4, Special
    Reports, Pt. 3, Coverage Evaluation. Washington, D.C.:
    U.S. Government Printing Office, 1978b.
_____. 1974 Census of Agriculture. Vol. 4, Special

Reports, Pt. 5, Corporations in Agricultural Production. Washington, D.C.: U.S. Government Printing Office, 1978c.

U.S. Department of Agriculture. 1978 Handbook of Agricultural Charts. Agriculture Handbook no. 551. Washington, D.C.: U.S. Government Printing Office, 1978.

Wardle, Christopher, and Boisvert, Richard N. Farm and Non-Farm Alternatives for Limited Resource Dairy Farmers in Central New York. A.E. Res. 74-6. Ithaca, N.Y.: Department of Agricultural Economics, Cornell University, 1974.

Wheelock, Gerald C. "Farm Size, Community Structure and Growth: Respecification of a Structural Equation Model." Paper delivered at the Annual Meeting of the Rural Sociological Society, Burlington, Vt., August 1979.

Whiting, Larry R., ed. Communities Left Behind: Alternatives for Development. Ames, Iowa: Iowa State University Press, 1974.

Wilkening, Eugene A., and Ahrens, Nancy. "Involvement of Wives in Farm Tasks as Related to Characteristics of the Farm, the Family and Work Off the Farm." Paper delivered at the Annual Meeting of the Rural Sociological Society, Burlington, Vt., August 1979.

Wunderlich, Gene. Who Owns America's Land: Problems in Preserving the Rural Landscape. Economic Research Service, U.S. Department of Agriculture. Washington, D.C., 1974.

Zeimetz, Kathryn A. et al. Dynamics of Land Use in Fast Growth Areas. Economic Research Service, U.S. Department of Agriculture, Agricultural Economic Report no. 325. Washington, D.C., 1976.

Thomas E. Till

5
Manufacturing Industry: Trends and Impacts

INTRODUCTION

Machines replaced men so quickly during the technological revolution on America's farms that the number of farm jobs (and, through multiplier effects, total employment) shrank drastically in recent decades. As a result, migratory streams swelled metro areas, often intensifying their problems; and the rural hinterland desperately sought jobs to replace those lost in farming. In most nonmetro areas, attracting factory employment became the primary strategy. The state of knowledge on this effort is the subject of this chapter. It will address the following questions: (1) What is the extent and pattern of employment changes, especially since 1960? (2) Why have these manufacturing patterns occurred? (3) What has been the impact of manufacturing growth, both on the nonmetro population in general and on the poor in particular? (4) Finally, what are the implications for policy?

To make this vast body of literature[1] manageable, several restrictions will be observed: (1) The topic of industrial development will be narrowed to that of manufacturing employment, rather than to any other Standard Industrial Classification (SIC) "one-digit" industry. Consequently, the impacts of the boom in mining and other energy employment, recreational jobs, growth of the service sector, and other base activities will not be covered. (2) Because recent changes seem more relevant to policy, the period of the 1960s and 1970s will be stressed. (3) Here, as elsewhere, nonmetro shall be used in preference to "rural." Not only are employment data more inadequate for any other definition, but also it seems functionally unwise to sepa-

Special thanks are due to Mr. Claude C. Haren of the Economics, Statistics and Cooperatives Service, U.S. Department of Agriculture. The data he has provided on nonmetropolitan employment are invaluable.

rate a hinterland from the nearby city of less than 50,000 population, which often acts as the chief place of employ- ment and the service center for surrounding open country and small town areas. (4) Nonmetro pertains to all counties not included in Standard Metropolitan Statistical Areas (SMSAs) as defined by the 1970 definition of the U.S. Bureau of the Census.

PATTERNS IN NONMETROPOLITAN
MANUFACTURING EMPLOYMENT, 1960-1978

During the 1960s there was considerable controversy about the extent of, and possibility for, manufacturing job growth in nonmetro areas. Prominent urban and regional economists and geographers (Berry 1968; Thompson 1965) doubted the extent of rural industrialization and held a theory of SMSA locational dominance. They cited as empirical evidence the more rapid growth of SMSAs during the 1940s and 1950s in population and total employment. As the causal factor, they advanced the agglomeration economics of SMSAs; for example, the more varied, skilled, and abundant labor supply, better business services, cultural amenities, and other advantages of large urban areas. But some agricultural economists and demographers--especially those associated with the Economic Research Service of the U.S. Department of Agriculture (Haren 1970; Beale 1969)--challenged the findings. The dispute was not without policy significance. If desirable factories could not be lured to rural areas without impractically large subsidies, the federal policies of infrastructure-building and business and industrial loans to attract industry were irrelevant. The debate also was relevant to the question of whether public job-creating investments should be located primarily in growth centers or in "worse-off" places. Also, those who admitted that some low-wage, labor-intensive factories could be attracted, questioned whether such jobs were worth the effort, a ques- tion to which we shall return in a later section of this chapter.
    At the time of the controversy, the empirical work was not of sufficient clarity to resolve the debate. Even though it could be shown that there was factory job growth in nonmetro counties, it was claimed that this could be occurring on the fringes of SMSAs, and so be due to large- city labor markets. Today, in the decade of the "rural

renaissance," the controversy seems mainly of historical
interest. An abundance of empirical work published in the
1970s (see, for example, Sternlieb and Hughes 1975; U.S.
Bureau of Census 1979) has confirmed three main locational
trends: (1) The intrametro shift from central city to suburban locations; (2) the regional movement from the old manufacturing belt of the Northeast and Midwest to the South and
West; and (3) finally, and most relevant to this paper, the
shift from metro to nonmetro locations. All three of these
shifts were part of a process of deconcentration of manufacturing employment from areas of previous concentration.

An important distinction divides employment into export
base and local service sectors. The export base is composed of firms (e.g., farms, mines, factories) that produce a product or services sold primarily to outsiders.
Businesses that produce mainly for local residents (e.g.,
barber shops, supermarket, drug stores) comprise the local
sector. Because the export base generates the demand for
the goods and services of the local sector, changes in its
industries are more crucial for the growth or decline of
communities.

It is well-known that employment losses in the extractive industries (especially agriculture) have been for
decades the main factor in population losses in nonmetro
areas: "In 1820 over 70 percent of all American workers
were employed in agriculture...By 1940 [this had declined
to] only 17.5 percent...The decline continued from 1950
to 1970: nonmetro employment in extractive industries
(agriculture, forestry, fisheries, mining) declined from
31.1 percent to 10.2 percent of the labor force, or by over
4 million jobs." (Zuiches and Brown, 1978: 64.)

During the 1960s, the loss was 2.5 million (Holt and
Fisher 1979). The striking fact about the decade of the
1970s is that extractive employment stabilized. Although
the figures for nonmetro areas are lacking, extractive
industries nationally during the 1972-78 period gained
147,000 jobs. Agriculture, forestry, and fishing suffered a
loss of only 84,000 jobs during this period, and from 1975
to 1978 seem to have reversed and experienced an increase
(U.S. Bureau of Census, 1979: 45).

Mining, another important base industry in nonmetro
areas, has also experienced declining employment for decades. This trend continued in the 1960s, with a drop from
1962 to 1970 of 32,000 jobs, or 7.4 percent. The energy
crisis helped bring about a boom in the 1970s, with employment increasing by 13.7 percent (55,000 jobs) from 1970 to

1978.[2] It is striking that this industry, despite its
importance in central Appalachia and the northern Great
Plains, represents relatively few jobs, and is a very small
employment sector even in nonmetro areas. In 1978, there
were more than eight factory workers for every miner. Job
gains in mining over the 1962-78 period were only 1 percent
of manufacturing's increase (see Table 5.1).

"Chasing smokestacks" has been a key development strategy in nonmetro areas. The record shows a considerable payoff: an addition of 1.8 million manufacturing jobs during
the 1962-78 period, a gain of 46.6 percent. However, two-
thirds of the increase came in the 1960s. Manufacturing
has been a less dynamic factor since 1974. In the 1970-74
period, the manufacturing gain amounted to 21.7 percent of
all nonmetro farm gains; from 1974 to 1978, the comparable
percentage was only 6.5. In this latter period, the service-
providing industries were the most dynamic. That the service
economy is becoming more dominant in nonmetro areas is
consistent with a passage from an industrial to a tertiary
stage of development. Also, the service sector should not
be regarded as merely passive in relation to changes in the
economic base. It contains important basic industries, such
as tourism, four-year colleges, retirement complexes, as
well as federal government programs.

Manufacturing historically has been concentrated in
large cities. As it routinizes its production process and
engages in pursuit of low-cost labor, this is becoming
increasingly untrue. Nonmetro areas outpaced the large
cities during the 1962-78 period by almost 400,000 factory
jobs, thereby increasing their share of manufacturing
employment from 24.3 to 26.1 percent.

Not only is the manufacturing sector shifting toward
nonmetro locations, but also it is (within nonmetro areas)
moving toward the Sunbelt. The South and West had the highest rates of increase--56.9 and 74 percent, respectively--
for the nonmetro regions. Nearly a million of this 1.8
million manufacturing increase was captured by the South.

This trend conjures up pictures of Frostbelt decline.
This is by no means true for nonmetro areas of the Northeast
and Midwest, as may be seen in Table 5.2. The nonmetro
Midwest gained more than one-half million jobs of the manufacturing sector increases. Even northeastern nonmetro areas
grew by 104,000 jobs in striking contrast to their metro
areas. It is apparent that the nonmetro locational trend is
occurring in the Northeast and Midwest, as well as the
Sunbelt.

Table 5.1. Nonfarm Employment In Metropolitan and
Nonmetropolitan Areas, 1962-1978

Area and Industry Group	Employment[a]		Change	
	1962 (000s)	1978 (000s)	No. (000s)	%
Metro	41,030	61,628	20,598	50.2
Goods-producing	14,823	16,955	2,132	14.4
Manufacturing	12,715	14,141	1,426	11.2
Construction	1,899	2,592	693	36.5
Mining	209	222	13	6.2
Service-providing	23,191	41,039	17,848	77.0
Private sector	16,935	29,794	12,859	75.9
Trade	8,606	13,924	5,318	61.8
Services	5,990	12,090	6,100	101.8
FIRE[b]	2,339	3,780	1,441	61.6
Government	6,256	11,245	4,989	79.8
TCU[c]	3,016	3,634	618	20.5
Nonmetro	13,162	21,695	8,533	64.8
Goods-producing	4,936	7,237	2,301	46.6
Manufacturing	3,907	5,729	1,822	46.6
Construction	596	1,052	456	76.5
Mining	433	456	23	5.3
Service-providing	7,381	13,398	6,017	81.5
Private sector	4,637	8,698	4,061	87.6
Trade	2,609	4,623	2,014	77.2
Services	1,613	3,330	1,717	106.4
FIRE[b]	415	745	330	79.5
Government	2,744	4,700	1,956	71.3
TCU[c]	845	1,060	215	25.4

Source: Haren and Holling, Table 1, p. 16.

[a]Adapted from BLS-Employment Security Estimates.

[b]Finance, Insurance, and Real Estate.

[c]Transportation, Communications, and Utilities.

The increasing nonfarm character of nonmetro America does not come without cost. Strength in the manufacturing sector implies increased vulnerability to recessions. During the severe 1974-75 decline, 711,000 manufacturing jobs were lost--which is the principal factor in accounting for an absolute decline in total nonfarm employment. Although the vigorous growth of service-producing industries has restored its job losses three times over since 1974, it took the manufacturing subsector until 1978 to reach its 1974 totals (Table 5.3).

Very little research has been performed on the cyclical behavior of employment in nonmetro areas. It is interesting that the 1970-71 recession affected nonmetro areas only slightly in comparison to the big cities. This is consistent with a hypothesis that older metro plants would be abandoned first. However, the 1974-75 decline affected nonmetro areas almost as severely as it did metro areas.

LOCATIONAL FACTORS

This section is an attempt to explain the employment patterns of the recent decades--to discover why industrialization does or does not take place in an area.

EMPIRICAL CONTRIBUTIONS

Because of the relatively nonoperational state of general location theory, most of the relevant work has been empirical (and mainly descriptive) in nature. The aim has not been to test classical location theory, but rather to understand location factors and patterns and to arrive at statistical explanations that might be useful for prediction and policy purposes.[3]

It is generally accepted that a firm's locational decision has two stages. First, a region is usually chosen for reasons that communities can do little about. Next, a specific city within the area is selected. For this, community-controlled factors play a key role. This distinction is summarized by Tweeten and Brinkman (1976: 246):

Locations factors generally can be grouped as (1) factors that communities have little control over and

Table 5.2. Changes in Nonfarm Employment by Regions,
1962-1978

Area and Industry Group	Northeast N (000s)	%	North Central N (000s)	%
Total	3,767	24.4	7,138	45.9
Metro	2,789	20.8	4,744	42.0
Goods-producing	-640	-12.2	555	12.1
Manufacturing	-578	-12.3	405	9.7
Construction	- 44	- 8.8	155	37.5
Mining	- 18	-72.0	- 5	-23.8
Service-providing	3,436	47.6	4,094	69.7
Private sector	2,409	43.7	3,003	68.0
Trade	808	30.8	1,270	55.0
Services	1,336	65.8	1,440	94.4
FIRE[a]	265	30.7	293	50.5
Government	1,027	60.3	1,091	74.7
TCU[b]	- 7	- 0.7	95	11.7
Nonmetro	978	48.2	2,394	56.1
Goods-producing	128	14.5	642	44.3
Manufacturing	104	13.4	564	47.8
Construction	32	43.2	96	55.2
Mining	- 8	-22.9	- 18	-19.1
Service-providing	832	81.1	1,716	68.0
Private sector	594	90.3	1,177	72.1
Trade	257	75.8	592	62.0
Services	297	114.7	494	92.7
FIRE[a]	40	66.7	91	63.2
Government	238	64.7	539	60.4
TCU[b]	18	14.9	36	12.2

Source: Haren and Holling, Table 8, p. 29.

[a]Finance, Insurance, and Real Estate

[b]Transportation, Communications, and Utilities.

South		West	
N	%	N	%
(000)s		(000s)	
11,315	77.1	6,911	81.0
7,692	82.2	5,373	77.0
1,462	51.8	755	34.8
1,029	48.5	570	33.0
417	72.0	165	40.7
16	12.8	20	52.6
5,906	102.0	4,412	102.5
4,193	104.5	3,254	108.8
1,865	86.9	1,375	90.0
1,835	136.5	1,489	136.5
493	94.4	390	104.6
1,713	96.2	1,158	88.1
324	43.4	206	40.7
3,623	68.2	1,538	99.2
1,220	55.9	311	73.7
966	56.9	188	74.0
236	91.1	93	103.3
19	8.4	30	38.5
2,293	81.1	1,176	117.2
1,512	84.8	778	138.2
793	79.4	372	117.7
594	95.7	332	166.0
125	76.2	74	157.4
781	74.8	398	90.5
110	36.2	51	40.8

Table 5.3. Changes in Nonfarm Wage and Salary Employment,
March 1970–1978

Area and Industry Group	Decline 1970–71		Upturn 1972–74	
	N (000s)	%	N (000s)	%
Total	− 704	−1.0	7,845	11.3
Metro	− 760	−1.4	5,354	10.2
Goods-producing	−1,241	−7.2	1,275	8.0
Manufacturing	−1,156	−7.9	822	6.1
Construction	− 81	−3.4	435	18.6
Mining	− 4	−1.9	18	8.8
Service-providing	516	1.6	3,933	11.9
Private sector	211	0.9	3,132	13.3
Trade	16	0.1	1,253	11.0
Services	145	1.6	1,499	16.5
FIRE[a]	50	1.6	380	12.2
Government	305	3.4	801	8.6
TCU[b]	− 35	− 1.0	146	4.2
Nonmetro	55	0.3	2,491	14.5
Goods-producing	− 212	−3.4	1,057	17.5
Manufacturing	− 209	−4.1	762	15.6
Construction	− 5	−0.7	258	34.7
Mining	2	0.5	37	9.2
Service-providing	258	2.6	1,341	13.2
Private sector	177	2.9	1,039	16.4
Trade	73	2.2	555	16.4
Services	91	4.0	374	15.6
FIRE[a]	13	2.5	110	20.3
Government	81	2.1	302	7.8
TCU[b]	9	1.0	93	1.0

Source: Haren and Holling, Table 5, p. 23.

[a]Finance, Insurance, and Real Estate.

[b]Transportation, Communications, and Utilities.

Decline 1974-75		Upturn 1975-78	
N	%	N	%
(000)s		(000s)	
-1,514	- 2.0	7,328	9.6
-1,133	- 2.0	4,918	8.7
-1,657	- 9.6	1,293	8.3
-1,243	- 8.7	1,064	8.1
- 427	-15.4	243	10.3
13	5.8	- 14	-5.9
645	1.8	3,514	9.4
182	0.7	2,876	10.7
- 23	- 0.2	1,306	10.4
207	2.0	1,282	11.9
- 2	- 0.1	288	8.3
463	4.6	638	6.0
- 121	- 3.3	111	3.2
- 381	- 1.9	2,410	12.5
- 777	-10.9	909	14.4
- 711	-12.6	777	15.7
- 106	-10.6	156	17.4
40	9.1	- 24	-5.0
424	3.7	1,429	11.9
238	3.2	1,084	14.2
75	1.9	597	14.8
148	5.3	410	14.0
15	2.3	77	11.5
186	4.5	345	7.9
- 28	- 2.8	72	7.3

(2) factors that can be affected by community actions.
Factors outside community control include nearness to
markets and raw materials, transportation routes, labor,
state laws and development policies, and special preferences of plant managers. Communities certainly can exploit such factors to attract industry, but they must
accept them essentially as they occur. Community-
controlled factors, on the other hand, can be modified
somewhat by community actions. They include the attitude
of the community toward developing industry, facilities
(land sites, buildings, utilities, etc., that can be
provided), financial assistance, taxes, community characteristics (schools, recreation, etc.), and special
incentives.

Although work has been done on the comparative locational advantages of areas (Lowry 1963; Chapman and Wells 1959),
most research efforts have been directed to identifying reasons for particular locational decisions. For that purpose
questionnaire surveys of area industrialists have been used
(Mueller, Wilkin, and Wood 1950; Katona and Morgan 1952;
Moeller 1959; McLaughlin and Robock 1949; McMillan 1965;
Bergin and Eagan 1961; Wallace and Ruttan 1961; Morgan
1967). A common finding in that body of research is that
regional factors—markets, labor, raw materials, and
transportation—exercise overriding influence. The results
of seventeen questionnaire and seven interview studies
conducted in the 1940s and 1950s are summarized in Table
5.4 by Morgan (1967). The minor importance given to taxes
and financial subsidies is a typical finding of these
studies.
The influence of community-controlled factors has been
observed by Wallace (1961) in an Indiana area. He discovered
that community actions were influential in locating six
firms that accounted for 17.2 percent (783 workers) of the
manufacturing jobs created by the new plants studied. Brinkman's (1973b) survey of plant managers in Kansas found the
same general results. It is summarized in Table 5.5. The
results show that three of the top five factors were under
community control: (1) availability of facilities for
business operations (land, buildings, utilities, etc.); (2)
financial assistance (primarily adequate private credit at
market rates); and (3) community attitudes favorable to
business. When the managers were asked which factors were
most important for overcoming other deficiencies, the same

Table 5.4. Significance of Location Factors According to
Business Opinion, as Revealed by Seventeen Questionnaire
Survey Studies and Seven Interview Survey Studies, 1945-1960

	Number of Studies		
Factor	Primary Significance	Some Significance	Little Significance
Markets	22	2	...
Labor	13	11	...
Raw materials	13	10	...
Transportation	7	16	1
Taxes	1	3	20
Financial inducements	...	...	20

Source: Morgan 1967; quoted in Tweeten and Brinkman,
1976: 247.

three were dominant. On the negative side, markets and
transportation were listed as the chief drawbacks of the
nonmetro locations.

For nonmetro areas specifically, most researchers
would agree with Kale and Lonsdale's conclusions (1979:
45-50): "The availability of low-cost labor has probably
been the most important attraction influencing industry
to locate in nonmetro America. Manufacturing plants locating in nonmetro areas are typically oriented to low-skilled
or medium-skilled labor....The absence of labor unions is
also considered a contributing factor to productivity by
many nonmetro employers. The possibility of avoiding labor
unions remains a highly attractive consideration to these
employers."

So far the discussion has been on location in terms of
current nonmetro community characteristics. A more dynamic
argument is presented by Alfred Eichner (1970). His basic
thesis is that state development agencies should upgrade
the skills of labor through manpower training in order to
attract high-wage, high-growth industry. Although plausible
on a priori grounds, the only evidence presented is a descriptive growth model that makes the rate of growth a function of possessing high-wage, high-growth industries, and
the latter a function in turn of a skilled labor force.

Table 5.5. Importance of Factors in
Locating Industry in Southeastern Kansas

Location Factor	Weighted Rankings
Labor	718
Facilities for business operation	612
Transportation	598
Financial assistance	534
Community attitude	528
Markets	509
Availability of shipped-in raw materials	478
Community characteristics	469
Taxes	440
Manager's personal preference	378
State and local legislation	355
Availability of local raw materials	327
Other	65

Source: Brinkman 1973b; quoted in Tweeten and
Brinkman, 1976: 248.

No data to support the model are given. The author does
describe the South Carolina Committee on Technical Education
that provides manpower training for prospective firms. But
again, its operations are merely detailed and no data are
given to evaluate the effectiveness of this approach in
attracting industry.

A second model of the process might be called the SMSA
Locational Dominance Model. According to this, business
services, amenities, skilled labor, and other advantages of
SMSAs are so great that few manufacturers could be induced
to locate in nonmetro areas. The empirical studies above
obviously do not support this theory. What the SMSA model
has failed to recognize is the well-known filtering hypothesis (Thompson 1969). According to this theory, new industries are spawned primarily in metro areas, where they can
draw upon vacant plant space and abundant business services.
Later on, as the product is standardized and mass production
is achieved, production is routinized and locations are
sought further down the city-size hierarchy, where less
industrial sophistication is present or required. In labor-
intensive industries, abundant supplies of low-wage labor

prove to be a top drawing card--a leading attraction of nonmetro locations. Thus, as an industry ages, locations "filter down" to smaller cities.

Because little empirical work has been done on this filtering hypothesis--with the exception of some recent studies by Erickson and Leinbach (Erickson 1977; Erickson and Leinbach 1979)--not much more can be said about it. Most of the empirical work concentrates on the section of the theory that states that most plants in small city areas will be in nationally slow-growth industries. The basis for this is the traditional S-curve theory of an industry's rate of growth; namely, first, slow growth until the product becomes popular; then mass production; finally, slower growth as the industry ages and declines. Several studies have established that nonmetro counties' growth has been primarily due to capturing increased shares of these slow-growth industries (Hansen 1970; USDA 1979; Till 1972). The same studies have shown that the nonmetro industrial mix contains less nationally fast-growth industries than in SMSAs. However, Till (1972) found that two of the three manufacturing industries with the largest job growth in the nonmetro South in the 1960s were higher-wage, fast-growth industries (i.e., electrical machinery and transportation equipment). Petrulis (USDA 1979) discovered that this trend increased nationwide during the early 1970s. This suggests one reason why the predicted stagnation for nonmetro counties, based on the slow-growth industry phenomenon, has not occurred.

DEVELOPING NEW VENTURES AND SMALL BUSINESS

In recent Senate testimony Carl Holman, president of the National Urban Coalition, stressed a topic that is rarely treated in the industrial development literature:

I want to expand on the three basic approaches to economic development which we are advocating: (1) Venture and equity capital to young, small, independent firms in distressed areas. A study recently completed by David Birch of MIT has some striking findings which, I believe, should affect development dollars. Birch found that young firms--those four years old or less--are generating about 80 percent of all new jobs and that this pattern held true across all sectors of the economy and all regions. But more important, small firms,

with 100 or fewer employees, generated 81.5 percent of
all new jobs in this country, virtually all new jobs in
the Northeast and 70.2 to 84.4 percent of new jobs in
other regions. Well over half of the jobs--56.2 percent
--were created by independent firms of this size. Large
corporations, on which conventional economic development
policy has relied, generate few new jobs. Furthermore,
because of their financial strength, they are the first
to redistribute their operations out of declining areas
and into growing ones. The public policy problem is that
the very firms which generate the most jobs are the
firms, which, because of their volatility, are the least
bankable. If, in addition, they are firms operating in
distressed communities, the problem of access to capital for business growth becomes paramount. We are talk-
ing now about the access to capital; what we are hearing
from healthy businesses in distressed communities, many
of them minority firms, is that they cannot get the
capital, not at any price. (Holman, 1979: 2.)

The data of Allaman and Birch (1975) for nonmetro areas
reveal several interesting patterns, even though the time
period is short (Table 5.6). The relocation of firms (in-
migration and out-migration) though a major factor in popular stereotypes, is a very minor source of job changes--
accounting for less than 1 percent. Establishment closings
("deaths") and contractions are more important, but are
very similar across regions. Consequently, it is the birth
of new establishments and the expansion of existing ones
that is responsible for the greater growth in regions of
the South and West.
    Birch (1979) also reported for the United States as a
whole: (1) Small firms (those with twenty or fewer employees) generated 66 percent of all new jobs generated in
the United States. (2) Small, independent firms generated
52 percent of the total. (3) Middle-sized and large firms
on balance provided relatively few new jobs. These findings
raise important policy questions. State and local industrial
development corporations have focused their efforts on attracting branch plants of large corporations. To increase
local jobs, the above data suggest that they should have
stressed helping existing firms to expand and aid new entrepreneurs to start operations and services. The argument
is apparently strengthened in areas that the larger corporations have tended to avoid, such as in south Texas and
the Black Belt of the South.

Table 5.6. Average Components of Manufacturing Employment Change for Metropolitan and Nonmetropolitan Areas by Region, 1970-1972

Region	Net Change %	Births %	Deaths %	Expansion %	Contraction %	In-migration %	Out-migration %
Metro							
Northeast	-6.6	4.5	-12.1	10.9	- 9.9	0.2	-0.3
North Central	-4.3	4.5	-10.2	10.6	- 9.3	0.2	-0.2
South	-0.0	7.8	-11.6	13.6	- 9.9	0.3	-0.2
West	-3.5	6.7	-13.9	14.2	-10.7	0.3	-0.2
Nonmetro							
Northeast	-2.3	5.4	-13.2	13.6	- 8.2	0.3	-0.2
North Central	1.4	6.6	-12.7	15.9	- 8.5	0.3	-0.2
South	1.2	7.4	-13.9	15.6	- 8.0	0.4	-0.2
West	7.7	10.4	-14.8	21.6	- 9.6	0.3	-0.2

Source: Allaman and Birch, Table 3, p. 13.

Several researchers besides Birch have used the Dun &
Bradstreet data on firms, such as Jusenius and Ledebur for
two reports on the New England economy (1978) and Ohio
(1977). An excellent survey of these D & B studies of the
components of employment change is provided by Wolman
(1979).

It is important to state that there is still considerable question among experts about the Birch studies. First,
his data are too highly aggregated to be sure of the implications for manufacturing in nonmetro areas. Nonmetro information needs to be broken out by industry, so that
changes in manufacturing are visible. We know, for example,
that small businesses are more prevalent in the service
sector (barber shops, beauty salons, etc.) than in the
manufacturing sector. Second, the contribution of small
firms to new jobs is a gross figure. Because the failure
rates for small firms are very high, we need to subtract
closures to determine a net change attributable to small
businesses. Nonmetro areas are interested in permanent, not
temporary, employment. Finally, we know that the Dun &
Bradstreet data underestimate relocations and certain
industries (Wolman, 1979: 45-47), though it is not clear
that corrections would reverse Birch's results. Briefly,
Birch's data raise major policy questions; but they are
still too uncertain and untested to support major policy
changes.

Another topic that has generated very little research
attention is the industrial development activity of community development corporations (CDCs) and cooperatives. Except for one article by Deaton (1975) on a CDC in Tennessee,
which later failed, the professional literature has largely
ignored them. This is unfortunate because CDCs can potentially play an important role, especially in areas that
corporate manufacturers have avoided.

Eighteen rural CDCs have been funded by the Community
Services Administration (CSA) through the Special Impact
Program. CSA allocations to those CDCs in fiscal year 1977
amounted to more than $15 million. One of them--Delta
Foundation in Greenville, Mississippi--placed fifty-seventh
(gross sales of $5.8 million) among black-owned businesses
for fiscal 1977. Another, Kentucky Highlands, has had
considerable success in starting new businesses in the
central Appalachian area. It is unfortunate that current
information about CDCs comes only from the popular press
(see, for example, the article on Delta Foundation in Black
Enterprise, June 1978), occasional reports to agencies

(Center for Community Economic Development 1977), and newsletters (CCED Review 1978-).

THE IMPACT OF NONMETROPOLITAN INDUSTRIALIZATION

ECONOMIC IMPACTS

Basically, impact studies supply an empirical basis for a general theory of growth. However, regional Harrod-Domar models or neoclassical growth models have been little used, mainly because of data deficiencies (no system of regional income and product statistics exists) and the high level of aggregation of the models. General equilibrium models have been avoided for similar reasons, although they are certainly relevant, especially when plant relocations occur. Growth pole theory has been investigated by Stevens et al. (1969), but vagueness inhibits its usefulness.

The methods most used have been multiplier analysis (and the closely related economic base theory) and input-output techniques. Output, income, and employment multipliers can be calculated, but usually the focus is on the last two.

A major group of early articles is centered on the "industrialization hypothesis." This states that the development of agricultural areas is directly proportional to their proximity to industrial-urban centers. First stated by Theodore Schultz (1953), it was developed by Nicholls (1961) in research on the eastern Tennessee Valley region and by Tang (1958).

The analysis held that both the agricultural factor and product markets functioned more efficiently near urban-industrial centers (e.g., farm labor had the alternative of off-farm earnings; more investment capital was available on better terms, etc.). The empirical test was made by time-series data. Neighboring agricultural counties initially similar in activity and culture were selected. Over a time period of nearly one hundred years, farm income, output, and investment per acre of the counties that had become industrialized were compared with those that had not, the latter thus serving as a control group. The marked differences supported the hypothesis. This line of argument runs into admitted ceteris paribus problems, but given this limitation, the handling was ingenious and competent. Efforts to test the theory on a national scale were made, with mixed results, by Hathaway et al. (1968). Other work,

with findings generally supporting this hypothesis, includes
Bryant (1966) and Ruttan (1955).

In contrast to the very long-run studies above, the
usual impact study tries to measure the short-run effect of
a new plant on the income and employment of the local community or county. Many of these are of varying quality.
From these, certain conclusions emerge. First, nonmetro
industrialization raises the income and employment of local
people. In Ruttan's words (1955: 185), "There is little
doubt...that the level of farm family income is closely
related to the extent of local urban-industrial development.
When the median income of rural farm families is plotted
on one axis and the proportion of the total population that
is nonfarm on the other axis of the chart the result for
most areas is a very clear positive relationship."[4]

Dale Hathaway (1963: 373-74) adds, "There is no doubt
that local industrial development which offers nonfarm
occupations without necessitating change in residence
offers an advantage to local agriculture as well as to
those who take nonfarm jobs. Analysis of part-time farming,
even at relatively low nonfarm wage rates, will result in
significant improvements in family income."

This result, although important, is rather obvious. If
subsidization is involved, however, it by no means follows
that the benefits are greater than the costs, especially
the opportunity costs of alternative uses of investment,
such as increased manpower training, education, health, and
relocation assistance. The case for such uses, especially
in light of the present inadequate preparation of migrants
for successful transition, is strongly made by Hansen
(1970).

An important benefit of rural industrial development
for farm families is accomplished through expansion of the
opportunities for part-time farming. Research shows that
many factory employees will not move to town, but will
continue to farm on a part-time basis (USDA 1967; Price et
al. 1958). This significantly raises household income
levels. Hathaway (1963: 374) comments that, "despite the
disdain of farm management economists for part-time farming, it appears that this provides an optimum way of integrating industrial development into local farm communities."

An example of the importance of off-farm employment to
farm families is provided by Sutherland's study of small
farms in the southern Piedmont of North Carolina. He found
that:

> In 1954, 41 percent of farmers in North Carolina were
> employed in off-farm work. Sixty-one percent of those
> so employed worked off the farm 100 or more days. In
> addition, 17 percent of the farmers reported that
> family members other than the farm operator worked off
> the farm. On 27 percent of the farms, income received
> from off-farm sources was greater than the value of
> farm products sold. An earlier study indicated that in
> 1949 approximately 46 percent of the net income re-
> ceived by North Carolina farm families was received by
> persons whose major occupation was in nonfarm employ-
> ment. (Sutherland, Bishop, and Hannuth, 1959: 3.)

His linear-programming examination of alternative combinations of resources concluded that if about $165,000 of in-
vestment capital was added, full-time farming became as
profitable as part-time or full-time nonfarming, but because
of the risks involved a combination of part-time farming and
a modest increase of investment seemed preferable. Similar
results came from Saunder's (1959) linear-programming analysis of part-time farming in Georgia. Given the limited
access of small southern farmers to investment capital,
part-time farming seems to be the most practical strategy.

A frequent objection is that much nonmetro industrialization is of little benefit because it mainly employs
women (e.g., in textile and apparel firms). It is true that
this can discriminate against men in areas where unemployed
men have no alternative occupations. But in the more usual
agricultural regions, the husband can continue farming. And
given the underemployment in farm families, jobs for wives
and daughters can raise farm-family income levels.

A second conclusion from impact studies is that the
number of jobs created for local people in a poverty area
depends, anmong other things, on the skill level demanded
by the factory. In this respect, the high-wage, high-skill
factory, so often regarded as the ideal project, is by no
means an unmixed blessing. Given the unskilled, poorly
educated labor supply in most depressed areas, the jobs in
a high-wage plant may go mainly to outsiders. An example of
this is the Kaiser Aluminum plant that located in rural
West Virginia in 1957, as described by Irwin Gray (1969).
He estimates that out of the four thousand jobs created by
the plant, only six hundred went to local people; the rest
were taken by more skilled outsiders.

The corollary of this is that the low-wage, labor-
intensive factory, often condemned for its low pay, has a

much higher local employment multiplier, because its labor demand fits the skill characteristics of the local labor supply. Analytically, the problem involves a double labor market: one skilled, the other unskilled. The labor demand from the Kaiser plant was pertinent to the skilled market, but the local labor supply pertained to the unskilled. Unless the skill levels of local people are improved, as recommended by Eichner and attempted by South Carolina and several other states, the barriers between these two markets will significantly reduce the impact high-wage factories can have on conditions of employment.

A third conclusion is that, for the above and other reasons, the size of the income and employment multipliers varies considerably. Factors such as the size of an area and the amount of excess capacity in the service sector as well as other facts will affect this. For example, Edgar Z. Palmer (1958) estimates multipliers for fourteen different communities. The one for the largest area (New York SMSA) was two and a half times that of the smallest (Auburn, Washington, population 6,500). Wadsworth and Conrad (1965) make the same point.[5]

Summers et al. (1976: 2-4) summarize the results of 186 studies described in their work: (1) In a clear majority of plant locations, the host community experiences population growth. (2) The initial source of population growth is likely to be increased in-migration coupled with unchanged or decreased out-migration. (3) The majority (two-thirds to three-fourths) of in-migrants move no farther than fifty miles. Those who move farther are probably managers and technical personnel. (4) Nonmetro workers often commute long distances for a period of time after employment, but in the long run they move closer to their place of work, or change jobs. (5) Employers prefer younger workers although in some instances, skill gained through experience may be competitive with youth. (6) There is considerable evidence that nonwhites are underrepresented in the work forces of nonmetro industrial plants. Where they are hired they are concentrated in unskilled and semiskilled jobs. This situation may indicate outright discriminatory hiring practices, or insufficient skill level among local nonwhites, or both. (7) There is virtually no evidence that industrial development increases the level of educational attainment in the host community. Where it does occur the evidence suggests it is due to changes in the age structure, younger adults generally having completed more years of schooling. (8) New jobs often do not go to the local unemployed,

underemployed, minorities, and marginally employable
persons likely to be near or below the poverty level. (9)
High-skill, high-wage industries, which are most likely
to increase the aggregate income and raise the percentage
of families above the poverty level, are least likely to
hire the local disadvantaged. The apparent gains in aggregate income and unemployment rate often hide the failure to
aid the local disadvantaged. (10) Low-skill, low-wage industries, are most likely to employ the disadvantaged. (11)
Worker dissatisfactions with wage work in industry are
offset by higher standards of living, job security, shorter
hours, easier work, and greater chances of advancement.
(12) Anticipated benefits to the local community generally
exceed perceived benefits after development. Even so, the
percentage of local citizens perceiving benefits outweighs
those expressing negative opinions. (13) Having experienced
industrial development, a majority of the local citizens
want more. (14) Many local residents express positive feelings about one or another aspect of industrial invasion;
for example, population growth, in-migrants, economic diversification, improved local shopping, and opportunity
for off-farm work. Although there are contrary feelings
expressed, the scale weighs more heavily in favor of
optimism and satisfaction.

Whereas impact studies reveal increases in local population, income, and employment, unfortunately the same cannot be said for the fiscal sector of the local community.
Communities often hope that a new plant will increase tax
revenues and allow tax rates to be lowered for their citizens. However, they tend to underestimate increased public
costs, such as sewer hookups, tax exemptions, school expansions, and the like. The main finding of fiscal impact studies is that the fiscal situation is worsened about as often
as it is helped by new factories. As Summers et al. (1976:
4) put it in their summary of the impact literature: "Increase in the fiscal resource base of the local community
often is outweighed by the increased costs of providing services to the new industry and the community. Net fiscal
gains to the local government do occur. This usually is when
no local subsidy was offered the industry, or the plant work
force is hired locally, or large proportions of the plant
work force live outside the community and commute to work."

As an example of fiscal impact, Shaffer and Tweeten
(1974) studied the annual impact of twelve firms that
recently located in six Oklahoma cities. Brinkman (1973a)
studied the cumulative impact (over ten years) of eight

firms locating in the small town of Parsons, Kansas between 1960 and 1970. Both studies found sizeable gains to local citizens from increased income and business sales. But they also found a ten-year loss of $330,000 each to the government and schools in Kansas, and a mixture of small gains and losses in Oklahoma. Given the uncertain fiscal impact, and the unimportance of tax and other purely financial inducements, it seems dubious whether local communities should offer tax exemptions and similar financial incentives.

Almost all impact studies have focused on fiscal effects or on employment and income results for the local population in general. Only a very few investigate the effect on local poor people.

One of the earliest of these studies was performed by what was formerly the Economic Research Service (USDA 1972). Four nonmetro growth areas were chosen: northeast Arizona (Apache and Navajo counties), Mississippi Appalachia (Alcorn and Tippah counties), northwest Arkansas Ozarks (Benton and Washington counties), and southeast Arkansas Delta (Cross, Lee, and St. Francis counties). The method used was the factory questionnaire, distributed during the winter of 1970-71 to 25 percent of the employees of factories that had either been established since 1964 or significantly expanded since 1965. However, because only twenty-seven of the fifty-six plants agreed to cooperate, and because various problems often made the sampling fraction less than 25 percent, the resulting samples were not strictly representative. Further, only the direct impact was measured (i.e., that of jobs provided in the new or expanded factory). The number and impact of jobs indirectly created (through input-output linkages) or induced (through the effects of increased incomes on employment in retail trade, etc.) were not measured. However, despite the limitations, the results are valuable.

First, as seen in Table 5.7, of the total sample, 26.8 percent of the plant workers previously were poor. However, the range was very great: from 49 percent in Arizona and 47 percent in the Arkansas Delta to 19 percent in Mississippi Appalachia and the Arkansas Ozarks. Beside the problem of sample representativeness, the range seemed to be due to the difference in underemployment and previous manufacturing development in these areas. The last two areas, having fewer underemployed persons and prior manufacturing growth, had a work force that was less poor.

The second finding refers to the direct impact of the jobs on the poor employees. Of the 266 previously poor

workers, 57 percent were raised out of poverty by 1970.
Here again the differences were great, ranging from 36
percent for Arizona to 57 percent for the Arkansas Delta
and 68 and 69 percent for the Ozarks and Appalachian areas
respectively. Higher wages and greater employment for other
family members appear to be the causal factors for the
latter two areas. In both Arizona and the Arkansas Delta, a
second earner was apparently necessary to keep the family
out of poverty.

Third, it is important to know whether the jobs are
going to women only, or to men as well. Again there were
great differences, with women holding 76 percent of the
jobs in Arizona, 47 percent in the Ozarks, 36 percent in
Appalachia, and 23 percent in the Delta.

Finally, because the local poor are often bypassed for
jobs, due to competition from more qualified in-migrants,
it is interesting to ask what proportion of the jobs were
filled by those who moved, not necessarily for the first
time, into the study areas between 1 June 1965 and 31
December 1970. An attempt was made to define the study
areas in terms of job-commuting radius. Thus the extent
ranged from three counties for the Delta to nine for the
Appalachian area. With these criteria, the percentage of
workers who were in-migrants ranged from 10 percent in the
Delta to 36 percent in the Ozarks, whereas Appalachia and
Arizona had 18 percent and 29 percent respectively. Although
several previous studies had found that a majority of jobs
went to nonresidents, in this study more than two-thirds of
the jobs were held by local people.

A more recent study (Deaton and Landes 1978) of 714
workers (a 20 percent sample) in thirty-five new factories
in rural Tennessee found that between the year before the
factory located and 1977 (the time of the survey), the
percentage of factory workers in poverty dropped from 13 to
3 percent. The main factor in a family's escaping from or
slipping into poverty proved to be the gain or loss of an
additional working member. The percentage of sample families
with both spouses working increased from 40 to 53 percent.
West (1978) examined the impact on poverty of manufacturing,
mining, and recreation growth in nine Ozark counties, from
1960 to 1970; but, because of a different definition of
poverty reduction, his results are not comparable.

Neither study (the Economic Research Service or Deaton
and Landes) extends its examination beyond the impact of
the direct hiring of the poor. Jobs gained by the poor
indirectly (i.e., by gaining employment left vacant by

Table 5.7. Impact of Job Development on Poverty Status,
Four Study Areas, 1965-1970

Poverty Status	Arizona		Mississippi Appalachia	
	Number of Jobs[a]	Determined Jobs[bc]	Number of Jobs[a]	Determined Jobs[bc]
		%		%
Total number of jobs	1,207	---	2,600	---
Number of determined jobs[bc]	373	100.0	2,368	100.0
Total previously poor	183	49.1	441	18.6
Residents previously poor	121	32.4	401	16.9
Total escaping poverty	93	24.9	315	13.3
Residents escaping poverty	58	15.5	281	11.8
Total slipping into poverty	8	2.2	69	2.9
Residents slipping into poverty	5	1.4	56	2.3

Source: USDA, Economic Research Service, Table 3, p. 7, 1972.

[a]Represents total jobs enumerated for which a poverty
status was associated.

[b]Jobs enumerated for which a poverty status in both time
periods was determined.

[c]Usage of these percentages assumes that sampled responses
were typical of unsampled employees and sampled refusals by plant.
Percentages are based on unrounded data.

Region					
Northwest Arkansas Ozark		Arkansas Delta		Four Study Areas Combined	
Number of Jobs[a]	Determined Jobs[bc]	Number of Jobs[a]	Determined Jobs[bc]	Number of Jobs[a]	Determined Jobs[bc]
	%		%		%
1,980	---	879	---	6,729	---
1,572	100.0	809	100.0	5,122	100.0
310	19.8	389	48.1	1,323	25.8
228	14.5	370	45.8	1,120	21.9
219	13.9	230	27.2	847	16.5
142	9.1	201	24.8	682	13.3
73	4.6	9	1.1	159	3.1
44	2.8	9	1.1	114	2.2

those taking jobs in the new factory) are not examined by
either study.

The picture that emerges is one where only a minority of
jobs in a new factory go to poor workers from poor families.
However, the majority of the poor hired will escape poverty.
Because most jobs are low-wage, the main mechanism seems to
be through multiple-earners or multiple jobholding.

Also rather rare are impact studies on the distribution
of income. These, of course, measure changes in inequality,
rather than changes in poverty. Most of the results show
improvement for the lowest quartile with respect to average
income for the whole distribution. Shaffer and Tweeten's
study of four Oklahoma counties (1974) found that that the
lowest quartiles' mean income had increased from a range of
10 to 32 percent of the counties' average in 1960 to a range
of 28 to 50 percent by 1970. The second quartile also had
relative gains. Reinshmiedt (1976) discovered mixed results.
West (1978) found no improvement in his manufacturing results compared with his control group. So, although the
lowest groups had relative gains, we cannot say that the
whole distribution of income became more equal. Also interesting are Clemente and Summers's (1973) results that those
over 65 and in female-headed families were relatively worse
off after industrialization in the one county studied.

As with poverty impact, so with the effect on unemployment. Summers et al. (1976) show that only a minority of
the unemployed are hired by a new plant (see Table 5.8). It
is striking that when receipt of federal loans was tied to
hiring the unemployed (the Area Redevelopment Authority
study), the percentage became much higher. Of course,
indirect effects on employment are not measured.

Relatively little attention has been given to the impact
of industrialization on minorities. Till (1972) observed
that by mapping rates of manufacturing growth in the South
in the 1960s, the bulk of the gains had gone to the white,
hill-country areas--primarily in the border South and
southern Appalachian regions. Heavily black areas were
largely bypassed. Walker's (1977) study of 244 heavily
black counties in the Deep South revealed that blacks had
benefited far less than whites from 1960s nonfarm job
growth in those counties, although manufacturing's record
was better than that of most other nonfarm industries. Only
in manufacturing (21 to 26 percent), mining (7 to 10
percent), and public administration (8 to 12 percent) did
blacks increase their share of total jobs from 1960 to
1970. Minority areas that were bypassed by manufacturing

Table 5.8. Percentage of New Plant Workers Previously Unemployed

Study Area	Industry	Number	Jobs Filled by Previously Unemployed
			%
Linton, Ind.	Aluminum chairs	100	25.0
Wynne, Ark.	Apparel; copper tubing	1,900	11.2
Rochester, Minn.	Business machines	1,862	14.0
Ravenwood, W.Va.	Aluminum	894	11.0
Eastern Oklahoma community	12 plants (mixed)	554	7.7
Area Redevelopment Administration area survey	33 plants (mixed)	1,262	43.0
Mt. Airy, N.C.	Appliances	435	8.0
Jefferson, Iowa	Stamping; athletic equipment	369	3.0
Orange City, Iowa	10 plants (mixed)	364	19.0
Creston, Iowa	Appliances; chemicals; oil filters	424	1.0
Grinnell, Iowa	Farm machinery; stadium bleachers; plastics	200	7.0
Decorah, Iowa	Screws	212	8.0
Star City, Ark.	Apparel (shifts)	336	9.5

Source: Summers et al., Table 5.1, p. 49.

development in the 1950s and 1960s remain a major national
policy problem for the future.

NONECONOMIC IMPACTS

Most studies on industrial development have stressed the
economic impacts. They have been conducted by economists,
with a sprinkling of geographers and planners. However, a
small body of literature exists on the social impacts,
primarily done by rural sociologists. A considerable percentage of this has been carried out by Gene Summers and
associates at the Center for Applied Sociology at the University of Wisconsin at Madison. The literature is too
extensive to be summarized here, but is usefully covered by
Summers et al. (1976: 106-25). Briefly, this survey examines
social participation and attitudes and opinions before and
after industrial development. On social participation (i.e.,
extent and characteristics of membership in formal and informal organizations), there is little change. Leadership
studies found leadership still concentrated, but with influence increasingly exercised by business groups and less
by large farmers. Regarding opinions and attitudes, industrial development was perceived as beneficial to the community by the majority of respondents, whether or not they
were factory employees. This is an inadequate picture of
the richness of research results, but space is lacking for
a more comprehensive treatment.

CONCLUSION

Many of the controversies in the late 1960s about industrial development had been settled by the late 1970s.
Earlier it was claimed that nonmetro areas were inferior
locations for factories, and policies to attract them were
useless. Empirical work has since proven that currently
nonmetro areas are generally more favorable than the larger
cities for manufacturing locations, as shown by the industry shift toward nonmetro areas.

In the 1960s it was claimed that rural poverty would
be little eased by industrialization, because the jobs
often would pay wages below the poverty line and most
would go to better-off in-migrants. We know now that the
main method by which nonmetro poor families in the labor

force have climbed out of poverty has been through the multiple-earner and multiple-job process, even if each job by itself pays low wages. We also know that the majority of employment goes to local workers, not in-migrants, and that as many as one-half of the in-migrants are returnees to the area often bringing back the important human capital skills of education and job-training that were lost by their migration. We also know that not all the jobs coming to rural areas are low-wage, and that the proportion of higher-paying firms is increasing. We also know that most local people consider the "industrial invasion" as beneficial, even though the very wealthy are often opposed (Hough and Clark 1969).

This gain in knowledge is important, but there are other things we know too little about. What is--and will be--the effect of the energy crisis on nonmetro manufacturing employment? What has been--and will be--the effect of international trade? The standardized labor-intensive products of nonmetro America, for example, are generally similar to those produced in less developed nations.

Just as importantly, what strategy can effectively address those areas bypassed by manufacturing growth? Will low-wage industries spin off in the 1980s from currently industrialized nonmetro areas and locate in those neglected areas in search of a surplus of cheap labor? Or will they locate abroad? What has been the record of CDCs and co-ops in developing jobs for those areas? Which have been successful? For what reasons? How can they be replicated?

Also, for all areas, should aid to the expansion of business and to new ventures be increased? What is the past record of these activities? If the 1980s can provide answers to those questions, it will have proved as productive as the 1970s.

NOTES

1. A recent bibliography (Smith 1978) contains 755 entries. Useful surveys of literature are Smith and Summers 1978; Tweeten and Brinkman 1976; and Summers 1976.

2. The following data analysis is based on Haren and Holling (1979) pp. 13-46.

3. An authoritative summary of methods of explaining locational decisions is provided by Walter Isard (1960).

4. Compare with discussion of off-farm employment in

Chapter 4.

5. Various estimates of the number of service jobs
created by 100 manufacturing jobs have been made by Tiebout
(1956), Hildebrand and Mace (1950), and Stevens and Wallace
(1964).

BIBLIOGRAPHY

Allaman, Peter M., and Birch, David L. "Components of
    Employment Change for Metropolitan and Rural Areas in
    the United States by Industry Group, 1970-1972." Inter-
    Area Migration Project. Cambridge, Mass.: Joint Center
    for Urban Studies of MIT and Harvard, September 1975.
Beale, Calvin L. "Demographic and Social Considerations for
    U.S. Rural Economic Policy." American Journal of
    Agricultural Economics 51 (1969): 410-27.
Bergin, Thomas P., and Eagan, William F. "Economic Growth
    and Community Facilities." Municipal Finance 33 (1961):
    146-49.
Berry, Brian. "Spatial Organization and Levels of Welfare:
    Degree of Metropolitan Labor Market Participation as a
    Variable in Economic Development." Paper prepared for
    the Economic Development Administration Research
    Conference, Washington, D.C., February 1968.
Birch, David L. The Job Generation Process: Summary.
    Cambridge, Mass.: MIT Program on Neighborhood and
    Regional Change, 1979.
_____. "The Processes Causing Economic Change in
    Cities." Paper presented at a U.S. Department of
    Commerce Round Table on Business Retention and
    Expansion, 22 February 1978.
Brinkman, George L. "Effects of Industrializing Small
    Communities." Journal of the Community Development
    Society 4 (1973a): 69-80.
_____. "Industrializing Small Communities in Kansas."
    Cooperative Extension Service. Economics Research Re-
    port. Manhattan, Kans.: Kansas State University, 1973b.
Bryant, W. Keith. "Causes of Inter-County Variations in
    Farmers' Earnings." Journal of Farm Economics 48
    (1966): 557-77.
Center for Community Economic Development. A Review of the
    ABT Associates, Inc. Cambridge, Mass.: Center for
    Community Economic Development, 1977.
Chapman, James E., and Wells, William H. "Factors in Indus-

trial Location in Atlanta, 1946-1955." Atlanta Economic Review 9 (1959): 3-8.

Clemente, Frank, and Summers, Gene F. Large Industries in Small Towns: Who Benefits? Working Paper RID 73.9. Madison, Wis.: University of Wisconsin, Department of Rural Sociology, Center of Applied Sociology, 1973.

Coppedge, Robert O., and Davis, Carlton G. Rural Poverty and the Policy Crisis. Ames, Iowa: Iowa State University, 1977.

Deaton, Brady J. "CDCs: A Development Alternative for Rural America." Growth and Change 6 (1975): 31-37.

_____, and Landes, Maurice R. "Rural Industrialization and the Changing Distribution of Family Incomes." American Journal of Agricultural Economics 60 (1978): 950-54.

Eichner, Alfred. State Development Agencies and Employment Expansion. Policy Paper in Human Resources and Industrial Relations 18, Institute of Labor and Industrial Relations. Ann Arbor, Mich.: University of Michigan, 1970.

Erickson, Rodney A. "Nonmetropolitan Industrial Expansion: Emerging Implications for Regional Development." Review of Regional Studies 6 (1977): 35-48.

_____, and Leinbach, Thomas R. "Characteristics of Branch Plants Attracted to Nonmetropolitan Areas." In Nonmetropolitan Industrialization, edited by Richard E. Lonsdale and H. L. Seyler, pp. 57-58. New York: John Wiley, 1979.

Experience, Inc. Experiences, Opinions, and Attitudes of Company Officials and Nonmetropolitan Branch Plants. Minneapolis, Minn.: Experience, Inc., undated.

Ford, Thomas R., ed. Rural U.S.A.: Persistence and Change. Ames, Iowa: Iowa State University Press, 1978.

Gray, Irwin. "New Industry in a Rural Area." Monthly Labor Review 92 (1969): 26-30.

Hamilton, William L. A Study of Rural Cooperatives, Final Report: Summary. Cambridge, Mass.: ABT Publishers, 1973.

Hansen, Niles M. Rural Poverty and the Urban Crisis. Bloomington, Ind.: Indiana University Press, 1970.

Haren, Claude C. "The Decentralization of U.S. Employment, 1969-1976." Paper presented at the Southern Regional Science Association, Nashville, Tenn., April 1979.

_____. "Rural Industrial Growth in the 1960's." American Journal of Agricultural Economics 52 (1970): 431-37.

_____, and Holling, Ronald W. "Industrial Development

in Nonmetropolitan America: A Locational Perspective."
In Nonmetropolitan Industrialization, edited by Richard
E. Lonsdale and H. L. Seyler. New York: John Wiley,
1979.

Hathaway, Dale E. Government and Agriculture. New York:
Macmillan, 1963.

_____; Beegle, J. Allan; and Bryant, W. Keith.
People of Rural America. Census Monograph Series.
Washington, D.C.: U.S. Government Printing Office,
1968.

Hildebrand, George H., and Mace, Arthur, "The Employment
Multiplier in an Expanding Industrial Market: Los
Angeles County 1940-1947." Review of Economics and
Statistics 32 (1950): 241-49.

Holman, M. Carl. "The National Public Works and Economic
Development Act of 1979: Testimony Before the Subcommittee on Regional and Community Development, Committee
on Environment and Public Works, U.S. Senate." Washington D.C.: National Urban Coalition, 24 April 1979.

Holt, James S., and Fisher, Dennis. "Introduction to the
Seasonal Farm Labor Problem." Unpublished manuscript.
Washington, D.C.: U.S. Department of Labor, 1979.

Hough, Richard L., and Clark, John P. Some Determinants of
Attitudes Toward Industrialization in a Rural Community.
Working Paper 69.3. Madison, Wis.: University of
Wisconsin, Department of Rural Sociology, Center of
Applied Sociology, 1969.

Isard, Walter. Methods of Regional Analysis: An Introduction to Regional Science. Cambridge, Mass.: MIT, 1960.

Jusenius, Carol L., and Ledebur, Larry. The Migration of
Firms and Workers in Ohio, 1970-1975. Columbus, Ohio:
Academy for Contemporary Problems, 1977.

_____. "Where Have All the Firms Gone: An Analysis
of the New England Economy." Office of Economic Research, Economic Development Administration, U.S.
Department of Commerce. Washington, D.C., 1978.

Kale, Steven R., and Lonsdale, Richard E. "Factors Encourag-
ing and Discouraging Plant Location in Nonmetropolitan
Areas. In Nonmetropolitan Industrialization, edited by
Richard E. Lonsdale and H. L. Seyler, pp. 47-56. New
York: John Wiley, 1979.

Katona, George, and Morgan, James N. "The Quantitative Study
of Factors Determining Business Decisions." Quarterly
Journal of Economics 66 (1952): 67-90.

Lonsdale, Richard E., and Seyler, H. L., eds. Nonmetropolitan Industrialization. New York: John Wiley, 1979.

Lowry, Ira S. Portrait of a Region. Pittsburgh Regional
    Planning Association. Pittsburgh, Pa.: University of
    Pittsburgh, 1963.
McLaughlin, Glenn E., and Robock, Stefan. Why Industry
    Moves South. Washington, D.C.: National Planning
    Association, 1949.
McMillan, T. E., Jr. "Why Manufacturers Chose Plant Loca-
    tions vs. Determinants of Plant Location." Journal of
    Land Economics 41 (1965): 239-46.
Marshall, F. Ray. "Low-Income Cooperatives and Economic
    Development." Washington, D.C.: EDA/U.S. Department of
    Commerce, 1972.
Miernyk, William N. "Local Labor Market Effects of New
    Plant Locations." In Essays in Regional Economics,
    edited by John F. Klein and J. R. Meyer. Cambridge,
    Mass.: Harvard University, 1971.
Moeller, Warren E. "Industrial Location Decisions." Oklahoma
    Business Bulletin 26 (1959): 1-4.
Morgan, William E. Taxes and the Location of Industry.
    University of Colorado Studies, Series in Economics,
    no. 4. Boulder, Colo.: University of Colorado, 1967.
Mueller, Eva; Wilken, Arnold; and Wood, Margaret. Location
    Decisions and Industrial Mobility in Michigan. Institute
    for Social Research. Ann Arbor, Mich., 1950.
Nicholls, William H. "Industrialization, Factor Markets and
    Agricultural Development." Journal of Political Economy
    49 (1961): 319-40.
Palmer, Edgar Z. The Community Economic Base and Multiplier.
    Publication 199. Lincoln, Neb.: University of Nebraska,
    1958.
Price, Paul; Bertrand, Alvin; and Osborne, Harold. The
    Effects of Industrialization on Rural Louisiana: A
    Study of Plant Employees. Louisiana Agricultural
    Experiment Station. Baton Rouge, La.: Louisiana State
    University, 1958.
Reinschmiedt, Lynn. "An Evaluation of Economic Benefits and
    Costs of Industrialization in Rural Communities in
    Texas." Ph.D. dissertation, Texas A & M University,
    1976.
Ruttan, Vernon W. "The Impact of Urban-Industrial Develop-
    ment in the Tennessee Valley." Journal of Farm Economics
    37 (1955): 38-56.
Saunders, Fred B. Economics Analysis of Part-Time Farming in
    Georgia. Bulletin 65. Athens, Ga.: University of
    Georgia, 1959.
Schultz, Theodore W. Economic Organization of Agriculture.

New York: McGraw-Hill, 1953.

Shaffer, Ronald E., and Tweeten, Luther. Economic Changes from Industrial Development in Eastern Oklahoma. Oklahoma Experiment Station, Bulletin B-715. Stillwater, Okla.: Oklahoma State University, 1974.

Smith, Eldon D. Industrialization of Rural Areas: A Bibliography. Rural Development Bibliography Series 1. Mississippi State, Miss.: Mississippi State University, 1978.

_____, and Summers, Gene F. How New Manufacturing Industry Affects Rural Areas. Rural Development Series 1A. Mississippi State, Miss.: Mississippi State University, 1978.

Stein, Barry A. Size, Efficiency and Community Enterprise. Cambridge, Mass.: Center for Community Economic Development, 1974.

Sternlieb, George, and Hughes, James, eds. Post-Industrial America: Metropolitan Decline and Inter-Regional Job Shifts. New Brunswick, N.J.: Center for Urban Policy Research, 1975.

Stevens, Benjamin H. et al. Trends in Industrial Location and Their Impact on Regional Development: A Report on Research in Progress. Discussion paper 31. Philadelphia, Pa.: Regional Science Research Institute, 1969.

Stevens, B. H., and Wallace, L. T. "The Impact of Industrial Development on Howard County, Indiana, 1947-1960." Research Bulletin no. 764. Purdue University Agricultural Experiment Station, August 1964.

Summers, Gene, F. et al. Industrial Invasion of Nonmetropolitan America: A Quarter Century of Experience. New York: Praeger, 1976.

Sutherland, J. Gwyn; Bishop, C. E.; and Hannuth, B. A. An Economic Analysis of Farm and Nonfarm Uses of Resources on Small Farms in the Southern Piedmont, North Carolina. Technical Bulletin 138. North Carolina Experiment Station, 1959.

Tang, Anthony M. Economic Development in the Southern Piedmont, 1860-1950. Chapel Hill, N.C.: University of North Carolina, 1958.

Thompson, Wilbur R. "The Economic Base of Urban Problems." In Contemporary Economic Issues, edited by Neil W. Chamberlin. Homewood, Ill.: Irwin, 1969.

_____. A Preface to Urban Economics. Baltimore: Johns Hopkins Press, 1965.

Tiebout, Charles. "The Community Income Multipliers." A paper presented at the Joint Conference of the Econometric Society and the American Statistical Association, September 1956.

Till, Thomas E. "Changes in Industries Located in the Non-metropolitan South, 1959-1969." American Journal of Agricultural Economics 56 (1974): 306-9.

_____. "The Extent of Industrialization in Southern Nonmetro Labor Markets in the 1960's." Journal of Regional Science 13 (1973): 456.

_____. "Industrialization and Poverty in Southern Nonmetropolitan Labor Markets." Growth and Change 5 (1974): 18-24.

_____. "Rural Industrialization and Southern Rural Poverty: Patterns of Labor Demand in Southern Nonmetropolitan Labor Markets: Their Impact on the Poor, 1959-69." Ph.D. dissertation, University of Texas, 1972.

Tweeten, Luther, and Brinkman, George L. Micropolitan Development. Ames, Iowa: Iowa State University, 1976.

U.S. Bureau of the Census. Current Population Reports, series P-20, no. 336. Population Profile of the United States: 1978. Washington, D.C.: U.S. Government Printing Office, 1979.

U.S. Department of Agriculture. Migrant Response to Industrialization in Four Rural Areas, 1965-1970. By Duane A. Olsen and John A. Kuehn. Agricultural Economic Report 270. Washington D.C.: USDA, 1974.

U.S. Department of Agriculture, Economic Research Service. Impact of Job Development on Poverty in Four Development Areas, 1970. By John A. Kuehn; Lloyd D. Bender; Bernal L. Green; and Herbert Hoover. Agricultural Economic Report 225. Washington, D.C.: USDA, 1972.

_____. Rural Industrialization in the Ozarks: Case Study of a New Shirt Plant in Gassville, Arkansas. Agricultural Economic Report 123. Washington, D.C.: USDA, 1967.

U.S. Department of Agriculture, Economics, Statistics and Cooperatives Service. Growth Patterns in Nonmetro-Metro Manufacturing Employment. By M. F. Petrulis. Rural Development Research Report no. 7. Washington, D.C.: USDA, ESCS, 1979.

Wadsworth, H. A., and Conrad, J. M. "Leakages Reducing Employment and Income Multipliers in Labor-Surplus Rural Areas." Journal of Farm Economics 47 (1965): 1197-1202.

Walker, James L. Economic Development and Black Employment in the Nonmetropolitan South. Austin, Tex.: Bureau of

Business Research, University of Texas, 1977.

Wallace, L. T. Factors Affecting Industrial Location in Southern Indiana, 1955-1958. Research Bulletin no. 724. Lafayette, Ind.: Purdue University Agricultural Experiment Station, 1961.

_____, and Ruttan, V. W. "The Role of the Community in Industrial Location." Regional Science Association Papers 7 (1961): 133-42.

West, Jerry G. "Consequences of Rural Industrialization in Terms of Income Distribution." Growth and Change 9 (1978): 15-21.

Wolman, Harold. Components of Employment Change in Local Economics: A Literature Review. Working Paper 1264-02. Washington, D.C.: Urban Institute, 1979.

Zuiches, James J., and Brown, David L. "The Changing Character of the Nonmetropolitan Population, 1950-1978." In Rural U.S.A.: Persistence and Change, edited by Thomas R. Ford, pp. 55-72. Ames, Iowa: Iowa State University Press, 1978.

Mark David Menchik

6

The Service Sector

INTRODUCTION

Both nationally and in rural America, the service sector is the fastest growing sector in the economy. It is also the least understood, which is unfortunate because its role in creating jobs and enhancing the quality of life may make it a prime component of rural development policies.

Other chapters in this volume consider specific service industries (such as health and government); we therefore cast a broader net here, examining trends and background concepts that are common among service industries and that distinguish the service sector from the rest of the economy. Next we raise issues underlying the service sector's rural roles. If (as is likely) the service sector continues to grow, how may rural economies and the other aspects of rural life be affected? What problems, opportunities, and choices does this pose for government decision makers? Finally, we explore how changing service technologies and transport cost may influence rural access to services.

I am indebted to members of the Future of Rural America Advisory Group, and also to my Rand colleagues Brent Bradley, Will Harriss, and Barbara Quint for their helpful comments. Preparation of this paper was supported by the Farmers Home Administration, the Rand Corporation, and grant number P-50-HD12639 awarded by the National Institute of Child Health and Human Development, U.S. Public Health Service.

TRENDS AND BACKGROUND

DEFINITION

The definition of the service sector is a matter of dispute, for it is usually a residual category. Some observers define services broadly to include all but the goods-producing industries; that is, they exclude agriculture, mining, construction, and manufacturing. Others narrow this definition, variously excluding transportation, communications, utilities, trade, government, and nonprofit activities. (Stigler, 1956: 47 and Fuchs, 1969: 14-17 discuss alternative definitions.) We use the broad definition here but disaggregate figures by specific service industries (see Table 6.1).

TRENDS

Using a broad definition of the service sector, Table 6.1 shows that national employment in the sector increased by 24 percent from 1970 to 1977. This is more than four times the growth in the goods sector. Each industry within the service sector grew faster than the average for all industries, except for the transport, communications and utilities industry, which is unusually capital intensive for the service sector. As mentioned, many analysts exclude this industry from the service sector.

In this period the nonmetro service sector grew far faster than the metro one: 32 versus 21 percent. In nonmetro America, each service industry grew at least 65 percent faster than the goods sector. The two service industries that grew the fastest were "finance, insurance, and real estate" and "other services." We will shortly see that these service industries are the most underrepresented in nonmetro areas, compared to the metro pattern. In nonmetro areas, service industries grew even faster than the population (see Table 6.2). Perhaps the best indicator of the service sector's importance to the nonmetro economy is the fact that service growth accounted for 74 percent of the period's net gain in nonmetro employment.

Service activity has traditionally been concentrated into densely settled areas. Table 6.2 shows this, using service employment relative to population as a simple yardstick. The most populous areas (metro areas of a million or more) had 304 service employees per 1,000 residents in 1977 whereas the smallest areas (nonmetro counties with no place of 2,500 or more persons) had 221. Smaller metro areas and nonmetro counties with larger places had a service sector of intermediate size. In fact, moving from left to right in Table 6.2 shows the service sector systematically shrinking with smaller places.[1] Theories of geography and regional economics (especially central place theory) help explain this, and show the geographic and economic advantages responsible for service location in populous places.[2]

CENTRAL PLACE THEORY

Developed by Walter Christaller (a geographer) and August Loesch (an economist), central place theory explains the patterns of the space economy, that is, what causes economic activity to locate in one type of place or another (for a summary see Berry 1967). It particularly shows variations in economic activity with size of place, such as the hierarchy of market towns serving an agricultural hinterland, but can also show manufacturing-based hierarchies. Central place theory best predicts the space-economy when there is regionally uniform access to transport and to raw materials as in the Great Plains, for example. Grossly oversimplifying central place theory, there are four determinants of spatial patterns. First, the higher the population density (actually, the demand density), the greater the size and number of market towns and the closer together they are located. Second, significant economies of scale cause larger establishments to be widely spaced, so that their service areas are large enough to support them. Third, low transport costs also cause the wide spacing of service establishments. The fourth locational determinant--the most elusive--is "agglomeration economies," which encourage establishments in the same or different industries to cluster in one town. Agglomeration economies include the efficiency of shopping for different goods and services at one place, and productive efficiencies.

The patterns of Table 6.2 are summarized in the indexes that appear in Table 6.3, which show the degree to which service industries are concentrated into the most populous areas. Some of the most concentrated of the service industries (e.g., wholesale trade; finance, insurance, and real estate; and business and repair services) are so specialized as to require a location in a populous area and are heavily

Table 6.1. Employment by Sector for Metropolitan and Nonmetropolitan Areas, 1970 and 1977

| Industrial Sector | Thousands of Employed Persons 16 and Older | | | | | |
| | Metro | | Nonmetro | | Total | |
	1970	1977	1970	1977	1970	1977
Goods						
Agriculture, forestries, and fisheries	805	844	2,012	2,180	2,818	3,025
Mining	246	305	367	421	613	726
Construction	2,960	3,101	1,527	1,841	4,487	4,943
Manufacturing	13,793	13,576	5,857	6,737	19,650	20,313
Total goods	17,804	17,826	9,763	11,179	27,568	29,007
Services						
Transport, communications, and utilities	3,818	4,088	1,273	1,583	5,091	5,671
Wholesale and retail trade	10,969	13,035	4,127	5,259	15,096	18,294
Finance, insurance, and real estate	3,143	3,967	672	963	3,815	4,930
Other services[a]	14,251	18,199	5,317	7,309	19,568	25,508
Public administration	3,135	3,565	989	1,246	4,124	4,811
Total services	35,316	42,854	12,378	16,360	47,694	59,214
Total goods and services	53,119	60,681	22,140	27,539	75,260	88,221

Industrial Sector	Percentage Change 1970 to 1977		
	Metro	Nonmetro	All
Goods			
Agriculture, forestries, and fisheries	4.8	8.3	7.3
Mining	24.4	14.7	18.4
Construction	4.8	20.6	10.2
Manufacturing	-1.6	15.0	3.4
All goods	0.1	14.5	5.2
Services			
Transport, communications, and utilities	7.1	24.4	11.4
Wholesale and retail trade	18.8	27.4	21.2
Finance, insurance, and real estate	26.2	43.3	29.2
Other services[a]	27.7	37.5	30.4
Public administration	13.7	26.0	16.7
All services	21.3	32.2	24.2
All goods and services	14.2	24.4	17.2

Source: U.S. Bureau of the Census, Current Population Reports, pp. 88–89.

Note: Employees classified by place of residence. Metro areas as of 1970. Details may not add to totals becaues of rounding.

[a]Major categories are business and repair services, personal services, entertainment and recreation services, and professional and related services.

Table 6.2. Service Employment per Thousand Residents Relative to Population, By Size of Place, 1970 and 1977

Service Industry	Population of Metro Area				Population of Largest Place in Nonmetro County					
	1,000,000 or More		Less Than 1,000,000		25,000 or More		2,500 to 24,999		Less than 2,500	
	1970	1977	1970	1977	1970	1977	1970	1977	1970	1977
Transport, communications, and utilities	39	29	25	28	22	24	20	22	17	22
Wholesale trade	19	20	16	18	12	14	9	11	8	9
Retail trade	62	71	62	74	60	67	56	64	48	60
Finance, insurance, and real estate	26	30	19	24	14	17	10	13	7	13
Business and repair services	16	20	11	14	9	11	7	9	5	8
Personal services	16	16	18	18	17	21	18	18	16	15
Entertainment and recreational services	4	5	3	4	3	3	2	2	1	4
Professional and related services	70	88	69	88	67	86	57	72	46	71
Public administration	23	25	22	24	17	18	15	18	16	19
Total	267	304	245	293	223	260	193	229	164	221

Source: U.S. Bureau of the Census, Current Population Reports, pp. 20–21, 88–89.

Note: Population and metropolitan status are as of 1970. Details may not add to totals because of rounding.

dependent on access to information. The least concentrated
service industries (retail trade and personal services) are
less esoteric and, generally speaking, have fewer economies
of scale. This allows relatively small establishments to be
located in a variety of areas.

When the four locational determinants change, so does
the geography of the service sector. For example, the
virtual desertion of some small market towns in the Great
Plains in the last half-century may be explained thereby.
The surrounding agricultural population declined, while
cheap automobile transportation allowed consumers to shop
in larger towns that were farther away and thereby realize
the economies of scale (compared to "Ma and Pa" groceries)
newly offered by supermarkets. These events moved shopping
to higher levels in the central place hierarchy (i.e., to
larger towns with more varied functions). Mail-order shopping had the same effect, enabling isolated consumers to
trade at large, distant market centers.

Table 6.3 shows a very different trend--a recent movement of service activites down the central place hierarchy.
This is particularly true of some of the most specialized
and urbanized service industries, that is, wholesale trade;
finance, insurance, and real estate; and business and
repair services. This recent trend may reduce many urban
advantages in access to services and in the "urbanity" that
specialized services provide. This topic will be explored
further below.

UNDERSTANDING THE SERVICE SECTOR

The service sector is heterogeneous, comprising lawyers and
maids, musicians and bootblacks, groceries and universities,
restaurants and garages, hospitals and parking lots. This
diversity is but one reason that data and research are more
lacking in this sector than in the rest of the economy.
Other reasons are the multiplicity of small firms and
establishments;[3] the nonstandardization of products and
diversity of production processes (even within detailed
industries), which deprives the Standard Industrial Classification of its primary organizing principles;[4] and the
role of other than market forces. Nonprofit activities,
both public and private, account for about one-third of
service-sector employment (Fuchs, 1968: 10), whereas many
profit-making activities are heavily regulated. Governments
regulate finance, utility, transportation, and insurance

Table 6.3. Index of Central Place Tendency For
Different Service Industries, 1970 and 1977

Service Industry	1970	1977
Transport, communications, and utilities	1.77	1.29
Wholesale trade	2.59	2.32
Retail trade	1.31	1.17
Finance, insurance, and real estate	3.51	2.32
Business and repair services	2.92	2.56
Personal services	1.03	1.07
Entertainment and recreational services	2.99	1.15
Professional and related services	1.53	1.25
Public administration	1.45	1.35
All services	1.63	1.38

Source: Table 6.2. Indexes here were calculated from
more detailed figures than appear in Table 6.2.

Note: The index of central place tendency is the
number of employed persons per thousand residents
for the largest areas (metro areas of a million or
more) divided by that figure for the smallest areas
(nonmetro counties with no place of 2,500 or more
persons).

companies, to cite a few; both professional organizations
and government licensure regulate legal, medical, and educational activities. Perhaps most important is the belief
of Adam Smith and other early economists that only the
primary (agriculture and extraction) and secondary (manufacturing) industries are productive and the service sector
is therefore parasitic. We will return to this attitude.
    Interest in the service (or tertiary) sector began in
the 1930s and 1940s, when Colin Clark (1940) and Allan
Fisher (1935) viewed service as an important cause and
consequence of economic growth. Economic development, thus
viewed, is the shift from an agrarian to an industrial to

(in recent language) a postindustrial or service economy,
less focused on material production or consumption than on
intellectual and leisure activities (Bell 1973).[5] It has
been long believed that, as capital formation and technological innovation increase incomes, consumer demand will
rise more for services than for food and manufactured goods.
Empirical research has questioned this assumption. The
sketchy data assembled by Gallman and Weiss (1969) suggest
that nineteenth-century American industrialization and
rising real incomes did not increase the role of the service sector. This is confirmed by Fuchs (1968: 39-40), who
finds that service sector output did not increase its share
of GNP in the first half of this century. Because the income
elasticity of demand for services (the percentage increase
in service demand caused by a 1 percent increase in income)
is greater than unity, income growth in fact induces proportionately larger expenditures on services. However, some
studies have found it not much larger than unity (see, e.g.,
Fuchs, 1968: 41-46, and Houthakker and Taylor, 1970: 145-
59.) If these findings are correct (and there is reason
to believe that they underestimate income elasticities),
then only a fraction of the growth in service employment
can be explained by demand growth in a mature, high-income
economy.[6]

   If service sector output has roughly kept pace with
GNP, then its disproportionate increase in employment can
be caused only by this sector's failing to match the productivity gains in the rest of the economy. Fuchs (1968:
3-4, 41-46) finds that in both 1929 and 1965 the service
sector's output was 48 percent of the GNP, by one measure.
(Other measures of output yield similar results.) In this
period, however, service sector employment increased from
40 to 55 percent of all employment, by Fuchs's definition.
He argues that increased consumer and business demand for
services accounts for only a small fraction of employment
growth. Instead, productivity (measured as output per worker) grew more slowly in services than elsewhere in the
economy: 1.1 percent annually, compared with 2.2 percent in
manufacturing and 3.4 percent in agriculture. Fuchs cites
four explanations for the slower productivity increase in
services compared with manufacturing. First, workers'
skills improved faster in manufacturing than in services.
Second, physical capital probably grew faster in manufacturing. Third, hours per worker decreased more in services
than in manufacturing, so that relatively more service workers were needed and the differential productivity per hour

was not as great as the differential productivity per worker. Fourth, the residual suggests that "pure" technological
improvement was slower in services than in manufacturing.

It is no surprise that the service sector has not matched productivity improvements in manufacturing or agriculture, but it may come as a surprise that productivity has
increased at all. Both these facts are important. Some of
the increases in service sector productivity stem from the
same causes as those in manufacturing and agriculture: mechanization, such as computerized bank transactions (Gorman
1969), and economies of scale gained through specialization,
increased volume of business, and increased size of individual transactions--the supermarket replacing the grocery,
for example (Schwartzman 1969). This is not true of all
service industries, however. Although electric clippers
somewhat improved the efficiency of barbershops, the trend
away from barbershop shaves reduced transaction size to
haircuts alone.

Other sources of productivity increase are specific to
the service sector and show the confusion caused by analyzing food sold at retail, bank withdrawals, and restaurant
meals as one would analyze the production of ball bearings.
The nature of many services has changed (particularly
because of segmentation and specialization), often resulting
in reductions of quality that are hard to quantify. Pharma-
cists and medical specialists (and their nurses) now answer
questions formerly posed to the family doctor. Whatever its
other consequences, segmenting medical care loses the
family doctor's overview of tangible and intangible aspects
of health. The "Ma and Pa" grocery was a source of credit
and news, and the butcher gave advice on cooking, but the
supermarket checkout clerk provides none of these services.
The comparison of checkout clerk with butcher also shows
the substitution of lower- for higher-skilled labor, another
way to increase apparent productivity. (The downgrading of
skills in the service sector, by the way, is in sharp contrast with agriculture and manufacturing, where mechanization, automation, and the elimination of many routine tasks
have raised skill requirements.) Another source of productivity increase is having the customer perform certain
tasks for himself--filling out his own deposit slip at the
bank and selecting his own foods at the supermarket.
Finally, certain tasks have been pushed backward in the
production process when scale economies allow efficiencies.
Food is packaged in the factory, not at the store, restaurants buy portion-controlled food, and the factory, not the

druggist, compounds drugs. Whereas the seller previously
guaranteed the product, the manufacturer often does now.

Consider the implications of slower productivity increase in the service than in the goods sector. Following
the arguments of Baumol and Bowen (1966), imagine a two-
sector economy in which farmers produce bread and poets
produce poems. Technological improvement helps the farmer
make more bread, raising his income. But the poet cannot
automate to increase his output; his income falls relative
to the farmer's and the price of poems rises relative to
bread, decreasing the demand for poems and poets. The
poetry industry is therefore in sorry straits, unless the
income elasticity of demand for poetry (and the increase in
farmers' incomes) exceeds the price effect, that is, the
reduction in demand caused by poems' high relative price.
Relatively slow productivity increases, all else being
equal, can therefore price a service activity out of the
market, as happened with mechanisms that are cheaper to
replace than repair, eliminating repair services.

CHARACTERIZING SERVICE ACTIVITIES

Production Processes

To understand the service sector's linkages with business and households, one must recognize that specific
economic activities associated with the service sector may
or may not be performed within that sector (Lengellé 1966;
Treadway 1969; also see note 4). A farm or factory may repair its machinery itself, or it may contract with a repair
firm. A household may cook at home, or it may dine out. At
any time, the technology and scale of production and consumption, a firm's "maturity," and accessibility to service
establishments (the last especially important in urban-rural
comparisons) can influence whether a service activity is
performed "in house" or not (Hoover and Vernon 1959; Jacobs
1969). A large, "mature" farm or factory will probably have
its own full-time accountant, but a small or growing one
cannot afford to. Instead, it will hire a piece of an
accountant's services, or perhaps even do its own nonpro-
fessional accounting. Standardization and segmentation of
production processes allow a service establishment to have
an adequately large market (Glisson 1978). To continue the
example, accountants apply "generally accepted" auditing
principles. The number and type of service establishments,
and therefore accessibility to them, is a function of the

spatial demand for service activities, that is, the number
of demanders and the distance they (or the service they
seek) will travel.

The foregoing, although apparent on reflection, is
important in understanding that trends in service demands
can change with production and consumption processes, their
scale, the location of service demanders, and transport
costs for services. The recent increase in service use by
households (Linden 1978)--in particular restaurant meals
and daycare centers--reflects a growing number of working
wives, the increased value of their time, and related
changes in what has been called the household production
function. Thus, restaurant meals are now a more widely
considered substitute for home cooking, as daycare is for
supervision by the mother or relatives.[7]

That service activities are a part of production and
consumption processes helps refute the lingering notion
that services are somehow parasitic. Service enterprises
can be efficient economic actors. Nonetheless, transferring
the performance of an activity from its parent business or
household to a free-standing service establishment does
raise the concern of self-reliance, which we will discuss.

Household Versus Business Clients

A service enterprise (e.g., restaurant, plumber) may
sell to households; or business bankers or freight forward-
ers may sell to businesses. At first glance, one might
assume that many providers of household services are taking
on tasks the household might do for itself, unlike business
services, which attract firms that need them. This is not
so--the situations are parallel. A household may need a
mortgage loan just as a factory may need to borrow for
plant expansion. Both households and factories may seek
specialists for repairs. And just as the local provision of
specific business services may attract, retain, and encourage the expansion of those businesses benefiting from them,
locally provided household services may also support and
sustain households.

Exported Versus Nonexported Services

In a given locality, a service may be "exported" to
outside businesses or households (e.g., nonlocal real
estate or financial services) or may not be, as lawyers or
supermarkets, for example, serve local clients. Tourism is
an export service, for its clients live away from the site
of service provision--an example showing that we must

consider clients who travel to service providers, as well as services shipped to clients. Some nonexported services act as import substitutes, for otherwise they would be sought outside the locality; alternatively, nonexported services may substitute for those that the client firms or households would otherwise provide for themselves, or do without.

Import substitution of services makes an area more self-reliant, because it is less dependent on outside service providers. Import substitution can also tailor services to local conditions, needs, and goals. Financial and medical services are obvious examples, for any locality may be reluctant to place such vital needs in the hands of outsiders.

The export of services brings new money into the locality. The fact that so many services are not exported, however, causes a concern that the service sector may merely shift money within the local economy, unlike most agriculture or manufacturing. This fear is a modern form of mercantilism, the mistaken notion that an area's economic health comes only from export and not from internal exchange. After all, the global economy does not export. It functions like the mythical Irish village where everyone lived by taking in everyone else's washing.

Other Locational Characteristics

The exact locations of service providers affect the length and frequency of trips for service consumption and, more generally, access to services. Consider the convenience afforded by easy access to services. For example, a shopping trip yields more than purchases: It provides the stimulation of new products and faces and the sight of old faces. These are some of the features of urbanity, but people do not have to live in town to enjoy them; they can be enjoyed on visits to town. Those who do live in town benefit from assured access to its services even when winter makes travel difficult, and a "reverse commuter" can enjoy town life while commuting to an outlying workplace.

THE SERVICE SECTOR'S ROLES IN THE RURAL ECONOMY AND QUALITY OF LIFE

The following paragraphs identify topics bearing on the service sector's roles in rural areas.

Because the service sector is growing nationally, attracting service activity to one area does not inevitably take the activity away from another area. In other words, a locality that seeks service activity is not pursuing the same "beggar thy neighbor" strategy as chasing after the smokestacks of another locality's factories.

Service-sector activities have many desirable features from the standpoint of public goals for rural areas. They are labor-intensive and generally nonpolluting, and they make few demands on local public utilities, unlike factories, which may require soft water or sewage treatment (Shapiro et al. 1977). They are also energy efficient, except for the transportation industry--only marginally a member of the service sector--and also except for the transportation of customers.

Some evidence (summarized by Fuchs 1968) suggests that the service sector is countercyclical, does not lay off workers during recessions, and can therefore help smooth fluctuations in employment when an area is dependent on cyclically sensitive manufacturing. More generally, an expanded service sector can reduce a rural area's economic dependence on a single crop or other specialized pursuit.

Growth in the local service sector can absorb unemployed local workers leaving agriculture or manufacturing (Pursell 1975). Although this is an oft-stated goal, there is little research on whether expansion of the local service sector in fact achieves it. There is little data on whether new jobs go to unemployed residents, already-employed residents, in-migrant workers, or to local residents newly entering the local labor force--housewives, for example. One study, however, found that new factories in small cities and rural areas draw only a minority of their workers from the local unemployed (Wright 1968; see also Edgren 1978; Judy and Jack 1974; King 1978; and Scott and Wahi 1974). The same may prove to be true for the service sector.

The service sector provides many opportunities for small entrepreneurs and family enterprises, which are rare in manufacturing and comparable only to the family farm of the past. Some research (Allaman and Birch 1975) suggests that far more jobs are created by new firms than by the expansion of existing ones. Employment in new firms, however, is less secure than it is in more mature ones. This is particularly true of new small proprietorships, frequently undercapitalized and with little hard knowledge of their market. Moreover, like family farms, family enterprises in the service sector may disguise underemployment by using workers inefficiently (Judy and Jack 1974).

Although the service sector includes doctors and lawyers, it has more busboys and checkout clerks--jobs generally regarded as dead-end. Dead-end jobs may still retain
residents and be useful to the economy, but they do not
advance disadvantaged groups. Moreover, many rural areas
are in a position to choose the economic activity they
want. Does it serve the locality's purposes? The theory of
the dual labor market (Gordon 1972) asserts that many
service-sector industries offer secondary labor market jobs
without the possibility of economic advancement, relegating
service-sector workers to permanently low incomes. However,
one empirical test, based on job histories in New York City
(Lowell 1978), found that jobs in the secondary labor
market did not impede economic advancement. Is this true of
rural economies as well?

The seasonality of many service activities (tourism
especially) is a disadvantage to those who want to work the
whole year, but an advantage to others, perhaps by allowing
them to combine service-sector employment with farming.
(This combination has scarcely been studied, but see Coughenour and Gabbard 1977.) Similarly, long hours and evening
and weekend work are disadvantageous for most people, but
the owner of a small enterprise can set his own schedule.

Service-sector activities that serve businesses can
help make them more efficient, attracting new firms and
inducing existing ones to stay. The resulting economic
opportunities help to retain existing residents and attract
recent out-migrants into returning. Multiplier analysis
quantifies linkages within the local economy. Recently,
multipliers have been estimated by Braschler and Kuehn
(1976), Conopask (1978), Elrod and Laferney (1970), Garrison
(1974), Jones (1978), Jones and Mustafa (1972), and Klindt
and Smith (1977). Those multipliers vary widely but generally increase with the local economy's size and diversity,
which tend to contain linkages.

Not only can broadened and varied economic opportunity
retain residents and attract return migrants, but also an
expanded service sector can enhance the quality of rural
life. Cities provide cultural activities and other forms of
entertainment, exciting and varied wares, restaurants, and
the like. Low spatial density of demand makes it difficult
for rural areas to do the same, but increasing transportation costs and new means of service provision may change
the current space-economy.

A FUTURE SCENARIO

Armed with central place theory and six reasonable assumptions (based on current trends), we will explore the implications for the future of the rural service sector. (1) Assume that the general deconcentration of population and manufacturing to smaller urban and open country areas, both adjacent and nonadjacent to big cities, continues to occur.[8] (2) Assume also a continued rise in real income, plus continued return migration of country folk back from cities and reverse migration of the city-born to the countryside. These two assumptions place people in rural areas who have been exposed to "citified" services (especially easy accessibility to them) and city incomes, for we additionally assume here a continued narrowing of the gap between urban and rural real incomes. (3) Moreover, assume that changes in the technology of production and consumption will continue to increase the demand for business and personal services (some quite sophisticated and esoteric) in rural as well as urban areas. In other words, services will continue to be segmented and standardized, and thus can be performed "out-of-house."

Having established conditions for the increased demand for services by rural firms and households, consider changes in the supply of services by rural providers. (4) Assume that energy costs sharply increase the relative price of transportation, particularly by automobile, which will remain the dominant rural mode for trips of any length, aside from goods shipments. All things being equal, the rise in transport costs can reduce the length of trips taken to purchase or consume services. Shorter trips would themselves be conducive to smaller, less specialized, more clustered services, which is the old Great Plains pattern, but this is not the only possible outcome. Alternatively, increased transport costs may reduce trip frequency or increase the number of multipurpose trips, possibilities worthy of consideration. (5) Assume that the cost of communication and information processing continues to drop sharply, resulting in a "wired society"--homes and businesses with computer terminals and cheap, long-distance communication channels. This is not farfetched. Satellites are now efficiently used for data transmission and telephone calls; light-beam communication and cheap memories are fast developing; and integrated circuitry has cut the cost of computation so much that a home-computer industry is emerging. Ten years ago, who would have predicted computerized toys?

The high and rising cost of transportation relative to communication will sharply divide services by the degree to which their costs (to service clients, as well as service providers) are dependent on transportation or on communications. Services that are totally communications dependent (routine bank transactions, for example) can be supplied and consumed essentially without regard to location. With electronic transfer of funds, the need for trips to the bank for ordinary transactions will all but cease, as will the need to centralize banks' processing operations.

Other services depend at least partially on transportation. Dining out requires transport of both diners and food to the restaurant. Shopping occupies an intermediate position. Communications alone can supply information about goods, check stocks, and make purchases, but the goods themselves must be shipped.[9]

Finally (6), there will be continued refinements in the technology of much of the service sector based on communications improvement and the routinization and segmentation of service functions. These refinements will reduce economies of scale in service provision, allowing many small but specialized providers to prosper. Physicians, for example, will be able to communicate at a distance with esoteric diagnostic apparatus and with specialist colleagues. Computerized inventories and catalogs will speed ordering and make small stores more efficient. A vastly expanded capability for information retrieval and transmission will reduce the need for large central libraries. Distributed data processing and "smart" computer terminals will decentralize computing and reduce its scale.

In our scenario, rural residents and businesses no longer have far less access than do urbanites to specialized but communications-dependent services. An exception is transportation-dependent services: city dwellers will still have much more access to restaurants and concert halls. Nevertheless, the frequent reduction of the necessary scale of service provision will allow greater access to such services for the residents of even low-density areas. Following the example of bookmobiles and mobile health facilities, specialized transportation-dependent services might themselves periodically travel to central places in low-density areas, for this is more transportation-efficient than moving clients to services. The delivery of some transportation-dependent services in the future may come to resemble medieval trade fairs and periodic markets in present-day underdeveloped countries, an efficient way to deliver many specialized services when transportation costs are high.[10] Coordinating the itineraries of traveling service providers so that related services travel together will enable agglomeration economies in production and consumption, the latter enabling consumers to make multi-purpose trips. A cluster of traveling service providers can also bring to small places the new faces, new activities, and general bustle of a big city.

CONCLUSIONS

In the hypothetical future sketched out, the traditional lack of rural access to specialized "citified" services is greatly reduced. A wired society gives country folk the same access to television, bank transactions, and professional consultation that city dwellers enjoy. There will still be an urban advantage for services that have bulky inputs or outputs, or that require customer presence for production or consumption, although technological advances that minimize economies of scale may reduce the urban advantage.

This process, we have seen, has already begun. In the late 1970s, services moved down the central place hierarchy, reducing relative urban concentrations. The trend is most pronounced in finance, insurance, and real estate, and in business and repair services, two service industries with a strong urban focus.

Bringing traditionally urban services to the countryside is not a new phenomenon in American history. Waves of migrants washing over the nation, population movements between city and country, and the spreading of new styles of consumer goods through mail-order catalogs—all of these have avoided many of the rural-versus-urban and interregional cultural differences that have occurred elsewhere (Boorstin 1973). Expanding rural access to traditionally urban services is yet another means of national unification.

In exploring the future of the rural service sector, this essay has identified gaps in knowledge, particularly the lack of detailed empirical information on current locational trends. Three specific questions are most important for future research. First, when a rural service industry expands, who gets the new jobs, current residents or in-migrants, those currently employed or the unemployed? One would expect that characteristics of the rural economy

and of the new service activities interact here, particularly the skill mix in the labor force, the skills required
by the new services, and the extent of local employment or
underemployment. Second, to what extent do specific types
of service-sector jobs provide opportunities for economic
advancement, as opposed to dead-end jobs? A growing local
economy with many job openings may help a worker transfer
the skills learned in one service sector job to a better
job. Third, to what extent do rural residents believe that
access to specific services, particularly specialized ones,
enhances their quality of life? Do migrants returning from
cities miss urban services and bring urban tastes for
services with them? Do reverse migrants, former city
dwellers, tend to establish new service enterprises?

This essay has also raised important issues. Specifically, how may localities guide service-sector growth to
attain their goals and avoid untoward consequences? How may
state and federal governments assist in this process, providing localities with the means to guide service-sector
growth?

By substituting for imported services, growth in local
services can integrate the local economy and orient it to
local goals, reducing dependence on other areas. This is
already the case with banking because many states limit
city banks' expansion into the countryside. On the other
hand, the use of service enterprises does militate against
the common rural tradition of doing for oneself. This
conflict may be more symbolic than real, however. After
all, the tradition of doing for oneself was likely born of
necessity, given the past rural inaccessibility to citified
services. As accessibility increases, the tradition may
wane.

Land-use policy, highway construction, lending policy,
and professional licensure plus other forms of regulation
are the prime means by which different levels of government
can guide the growth of the rural service sector. Controls
on land use and highways strongly influence the location of
the many service activities (such as retail trade) that
depend heavily on accessibility to their clientele. Such
controls can channel service establishments into the most
appropriate locations, gaining shopping efficiency and
avoiding sprawled commercialization. Lending policies
(e.g., for public funds or loan guarantees) may affect the
competitive standing of new, existing, or newly enlarged
service establishments. Licensure and other regulatory
practices can, for example, influence the spread of banks'

branch offices or require minimum-sized facilities and thus
discourage service establishments in sparsely settled areas.
    The automobile has taken business away from many small-
town main streets. Current growth in the service sector,
guided away from forming new, peripheral shopping centers,
can revitalize main street. Revitalization would exploit
existing physical capital, central locations, and (for
small towns with low densities of businesses) good automobile access and parking facilities.

NOTES

    1. Exceptions: Personal services (e.g., laundries,
beauty, barber, and shoe repair shops; and funeral parlors)
do not show the usual variation with size of place. Only in
1977 was there somewhat more retail trade in small than
large metro areas. Also in 1977, the smallest nonmetro
counties violated the pattern for public administration and
entertainment and recreational service. (Is the sharp
increase in the latter a recreational spurt in the most
rural counties?)
    2. Unfortunately, there appears to be little literature
on recent locational trends in the rural service sector
(but see Johnson 1979 for retail trade). No one has updated
the classic study of Perloff et al. (1960). The important
work by Fuchs (1968) considers no locational matters,
examining instead aspatial questions of productivity, for
example. Clearly, empirical research should fill this
gap.
    3. For example, about two-thirds of the manufacturing
labor force works in firms with 500 or more employees.
Although this figure varies in service industries, it is 7
percent in wholesale trade and one-third in finance, insurance, and real estate. Even in those service industries
where employment is most concentrated into large establish-
ments--nongovernmental hospitals and local government--
employers of 500 or more account for only one-half of the
labor force. Moreover, profit-making service firms are
usually owner managed, and are often noncorporate (Fuchs,
1968: 10, 190).
    4. As an example of resulting anomalies, automobile
repair services are classified under "other services" (a
category that includes "miscellaneous repair services");
railroad repair shops are in the railroad transportation

category (part of "transport, communications, and utilities"); and ship and boat repair appear under manufacturing,
as part of "transportation equipment." Moreover, certain
"agricultural services" (e.g., soil preparation, crop protection, crop harvesting, crop preparation, veterinary care,
and farm labor contractors) are grouped with agriculture.

5. A phenomenon emergent in the last decade may, however, belie the notion that economic growth is necessarily
a transition from primary to secondary and tertiary activities. For the first time in this century, worldwide prices
of primary products have grown relative to secondary pro-
ducts--manufactured goods. Oil is only the most striking
example of a phenomenon that includes many mining, farm,
and fishery products.

6. Without going into detail, it is sobering to sketch
some difficulties of analytical research in this area. To
measure "real" service output and consumption, one must
control for the price inflation of unstandardized services
undergoing changes in quality, as well as the invention of
new services and the demise of outmoded ones. At the
extreme of difficulty, government output is currently
simply defined as the cost of its inputs, preventing any
measurement of productivity. See Fuchs (1969).

7. Not only are households consuming more services, but
a growing fraction of services is unrelated to care of the
home (Linden 1978).

8. A cautionary reminder is in order here. The current
variation in population trends across nonmetro areas (noted
in Chapters 1 and 2) means that, e.g., the Great Plains
counties, particularly those in which large-scale agriculture prevails, continue to lose population and, therefore,
service activity. That experience also may lie in the
offing for poverty counties that have scant resources. But
where population growth has resumed it seems to have taken
place within short commuting radii of small- and medium-
sized service centers. Thus, the future provision of services in most nonmetro areas should contend with increases
of population or with moderate reductions, the latter
perhaps only in the short-run.

9. Of course, the purchase of material goods is assumed,
not information (e.g., books or music) that may be shipped
via communication channels.

10. In developed countries, touring orchestras and
lecturers already practice this mode of service delivery.
Their services are so specialized that no one service area
can continuously support them.

BIBLIOGRAPHY

Allaman, Peter M., and Birch, David L. "Components of
   Employment Change for Metropolitan and Rural Areas in
   the United States by Industry Group, 1970-1972."
   Inter-Area Migration Project. Cambridge, Mass.: Joint
   Center for Urban Studies of MIT and Harvard, September
   1975.
Baumol, William J., and Bowen, William G., Performing Arts--
   The Economic Dilemma. New York: Twentieth Century Fund,
   1966.
Bell, Daniel. The Coming of Post-Industrial Society. New
   York: Basic Books, 1973.
Berry, Brian J. L. The Geography of Market Centers and
   Retail Distribution. Englewood Cliffs, N.J.: Prentice-
   Hall, 1967.
Boorstin, Daniel J. The Americans: The Democratic Experi-
   ence. New York: Random House, 1973.
Braschler, Curtis, and Kuehn, John A. "Estimation of Em-
   ployment Multipliers for Planning in Ozarks Nonmetro-
   politan Counties." Southern Journal of Agricultural
   Economics 8 (1976): 187-92.
Clark, Colin. The Conditions of Economic Progress. 1st ed.
   London, 1940.
Conopask, Jeff V. A Data-Pooling Approach to Estimate
   Employment Multipliers for Small Regional Economies.
   U.S. Department of Agriculture, Economics, Statistics,
   and Cooperatives Service. Washington, D.C., 1978.
Coughenour, C. Milton, and Gabbard, Anne V. Part-Time
   Farmers in Kentucky in the Early 1970's: The Development
   of Dual Careers. Lexington, Ky.: University of Kentucky,
   1977.
Edgren, Gus. "Employment Adjustment to Trade Under Condi-
   tions of Stagnating Growth." International Labor Review
   117 (1978): 289-303.
Elrod, Robert H., and Laferney, Preston E. Sector Income
   and Employment Multipliers. U.S. Department of Agricul-
   ture, Technical Bulletin no. 1421. Washington, D.C.,
   1970.
Fisher, Allan G. B. The Clash of Progress and Security.
   London: 1935.
Fuchs, Victor R. The Service Economy. New York: National
   Bureau of Economic Research, 1968.
_____, ed. Production and Productivity in the Service
   Industries. New York: National Bureau of Economic
   Research, 1969.

Gallman, Robert E., and Weiss, Thomas J. "The Service Industries in the Nineteenth Century." In Production and Productivity in the Service Industries, edited by Victor R. Fuchs, pp. 287-351. New York: National Bureau of Economic Research, 1969.

Garrison, Charles B. "Industrial Growth in the Tennessee Valley Region, 1959 to 1968." American Journal of Agricultural Economics 56 (1974): 50-60.

Glisson, Charles A. "Dependence of Technological Routinization on Structural Variables in Human Service Organizations." Human Behavior 23 (1978): 383-95.

Gordon, D. M. Theories of Poverty and Underemployment: Orthodox, Radical, and Dual Labor Market Perspectives. Lexington, Mass.: D. C. Heath, 1972.

Gorman, John A. "Alternative Measures of the Real Output and Productivity of Commercial Banks." In Production and Productivity in the Service Industries, edited by Victor R. Fuchs, pp. 155-88. New York: National Bureau of Economic Research, 1969.

Hoover, Edgar M., and Vernon, Raymond. Anatomy of a Metropolis. Cambridge: Harvard University Press, 1959.

Houthakker, H. S., and Taylor, Lester D. Consumer Demand in the United States. 2nd ed. Cambridge: Harvard University Press, 1970.

Jacobs, Jane. The Economy of Cities. New York: Random House, 1969.

Johnson, Kenneth. The Impact of Population Decline on Organizational Structure of American Counties, 1920-1970. Ph.D. dissertation, University of North Carolina at Chapel Hill, 1979.

Jones, C. D., Jr. Input-Output Analysis Applied to Rural Resources Development Planning. U.S. Department of Agriculture, Economics, Statistics, and Cooperatives Service. Washington, D.C., March 1978.

Jones, Lonnie L., and Mustafa, Gholam. Structure of the Texas Economy: Emphasis on Agriculture. Texas Agricultural Experiment Station, May 1972.

Judy, Kerlin R., and Jack, Robert L. Impact of a New Greenhouse Complex on Income and Employment in a Rural Community in West Virginia. Morgantown, W.Va.: West Virginia Agricultural Experiment Station, November 1974.

King, Allan G. "Industrial Structure, the Flexibility of Working Hours, and Women's Labor Force Participation." Review of Economics and Statistics 60 (1978): 399-407.

Klindt, T. H., and Smith, G. F. "Economic Interrelationships in a Rural Tennessee Economy." Bulletin of the University of Tennessee Agricultural Experiment Station, no. 570, June 1977.

Lengellé, Maurice. "Growth of the Commerce and Services Sector in Western Europe." Manpower Problems in the Service Sector. Paris: OECD, 1966.

Linden, Fabian. "Service, Please!" Across the Board 15 (1978): 42–45.

Lowell, R. F. "Testing a Dual Labor-Market Classification of Jobs." Journal of Regional Science 18 (1978): 95–103.

Perloff, Harvey S. et al. Regions, Resources, and Economic Growth. Baltimore: Johns Hopkins University Press, 1960.

Pursell, Donald E. et al. Trade Adjustment Assistance: An Analysis of Impacted Worker Benefits of Displaced Workers in the Electronics Industry. Center for Manpower Studies. Memphis, Tenn.: Memphis State University, 1975.

Schwartzman, David. "The Growth of Sales Per Man-Hour in Retail Trade, 1929–1963." In Production and Productivity in the Service Industries, edited by Victor R. Fuchs, pp. 201–29. New York: National Bureau of Economic Research, 1969.

Scott, John T., Jr., and Wahi, P. L. "Factors Affecting the Labor Supply Schedule in an Industrializing Rural Area." Illinois Journal of Agricultural Economics 14 (1974): 31–35.

Shapiro, B. I. et al. "The Impact of Employment Expansion on Rural Community Services Expenditures: A Small Area Model." Southern Journal of Agricultural Economics 9 (1977): 57–62.

Stigler, George J. Trends in Employment in the Service Industries. New York: National Bureau of Economic Research, 1956.

Treadway, Arthur B. "What is Output? Problems of Concept and Measurement." In Production and Productivity in the Service Industries, edited by Victor R. Fuchs, pp. 55–83. New York: National Bureau of Economic Research, 1969.

U.S. Bureau of the Census. Social and Economic Characteristics of the Metropolitan and Nonmetropolitan Population: 1970 and 1977. Special Studies, series P-23, no. 75. Washington, D.C.: U.S. Government Printing Office, 1978.

Wright, Emmett Earl. Industrial Experience in Small City Job Markets. Ph.D. dissertation, University of Arkansas, 1968.

Arthur Saltzman
Lawrence W. Newlin

7

The Availability of
Passenger Transportation

INTRODUCTION

Passenger transportation in nonmetro America is currently
in a state of flux. Energy shortages coupled with soaring
inflation are hampering the mobility of residents in nonmetro areas. A number of communities have experienced
recent cutbacks or abandonment of scheduled air, passenger
rail, and intercity bus service. On the other hand, there
are positive trends including the enactment of a new passenger transportation program at the federal level to encourage
the development and expansion of innovative paratransit
systems, and the launching of a set of interagency agreements by the White House to help improve a variety of transportation programs for small cities and towns.

From a longer-term perspective, improvements in transportation facilities and services during this century have
assisted in removing the barriers of nonmetro isolation. The
private automobile has afforded an unprecedented degree of
mobility. Yet, despite these gains, the problems of isolation persist among the poor, elderly, handicapped, and youth
in nonmetro areas. The current energy situation has extended
these problems to the general nonmetro populace with major
impacts on those living and working in recreation communities, residents of bedroom communities within commuting
distance of metro employment locations, and low-income residents of communities with little or no economic opportunity.

The future of settlement patterns in nonmetro areas is
likely to be significantly influenced by the future of the
transportation system found in these areas. The development
of new technologies in the automobile transportation system
coupled with the expansion of alternative transportation
modes could help to offset the adverse impact of the energy
crisis. Similarly, new patterns of land use, as well as the
application of innovative telecommunications technology,
could help counterbalance some of the current trends. Un-

doubtedly, transportation and these related concerns will
be of increasing importance during the years to come.

This chapter addresses the mobility characteristics,
needs, and problems of people living in nonmetro America,
and the passenger transportation system that the nonmetro
population uses. Both intercity and local passenger modes
will be discussed. Other important transportation issues
such as the transportation of goods, energy, and information
are also of critical importance to rural America but are
beyond the scope of this presentation.

NONMETROPOLITAN PASSENGER
TRANSPORTATION SYSTEM--AUTO DOMINANCE

In order to get to the job, to shop, to visit the doctor, or
go to the city, the resident of nonmetro areas potentially
has available a transportation system consisting of four
major modes, the automobile, bus, train, and airplane. Each
mode tends to serve different but overlapping functions.

As in metro areas, the automobile has become the predominant mode of personal transportation in nonmetro areas
during this century. Public policies have generally encouraged the automobile transportation system to gain dominance
in nonmetro America and the nation by placing controls on
gasoline prices, financing an extensive network of highways,
and other means. An improved and expanded road and street
system has also encouraged this trend, fulfilling the
mobility needs of nonmetro people and reducing problems of
rural isolation. Meanwhile, alternative passenger modes
such as rail, public transit, and intercity bus have been
allowed to deteriorate.

Figure 7.1 illustrates the historical trend for the
intercity modes from 1962 to 1972. Although the automobile
and air carriers have made large gains in passenger miles,
the intercity bus system has only modestly increased its
absolute ridership and has a smaller part of the market.
Rail passenger miles have been lost to other modes both in
relative and absolute terms. Generally, both bus and rail
service to small communities have been reduced.

Automobile ownership in nonmetro areas is high. Eighty-
seven percent of nonmetro households own at least one automobile or truck compared to 84.3 percent of all American
households (U.S. Department of Transportation, hereafter
DOT, 1977: 350). Nonmetro people travel more often and far-

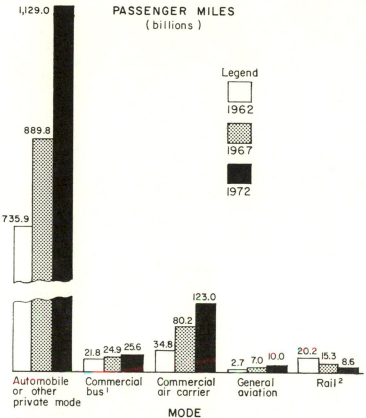

PASSENGER MILES
(billions)

1,129.0

889.8

735.9

Legend

1962

1967

1972

123.0

80.2

34.8

21.8 24.9 25.6

2.7 7.0 10.0

20.2 15.3 8.6

Automobile   Commercial   Commercial   General   Rail²
or other   bus¹   air carrier   aviation
private mode

MODE

¹ Includes all class I, II, and III intercity bus travel.
² Includes all class I and II intercity rail travel.

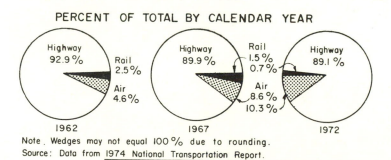

PERCENT OF TOTAL BY CALENDAR YEAR

Highway 92.9%   Rail 2.5%   Air 4.6%

1962

Highway 89.9%   Rail 1.5% 0.7%   Air 8.6% 10.3%

1967

Highway 89.1%

1972

Note. Wedges may not equal 100% due to rounding.
Source: Data from 1974 National Transportation Report.

Figure 7.1 Nonmetropolitan Passenger Transportation in 1962, 1967, and 1972

ther than their metro counterparts. In particular, persons
living in communities of 5,000 to 24,999 make more trips
(1,870) and log more vehicle miles (14,696) annually than
residents of other sized communities (Rupprecht, 1976: 221).

Although traveling on open roads provides better gas
mileage than driving in congested urban areas, the greater
frequency of travel and the greater distances covered by
nonmetro residents make owning and operating a vehicle
generally more expensive in nonmetro than metro areas. It
is estimated that nonmetro households consume approximately
1,000 gallons annually, whereas urban households use about
700 gallons (Rupprecht, 1976: 222).

Interestingly, residents of rural areas within metro
areas spent more money than residents of any other type
of community, indicating long-distance commuting to work.
Residents of urban places with over 2,500 population outside
of SMSAs spent less than urban residents as a whole though
more than residents of central cities.

Despite the high rates of automobile ownership in nonmetro areas, the nonmetro population contains a disproportionate share of the transportation disadvantaged. Because
of the overwhelming dominance of the automobile as the major
mode of transportation in nonmetro areas, people without a
car have severely restricted mobility. Lack of access may
be a function of any of several factors. There is a higher
incidence of poverty and disability in nonmetro areas than
in either suburban or urban areas. And nationally, in 1973,
54.7 percent of households with incomes less than $3,000
and 32.2 percent of households with incomes between $5,000
and $7,499 were without an automobile. It has been estimated
that the rural poor make only 15 percent of the total trips
made by the average American (Burkhardt et al., 1972: 1).
The nonmetro population also contains a higher proportion
of young and old than does the metro population. In 1973,
38.4 percent of household heads sixty-five years of age and
older were without automobiles (DOT, 1976: 8).

Also included among the ranks of the transportation
disadvantaged are single-car households in which family
members are often left behind when the principal wage
earner uses the family car to travel to and from work. The
percentage of nonmetro households in this category is 52.4
percent (DOT, 1976: 8). It is estimated (Brown 1977) that
as many as twenty million nonmetro residents lack access to
transportation because the family car is used by the principal wage earner. Furthermore, data on automobile ownership do not indicate the reliability of a household's auto-

mobile. In 1970, 40.7 percent of all nonmetro households
purchased their newest car at least four years earlier
(Hauser et al., 1974: 3-19).

The elderly, poor, and handicapped in nonmetro areas
are in particular need of access to health care and social
services. Health care facilities, recreation centers, and
governmental activities are usually centrally located in
towns and cities and are often inaccessible to many of the
transportation disadvantaged living in outlying areas. By
some standards of the U.S. Department of Health and Human
Services, twenty-seven million nonmetro residents live in
areas with inadequate access to health facilities. Moreover,
the nonmetro poor participate in the Food Stamp Program at
a lower rate than the metro poor.

The lack of alternatives to the automobile is a major
problem for many nonmetro residents eligible for such services, though the situation varies according to size and
location of communities. Jackson and McKelvey (1978) found
that less than 10 percent of communities under 2,500 population are served by taxi service and less than 20 percent
are served by specialized transportation systems, compared
to 79 percent and 34 percent respectively for communities
between 2,500 and 10,000 population.

The automobile transportation system has had varying
levels of success in meeting the needs of different types
of rural communities. It has played an important role in
encouraging growth in some industries, such as tourism and
recreation, and improvements in the interstate and primary
highway system have enabled residents of counties adjacent
to metro areas to take advantage of employment opportunities
in central cities and suburbs. There is evidence, however,
(U.S. Economic Development Administration 1979) that the
lack of public transportation has denied residents of outlying distressed areas access to new employment opportunities
in urban nodes designated as growth centers. Similarly,
although many small farmers have been able to secure off-
farm employment, the disproportionate number of farmers
living in poverty suggests that access to jobs at an acceptable salary level is limited.

The road system on which nonmetro residents travel contains 3.2 million miles of the nation's total 3.8 million
miles of roads and streets. In recent years the overall
quality of these roads has been improved as measured by a
gain in surfaced road mileage (Senate Committee on Agriculture and Forestry, 1975: 40-41). The nearly completed interstate highway system has greatly improved travel for some

nonmetro residents and enhanced the economy of many communities located on or near the system.

This network of roads and highways is not without its
problems, however. Twenty-three percent of nonmetro roads
remain unsurfaced, some of which are considered intolerable
(Senate Committee on Agriculture and Forestry, 1975: 41).
Increases in the average load on nonmetro roads due in large
part to increased trucking activity, have accentuated the
need for improved maintenance of the road system. And some
communities have been adversely affected by the interstate
highway system as traffic from other routes intersecting
their boundaries has been diverted to the new route.

In summary, the passenger transportation system in
nonmetro areas is dominated by the private automobile, but
the benefits of this system have not been shared equally by
all residents in the cities, towns, and open country of
nonmetro areas.

JOURNEY TO WORK IN NONMETROPOLITAN AMERICA

The expansion of the automobile transportation system
within metro as well as nonmetro areas has effectively
expanded the labor markets accessible to the nonmetro
population. Long-distance commuting has offered an alternative to out-migration for many nonmetro residents and
has enabled many new in-migrants to enjoy the amenities of
rural living while taking advantage of economic opportunities in metro areas.

Commuting patterns vary according to community size and
region of the country. Data from the 1970 Census indicate
that of those commuting across county lines to work, the
residents of the open country and small towns comprise a
larger proportion (24 percent) than either residents in
places of 2,500 to 9,999 population (16 percent) or residents in nonsuburban cities of 10,000 to 49,999 population
(11 percent). Moreover, two of every five nonmetro residents
commuting outside their county of residence also commute
to work outside the region (Hansen, 1976: 119). Nonmetro
workers commuting long distances to work tend to be located
primarily in the South and East.

According to the 1975 housing survey (U.S. Bureau of
the Census 1979), the number of nonmetro residents (just
over 2.087 million) commuting to work within metro areas
was roughly double the number of metro residents (1.005

million) commuting to work within nonmetro areas. Nonmetro
workers commuting to central city jobs comprised 4.5 percent
of the nonmetro work force, averaging 30.1 miles one way,
whereas those working in metro suburbs comprised 4.9
percent of the rural work force, averaging 25.3 miles.

Those nonmetro residents working away from home but
within nonmetro areas actually commuted shorter distances
than their metro counterparts. This shorter commuting distance is due in part to the fact that nonmetro cities of
10,000 to 49,999 population have less intercounty job
commuting than either larger or smaller communities. It is
also consistent with evidence that economic opportunities
within nonmetro communities are expanding.

The primary means of transportation to work in nonmetro
America and the nation is the private automobile. However,
as indicated in Table 7.1, a larger proportion of nonmetro
workers carpool to work than either suburban or central
city workers. In addition, a greater percentage of nonmetro
workers commute by bicycle, motorcycle or foot than either
their suburban or central city counterparts. The high percentage of nonmetro residents working at home is accounted
for primarily by farm residents.

The low use of public transportation to get to work
indicates both its current lack of availability as well as
resistance to its use. Transit service is generally unavailable in nonmetro areas, and even for the many counties
that report some local passenger service, it is often restricted to clients of social service agencies and thus is
not used for the journey to work. However, this situation
is changing as indicated by a survey of forty-eight rural
public transportation systems funded under a Department of
Transportation (DOT) demonstration program (Federal Highway
Administration 1978). It indicates in the first quarter of
1978 that 18.6 percent of the total trips made by those
systems were to work. The proportion is even higher (23
percent) for those systems with five or more vehicles
operating in areas with less than fifty persons per square
mile. Early indications are that many of the most successful demonstration projects are providing a substantial
share of work trips as part of their overall service.

The lack of public transportation availability in nonmetro areas for commuting purposes appears to have its
greatest impact on the poor in nonmetro areas. Although 40
percent of the poor use carpools, Hauser et al. (1974: 3-35)
cite problems with this means of transportation. "Often the
vehicle is old, maintenance is poor or non-existent, repairs

Table 7.1. Principal Mode of Transportation to Work,
by Type of Residence, 1975.

| Mode of Transportation | Residence of Workers | | |
| | Nonmetro | Metro | |
		Suburban	Central City
	%	%	%
Drive alone	64.4	69.7	59.9
Carpool	22.1	18.9	17.3
Public transit	0.8	4.4	14.0
Other means	6.6	4.8	2.2
Work at home	6.1	2.2	1.6
All modes	100.0	100.0	100.0

Source: Compiled from U.S. Bureau of the Census, 1979.

and good tires are too expensive. With the reliability of
this pool of shared-ride vehicles so low, the entry-level
worker is likely to be replaced by another employee if he
is late or fails to show for work too often." Many of the
nonmetro transportation demonstration projects that have
successfully provided commuter work trips have drawn heavily
from the ranks of those carpooling, represented in large
part by poor persons and women.

In addition to carpooling and public transportation,
vanpooling offers an increasingly important work trip
alternative. Various states are carrying out promotional
campaigns to attract vanpool ridership, and anecdotal
evidence suggests that interest in these activities increased dramatically during energy shortages of 1979.
Ridesharing incentives were also included in the interagency agreements announced as part of the White House
Rural Initiatives in June 1979.

The impact of gas shortages and increased gasoline
prices on nonmetro commuters is still uncertain, but it is
assumed to be adverse. The impact is expected to be greatest for the poor and those workers traveling substantial
distances to work. A recent article from the Wall Street
Journal illustrates the problem. "Mrs. Wallace (of Crystal
Springs, Mississippi) recently quit a job at another shirt
factory in order to cut her daily commuting by about 26
miles, but she still faces a 40-mile round trip each day.

Gasoline for her 1975 Chrysler, which she says gets 'mighty bad' mileage, is taking a big chunk out of her $3-an-hour pay." Increased availability of public transportation in nonmetro areas will help ease the burden of the energy crisis as will further gains in ridesharing activities. However, such change will not occur quickly. The residents of the cities, towns, and countryside may find it necessary to change jobs or residence, creating significant alterations in both economic and demographic patterns in nonmetro areas.

INSTITUTIONAL, REGULATORY, AND FINANCIAL CONTEXT

The passenger transportation system in nonmetro areas functions in a complex set of multilayered and overlapping administrative, regulatory, and funding agencies. Passenger travel on roads, trains, and airlines has both public and private sector components in that transportation facilities are planned, constructed, and owned by both the public and private sector and are regulated by agencies at every level of government.

The primary areas of regulatory activity are rate setting and control of entry to and exit from the market. Legislative authority for regulation is included in many statutes and administrative codes promulgated by various levels of government, although financial assistance comes from various sources.

In the past the federal government set the regulatory tone whereas the states and localities were primary providers of the facilities. Even in the building of the interstate highway system, the states have had the responsibility for building those segments within their jurisdiction. Each state exercises considerable regulatory power, but the tone of federal regulation is usually reflected by the states. This situation is illustrated by the following statement: "The difference between Federal ascendancy in transportation regulation and state and local primacy in the provision of transportation facilities is quite clearly attributable to the fact that regulation involves transportation operations which frequently cross State lines, whereas funding for facilities can be categorized for areas located within a State" (Senate Committee on Commerce, Science and Transportation, 1977: 26).

HIGHWAYS AND AUTOS

Just as private automobiles dominate the passenger transportation scene in nonmetro areas, the institutions that affect
roads and private automobiles are pervasive. The largest
federal agency in transportation is the Federal Highway
Administration (FHWA), which is responsible for implementation of the Federal-Aid Highway Program and the administration of highway planning, research and safety programs.
    In every state corresponding highway/transportation
departments plan the intercity and rural networks. Although
all interstate highway system activites are performed by
state agencies, the planning, programming, and funding
functions for other arterial systems are not handled the
same way in all states. Various combinations of state,
county, and local agencies are involved so that in a few
states the counties have no role, whereas in most the
county transportation agency is solely responsible for
rural roads. Localities usually build and maintain the
local collector system, and as with the states the actual
construction is generally performed by the private sector.
    Federal financial involvement in highway construction
varies according to program category--for the interstate
system the maximum share is 90 percent and for other
arterial systems it is 70 percent.
    Federal assistance derives primarily from the Highway
Trust Fund, which is supported by user charge revenues. In
1975 the federal government disbursed about $2 billion more
for highways than it received in user charges, and state
and local governments provided almost $7.5 billion (National
Transportation Policy Study Commission 1979). Nonmetro road
expenditures from the Highway Trust Fund exceed rural user-
charge revenues in rural areas, whereas urban road revenues
from users exceed road expenditures from the same source
(Urban Institute 1977). Hence, federal policy and many
state policies serve to subsidize intercity auto travel in
rural areas.
    Road maintenance, however, is supported wholly by local
and state resources. The highway system, though it needs
only minor expansion, continues to require substantial
investment in the maintenance and improvement of existing
facilities, and these costs are consuming an increasing
proportion of highway expenditures at the state level. In
the 1974 National Transportation Report (DOT 1975) the
states estimated that the maintenance and administration

cost per mile of rural highway would increase by 64 percent between 1971 and 1989.

Although the provision of the arterial network is a public function, most of the passenger vehicles that use the system are provided by the private sector. For this reason, there is little regulatory activity aside from licensing drivers. (Other regulatory functions such as environmental control and regulation of fuel supply are performed, but these are beyond the scope of this chapter.)

RAIL

As the use of automobiles and airlines for intercity and rural trips has grown in absolute and relative terms, the number of passengers using railroads has declined precipitously since the end of World War I. The decline in revenues caused by this loss of passengers has not been matched by reductions in operating costs. The increasing deficit led to the assumption of almost all intercity rail operations by Amtrak in 1971. The statutes that created the quasi-public Amtrak Corporation withdrew jurisdiction over rates, entry, and exit from the Interstate Commerce Commission and gave it to Amtrak. Thus the rail passenger sector is almost totally in the public domain, and little state or local regulatory activity is evident.

In addition to Amtrak the major institution involved in rail passenger transportation is the Federal Railroad Administration (FRA), which administers programs providing grants and low-interest loans to railroad lines. These programs should result in major physical plant rehabilitation over much of the system used by Amtrak (Senate Committee on Commerce, Science and Transportation, 1977: 315).

INTERCITY BUS

The intercity bus industry is regulated by the Interstate Commerce Commission (ICC). Rate setting and market entry and exit for all interstate carriers are controlled by the ICC, whereas intrastate and regional carriers are under the jurisdiction of state public utilities commissions.

Rate changes in the intercity bus industry are usually proposed by an industrywide rate bureau--the National Bus Traffic Association--that serves as the rate-making bureau

for nearly 400 intercity carriers accounting for more than
90 percent of intercity bus revenues (Senate Committee on
Commerce, Science and Transportation 1977). The ICC, which
is charged by the Interstate Commerce Act with determining
whether fares are "just and reasonable," can investigate or
reject proposed increases. The trend, however, has been for
the ICC to accept all proposed fare changes that are not
protested.

Entry into the intercity bus industry tends to be inhibited by the ICC. Some applications are approved, but the
burden is on the carrier to show that the proposed service
is justified by public convenience and necessity. When
another carrier is already serving essentially the same
route, the application is usually denied.

AIRLINES

The certificated and commuter carriers together serve the
cities and towns in nonmetro America. Prior to 1978 the
Civil Aeronautics Board (CAB) regulated the fares of all
certificated carriers, that is airlines using aircraft over
a certain weight for scheduled flights. It also controlled
the certificated carriers' entry into and exit from the
industry and in and out of specific routes. Meanwhile,
commuter air carriers with scheduled flights on a lighter
weight class of plane remained free of CAB regulation.

In 1978, on the recommendation of the CAB, Congress
passed the Airlines Deregulation Act of 1978, essentially
removing barriers to market entry and exit, and deregulating
the rate structure for certified carriers over a period of
time.

When taken as a whole, the set of institutions, both
private and public, which influences the availability of
passenger transportation in nonmetro areas, is far from
coherent. This explains in part the rather uneven manner in
which the transportation system, both its intercity and
local transit components, meets the needs of the people and
places in nonmetro areas.

INTERCITY NONMETROPOLITAN PASSENGER TRANSPORTATION

The intercity transportation system in the United States
serves a vast network of small and large communities, and

the private automobile is clearly the principal means of
intercity travel, followed next by the commercial air
carrier. However, small community air service has had a
mixed record as trunk and regional air carriers have exited
from the nonmetro market and commuter air carriers have
come to play an increasingly important role. The two remaining major passenger modes, bus and rail, have generally
reduced service to small communities. In this light, the
degree to which intercity passenger transportation should
be regulated to insure service to smaller communities and
subsidized to insure service when it is uneconomical is
crucial in determining the availability of passenger
transportation in nonmetro areas.

The extensive network of highways and the convenience
and economy of the private automobile have served to replace
much of the intercity service previously provided by other
intercity passenger modes. Eighty-five percent of intercity
passenger mileage in America is traveled by private automobile on the nation's highways. The principal arterial
network carries 40 percent of travel in nonmetro areas but
accounts for only 2.5 percent of the total nonmetro road
and highway mileage (National Transportation Policy Study
Commission, 1979: 13).

The remaining three primary intercity modes, air, rail,
and bus, have traditionally served different elements of
the nonmetro market. The airlines provided long-distance
travel; railroads served intermediate distances; and buses
served short trips. These distinctions are no longer as
clear. Since the deregulation of certified air carriers in
1978, the decline of regional air carriers as a class of
certificated carriers serving a limited area of the country
and the emergence of commuter air carriers serving the
nonmetro market have generally lowered the average trip
distance for air carrier trips to and from small communities. However, the ultimate trip distance for the passenger may not have changed. The average trip distance for
regional air carriers in 1974 was 300 miles compared with
102 miles for commuter carriers (DOT, 1977: 151). By comparison, the average trip length over the entire Amtrak
rail passenger system is 225.8 miles, but the short and
intermediate trips serve the bulk of Amtrak passengers in
the highly urbanized Northeast corridor linking Boston, New
York, and Washington, D.C. Elsewhere, the long-distance
train routes have high proportions of average trip length
to total trip route length. For example, the average passenger on the Chicago to New Orleans route, which serves

over a dozen nonmetro stations, traveled 71 percent of
the total route distance (DOT, 1978: 3-10). The average
intercity bus trip is still short (112 miles in 1976), but
there has been increased competition from rail passenger
service in the Northeast for intermediate trips in recent
years.

Intercity rail and bus passenger service are primarily
utilized for recreation and personal visitation, though
rail passengers are more inclined than bus passengers to
take business or work trips. Amtrak's passengers are drawn
from a broad cross section of the American public with 14
percent of riders in the upper income bracket and 46 percent
with lower than average incomes (DOT 1978: 7-14). Intercity
bus ridership is much more likely to serve the transportation disadvantaged than either rail or air service. Nearly
one-half of the total bus ridership in 1972 on trips of 100
miles or more was comprised of persons less than eighteen
years of age or more than sixty-five; nearly 60 percent
were females; 20 percent were nonwhite; and more than one-
half had household incomes of less than $10,000 (Interstate
Commerce Commission, 1978).

SERVICE AVAILABILITY AND QUALITY

A growing trend for all three public passenger modes has
been the curtailment of service to small communities.
Victims of low volume and lacking economy of scale, these
small communities lose important access to larger centers
of economic and social activity. The CAB attempted to promote service to small communities by subsidizing regional
air carriers and strengthening those carriers' routes. An
unforeseen consequence of these efforts was to encourage
regional carriers to purchase faster, larger, and more
expensive aircraft, making service to small communities
less economical. Thus, between 1970 and 1975, thirty-three
communities with populations less than 50,000 lost service
from regional carriers, repeating a trend that had occurred
after World War II with the major domestic airlines.

The results of airline deregulation in 1978 are still
being debated. All output measures indicate that there is a
boom in the industry as a whole since deregulation. Ridership is up and widespread discounting is bringing many new
passengers. Arguments against deregulation suggest that
the quality of service has deteriorated and that increased
airport congestion, jammed reservation lines, and potential-

ly reduced safety are factors that should be weighed
against its benefits.

From the perspective of nonmetro residents, deregulation
may eventually provide more service to their cities and
towns. The immediate impact, however, has been to further
accelerate the curtailment of service to small communities
by some regional carriers without replacement by commuter
airlines.

The frequency of commuter carrier service to small communities is about twice that of certificated carriers at
points with the same volume of traffic, and commuter fares
have ordinarily been lower than those of certificated carriers for distances of up to 100 miles. Between 1965 and
1975, commuter carriers replaced certificated carriers at
63 of the airports they abandoned and were serving 111
airports that would not otherwise have received service.
Overall, 312 communities with less than 50,000 population
had scheduled air service as of 1975.

The decline of the rail passenger industry has drastically affected service to small communities. Prior to the
most recent cutback of Amtrak routes, 21 major city pairs
were connected serving 532 stations, a number of which are
in nonmetro areas. In January 1979, then Secretary of Transportation Brock Adams proposed reductions in the Amtrak
system by 43 percent, but the upsurge of ridership during
the spring and summer of 1979 caused a modification of the
original proposal, resulting in a cutback of approximately
20 percent of the current system. This would entail elimination of direct service to over 60 small communities.

For many of the small communities and surrounding areas
served by the existing system, rail service is often inaccessible during peak periods because capacity is reached
at major metro points. Problems with rail passenger service
in general include outdated equipment, deteriorated tracks,
low average speed, and poor on-time performance, and the
prospects for improved rail passenger service to the nonmetro population appear bleak.

As with rail service in recent years there has been a
decline in bus service to nonmetro cities and towns. During
the 1970s almost 1,800 nonmetro communities lost intercity
bus service. An inventory taken in 1978 of 380 communities
between 2,500 and 10,000 population found that only 42
percent of the places sampled were served by intercity bus,
and a mere 11 percent of the 291 communities with less than
2,500 population were served by intercity bus (Jackson and
McKelvey 1978). This appears to contradict previous esti-

mates (DOT 1977) that claim that 96 percent of the communities between 2,500 and 5,000 population and 100 percent of communities with more than 5,000 population are served by intercity bus. The industry claims to serve some 15,000 points, of which 14,000 receive no other form of common carrier intercity passenger service. It also claims that 31 percent of intercity bus passengers are rural residents, compared with 18 percent for Amtrak and 12 percent for airlines (American Bus Association, 1978).

Flagstop service is generally available on routes that are not scheduled as express, but inclement weather and poor information about this service make it an underutilized feature of the bus industry. General criticism of the industry focuses on a lack of information about schedules and fares, inconvenient and infrequent departure times, missed connections and long layovers, and dilapidated terminals.

Legislative proposals are currently being developed for the phased deregulation of the intercity bus industry. The liberalization of entry and exit regulation could further exacerbate the trend in service curtailment for small communities, and more freedom to raise fares could place service out of the reach of some disadvantaged groups, especially if the industry continues to expand into the charter and small freight markets. The management of Greyhound and Trailways--bus companies with 75 percent of the national market--have indicated that cuts in service to nonmetro areas are necessary because service to these areas is straining the main service on primary routes (Senate Committee on Commerce, Science, and Transportation, 1978: 17).

To the extent that deregulation is gradual and encourages competition among Greyhound, Trailways, and the other 1,000 carriers, drastic cuts in service are not likely to ensue, and indeed, service to some small communities might be improved and expanded. A recent study of bus service to small communities (Senate Commerce Committee, 1978) reveals that the most profitable carriers serve a well-defined region and provide a considerable amount of service to small communities in contrast to the least profitable carriers, which primarily operate in the highly urbanized areas of the Middle Atlantic. Thus, service to small communities can be profitable, and increased competition within the industry, particularly during the current energy situation, could counterbalance adverse impacts due to changes in the regulatory environment.

SUBSIDIZING SERVICE TO NONMETROPOLITAN AREAS

Pressures to hold down public expenditures coupled with a
general reluctance to fund operating deficits conflict with
counterforces to continue transportation service to more
isolated communities at a reasonable cost to their residents. Attention must be given to the appropriate and
economically feasible mix of transportation services required to serve both nonmetro and metro populations.

For fiscal year 1979 subsidies to regional air carriers
were estimated at $51.5 million--the bulk of which went to
six carriers. A second subsidy program was authorized by
the Airline Deregulation Act of 1978 to insure essential
service to every community certificated as of October 1978,
but the subsidy requirements under this program are as yet
undetermined. Loan guarantees by the Federal Aviation
Administration to commuter carriers, estimated at $50
million in fiscal year 1979, were to double in 1980.

The Federal Aviation Administration's Airport Development Aid Program has assisted in the improvement of small
community airports, though only 11 percent of the program's
funds benefited nonmetro areas in fiscal year 1976. Proposed
legislation would extend and expand the program, providing
approximately 25 percent of the program's funds to foster
small community air service. In addition, the White House
rural transportation initiative (Improving Transportation
in Rural America 1979) allocates $200 million in funds from
the Economic Development Administration, Farmers Home Administration, and Small Business Administration for airport
improvements and assistance to commuter airlines.

The passenger rail system now run by Amtrak has operated
at a deficit for many years. The federal government subsi-
dizes this deficit that more than doubled per passenger
mile between fiscal years 1972 and 1978, and reached a
total of $578 million in fiscal 1978.

From a nonmetro perspective, this level of subsidy is
disproportionate to the amount of service available to the
vast majority of nonmetro Americans. For example, DOT has
recommended retaining the northern route from Chicago to
Seattle, despite its poor economic performance, because no
alternative passenger service is available to 40 percent of
the route's patrons--some 80,000 people. The DOT (1979: 4-
18) has found that it is the only passenger transportation
alternative to several tourist attractions in the northern
Great Plains, and offers a major alternative to a two-lane

highway during the inclement weather. In instances such as
this, subsidies may be warranted to maintain service to
nonmetro communities. Moreover, unlike the intercity bus
industry, the rail industry does not have the advantage of
a publicly owned and maintained infrastructure resulting in
large roadbed maintenance costs. Nevertheless, justification
for Amtrak subsidies must generally rely on arguments other
than the importance of passenger rail service to nonmetro
communities.

The intercity bus industry has not fared nearly as well
as the other modes of passenger transportation in obtaining
assistance from the federal government. Although states
such as New York, New Jersey, and Pennsylvania are subsidizing intercity bus operations, the federal government has
not provided such assistance. The Surface Transportation
Assistance Act of 1978 made bus companies eligible for
funds under the Nonurbanized Public Transportation Program,
but only a few states are apt to divert funds away from
local public transportation projects. Although operating
costs for the bus industry have risen dramatically in recent
years and competition from Amtrak has had an adverse impact,
the duopolistic position of the industry makes subsidy an
undesirable alternative to many policymakers. Policies that
would target assistance to bus operations smaller than
Greyhound or Trailways might receive a more favorable
reception from policymakers.

The picture that emerges after looking at the total
intercity passenger transportation system is full of gaps.
Automobile transportation meets the needs of many but far
from all nonmetro residents. Air service, although very
important, is not found in many nonmetro places. Nonmetro
rail service is very limited and its future is in doubt.
Finally, the prospect of deregulation of the intercity bus
industry raises questions about the future of service to
small nonmetro communities. Whether the gaps in the service
to nonmetro areas are filled will depend in large part on
whether the federal government tries to ensure that some
type of intercity transportation service is available in
nonmetro communities even when it is not economical. Various
subsidy programs, as described above, do promote such service but an overall transportation plan or strategy coordinating all modes does not exist. The result is the
incomplete intercity transportation system now found in
nonmetro areas.

CONVENTIONAL TRANSIT AND
PARATRANSIT IN NONMETROPOLITAN AREAS

Conventional public transit systems were prevalent in small
towns before the advent of widespread ownership of automobiles. Private operators served most areas as long as the
residents needed and used the service enough to make it
profitable. But the demise of the local transit operator in
nonmetro areas is almost complete.

Virtually the only currently existing public transportation in nonmetro areas consists of paratransit modes:
taxis, carpools, jitneys, and demand-responsive and sub-
scription buses. This situation is logical and should be
expected because conventional fixed-route transit did not
meet the mobility needs of residents. The nature of nonmetro
travel demands, that is, a low volume of people wanting to
get to different places at different times, tends to mitigate against fixed-route transit, and thus, few conventional
operators currently provide transit services in nonmetro
areas.

The development of the paratransit mode started in
nonmetro areas about a decade ago. Voluntary drivers and
agency staff of local human service agencies have helped
clients meet their mobility needs for many more years. But
it was not until the dramatic increase in social welfare
and health programs of the 1960s that agencies began to develop systematic techniques for transporting their clients.
The motivation to develop the systems came from agency
directors who became aware of their clients' mobility problems. Agencies found that they were able to serve only a
fraction of their potential client group because of access
problems. Their clients--especially elderly, handicapped,
and poor persons--were often without access to an automobile
or adequate public transportation and simply had no way to
get to the agency (Saltzman 1976).

During the 1960s, the Office of Economic Opportunity
(OEO), now the Community Services Administration (CSA),
initiated a variety of programs in nonmetro areas that were
designed to help take people out of the poverty cycle.
Local OEO-funded community action agencies (CAAs) had
consistently identified transportation as a major problem
area that hampered the effective delivery of social and
health services to their clients. Community workers in the
CAAs spent a large portion of their time transporting poor
people to and from the agency. In response to these needs
many rural transit systems were started with demonstration

grants from OEO. By 1972 more than fifty rural transportation projects had been funded by OEO (Kaye 1972). Kidder
(1979) notes that these paratransit systems are now widespread, with 65 percent of the most agricultural counties
in the United States reporting some form of specialized
transportation services available.

These systems were small and personalized, offering
door-to-door service. The vehicles used initially were
large government-surplus buses that provided trips connecting the nonmetro areas and the small towns where the various
health and social service agencies are located. These paratransit services were sometimes operated along a fixed
route with designated stops but more often deviated from
the route to provide door-to-door service.

Community action agencies were the first to develop
these social service delivery systems, but other government
agencies, including the U.S. Department of Agriculture, and
the Appalachian Regional Commission, have established paratransit services for their clients. Most active has been
the Administration of Aging (AOA) of HEW, which was authorized to conduct transportation research and demonstration
programs under Titles III and VII of the Older Americans
Act.

Notably absent from the nonmetro transit scene until
recently has been DOT. Because of the initial legislative
focus on large urban areas, there was little DOT activity
in nonmetro transit until Section 147 of the Federal Aid
Highway Act of 1973 authorized a Rural Highway Public Transportation Demonstration Program. The National Mass Transportation Assistance Act of 1974 provided for some capital
assistance to rural (nonurbanized) communities, but less
than $25 million of the $500 million set-aside authorized
in the bill reached nonurbanized areas, and much of that
went to small cities that were closest to the 50,000
population cutoff. The 16(b)2 program of the Urban Mass
Transportation Administration provides grants to private
nonprofit agencies to purchase capital equipment and has
been used by many nonmetro agencies to purchase vehicles.

The passage of the Nonurbanized Public Transportation
Program (Section 18) of the Surface Transportation Assistance Act of 1978 marked the coming of age of nonmetro
transit. It moved nonmetro transit out of the research and
demonstration phase with a clear legislative mandate and an
initial $75 million annual appropriation to develop an
ongoing program that provides capital as well as operating,
administrative, and technical assistance. However, many

problems remain before this new program can be effectively implemented.

SYSTEMS DIVERSITY

As nonmetro transit has moved from early small human service agency systems to larger more diversified operations, many of their characteristics have changed. Systems vary somewhat according to the program under which they were developed. In general, the Section 147 grants and Section 18 projects involved systems that are larger, more stable, and more intensely evaluated than other projects.

Early nonmetro transit systems began when a human service agency director perceived the need for better client transportation. Vehicles were bought after little previous planning, and funds were usually not included in the continuation budget, thus contributing to the ad hoc nature of most of the non-Section 147 projects. On the other hand, the plans for the Section 147 and Section 18 systems have been scrutinized by many agencies. They are well planned and are therefore more likely to be stable.

However, most nonmetro transit operations have not had a long enough history to become stable. Typically, the systems are between one and three years old and small. As Kidder et al. point out (1976: 6), most of the 400 systems they surveyed consisted of between one and two vehicles. This is particularly true of the rural projects that have been initiated as a result of the 16(b)2 grant program.

The clients of nonmetro transit operations tend to be elderly, handicapped, poor, or otherwise disadvantaged. The nature of most trips in nonmetro transit is to provide accessibility to basic services for their passengers. Frequently this means each trip has a significant impact on the passenger's social or economic well-being.

For a number of reasons the management expertise that has been attracted to nonmetro transit has not been of high quality. There are many exceptions to this, but serious management problems are often evident in the systems, resulting in a lack of proper data collection for either internal management function or presentation to outside sources.

The early systems were usually at least initially part of a human service agency. More recent systems are finding a separate identity as legislation for nonmetro transit has been enacted.

Being part of another unit complicates the bookkeeping and proper allocation of costs. Although records are usually kept of all operational expenses that are directly attributable to the transit system, the appropriate administrative and other overhead costs are frequently not included as a transportation expense.

The nonmetro transit operations tend to live on a month-to-month budget, and rarely can project an operating budget for more than six months. Operators, in fact, have frequently started a system before secure finances are available, causing them to be in a continual catch-up position. This is not the case with the Section 147 and Section 18 programs, which receive grants of longer duration than others.

Because many operations receive funds from more than one agency, they are not likely to be as accountable as those that are funded by a single agency. In addition, the overlay of various accounting and data requirements can complicate the management and flexible use of funds of these systems.

FROM SPECIALIZED TO PUBLIC TRANSIT

Public transit in large metro areas is oriented to the journey to work. Its radial route structure and severe peaks of ridership are characteristic of a system whose major function is to provide home to job transportation for commuters. Because the roots of most nonmetro transit were human service agencies, it has until recently served predominantly nonwork trips.

However, many nonmetro transit operators have been aware that this focus on nonwork trips and especially the orientation towards the transportation disadvantaged has had some negative consequences. Political officials at all levels of government have been reluctant to provide public funds for systems that were not available to the general public. Furthermore, one reason the ridership on these systems has been low is that passengers have been attracted from a small segment of the population.

Thus, the Section 147 and Section 18 programs have moved nonmetro transit toward a broader passenger base. Although these programs recognize that the transportation disadvantaged are a primary target of nonmetro transit, DOT has insisted that they also provide service for the general public. In the Section 147 demonstrations there was a clear

trend toward serving a larger proportion of work trips than
had been served by previous systems. As nonmetro transit
becomes an operating program under Section 18, it will
certainly be serving a broader clientele. This hopefully
will provide for more long-term viability for nonmetro
public transportation.

SCHOOL BUSES

During the planning of nonmetro transit systems, it is often
suggested that school buses be utilized for providing specialized transportation. These buses are idle during most of
the day, and thus would seem to be available to transport
elderly, handicapped, and other special population groups
when they are not in use for student transportation.

Although in some special situations this use of school
buses has been tried and proven successful, it is usually
not feasible. Availability, vehicle size, unsuitability for
use by elderly and handicapped, legal restrictions on use,
and problems with school and community officials are cited
(DOT, 1976: 14-15) as reasons why school buses have not
been utilized for nonmetro transit.

COORDINATION OF RURAL TRANSIT

Inventories of human service agency facilities have confirmed that there are a large number of agencies that
provide transportation for their clients. Nonmetro transit
has developed out of categorical grant programs, and therefore, the norm is that in any area the systems are overlapping, uncoordinated, and duplicative.

Laws affecting nonmetro transit are developed by many
different Congressional committees, and these various pieces
of legislation have not been coordinated to see that they
do not create overlapping programs or to ensure that they
allow for sufficient flexibility for consolidation when
advisable. Of course, this is not unique to the area of
transportation, as the interfacing of many federal social
service programs is made difficult by the uncoordinated
nature of the Congressional committee structure.

But recent studies (Cutler and Knapp 1979; U.S. General
Accounting Office 1977) have concluded that federal legis-
lation and regulations provide few barriers to coordination.
Arbitrarily restrictive interpretations and false percep-

tions of the legal barriers are cited as being problems
that inhibit local level attempts at coordination. There
are some barriers, but the fact that many areas have been
coordinated proves that these barriers are not insurmountable.

Policy deliberation on the coordination issue concentrates on economic efficiency improvements. Revis (1976)
suggests that it is axiomatic that cost savings will result
from coordination among transportation projects serving the
elderly, handicapped, and other disadvantaged persons.
However, these assumed net benefits have been questioned in
more recent studies. Ketola (1979) voiced concern that
agencies believed that simply agreeing to coordinate will
create new transportation funds. Burkhardt (1979) concludes
that it is in only very special circumstances that coordination costs less but that there are often substantial increases in the amount and quality of transportation services provided by a coordinated system.

Another view of efficiency is found in the guidelines
developed by Rosenbloom and Cox (1978) to aid agencies in
their evaluation of whether it is cost-effective to coordinate. Based on an analysis of social service agencies in
Texas, they conclude that the extent of transportation
needs will influence the preferred alternative. For less
than 350 client trips per month contracting with an alternative provider is probably most cost-effective whereas for
more than 500 monthly trips direct provision may be reasonable. For a demand between 350 and 500 trips per month all
options should be evaluated.

These authors note that costs as well as benefits will
result from a coordination effort. Agency directors will
have to consider more than the cost-effectiveness criteria
in deciding whether to provide direct transport service
conditions. Moreover, specific trip needs of clients will
often be more influential than relative costs in determining the alternative chosen by an agency (Rosenbloom and
Cox 1978).

TRANSPORTATION AND NONMETROPOLITAN DEVELOPMENT

Improved transportation facilities have played an important
role in enhancing the development potential for many communities seeking new industry. Although not a sole determinant
of industrial location, transportation for the movement of

goods and people is often a necessary ingredient in promoting economic growth.

Small community air service is considered important to attract and maintain business and industry. Several of the Regional Action Planning Commissions have taken an interest in retaining and improving air service to small communities. A study commissioned by the Old West Regional Commission found "Because of . . . large distances, the lack of alternative ground transportation modes, and winter weather factors, air service is not only desired but also often critically needed for business, medical, airline connection, shopping, and recreational travel purposes." (Aerospace Corporation, 1975: 5.) The region encompasses the sparsely settled states of Montana, Nebraska, North and South Dakota, and Wyoming.

Another study conducted for the Four Corners Regional Commission cited the importance of air service for the recreation and resort industries of New Mexico, Arizona, Utah, and Colorado (R. Dixon Speas Associates 1971). Because a number of retirement communities have also sprung up in those states, air service is important in providing convenient travel for older residents of outlying communities.

The widespread use for business purposes of scheduled air service, as well as general aviation, to and from non-metro communities further underscores the role of air transportation in economic development. For example, 3,000 manufacturing firms were surveyed to determine the importance of various community characteristics on industrial location (U.S. Economic Development Administration 1973), and scheduled air passenger service was found to be a critical factor to 12 percent of the respondents. Another 52 percent ranked it as significant. A survey of business and industry located in three nonmetro regions of Iowa (Iowa State University 1975) found that the personnel of the 171 respondents made an average of 18.6 business trips per month utilizing commercial airlines 11.3 percent of the time, company-owned or leased aircraft 1.4 percent, and chartered air service 0.7 percent. The bulk of travel was by private automobile. Thus, although additional research is needed on the relationship between small community air service and growth and development, it appears that this service plays an important role in industrial location decisions.

Highway development has been an important strategy for encouraging economic development in some nonmetro areas but has evoked considerable controversy among policymakers and planners. This debate has become especially important in

Appalachian states where the Appalachian Regional Commission has assisted the thirteen states in the region with the development of major highways to enhance Appalachia's economic potential.

Hansen (1973) has found that those nonmetro counties experiencing population growth in the 1950s and accelerated growth in the 1960s were likely to contain one or more highways. However, proximity of the counties to metro areas had a much greater effect on growth. Nonmetro counties experiencing population decline during the 1950s but pop- ulation growth during the 1960s had no advantage over other counties in terms of access to highways, suggesting the explanation for their population reversal is unrelated to the availability of major highways. Hansen (1973: 31) con- cludes, "Although no doubt there are isolated success stories, emphasis on the causal efficacy of highways with respect to development has diminished in favor of greater emphasis on their permissive role. This has been the case not only in the scholarly literature but also in some de- velopment programs, notably that for Appalachia." Obviously, highway development has had a major influence on settlement patterns, but its role in the development process remains a subject of policy debate.

PASSENGER TRANSPORTATION RESEARCH

There is an increasing awareness in the policy community that transportation policies, or the lack thereof, are re- emerging as dominant forces in shaping settlement patterns and directing economic activity. The energy situation has created a climate of uncertainty regarding the direction of transportation policies. Gasoline rationing, deregulation of passenger modes, transportation subsidies, and diversion of highway funds to public transportation are policy issues that are likely to have a direct impact on the mobility of rural citizens.

Ideally, policy decisions made during the 1980s and beyond should recognize the diversity of nonmetro America, address problems on a intermodal basis, and enhance the de- velopment and application of new and creative technologies. The realization of this scenario is doubtful not only be- cause the policymaking process lacks rationality but also because decisions made in this arena must be made in a virtual void of information. The challenge to policymakers lies not only in making important decisions but also in encouraging necessary research to lay the groundwork for intelligent decisions.

The research field of nonmetro passenger transportation is quite young. It was not until 1977 that a rural transportation committee was formed under the aegis of the Transportation Research Board, an organization affiliated with the National Academy of Sciences. Most of the research has been sponsored by either Congress or federal agencies, but the research that has been conducted has rarely examined topics on an intermodal basis. Similarly, passenger transportation's role in community development, economic development, and social service delivery has been widely recognized but poorly examined on a comprehensive basis.

The potential for productive research is virtually unlimited. For example, future policy research should address the degree to which commuting costs limit labor force participation by the poor. The impact of higher energy costs on the delivery of governmental and social services should be examined. The economic feasibility of providing intercity passenger service to small communities that have been abandoned should be explored as well as the potential trade-offs of subsidizing various intercity modes. In addition, the potential of substituting telecommunications such as teleconferencing, telehealth, and similar innovative applications of technology for personal travel should be studied in greater depth.

These and numerous other issues deserve attention from researchers interested in the future of nonmetro America. Applied research, which is of direct utility to planners and development practitioners, is also needed on a broader scale. If a balanced national transportation policy is to be forged, increased attention to nonmetro passenger transportation issues will be required from both researchers and policymakers.

BIBLIOGRAPHY

Aerospace Corporation. Old West Regional Commuter Air Service Feasibility Study, Summary Report. Old West Regional Commission. El Segundo, Calif., 1975.

American Bus Association. America's Number 1 Passenger Transportation Service. Washington, D.C., 1978.

Brown, David L. "Passenger Transportation in Nonmetropolitan

America." Paper prepared for the Economic Development
Division, ESCS (USDA), 1977.

Burkhardt, Jon E. "Coordinated Transportation Systems:
Potential Costs and Benefits." Paper presented at the
Fourth National Conference on Rural Public Transpor-
tation, Vail, Colo., June 1979.

_____ et al. A Study of the Transportation Problems
of the Rural Poor, vol. 1. Bethesda, Md.: Resource
Management Cooperation for the U.S. Office of Economic
Opportunity, 1972.

Cutler, Delores, and Knapp, Sue. Coordinating Transportation
Services for the Elderly and Handicapped: Executive
Summary. Prepared by Econometrics for the U.S. Depart-
ment of Transportation Office of Environment and
Safety. Washington, D.C., May 1979.

Hansen, Niles M. The Future of Nonmetropolitan America:
Studies in the Reversal of Rural and Small Town Population Decline. Lexington, Mass.: Lexington Books, 1973.

_____ . Improving Access to Economic Opportunity:
Nonmetropolitan Labor Markets in an Urban Society.
Cambridge, Mass.: Ballinger Publishing Co., 1976.

Hauser, E. W.; Martin, R. L.; Brooks, E. H.; Johnson, S. A.;
and MacGillivray, L. Use of Existing Facilities for
Transportation Disadvantaged Residents of Rural Areas.
Prepared for the U.S. Department of Transportation.
Washington, D.C., 1974.

Interstate Commerce Commission. The Intercity Bus Industry:
A Preliminary Study. Washington, D.C.: U.S. Government
Printing Office, 1978.

Iowa State University. Integrated Analysis of Small Cities
Intercity Transportation to Facilitate the Achievement
of Regional Urban Goals, Final Report. Prepared for the
U.S. Department of Transportation. Washington, D.C.,
1975.

Jackson, Arthur F., and McKelvey, Douglas J. An Inventory
of Transportation Services in Places of Less than Ten
Thousand Population Outside of Urbanized Areas. Prepared
for the U.S. Department of Transportation. Washington,
D.C., 1978.

Kaye, Ira. "Transportation Problems of the Older American
in Rural Areas," in Rural Development. A report printed
for use of the U.S. Senate Committee on Agriculture and
Forestry. Washington, D.C.: U.S. Government Printing
Office, 1972.

Ketola, Norman. "Assessing the Potential for Coordination,"
presented at the Fourth National Conference on Rural

Public Transportation, Vail, Colo., June 1979.

Kidder, Alice E. Accessibility of Passenger Transportation Facilities in Rural Areas of the United States. Transportation Institute, North Carolina A&T State University, Greensboro, N.C., 1979.

_____; Lalita, Sen; McKelvey, Douglas; Amedee, George. Costs of Alternative Systems to Serve Elderly and Handicapped in Small Urban Areas. Transportation Institute, North Carolina A&T State University, Greensboro, N.C., 1976.

National Transportation Policy Study Commission. National Transportation Policies Through the Year 2000. Washington, D.C.: U.S. Government Printing Office, 1979.

R. Dixon Speas Associates. Regional Air Transportation Study: The Demand for Scheduled Air Service 1971-79. Prepared for the Four Corners Regional Commission, 1971.

Revis, Joseph. Coordinating Transportation for the Elderly and Handicapped: A State of the Art Report. Prepared by the Institute of Public Administration for the U.S. Department of Transportation, Urban Mass Transportation Administration, Washington, D.C., November 1976.

_____. Transportation for the Elderly: The State of the Art. Prepared by the Institute of Public Administration for the Administration on Aging, Washington, D.C., 1975.

Rosenbloom, Sandra, and Cox, Walter. "Social Service Agencies Transportation Services in Texas: The Potential for Other Paratransit Modes." Presented at the Annual Meeting of the Transportation Research Board, Washington, D.C., January 1978.

Rupprecht, Erhard O. "Impacts of Energy Costs on Rural Mobility," in Proceedings of the National Symposium on Transportation for Agriculture and Rural America. Edited by John O. Gerald, et al. Washington, D.C., 1976.

Saltzman, Arthur. "Role of Paratransit in Rural Transportation." Paratransit. Proceedings of a Conference on Paratransit, Williamsburg, Va., November 1975. Special Report 164, Transportation Research Board, Washington, D.C., 1976.

Senate Committee on Agriculture and Forestry. Rural Development. Washington, D.C.: U.S. Government Printing Office, 1972.

_____. Transportation in Rural America: An Analysis of the Current Crisis in Rural Transportation, Part 2.

Prepared for the committee by the Economic Research
Service of the U.S. Department of Agriculture and the
National Area Development Institute. Washington, D.C.:
U.S. Government Printing Office, 1975.
Senate Committee on Commerce, Science and Transportation.
Intercity Bus Service in Small Communities. Washington,
D.C.: U.S. Government Printing Office, 1978.
_____. Intercity Domestic Transportation System for
Passenger and Freight. Prepared by Harbridge House,
Inc. Washington, D.C.: U.S. Government Printing Office,
1977.
Urban Institute. An Analysis of Road Expenditures and
Payments by Vehicle Class (1956-1975). Washington,
D.C., 1977.
U.S. Bureau of the Census. The Journey to Work in the
United States: 1975. Washington, D.C.: U.S. Government
Printing Office, 1979.
U.S. Department of Transportation. Final Report to Congress
on the Amtrak Route System. Washington, D.C., 1979.
_____. National Transportation Trends and Choices
(To the Year 2000). Washington, D.C.: U.S. Government
Printing Office, 1977.
_____. 1974 National Transportation Report: Current
Performance and Future Prospects. Washington, D.C.:
U.S. Government Printing Office, 1975.
_____. Preliminary Report to Congress on the Amtrak
Route System. Washington, D.C., 1978.
_____. Rural Passenger Transportation: State-of-the-
Art Overview. Transportation Systems Center. Cambridge,
Mass.: U.S. Department of Transportation,1976.
U.S. Economic Development Administration. "Industrial
Location Determinants, 1971-75." Washington, D.C.,
1979.
U.S. Federal Highway Administration, 1978 first quarter
profile of the Section 147 demonstration.
U.S. General Accounting Office. Hindrances to Coordinating
Transportation of People Participating in Federally
Funded Grant Programs. Vol. 1. Washington, D.C.,
October 1977.
White House Rural Development Initiatives. Improving
Transportation in Rural America. Washington, D.C.,
1979.

Irving Hoch

8
Energy and Location

INTRODUCTION

PURPOSE

It is a plausible and appealing hypothesis that higher
energy prices have considerable impact on geographic
distributions of population and economic activity. This
paper considers aspects of that basic hypothesis, focusing
particularly on nonmetro and rural impact. Some caveats
should be noted immediately. First, good data are sparse,
and probably even sparser than usual in social science
research. Second, the perception of energy price increases
tends to be exaggerated because deflation by an index of
the general price level is not always carried out; because
energy price controls have had some impact; and because
nonenergy margins (middlemen markups) can comprise a large
portion of the price facing the consumer. Finally, many
energy impacts seem only weakly related to geography. Thus,
responses to higher gasoline prices include: (1) mandated
increases in auto fuel efficiency; (2) a switch to smaller
cars; (3) carpooling; (4) less social-recreational travel;
(5) more work at home; and (6) reduction of distance
between residence and workplace, by changing one or both of
those locations. Only some of these items are strongly
related to geography, and their relative importance is not
obvious.

However, some recent changes at the regional level are
relatively easy to document, and seem to fit the hypothesis
of significant impacts on location from energy price
changes.

A consideration of the regional evidence will be followed by a discussion of rural and nonmetro impacts, first in

I benefited from constructive comments by Amos Hawley, Sara
Mazie, and Wilbur Zelinsky. John Mankin typed the several
drafts of the manuscript.

terms of consumption, and then of production. A concluding
section contains a summary of results and a brief consideration of major policy issues. There are two technical
appendixes. Appendix A applies economic theory to the
question of user responses to higher energy prices, while
Appendix B presents details on a statistical analysis of
impacts of energy production on producing county income and
population.

THE REGIONAL SETTING

It seems useful to consider likely regional impacts because
they furnish both background and consequences for energy
impacts at the local level. In this discussion, material
from three earlier papers is summarized (Hoch, 1978, 1980a,
1980b).

First, consider the annual growth rate of population,
r, for the 1970-72 period versus the 1972-77 period, as if
all changes in rate could be attributed solely to changes
in energy prices. Of course, this is a gross simplification,
because other underlying changes were at work, but it nevertheless seems to have merit in reflecting an underlying
reality. One forms (1+r) for each U.S. region, divides by
(1+r) for the U.S. as a whole, and obtains the growth
indicators in Table 8.1. A reading for index (3) of more
than 100 implies that the rate of growth rose in the later
period relative to the earlier, after accounting for the
national growth rate. Percentage changes in population over
the 1972-77 period, given the change in growth rate, appear
in column (4). Thus, New England's 1977 population was 2
percent below what it would have been if its 1970-72
relative growth rate had remained in effect from 1972 to
1977. Corresponding readings on indicator (4) for selected
states were:

Delaware	-5.8%	Alaska	+4.5%	California	+3.6%
Massachusetts	-2.3	Texas	+3.3	Florida	-4.1
New York	-1.9	Oklahoma	+1.6	Arizona	-8.7
Illinois	-0.3	Louisiana	+0.7	Colorado	-5.6
		Wyoming	+13.3		
		Montana	+0.7		

It seems reasonable to see an energy connection in these
indicators. Energy-producing states and regions should have

Table 8.1. Percentage Changes in Population, by Region, for 1972-1977

Region	(1) Index of Annual Growth (U.S.=100) $\frac{1+r(region)}{1+r(U.S.)}$ x 100 1970-72	(2) 1972-77	(3) $\frac{(2)}{(1)}$ x 100	(4) Percentage Change in Population, 1972-77, Given Change in Growth rate
New England	99.88	99.46	99.58	-2.0
Mid-Atlantic	99.34	98.93	99.59	-1.9
East North Central	99.44	99.36	99.92	-0.2
West North Central	99.68	99.55	99.87	-0.3
South Atlantic	100.78	100.68	99.90	-0.7
East South Central	100.13	100.24	100.11	+0.7
West South Central	100.47	100.89	100.42	+2.3
Rocky Mountain	102.30	101.68	99.39	-3.0
Far West	99.96	100.71	100.75	+3.6
United States	100.00	100.00	100.00	0.0

Source: Data from Hoch 1980b.

increased economic activity and population growth associated
with that production. On the consumption side, states and
regions faced with relatively high prices initially, or
that are heavily dependent on energy consumption, should be
adversely affected and tend to lose population. The indicators furnish support for these hypotheses. Major energy-
producing states generally had an increasing growth rate,
with maximum gains in the expanding production states of
Alaska and Wyoming. Eastern nonproducing regions and states
generally had declines in growth rate, with greatest percentage losses occurring along the Atlantic Coast, where
there is considerable reliance on oil in energy consumption.
Though the overall pattern involves some acceleration of
the Frostbelt to Sunbelt shift, this change is selective,
as can be seen in the case of California versus Florida and
Arizona. Consumers in the latter states are much more re-
liant on electricity for air conditioning than are those
in California, with its generally mild climate. The decline
in the Rocky Mountain regional growth rate seems explainable
as the consumption effect outweighing the production effect.
A decline in growth rate for Colorado, perhaps because of
inhibited tourism with higher energy prices, along with the
decline for Arizona, more than covered the increases in the
states involved in the western coal boom.

As a next step, the underlying energy parameters that
seem related to the observed population changes will be
examined, considering energy consumption and production, in
turn.

Consumption Impacts

Table 8.2 exhibits estimates of energy consumption in
physical terms (BTU) and in dollars, and price indexes for
energy, by region. Data appear for the household sector and
for all sectors of the economy, which includes government
and business, as well as households.

There is a general decline in energy use with movement
southwestward from New England, explainable primarily by
lower residential heating. This decline occurs despite a
general decline in price in the same geographic direction.
Hence, there is a reinforcement of quantity and price
differentials when expenditures are calculated.

Given higher energy prices, a fairly substantial new
differential emerges between high and low expenditure
states and regions. Thus, by rough estimate, between 1972
and 1979 per capita household energy costs in Massachusetts
increased by about $40 relative to those in California (in

Table 8.2. Energy Use in 1972

| Region | Household Use | | | All Sector Use | | |
| | Per Capita Consumption and Expenditures | | Price Indexes | Per Capita Consumption and Expenditures | | Price Indexes |
	Million BTU	$	U.S.=100	Million BTU	$	U.S.=100
New England	116.1	297.0	113.7	270.1	514.1	120.5
Mid-Atlantic	103.2	256.7	109.6	291.2	484.9	112.7
East North Central	112.5	256.6	97.4	369.4	512.6	100.9
West North Central	104.4	244.9	96.0	336.8	482.0	98.7
South Atlantic	82.4	238.1	101.4	299.8	480.2	101.0
East South Central	85.1	223.7	92.6	385.8	483.2	90.9
West South Central	88.6	222.9	89.5	565.4	519.3	82.6
Rocky Mountain	95.5	232.0	98.6	403.6	514.0	94.0
Far West	86.9	211.5	97.5	322.9	443.2	90.7
United States	97.7	243.0	100.0	351.5	490.1	100.0

Source: Hoch 1978.

1979 dollars). In turn, this amounts to about $125 per
household. Because these are annual amounts, they could be
capitalized by the household and treated as an offset to
the costs of moving from Massachusetts to California.
Capitalized value, at a "real" interest rate of 10 percent,
is $1,250; this would appear to be enough of a financial
incentive to cause a significant number of households to
move from Massachusetts to California. The addition of some
details can increase the plausibility of this behavioral
hypothesis. First, the financial incentive will be most
attractive and effective for those thinking of making the
move, in any event, for then it can tip the balance in
favor of migration. Second, although some households may
well go through an elaborate bookkeeping exercise in making
their location decisions, all we need assume is that prospective migrants have a general awareness that they will
be better off given the move, and enough better off so that
they expect to more than offset the various costs of
moving.

The scenario for nonhousehold use and impacts is not
so obvious, because low energy prices are associated (un-
surprisingly) with high energy use. A given percentage increase in energy prices should then mean a higher absolute
jump in energy prices in high price regions, but might also
involve a relatively greater increase in total energy costs
in low price regions. Hence, some observers have speculated
that regions with high energy prices will do well, given an
energy price increase, because they have historically econ-
omized on energy use. A counter speculation is that the
advantage resides with energy-producing regions.

An examination of the ratio of employment in manufactures to total population in 1977 relative to that ratio
in 1972 may be of some help in considering the question.
Results are shown in Table 8.3. Because the West South
Central and Rocky Mountain regions are major energy producers, there seems a strong suggestion here that manufacturing expansion is tied to availability of energy. The
"historically economizing" scenario receives some support
from the results for New England, however, suggesting that
reality may partake of both scenarios.

The question of consumption response to higher energy
prices merits a deeper theoretical probing than can be
attempted in this chapter. However, a modest application of
economic theory can yield some useful insights, which are
summarized here, whereas a technical statement of the
application appears as Appendix A.

Table 8.3. Ratio of Employment in Manufactures to
Total Employment for 1972 and 1977

Region	Change in Ratio of Employment in Manufactures to Population: 1977 Ratio Divided by 1972 Ratio
New England	1.0169
Mid-Atlantic	0.9428
East North Central	0.9977
West North Central	1.0525
South Atlantic	0.9599
East South Central	1.0092
West South Central	1.0829
Rocky Mountain	1.0323
Far West	1.0413
United States	0.9908

Source: Based on data in Hoch 1978.

    Given that energy is one of several inputs employed
("consumed") in producing a standardized output by the
typical firm in each of two regions, say that one wishes to
compare production between those regions, and determine how
production will respond to higher energy prices. The technical relationship describing how output is obtained from
inputs is labeled the production function, and for a "standard" form of that relationship (the Cobb-Douglas function),
the following conclusions hold.

    If both regions have the same production function,
then even with an initial energy price differential between regions, a given percentage energy price increase
will cause both regions to reduce output in the same proportion, so that the impact of an energy price increase
is neutral. In this case, if energy price initially is
lower in region I than in region II, region I will consume
more energy in physical terms (BTU) than region II, both
before and after the price change. However, the ratio of
expenditures on energy to revenue from sales of output will
be the same between regions; expenditures equals physical
use (BTU) times price per BTU, and region I's higher energy
quantity is in effect balanced by its lower price. The

expenditure ratio can be interpreted as a measure of energy dependence.

In contrast, if the regions have _different_ production functions, with region I more dependent on energy, as indicated by a higher expenditure ratio, than a given percentage energy price increase will cause a greater proportionate reduction in the output of region I than in that of region II. The higher the expenditure ratio, the greater the dependence, and the more adverse the impact of an energy price increase.

This theoretical development can have empirical payoff in terms of impact predictions if expenditure ratios can be observed in practice. Thus, returning to Table 8.1, if the theory is extended and household use of energy is treated as if it were part of a production process that produces household well-being, then one can infer that household dependence on energy, and potential adverse impacts from energy price increases, diminish with movement in a south-westward direction from New England. It is assumed here that _real_ income per capita corresponds to expenditures, and does not vary much between states. The question of industrial dependence and impacts could be addressed in similar fashion, given good estimates of energy expenditures and the value of output. The data on all sector use in Table 8.1, if combined with value of output data, could furnish a starting point. Those data suggest that regional industrial impacts tend to be neutral. The further development and application of such data should be a useful avenue of inquiry in impact analysis.

Production Impacts

On the production side, there has been considerable expansion in fuel extraction employment, wage rates, and earnings (labor and proprietor income) since 1972, as summarized by the data in Table 8.4. Those data also show the relatively small share of fuel extraction in all employment and income, amounting to roughly 1 percent of the total. Thus, labor and proprietor income as a percentage of the U.S. total increased from .0068 to .0124 between 1972 and 1977.

Even in major producing states, the fuel extraction share in state earnings is generally below 10 percent. However, a regression analysis comparing 1972 to 1975 per capita income changes between states yielded the inference that the expansion in the fuel extraction sectors has had considerable multiplier effects. In that period, per capita

Table 8.4. Expansion of Fuel Extraction Employment,
Wage Rates, and Earnings Since 1972

	1972	1977	1977/1972
U.S. employment in thousands			
Coal	159	240	1.51
Oil and gas	258	365	1.41
All other industries	71,931	78,903	1.10
Wage rates relative to U.S. average (U.S.=100)			
Coal	128	146	1.14
Oil and gas	125	144	1.15
Earnings in billions of dollars			
Coal	2.1	4.9	2.36
Oil and gas	3.0	9.5	3.21
All other industries	759.4	1,148.8	1.51

Source: Hoch 1980b.

incomes grew 4 percent more in major fuel producing states
than in the rest of the country, and more than one-half of
that gain appeared to involve the indirect impacts of
multiplier effects.

Fuel extraction is regionally specialized, as suggested
by Table 8.5 that lists the total of petroleum, natural gas
plus coal production, in trillion BTU and in million BTU,
per capita, by region for 1978.

In contrast to the growth in employment and earnings,
fuel extraction output has shown little total growth since
1972. In 1977, U.S. coal output was about 10 percent above
its 1972 level while oil and gas production were both
roughly 10 percent below their 1972 levels. Eastern coal
production showed little change, with almost all of the
increase in coal output attributable to western expansion.
Coal production by states west of the Mississippi amounted
to 10 percent of the United States total in 1972, to 25
percent in 1977, and to 28 percent in 1978. The switch to
western coal is not surprising because it is cheaper and
cleaner (lower sulfur content) than eastern. Most western
coal is strip-mined, and strip-mined coal typically is much
cheaper than that mined underground, making it competitive

Table 8.5. Fuel Extraction by Region for 1978

Region	Trillion BTU	Million BTU per Capita
New England	0.0	0.0
Mid-Atlantic	1,862.4	50.6
East North Central	3,269.7	79.3
West North Central	1,871.8	110.0
South Atlantic	3,140.5	90.8
East South Central	4,222.7	301.6
West South Central	26,862.1	1,218.5
Rocky Mountain	6,573.1	638.8
Far West	5,316.1	178.4
United States	53,118.9	243.6

Source: Hoch 1978.

even though its length of haul typically is much greater. However, that competitive position shows some signs of erosion by increased railroad rates.[1] Around 1975, the transportation share of delivered coal prices was roughly 25 percent for eastern coal and as much as 75 percent for western coal. Since then, the Interstate Commerce Commission has allowed railroads hauling western coal to increase their rates substantially, almost doubling the charge per ton on coal hauled from Gillette, Wyoming to San Antonio, Texas. The Congress has rejected "eminent domain" legislation that would enable coal slurry lines to compete with the railroads, though there are predictions that such lines eventually will be built.

The Clean Air Act amendments of 1977 involved a tilt toward eastern coal, by imposing a uniform percentage reduction in sulfur emissions; an explicit argument for that feature was that it would help protect eastern jobs from western competition. In conjunction with the rail rate increases, this may help slow the trend to western coal, but the trend seems unlikely to be reversed or stopped.

A likely factor in the shift to western coal is an avoidance of union power, because most western operations are nonunionized, and the United Mine Workers has not been very successful in organizing the western coal mines. The unionized share of coal output has dropped from 67 percent in 1974 to 52 percent in 1979 (Wall Street Journal, 18 Oct. 1979). Unionized eastern coal companies pay a considerable amount in pensions and health benefits to 80,000 retirees, which amounts to several thousand dollars per year for each of the 180,000 active miners; nonunionized western coal companies have few retirees, and so can afford to pay higher wage rates than the eastern companies, and yet have lower labor costs per worker (Business Week, 24 Sept., p. 109). The eastern retirement benefit burden is likely to grow in the future, which in turn may put additional pressure on a slowly growing or even contracting eastern industry, perhaps eventually putting the retirement benefits in jeopardy. A national welfare problem could be in the making.

Shifting the focus to oil and gas, it was noted that employment has increased though output has declined. This could be interpreted as a sign of depletion of resources; alternatively, the decline in output may reflect price controls on "old" output, whereas the increase in employment reflects exploration and development of "new" output, which usually involves a considerable lag before production comes on stream. Again, some of the decline in oil production is now being offset by increased Alaskan output. Further, if price controls on both oil and gas are actually phased out by 1981 for oil and 1985 for gas (despite the doubts of some observers, e.g., Wright 1979), then at least some expansion in gas and oil production should occur, though a high enough excess profits tax can be as inhibiting to supply as price controls.

Finally, considerable expansion of output and employment may occur through synthetic fuel development involving coal gasification and liquefaction, and shale oil extraction and processing.

The ultimate impact appears to be a much greater impetus to Rocky Mountain employment and population growth than has occurred and will occur elsewhere. Coal extraction employment has tripled in Montana and Wyoming since 1972, and increased by only 20 to 40 percent in West Virginia, Kentucky, and Pennsylvania. Conventional oil and gas reserves are estimated to be distributed about equally among Alaskan, offshore, and continental United States fields (Schurr et al., 1979: 230); much of the latter reserves appear to be in the Rocky Mountain "overthrust belt" (Wall Street Journal, 27 Aug. 1979). And, of course, shale oil is a Rocky Mountain resource. There are qualifiers, which suggest some growth elsewhere, as well: expansion could occur in Texas and Louisiana with the elimination of price controls; there is some potential for offshore production on the East Coast; and a number of "unconventional" resources, such as heavy oil in California, may yield considerable increments of output.

Given the sparse population of the Rocky Mountain region, and the tendency of fuel extraction to take place in nonmetro areas, a considerable impetus to nonmetro growth has occurred and should continue. However, given the evidence on Rocky Mountain growth in the 1972–77 period, a final caution must be noted. It seems likely that growth will be selective and concentrated in major energy-producing localities and states.

RURAL AND NONMETROPOLITAN CONSUMPTION

This section reviews rural and nonmetro energy consumption in some detail, first considering overall patterns and then focusing on specific forms of consumption. Unless otherwise noted, standard definitions are employed for geographic areas; thus, "metro" refers to the SMSA or Standard Metropolitan Statistical Area.

A useful table showing household energy consumption expenditures by locale was compiled by Wilbur Zelinsky from the 1972–73 Bureau of Labor Statistics Consumer Expenditure Survey, and is presented here as Table 8.6. The table shows rural expenditures exceeding urban for both metro and nonmetro populations. This pattern also holds for the subcategories of consumption that are labeled "household" energy (for residential use) and travel energy. Further, when energy expenditures are expressed as a fraction of total expenditures, the nonmetro fraction exceeds the metro for all corresponding cases (total, urban, and rural).

On the basis of this evidence, it might be inferred that increased energy prices have a stronger negative impact on rural than on urban residents, and on nonmetro than on metro residents. That conclusion would follow from the argument developed above that the impact of changes in energy price is a function of energy dependence.

However, caution must be exercised in drawing that inference. First, "direct expenditures" omits such "indirect" items as spending on public transportation, taxis, rental cars, rail and air fares; it also tends to exclude heating and utility costs paid for by landlords rather than by

Table 8.6. Mean Annual Direct Expenditures On Energy, per Family, by Type of Area, 1972 to 1973

	All Families	Inside SMSAs					Outside SMSAs		
		Total	Total Urban	Central City Urban	Other Urban	Rural	Total	Urban	Rural
	$	$	$	$	$	$	$	$	$
Gas, total	92.86	91.37	91.20	86.69	95.93	92.89	96.33	98.72	94.54
Delivered in mains	77.64	85.02	88.74	85.31	92.35	53.47	60.47	90.44	38.16
Bottled or tank	15.22	6.35	2.46	1.38	3.59	39.42	35.85	8.28	56.38
Electricity	156.80	146.36	137.44	118.63	157.24	222.08	181.08	152.93	202.04
Gas & electricity, combined bills	40.47	50.35	52.53	46.43	58.95	31.87	17.47	29.33	8.65
Fuel oil & kerosene	51.19	44.98	38.76	25.59	52.61	97.84	65.63	43.44	82.14
Other fuels, coal & wood	4.97	3.15	2.61	1.89	3.37	7.71	9.19	5.05	12.28
Total: Household energy	439.15	427.58	413.74	365.93	464.04	545.28	466.02	428.19	494.19
Gasoline & other vehicular fuels	347.61	340.92	324.91	269.80	382.90	476.82	363.20	318.41	396.55
Gasoline purchased on vacation & pleasure trips	32.03	32.41	31.81	26.45	37.45	37.51	31.14	34.43	28.70
Total: Travel energy	379.64	373.33	356.72	296.25	420.35	514.33	394.34	352.84	425.25
Total energy expenditures	818.79	800.91	770.46	662.18	884.39	1,059.61	860.36	781.03	919.44
Total current consumption expenditures	8,270.48	8,769.36	8,731.63	7,779.79	9,747.68	9,089.73	7,119.00	7,225.34	7,038.16
Energy expenditures as % of total expenditures	9.90%	9.13%	8.82%	8.51%	9.07%	11.66%	12.09%	10.81%	13.06%

Source: Compiled by Wilbur Zelinsky from data in Bureau of Labor Statistics, Consumer Expenditure Survey: 1972-73 (1978).

tenants. Spending on all of these expenditure items can be
expected to be greater in urban than in rural areas, and
similarly, of course, in metro than in nonmetro areas.
Accounting for these factors would, at least, narrow the
observed differentials. Evidence on recent residential
energy use, presented below, shows landlord-borne costs are
quite significant.

Second, as hinted at earlier, it may be expedient to
distinguish between money versus "real" income and expenditures. There is considerable evidence that wage rates for
the same work increase with population size of settlement
(e.g., Fuchs 1959; Alonso 1971; Hoch 1972 and 1976; Izraeli
1973; and Danziger 1976). A major part of the increase can
be accounted for by increases in the cost of living, as
measured by the conventional market basket index. Thus,
roughly a 9 percent increase has been estimated in wage
rates per order of magnitude of population for performing
the same work; for example, if a place of one hundred
thousand population paid $10.00 per hour for a given job, a
place of one million population would pay $10.90 per hour
for the same job. About one-half the increase with population size can be accounted for by increases in the cost of
living. There is also evidence that these money wage
differentials hold for nonmetro populations and for rural
occupations (Hoch 1979). Further, the cost-of-living effect
varies among commodities (Hoch 1972; Izraeli 1973). This
can be viewed as a variant of Tolley's distinction (1969)
between local goods (with a local price level) and national
goods (with price set nationally). In particular, gasoline
prices tend to be fairly uniform among regions of the
country, and there is evidence that prices are essentially
invariant between SMSAs and contiguous nonmetro counties
(Foster Associates 1974). Prices for other sources of
energy show marked regional variation but little variation
by size of place. (More detail on prices appears at several
points, below.) The upshot of the argument is that if both
energy and expenditures are deflated, the latter is likely
to deflate more with settlement size than the former, again
reducing the urban-rural and SMSA-nonSMSA differentials
observed in Zelinsky's compilation. Though the wage and
cost-of-living differential is subject to controversy and
differences of interpretation (e.g., Alonso 1976), it can
be useful in future work aimed at refining energy-expendi-
ture ratios.

The question of likely location impacts of higher energy
prices will be explored in detail by considering local

transportation, focusing on the journey to work; residential
use of energy; nonhousehold use of energy, including agricultural and industrial use; and outdoor recreation dependent on long-distance travel. The section concludes
with some speculation on the relations among energy price
increases, inflation, and location impacts.

TRANSPORTATION

Several writers (Beale 1978; Doherty 1979; and Pierce 1979)
note the heavier reliance of rural than of urban residents
on cars (and trucks), and suggest that this can have an
adverse or limiting effect on rural growth, and conversely,
that rural growth will imply more pressure on energy supplies. Documentation on that greater reliance shows that
rural residents make more passenger car trips and travel
more miles per trip than do their urban counterparts, so
that car travel of the rural household is about 40 percent
higher than that of the urban household (from Federal
Highway Administration data cited in Shonka, Loebl, and
Patterson, 1977, p. 10). Here "rural" refers to unincorporated places, and "urban" to incorporated. Additional
comparisons, from the same source, are presented in Table
8.7.
    A fairly obvious difficulty in the comparisons here is
that mass transit and taxi trips are excluded, perhaps on
the grounds they are purchased services, so the energy use
involved is "indirect." Of course, transit tends to be a
metro service, and so metro energy use tends to be understated. Mass transit is subsidized, and higher energy costs
may not get passed along immediately or fully to the transit
passenger. A case might be made that there is an urban net
benefit on those grounds, but the central argument seems at
least somewhat questionable because of the omission of the
transit energy component.
    Work-related trips account for about 40 percent of both
urban and rural trip making in the comparisons above, with
family business, social-recreation, and education, civic,
and religious trips accounting for the remainder. Because
there is little discretion in choosing to make work trips,
they are likely to be more important than nonwork trips in
the perceived impact of higher energy prices. Some detailed
information is available on metro versus nonmetro work
trips, and it turns out that differences between SMSA and
nonSMSA are relatively minor, at least in terms of averages.

Table 8.7. Comparison Between Urban and Rural
Passenger Car Transportation

	Urban	Rural	Rural Divided by Urban
Average trip length, in miles	8.4	9.8	1.17
Average work-related trip length, in miles	9.5	11.5	1.21
Annual number of trips	1,321	1,568	1.19
Vehicle miles per year	11,105	15,387	1.39

Table 8.8 shows the percentage distribution of work trips
by transportation mode, and it can be seen that commuting
by automobile or truck accounts for roughly 85 percent of
work trips both for the nonmetro and the "all SMSA" categories. The larger percentage relying on transit in SMSAs
is almost balanced by greater percentages working at home
and walking to work in nonSMSAs. (Many of those working at
home are engaged in farming.)

Table 8.9 presents distributions of distance and travel
time in the journey to work of household heads, as of 1976.
It turns out that nonSMSA residents had shorter trip
lengths and travel time, on average, than SMSA residents,
as a whole, though the nonSMSA trip length did exceed that
of the central city residents. However, the nonmetro
distribution is higher at the extremes than the metro, with
greater percentages making very short trips (less than four
miles, or working at home) or very long trips (more than
thirty miles).

Bowles and Beale (1980) present similar distributions
for household heads as of 1975; and reach similar conclusions. Employing their data[2] and those of Table 8.9 these
comparisons, presented in Table 8.10, are obtained.

The percentages for the long trips suggest that for
those making such trips, the typical nonSMSA resident
travels a longer distance, but at higher speeds than does
his SMSA counterpart, presumably because of more highway
driving, with less congestion and "stop and go" traffic.
For the very long trip distances of thirty miles and over,

Table 8.8. Transportation Mode to Work, by Residence, 1975

Principal Mode of Transportation	Residence of Workers			
	SMSAs		All SMSA	Nonmetro Areas
	Central City	Noncen- tral City		
	%	%	%	%
Working at home	1.6	2.2	2.0	6.1
Commuting by:				
Auto or truck	77.2	88.6	84.0	86.6
Public transit	13.9	4.4	8.3	0.8
Walking	6.0	3.4	4.4	5.2
Other	1.3	1.4	1.3	1.3
Total	100.0	100.0	100.0	100.0

Source: Journey to work survey for DOT, collected as supplement to Annual Housing Survey by Bureau of Census for HUD, 1975, as reported in Diane N. Westcott, "Employment and Commuting Patterns," Monthly Labor Review, July 1979, p. 8, and U.S. Bureau of the Census, Current Population Reports, "The Journey to Work," series P-23, no. 99, 1979.

the nonSMSA versus SMSA percentages were approximately 8 percent and 5 percent, respectively, in both years.

Bowles and Beale present data on "commuters," defined as persons who live in one county and work in another. For commuters, some comparisons of note are presented in Table 8.11. The higher percentages for long-distance trips in nonSMSAs than in SMSAs can be viewed as a source of vulnerability to higher energy prices, particularly if long-distance commuters have limited alternative job opportunities. But in practice, there must be a narrower difference in gasoline consumption because of differences in driving conditions that make miles per gallon higher for nonSMSA than for SMSA commuters.

Some additional sets of data can be of help in the transportation comparisons. Thus, a Gallup Poll taken in February 1979 measured public perceptions of the energy problem almost exclusively in terms of attitudes on policies affecting gasoline consumption, and the poll results can be used to draw inferences on the impacts of higher gasoline prices. Table 8.12 presents the poll results

Table 8.9. Information on Journey to Work of Heads of Households, 1976

Distance and Time	Assumed Class Averages	Total U.S.	Inside SMSAs In Central Cities	Inside SMSAs Not in Central Cities	Total SMSAs	Out- side SMSAs
One way distance	Miles	%	%	%	%	%
Works at home	0.0	2.6	1.1	1.6	1.4	5.4
< 1 mile	0.6	8.2	7.5	5.1	6.1	13.1
1-4 miles	2.0	26.4	32.9	20.5	25.7	27.9
5-9 miles	6.5	17.4	21.8	18.0	19.6	12.3
10-29 miles	18.0	27.1	23.4	35.4	30.4	19.7
30-49 miles	36.0	4.2	1.7	5.0	3.6	5.4
> 50 miles	60.0	1.3	0.6	1.1	0.9	2.4
No fixed place of work	-	11.2	9.2	12.0	10.8	12.0
Not reported	-	1.6	1.8	1.2	1.5	1.7
Total[a]		100.0	100.0	100.0	100.0	100.0
Travel time	Minutes	%	%	%	%	%
Works at home	0.0	2.6	1.1	1.6	1.4	5.4
< 15 minutes	9.0	31.3	29.4	25.6	27.4	40.6
15-29 minutes	22.5	30.7	36.4	32.9	34.2	22.6
30-44 minutes	36.0	13.7	13.8	16.7	15.5	9.7
45-59 minutes	50.0	4.8	4.6	5.7	5.2	3.8
60-89 minutes	70.0	3.4	3.5	3.7	3.6	3.0
> 90 minutes	110.0	1.0	1.0	0.9	1.0	1.2
No fixed place of work	-	11.2	9.2	12.0	10.8	12.0
Not reported	-	1.2	1.0	1.1	1.0	1.6
Total[a]		100.0	100.0	100.0	100.0	100.0
Weighted average						
Miles		10.18	8.21	12.05	10.41	9.71
Minutes		23.55	24.33	25.55	25.02	20.36

Source: Motor Vehicle Manufacturers Association, 1979, p. 53; original data from U.S. Bureau of the Census, Current Housing Reports, Annual Housing Survey 1976.

Note: Weighted averages from preceding data in table. Class averages for miles and for minutes assumed to differ somewhat from midpoint of range, based upon experience with similar distributions, e.g., income distributions. This assumption does not greatly affect estimates.

[a]Actual totals may differ slightly from 100.0 because of rounding.

Table 8.10. Comparison Between SMSA and NonSMSA Travel, 1975 and 1976

	1975		1976	
	SMSA	Non-SMSA	SMSA	Non-SMSA
Average distance, miles	10.1	8.6	10.4	9.7
Average time, minutes	25.1	19.4	25.0	20.4
Trips 30 miles and more, as percentage of all trips	5.5	7.5	4.5	7.8
Trips 45 minutes and more, as percentage of all trips	11.7	8.5	9.8	8.0
Trips 60 minutes and more, as percentage of all trips	5.3	4.6	4.6	4.2

Table 8.11. Comparison Between SMSA and NonSMSA Commuters

	SMSA	NonSMSA
Commuting as percentage of all work trips	22.7	19.5
Trips 30 miles and more as percentage of all commuter trips	19.3	34.4
Trips 60 minutes and more as percentage of all commuter trips	17.5	20.6

obtained for settlement size categories (labeled "city size" in the Gallup Report), whereas Table 8.13 attempts to summarize the information, by presenting aggregated measures of responses in index form, relative to a national response pattern defined as 100.

Identifying the nonmetro population as more or less coincident with the two smallest population size categories, the following conclusions can be based on Tables 8.12 and 8.13. It must first be noted that there seems basic agree-

Table 8.12. Poll Results of Public Views on Energy,
by Settlement Size, 23–26 February 1979

Public Opinion Question and Possible Responses	Settlement Size (City Size) Population in 000s					
	National	>1,000	500–<1,000	50–<500	2.5–<50	<2.5–Rural
	%	%	%	%	%	%
Seriousness of energy crisis						
Very serious	43	44	49	42	42	40
Fairly serious	42	40	40	42	42	45
Not at all serious	13	14	10	14	14	14
No opinion	2	2	1	2	2	1
Likelihood of gasoline shortage						
Very likely	34	33	41	30	32	36
Fairly likely	40	39	37	41	41	41
Not too likely	17	18	16	16	16	17
Not at all likely	5	5	4	6	7	3
No opinion	4	5	2	7	4	3
On keeping 55 mph speed limit						
Favor	71	67	74	71	70	72
Oppose	26	28	23	26	28	25
No opinion	3	5	3	3	2	3
On raising limit to 65 mph						
Favor	34	33	31	34	39	32
Oppose	62	58	68	63	58	65
No opinion	4	9	1	3	3	3
On lowering limit to 50 mph						
Favor	9	11	9	11	5	7
Oppose	87	80	88	86	93	89
No opinion	4	9	3	3	2	4
On a gasoline rationing law to require one-fourth less driving						
Favor	40	41	47	41	38	38
Oppose	52	51	46	51	57	52
No opinion	8	8	7	8	5	10

Source: The Gallup Opinion Index, pp. 14–16, 18–20.

Table 8.13. Poll Results in Index Form

Public Opinion Question and Explanation of Scoring	Settlement Size (City Size) Population in 000s				
	>1,000	500- <1,000	50- <500	2.5- <50	<2.5- Rural
	Estimated indexes, national = 100				
Seriousness of energy crisis.					
Higher score = more serious	98	116	96	96	95
Likelihood of gasoline shortage.					
Higher score = greater likelihood	96	114	92	94	109
On 55 mph limit. Higher score = greater agreement with majority opinion					
Keep as is	94	106	100	97	102
Oppose raising limit	97	109	101	91	105
Oppose lowering limit to 50 mph	91	101	97	110	104
Oppose gasoline rationing law.					
Higher score = greater agreement with majority opinion	98	87	98	107	102

Source: Table 8.12. For the first question, the responses (in order) were weighted +2, +1, -2, and 0. For the second question, the responses (in order were weighted +2, +1, -1, -2, and 0. For the last set of questions a response obtaining a majority vote was assigned a weight of +1, and the minority vote response was assigned a weight of -1. Then differences from the corresponding national percentages were obtained and multiplied by the weights. Finally, these products were summed and added to 100. For example, consider size group ">1,000" and question "on 55 mph limit, keep as is." From Table 8.12, we subtract the national percent responses from the group responses to obtain: 67-71 = -4, and -28-(-26) = -2; then 100+(-4-2) = 94, which is entered in the table, above. A higher score than 100 is interpreted as greater support than held nationally for the position receiving the majority of responses, and a lower score as indicating less support than held nationally.

ment on all the questions, across categories; this holds for all other classifications, as well (education, income, sex, politics, region, etc.). Hence, the following differences in pattern are not particularly pronounced and seem to involve slight shifts within an overall consensus. The nonmetro population perceives the energy crisis as somewhat less serious than does the metro. Somewhat surprisingly, the most concerned group was the population in middle-sized cities (one-half million to one million population). That

group's concern translated into the highest perceived likelihood of another gasoline shortage (which was rather pre-
scient before the spring of 1979); a greater satisfaction
with the 55 mph speed limit than expressed by the other
groups, and a greater willingness to lower that limit; and
a greater inclination to accept gasoline rationing. Although
the two small-size population groups were least exercised
about the energy crisis, and were most strongly opposed to
gasoline rationing, they showed some divergence on other
questions. Relative to the national pattern of response,
the smallest size group, which includes the rural population,
saw another gasoline shortage as more likely and expressed
greater acceptance of the 55 mph limit; the small city
group differed from the national pattern in the opposite
direction.

Inferences must be highly speculative, of course, but
it appears that perceived negative impacts of higher energy
price on consumers are distributed in fairly uniform fashion, by settlement size. The greater concern of the middle-
size city group suggests a somewhat more adverse impact in
such places, perhaps because of a combination of limited
reliance on mass transit and a relatively long work trip.
(There is considerable evidence that both time and distance
of the journey to work increase with size of place.) In
contrast, consumers in smaller places appear to be doing as
well as, or better than, their metro counterparts.

The attitudes on lowering versus raising the speed
limit should reflect the amounts of high-speed travel by
the respondents on rural highways or urban freeways, plus
their rough calculation of additional time costs versus
accident reduction benefits of the lower speed limit.

Highway fatality rates (deaths per 100 million vehicle
miles) have been reduced considerably since 1972, probably
in large part because of the 55 mph limit imposed to save
gasoline. It seems clear that rural areas have had more of
a reduction than urban, on the basis of the following ratios
of 1976 to 1972 highway fatality rates presented in Table
8.14 (Motor Vehicle Manufacturers Association, 1977 and
1979). Of course, the travel of urban and rural residents
is not limited to the roads in their respective areas;
however, it seems plausible that the benefits of accident
reduction have been greater for rural than for urban
residents, because considerable correlation is to be
expected between location of travel and residence.

Considered in concert, the evidence of this section
yields a more complex set of inferences than the initial

Table 8.14. Ratio of Urban to Rural Highway Fatality Rates

	Rural Areas	Urban Areas
Total, all systems	0.73	0.81
Interstate system	0.55	0.61
Local roads and streets	0.80	0.92

notion that rural areas are more disadvantaged than urban by higher energy prices. From that evidence, it appears that nonSMSA small-city residents as a group suffer least from higher gasoline prices; that nonSMSA rural and SMSA central-city residents follow in order of distress; and that SMSA suburban and SMSA rural residents are most disadvantaged by higher gasoline prices.

There is some additional support for this ordering when we consider the workings of the federal gasoline allocation system and the gasoline lines that occurred both in the 1973-74 period and in 1979. In both cases, the lines were essentially a metro phenomenon, for nonmetro areas were generally well-supplied. In the allocation system, farmers have priority in access to supplies, as do rural jobbers claiming to serve farmers (New York Times, 30 June 1979; Washington Post, 10 June 1979 and 3 July 1979). In 1974, John Sawhill, then deputy administrator of the Federal Energy Office, testified before a subcommittee of the Joint Economic Committee that federal gasoline regulations meant that "Farmers get 100 percent of their current needs, period. In other words, they get all they want." He added: "We have got to serve rural America. Our no. 1 priority is to provide sufficient fuel that will be consistent. . .with the demands we are making on our farmers." (U.S. Joint Economic Committee, 1974: 73, 74.) Justifications for this priority include the rationalizations that agricultural production is particularly vulnerable to fuel shortfalls, and that farm products are especially important in foreign trade. Current policy is to give precedence and priority to both agricultural areas and predominantly rural states, on the explicit argument that residents are more dependent on the automobile (Executive Office of the President, 1979: 5).

Of course, future supply interruptions or gas lines

Table 8.15. Place of Residence by Place of Work for Workers Using Vehicles in the Journey to Work

Number of workers, in 000s[b]

Place of Residence	Place of Work 1970				Place of Work 1975			
	Central Cities	Suburbs and Other SMSAs[a]	Non-metro	All Locales	Central Cities	Suburbs and Other SMSAs[a]	Non-metro	All Locales
Metropolitan								
Central cities	16,093	3,951	200	20,244	14,704	4,198	267	19,169
Suburbs	8,485	15,466	465	24,416	8,909	18,207	687	27,803
Nonmetropolitan	861	810	15,448	17,119	987	1,079	17,493	19,559
All locales	25,439	20,227	16,113	61,779	24,600	23,484	18,447	66,531

Source: Data from U.S. Bureau of the Census, Current Population Reports, "The Journey to Work," series P-23, no. 99, 1979.

aWorking in another SMSA than SMSA of residence.

bBased on sample data expanded to estimate entire population. Excludes workers with no fixed place of work, and workers who did not report a place of work. The 1970 data cover workers 16 years old and more; 1975 data cover workers 14 years old and more.

Table 8.16. Rural Turnaround Between 1970 and 1975

| | 1975/1970 | |
	Residence	Place of Work
Metro		
Central cities	0.947	0.967
Suburbs	1.139	1.161
Nonmetro	1.143	1.145
All	1.079	1.079

Table 8.17. Percentage Distributions of Nonmetropolitan Workers' Residences and Place of Work, 1970 and 1975

| | Where Nonmetro Residents Worked | | Where Nonmetro Workers Resided | |
	1970	1975	1970	1975
	%	%	%	%
In central cities	5.03	5.05	1.24	1.45
In suburbs	4.73	5.52	2.89	3.72
In nonmetro areas	90.24	89.44	95.87	94.83

are likely to lead to a coupon rationing system, and then the rural advantage should be reduced, if not eliminated.

In this discussion, location categories have been treated as distinct and separate, but overlap (by way of transportation) is exhibited when there is a cross-classification of place of residence by place of work, as shown in Table 8.15. (Coverage in Table 8.15 is limited to workers using vehicles in the journey to work, including public transportation.)

Table 8.15 is useful not only in showing that some metro residents work in nonmetro places (and vice versa), but also in exhibiting some important shifts between 1970 and 1975. Thus, the following population ratios, which exhibit the rural turnaround, can be derived, as shown in Table 8.16.

Again, consider Table 8.17 that shows percentage distributions indicating where nonmetro residents worked and
resided.

Wardwell and Gilchrist (1979) suggest that higher energy
prices mean that the friction of space will increase, in
turn implying system contraction and reconcentration of
activities in spatial terms. A plausible corollary is that
metro-nonmetro interactions should decline; yet the percentage distributions shown above indicate the opposite, at
least in terms of the work force. Admittedly, it is possible
there was a peaking of this trend between 1970 and 1975, or
that there will be a trend reverssal post-1975. Later data
should be applied to this question.

In metro areas, the spatial impacts of higher transportation costs can be expected to increase density of settlement, though this can occur in several ways, including
greater centrality or greater clustering at nodes of development in the suburbs ("multinucleation"). Presumably, there
will be nonmetro analogues--for example, more concentration
in a smaller number of small towns that would otherwise
occur. In all cases, the processes will probably be rather
slow moving and long term, given the long life of infrastructure (water systems, streets and roads, etc.). Further,
transportation effects will occur by way of commercial as
well as personal transport, though very little evidence
appears available on the former. The National Transportation Policy Study Commission (1979: 164) presents some
rough estimates of local goods movement by truck in urban
versus rural areas, and the estimated levels of ton-miles
are approximately proportional to population levels, perhaps indicating similar levels of energy dependence for
that form of transportation. Turning to "external" transport, we can speculate that some withering of prospects
will occur for isolated communities located at a considerable remove from sources of supply or trade, and that some
communities could be hurt by a general reduction in access
if there are cutbacks in rail, air, or trucking services as
a response to higher energy prices. In considering this
speculation, note a distinction between small size and
isolation, as well as between local, primarily personal
transport and "external" transport. Small places are not
necessarily isolated, though there may be some correlation
between those characteristics; and benefits to some small
towns of short journeys to work can be negated by costs of
a long haul for supplies coming in or for shipments going
out. The strength of these respective factors will vary

from place to place, and hence, how they vary should be an important topic for future research.

RESIDENTIAL USE OF ENERGY

Table 8.18 presents data on residential energy use per household in the 1978-79 period, comparing both urban to rural use, and SMSA to nonSMSA use.

Table 8.18 shows more energy use, in BTU, for urban than for rural households, and for SMSA than for nonSMSA households. A similar pattern holds for SMSA versus nonSMSA expenditures, but rural spending exceeds urban. The remainder of the table makes clear why rural expenditures exceed urban, though usage is lower. In all areas, natural gas is the cheapest fuel, by far, and its share of total fuel use is much higher in urban than in rural areas, but only somewhat higher in SMSAs than in nonSMSAs. Note the 10 percent share devoted to liquid petroleum gas (LPG) in rural areas versus the roughly 1 percent in the other areas, and the much higher price for LPG than for piped natural gas. Clearly, access to natural gas lines is much more limited for rural than for nonSMSA residents. Presumably, residents of small cities are relatively well supplied with natural gas.

Table 8.6, above, contains information on SMSA and nonSMSA residential use of energy, as of the 1972-73 period. If corresponding entries in that table are scaled to 1978 dollars, the following comparisons, illustrated in Table 8.19, can be made to the data of Table 8.18.

The increase in SMSA spending is considerably above that for nonSMSA use. However, it is likely that this difference is more apparent than real, because the 1978-79 estimates contain imputed energy costs paid for by landlords rather than tenants (U.S. Energy Information Administration, 1980: 184), and the 1972-73 estimates do not. Hence, it seems quite possible that accounting for landlord payments would make the 1972-73 pattern consistent with the 1978-79 pattern, so that SMSA expenditures would exceed those for nonSMSAs in both cases. This inference receives some confirmation when Table 8.6 expenditures for rural areas within SMSAs ($791) are compared to those within nonSMSAs ($717), again presented in terms of 1978 dollars. Presumably, landlord payments for energy are minor in both cases.

A caution must be noted in these comparisons. They are

Table 8.18. Information on Residential Energy Use
by Locale, 1978-1979

Category of Use	Urban	Rural	SMSA	NonSMSA
Fuel use per household in million BTU, all fuels	141.4	127.8	142.0	129.1
Expenditures on fuels, per household	$715.9	$747.7	$733.5	$704.4
Percentage distribution of BTU used				
Natural gas	60.1	29.3	56.7	43.9
Electricity	20.1	33.8	20.4	30.2
Fuel oil and kerosene	19.0	26.5	21.4	19.2
Liquid petroleum gas	0.8	10.4	1.5	6.7
	100.0	100.0	100.0	100.0
Percentage distribution of expenditures				
Natural gas	32.9	13.0	30.5	21.2
Electricity	51.4	60.6	51.3	59.3
Fuel oil and kerosene	14.8	17.6	16.5	13.6
Liquid petroleum gas	0.9	8.8	1.7	5.9
	100.0	100.0	100.0	100.0
Energy prices--dollars per million BTU[a]				
All fuels	5.06	5.85	5.16	5.46
Natural gas	2.76	2.60	2.78	2.64
Electricity	12.95	10.50	13.01	10.71
Fuel oil and kerosene	3.96	3.88	3.97	3.86
Liquid petroleum gas	5.87	4.91	5.69	4.79

Source: U.S. Energy Information Administration.

[a]Obtained by dividing total expenditures by total BTU
consumed.

averages over broad categories, without controlling for
other sources of variation in energy use. In particular,
the higher energy quantities consumed in urban than in
rural areas, and in SMSAs than in nonSMSAs, may be in part
a regional mix effect. Consider 1978-79 residential use by

Table 8.19. SMSA and NonSMSA Residential Energy Use
for 1972-1973 and 1978-1979

	Average Household Use		
	(1) Estimated 1972-73 in 1978 Dollars	(2) Estimated 1978-79	(3) (2)/(1)
	$	$	
U.S.	637	724	1.14
SMSA	620	734	1.18
NonSMSA	675	704	1.04

regions, in million BTU per household (U.S. Energy Information Administration, 1980):

U.S.	138
Northeast	166
North Central	180
South	99
West	110

The variations here are consistent with those shown in
Table 8.2, above, for all household use per capita.

Because rural and nonmetro population is proportionately
greater in the South than in the rest of the country, rural
and nonmetro average energy use will have some tendency to
be lower than corresponding urban and metro use. If one
were interested in eliminating the effect of regional mix,
one would need comparisons holding the regional effect
constant. Data for such comparisons appear limited, at best.
(In its most general formulation, controlling the regional
effect would involve control of all geographic influences
other than those that interest us here, perhaps best approximated by comparisons of contiguous geographic areas.)

Other factors that can cause area differences in energy
use include form and size of dwelling unit, the urban "heat
island" effect, income, and price.

Buildings with multiple dwelling units are obviously
much more common in urban than in rural areas. The dwelling
in multiple units probably uses less energy for given floor

space than the single-family unit because of less exposure
to the elements and some transmission of neighbors' heat in
the winter. On the other hand, heating of common space
(hallways, foyers) and energy required for elevators are
sources of additional energy use.

Smaller dwelling units should consume less energy than
larger ones, and size is often associated with locale.
Central city dwellings typically are smaller than suburban
ones, and Beale (1978) suggests that rural homes tend to be
smaller than urban.

Considering the city versus the surrounding countryside,
the urban heat island effect can be substantial, with a
temperature at the city center that is 5° F. to 10° F.
above that in contiguous rural areas. The heat island
effect tends to be a nighttime phenomenon, and so may be
benign in net impact, reducing heating costs more than it
raises those for air conditioning.

Higher real income implies larger dwelling units and
greater use of appliances, and could be a factor in the
observed differences in use between areas.

Finally, as noted in discussing Table 8.18, above, the
average price for all fuels combined is higher in rural
than in urban areas, and in nonSMSAs than in SMSAs, because
of the different shares for natural gas use. Table 8.18
also shows that the opposite price pattern holds for all
individual fuels, although the price differentials for
natural gas, and for fuel oil and kerosene, are rather
small. The major differences occur in electricity rates,
and to some extent, this may again be a regional effect,
because the low electricity rate areas of the TVA and
Pacific Northwest are more nonmetro and nonurban than the
nation as a whole. A smaller but similar effect may occur
in oil and gas because of southern proximity to major
sources of supply.

Regional effects are controlled in some data series,
but the available information is limited. In one study,
Foster Associates (1974) found little difference in fuel
oil prices between rural areas contiguous to SMSAs, and the
central cities of those SMSAs. In comparing 1972 electricity
and natural gas space heating bills, considerable variability occurred between members of twenty-four matched pairs
of SMSAs and rural areas of contiguous nonSMSA counties.
However, the average effect involved a slight price advantage to rural areas. In both natural gas and electricity,
these totals were obtained:

Urban prices higher: 11 cases
Rural prices higher: 7 cases
Same price: 6 cases

The ratios of average rural price to average urban price were:

Natural gas: .965
Electricity: .986

In a study in progress (with results not yet available for general use), Mikesell (1979) has developed data comparing residential energy costs by fuel type, housing type, and region for 1974 and 1975. The data, from the Annual Housing Survey, consist of average monthly bills paid by owners of single family or mobile homes, and so involve both energy price and quantity used per housing unit. Because the data are classified by region, regional effects can be controlled by forming cost ratios within regions and then averaging those ratios. This procedure was carried out for single family homes to obtain the ratio of the nonSMSA bill to the SMSA bill; comparable ratios were obtained from Table 8.18 by dividing nonSMSA expenditures by SMSA expenditures derived from entries in the table. The corresponding results were:

| | NonSMSA/SMSA Expenditures | |
	Mikesell Data	Table 8.18
Natural gas	0.97	0.67
Electricity	0.94	1.11
Heating oil	0.92	0.79
LPG (propane)	1.15	3.33

Controlling for regional effect removes much of the SMSA-nonSMSA variability within individual fuels. If the Mikesell ratios are applied to the SMSA expenditures obtained from Table 8.18, in effect holding region constant, the nonSMSA fuel bill becomes $696, compared to the listed $704. Hence, one can conclude that here, regional effects do not greatly affect the metro-nonmetro comparisons.

Some additional data developed by Mikesell (1979), and summarized in Table 8.20, show that the percentage of single family home owners installing energy conservation devices was higher in rural than in urban areas; it was also generally higher in nonmetro than in metro areas, though the difference was not as great as the urban-rural difference,

Table 8.20. Percentage of Owner-Occupied Single Family
Detached Units Installing Energy Conservation Items, 1975

Item	Urban	Rural	SMSA	NonSMSA
Storm windows	5.0	7.2	5.1	6.8
Storm doors	5.3	6.5	5.6	5.8
Insulation added	6.6	8.5	7.0	7.6
Attic insulation	4.8	6.1	5.1	5.4
Wall insulation	2.9	5.1	3.1	4.5
Weather stripping	14.0	14.6	14.8	13.2

Source: James J. Mikesell, ESCS, USDA, unpublished data
derived from computer tapes of Annual Housing Survey.

and there was an important exception (weather stripping).
This suggests greater exposure and "need" for insulation in
the areas of higher percentage of installation.

It is possible that the percentage differences reflect
some other cause, for example, rural residents are more
likely to be handy with tools, and so more likely to engage
in do-it-yourself installation of conservation devices.
However, Mikesell's regional data show that northeastern
and north-central rates of installation were well above
southern and western, again suggesting that conservation
behavior increases given the potential for greater savings.

The relative impacts of higher energy prices are not
obvious, but, in conjunction, the evidence of this section
might be read as indicating greater energy dependence in
rural than in urban areas, and also as suggesting approximately equal dependence for metro and nonmetro areas. In
any event, the small town appears to be in a relatively
advantageous position.

Given higher energy prices, the following forecasts seem
reasonable. New housing is likely to feature reduced floor
space, there is likely to be more clustering of housing,
and small towns are likely to have greater viability than
open country settlement. The latter forecasts seem reinforced by the similar effects, noted earlier, to be expected
from higher gasoline prices.

Table 8.21. Percentage of Manufacturing Employment in
Nonmetropolitan Areas, by Region

Region	Energy Intensive Industries	All Manufactures
New England	40.1	14.0
Mid-Atlantic	19.6	13.3
East North Central	32.3	22.6
West North Central	57.4	36.3
South Atlantic	43.4	44.7
East South Central	47.6	51.0
West South Central	29.2	28.7
Rocky Mountain	69.8	32.1
Far West	27.7	9.5
United States	35.8	25.8

NONHOUSEHOLD ENERGY USE

The USDA has developed a table exhibiting energy consumption
in U.S. agricultural production, with a detailed breakdown
by activity, cross-classified by source of energy (obtained
from Yeck 1979). Total 1976 consumption by agriculture is
estimated as 1,251.2 trillion BTU, which amounts to 1.7
percent of total U.S. consumption for that year of 74,000
trillion BTU.

Edward J. Smith (1980) has examined industrial use of
energy in nonmetro areas, noting that in 1970, manufactures
employed more than five million people in nonmetro areas,
making it the leading source of employment. He classified
manufacturing industries by energy intensity, measured by
the ratio of energy use to production labor, and developed
information on the most energy intensive class; this group
of thirty-two industries employs only 4.8 percent of all
workers in manufactures, but accounts for 50.8 percent of
energy use. Nonmetro areas had a greater than proportionate
share of this group, with 35.8 percent of all employment in
the group as opposed to 25.6 percent of all manufacturing
employment.

By region, the percentages of manufacturing employment
located in nonmetro areas are presented in Table 8.21.
Rough equality of the percentages holds for the three

Table 8.22. Indicators of Outdoor Recreation Activity, 1970, 1972, and 1977

Outdoor Activity and Unit of Use	Use Levels			Annual Percentage Growth	
	1970	1972	1977	1970-72	1972-77
National park system,[a] visits in millions	172.0	211.6	262.6	11.5	4.8
National parks, visits in millions	45.9	54.4	62.0	8.2	2.8
National forests, visitor days	172.6	188.2	204.8	4.4	1.8
Outboard motors in use, in thousands	7,215.0	7,400.0	7,760.0	1.3	1.0
Outboard motorboats sold, in thousands	276.0	375.0	336.0	17.9	-2.3
Fishing licenses, millions	31.1	33.0	34.9[c]	3.1	1.4
Hunting licenses, millions	22.2	23.3[b]	25.3[c]	1.7	2.8
Federal duck stamps sold, in thousands	2,072.0	2,442.0	2,170.0	8.9	-2.8

Source: U.S. Bureau of the Census, Statistical Abstract of the United States, 1971, 1973, and 1978 editions, section "Public Lands, Parks, Recreation and Travel."

[a]Includes national parks, monuments, parkways, seashores, etc.

[b]1973 data.

[c]1976 data.

southern regions, but for the remaining regions the energy intensive share is above the all manufactures share.

If level of production labor is well correlated with value of output, and if energy prices are fairly invariant within regions, then Smith's measure of energy intensity corresponds to what has been termed here as energy dependence. In turn, this suggests that within the South, nonmetro industries have roughly the same dependence and vulnerability as metro; however, outside the South, nonmetro industries would appear to be more dependent and vulnerable to energy price increases than their metro counterparts.

OUTDOOR RECREATION

Wardwell and Gilchrist (1979) argue that growth in recreation, including second homes in rural areas, has accounted for a significant portion of nonmetro repopulation trends. And they predict that areas dependent on recreation-tourism will experience declining rates of growth, given higher fuel costs. (Because of the strong dependence of outdoor recreation use on transportation, the topic could have been included in the earlier discussion of transportation impacts, but it seemed important enough to treat separately.)

Gasoline shortages have had some obvious short-term reductions in tourism and use of recreation areas (New York Times, 27 July 1979) but higher prices also seem to imply a considerable long-term slowdown in growth. Evidence for this conclusion appears in Table 8.22, which shows use levels over time for a variety of outdoor recreation activities. Almost all show a pronounced downturn since 1972. It seems plausible that such downturns hold generally for outdoor recreation activities with a nonlocal clientele, and because such activities tend to be located in nonmetro areas, there will be a disproportionate impact on nonmetro economies.

ENERGY, INFLATION, AND LOCATION

It is hypothesized here that higher energy prices have indirectly helped bring about inflation, and that inflation plus the progressive income tax helps to induce migration from metro to nonmetro places. Higher energy prices, per se, do not imply inflation (or a rise in the general price level), but rather a change in relative prices. If energy

prices go up, something else can go down. But the Consumer
Price Index (CPI) will indeed register energy price increases as a form of inflation. There are two problems with
the CPI: (1) it is always somewhat flawed by overstatement,
because it assumes a fixed market basket; and (2) it cannot
distinguish between a general price increase with no change
in real income, and a loss in real income, which is what
the OPEC energy "tax" involves. However, energy price rises
may well have generated inflation in two ways: (1) a number
of wage contracts and social security payments are formally
tied to the CPI, and a great many other transactions are
informally tied to the CPI, so that there is some compound-
ing of any CPI reading of "inflation"; and (2) Congress or
the directors of the Federal Reserve System may well have
believed that inflating the economy was the way to reduce
the OPEC tax bite, or to avoid a recession brought about by
that tax bite. (Congressman David Stockman of Michigan
expressed belief in the latter scenario in 1979.)

As noted earlier, there is also considerable evidence
that wage rates for the same work increase by size of
place, and there is good reason to interpret these differentials as compensatory payments.

In periods of inflation, the progressive income tax
moves people into higher tax brackets, and the effect is to
increase the real tax burden. An analysis of tax tables
that were applicable over the past decade leads to the
conclusion that the increased tax burden, in percentage
terms, tends to be greater the higher the initial level of
money income. (This is not an obvious concomitant of pro-
gressivity; in fact, at high enough income levels, there
is a drop in burden.) This suggests a built-in financial
incentive for people to move from larger to smaller places,
given inflation. It may well be that a good portion of the
rural turnaround is attributable to this effect.

This argument does not assume that people pore over
tax tables and make location decisions accordingly; rather,
if there is a tilt in economic advantage toward smaller
places, people can discover that tilt in a variety of ways.
One way can be random migrations: if one is better off in
the new locale, one stays put; if one is not, one moves on.
And one may tell others about what has been learned.

If current and future energy price increases are matched
by more general price level inflation, the hypothesized tax
effect can be expected to continue.

RURAL AND NONMETROPOLITAN PRODUCTION

This section considers production impacts under three headings: (1) growth in county income and population related to
energy production, for a sample of producing states; (2)
boom towns and similar local production sites; and (3)
location impacts from the development of "unconventional"
energy sources.

GROWTH IN COUNTY POPULATION AND PER CAPITA
INCOME RELATED TO LEVEL OF ENERGY PRODUCTION

What follows is a report on some original research carried
out for this paper to gauge the effects of energy production
on local income and population growth. Although there is
the not-too-surprising conclusion that positive impacts
indeed exist, there were some surprises; for example, there
have been some reversals in income gains. These results are
summarized here, and some details of the work are presented
in Appendix B.
    County data on per capita income, population, and energy
output were developed for five energy-producing states:
Kentucky, Montana, Oklahoma, Pennsylvania, and Wyoming.
Income and population data for the 1969-77 period were
obtained from a U.S. Bureau of Economic Analysis computer
data tape. (Some corresponding tables appear in U.S. Department of Commerce, 1979.) Estimates of annual energy
production by county were obtained from Drysdale and Calef
(1977), with coverage limited to one point in time (the
1972-73 period for the major fuels), so that changes in
income and population could be related only to base levels
of production. The number of counties covered was 343, of
which 281 were nonmetro. Counties were further classified
in terms of area characteristics, reflecting both size of
central place and location vis-à-vis an SMSA. A series of
regression equations then related both per capita income
and population to energy production, state, and area
characteristic. Results for income and population will be
summarized in turn.

Impacts on per Capita Income
    Both per capita income (in constant 1967 dollars) and
annual growth rate in per capita income were related to the
explanatory variables. Estimated growth rate effects were
embodied in the coefficients appearing in the growth rate

Table 8.23. Effects of Energy Production on Estimated
per Capita Income Growth Rate

Production in Billion BTU per Capita	Coefficients		
	Additions to Growth Rate (in Percent)		
	1969–72	1972–75	1975–77
Coal	0.192	0.529*	-0.283*
Oil	-0.052	0.206*	0.153
Natural gas	0.534*	-0.329	-0.371*

*Indicates statistically significant case.

equation in Table 8.23. The coefficients can be interpreted
as the addition to a county's annual percentage rate of
growth in per capita income per billion BTU of fuel production per capita in the base period. Thus, if the annual
rate of growth were 1.0 percent in nonproducing counties,
then in the 1972–75 period, a county producing one billion
BTU of coal per capita would have a growth rate of 1.529
percent. The regression results yielded the following
interpretations.

There was a substantial increase in the contribution
of coal and oil to per capita income when comparing the
1972–75 and 1969–72 periods. However, natural gas shows a
declining contribution when those time periods are compared.
The coal and oil results fit expectations. Perhaps the natural gas results reflect relatively strong price controls
on existing gas production, limiting price, and income,
increases. A corollary argument is that the impact of price
controls on oil appears to have been less binding.

An important caveat in these inferences stems from the
assumption that higher income from energy occurs only in
the locales of base production; if new production occurred
in other counties, or at least in different proportions
from the base levels, errors could be introduced into the
results and the inferences.

There was a downturn in the contribution of coal, oil,
and natural gas to per capita income when the 1975–77 period
is compared to the 1972–75 period; but the 1975–77 period
was one of relative energy "glut," involving some fall in
real energy prices. It appears that price change was translated into income change in relatively quick fashion.

Table 8.24. Effects of Energy Production and Change in
Population Growth Rate

Production in Billion BTU per Capita	Coefficients		
	(1) Additions to Growth Rate 1969-72	(2) Additions to Growth Rate 1972-75	(3) Change in Growth Rate (2)/(1)
Coal	0.095*	0.265*	0.165*
Oil	-0.155*	-0.017	0.142*
Natural gas	-0.057	0.031	0.087*

*Indicates statistically significant case.

The results for the combined state samples were checked
by fitting equations for each state. Parallel results were
obtained save for Wyoming, where the impact of coal on per
capita income increased in every period.
Not surprisingly, energy production per capita is much
higher in nonmetro than in metro areas, and consequently
nonSMSA income appeared much more affected by increased
energy prices. Applications of the fitted equations yielded
these estimates of the share of energy production in
income:

Energy portion all income	NonSMSA	SMSA
1969	.0098	.0007
1972	.0273	.0022
1975	.0305	.0030
1977	.0247	.0024

Impacts on Population
The effect of energy production on population was also
examined by regressing population growth rates on energy
production per capita and the location variables, parallel-
ing the income analysis. The population results were more
clearcut than those for income, because there was strong
evidence of a significant impact of energy on growth.
Again, estimated growth rate effects were embodied in
the coefficients, in Table 8.24, which show both additions

to the population growth rate and relative changes in growth
rate. As before, if the nonproducing county growth rate were
1 percent, the production of one billion BTU of coal would
correspond to an annual growth rate of 1.265 percent in the
1972-77 period.

The following inferences were obtained from the regression results.

All of the specific forms of energy had a positive
impact on population growth in relative terms (i.e., growth
in the second period is greater than in the first if energy
is produced), and the greater the production the greater
the relative increase in growth. The effect is statistically significant for all the fossil fuels.

Coal had the greatest impact, both in terms of population growth rates and relative growth. Oil had a strongly
<u>negative</u> effect in the first period, and this became a mild-
ly negative effect in the second. The natural gas impact
changed from mildly negative in the first period to mildly
positive in the second. Hence, though natural gas was associated with per capita income declines in the work reported
above, it nevertheless is also associated with population
increases. It might be hypothesized that the income decline
exhibits the negative impact of regulation on "old" gas production, while the population increase reflects expansion
of "new" production in previously producing counties.

Given the per capita income decline in the 1975-77
period, there was a check for a possible parallel decline
in population growth, but such was not apparent. Perhaps
there is a lag between income change and population growth.

The results were also extended by analyzing county
population growth for each state individually, limiting the
observations to nonmetro counties, and the explanatory
variable to all energy production.

In all cases, there was a positive association between
energy production and relative population growth (using
growth in the second period relative to that in the first
as the variable to be explained). Although the association
was always positive, it was statistically significant only
for Montana and Wyoming, which fits the patterns noted
earlier in the discussion of regional developments.

The investigation of individual state impacts was carried out both by relating population growth rate to billion
BTU per capita measured as a continuous variable and as a
discrete variable, with four levels of output specified in
the latter case. Results for the former approach appear in
Appendix B, whereas those for the latter are in Table 8.25.

Table 8.25. Energy Production Level and Relative
Population Growth Rates

Production Level	Billion BTU per Capita	Relative Population Growth Rates[a]				
		Ky.	Mont.	Okla.	Pa.	Wyo.
Level 1	zero	100.4	99.7	100.0	99.1	100.5
Level 2	0 - <1	100.4	100.3	100.6	99.1	101.7
Level 3	1 - <10	100.5	101.1	101.2	99.8	101.8
Level 4	$\geq$ 10	100.0	104.4	101.4	--	103.1

[a]1972-77 rate relative to 1969-72 rate times 100.

BOOM TOWNS AND SIMILAR LOCAL PRODUCTION SITES

A concentration of energy development at a particular
locale can generate very rapid growth and boom conditions;
this is sometimes a source of concern and complaint, but it
seems that much of that involves "crying all the way to the
bank."

In this section some of the literature on boom towns
and related production sites is reviewed, including western
coal boom towns, Indian reservations with energy resources,
and small towns housing nuclear power plants. In all cases,
it seems that energy development yields net benefits for
the local "impacted" population, and that growth problems
tend to get solved, though there are some qualifications to
both these conclusions.

Western Coal Boom Towns

Boom town conditions cause several kinds of disruptions:
(1) A surge in population puts great pressure on infrastructure: roads, water systems, schools, etc.; (2) There
are perceived inequities as some long-term residents are
stuck with more in the way of new costs than they receive
in new benefits; (3) There are putative problems of social
disorganization, such as delinquency, drunkeness, and
divorce.

But some case studies suggest that the pressure on
infrastructure can be ameliorated rather quickly, and that
long-term local residents generally (though not always)
benefit from the boom. Finally, it is likely that some of
the social disorganization occurs because "disorganized" or

disreputable people are attracted to boom areas, and they would be likely to have trouble wherever they were located. Admittedly, some of their difficulties are imposed on local innocent bystanders.

Kroll (forthcoming) has carried out an instructive case study of five boom counties in the Powder River basin in Wyoming, including Campbell and Converse counties, which are major energy producers. Campbell includes the town of Gillette, a major strip-mining center.

Within the region, wage rates are highest and unemployment lowest in Campbell County. In that county, high wages occur not only in mining and construction, but also in services and trade, which have increased substantially over time. In the other counties, mining and construction wage rates are on a par with Campbell County's, but those in other occupations have lagged behind. Jobs in mining, construction, power generation, and government tend to be filled by outsiders, but trade and services draw on local residents. There was considerable inflation of local price levels; housing values, in particular, rose from 76 percent of those in Laramie in 1960 to 110 percent in 1978. Between 1970 and 1977, property values rose about 50 percent in the three counties that were not major fuel producers, and roughly tripled in Campbell and Converse counties.

Some local ranchers gained by sale or lease of land for residential use, or from mining royalties; but many were hurt by higher wages they had to pay their hired farm labor.

There appeared to be numerous multiplier effects of energy development, often occurring outside the fuel extractive counties, per se. Thus, some contiguous counties contain a coal-fired power plant, oil refineries, and secondary industries related to coal mining and to refining. Others have had substantial residential growth, furnishing housing for some of the workers in fuel extraction.

Initially, police and fire services were understaffed, and there was great pressure on the infrastructure. But with the great rise in property values and property taxes, and the imposition of local sales taxes, there were great increases in local government and employment. As of 1978, schools were adequate, mental health services were being provided, and Campbell County had invested in major road work, a water treatment facility, and a recreation center. There are a variety of state programs funded by general state revenues and mineral royalties that offer local aid in the form of grants and loans.

On the basis of an analysis of crime rates and wildlife
depletion, Brookshire and d'Arge (1980) also raise doubts
that boom towns are necessarily bad. They find evidence of
a change in the mix of crimes in boom towns (higher incidence of murder and larceny), but little evidence of an
appreciable increase in overall crime rates. In the case of
the Power River Basin, Wyoming, a 25 percent growth in the
human population implied only a small reduction in wild
herds of deer and antelope.

Western coal-producing states have raised a great deal
of revenue from taxes on coal production. Yet the governors
of Montana and North Dakota have argued that the federal
government has an obligation to help communities impacted
by federally mandated energy development policies, and in a
1977 Senate committee hearing, they requested a billion
dollars in aid to impacted areas in their states (Land Use
Planning Report, 15 Aug. 1977: 258). Such relatively massive funding may eventually be approved by Congress (Land
Use Planning Report, 2 July 1979: 205). Obviously, a case
could be made, instead, for internalizing negative impacts
through use of state severance taxes on local production.
Brookshire and d'Arge (1980: 542) reach a similar conclusion, raising doubts as to why federal or state government
should subsidize energy impacted communities.

Indian Reservations

Recent newspaper accounts note that Indian reservations
contain the largest pool of underdeveloped energy resources
in the United States, variously estimated as involving 25
to 50 percent (or more) of its uranium; 15 percent of its
coal; from 2 to 4 percent of its oil and gas; and considerable amounts of shale oil and geothermal energy. (New York
Times, 7 Aug. 1979, cites the Department of Interior for
the more conservative of these estimates.) But there is a
great deal of guesswork involved, and interested observers
cite a pressing need for an inventory of holdings (Harris
1979). There is also considerable concern that the energy
resources will not yield a "proper" return to the tribes,
or will impose a variety of burdens as well as financial
benefits.

Twenty-five major producing tribes (actual and potential) have formed a Council of Energy Resource Tribes (CERT)
aimed at advancing tribal interests in development and negotiations with business and government. All of the CERT
tribes are located in the western states, including seven of
eight Rocky Mountain states and the state of Washington.

One complaint is that past contracts, negotiated for
the tribes by the Bureau of Indian Affairs, contained no
escalator clauses, so royalties remained at low, fixed
levels (e.g., 17.5 cents per ton of coal) even though fuel
prices soared. Some contracts have been renegotiated, and
new coal contracts must receive the minimum 12.5 percent
royalty now required for coal mined on federal land, a
policy that was also applied to Indian lands in a 1977
policy decision by the Secretary of Interior (New York
Times, 8 Jan. 1978).

There are a number of Indian concerns beyond "proper"
pricing of their resources. For example, Feighter and
Nordstrom (1977) found the Crow Tribe seriously split over
coal development on the reservation; the most frequently
cited concern was a likely influx of outsiders, resulting
in "overpopulation" and a perceived loss of control over
the reservation.

The Navajo Tribe, with 160,000 members, is America's
largest, and one of the most important in terms of energy
resources. Natwig and Godoff (1976) list these areas of
Navajo concern: (1) employment and "life-style" problems,
(2) capital limitations and taxation problems, and (3)
environmental problems.

There is high unemployment and the labor force is generally unskilled, so the tribe maintains that it must be
able to obtain a significant percentage of the new employment involved in energy development. However, the trade-
offs may not be palatable, for there is also concern about
changes in Navajo life-style and induced social problems if
Navajo are employed by developers.

The tribe does not have the financial resources to make
massive direct investments. In part, this involves institutional constraints. The federal government has not provided
the legal mechanisms to give tax exempt status to bonds
floated by Indian tribes; further, under existing legislation, New Mexico cannot pass on revenue-sharing funds to
unincorporated subdivisions of the state, and the tribe
fears it would jeopardize its sovereignty by allowing incorporation of a community on the reservation. The Navajo
have attempted to levy new taxes on energy companies operating on tribal land, but because those companies already
pay state taxes they feel they are being doubly taxed by
overlapping governments, and twenty of the companies have
filed suit against the taxes (Wall Street Journal, 20 Sept.
1979).

Environmental conflicts can be exacerbated because of

differences between environmental regulations of the state
and those of the tribe. As a case in point, Kneese and
Williams (1979) note that the Navajo tribal council has
become the first government in the world to set a fee on
sources of sulfur emissions, which will impose costs on the
Four Corners plant, a large coal-fired electric power plant
located on the reservation. Currently, the fee is the
subject of litigation.

Howes and Markusen (see Chapter 11) hypothesize that
there is fear that coal production will not alleviate poverty but may in fact worsen economic conditions, and consequently, several tribes have decided to limit or stop
energy resource development. But one can read the evidence,
instead, to indicate that the tribes are attempting to maximize returns by holding out for the best possible price.
There are active negotiations with many coal developers and
users, including the TVA; and CERT has called for exclusion
of the tribes from an excess profits tax because the tribes
are sovereign governments (Harris 1979)--hardly an expression of disinterest in production.

Nuclear Power Plant Siting
    A number of studies show that nuclear power plants
bring considerable financial benefits to the communities in
which they are located, because the property taxes they pay
are a considerable financial relief to the community and
its residents, and they are also a source of new employment.
For example, Gamble, Downing, and Sauerlender (1979) found
that nuclear power plants tended to increase property
values in the municipalities in which they were located.
Similar results were obtained by Purdy et al. (1977).

Nuclear power plants tend to be located on the fringes
of metro areas, so that seventy-eight of the one hundred
largest cities are located within fifty miles of one of the
seventy existing plants (Burwell, Ohanian, and Weinberg,
1979, p. 1049). The ninety plants under construction also
show some spatial orientation toward large metro markets,
though an inspection of a map showing both sets of plants
suggests that those under construction tend to be somewhat
more removed from SMSAs (Burwell, Ohanian, and Weinberg,
Figure 2). Even before the Three Mile Island accident,
there had been few orders for new nuclear reactors for
several years; this reflected both lower than expected
growth in electricity demand, given higher prices, and a
costly licensing and construction process that took twelve
or more years. With postaccident concern expressed in even

more litigation and regulation, it seems unlikely that any
new plants will be started for some years to come, whereas
some of those under construction may be shifted to coal, or
never completed.

Some shifting away from metro areas can also be expected. There is a possibility that some existing nuclear plants
near large cities will be closed (New York Times, 6 Nov.
1979), and it is likely that when new plants are initiated,
they will be considerably more removed from population centers than is currently the case. A New York Times editorial
of 23 December 1979 called for new siting in rural areas
more than fifty miles from population centers, arguing that
increased transmission costs might be balanced by less
opposition, though it was recognized that rural residents
might resist such siting.

However, nuclear power seems acceptable in some parts
of the country, and hence, some concentration of activity
may occur in those places, for example, eastern Washington.

Burwell, Ohanian, and Weinberg (1979) recommend the
concentration of new nuclear reactors at existing sites,
with about five reactors at each site. They suggest this
would reduce the nuclear waste disposal problem, simplify
security and site inspection, and help the technical pro-
ficiency of plant workers and management. We may see a
variant of such clustering in sparsely settled localities
where the populace finds nuclear power congenial. But tax
benefits, noted above, and the general economic advantages
of cheaper power could attract more residents to those
areas. Many of the newer residents might be less kindly
disposed to nuclear power, and this could be a source of
friction. (Similar problems occur for airports, which induce nearby development and complaints about noise externalities from some of the new residents.)

In sum, the likely nuclear future outlined here should
entail a small shift in economic advantage from metro to
nonmetro areas.

UNCONVENTIONAL ENERGY SOURCES

There are large numbers of unconventional energy sources
that could yield significant future amounts of energy. Four
such sources are considered here because of their likely
nonmetro impacts: (1) synthetic liquids and gases based on
coal or shale oil, (2) solar energy, (3) wood and biomass
generally, and (4) ethanol alcohol from agricultural pro-

ducts. (Some of the general interest in solar and alcohol reflects presumed benign effects on the environment.)

Synthetic Liquids and Gases Based on Coal or Shale Oil

The United States appears on the verge of embarking on a massive synthetic fuels program that can involve the production of liquid or gaseous fuels from coal or of oil from shale. The economics of the endeavor are questionable, for at the least, the timing is premature. Landsberg (1979), for example, argues that smaller scale experimental efforts at synthetic fuel production make sense in terms of developing knowledge and technology to be used when the economics are right; but a $50 billion or $100 billion program seems much too much too soon. Given the questionable economics, it is likely that, in practice, the program will be considerably smaller and take much longer than the current scenario suggests: the real world does interpose its objections.

But even under such a scaled-down version, considerable location impacts are to be expected. Most of those impacts are to be expected in nonmetro areas located primarily, but not exclusively, in the Rocky Mountain region. Some notion of the locus of impacts can be obtained from a DOE report (Williams 1979), which applied screening factors (availability of energy resources, various air quality constraints and water availability) to identify forty-four counties that could support a synthetic fuel plant. The counties had this distribution by state: Colorado (five); Illinois (eight); Montana (ten); North Dakota (seven); West Virginia (five); Wyoming (six); and one each in Pennsylvania, Texas, and Utah. All but one of the counties are nonmetro.

Lloyd Bender et al. (1979) applied an impact model to predict effects on specific county employment and population of both a coal gasification plant and of a coal liquefaction plant. The gasification plant was assumed to produce 250 million cubic feet of gas per day, with an employment of 600 workers, whereas the liquefaction plant was assumed to produce 100,000 barrels of oil per day, with an employment of 1,600 workers. Estimated impacts were obtained for three northern Great Plains counties, with the results for the liquefaction plant presented in Table 8.26. Employment gains per county averaged around 3,500 ranging from 3,400 to 3,800; population gains averaged around 7,700, and showed more spread than the employment results, ranging from around 6,000 to 9,500.

Production targets for the synthetic fuels program are roughly 2 million barrels per day, equivalent, then, to

Table 8.26. Estimated Impact of Coal Liquefaction Plant

| County | State | 1990 Employment | | 1990 Population | |
		Base Case[a]	With Plant	Base Case[a]	With Plant
Campbell	Wyo.	18,260	21,660	28,800	34,940
Rosebud	Mont.	7,130	10,600	14,630	22,000
Mercer	N.Dak.	5,240	9,000	10,470	20,125

[a]Assuming current expansion continues.

twenty plants at 100,000 barrels each. Applying the Bender estimated averages, we get a total employment gain of 70,000 workers, and a total growth in population of 154,000 persons for our estimated impacts.

Solar Energy
     Cool observers of the energy scene are dubious about widespread use of solar energy at any time in the near future. For example, Schurr et al. (1979: 532) conclude that solar economics are not particularly attractive, given relative costs of solar versus fossil fuel alternatives, and they add that even if fossil fuel prices rise markedly, a variety of institutional barriers will inhibit solar energy use.
     Electricity from solar power is seen by most observers as decades away; solar space heating and water heating are closer to competitive status, but both applications still are generally uneconomic. Solar water heaters, for example, typically take eighteen to twenty years to recover costs, hardly an exciting investment opportunity, at present. And space heating installations almost always have to be coupled with a conventional backup system, given the intermittent nature of sunshine. (For some detailed cost data, see Schurr et al., 1979: 328-29; Wall Street Journal, 13 Nov. 1979; U.S. House Committee on Science and Technology, 1976: 171; Cartee, 1976: 25; and Norman 1978.)
     Institutional barriers include: (1) the absence of general legal protection for sun rights, (2) lending policies that discriminate against solar technologies, and (3) utility policies that limit availability of backup service, or make it excessively expensive (Schurr et al., 1979: 528).

Although some have argued that solar power can be economic in northern climates (e.g., Schulze, Ben-David, and Balcomb, 1977; and Farber, 1978), there appears more truth than whimsey in the negative evaluation, "Maine is too far from the sun" (Solar Action, 1978: 190), and as Maine goes, it appears, so goes a good deal of the nation. Solar heating appears clustered in New Mexico, Colorado, and California, with the latter state possessing one-half the nation's solar devices (including swimming pool heaters). In order, the following Sunbelt states (rather naturally) are estimated as having the highest annual amounts of solar energy available: Arizona, New Mexico, Hawaii, Nevada, California, Utah, and Florida (Solar Action, Appendix, 1978: 14). Despite less promising conditions elsewhere, most states encourage installation of solar units, often through tax breaks on the cost of installation. Types of encouragement, and number of states using each type are (New York Times, 13 Aug. 1979):

Income tax incentives:	19
Property tax incentives:	25
Local option for property tax incentives:	5
Sales tax incentives:	10
Grants or loans:	5
Provision allowing solar easement:	12
States with none of above:	9

In California, the San Diego County Board of Supervision passed an ordinance in December 1978, requiring solar hot water systems in all new homes built in unincorporated areas after 1 October 1980. Federal law currently allows homeowners an income tax credit of up to $2,200 for solar installations.

The USDA and the DOE are cooperating in a program to adapt solar energy for on-farm uses in agriculture; a series of experiments and pilot projects are being conducted, such as solar heating of poultry houses and crop drying (Executive Office of the President, 1979: 9). The Farmers Home Administration shows something of a shift in policy stance on solar installations. In 1977, the agency refused to finance solar installations on the grounds they were too experimental (Washington Post, 25 June 1977); but the next year, it considered requiring that all homes financed by the agency include solar heating or other alternative fuel sources (Washington Post, 25 Mar. 1978). However, at this date, those plans apparently have not moved beyond the preliminary stage.

   Because rural and nonmetro residences typically are
sited with more open space, they should be more congenial
to solar installations than residences in large urban areas. A major objective in solar energy use is to maximize
southern exposure, thus maximizing access to sunlight.
Another is to avoid having the owner of adjacent property
erect a building or plant a tree that shades the solar
collector, because American law has no property right in
sunlight falling on one's property (Jaffe 1978). Both
objectives should be easier to accomplish in low-density
nonmetro locations than in high-density metro places.

Wood (and Biomass)

   As late as 1940, nearly 25 percent of American households used wood as the primary fuel in heating their homes;
the percentage dropped to 10 percent by 1950, and to roughly
1 percent by 1975. Use was concentrated in the rural areas
of the South, the Upper Midwest, the Pacific Northwest, and
parts of Arizona and New Mexico (U.S. Bureau of the Census
1978). Wood has now made something of a comeback, particularly as pellets, which is wood processed into uniform size
and shape. In 1978, fuel costs for pellets appeared competitive with oil, if not natural gas (Mazzeo 1978). Fuel
wood typically has to be used close to its point of origin
because of transport costs, implying some concentration of
use in rural areas.
   More generally, biomass from forests or crops is
relatively low in energy density, and, hence, either
high fuel-transport costs must be incurred, or economies
of scale in plant size probably will be foregone (Schurr
et al., 1979: 264). Zeimetz (1979) reviews the literature
on energy from biomass, classified under the headings of
silviculture, field crops, and aquaculture. She notes
that many cost estimates are based on optimistic assumptions regarding yield, economies of scale, and management
abilities; and she concludes that under present technology
the cost of energy contained in biomass to be grown on
energy farms is several times the current cost of energy
in crude oil or coal. Further, two long-term factors
militate against such production: (1) likely cost increases in inputs themselves strongly dependent on energy
in their manufacture or transport, and (2) increasing
environmental constraints.

Ethanol Alcohol from Agricultural Products[3]

Ethanol alcohol can be fermented from grain, sugar beets, sugar cane, and potatoes; in its use for industrial alcohol, 93 percent of ethanol is derived from ethylene, in turn obtained from petroleum or natural gas, and 7 percent is obtained from other sources, including grains and fruits. Alcohol can be used with gasoline, in a mixture that is 10 percent alcohol and 90 percent gasoline, commonly referred to as gasohol; or it can substitute fully for gasoline as an automotive fuel. There is considerable agreement on the relative costs of alcohol from agricultural products versus gasoline, but optimists and pessimists diverge considerably on the implications of those figures. Costs of producing ethanol are estimated in the range of $1.00 to $1.50 per gallon, with hopes of a price as low as $.75 per gallon. The refinery cost of gasoline was around $.40 per gallon in 1978, and pessimists see the price differential as insurmountable, arguing that using alcohol to stretch gasoline is like using filet mignon to stretch hamburger. Optimists feel that the cost differential as of late 1979, had become quite thin, and that likely technological advances will make ethanol competitive in the near future. The pessimists are probably more realistic than the optimists. However, recent energy price increases have also brightened alcohol's prospects; and even in 1978, it appeared that alcohol from agricultural products was a competitive form of industrial alcohol. Let us now focus on specifics of the cost estimates, and then consider implications for population distribution, given the optimistic scenario.

A recent optimistic appraisal (Converse et al. 1979) estimates cost per gallon of corn-based ethanol as:

Operating costs	$0.315
Fixed cost (interest & depreciation)	0.165
Feed stock (corn at $2.30 per bushel)	0.885
Total	$1.365

Salable byproducts obtained in the distilling process are estimated as ranging from $.36 to $.684 per gallon; treated as an offset, they reduce the net cost to $.68 to $1.00 per gallon. The primary byproduct is "distiller's

dried grain," but other byproducts include corn oil, meal,
yeast, and fusel oil.

Converse et al. (1979) take $.75 per gallon as a
best estimate of current cost and argue that this is
comparable to the wholesale price of gasoline, which rose
from $.41 to $.75 per gallon during 1979. It is admitted
that the BTU content of alcohol is only 70 percent that
of gasoline, but it is argued (rather too hopefully) that
because engine performance may be improved when a gasohol
mixture is used, the comparative BTU effect may be reduced,
if not eliminated. But this effect appears to be relatively
minor, and may be balanced by occasional performance problems. Further, the price comparison made is of alcohol
at the distillery and of gasoline at the wholesale terminal,
which should include freight costs from the refinery to
the terminal.

Most proponents of agricultural ethanol recognize the
importance of the feedstock component in price; they also
envision massive production of ethanol. But any substantial
amount of production may well bring about considerable
price rises for the feedstock input, and price declines
for the byproduct output.

At present, gasohol has a federal subsidy of four
cents a gallon because the federal gasoline tax is not
applied to the product; in effect, this amounts to a
subsidy of forty cents a gallon for alcohol, given alcohol's 10 percent share of the product (i.e., the subsidy is applied to the full gallon of gasohol), which
amounts to four cents per one-tenth gallon of alcohol.
In addition, several agricultural states (including Kansas
and Louisiana) exempt state taxes also, which implies
another eighty cents per gallon subsidy. The Energy Tax
Act of 1978 included an enhanced investment tax credit
of 10 percent for alcohol production; three federal agencies
(DOE, EDA, and CSA) have an agreement to provide technical
and financial assistance for the construction of up to
one hundred small-scale gasohol plants by June 1981; and
there is a presidential directive to simplify licensing
and reporting of alcohol for transportation fuel purposes
(Executive Office of the President, 1979: 2, 7). It is
likely that there will be additional federal subsidies;
thus, the omnibus energy bill of 1979 authorized $20 bil-
lion in government loans and guarantees for synthetic fuel
production; the bill also authorized a gasohol program
(Washington Post, 25 Oct. 1979).

Corn and molasses appear to be the agricultural products

with best prospects for alcohol production, implying some
localization of production to the Midwest and North Central
states (for corn) and the Gulf Coast states (for sugar
cane). Distilleries will probably be fairly small scale and
service limited to producing areas because of transportation
costs of the raw material; Converse et al. (1979) envision
a plant at the center of a twenty-five-mile diameter production area. Hence, a considerable manufacturing activity
could emerge in nonmetro areas if the most sanguine hopes
of the optimists are fulfilled. Given subsidies and promotion, some such activity can be anticipated.

With enough plants at small enough scale, perhaps there
will be some enhanced opportunities for bootlegging, which
can involve a variety of putative social problems as well
as tax losses. In any event, perhaps the most important
aspect of ethanol is that its availability from renewable
resources implies there <u>is</u> a long-term upper bound to
energy prices.

CONCLUSION

This concluding section draws together the strands of
the discussion, and, in the process, presents some final
evaluations as well as a summary of the major points of
the chapter.

At the most general level of discourse, this chapter
has touched on some underlying theory that needs further
development and application to gain understanding of energy
impacts. Production function analysis implies that a measure of "energy dependence" can be defined and calculated,
with the ratio of energy expenditures to revenue (or to
income) a contender for that role. The greater the dependence, the more adverse the impact of higher energy prices.
Again, there is concurrence with the perception of most
location analysts that such price increases will increase
the friction of space, and cause a general contraction of
settlement patterns, as economic activities get an increased
incentive to move closer together. Places that are "isolated" or "peripheral," those that are faced with long
hauls for their imports and exports, will be at some disadvantage. There may be some correlation between isolation
and size of place because isolated places may tend to be
small, by virtue of the higher transportation costs they
face for goods movement, but small places certainly need

Table 8.27. Population Change by Region, 1972-1977

Region	Thousands of Persons
New England	-250
Mid-Atlantic	-700
East North Central	-100
West North Central	-50
South Atlantic	-250
East South Central	+100
West South Central	+500
Rocky Mountain	-300
Far West	+1,050
Total United States	0

not be isolated. It has also been speculated that higher
energy prices will bring about reductions in travel to
work, either by shifts in residences, work places or work
trip patterns; greater density of settlement and more
clustering; smaller housing units (perhaps smaller structures, generally); and less outdoor recreation involving
long-distance travel. On the production side, the initial
premise that there will be both direct and indirect impacts
of expanded energy production on income, employment, and
population has been supported by the evidence, including
some preliminary estimates of growth in county employment
and population as a function of energy output. The brief
discussion on the likely sequence of multiplier effects
involved in that growth was included because fuel extraction
can attract not only input suppliers (e.g., services to
miners) but output users, as well (e.g., chemical industries). All of these topics seem deserving of intensive
investigation in future research.

Turning to specific applications, the major empirical
question addressed is that of comparative impact: given
higher energy prices, how adverse is the impact on consumers, and how beneficial the impact on producers, for
particular locales, relative to others? In turn, what can
be said about changes in income and population?

At the regional level, both consumption and production
relations suggest pain in the Northeast and gain in the
Southwest, implying an acceleration of the Frostbelt to

Sunbelt shift. However, evidence on migration patterns
suggests that the shift attributable to energy is highly
selective. When actual 1977 population was compared to the
population that would have occurred if 1970-72 trends had
continued from 1972, after accounting for a lower national
growth rate, it seemed clear that both energy production
and mild climate were involved in the percentage changes
that were calculated. (See Introduction for details.) Those
percentage changes correspond to the changes in number of
persons, by region, in Table 8.27.

Of the total positive shift of about 1.6 million persons, there was a gain of about 0.8 million in California,
and 0.4 million in Texas, indicating the concentrated nature
of these shifts. In the 1972-77 period, total interstate
migration amounted to about 20 million persons, with about
12 million of that shift representing movement among regions
(estimated from U.S. Bureau of the Census, Current Population Reports, P-20, no. 273, 1974 and no. 350, 1980). Hence,
if we dare assume that all of the change in trend was energy
related, it appears that roughly 10 to 15 percent of recent
interregional migration is a response to higher energy
prices.

Rural and nonmetro impacts do not seem as obvious as
regional impacts. Aside from sparsity of data, there are
various measurement problems in making comparisons, discussed at some length above. Further, the available evidence
suggests that differences in energy consumption impacts are
relatively mild among different forms of settlement. On the
whole, however, it seems likely that those consumption impacts favor small towns (nonmetro urban areas), which appear
less adversely affected than other localities, whereas open
country rural areas are more adversely affected. Production
impacts appear generally favorable to nonSMSAs relative to
SMSAs, though, of course, this conclusion applies only to
producing areas.

Table 8.28 summarizes relative advantage (+), disadvantage (-) or neutral impact (0) for settlements by
category of consumption effects, based on the earlier,
detailed discussion of consumption. Of course, these
evaluations in Table 8.28 are impressionistic, at best, and
the weights to attach to them are hardly obvious. If we
arbitrarily sum the pluses and minuses we obtain:

Table 8.28. Impact of Energy Consumption for SMSAs
and NonSMSAs

Energy Use	SMSA			NonSMSA	
	Central City	Suburbs	Rural	Urban	Rural
Personal transportation					
Journey to work	+	–	–	+	0
Long-distance drivers	0	0	0	0	–
Other auto trips	0	–	–	0	–
Gasoline lines, shortages	–	–	–	0	0
Accident reductions	0	0	0	+	+
Housing use of energy					
Access to natural gas lines	+	+	–	0	–
Single-family housing	+	–	–	0	–
Energy prices, individual fuels	–	–	–	+	+
Energy conservation investment as indicator of disadvantage	+	0	0	0	–
Manufacturing	0	0	0	–	–
Outdoor recreation	0	0	0	0	–
Impact of inflation	0	0	0	+	+

SMSA		NonSMSA	
Central city	+2	Urban	+3
Suburbs	–4	Rural	–4
Rural	–6		

The corresponding list for production impacts is illustrated

Table 8.29. Impact of Production for SMSAs and NonSMSAs

	SMSA			NonSMSA	
	Central City	Suburbs	Rural	Urban	Rural
Fuel extraction	0	0	0	+	+
Western boom towns	0	0	0	+	0
Indian reservations	0	0	0	0	+
Nuclear siting	0	0	0	+	0
Synthetic fuel	0	0	0	+	+
Solar energy	0	0	0	+	+
Biomass energy	0	0	0	0	+
Gasohol	0	0	0	0	+

in Table 8.29. Production impacts seem strongly favorable to nonmetro areas. Arbitrarily combining the two sets of estimated impacts yields this ordering by increasing adversity:

NonSMSA urban
SMSA central city
NonSMSA rural
SMSA suburbs
SMSA rural

Hence, we can conclude that the nonSMSA fares better than the SMSA, but that the urban fares better than the rural settlement, as a consequence of higher energy prices.

Some of these evaluations are implicitly predicated on the continuation of current policies, and changes in those policies could affect several of the orderings. Thus, if natural gas price decontrol in fact occurs by 1985, as scheduled, there will be some reduction in the current disadvantage to rural areas not having access to natural gas. A variety of public policies can affect the western coal boom, including rail deregulation, coal slurry pipeline rights-of-way, federal coal leasing policy, and level of severance taxes. Of more direct significance, population shifts set in motion by changed energy conditions will often be viewed as a source of pain, followed by attempts to alleviate that pain through public policy. Such alle-

viation of pain is also likely to inhibit the adjustment
process that the population shifts represent. It would be a
pleasant outcome if a great deal of pain alleviation could
be had for only a little inhibition of adjustment. Unfortunately, the trade-off is often less benign. Spelling out
the trade-off in practice seems an important goal for
future research.

The question of policy is only one of many uncertainties
affecting this appraisal. Nevertheless, it appears that the
energy problem is likely to reinforce the "rural turnaround"
in the sense that it will accelerate the relative growth of
nonmetro America.

APPENDIX A

APPLYING THE COBB-DOUGLAS PRODUCTION
FUNCTION TO ENERGY IMPACT QUESTIONS

This appendix applies the Cobb-Douglas production function
to the question of how a firm responds to higher energy
prices. Assume that production of output by the typical
firm is described by this form of the Cobb-Douglas function:
$x = ka^{\alpha}b^{\beta}$, where x is output, a is energy input and b is
all other input. If the firm maximizes profit, it follows
that

$$\left(\frac{aP_a}{xP_x}\right) = \alpha \text{ and } \left(\frac{bP_b}{xP_x}\right) = \beta$$

where P_a, P_b, and P_x are prices of inputs and output, respectively. Maximization involves the condition that
$\alpha + \beta < 1$. We can now solve for x in terms of prices and
parameters; let the solved value of x be $\overset{o}{x}$. We obtain

$$\overset{o}{x} = [k\alpha^{\alpha}\beta^{\beta} \; P_a^{-\alpha} \; P_b^{-\beta} \; P_x^{\alpha+\beta}]^{\frac{1}{1-\alpha-\beta}}$$

Now, let energy price increase, so that

$$P_{a_2} = CP_{a_1},$$ where

numerical subscript denotes time period, and C is a constant, e.g., C=2. It follows that

$$\overset{o}{x}_2/\overset{o}{x}_1 = \frac{-\alpha}{c^{1-\alpha-\beta}},$$

i.e. this is the ratio of solved x in period 2 to that in period 1. We can also write the elasticity of $\overset{o}{x}$ with respect to P_a as

$$- \frac{\alpha}{1-\alpha-\beta}.$$

Say we are comparing output response between two regions, I and II, assuming each has a Cobb-Douglas function. We can show the following:

(1) If energy prices differ initially between the regions, but both have the same production function, then a given percentage increase in energy price will cause the same proportionate decline in output between the two regions. The effect is <u>neutral</u>.

(2) If the percentage increase in energy price is greater in region I than in II, I will reduce output more than II.

(3) If region I is more "dependent" on energy than region II, it will have a greater proportionate reduction in output. Dependence on energy can be measured by

$$\frac{\alpha}{1-\alpha-\beta};$$

if $\alpha+\beta$ is assumed invariant, then dependence can be measured directly by α. Empirically, we can treat

$$\frac{aP_a}{xP_x}$$

as an estimate of α. For example, say $\alpha+\beta= .9$, $\alpha = .1$ in I and $\alpha = .2$ in II. For C = 2, $\overset{o}{x}_2/\overset{o}{x}_1 = 1/2$ in I and 1/4 in II.

(4) The greater the invariability or fixity of other inputs, or the greater the contribution of such "fixed" factors as land and entrepreneurial capacity, the less the impact of increased energy prices. Fixity can be viewed as reducing the level of β in $\overset{o}{x}$. In the simplest case, assume b is fixed at a constant value, b_0; then $x = (kb^\beta)a^\alpha = k*a^\alpha$ and $\overset{o}{x}_2/\overset{o}{x}_1$ becomes

$$\frac{-\alpha}{c^{1-\alpha}}.$$

(5) Given an increase in P_a, we can expect some long-term increases in P_x and decreases in P_b. The greater these counteracting changes, the less the impact of energy price increases.

APPENDIX B

DETAILS ON REGRESSION EQUATIONS
FOR COUNTY ENERGY PRODUCTION IMPACTS

This appendix presents some detailed information on the regression equations relating changes in county income and population to level of county energy production. The sample employed covered five producing states, and energy production included hydropower generation as well as fuel extraction. In the source document for energy data (Drysdale and Calef 1977), total energy was defined as the sum of the fossil fuels plus three times hydropower, the latter corresponding to the fossil fuel equivalent employed to produce electricity.

The number of observations (counties) and average levels of energy production per capita (using 1972 population) are illustrated in Table B.1. A number of counties had energy per capita levels above 10 billion BTU; the highest observed value was 34 billion BTU per capita in a Wyoming county.

The SMSA versus nonSMSA classification was extended to a finer classification system on the basis of location and population criteria, as shown in Table B.2.

This classification was developed from an inspection of maps for each state appearing in respective issues of U.S. Census Bureau, Current Population Reports, Population Estimates, Series P-26, 1978. The number of cases for each area in the sample was:

Nonmetropolitan		Metropolitan	
Area 1:	171	Area 5:	1
Area 2:	96	Area 6:	8
Area 3:	6	Area 7:	29
Area 4:	8	Area 8:	4
Subtotal:	281	Area 9:	11
		Area 10:	9
		Subtotal:	62

Table B.1. Average Level of Energy Production by State

	All Five States	Ky.	Mont.	Okla.	Pa.	Wyo.
Number of counties	343	120	58	77	67	23
NonSMSA counties	281	103	54	63	39	22
Billion BTU per capita All energy per capita	1.683	0.912	1.707	2.703	0.362	6.086
Coal per capita	0.477	0.855	0.336	0.047	0.320	0.749
Oil per capita	0.594	0.030	0.983	0.762	0.007	3.742
Natural gas per capita	0.563	0.000	0.182	1.889	0.026	1.560
Hydropower per capita	0.016	0.009	0.069	0.002	0.003	0.011

Table B.3 exhibits results obtained by regressing per capita income on output of specific forms of energy, per capita, as well as on dummy variables for states and areas. Further, the annual rates of growth in per capita income for the periods of interest were also employed as dependent variables, and were regressed on the same set of explanatories, with results in Table B.4.

Energy production per capita is much higher in non-metro than metro areas, as indicated by these summary data:

Area	Energy per capita
Area 1	2.524
Area 2	1.318
Area 3	0.534
Area 4	0.128
All nonSMSA	2.001
SMSA	0.242

Table B.2. County Classification by Population and Location

Area	Metro/ Nonmetro	Location Criteria	Population Criteria
1	nonmetro	noncontiguous to SMSA	contains no place > 25,000
2	nonmetro	contiguous to SMSA	contains no place > 25,000
3	nonmetro	noncontiguous to SMSA	contains a place of 25,000 to 50,000
4	nonmetro	contiguous to SMSA	contains a place of 25,000 to 50,000
5	metro	outlying county	central city population < 50,000
6	metro	outlying county	central city population 50,000- 100,000
7	metro	outlying county	central city population > 100,000
8	metro	county with central city of SMSA	central city population < 50,000
9	metro	county with central city of SMSA	central city population 50,000- 100,000
10	metro	county with central city of SMSA	central city population > 100,000

Given these data (and corresponding levels of specific energy sources), regression equations were applied to estimate the contribution of energy production to per capita income, by area, with results shown in Table B.5.

Table B.6 exhibits results when population growth was related to the explanatory variables. Here, define r as the annual rate of growth in population; then (1+r) was formed for the 1969-72 period and the 1972-77 period, and each was regressed on output per capita of specific forms of energy, and on dummy variables for states and areas. Finally, the ratio of those annual growth rates was formed, and multi-

Table B.3. Regression Equations Explaining Income per Capita, Pooled Samples

	1969	1972	1975	1977	Number of Statistically Significant Cases
Constant	3,983.0	4,332.9	4,451.0	4,893.0	4
Coal per capita	-19.1	-11.2	27.3	14.8	0
Oil per capita	-8.0	-13.1	8.3	22.5	0
Natural gas per capita	43.6	106.2	71.7	45.1	4
Hydropower per capita	-31.6	150.8	104.9	190.2	0
Kentucky	-1,024.5	-1,070.0	-1,020.4	-1,112.4	4
Montana	-225.0	-144.1	-143.8	-744.1	2
Oklahoma	-899.1	-923.8	-870.5	-1,065.3	4
Pennsylvania	-449.7	-527.0	-529.1	-681.3	4
Wyoming	0.0	0.0	0.0	0.0	-
Nonmetro areas[a]					
Area 1	-1,015.1	-1,035.9	-1,049.9	-1,196.5	4
Area 2	-816.4	-891.1	-949.9	-1,040.9	4
Area 3	-440.5	-577.4	-478.8	-415.5	2
Area 4	-245.2	-337.1	-370.1	-413.2	0
Metro areas[a]					
Area 5	-1,090.2	-1,042.5	-880.1	-906.3	2
Area 6	-725.8	-850.1	-869.0	-904.6	4
Area 7	-236.6	-337.9	-412.9	-449.7	3
Area 8	-597.0	-587.7	-574.3	-651.1	3
Area 9	-356.1	-379.0	-475.3	-439.1	3
Area 10	0.0	0.0	0.0	0.0	-
$\bar{R}^2$: explained variance	.460	.457	.327	.378	

[a]See Table B.2 for classification of areas.

Table B.4. Regression Equations Explaining Annual Growth Rates In Income,[a] Pooled Samples

	Estimated Coefficients				Number of Statistically Significant Cases
	1969–72	1972–75	1975–77	1972–77	
Constant	102.403	100.244	105.165	102.187	4
Coal per capita	0.192	0.529	-0.283	0.195	3
Oil per capita	-0.052	0.206	0.153	0.187	1
Natural gas per capita	0.534	-0.329	-0.371	-0.347	3
Hydropower per capita	1.758	-0.411	0.988	0.276	0
Kentucky	1.338	1.645	-0.064	0.962	2
Montana	1.204	-0.395	-7.426	-3.412	2
Oklahoma	1.064	1.322	-1.943	0.029	1
Pennsylvania	-0.086	0.571	-1.612	-0.283	0
Wyoming	0.000	0.000	0.000	0.000	–
Nonmetro areas[b]					
Area 1	1.299	0.692	-0.948	0.308	0
Area 2	0.089	-0.172	-0.122	-1.711	0
Area 3	-1.035	0.998	0.902	1.001	0
Area 4	-0.687	-0.311	-0.079	-0.246	0
Metro areas[b]					
Area 5	1.811	2.342	0.752	1.722	0
Area 6	-0.778	0.319	0.513	0.398	0
Area 7	-0.921	-0.521	-0.051	-0.336	0
Area 8	0.705	0.508	-0.318	0.183	0
Area 9	0.201	0.529	0.372	0.065	0
Area 10	0.000	0.000	0.000	0.000	–
$\overline{R}^2$: explained variance	.247	.117	.260	.380	

[a]Let r = observed annual growth rate in per capita income; then $(1+r)(100)$ is dependent variable employed in equations. Specifically, let $\overline{Y}_t$ = per capita income in year t. Then $(\overline{Y}_{72}/\overline{Y}_{69})^{1/3} = (1+r)$ for the 1969–72 period.

[b]See Table B.2 for classification of areas.

Table B.5. Deflated Income by Area, and Estimated Contribution of Energy Production to That Income

Category and Year	Nonmetro Areas					SMSA
	Area 1	Area 2	Area 3	Area 4	All nonSMSA	
Deflated per capita income, 1967 dollars						
1969	2,347.1	2,414.3	2,844.3	2,990.0	2,399.4	2,965.3
1972	2,732.8	2,680.4	3,049.7	3,201.3	2,735.0	3,203.2
1975	2,873.3	2,793.8	3,304.8	3,322.0	2,868.2	3,297.9
1977	2,925.2	2,939.2	3,635.1	3,555.4	2,963.2	3,561.0
Estimated income attributable to energy production[a]						
1969	52.5	0.6	17.9	0.9	23.5	2.0
1972	118.2	25.1	25.1	1.3	74.6	6.9
1975	125.2	47.8	29.1	4.7	87.5	9.9
1977	111.6	41.1	31.2	5.3	73.2	8.7
Energy portion/all income						
1969	.0224	.0002	.0063	.0003	.0098	.0007
1972	.0433	.0094	.0082	.0004	.0273	.0022
1975	.0436	.0171	.0088	.0014	.0305	.0030
1977	.0382	.0140	.0086	.0015	.0247	.0024

[a]Obtained by regression of deflated income on specific forms of energy per capita and on areas, and then by setting energy outputs equal to zero in the fitted equations to obtain income net of energy. Subtraction of that net figure from average income (shown above) yielded income attributable to energy production.

Table B.6. Regression Equations Explaining Annual Growth Rates
in Population, and Changes in Growth Rates, Pooled Samples

Variable	(1) Annual Population Growth Rates: $(1+r)(100)$[a] 1969-72	(2) 1972-77	(3) Relative Growth Rates (2)/(1) X 100
Constant	101.151*	102.836	100.644
Coal per capita[b]	0.095*	0.265*	0.165*
Oil per capita[b]	-0.155*	-0.017	0.142*
Natural gas per capita[b]	-0.057	0.031	0.087*
Hydropower per capita[b]	-0.419	0.351	0.785
Kentucky	-1.409*	-2.329*	-0.877*
Montana	-1.521*	-2.535*	-0.967*
Oklahoma	-1.495*	-2.178*	-0.610
Pennsylvania	-1.462*	-3.423*	-1.916*
Wyoming	0	0	0
Nonmetro areas[c]			
Area 1	-0.046	0.427	0.481
Area 2	0.305	0.707	0.408
Area 3	0.186	0.708	0.547
Area 4	-0.025	0.849	0.874
Metro areas[c]			
Area 5	0.289	0.588	0.309
Area 6	1.021	1.289*	0.267
Area 7	1.281*	1.948*	0.665
Area 8	-0.719	0.236	0.319
Area 9	-0.220	0.816	1.059
Area 10	0	0	0
$\bar{R}^2$: explained variance	.103	.331	.179

*Indicates statistical significance at 10 percent level.

[a]Let P = population of county, with P_{69} = 1969 population, etc.
Then $P_{72}/P_{69} = (1+r)^3$ for column (1) use; here, label the growth
rate as $r(1)$, with $[1+r(1)]$ (100) the dependent variable for the
equation of column (1). Similarly, $P_{77}/P_{72} = (1+r)^5$ for column (2),
with $[1+r(2)]$ (100) the dependent variable for the equation of
column (2). Finally, $[1+r(2)/1+r(1)]$ (100) is the dependent
variable for the equation of column 3.

[b]In billion BTU per capita.

[c]See Table B.2 for classification of areas.

Table B.7. Regression of Relative Population Growth Rates
(Times 100) on Energy per Capita (Billion BTU per Capita)

	Ky.	Mont.	Okla.	Pa.	Wyo.
Constant	100.354	100.006	100.640	99.096	101.165
Coefficient	0.029	0.260	0.072	0.157	0.136
t ratio	0.590	4.826	1.441	1.455	2.703

plied by 100 to obtain an index of growth in the second
period relative to the first; then that growth index was
also employed as a dependent variable using the same set of
explanatory variables.

Individual state regression equations were also obtained
in which the population growth index was related to energy
production per capita as a continuous variable. Results are
shown in Table B.7. Results for energy as a discrete variable are presented in text, above.

NOTES

1. The discussion here draws on U.S. General Accounting
Office, 1977: 5.4; New York Times, 27 Oct. 1979; and
Business Week, 24 Sept. 1979, p. 109.

2. The assumed class averages used in Table 8.9 were
also applied to the Bowles and Beale data.

3. This section draws on Schurr et al. 1979: 265-68;
Lipinsky 1978; Converse et al. 1979; U.S. Department of
Energy position paper in Biomass 1978; Nadkarni as cited in
Gamsin 1979; New York Times 28 Aug. 1979; and Perry 1979.

BIBLIOGRAPHY

Alonso, William. "The Economics of Urban Size." Papers and
    Proceedings of the Regional Science Association 26
    (1971): 67-83.
_____. "Urban Disamenities." Society May/June (1976):
    51-53.
Beale, Calvin. "Recent U.S. Rural Population Trends and

Selected Economic Implications." Statement before the
Joint Economic Committee, 31 May 1978.

Bender, Lloyd et al. "Local Impact of Coal Gasification and
Liquefaction Plants in Northern Great Plains Sites."
Unpublished manuscript, 1979.

Bowles, Gladys K., and Beale, Calvin L. "Commuting and
Migration Status in Nonmetro Areas." Agricultural
Economics Research 32 (1980): 8-20.

Brookshire, David S., and d'Arge, Ralph C. "Adjustment
Issues of Impacted Communities or Are Boomtowns Bad?"
Natural Resources Journal 20 (1980): 523-46.

Burwell, C. C.; Ohanian, M. J.; and Weinberg, A. M. "A
Siting Policy for an Acceptable Nuclear Future." Science
204 (1979): 1043-51.

Business Week. 24 Sept. 1979, p. 109.

Cartee, Charles. "Solar Energy Installations: Trends and
Lender Attitudes." Journal of Property Management
Jan./Feb., 1976.

Converse, J. C. et al., Ethanol Production From Biomass
with Emphasis on Corn. Ethanol Study Committee. Madison,
Wis.: College of Agricultural and Life Sciences,
University of Wisconsin, 1979.

Danziger, Sheldon. "Determinants of the Level and Distribution of Family Income in Metropolitan Areas, 1969."
Land Economics Nov. (1976): 467-78.

Doherty, Joseph C. "Public and Private Issues in Nonmetropolitan Government." In Growth and Change in Rural
America. Urban Land Institute, 1979.

Drysdale, Frank R., and Calef, Charles E. The Energetics of
the United States of America: An Atlas. Upton, N.Y.:
Brookhaven National Laboratory, 1977.

Executive Office of the President. Rural Development Initiatives: Energy for Rural America. Washington, D.C., May
1979.

Farber, Erich A. "Solar Energy." Building System Design
June/July, 1978.

Feighter, Yvonne, and Nordstrom, J. A Social, Economic and
Cultural Study of the Crow Reservation: Implications
for Energy Development. Billings, Mont.: Crow Impact
Study Office, Old West Regional Commission, 1977.

Foster Associates, Inc. Energy Prices, 1960-73. Cambridge,
Mass.: Ballinger, 1974.

Fuchs, Victor R. Differentials in Hourly Earnings by Region
and City Size, 1959. Occasional Paper 101. New York:
National Bureau of Economic Research, 1967.

The Gallup Opinion Index. Report no. 164. March 1979.

Gamble, Hays B.; Downing, R. H.; and Sauerlender, O. H.
Effects of Nuclear Power Plants on Community Growth
and Residential Property Values. University Park, Pa.:
Pennsylvania State University Institute for Research on
Land and Water Resources, 1979.
Harris, La Donna. Interview, WRC Radio, Washington, D.C.,
6 Dec. 1979.
Hoch, Irving. "City Size Effects, Trends and Policies."
Science 3 Sept. (1976): 856-63.
_____. "Energy, Regions and Highway Finance." In
State Transportation Issues and Actions: Proceeding of
Second TRB Conference on Statewide Transportation
Planning, pp. 18-36. Transportation Research Board
Special Report 189. Washington, D.C., 1980b.
_____. Energy Use in the United States, by State
and Region. Washington, D.C.: Resources for the Future,
1978.
_____. "Income and City Size." Urban Studies Oct.
(1972): 299-328.
_____. "The Role of Energy in the Regional Distri-
bution of Economic Activity." In Alternatives to
Confrontation: A National Policy Toward Regional
Change, edited by Victor Arnold, pp. 227-326. Lexing-
ton, Mass.: Lexington Books, D. C. Heath & Co., 1980a.
_____. "Settlement Size, Real Income, and the Rural
Turnaround." American Journal of Agricultural Economics
Dec. (1979): 953-59.
Izraeli, Oded. "Differentials in Nominal Wages and Prices
Between Cities." Ph.D. dissertation, University of
Chicago, 1973.
Jaffe, Martin. "Protecting Solar Access." Environmental
Comment, Urban Land Institute Journal, May 1978.
Kneese, Allen, and Williams, Michael. "Environmental
Aspects of Resources Policy in a Regional Setting." In
Regional Environmental Policy: The Economic Issues, by
H. Siebert, I. Walter, and K. Zimmermann, pp. 187-220.
New York: New York University Press, 1979.
Kroll, Cynthia. "Community Disruption." In Minerals
Economics for Natural Resource Planning, by E. Thor and
G. Elsner. USDA, Forest Service, Pacific Southwest Range
and Experiment Station, Berkeley, Calif., forthcoming.
Landsberg, Hans. "Energy Realities." Washington Post, 7
Aug. 1979.
Land Use Planning Report. "Slants and Trends," 2 July
1979.
_____. "Western States Back Energy Impact Funds,"

15 Aug. 1977.

Lipinsky, Edward. Battelle Memorial Institute. "Sugar Cane vs. Corn vs. Ethylene as Sources of Ethanol for Motor Fuels and Chemicals." In U.S. House of Representatives, 95th Congress, Second Session, Committee on Government Operations, Biomass Conversion, 14 Apr. 1978. Washington, D.C., 1978, pp. 99-103.

McDonald, Steven. Cited in "Energy Shortage Is Said to Pose Lasting Economic Threat to North." New York Times, 1 Feb. 1977.

Mazzeo, D. "Wood as an Energy Source." Building System Design Aug./Sept. 1978.

Miernyk, William H. "Rising Energy Prices and Regional Economic Development." Growth and Change July 1977.

Mikesell, James J. Housing Program Area, ESCS, USDA, unpublished data developed from computer tape of U.S. Dept. of Commerce, 1974 and 1975. Annual Housing Survey, 1979.

Motor Vehicle Manufacturers Association. Motor Vehicle Facts & Figures. Detroit, Mich.: 1977 and 1979 editions.

Nadkarni, Ravindra. Unpublished study for DOE conducted by Arthur D. Little, Inc., cited in Sharon Gamsin, The Oil Daily, 18 June 1979.

National Transportation Policy Study Commission. National Transportation Policies Through the Year 2000. Washington, D.C., 1979.

Natwig, Eric, and Godoff, Stephen. "Energy Development and the Navajo Tribe." New Mexico Business Sept. (1976): 3-5.

New York Times. 8 Jan. 1978; 30 June, 27 July, 7 Aug., 13 Aug., 28 Aug., 27 Oct., 6 Nov., and 23 Dec. 1979.

Norman, James. "Application of Solar Collectors to Residential Systems." Building Systems Design June/July, 1978.

Perry, Harry. Personal communication, Oct. 1979.

Pierce, Neal R. "The Countrified City." Washington Post, 6 Oct. 1979.

Purdy, Bruce J. et al. A Post Licensing Study of Community Effects at Two Operating Nuclear Power Plants. Oak Ridge, Tenn.: Oak Ridge National Laboratory, 1977.

Schulze, W. D.; Ben-David, S.; and Balcomb, J. D. The Economics of Solar Home Heating. Prepared for the Joint Economic Committee, 95th Congress, 13 Mar. 1977.

Schurr, Sam H. et al. Energy in America's Future. Baltimore, Md.: Johns Hopkins Press for Resources for the

Future, 1979.

Shonka, D. B.; Loebl, A. S.; and Patterson, P. D. Trans-
    portation Energy Conservation Data Book: Edition 2. Oak
    Ridge, Tenn.: Oak Ridge National Laboratory, 1977.

Smith, Edward. Energy and Labor Use by Manufacturing
    Industries. Rural Development Research Report, EDD-
    ESCS, USDA, 1980.

Solar Action. Citizens' Solar Program: State Reports on
    Barriers and Strategies to Renewable Energy Develop-
    ment. Washington, D.C., 1978.

Stockman, David. Cited in George Will column, Washington
    Post, 1 Apr. 1979.

Tolley, George. "Economic Policy Toward City Bigness." In
    Proceedings of Inter-University Committee on Urban
    Economics. Cambridge, Mass., 1969.

U.S. Bureau of the Census. Current Housing Reports, series
    H-123. "Residential Energy Uses," H-123-77. Washington,
    D.C.: U.S. Government Printing Office, 1978.

_____. Current Population Reports, series P-20, no.
    273. "Mobility of the Population of the United States:
    March 1970 to March 1974." Washington, D.C., 1974.

_____. Current Population Reports, series P-20, no.
    350. "Population Profile of the United States: 1979."
    Washington, D.C., 1980.

U.S. Department of Commerce. Bureau of Economic Analysis,
    Regional Economic Measurement Division, "County and
    Metropolitan Area Personal Income." Survey of Current
    Business Apr. (1979): 25-47.

U.S. Department of Energy. Position paper, appendix in U.S.
    House of Representatives, 95th Congress, Second Ses-
    sion, Committee on Government Operations, Biomass
    Conversion, 14 Apr. 1978. Washington, D.C., 1978, pp.
    151-53.

U.S. Energy Information Administration. Residential Energy
    Consumption Survey: Consumption and Expenditures, April
    1978 Through March 1979. DOE/EIA-0207/5. Washington,
    D.C., 1980.

U.S. General Accounting Office. U.S. Coal Development--
    Promises, Uncertainties. Washington, D.C., 22 Sept.
    1977.

U.S. House Committee on Science and Technology. Hearings
    on Energy Conservation in Buildings Act of 1976. 94th
    Congress, Aug. 1976.

U.S. Joint Economic Committee. Gasoline Distribution.
    Hearings before the Subcommittee on Consumer Economics,
    93rd Congress, Second Session, 12 and 14 Mar. 1974.

Washington, D.C., 1974.

Wall Street Journal. 27 Aug., 20 Sept., 18 Oct., and 13
Nov. 1979.

Wardwell, John M., and Gilchrist, C. Jack. "The Distribution of Population and Energy: Confluence and Divergence." Paper presented at Rural Sociological Society
Annual Meetings, Burlington, Vt., August 1979.

Washington Post. 25 June 1977; 25 Mar. 1978; 10 June, 25
June, 3 July, and 25 Oct. 1979.

Williams, Edward. Environmental Analysis of Synthetic
Liquid Fuels. Washington, D.C., U.S. Department of
Energy, 1979.

Wright, Arthur. "Energy Policy and Deregulation: Two Hot
Topics, or Does Smoke Necessarily Mean There Is a
Fire?" Growth and Change, 10 (1979).

Yeck, Robert G. Personal communication, November 1979, of
table developed in "Energy Consumption in Agricultural
Production," U.S. Department of Agriculture, 1976.

Zeimetz, Kathryn A. Growing Energy: Land for Biomass Farms.
U.S. Economics, Statistics and Cooperatives Service,
Agricultural Economic Report no. 425. Washington, D.C.,
1979.

III.

The Differential Access
to Opportunity

Vernon M. Briggs, Jr.

9
Unemployment and Underemployment

INTRODUCTION

Despite both the size and importance of the nonmetro sector
of the economy, its human resource needs have long been
neglected. As of 1976, almost one-quarter of the nation's
population lived in nonmetro areas and one-third of its
labor force worked there. Of even greater long-run consequence is that the nonmetro population, which was relatively stable between 1940 and 1970, has shown signs of
increasing both its absolute size and relative share of the
nation's population since 1970. This has led some observers
to speak of a "rural renaissance" (Martin, 1977: 217). The
rapid rise of the rural nonfarm sector as a source both of
residences and of employment has sparked the revival of the
nonmetro economy, and this has led to a demand for more
knowledge about both nonmetro workers and nonmetro labor
markets.

To interpret the effectiveness of nonmetro labor markets
for nonmetro workers, certain definitional concepts must be
established. These concepts enable analysts to discern
trends over time and policymakers to make decisions. The
economic and political utility of these concepts, therefore,
has often become intertwined. Unfortunately, the concepts
used for analysis of nonmetro labor markets have tended to
be transplanted from the study of the dominant metro economy, and the general result has been detrimental to the
welfare of nonmetro workers and to an adequate understanding
of the needs of nonmetro America.

The unemployment rate has become by far the most important of the economic indicators. It has been referred to as
"the most important single statistic published by the federal government" (President's Committee to Appraise Employment and Unemployment Statistics, 1962: 9). Not only has it
become the standard for determining the inadequacy of the
demand for labor and the slack utilization of the available
labor supply, but, especially since the early 1970s, it

also has evolved into a role as a primary allocator of
federal funds for human resource development policies
(Shiskin 1977; Norwood 1977). As of fiscal year 1977,
unemployment data were used to allocate more than $13
billion to more than 6,000 political and geographic subdivisions of the nation (National Commission on Employment
and Unemployment Statistics, 1979: 12, 28). Thus, the
"officially" undefined unemployment rate has become more
than simply a subject of academic interest. It has become a
topic of practical importance in both the formulation and
the implementation of public policymaking.

Yet since the early 1960s there has been growing concern
by some labor economists and by many public officials that
the unemployment rate itself is an inadequate indicator for
understanding the actual condition of local labor markets.
In addition to questions about whether the official definition of unemployment truly measures the availability of
labor, concerns have also developed over the adequacy of
existing jobs to provide "a minimally decent standard of
living" for those who hold them (Levitan and Taggart, 1974:
xii). In response to these issues, federal legislation was
enacted in 1976 that created the National Commission on
Employment and Unemployment Statistics. Among its duties,
the commission was mandated to examine whether: "the
current method of data collection and the form of its
presentation, at national, regional, and subregional levels
may not fully reflect unemployment and employment trends
and may produce incomplete and, therefore misleading
conclusions, thus impairing the validity of this critical
economic indicator." (P.L. 94-444: Section 13, a 1E.) In
the final conference report pertaining to the passage of
this legislation, the congressional committee elaborated
upon its instructions to the commission as follows:

> The Committee has been concerned for some time with the
> development of labor force data that would measure the
> degree of economic hardship experience by individuals
> both in and out of the labor force. In the Comprehensive
> Employment Act of 1973, the Secretary of Labor was
> directed to develop such data, including measures of
> "unemployment, labor force participation, involuntary
> part-time employment, and full-time employment at less
> than poverty wages." No agreed-upon measurement system
> has yet been developed.
>
> The Commission is directed in the bill to examine
> this issue and is expected by the Committee to make

specific recommendations for implementing the directive
expressed in CETA. (Emergency Jobs Programs Extension
Act of 1976, Report No. 94-833: 347.)

The conceptual concerns in the term "hardship" as used
by the conference committee are essentially the same ones
raised by scholars and public officials to address the
issue of underemployment or subemployment in the 1960s
(Spring, 1972: 187-94). Actually, as will be seen, there
are both substantial as well as subtle differences in the
terms "underemployment," "subemployment," or "hardship
index" in the literature. Indeed, the lack of clarity among
these terms has been a major impediment to the development
of a formal measure of underutilization of labor. For this
reason, it will be necessary to trace the general development of these concepts and to note the differences independent of the specific discussion of their usefulness to
rural labor market analysis. Nonetheless, despite their
conceptual variations, they collectively represent a singular purpose: an effort to broaden significantly the scope
of the standard labor market indicators.

THE DEFINITION AND STATUS
OF THE CONCEPT OF UNEMPLOYMENT

The official definitions of the civilian labor force--those
employed plus those unemployed--have not been substantially
altered since they were set forth during the Depression
(National Commission on Employment and Unemployment Statistics, 1979: 23). The definitions used by the U.S. Bureau of
the Census in its monthly "Current Population Survey" state
that employed persons are those civilians more than sixteen
years of age who are not institutionally confined and who
either work for pay at any time or who worked unpaid for at
least fifteen hours in a family-operated enterprise during
the week in which the monthly sample count is conducted.
Those persons who were temporarily absent from regular jobs
because of illness, vacation, industrial dispute or similar
reason are also counted as being employed. A person with
more than one job is counted only in the job at which he or
she worked the greatest number of hours. Unemployed persons
are those civilians above the age of sixteen who are not
institutionally confined who did not work at all during the
survey week but who claim to be available for work and who

searched for a job during the preceding four weeks. The
official unemployment rate, therefore, is simply a ratio of
the unemployed to the combined number of employed and
unemployed. Only civilians (as opposed to those in the
military) are presently included. The monthly figures and
the resulting annual averages are adjusted to correct for
estimating errors after each decennial census. Thus, the
definitions used to determine the official unemployment are
statistically explicit. Aside from a few minor suggestions,
the National Commission on Employment and Unemployment
Statistics recommended that no changes be made in the
current definition of employment. The commission, in a five
to four split vote, specifically rejected a proposal that
discouraged workers should be counted as being unemployed
(National Commission of Employment and Unemployment Statistics, 1979: 56). As will be discussed subsequently, the
continued exclusion of discouraged workers has disproportionately adverse significance to the evaluation of rural
labor markets relative to urban labor markets.

THE DEFINITION AND STATUS OF
THE CONCEPT OF UNDEREMPLOYMENT

During the 1930s when the procedures and terms used to
measure unemployment were being largely perfected, there
was a close relationship between unemployment and economic
deprivation. Unemployment was pervasive among all regions,
races, sexes, and classes. In subsequent years as the unemployment rate has fallen considerably from its Depression
heights, there has been growing concern that the unemployment rate no longer is a satisfactory proxy for economic
deprivation. As an aggregate figure, the unemployment rate
is a composite of the vast amount of diverse individual
experiences. Hence, even a low unemployment rate can mask
the fact that subgroups in the population may still be
experiencing very high levels of unemployment. Average
figures often conceal more than they reveal.
    Indeed, during the 1960s as the civil rights movement
progressed from its initial preoccupation with the social
and political indignities of overt segregation in the South
to becoming a national movement for equal economic opportunity, the shortcomings of the unemployment rate became
painfully obvious. Unemployment rates during the mid-1960s
fell to their lowest levels since World War II. Yet a rash

of civil disorders erupted in a number of urban areas
throughout the nation. Analysis of the causes of these
upheavals centered upon the deterioration of urban black
employment opportunities despite opposite national trends
(Report of the National Advisory Commission on Civil Disorders, 1968: 251-65). Many of these urban blacks were either
migrants from the rural South or children of families who
themselves had migrated from the rural South (Fuller 1970).
Unemployment rates for blacks were more than twice those of
whites and the rates for black women and black youth were
even higher. But to make things even worse, labor market
experts noted that the economic plight of blacks was also
adversely affected by declining labor force participation
rates and by the fact that many fully employed blacks were
unable to earn incomes that would bring them above nationally defined poverty levels. Contrary to popular beliefs at
the time, the economic status of the black population in
the 1960s was deteriorating from advances made in the 1940s
and early 1950s (Killingsworth 1968).

Thus, the stage was set for a departure from sole reliance upon the unemployment rate as the principal determinant of the adequacy of labor markets. In 1966, the U.S.
Department of Labor (DOL) launched its "slum survey" in ten
large urban areas. No nonmetro areas were included. The
study found that in slum areas where minorities were disproportionately concentrated, considerably higher unemployment rates prevailed than in the surrounding metro areas.
But the level of analysis was broadened by the introduction
of the new concept of a "subemployment" measure (Manpower
Report of the President, 1967: 73-75), containing the
following: (1) People classed as unemployed because they
were jobless and looking for work during the survey week.
(2) Those working only part time though they wanted full-
time work. (3) Heads of households under sixty-five who
earn less than $60 a week though working full time; also
individuals less than sixty-five years of age, not heads of
households, who earn less than $56 a week on a full-time
job (the equivalent of $1.40 an hour for a forty-hour week).
(4) Half the number of "nonparticipants" in the labor force
among men aged twenty to sixty-four (on the assumption that
the other half are not potential workers, chiefly because
of physical or mental disabilities or severe personal problems). (5) An estimate of the male "undercount" group (based
on the assumption that the number of men in the area should
bear the same relation to the number of women in the population generally; also that half of the unfound men are

in the four groups of subemployed people just listed--the others being either employed or not potential workers). The average rate of subemployment in the ten urban slum areas was computed to be 34 percent with the range being from 24 to 47 percent.

The subemployment index, therefore, was developed in response to the need for a better yardstick to measure the utilization of available urban labor, following the violent eruption of a number of the nation's urban slums. No consideration was given at the time to the application of the concept to rural labor markets. The obvious explanation is that rural workers suffer from the lack of a public voice. Their needs at the time that the subemployment index was conceived were as severe as those of urban workers, if not more so. But because rural workers are geographically dispersed and they lack media coverage (relative to what is available to urban workers), it is almost impossible for their needs to be articulated and publicized or for their frustrations to be manifested in ways that are available to urban workers. Hence, no research or policy effort was made to include rural workers in the conceptual design of the index by DOL. In passing it should be noted that in 1967 the final report of the President's National Advisory Commission on Rural Poverty did make reference to the severity of underemployment in rural areas. Its report, however, did not attempt to measure the magnitude of underemployment or to offer a preferred way to measure its dimension (President's National Advisory Commission on Rural Poverty, 1967: X).

In 1968, DOL reiterated its belief that a subemployment index should be developed and expanded (Manpower Report of the President, 1968: 24). DOL announced that further surveys were underway and suggested that "impoverished rural areas" should also be studied in light of this expanded definitional concept. But with the change in political leadership and philosophy at the federal level that occurred in late 1968, the official interest in the subject of underemployment concepts was abandoned (Spring: 1972).

In 1972, the staff of the Subcommittee on Employment, Manpower, and Poverty of the Senate Committee on Labor and Public Welfare undertook the task of compiling a subemployment index for fifty-one urban areas (U.S. Senate, 1972: 2276-80). Again, the concern of the subcommittee was to find a better way "to understand economic conditions in inner-city slums" (Ginsburg, 1975: 96). The subcommittee relied, however, not on a sampling technique but rather on

the data collected in the 1970 count of the entire population of these low income areas by the census. It found that
although the national unemployment rate was between 5 and 6
percent, the unemployment rate in these inner-city areas
was 10 percent and that the subemployment rate was 30 percent. The subemployment concept was essentially the same
as that used in 1967 by DOL. Again, no effort was made to
include any rural areas.

Interest among academicians in the subject of an expanded definitional concept remained strong. In 1973,
Miller pointed out that "statistical concepts do not exist
in a vacuum" and, although the traditional reliance upon
unemployment was "still extremely useful as an economic
indicator," that "it has serious defects as a social indicator for which it is often used" (Miller, 1973: 10).
Miller proposed his own version of a measure of subemployment that seemed "to be more appropriate to the employment
problems of today." It counted as subemployed all persons
twenty-one to sixty-four years old or sixteen to twenty-one
years old if not enrolled full time in school or in a training program who are also either: (1) unemployed; (2) not
looking for work because they believe no work is available
(i.e., discouraged workers); (3) working part time involuntarily; or (4) family heads or unrelated individuals
working full time for less than the minimum wage or work
full time but not earning enough to provide their families
income above the poverty line (as defined by the Social
Security Administration whose income standards vary with
family size). Miller anticipated that "many economists"
would criticize such a measure because of its subjective
judgments about what constitutes a decent wage or income
level. He responded by observing that "all social and
economic measures require judgments" and that "they become
accepted and used only when a concensus is reached that the
judgments are reasonable" (Miller, 1973: 11). Miller's
study applied to twelve cities and it computed a subemployment index of 19 percent--or two and one-half times the
tabulated unemployment rate for these same cities.

Also in 1973, Levitan and Taggart set forth the outlines
of a proposed index of Employment and Earnings Inadequacy
(EEI). The EEI builds "on previous subemployment concepts"
and "a range of separate labor market statistics" (Levitan
and Taggart: 1973). The derivation of the EEI involved a
three-stage process: first, the subemployed are counted;
second, all subemployed persons in a household with income
above the upper-income bounds used to define adequacy are

excluded; and third, the remainder is divided by the number
of actual and discouraged labor force participants to derive
a single index. The definitions of the subemployed in the
EEI differ in important ways from the original DOL subemployment index. In both, the unemployed and involuntary
part-time employed persons were treated similarly. But the
EEI included discouraged workers of both sexes. Moreover,
EEI included all employed family heads and unrelated individuals who were employed full time for a year but whose
incomes were insufficient to lift their households above
the federal poverty thresholds. It also included household
heads earning below poverty level incomes because of inter-
mittent employment. EEI excluded all persons between sixteen
and twenty-one years old and all those more than sixty-five.
Working wives in husband-wife families and other relatives
are also excluded from the two earnings group in the EEI
regardless of their work patterns or family income. The
result was that, when applied to the month of March 1972
when the official unemployment rate was 6.1 percent, the
EEI for the nation was 11.5 percent. There was no effort to
disaggregate the EEI in any way; it was designed to be an
aggregate national indicator. Also, no direct effort was
made to relate EEI to rural workers, and no mention was
made of the problem of statistical undercount as stated in
the original DOL concept.

In 1973, the passage of the Comprehensive Employment
and Training Act (CETA) mandated that DOL develop data that
closely resemble those needed to construct either a subemployment or an EEI index. The act also required that funds
be allocated on the basis of local labor market data on
unemployment--even though no such local labor market data
existed at that time (Norwood 1977). The Bureau of Labor
Statistics (BLS) of DOL was given the responsibility to
develop all such data. In 1975, the commissioner of BLS
outlined the extreme difficulty encountered in the collection and tabulation of subemployment data (Shiskin 1975).
Because there was no consensus among policymakers, academicians, and the public, the commissioner requested that an
independent and impartial review committee be established
to examine the definitional issues involved.

In the meantime, in 1976, BLS announced that it would
begin tabulation and publication of seven separate "measures
of unemployment." One would be the official defined rate
whereas the other six were various measures that were either
tighter or looser constructions of labor market conditions

Table 9.1. Published Unemployment Figures,
First Quarter 1979

Measure	Percentage
U_1 Persons unemployed 15 weeks or longer as a percentage of civilian labor force	1.2
U_2 Job losers as a percentage of civilian labor force	2.4
U_3 Unemployed persons 25 years and older as a percentage of civilian labor force 25 years and older	3.9
U_4 Unemployed full-time job seekers as a percentage of full-time labor force	5.2
U_5 Official unemployment rate--persons 16 years and older as a percentage of civilian labor force 16 years and older	5.7
U_6 Full-time job seekers plus 1/2 part-time job seekers plus 1/2 total on part-time for economic reasons as a percentage of civilian labor force, less 1/2 of part-time labor force	7.2
U_7 Numerator of U_6 plus discouraged workers as a percentage of denominator of U_6 plus discouraged workers	7.9

Source: U.S. Department of Labor, Bureau of Labor
Statistics, The Employment Situation, Table A-7.

(Shiskin 1976). Table 9.1 p   s these seven concepts
with the appropriate rates f   1979. The measures U_1-U_6 are
straightforward classifications of the employed and unemployed. Only U_7, which includes discouraged workers, introduces some ambiguities because it requires a judgment rather
than being the actual result of specific activity as is the
case with all of the others. All of the indicators are
national aggregates.

Also in 1976, as indicated earlier, legislation was
enacted that established the National Commission on Employment and Unemployment Statistics. This presidential commission of nine nongovernmental persons was charged to proceed
with the development of broader labor market concepts. A
specific request was made to study the issue of economic

hardship. Sar Levitan, one of the authors of the EEI
concept, was appointed chairman of the new commission.

In its final report, the Levitan Commission did find
"that the present system falls short of meeting the information needs of labor market analysts" who are concerned with
the usefulness of the data for policy development (National
Commission on Employment and Unemployment Statistics, 1979:
38). The commission noted that "economic hardship" may come
from low wages among employed persons, unemployment (including partial unemployment due to slack work) among those in
the labor force, and limited participation in the labor
force by persons who desire more participation. The commission recommended the development of "multiple indicators"
of hardship. In its final report, however, the commission
rejected the idea of a single composite index of labor market hardship. Such a composite index had been contained in
the preliminary draft issued nine months prior to the final
report. The decision not to recommend such a single index
was based on an eight to one vote with Chairman Levitan
casting the single dissent (National Commission on Employment and Unemployment Statistics, 1979: 59-60 and 71-72).
The majority of the commission concluded that "the issues
associated with defining labor market hardship reveal the
inherent complexity and multidimensional nature of the
concept." The commission did recommend that distinct
indicators corresponding to various types of hardship be
developed and published in an annual hardship report that
would separately discuss employed persons earning low
wages, unemployment, and nonparticipation in the labor
force (National Commission on Employment and Unemployment
Statistics, 1979: 63-71). In an appendix to its report, the
pros and cons of a single composite index are set forth.

It is significant that the commission explicitly recognized the lack of useful labor market indicators for measuring the adequacy of employment for rural workers. It
discussed the need for better indicators other than simply
unemployment. Hence, it did recommend "that the rural population be an identifiable population group in indicators
of labor market related hardships" (National Commission on
Employment and Unemployment Statistics, 1979: 97). But, as
should be apparent, the evolution of most of the efforts to
measure underemployment has had little explicit recognition
of rural labor market behavior. Either the concepts were
based largely upon urban market studies or upon national
data series that are heavily biased toward urban concepts.

RELEVANCE OF AVAILABLE UNEMPLOYMENT
AND UNDEREMPLOYMENT TO RURAL AREAS

The incidence of underemployment and unemployment, in 1974, provided by the U.S. Bureau of Census from its Current Population Survey is shown in Table 9.2. Although these data are useful as a first approximation, their interpretation is hazardous. Nonmetro workers were more frequently underemployed than metro workers and their unemployment rates were nearly twice the metro rates. But the high incidence of underemployment and low relative frequency of unemployment in some nonmetro counties seems to point to measurement problems. In metro areas employed black females were more fully employed than were white females, yet wage differentials are such as to suggest subemployment of blacks. The need for research in depth on the nature of underemployment is clearly indicated.

Research that is explicitly concerned with rural labor market operation and the job-seeking behavior of rural workers is very limited relative to that available for urban areas and urban workers. Moreover, the findings of this relatively small body of rural research are not always consistent on all matters. But on one key issue there is singular agreement in the rural labor market literature: the official government unemployment rate is a very poor measure of both underutilization of labor supply and job adequacy in rural areas. Perhaps the most emphatic statement to this effect was made by Tweeten in his background paper prepared for the Levitan Commission: "The ineluctable conclusion from the foregoing examination of issues is that no amount of massaging of unemployment statistics will provide appropriate measures of employment needs in rural areas. Refinement of data gathering and processing techniques will not salvage the situation. Unemployment is simply the wrong concept" (Tweeten, 1978: 21). Other scholars have forcefully expressed similar concerns, including Hathaway, who says that unemployment rates "aren't relevant at all" as a measure of economic welfare in rural areas (Hathaway, 1972: 43). Also, Marshall contends that unemployment data "is an unsatisfactory measure of the looseness or tightness of a labor market" in rural areas (Marshall, 1974: 78), and Nilsen says that "this labor market statistic [i.e., the unemployment rate] does not accurately portray conditions in non-metropolitan areas" (Nilsen, 1979: 31). Martin writes that rural labor market needs are "underestimated" by officially defined unemployment rates

Table 9.2. Labor Force Status and Number of Weeks Worked
by Employed Workers Sixteen Years of Age and Older, by Residence,
Sex, and Race, 1974

Residence	Weeks Worked						
	Total	50-52	40-49	27-39	14-26	<13	Unem-ployed
	White Males						
Metro	100.0	70.7	7.9	5.2	6.1	6.2	4.0
Central cities	100.0	69.3	8.1	5.4	6.5	6.1	4.4
Remainder	100.0	71.5	7.7	5.0	5.8	6.3	3.6
Counties added since 1970	100.0	70.6	7.6	6.2	6.0	6.4	3.3
Nonmetro	100.0	68.9	8.3	6.1	6.0	7.0	3.6
Counties with cities 25,000 and more	100.0	68.4	9.0	6.4	5.3	7.0	3.8
Counties with cities 2,500-25,000	100.0	69.4	8.0	5.8	6.2	7.1	3.6
Counties with no cities of 2,500 or more	100.0	67.6	8.4	7.6	6.4	6.8	3.2
	White Females						
Metro	100.0	51.3	9.3	9.2	12.6	12.9	4.6
Central cities	100.0	53.8	8.8	9.4	11.6	11.6	4.8
Remainder	100.0	49.6	9.7	9.1	13.3	13.8	4.5
Counties added since 1970	100.0	48.8	10.6	9.5	12.7	14.0	4.4
Nonmetro	100.0	47.6	9.7	10.0	13.3	15.2	4.1
Counties with cities 25,000 and more	100.0	49.2	10.0	9.3	13.2	15.4	4.4
Counties with cities 2,500-25,000	100.0	47.3	9.7	10.2	13.3	15.3	4.2
Counties with no cities of 2,500 or more	100.0	46.0	9.4	10.8	15.0	15.6	3.3

Table 9.2 (continued)

Residence	Weeks Worked						
	Total	50-52	40-49	27-39	14-26	<13	Unem-ployed
	Black Males						
Metro	100.0	60.4	7.7	7.1	8.1	7.4	9.1
Central cities	100.0	59.6	8.1	7.7	7.7	7.7	9.1
Remainder	100.0	62.8	6.7	5.2	9.6	6.6	9.3
Counties added since 1970	100.0	65.9	3.5	8.2	9.4	9.4	3.5
Nonmetro	100.0	56.2	8.8	7.0	8.2	12.9	6.7
Counties with cities 25,000 and more	100.0	61.6	8.6	8.2	5.8	8.6	7.2
Counties with cities 2,500-25,000	100.0	58.0	6.8	7.1	8.3	13.8	5.9
Counties with no cities of 2,500 or more	100.0	43.6	15.4	5.8	10.4	15.0	9.3
	Black Females						
Metro	100.0	52.0	8.2	8.3	11.4	12.6	7.6
Central cities	100.0	52.3	7.8	8.9	10.6	13.0	7.4
Remainder	100.0	50.8	9.3	6.1	14.3	11.5	8.0
Counties added since 1970	100.0	44.4	7.8	10.4	20.3	10.4	8.5
Nonmetro	100.0	41.7	7.8	11.4	12.6	18.6	7.8
Counties with cities 25,000 and more	100.0	45.6	10.4	10.7	12.1	13.1	8.0
Counties with cities 2,500-25,000	100.0	41.4	6.5	11.0	12.0	21.0	8.1
Counties with no cities of 2,500 or more	100.0	36.1	8.9	14.6	15.8	17.7	6.3

Source: U.S. Bureau of the Census, Current Population Reports, series P-23, no. 55.

(Martin, 1977: 223), and Rungeling et al. argue that unemployment measures not only "fail to reflect accurately the extent of economic difficulties for rural areas" but that "they actually mask the nature as well as the magnitude of the problem" (Rungeling et al., 1977: 146).

Each of the authors cited above has directed his research specifically to rural labor market operations and rural workers, and each has strongly recommended that some measure of underemployment would be a far more appropriate descriptor. The reasons given for the need for such a measure are complex but they do reflect careful analysis of nonmetro phenomena.

The incidence of self-employment in 1975 was twice as high in nonmetro areas (17.4 percent of the labor force) as it was in metro areas (8.9 percent) (Nilsen, 1979: 11). It was most common in the North Central states (21.5 percent) and least common in the northeastern nonmetro areas (11.2 percent). Of those self-employed in all nonmetro areas, 61.4 percent reported such work was their sole source of earned income. It is farm activity in rural areas that accounts for most of the difference in the degree of self-employment between metro and nonmetro areas. Self-employed persons represent an entirely different group than those who work for wages and salaries. Income from self-employment is subject to greater fluctuations and the earnings derived from such work are often low. Also, as Nilsen noted, "unlike wage and salary jobs, unemployment from self-employment activities generally requires that the enterprise fails" (Nilsen, 1979: 13).

It is also of consequence that involuntary part-time employment is higher in nonmetro than in metro areas. In 1975, the difference was 4.8 percent to 3.7 percent or almost 30 percent higher (Nilsen, 1979: 17). The main reasons for this difference are that many rural industries are more sensitive to unfavorable weather conditions and the employment mix in rural areas is disproportionately composed of industries with unstable labor requirements.

In addition, casual employment, unpaid family labor, multiple-job holders, as well as seasonal and migratory work are all more common in rural areas than in nonrural areas (Tweeten, 1978: 4). As a result nonmetro areas have a much higher proportion of low earnings occupations than do metro areas. The occupational categories of operatives, laborers, and farm occupations are proportionately higher. These three occupations in 1973 represented 41 percent of all male employment in nonmetro areas as opposed to only 25 percent in metro areas (Nilsen, 1979: 22-25).

With regard to income, median family incomes in rural areas are rising but they remain considerably below those of urban families. In 1975, nonmetro family income averaged $11,600 as opposed to $14,909 for metro incomes (Tweeten, 1978: 3). For present purposes, it is highly significant that the incidence of poverty was considerably greater in rural areas (17 percent) as opposed to metro areas (11 percent) in 1975. Moreover, the depth of poverty as indicated by the gap between actual income and the poverty threshold is greater in rural than urban areas (Tweeten, 1978: 3). The distribution of poverty families in the nation is quite unequal with the nonmetro South accounting for not only 41 percent of the nation's nonmetro population but also 60 percent of all nonmetro poor persons. Although in absolute terms, there are more Anglos in nonmetro poverty than any other racial group, the proportionate incidence of poverty among nonmetro blacks, Chicanos, and native Americans is much higher than the similar rate for nonmetro Anglos. Participation in social programs (e.g., unemployment insurance coverage, minimum wage coverage, and disability insurance) for needy persons, however, is lower in nonmetro areas than in metro areas (Tweeten, 1978: 5). The fact that the population is geographically dispersed in nonmetro areas also adds to the difficulty of providing labor market information and of delivering employment assistance services. Likewise, the general scarcity of employment alternatives in nonmetro areas often leads to shorter job search activity.

As a result of these uniquely nonmetro labor market characteristics, the available research is uniform in its findings. The statistical representation of unemployment is actually lower than the real number of persons wanting jobs. Many persons who are involuntarily employed part time are counted as being fully employed. Labor force participation rates for both men and women are lower in nonmetro than metro areas. In 1970, for instance, 73.8 percent of the males and 41.1 percent of females in nonmetro areas were in the labor force as opposed to 77.5 percent of the males and 43.4 percent of all females in metro areas (Tweeten, 1978: 3-4). The explanation is partly due to differences in the respective age profiles of the sectors and partly because workers become more easily discouraged from actively seeking jobs. There are considerably fewer

job alternatives available in rural areas and low wages
dampen the enthusiasm for prolonged searches (Rungeling et
al. 1975). The lower wage levels, the presence of fewer
capital intensive industries, the seasonal employment
opportunities, and the reduced access to income assistance
programs all contribute to the fact that the working poor
are proportionately more numerous in nonmetro than metro
areas.

Thus, it is not surprising that nonmetro labor market
researchers are in complete agreement that underemployment
measures are mandatory for an adequate depiction of nonmetro
labor market reality. These conclusions have also been recognized by the National Governors Association (NGA). Increasingly since the inception of CETA, the nation's governors have been assigned the responsibility for human resource problems in nonmetro areas. Hence, NGA has strongly
criticized the use of unemployment rates as a basis for
fund allocations and it has sought to have some form of
subemployment formula substituted in its place (National
Governors Association, 1979: 43-104). The NGA, however, is
very concerned that so little research has actually been
done on the critical problems of the working poor and discouraged workers in nonmetro areas, and that the economics
profession has been unable to develop a measure of underemployment that can be disaggregated to nonmetro labor
markets (National Governors Association, 1979: 48-49).

One crude effort was made by Marshall to construct a
subemployment index for the aggregate nonmetro economy in
1970 (Marshall, 1974: 80-81). He took the number of men and
women who were unemployed in nonmetro areas in 1970 and
then added an adjustment that would account for their lower
labor force participation. For males less than age sixty-
five, the adjustment was 50 percent; for females less than
age sixty-five it was 10 percent. To these adjusted figures,
the number of working-poor family heads was added. The
result was that the nonmetro subemployment rate for men was
25 percent and for women 17.3 percent. The subemployment
rate for men was 6.1 times greater than their unemployment
rate; for women it was 3.0 times greater. The major limitation of Marshall's work was that it is based entirely on
the use of secondary data--that is, census data.

Only one study of nonmetro labor markets has attempted
to compute a subemployment index that was drawn from a
primary household survey (Rungeling et al. 1977). The
strength of this study is that it was based on 3,422
interviews that were randomly selected from the population

of four geographically separated southern nonmetro counties. The questionnaire was able to probe more deeply into participation and nonparticipation than has any other source of labor market information currently available (including census reports). It was possible to identify precisely who was involuntarily employed part time, who was a discouraged worker, and who were the working poor. This information was compiled and used to prepare a subemployment index that was constructed with exactly the same standards used by Levitan and Taggart in their EEI that was discussed earlier. The result was that although Levitan and Taggart found a subemployment index of 11.5 percent for the nation in 1972, Rungeling et al. found a rate of 41.0 percent for the combined four nonmetro counties for roughly the same time period.

The limitation of this study, however, is that the four nonmetro counties were all from the South. Moreover, the counties were preselected partly because of their known high incidence of poverty. The study was originally designed to serve as a baseline for measuring the impact of proposed welfare reform changes in 1972. But when the reform effort was abandoned, the DOL decided to continue support for the study because so little was known about the dynamics of rural labor markets. The authors do contend that "each [county] is roughly representative of large segments of the rural South" (Rungeling et al., 1977: 12). Nonetheless, the subemployment rate of 41.0 percent is certainly extreme as a depiction of the total nonmetro economy of the nation (and, perhaps, of the total nonmetro South). The study, however, did reveal numerous ways in which nonmetro labor markets are distinguishably different from metro labor markets. For instance, the official unemployment rate for the four counties, computed from the interviews, was only 2.7 percent. But the combined labor force participation rate of the counties was an incredibly low 42.3 percent (the comparable national rate was 61.8 percent in 1972). In standard labor market analysis, low unemployment rates are usually accompanied by higher than average (not lower than average) labor force participation. The study was able to identify exactly why the labor force participation was so low. It found that the unemployment rate would have been 11 percent higher if discouraged workers were included and another 8 percent higher if those working involuntarily on a part-time basis were included (Briggs et al., 1977: 228). Also, whereas 43.1 percent of the households surveyed were living in poverty, fully 34 percent of those poverty house-

holds had a head who was employed full time. Thus, there
were many nonmetro workers who were poor despite the fact
that they were regularly employed. Notwithstanding the
limitations of the study, the magnitude of the revealed
problems accentuates the necessity of a more realistic
measure of labor utilization than mere reliance upon the
standard definition of unemployment.

THE DATA BARRIER TO EFFECTIVE RESEARCH

To collect primary data, however, is a costly undertaking.
It is not surprising, therefore, that most of the limited
amount of available research is based upon secondary data.
But the use of secondary data sources is often confusing.
One of the factors that has retarded research in nonmetro
labor market operations and has hampered the formulation of
effective public remedies for nonmetro human resource
problems has been the lack of a consistent definition of
the term "nonmetro."
    The Bureau of the Census has two separate data series
that are most commonly used to define the rural population.
One, used in the "Current Population Survey," includes in
the metro population all persons living in a Standard Metropolitan Statistical Area (SMSA) of 50,000 persons or more;
those living in the county in which an SMSA is located;
and those counties tied to an SMSA by daily communication
links. The nonmetro population includes those people living
in the counties that remain. In 1970, 2,485 counties out of
3,097 were classified as nonmetro counties. The Census
Bureau, in its decennial count of the population, however,
uses a definition of the rural population that defines
rural persons as those living in open country as well as
small towns of less than 2,500 persons, unless inside the
urban fringe of metropolitan areas.
    "Rural" and "nonmetro" are sometimes used interchange-
ably. This is misleading because the land areas classified
as nonmetro greatly exceed the areas classified as rural.
Moreover, it is estimated that about 30 percent of those
classified as "rural" reside in open areas within the boundaries of metro areas. In 1970, one series listed 62.8 million persons living in nonmetro areas and the other series
reported 53.9 million persons living in rural areas. As yet
there has been no study of the effect of the different

definitions although it is obvious that there is a considerable numerical difference.

The U.S. Department of Labor, in turn, defines as rural counties those in which a majority of the people live in places with populations less than 2,500. Because the definition includes people living in places with more than 2,500 if those places were in counties where a majority of the people lived in places with populations of less than 2,500, the DOL definition is more inclusive than is the definition of the Census Bureau.

The nonmetro definition of rural is often used by the U.S. Department of Health, Education and Welfare in its rural programs. In addition, there are other definitions used by the U.S. Department of Agriculture (some of its programs define as rural areas the open country plus places with population of 10,000 or less). All of these (plus a few more that could be cited) are "official" definitions of one government agency or another. Until the population is uniformly defined, it is very difficult to address the derivative labor market data problems in an unambigious manner from secondary data sources.

THE STATUS OF UNDEREMPLOYMENT MEASURES

Although the final report of the National Commission on Employment and Unemployment Statistics did not explicitly recommend the tabulation of an economic hardship measure, the reluctance was due more to methodological problems than to principle. If the recommendation to prepare annual reports on low wage workers, unemployment, and nonparticipation in the labor market actually is implemented and the rural population is identifiable within these indicators, it can only be a matter of time until the mechanical difficulties of making a hardship index useful at the local level can be worked out.

The report of the Levitan Commission may prove to be of significance for improved human resources policies in rural areas because it discusses many of the basic data problems confronting contemporary labor market analysis in these areas. For instance, it noted that all of the available government data series define nonmetro areas as residuals of metro data definitions. Also, it argues for a consistent definition among government agencies that collect

and publish nonmetro labor market data. The report observes
that "unemployment rates in rural areas are consistently
low relative to urban areas." Taking note of the inordinately high incidence of poverty in nonmetro areas and the general scarcity of jobs relative to metro areas, the commission also mentions that the problems of worker discouragement, involuntary part-time employment, and the working
poor are especially severe in many nonmetro areas. The
commission states that "the diverse circumstances of rural
workers and the unique characteristics of rural labor markets" underscore the need for new measures of earnings
and income adequacy (National Commission on Employment and
Unemployment Statistics, 1979: 97). Hence, despite its
hesitation to endorse the need for hardship measures explicitly, the commission's discussion of nonmetro labor
market problems certainly contributes to the drive by other
scholars and policymakers for the collection of such data.
Throughout the literature on nonmetro labor markets, there
is unanimous opinion that underemployment measures are
essential for both understanding the nonmetro economy and
the development of appropriate policy actions to address
nonmetro human resource needs.

CONCLUDING OBSERVATIONS

The preponderance of research pertaining to labor market
operations and worker behavior has been based upon exclusively metro studies or national studies that contain extensive metro biases. Few studies have explicitly sought
to study nonmetro labor markets. As a result, the major
conceptual measures used for policy formulations have
assumed statistical definitions that appear to have little
real relevance to the nonmetro economy. Specifically, unemployment and labor force participation rates have become
the standard barometers of labor utilization at the national, regional, and local level.
    Although the available research from primary data is
sparse and that from secondary data is limited, the singular
conclusion that underemployment is a far more prevalent
issue in nonmetro areas is sufficient to warrant acceptance
until other studies can prove otherwise. An underemployment
index should be added to the existing federal labor market
data collection system, and this measure needs to be disaggregated to the county level and based upon the regular

decennial census or the proposed five-year population
census.

It can be expected that, if underemployment measures
are actually developed and if they are included in formulas
that allocate funds for federal programs, there would be a
considerable increase in assistance provided under most
programs to rural areas. As such increases will probably
mean decreases elsewhere, it is likely that there will be
immense political opposition to any effort to change the
prevailing urban bias that accentuates unemployment as the
key allocator (National Governors Association, 1979: 86-87).
Thus, part of the resistance to the wider adoption of economic hardship measures would stem not from logic or methodological restraints but from political awareness of what
the results might be.

BIBLIOGRAPHY

Briggs, Vernon, M., Jr.; Rungeling, Brian; and Smith, Lewis
H. "The Significance of Welfare Reform for the Rural
South." In Proceedings of the Thirtieth Annual Winter
Meetings of the Industrial Relations Research Associa-
tion, pp. 226-34. Madison, Wis.: Industrial Relations
Research Association, 1977.
Emergency Jobs Programs Extension Act of 1976. U.S. Senate
Report no. 94-883.
Fuller, Varden. Rural Work Adjustment to Urban Life. Ann
Arbor, Mich.: The Institute of Labor and Industrial
Relations, 1970.
Ginsburg, Helen. Unemployment, Subemployment, and Public
Policy. New York: Center for Studies in Income Main-
tenance Policy, New York University School of Social
Work, 1975.
Hathaway, Dale. "Discussion of Session I." In Labor Market
Information in Rural Areas, edited by Collette Moser.
East Lansing, Mich.: Center for Rural Manpower and
Public Affairs, Michigan State University, 1972.
Killingsworth, Charles G. Jobs and Income for Negroes.
Policy paper no. 6. Ann Arbor, Mich.: Institute of
Labor and Industrial Relations at the University of
Michigan, 1968.
Levitan, Sar, and Taggart, Robert. "Employment and Earnings
Inadequacy: A Measure of Worker Welfare." Monthly Labor
Review 96 (1973): 19-27.

_____. Employment and Earnings Inadequacy: A New
Social Indicator. Baltimore, Md.: Johns Hopkins Univer-
sity Press, 1974.
Manpower Report of the President: 1967. Part II. Washington,
D.C.: U.S. Government Printing Office, 1967.
Manpower Report of the President: 1968. Washington, D.C.:
U.S. Government Printing Office, 1968.
Marshall, Ray. Rural Workers in Rural Labor Markets. Salt
Lake City, Utah: Olympus Publishing Company, 1974.
Martin, Philip L. "Rural Labor Markets and Rural Manpower
Policy." In Proceedings of the Thirtieth Annual Winter
Meetings of the Industrial Relations Research Associa-
tion. Madison, Wis.: Industrial Relations Research
Association, 1977.
Miller, Herman P. "Subemployment in Poverty Areas of Large
U.S. Cities." Monthly Labor Review 96 (1973): 10-18.
National Commission on Employment and Unemployment Statis-
tics. Counting the Labor Force. Washington, D.C.:
National Commission on Employment and Unemployment
Statistics, 1979.
National Governors Association. CETA and Rural Places.
Washington, D.C.: National Governors Association, 1979.
Nilsen, Sigurd R. Employment and Unemployment Statistics for
Nonmetropolitan Areas. Background Paper no. 33. Washing-
ton, D.C.: National Commission on Employment and
Unemployment Statistics, 1979.
Norwood, Janet. "Reshaping a Statistical Program to Meet
Legislative Priorities." Monthly Labor Review 100
(1977): 6-11.
President's Committee to Appraise Employment and Unemploy-
ment Statistics. Measuring Employment and Unemployment.
Washington, D.C.: U.S. Government Printing Office,
1962.
President's National Advisory Commission on Rural Poverty.
The People Left Behind. Washington, D.C.: U.S. Govern-
ment Printing Office, 1967.
Public Law 94-444. Section 13. (1 October 1976).
Report of the National Advisory Commission on Civil Dis-
orders. New York: Bantam Books, 1968.
Rungeling, Brian et al. Employment, Income and Welfare in
the Rural South. New York: Praeger Publishing Co., 1977.
Rungeling, Brian; Smith, Lewis H.; and Scott, Loren. "Job
Search in Rural Areas." In Proceedings of the Twenty-
Eighth Annual Winter Meetings of the Industrial Rela-
tions Research Association, pp. 20-135. Madison, Wis.:
Industrial Relations Research Association, 1975.

Shiskin, Julius. "Employment and Unemployment: The Doughnut or the Hole." Monthly Labor Review 99 (1976): 3-10.
_____. "A New Role for Economic Indicators." Monthly Labor Review 100 (1977): 3-5.
_____, and Stein, Robert L. "Problems in Measuring Unemployment." Monthly Labor Review 98 (1975): 3-10.
Spring, William J. "Underemployment: The Measure We Refuse to Take." In The Political Economy of Public Service Employment, edited by Harold L. Sheppard, Bennett Harrison, and William J. Spring. Lexington, Mass.: D. C. Heath Company, 1972.
Tweeten, Luther. Rural Employment and Unemployment Statistics. Background Paper no. 4. Washington, D.C.: National Commission on Employment and Unemployment Statistics, 1978.
U.S. Bureau of the Census. Current Population Reports, series P-23, no. 55. "Social and Economic Characteristics of the Metropolitan and Nonmetropolitan Population, 1974 and 1970." Washington, D.C.: U.S. Government Printing Office, 1975.
U.S. Department of Labor, Bureau of Labor Statistics. The Unemployment Situation. 1 June 1979.
U.S. Senate, Committee on Labor and Public Welfare, Subcommittee on Employment, Manpower, and Poverty. Comprehensive Manpower Reform. Hearings, pt. 5, 92nd Congress, 2nd Session, pp. 2276-80. Washington, D.C: U.S. Government Printing Office, 1972.
Werneke, Diane. "Measuring Economic Hardship in the Labor Market." The American Economic Review 69 (1979): 43-7.

Stephen F. Seninger
Timothy M. Smeeding

10

Poverty: A Human Resource-Income Maintenance Perspective

INTRODUCTION

Fourteen years ago, the President's National Advisory
Commission on Rural Poverty (1967) published its report,
The People Left Behind. At that time fully one-half of all
poor Americans lived in nonmetro areas, although only one
in three of all (poor and nonpoor) Americans lived in such
places. By 1977--the latest year for which data are avail-
able--the percentage of the poor in nonmetro areas had
decreased to 40 percent although the proportion of all
Americans living in rural places remained at about one-
third. Between 1959 and 1977 the nonmetro poverty rate
dropped 58 percent (from 33.2 to 13.9 percent) as compared
to only a 32 percent decline in metro poverty rates as
illustrated in Table 10.1.

However, such signs of progress against nonmetro poverty
must be tempered by other less encouraging observations.
The poverty rate in nonmetro America (13.9 percent) is
still one-third higher than the poverty rate in metro areas
(10.4 percent), and the poverty income gap (the difference
between income and the poverty threshold) is greater for
the nonmetro poor than for the metro poor. The large decline in poverty in nonmetro areas (and in contrast the
less rapid decline in central city poverty) over this

This research was supported in part by funds granted to the
Institute for Research on Poverty at the University of
Wisconsin-Madison by the Department of Health, Education
and Welfare pursuant to the provisions of the Economic
Opportunity Act of 1964. Helpful comments on an earlier
draft were made by William Alonso, David L. Brown, Sheldon
Danziger, Garth Magnum, and Peter Morrison. We would also
like to thank Kate Samolyk, Marian Lewin, Richard Anderson,
and especially Nancy Williamson for the valuable research
and computational assistance, and Catherine Ersland for
typing and patience.

Table 10.1. Number and Percentage of Persons Below the Poverty Level by Place of Residence, 1959–1977

Year	Total		Metro		Nonmetro		Central Cities		Living on Farms	
	(000,000s)	%	(000,000s)	%	(000,000s)	%	(000,000s)	%	(000,000s)	%
1959	38.87	22.0	17.02	15.3	21.75	33.2	10.44	18.3	7.4[a]	45.0[a]
1967	27.77	14.2	13.83	10.9	13.94	20.2	8.65	15.0	2.71	25.9
1969	24.15	12.0	13.08	9.5	11.06	17.9	7.99	12.7	2.00	20.7
1971	25.56	12.2	14.45	10.4	11.00	17.2	8.91	14.2	2.07	20.9
1973	22.97	11.1	13.76	9.7	9.21	14.0	8.51	14.0	1.28	13.4
1974	23.37	11.2	13.85	9.7	9.52	14.2	8.37	13.7	1.46	16.2
1975	25.88	12.3	15.34	10.8	10.53	15.4	9.09	15.0	1.32	16.4
1976	24.98	11.8	15.23	10.7	9.75	14.0	9.48	15.8	1.26	15.9
1977	24.72	11.6	14.86	10.4	9.86	13.9	9.20	15.4	1.34	17.1
Percentage change: 1959–1977	-47.3		-32.0		-58.1		-15.8		-62.0	

Source: U.S. Bureau of the Census, Current Population Reports, series P-60, no. 98, no. 115, and no. 119, Table 3 from each.

[a]Author's estimate based on unpublished census data.

period was in large part due to the migration of poor
families to larger cities in search of better jobs rather
than widespread economic growth in the poverty pockets of
rural America. Nonmetro population dispersion suggests that
nonmetro poverty is much more diverse and heterogeneous
than metro poverty, which is primarily found in the ghettos
of large central cities. Such a statement, however, needs
to be qualified. Nonmetro poverty also has its areas of
concentration. A full 60 percent of all nonmetro poor still
reside in the South, mainly in the Mississippi Delta, along
the southeastern Coastal Plain, in Appalachia, and on the
Ozark Plateau. Relatively new poverty pockets primarily
consisting of Chicanos are appearing in southern Texas and
New Mexico (see Chapter 13). Moreover, since 1973 there has
been no overall progress against poverty in America--as the
official poverty figures in Table 10.1 suggest.[1]

Going beyond such generalizations to an analysis of
the causes of (and cures for) nonmetro poverty is a somewhat
more difficult task. Recent shifts in regional economic
development patterns--the snowbelt/sunbelt phenomenon--and
net migration from metro areas to nonmetro places (Beale
1975, 1976; Clawson 1976a; Martin 1977) make it hazardous
to summarize the current state of knowledge regarding rural
poverty, much less to predict future patterns of poverty in
rural areas.

However, despite the heterogeneity and diversity of
ongoing trends in rural areas, several facts seem to stand
out: (1) The recent migration from metro to nonmetro areas
has so far had little effect on the broad typology of rural
poverty in the United States. In particular, it has had
little effect on the low incomes and the high incidence of
poverty in the rural South. Based on an income concept that
includes the effects of in-kind transfers on poverty, the
poverty rate in rural America is still more than 20 percent
higher than in central city areas--the place where the poverty conditions are supposedly the worst. (2) As educational
attainment among younger nonmetro residents approaches that
of metro residents, these more mobile nonmetro people (particularly in the South) are moving to areas where economic
growth has made jobs available (Zuiches and Brown 1978:
U.S. Department of Agriculture 1975). However, underemployment and low wages, particularly among middle-age and older
residents in depressed nonmetro areas, are still persistent
problems that call for innovative public manpower policies.
So far, there have been few successful strategies. In particular, recent manpower policy efforts (e.g., the CETA

program) have had little effect on nonmetro labor markets and nonmetro poverty. (3) Comprehensive welfare reform of the type recently suggested by President Carter would enormously and undeniably benefit the nonmetro areas of the country, particularly the nonmetro South. However, powerful political forces and antigovernment feeling make passage of such legislation unlikely at this time.

The remaining sections of this chapter will present and examine evidence to support these facts by reviewing the conditions and problems of poverty, manpower programs, and welfare systems in nonmetro areas. The next section identifies the descriptive characteristics of poverty according to the typology of nonmetro areas. A simple framework for understanding the underlying factors of low income and its attributes is presented in the third section of the chapter. This framework serves as an organizational vehicle for the remaining two sections: the fourth section on poverty and its relationship to human resources (human capital, labor mobility, and other labor market problems of rural low-wage earners), and the fifth section on the current welfare system and welfare reform.

Several socioeconomic issues that indirectly affect nonmetro poverty are not included within the scope of this discussion. Deavers (1978: 1) has described "rural development" as the existence of viable opportunities for a large majority of individuals to choose among a wide range of decent opportunities to live and work in nonmetro (or metro) areas. The following discussion omits the direct and traditional concept of nonmetro development as it relates to the regional nonmetro industrial infrastructure--the demand side of nonmetro labor markets.[2] Instead, the emphasis will be on the ways in which nonmetro development relates to labor mobility and human resources--the supply side of the nonmetro job market. In order to develop some general perspectives on the relevant nonmetro poverty literature, a detailed examination of all of the demographic features of nonmetro versus metro poverty will not be attempted.[3] Also, the poverty status of specific nonmetro groups (e.g., American Indians and several Hispanic minorities) will not be reviewed.

THE TYPOLOGY OF POVERTY IN NONMETROPOLITAN AREAS

The purpose of this section is to describe the level of and
trend in nonmetro poverty according to the typology of
nonmetro areas. The typology of nonmetro areas is broken
down into five groupings: regional context, size of community, rate of population change, structure of settlement
patterns (concentrated or dispersed), and degree of urban
access (influence). Unless otherwise specified the terms
"nonmetro" and "metro" will be used in preference to
"rural" and "urban" in this chapter.[4]
     Poverty has several dimensions and definitions (Davis
1977; Deavers 1978; Tweeten and Brinkman 1976; Howes and
Markusen, Chapter 11 in this volume). Yet the poverty data
presented here focus on only one of these dimensions: income
inadequacy. However, income inadequacy is probably the most
important determinant of poverty. Other dimensions of poverty such as inadequate assets, lack of social mobility,
low socioeconomic status, and lack of political power are
highly correlated with inadequate incomes. In addition,
individual low income is typically reflected by poor housing, inadequate nutrition, and poor health, while concentrations of low-income people (such as those found in the
rural South) create communities in which basic public services (education, sanitation, police, fire, utilities) are
poor or nonexistent (Coelen and Fox, in Chapter 15 in this
volume). It seems reasonable to argue that, in general,
patterns of income poverty and low incomes serve as proxies
for all of the other dimensions of poverty.

POVERTY UNDER THREE DEFINITIONS OF INCOME

As a preface to the typological analysis of poverty presented below and in contrast to the official census poverty
estimates on which this is generally based, nonmetro poverty
will be examined first under three different definitions of
income: official income, pretransfer income, and final or
adjusted income. It will be shown that depending on those
receipts that are counted as income, very different pictures
of nonmetro versus metro poverty emerge.
     The inadequacies of the Census Bureau's poverty statis-
tics are by now widely known (Smeeding 1977; Congressional
Budget Office 1977). The official income measure used by
the census includes only before tax cash income—earnings,
property income, and transfers. Because the official census

poverty line[5] is a consumption needs standard, income must
be adjusted to reflect ability to meet the given consumption
floor; thus, direct federal income taxes and Social Security
payroll taxes need to be subtracted from income. Moreover,
census income figures are derived from Current Population
Survey (CPS) data that are on average substantially under-
reported. For instance, in any one year only about 75 percent of the cash public assistance actually received is
reported in the CPS. Most importantly, census poverty data
completely ignore the antipoverty effect of in-kind transfers in the form of food, housing, and medical care. Although these transfers are less valuable to most recipients
than equal amounts of cash income, they should in some way
be accounted for. Clearly they add to the economic well-
being of recipients and substitute for out-of-pocket expenses. Given the rapid growth of in-kind transfer programs
in recent years, this is a most serious omission. In-kind
transfers from medicare, medicaid, and food stamps totaled
$48.5 billion in 1977, whereas cash public assistance ben-
efits, Aid to Families with Dependent Children (AFDC),
Supplemental Security Income (SSI), and General Assistance
were only $17.9 billion in this same year (Danziger et al.
1979). In-kind transfers are included based on an estimate
of their cash equivalent value to recipient households.
This value is equal to the amount of cash income that would
leave the recipient family equally as well off as the in-
kind subsidy (Smeeding 1977). Having adjusted the data for
income underreporting, federal income and payroll tax
liability, and in-kind transfers, we arrive at an adjusted
or final income measure. On this basis the poverty count
declines by a substantial amount, particularly in metro
areas and central cities where the number and generosity of
in-kind benefits is highest (Tables 10.2 and 10.4). In
1974, these adjustments reduced the official poverty count
by 37.9 percent in central cities versus only 26.1 percent
in nonmetro areas. Given the relatively low levels of transfer benefits and widespread racial discrimination in the
nonmetro South, where black poverty is highly concentrated,
the differential effect of in-kind transfers is especially
pronounced for nonwhites, reducing central-city nonwhite
poverty by almost twice as much (43.5 percent) as nonmetro
nonwhite poverty (23.2 percent).

A third way to look at poverty is to consider the poverty position of families based on pretransfer income (or
factor income) only, that is, before receiving any transfers. Because larger numbers of rural persons are "working

Table 10.2. Number of Poor and Incidence of Poverty by Residence, Race, and Type of Income, 1974

Income and Race	Total		Metro				Nonmetro[c]	
			Central City[a]		Suburb[b]			
	(000,000s)	%	(000,000s)	%	(000,000s)	%	(000,000s)	%
Official census income[d]								
(1) Total	23.37	11.5	8.37	13.7	5.48	6.7	9.52	14.2
(2) Whites	15.74	8.8	4.23	9.2	4.45	5.8	6.93	11.4
(3) Nonwhites	7.63	30.3	4.14	18.3	1.03	19.0	2.59	40.6
Pretransfer income[e]								
(4) Total	38.64	18.5	13.75	22.5	9.84	12.1	15.04	22.5
(5) Whites	28.44	15.6	8.06	17.6	8.46	11.1	11.92	19.7
(6) Nonwhites	10.19	39.5	5.69	38.9	1.39	26.9	3.12	49.2
Final income[f]								
(7) Total	16.37	7.8	5.20	8.5	4.14	5.1	7.03	10.5
(8) Whites	11.29	6.3	2.86	6.2	3.39	4.5	5.04	8.3
(9) Nonwhites	5.07	19.0	2.34	16.0	.75	14.4	1.99	30.2
			Percentage Reductions in Poverty by Income					
Pretransfer poor to final poor								
Total [(4)-(7)]/(4)	57.6		62.2		57.9		53.3	
Whites [(5)-(8)]/(5)	60.3		64.8		59.5		57.9	
Nonwhites [(6)-(9)]/(6)	51.9		58.9		46.0		36.2	
Official census poor to final poor								
Total [(1)-(7)]/(1)	30.0		37.9		23.9		26.1	
Whites [(2)-(8)]/(2)	28.3		32.4		23.8		27.2	
Nonwhites [(3)-(9)]/(3)	33.6		43.5		27.2		23.2	

Source: Tabulations based on U.S. Bureau of the Census, Current Population Survey, March 1975.

a"Central City" includes persons living in city centers of Standard Metropolitan Statistical Areas (SMSAs) with cities of 50,000 or more inhabitants.

b"Suburb" includes all persons living in metro areas but outside of central cities as defined above.

c"Nonmetro" includes all persons not residing in SMSAs as defined above.

d"Official census income" is the same income measure used by the Bureau of the Census in the P-60 income and poverty series.

e"Pretransfer income" includes all taxable factor income except for capital gains plus non-Social Security pensions, gross of personal income and payroll taxes.

f"Final income" is census income, adjusted for underreporting of survey income, federal income, and payroll taxes, and the cash equivalent value of in-kind food and medical care transfers. For more detail, see Smeeding 1977.

Table 10.3. Residence and Race of the Poor by Various
Income Measures, 1974

| Income and Race | Total[a] | Metro | | | Nonmetro |
		Total	Central City	Suburb	
	%	%	%	%	%
Official census income[b]					
Total	100.0	59.6	35.8	23.8	40.4
Whites	100.0	56.0	26.1	29.9	44.0
Nonwhites	100.0	67.8	54.5	13.3	33.2
Pretransfer income[b]					
Total	100.0	61.1	35.6	25.5	38.9
Whites	100.0	58.1	28.3	29.8	41.9
Nonwhites	100.0	59.4	55.8	3.6	30.6
Final income[b]					
Total	100.0	57.1	31.8	25.2	42.9
Whites	100.0	55.4	25.3	30.0	44.6
Nonwhites	100.0	60.8	46.1	14.7	39.2

Source: Tabulations based on U.S. Bureau of the Census,
Current Population Survey, March 1975.

[a]Totals may not add to 100% due to rounding error.

[b]See notes to Table 10.2 for definitions of income.

poor," the percentage of all poor pretransfer persons who
live in nonmetro areas is considerably less than when poverty is measured on the basis of either official or adjusted income (Table 10.3). Once more, this effect is most
pronounced for nonwhites. Although our latest data are
for 1974, unpublished Congressional Budget Office data for
1976, using a similar adjusted income measure, show an even
more pronounced preurban bias in the antipoverty effect of
the current income transfer system. Thus, although these
data adjustments sharply reduce the incidence of poverty
regardless of place of residence, their effect is most
pronounced in metro areas. This issue is discussed more
fully in the fifth section.

Table 10.4. Number and Percentage of Persons Below the
Poverty Level by Region and Place of Residence,
1968 and 1974

Year and Region	Residence					
	Central City[a]		Nonmetro[b]		Total[c]	
	(000,000s)	%	(000,000s)	%	(000,000s)	%
	Official Census Income[d]					
1974						
New England	.369	11.5	.354	9.7	.945	7.8
Middle Atlantic	1.951	15.4	.389	6.0	3.322	9.4
East North Central	1.528	12.6	.961	9.1	3.289	8.2
West North Central	.406	11.7	.885	10.3	1.473	9.2
South Atlantic	1.039	15.0	2.127	16.3	4.170	13.2
East South Central	.586	17.7	1.689	21.6	2.502	17.1
West South Central	1.190	15.8	2.048	24.8	3.895	18.7
Mountain	.268	10.0	.702	16.2	1.147	11.8
Pacific	1.033	11.5	.368	9.1	2.623	9.5
Total	8.370	13.7	9.523	14.2	23.366	11.2
1968						
New England	.213	7.0	.300	8.2	.753	6.5
Middle Atlantic	1.712	12.9	.621	9.3	3.465	9.6
East North Central	1.360	10.6	1.241	9.7	3.322	8.2
West North Central	.353	11.2	1.130	13.3	1.637	10.7
South Atlantic	1.059	18.7	3.341	23.4	5.162	17.7
East South Central	.365	16.4	2.403	32.2	3.107	25.9
West South Central	1.101	15.4	1.963	27.5	3.409	19.6
Mountain	.250	12.7	.719	16.6	1.097	12.7
Pacific	.751	10.3	.549	10.8	2.219	8.7
Total	7.164	12.8	12.267	17.6	24.171	12.3

Table 10.4 (continued)

Year and Region	Residence					
	Central City[a]		Nonmetro[b]		Total[c]	
	(000,000s)	%	(000,000s)	%	(000,000s)	%
	Pretransfer Income[e]					
1974						
New England	.641	20.0	.609	16.6	1.870	15.3
Middle Atlantic	3.428	27.0	.958	14.8	6.275	17.5
East North Central	2.469	20.2	1.787	16.8	5.740	14.2
West North Central	.719	20.2	1.638	19.1	2.667	16.6
South Atlantic	1.591	22.9	3.213	24.5	6.452	20.1
East South Central	.838	25.2	2.380	30.4	3.646	26.2
West South Central	1.664	22.1	2.721	33.1	5.196	24.8
Mountain	.452	16.8	.925	21.3	1.761	18.0
Pacific	1.947	21.5	.810	19.9	5.027	18.1
Total	13.749	22.5	15.041	22.5	38.634	18.5
1968						
New England	.409	13.5	.398	10.3	1.210	10.5
Middle Atlantic	2.448	18.5	.833	12.5	4.858	13.5
East North Central	2.029	15.8	1.638	12.8	4.782	11.9
West North Central	.548	17.3	1.423	17.6	2.203	14.4
South Atlantic	1.299	22.9	3.652	26.4	6.080	20.8
East South Central	.488	21.9	2.682	35.9	3.601	30.0
West South Central	1.232	17.3	2.295	32.1	3.933	22.6
Mountain	.299	15.3	.843	19.6	1.322	15.4
Pacific	1.193	16.3	.875	17.3	3.495	13.7
Total	9.945	17.6	14.639	21.2	31.484	16.1

Table 10.4 (continued)

Year and Region	Residence					
	Central City[a]		Nonmetro[b]		Total[c]	
	(000,000s)	%	(000,000s)	%	(000,000s)	%
	Final Income[f]					
1974						
New England	.133	4.2	.202	5.5	.481	3.9
Middle Atlantic	.863	6.8	.245	3.8	1.689	4.7
East North Central	.801	6.6	.676	6.4	1.998	4.9
West North Central	.258	7.4	.674	7.9	1.051	6.6
South Atlantic	.782	11.3	1.629	12.4	3.343	10.4
East South Central	.438	13.2	1.248	16.0	1.870	13.4
West South Central	.977	13.0	1.510	18.3	3.073	14.7
Mountain	.229	8.5	.671	12.9	.935	9.6
Pacific	.714	7.9	.284	7.0	1.925	6.9
Total	5.195	8.5	7.139	10.5	16.365	7.8
1968						
New England	.140	4.6	.218	6.0	.529	4.6
Middle Atlantic	1.046	7.9	.430	6.4	.233	6.5
East North Central	1.064	8.3	.875	6.9	2.527	7.3
West North Central	.282	8.9	.846	10.4	1.229	8.0
South Atlantic	.930	16.4	2.940	21.2	4.658	15.9
East South Central	.359	16.1	2.187	29.3	2.869	23.9
West South Central	.987	13.8	1.676	23.4	2.975	17.1
Mountain	.213	10.9	.610	14.1	.961	11.2
Pacific	.545	7.4	.415	8.2	1.548	6.1
Total	5.566	9.8	10.197	14.8	17.529	10.0

Table 10.4 (continued)

Source: Tabulations based on U.S. Bureau of the Census, Current Population Survey, March 1975.

Note: The states included in each region are:
New England--Conn., Maine. Mass., N.H., R.I., and Vt.; Middle Atlantic--N.Y., N.J., and Pa.; East North Central --Ohio, Mich., Ind., Ill., and Wis.; West North Central --Minn., Iowa, Mo., Kans., Nebr., N.Dak., and S.Dak.; South Atlantic--Del., D.C., Md., Va., W.Va., N.C., S.C., Ga., and Fla.; East South Central--Ky., Tenn., Ala., and Miss.; West South Central--Ark., Okla., La., and Tex.; Mountain--Ariz., Colo., Idaho, N.Mex., Utah, Nev., Wyo., and Mont.; Pacific--Alaska, Wash., Oreg., Hawaii, and Calif.

[a]"Central City" includes persons living in city centers of Standard Metropolitan Statistical Areas (SMSAs) with cities of 50,000 or more inhabitants.

[b]"Nonmetro" includes all persons not residing in SMSAs as defined above.

[c]"Total" includes all poor in metropolitan areas (central cities plus suburbs) and nonmetropolitan areas. Note that due to the omission of suburbs, "Central City" and "Nonmetro" do not sum to "Total."

[d]"Official Census Income" is the same income measure used by the Bureau of the Census in the P-60 income and poverty series.

[e]"Pretransfer Income" includes all taxable factor income except for capital gains plus non-Social Security pensions, gross of personal income and payroll taxes.

[f]"Final Income" is census income, adjusted for underreporting of survey income, federal income, and payroll taxes, and the cash equivalent value of in-kind food and medical care transfers. For more detail, see Smeeding 1977.

REGIONAL POVERTY

The first typological characteristic of interest is nonmetro poverty differentiated by region of the country

(Table 10.4). Regional poverty patterns are of interest due
to the widely divergent locational and racial dimensions of
poverty in each area of the country. Outside of the South,
extensive poverty is found mainly in the central cities of
large metro areas while in both the South and the Mountain
states poverty is concentrated in nonmetro areas. The nonmetro South holds more than 61 percent of all rural poor
and nearly one of every four poor persons in the country as
a whole. Within the South, the incidence of rural poverty
in 1974 was highest (24.1 percent) in the West South Central
division that includes the states of Arkansas, Oklahoma,
Louisiana, and Texas. Nonmetro poverty incidence in the
rest of the South is not much lower. For instance, in 1968,
poverty incidence in the East South Central region (including Mississippi, Alabama, Kentucky, and Tennessee) was the
highest in the country. Official poverty figures reveal
that almost one in three nonmetro persons was poor in that
region in 1968. Together, the eight states in the West and
East South Central division encompass the Ozark Plateau and
the Mississippi Delta (traditionally two of the poorest
areas of the country), and account for almost 40 percent of
all poor nonmetro persons. In 1975, only three nonsouthern
states (Arizona, New Mexico, and Missouri) had nonmetro
poverty incidence rates exceeding 15 percent, while all
southern states (excluding the border states of Delaware
and Maryland) had in excess of 15 percent of their rural
population in poverty (U.S. Bureau of the Census 1979;
Hoppe 1979).

Although these general characteristics of regional
poverty hold under all three income concepts, they are most
pronounced when using the adjusted or final income figures
(Table 10.4). After taking in-kind transfers and other
adjustments into consideration for 1974, the incidence of
nonmetro poverty in the West South Central region (18.3
percent) was more than twice the national average (7.8
percent) and almost 75 percent above the overall nonmetro
poverty rate.

These regional patterns of poverty also have a clear
racial dimension as well. About three of every five poor
nonwhites live in the South—more than one-half of these in
nonmetro areas. Almost three-quarters of the remaining black
poor live in the metro central cities of the Northeast and
the North Central regions of the country. Together the
northern ghettos and the nonmetro South virtually exhaust
the geographic locations of nonwhite poverty in the U.S.
today.

SIZE OF COMMUNITY AND DEGREE OF URBAN INFLUENCE

The size of a community and its proximity and accessibility
to urban job centers exerts a significant force on the
spatial pattern of nonmetro poverty. In general, the smaller
and more remote the nonmetro place, the less the opportunity
to find a good job (National Rural Center 1978). And, where
commuting and job search costs are excessive, weak systems
of social services, underemployment, low wages, and working
poor families can be found (Berry 1970). Further, due to
the isolated nature of these areas, public assistance benefits, supportive social services, and other transfers,
including food and medical care, are also in short supply
because of the high transportation costs necessary to file
for or to provide benefits. The poverty rate in nonmetro
counties with no community of 2,500 population or more is
substantially above that found in nonmetro counties with a
town of 25,000 or more (Table 10.5). This pattern holds
especially true for the working poor. Of all poor family
heads who worked a full year in 1976, the poverty rate in
the most sparsely populated nonmetro areas was twice that in
those nonmetro areas with the largest towns (U.S. Department
of Agriculture, hereafter USDA, June 1979). Further, over
67 percent of all nonmetro poor families had at least one
earner in 1975; compared to only 48 percent of all poor
metro families (National Rural Center, 1978: 59). In fact,
overall poverty rates for the working poor in all nonmetro
areas are 25 to 75 percent greater than similar families in
metro areas. Quite possibly, the overrepresentation of the
working poor in nonmetro versus metro areas is the result
of the movement of low-skill, low-wage manufacturing enterprises (e.g., textiles, shoes) to nonmetro areas (particularly in the South) in order to take advantage of low labor
costs (declining farm labor demand, underemployed female
labor force, cheap land, etc.) as is suggested by Beale
(1976: 955), and Roy and Bordelon (1974: 82).

If poverty figures are compared for 1969 and 1976, despite the fact that smaller nonmetro areas have the highest
rate of poverty incidence in both years, they have also
shown the greatest percentage decline in that rate over
this period. One possible reason for this decrease is the
migration of younger, better-educated, low-income families
to more urbanized areas. This seems particularly true for
younger nonwhites who continued to migrate on a net basis
to metro areas in the 1970s where they are at a lesser income disadvantage to whites (Brown 1978), despite the re-

versal of this nonmetro to metro migration trend for the
population as a whole (Zuiches and Brown, 1978: 66). However, there are still more than 1.4 million poor people
in small nonmetro places (Table 10.5) and another 6.1 million in nonmetro counties with at least one town between
2,500 and 24,999 in population.

STRUCTURE OF SETTLEMENT PATTERNS

The structure or compactness of settlement patterns is an
important geographic aspect of nonmetro poverty. If the
nonmetro poor are widely dispersed across large geographic
areas, it will be more difficult to effectively implement
all types of antipoverty policies, particularly manpower
programs, industrial location subsidies, and health care
programs. On the other hand, to the extent to which the
poor are clustered in fairly compact areas, such policies
are more likely to succeed. The U.S. Bureau of the Census
(1979) publishes data on the poor for various nonmetro
places according to the proportion of the poor living in
"poverty areas" that are defined as: "nonmetropolitan civil
divisions (townships, districts, etc.) in which at least 20
percent or more of the population was poor in 1969" (Klein
1975). These poverty areas are disproportionately (60 percent) located not in metro central cities, but in nonmetro
areas. They contain poor families that are mainly white (63
percent in 1973), older, and less likely to be female headed than the poor in metro poverty areas. There is a clear
regional dimension to poverty areas as well. In the South
over three-fourths of all nonmetro poor live in poverty
areas, versus 38 percent in the West and smaller percentages
in other areas (Hoppe 1979). Table 10.6 shows the extent to
which the poor are clustered in various metro and nonmetro
places. The smaller the nonmetro place the greater the concentration of the poor in poverty areas. Over two-thirds
of all nonwhite poor live in poverty areas, while seven of
every eight poor nonmetro nonwhites in isolated places
(less than 2,500) live in poverty areas. However, the relevance of these statistics for poverty policy remains to
be seen. Poverty areas are places with at least a 20 percent poverty rate in 1969. But the average poverty rate
for nonmetro nonwhites was 52.6 percent in 1969. In other
words, virtually all nonmetro areas that had high proportions of nonwhite residents were also poverty areas in
1969. In fact, 36.8 percent of all nonmetro places are

Table 10.5. Number and Percentage of Incidence of Poverty
by Size of Place and Work Status, 1969 and 1976

Year and Work Status	All Places		Metro			
			Total		Central City	
	Total	%	Total	%		%
	(000,000s)	%	(000,000s)	%	(000,000s)	%
1969						
Total	27.20	13.8	15.22	11.2	9.25	14.9
Family head:						
Worked	2.83	6.6	1.46	4.9	.82	6.3
Worked 50-						
52 weeks	1.27	3.9	.61	2.7	.33	3.4
1976						
Total	24.98	11.8	15.23	10.7	9.48	15.8
Family head:						
Worked	2.55	5.7	1.37	4.5	.76	6.5
Worked 50-						
52 weeks	1.04	3.0	.46	2.0	.26	2.9

Source: U.S. Bureau of the Census, Current Population Reports, 1978.

classified as poverty areas. Although several well-defined and fairly compact pockets of poverty exist in various parts of the country,[6] there are still 16,776 nonmetro poverty areas in the United States. Such a large number of poor areas would seem to negate the usefulness of using poverty area data to target funds for nonmetro development.[7] However, large clusters of adjoining nonmetro poverty areas, such as those in the South, might be useful geographic guides for antipoverty policy (see Chapter 1, Figure 1.4).

RATE OF POPULATION GROWTH

According to many observers (Clawson 1976; Beale 1976, 1979; Deavers 1978), the sudden recent increase in migration to nonmetro areas and the resultant widespread and substan-

		Nonmetro					
				Size of Place			
Total		No Place 2,500 or More		One Place 2,500-24,999		One Place 25,000 or More	
(000,000s)	%	(000,000s)	%	(000,000s)	%	(000,000s)	%
11.98	19.3	1.90	27.2	7.73	20.3	2.35	13.9
1.37	10.4	.23	16.0	.89	11.0	.25	6.8
.66	6.7	.12	11.5	.43	7.1	.12	4.1
9.75	14.0	1.44	16.8	6.08	14.0	2.25	12.8
1.18	8.0	.19	10.3	.72	7.8	.27	7.3
.58	5.2	.11	8.2	.35	5.1	.12	4.2

tial growth of the nonmetro population heralds a nonmetro renaissance. The following interrelated demographic and economic trends have been noted: First, ever increasing numbers of retirees are moving to sunbelt and other retirement counties that offer amenities such as scenery, water recreation, and pleasant climate. Most of these counties are nonmetro. Because of their "portable incomes" (pensions, annuities, Social Security) and low labor supply, these retirees provide a stable and dependable income base for the area. In theory, this income injection should produce multiplier effects creating jobs and higher incomes in rural areas. However, retirees are still only a small percentage (10 percent) of total net migration to rural areas. Second, the South has in recent years achieved unprecedented rates of economic growth. In particular, the energy and defense industries in the South have grown substantially over the last decade, and metro areas have expanded quite

Table 10.6. Number and Percentage Composition of Poverty by
Size of Place, Race, and Poverty Area Status, 1969 and 1976

| Year, Race, and Area Status | All Places | | Metro | | | |
| | Total | | Total | | Central City | |
	(000,000s)	%	(000,000s)	%	(000,000s)	%
All persons						
1969						
Poverty areas	13.75	50.5	6.41	42.1	5.03	54.4
Nonpoverty areas	13.45	49.5	8.81	57.9	4.22	45.6
Total	27.20	100.0	15.22	100.0	9.25	100.0
1976						
Poverty areas	10.53	42.2	5.30	34.8	4.31	45.4
Nonpoverty areas	14.45	57.8	9.93	65.2	5.17	54.6
Total	24.98	100.0	15.23	100.0	9.48	100.0
Nonwhites						
1969						
Poverty areas	6.21	80.5	3.61	76.7	3.00	80.4
Nonpoverty areas	1.50	19.5	1.12	23.3	.73	19.6
Total	7.71	100.0	4.73	100.0	3.73	100.0
1976						
Poverty areas	5.08	66.9	3.11	60.5	2.65	63.7
Nonpoverty areas	2.51	33.1	2.03	39.5	1.51	36.3
Total	7.59	100.0	5.14	100.0	4.16	100.0

Source: U.S. Bureau of the Census, Current Population
Reports, 1978.

Total		No Place 2,500 or More		One Place 2,500-24,999		One Place 25,000 or More	
(000,000s)	%	(000,000s)	%	(000,000s)	%	(000,000s)	%
7.34	61.3	1.54	81.1	4.90	63.4	.90	38.3
4.64	38.7	.36	18.9	2.83	36.6	1.45	61.7
11.98	100.0	1.90	100.0	7.73	100.0	2.35	100.0
5.23	53.5	1.07	74.3	3.31	54.5	.86	100.0
4.52	46.5	.37	25.7	2.77	45.5	1.39	100.0
9.75	100.0	1.44	100.0	6.08	100.0	2.25	100.0
2.60	87.2	.41	95.3	1.83	88.4	.37	74.0
.38	12.8	.02	4.7	.24	11.6	.13	26.0
2.98	100.0	.43	100.0	2.07	100.0	.50	100.0
1.97	80.7	.30	90.9	1.25	84.5	.43	67.2
.47	19.3	.03	9.1	.23	15.5	.21	32.8
2.44	100.0	.33	100.0	1.48	100.0	.64	100.0

Nonmetro — Size of Place

rapidly. Although a large part of this growth is due to net migration of residents from other areas of the country, strong pull effects are exerted on the mobile population in nearby rural southern counties, many of which are quite poor (Engels and Healy 1979). Third, the net migration of the poor from the nonmetro South to other areas of the country in search of jobs has been reversed (Long 1978). Recent data (U.S. Bureau of the Census, 1978: 7) indicate that mobile black nonmetro residents in the South--those who are younger and better educated--are migrating to metro areas in the South in search of jobs.

Although these population developments would seem to translate into rapidly declining poverty levels, particular- ly in the South, many researchers (e.g., Engels and Healy 1979), the authors included, remain skeptical for several reasons. First of all, a full 28 percent of the growth in nonmetro areas between 1970 and 1975 took place in counties that, by 1975, had been redesignated as metro (Zuiches and Brown, 1978: 65). Hence, a good deal of nonmetro resurgence is really only "metro spillover"--the outward expansion of metro suburban areas due to greater accessibility (Morrison 1979). Further, between 1970 and 1976, only the largest metro areas (those with cities of greater than three million population) actually lost population. In fact, metro areas of less than two million grew faster than nonmetro areas in percentage terms, and by twice as much in terms of the total number of net in-migrants (Engels and Healy, 1979: 17).[8] Although a majority of people express a desire to live in nonmetro rather than metro areas, the process of actualizing these desires may be constrained by several forces. In particular, the continuing energy crisis and the growth of location problems for two wage earners in highly educated husband-wife households, argue against future rapid growth of nonmetro areas. Hence the "nonmetro renaissance" and its effects on poverty may be suspect. Let us pursue this dichotomy by examining the effect of the three trends noted above on nonmetro poverty.

Due to increasing private and public pensions, and in- come tax changes on taxation of capital gains from the sale of homes for those age fifty-five and older, the tendency for the elderly to migrate may be expected to continue on into the 1980s. However, the retirement effect cited above has so far had little impact on poverty in nonmetro areas. The most rapidly growing states in the country are the retirement states of Arizona and Florida (and also the Mountain states, such as Nevada, Colorado, Utah, etc.). In

neither of these two retirement states has the decline in
the overall poverty rate from 1969 to 1975 equaled that of
the U.S. as a whole. In fact, the total number of poor
persons in Arizona and Florida increased by 19 and 13 percent respectively from 1969 to 1975. Moreover, considering
both elderly and nonelderly population growth, none of the
ten fastest growing states in the U.S. has substantial
numbers of nonmetro poor. Taking all of the ten fastest
growing states together,[9] only 920,000 of the nonmetro
poor are included--less than 10 percent of the total.

Looking at regional migration patterns, the South
appears to have benefited greatly. The southern region
achieved the greatest overall reduction in poverty between
1969 and 1975, with the number of poor falling by 16 percent
versus 13 percent nationally. The net change in population
for the southern states from 1969 to 1975 (8.3 percent),
although not as high as the top ten states, was still far
above the average U.S. rate of population change (4.8 percent) for this same period. Yet the majority of this growth
was due to younger nonpoor in-migrants to southern metro
areas. In contrast, southern nonmetro areas grew due to
natural population increase and lesser out-migration (Engels
and Healy 1979), not because of in-migration per se. To
many, such a growth pattern in the nonmetro South would
seem to signify stagnation more than resurgence. In fact,
white retiree in-migration to Florida and other southern
states had disguised much of the substantial and persistent
poverty among the indigenous and largely black southern
aged population located in poverty areas (Thomas 1973). The
migration of younger nonmetro southern families to the
metro South cannot be seen as an encouraging development.
If anything, economically disadvantaged nonmetro areas
(e.g., Mississippi Delta) will become even worse off and,
with them, the remaining older and more disadvantaged poor.
Earlier it was mentioned that between 1969 and 1975, the
southern region experienced the largest decline in overall
poverty of any region in the country. The South also had
the smallest percentage decline in aged poor, 27 percent
versus 42 percent nationally, over this same period.

Despite some progress made against poverty in the nonmetro South during the past decade, poverty rates in southern states remain intolerably high (Table 10.7). Since
1959, the same ten to twelve southern states[10] have led
the nation in the percentage of residents--total or nonmetro
only--who are poor. The poor in these same states are heavily, over 60 percent, nonmetro. Perhaps the extreme impov-

Table 10.7. Ten Poorest States by Percentage of Poor Persons, 1959–1975

Rank	Overall Poverty								Rural Poverty	
	1959		1969		1975				1975	
	State	%	State	%	State	%	Population Change[a] %	Poor Who Are Rural %	State	%
1	Miss.	54.5	Miss.	35.4	Miss.	26.1	5.6	83.6	Miss.	27.6
2	Ark.	47.5	Ark.	27.8	La.	19.3	4.4	54.7	La.	25.0
3	S.C.	45.4	La.	26.3	N.Mex.	19.3	12.5	86.4	N.Mex.	24.4
4	Ala.	42.5	Ala.	25.4	Ark.	18.5	9.7	71.8	Ga.	23.2
5	N.C.	40.6	S.C.	23.9	Ga.	18.0	7.5	73.6	Ky.	22.2
6	La.	39.5	Ky.	22.9	Ky.	17.7	5.2	71.7	Ala.	21.3
7	Tenn.	39.3	N.Mex.	22.8	S.C.	17.2	8.7	68.8	S.C.	21.2
8	Ga.	39.0	W.Va.	22.2	Ala.	16.4	5.0	55.9	Tex.	20.3
9	Ky.	38.3	Tenn.	21.8	Tenn.	15.8	6.3	54.5	Ark.	19.8
10	W.Va.	34.6	Ga.	20.7	Tex.	15.2	9.3	42.3	W.Va.	17.5
U.S. Average		22.1		13.7		11.4	4.8	39.5		14.3

Source: U.S. Bureau of the Census, Current Population Reports, 1978.

[a] Population change equals the percentage change in state population from 1969 to 1975.

erishment of the nonmetro South can best be brought out by the following observation by Deavers (1978: 5): "There are in the U.S. (as of 1975) 255 nonmetro counties which have been in the lowest per capita income quintile of all nonmetro counties for 25 years; 237 of these are in the South."

A comparison of the poorest states at different poverty levels further enforces these observations (U.S. Bureau of the Census, 1979: 21). Many researchers (Fuchs 1969; Piven and Cloward 1971) have argued for relative poverty standards that reflect the economic status of low-income families relative to the incomes of the rest of the population. Most often, these researchers refer to a poverty line of one-half median family income (MFI) as a reasonable poverty cutoff. The official poverty line for a family of four was $5,470 in 1975. One-half MFI was $6,860--just about 25 percent larger. If a relative poverty standard were adopted for 1975, and adjusted for family size, the poverty estimate would be very close to the alternative poverty level data for persons living below 125 percent of the official poverty line that the census publishes. As might be expected, all but one of the ten poorest states on this basis are again southern states with large, impoverished, nonmetro populations. Although relative and absolute poverty levels produce different numbers of poor people, both poverty perspectives point to the nonmetro South as the area where poverty remains most prevalent and intractable.[11]

CONCLUSION

This typological analysis has pinpointed several persistent and important regional differences in nonmetro poverty. Although progress against nonmetro poverty is being made, nonmetro poverty levels, particularly in the South, remain intolerably high. The eight states in the West and East South Central regions of the country contain 40 percent of all nonmetro poor, but only 22.5 percent of the entire non-metro population. Three-quarters of the nonmetro southern poor live in remote poverty areas. Many are aged and/or disabled and in poor health. Rapid sunbelt economic expansion and the recent nonmetro renaissance had little impact on the economic well-being of these people.

Although the specific solutions to these long-standing poverty problems remain to be found, the prime contributing factors--lack of good jobs for the younger poor and inade-

quate support from income transfers for the older and disabled poor--will be considered in the following sections.

UNDERLYING FACTORS OF RURAL POVERTY AND LOW INCOME

Whereas the existence of widespread nonmetro poverty is
clear and well documented, the basic causes are not. Poverty
in the form of substandard earnings is, of course, partly
dependent on market determined forces.

In both metro and nonmetro labor markets income is
derived from market-determined returns on factor endowments
of human and physical capital. Because most nonmetro nonfarm
people have very little physical capital (other than owner-
occupied housing) they must rely on their human resources
to generate earned income. Earned income is dependent on
several elements, the most important of which include: (1)
the skills, knowledge, and experience of the worker (quantity and quality of human capital); (2) the mobility of the
worker, both physical (ability to migrate or commute to
areas where decent jobs are found) and social (lack of
racial and sexual discrimination barriers); and (3) the
nature of labor demand (location, wage structure, and skill
requirements). Adequate earnings depend on the ability to
synthesize effectively all three of these elements. Although
we do not concentrate on the nature of labor demand in nonmetro areas (see Chapter 11), a major aspect of chronic poverty is, and will most likely continue to be, the inability
to adjust to changing economic development patterns, a
shortcoming that can be traced to labor immobility (Tweeten
and Brinkman 1976) and deficiencies in human capital attainment. Clearly, impoverished nonmetro areas do not offer
much in the way of decent job opportunities. The industrial
structure of such places is usually based on a few technologically obsolete and often declining industries--usually
low-skill manufacturing industries. In order to increase
earnings, the worker must be able to migrate or commute to
areas that offer higher wages and better opportunities.
This physical mobility is a necessary prerequisite to escaping poverty although it alone is insufficient. The capacity
to adjust one's situation also depends on the individual's
stock of human capital. Without the skills, knowledge, or
experience required for a good job, migration to a metro-
industrial complex offers little payoff as was evident by
southern migration to the northern metro central cities in

the 1960s (Long 1978). Finally, for minorities and many female-headed, single-parent families, racial and sexual discrimination barriers must also be overcome in order to escape poverty. However, increased earnings are not the only way, at least for a short period, to escape poverty.

Under welfare-state capitalism, inability to generate sufficient factor income is often tempered by the availability of transfer payments. Social insurance transfer programs such as Social Security (OASDI) and Unemployment and Workers' Compensation are designed to replace losses in earned income due to old age, disability, or involuntary unemployment. These transfers are usually independent of other nonlabor income of the earner. Unfortunately, many poor do not qualify for adequate social insurance benefits due to poor work histories, and chronic illness or disability. In order to provide for the needs of these people, and others, public assistance programs are designed to put a floor under incomes by catching those who fall through the cracks of the social insurance structure. For instance, SSI benefits poor elderly, blind, and disabled people who have too little income (usually inadequate OASDI) to escape poverty. A third type of transfer, intended to maintain and enhance human capital, consists of education transfers, nutritional programs (e.g., school lunch program), and health care transfers (e.g., medicaid).

It is important to note that transfer programs only offer a permanent solution for the chronic poverty of the aged, and the permanently and/or totally disabled. For younger able-bodied persons who are poor, income transfers are intended to provide only temporary aid until suitable jobs can be found. Transfers alone are not the solution to the poverty problem for these individuals.

In sum, the ability to escape poverty depends on the ability to either generate adequate earnings or the sufficiency of the transfer system to provide at least temporary help for those whose ability to earn is impaired by home responsibilities, sickness, old age, or involuntary unemployment. If earnings and/or transfers are inadequate, poverty results. In the following sections these two prime determinants of nonmetro poverty will be reviewed.

NONMETROPOLITAN POVERTY, HUMAN RESOURCES, AND EARNINGS

Although a number of socioeconomic factors contribute to
nonmetro poverty, many observers single out the inadequate
level of human capital investment in the nonmetro labor
force as either a basic symptom or a cause of poverty. The
human resource interpretation of nonmetro poverty is based
on the premise that nonmetro America has traditionally
experienced a serious underinvestment in human capital due
to inferior schooling, lack of individual incentives for
educational self-investment, and a disproportionately small
share of training funds via established manpower programs.
The result, according to Hansen (1970) and others, is a
nonmetro concentration of underdeveloped and immobile human
resources characterized by underemployment, substandard
wages, and below poverty level earnings for rural households. A corollary of this deficient human resource approach
is the pronounced selectivity of out-migration by age and
education levels (Engels and Healy 1979).

Educational attainment categorized by elementary, high
school, and postsecondary education is the standard, qualitative indicator of human capital development.[12] Available
educational data for metro and nonmetro population show a
pattern consistent with our earlier observations that nonmetro America contains a disproportionate share of the
nation's poverty population in contrast to its share of
total population. Geographic variation in median years of
schooling measured by the Census Bureau for 1974 reveals
lower educational levels and, by implication, a less developed stock of human capital for the nonmetro poor in comparison to central city poverty populations. This disparity
holds for every region with the exception of the New England
and Mid-Atlantic regions (Table 10.8). Some of these differences reflect a comparative paucity of opportunities
(job alternatives) in nonmetro areas. Martin (1977) points
out that nonmetro wages tend to be lower than metro wages
for the same job and skill levels. Yet educational deficiencies per se are a serious nonmetro problem. In 1974,
over two million rural adults--8 percent of that population
--had less than five years of schooling and thus were considered to be functionally illiterate. Nationally only
5.3 percent of adults are in this category (Parham, 1978:
551).

A nationwide difference of one median year of schooling
between urban and rural poor conforms to differentials in
educational attainment for total metro and nonmetro popula-

Table 10.8. Median Education Levels (Years of Schooling) for the Poor, by Region

Region	Central City	Nonmetro
United States	9.4	8.4
New England	8.5	10.3
Middle Atlantic	9.3	9.5
East North Central	10.1	9.6
West North Central	10.5	10.1
South Atlantic	9.3	7.9
East South Central	8.6	7.6
West South Central	8.7	7.5
Mountain	11.0	9.0
Pacific	9.7	9.6

Source: Compiled from U.S. Bureau of the Census, Current Population Survey, March 1975.

tions during the current decade (U.S. Bureau of the Census 1978). In 1970, roughly 75 percent of metro residents (twenty-five years and older) attained some postelementary education in contrast to 65 percent of nonmetro residents. This difference narrowed slightly by 1977 with 83 percent of the metro and 75 percent of the nonmetro population respectively attaining an elementary level of education. Moreover, a given level of education in nonmetro areas offers less protection from poverty status by contrast to metro areas. Poverty incidence in 1975 (U.S. Bureau of the Census 1979) for metro families headed by a person with less than eight years of education was lower in comparison with nonmetro households with the same education. One-fourth of the latter were below the 1975 poverty level ($5,500 for a nonfarm family of four persons) whereas only 18 percent of the metro households in this educational cohort were below poverty level. At any given education level, a higher incidence of poverty was also characteristic of nonmetro versus metro households.

These patterns are descriptive, only suggesting an association between lower educational attainment in nonmetro areas and a disproportionately high incidence of poverty for nonmetro households. Systematic attempts to specify and estimate the relationships between a substan-

dard stock of human capital and nonmetro poverty are
virtually nonexistent.[13] Fishelson (1971) estimated
returns to human capital investment for farm earners using
public expenditure per pupil in nonmetro areas as a proxy
variable for human capital produced by schooling. Those
estimates were not statistically significant nor did they
pertain to the nonfarm nonmetro sector.[14]

Education and out-migration of labor is another aspect
of the human resource interpretation of nonmetro poverty.
Tweeten and Brinkman (1976) argue that out-migrants from
nonmetro America during the 1960s consisted of the better-
educated, young, and more productive component of nonmetro
labor forces. More recent evidence (Zuiches and Brown,
1978: 67) indicates that this net out-migration of better-
educated, younger persons is continuing, particularly for
younger nonwhites. Although many younger white families
have been moving to nonmetro areas in recent years, increases in nonmetro in-migration rates are mainly among
retired persons. In general, this selective outflow has
left a residual nonmetro stock of less developed human
resources with lower educational levels and earnings. The
selective nature of this process is reinforced by a comp-
lementarity between individual differentials in human capital and propensities to out-migrate. Schultz (1975: 835)
makes a general argument in favor of a positive association
between levels of human capital investment and migration,
suggesting that "geographical relocations of human resources
are responses to incentives that arise as a consequence of
disequilibria and that education increases the efficiency
of migrants in relocating themselves." Greenwood (1975)
surveys several studies that suggest that education levels
are an important factor in out-migration from distressed
areas, and that the dominant migration streams--movement
out of the Deep South and off the farm--have been most
profitable for more educated movers. These studies do not
directly confirm a lower-educated, less productive postmigration residual in nonmetro areas, but the results are
highly suggestive in that direction. Although the recent
net reversal of overall population migration streams to
selective nonmetro areas may change this situation in coming
years (Beale 1977), the selective out-migration process
continues today in many poor areas (e.g., the Mississippi
Delta).

POLICY EFFORTS TO UPGRADE HUMAN CAPITAL IN RURAL AREAS

The education and migration dimensions of the human capital
interpretation of nonmetro poverty lead to the chronic
underinvestment in human resources syndrome that is both
cause and symptom of the problem. A policy strategy of
greater investment in human resources has been the traditional reaction (e.g., Marshall 1974; Hansen, 1973). The
actual manpower policy response to nonmetro poverty includes
programs implemented under the Manpower Development and
Training Act (MDTA), and its successor the Comprehensive
Employment and Training Act (CETA), as well as other family-
based programs and labor mobility demonstration projects.
    The Rural Manpower Service established under the MDTA
in 1971 was designed to provide equal access to manpower
services for nonmetro groups. A number of other pilot programs were formulated in the early 1970s to improve the
delivery of manpower services and training to sparsely
populated nonmetro areas. These included the Smaller Communities Program where traveling teams of specialists delivered manpower services into nonmetro areas, and the Concerted Services in Training and Education project to identify (1) employment opportunities and occupational education for the nonmetro poor, and (2) ways in which rural
communities can promote human resource development. Deliverability of manpower programs to nonmetro areas has been
the major policy concern of all these programs including
the Concentrated Employment Programs that operated in thirteen nonmetro communities in 1970 and only four communities
by 1978. Marshall (1974) points out that the deliverability
factor for most of these programs has resulted in higher
program costs that, in turn, have raised some controversy
about the feasibility and effectiveness of nonmetro manpower
programs.
    Rural manpower programs under CETA have been primarily
developed under Title III (Special Federal Responsibilities)
and are focused on migrant and seasonal farm workers. Nonmetro underemployed and unemployed workers are, of course,
included in other portions of CETA, although Hansen (1976)
suggests that CETA is geographically biased toward prime
sponsors in metro areas. Hansen attributes this urban bias
to the politically and economically low visibility of small
towns and nonmetro residents, and to a lack of managerial
capability at the local, nonmetro level where prime sponsorship operates out of state executive offices in the majority
of states.

The metro bias of CETA also stems from the funding formulas used for the distribution of funds. Coltrane, King, and Barnow (1978) simulate the geographic distribution of CETA funds using formulas based on countercyclical unemployment, structural unemployment, and income maintenance needs. Their analysis shows a metro bias in fund distribution using countercyclical and structural unemployment measures, but a nonmetro bias for distribution formulas based on income needs. This latter prorural distribution pattern reflects areas that have either relatively low or incomplete unemployment rates, but high proportions of low-earnings families and underemployed workers, that is, the working poor.

The bias in the existing distribution of manpower programs is explicitly identified by Tweeten (1978), who calculates that 88.3 percent of all CETA funds (Table 10.9) were distributed to metro areas in 1975. A comparatively larger proportion of Title III funds was distributed in nonmetro areas and reflects the rurally based target groups of Indians and migrant-seasonal farm workers. Job Corps outlays (Title IV) also displayed a nonmetro tendency although the target group for this program area is composed of both metro and nonmetro hard-to-employ individuals.

Other manpower policy responses to chronic underinvestment in nonmetro human resources include family-based programs and labor mobility projects. The former have been implemented on a pilot basis during the current decade and have involved the relocation of low-income, nonmetro families to a residential training site. The National Institute of Education has funded a limited number of such projects where unemployed and underemployed household heads enroll in a vocational training program to acquire some job-related skills. Spouses are encouraged to participate in career education and are required to participate in a family-core curriculum to teach basic household skills, while school-age children receive education to advance them to the proper level for their age. This program's strategy of breaking the poverty syndrome by dealing with the family unit is noteworthy although the effectiveness of such an approach has not been thoroughly examined (Seninger and Stevenson 1979).[15]

Labor mobility projects reflect a different manpower policy strategy aimed at relocating unemployed and underemployed workers from depressed nonmetro labor markets to other areas. Morrison et al. (1974) point out that no direct reference to relocation assistance is included in CETA al-

Table 10.9. Percentage of Distribution of Federal Outlays for Human Resource Development in Metropolitan and Non-metropolitan Counties, Fiscal Year 1975

Program	Total	Metro	Nonmetro
	$a	%	%
Department of Labor:			
CETA Title I, comprehensive manpower (ETA)	1,915.5	89.6	10.4
CETA Title II, public employment (ETA)	642.3	86.6	13.4
CETA Title III, special Federal response (ETA)	244.5	84.0	16.0
CETA Title IV, Job Corps (ETA)	166.0	81.0	19.0
CETA Title VI, emergency jobs program (ETA)	842.3	92.1	7.9
Older Americans community service employment	12.0	99.9	.1
Work incentives program	129.8	91.0	9.0
Placement services (ETA)	493.6	82.6	17.4
Total	4,446.0	88.4	11.7
Unemployment insurance (ETA)	1,453.0	79.2	20.8

Source: President of the United States 1977 and Tweeten, 1978: 6.

Note: Of the total population in 1974, 72.3 percent was metro and 27.6 percent was nonmetro.

[a]In millions.

though implicit authority is provided to local governments for establishing mobility assistance programs. This type of program has been implemented in the Wisconsin-Michigan area, rural Mississippi, and other regions. The aim is to relocate potentially productive labor where it can be ef-fectively employed—the problem, as Marshall (1974) points out, is the result such an approach can have on that portion of the population not relocated. He suggests that relocation assistance as a component of manpower policy may be impor-tant for younger, better-educated workers and that, in fact, those who benefit from relocation are the ones who have the greatest tendency to migrate without assistance. Again, recent evidence (Zuiches and Brown 1978) bears out this hypothesis.

In sum, the nonmetro poor suffer disproportionately from low earnings. These are attributable to deficiencies in human capital caused by low educational attainment and/or lack of good job opportunities in nonmetro areas. The most mobile of those in low-income areas—the younger and more educated and those relocated by labor mobility projects—are migrating to better jobs. Policy efforts to upgrade the skills and marketability of nonmetro workers have met with little or mixed success, a deficiency that suggests that more attention should be paid to the problems of nonmetro labor markets and nonmetro workers during the 1980s.

TRANSFER PROGRAMS: WELFARE POLICY
AND NONMETROPOLITAN AREAS

Comparative metro-nonmetro research on the U.S. transfer system (Bawden 1977, 1974, 1972; Owens 1977, 1972; Huffman 1977; Briggs et al. 1977; National Rural Center 1978; Chernick and Holmer 1979; Lyday 1971; Pryor 1979) has unequivocally found that the nonmetro poor, particularly those in the South, are disproportionately served by the current transfer system and would benefit substantially from welfare reform. This final major section of the chapter explains how the current income transfer system affects nonmetro families in general and the nonmetro South in particular, and how welfare reform would benefit these same individuals.

Although the remainder of this discussion will deal specifically with transfer programs designed to benefit low-income families, that is, income- or means-tested programs, the nonincome-tested portion of the transfer system —the social insurance system—deserves mention as well. Only meager amounts of research on the distributional effect of social insurance benefits on rural poor families are available. The research that does exist suggests that the largest source of growth in personal income in the 1970s for 800 nonmetro counties (mainly underdeveloped southern counties) was transfer benefits in general, and Social Security (OASDI) benefits in particular (USDA, June 1979: 34). Yet, Hines and Reid (1977) found that the nonmetro aged received less than their fair share of OASDI benefits,

an inequity that can be traced to several sources. Many of
the nonmetro elderly were not eligible for OASDI for much
of their working lives--only in relatively recent years
have farmers and the self-employed been covered by Social
Security. To the extent to which low-income rural residents
have poor work histories marked by long spells of unemployment and low wages, OASDI retirement benefits will also be
low. Yet the fact remains that in several nonmetro areas
from which younger, more mobile families have emigrated,
OASDI benefits still provide much of the economic base.

Low wages and long periods of unemployment also lead
to lower Unemployment Insurance (UI) benefits for those
workers who are eligible. The UI benefits are usually lowest, both in terms of weekly benefits and number of weeks
before benefits are exhausted, in the South where most of
the nonmetro poor are located (U.S. Congress, Joint Economic
Committee, 1974). Ancillary facilities and services for the
unemployed are also in short supply in nonmetro areas. For
instance, Rural Job Service employment centers are few and
far between, providing little aid to the job search of the
nonmetro unemployed (Tweeten 1978; Marshall 1974).

THE CURRENT WELFARE SYSTEM

The inconsistencies in the current welfare system are well
known although little recent analysis of their effect on
the nonmetro poor is available.[16] On average the cash
welfare system covers only about one-half of the poor,
lifting only one-quarter from poverty (Bawden 1979). However, the picture is even more bleak in nonmetro areas.
Traditionally, those states with the highest number and/or
proportion of nonmetro poor have discouraged welfare by
keeping benefits low, making application for benefits difficult, and maintaining stringent eligibility qualifications.
Table 10.10 presents several facets of the current welfare
system for those thirteen states that ranked in the top ten
of the number or percentage of nonmetro poor in 1975.[17]
Together these thirteen states contain 55 percent of all
poor nonmetro persons. It is immediately obvious that twelve
of the thirteen states listed in Table 10.10 (all but New
Mexico)[18] are southern states. In fact, while all southern
states (except for the border states of Delaware and Maryland) had nonmetro poverty rates of 15 percent or greater
in 1975, only three nonsouthern states can be so designated
(Arizona, New Mexico, and Missouri).

Table 10.10. Characteristics of the Public Assistance
System in the Poorest Rural States

State	Number[a] and Percentage[b] of Rural Persons Who Were Poor in 1975				Food Stamp Participation 1974[c] 1978[d]		Maximum AFDC July 1975[e]
	(000,000s)	Rank	%	Rank	%	%	$
Texas	.658	1	20.3	8	35.2	29.4	140
Georgia	.560	2	23.2	4	32.2	35.7	153
North Carolina	.528	3	15.8	16	23.0	37.8	200
Mississippi	.513	4	27.6	1	34.5	44.5	60
Kentucky	.426	5	22.2	5	38.1	51.4	235
Florida	.414	6	16.7	14	30.0	48.8	170
Louisiana	.394	7	25.0	2	41.8	46.1	158
Tennessee	.355	8	17.0	12	26.4	49.5	132
South Carolina	.330	9	21.2	7	41.3	40.2	117
Alabama	.329	10	21.3	6	28.8	40.2	135
Arkansas	.279	12	19.8	9	33.0	37.4	140
West Virginia	.218	19	17.5	10	38.3	55.2	249
New Mexico	.186	21	24.4	3	42.6	39.9	206
U.S. Totals/ Averages	9.480		14.3		37.5	46.9	278

[a]National Rural Center, 1978: 50.

[b]U.S. Bureau of the Census, Survey of Income and Education, 1976; special tabulation by authors.

[c]MacDonald, 1978: 94-95 (percentage of all eligible households that participate).

[d]U.S. Department of Agriculture, Sept. 1979: 36 (percentage of all eligible households that participate).

[e]U.S. Department of Health, Education, and Welfare, 1976: 9.

Cash Public Assistance			Medicaid		
AFDC-UP[f]	SSI[g]	Recipients as Percentage of State Poor[h]	Average Payment[i]	Recipients as Percentage of State Poor[j]	Welfare Percentage of State Budget[k]
		%	$	%	%
No	No	34.4	632	18	15.5
No	No	56.7	497	35	16.8
No	No	43.4	496	na	10.5
No	No	50.5	326	16	12.4
Yes	No	47.5	281	43	17.2
No	No	33.1	448	27	9.7
No	No	53.0	361	23	13.1
No	No	52.2	384	19	15.0
No	No	46.2	284	16	9.9
No	No	53.3	406	17	13.3
No	No	49.7	505	10	16.2
Yes	No	43.0	231	35	11.8
No	No	39.0	381	28	9.5
Yes=26 states		59.2	549	59	19.3

[f]National Rural Center, 1978: 94.

[g]National Rural Center, 1978: 101 (states that supplement payments to the aged maintaining their own residences).

[h]National Rural Center, 1978: 124-25 (includes AFDC, AFDC-UP, or SSI recipients as Public Assistance recipients).

[i]Author's computation based on unpublished U.S. Department of Health, Education, and Welfare data.

[j]Davis and Schoen, 1978: 68 (1970 estimate).

[k]National Rural Center, 1978: 70.

The major cash welfare program in the United States is AFDC. Yet the nonmetro poor fare less well in this program than their metro counterparts, because maximum benefit levels in poor states are far below the national median (Table 10.10). In July 1975, average AFDC benefit levels were only $50 in Mississippi, $90 in South Carolina, $95 in Louisiana, and $108 in Texas compared to a national average of $205 (U.S. Congress, Joint Economic Committee, 1974: 166). Briggs et al. (1977) in their study of four nonmetro southern poverty areas found average monthly AFDC benefits were $100 in 1973, less than one-half the national average. In fact, more than 70 percent of the nonmetro poor live in states whose maximum AFDC benefits are below the national median. In isolated areas throughout the country information on program rules and available benefits are scarce. Hence most nonmetro states have below average participation rates in the AFDC program. Few states have rural outreach programs to instruct potentially eligible families about applying for benefits. Even if the family is eligible and knows where to apply for benefits, transportation costs in terms of both time and money are high. Often welfare benefit offices are open only on specific days (Pryor 1979). In any case, only 36 percent of all nonmetro poor children live in female-headed families as compared to 61 percent of all metro poor children.

Although all states are required to have an AFDC program, states are free to extend benefits to unemployed fathers in two-parent families through the AFDC-UP program if they so desire. However, among the southern states only West Virginia and Kentucky have taken advantage of this provision (Table 10.10). Nearly three-fourths of the non-metro poor live in states without AFDC-UP programs. Because nonmetro poor families are typically two-parent families-- almost 65 percent of all nonmetro poor children (60 perent of all nonmetro poor) come from husband-wife families--the absence of AFDC-UP in predominantly nonmetro states has resulted in little welfare aid being available in time of need (National Rural Center 1978). All in all, less than 5 percent of nonmetro two-parent families with children receive AFDC-UP.

Typically, existing welfare programs have provided little help for the working poor who are ineligible for most cash assistance programs and most worker training programs, because they are not unemployed (Briggs et al. 1977).[19] One program that has provided a good deal of aid to the nonmetro poor in general, and especially the working poor (Kotz 1979), is the Food Stamp Program. In effect, food stamps provide a national income floor in food vouchers instead of cash.[20] Nationwide, in 1974, approximately one-fifth of the population was eligible for food stamps. In the nonmetro, poverty-stricken East and West South Central regions, almost one-third of the population was eligible for food stamps. At the same time, participation in the Food Stamp Program was typically lowest in the South (Table 10.10), presumably due to transportation costs (especially for the elderly), local administration discouragement, and general confusion on how the program operates (Kotz 1979; MacDonald 1978; Rungeling and Smith 1975). Among the thirteen poorest states in Table 10.10, nine had food stamp participation rates below the national average in both 1974 (Bickel and MacDonald 1975) and 1978 (USDA, Sept. 1979: 36).[21] Not only are program participation rates lower, but average food stamp benefits in nonmetro areas are also below those in metro areas (Martin and Lane 1977), despite the facts that fewer nonmetro families receive AFDC benefits and nonmetro families are typically larger than metro families (both of which would tend to increase the value of food stamps).

Medicaid also benefits poor families if they qualify for benefits and if adequate medical care is available. Unfortunately, few nonmetro residents qualify. In virtually every state, AFDC, AFDC-UP, and SSI recipients are automatically "categorically eligible" for medicaid, but because few nonmetro families receive AFDC and many southern states do not have AFDC-UP programs, not many of the nonmetro poor qualify for medicaid. Although nationwide 59 percent of the poor persons were medicaid recipients in 1970, the highest percentage for the thirteen states with severe poverty problems was 43 percent in Table 10.10. Moreover, Davis and Schoen (1978: 81) point to the fact that average medicaid benefits in nonmetro areas are only 50 to 60 percent as high as benefits in metro areas, a discrepancy that exists not only because southern states spend little on medicaid (Table 10.10), but also because the availability of medical care in nonmetro areas is so limited. Even if all low-income residents were eligible for equal amounts of subsidized medical care, nonmetro areas would receive smaller benefits due to the unavailability of health care in such areas. Given the generally poorer health status and higher proportion of elderly residents in nonmetro areas, one expects a higher than average demand for health care services. However, of 2,600 nonmetro counties

in 1976, 1,888 or almost three-quarters were in whole or in
part medically underserved according to the Department of
Health, Education and Welfare (Parham, 1978: 551).

The federal SSI program for poor aged, blind, and disabled persons provides a good example of the effect of
welfare reform on the nonmetro poor. In 1974, the federal
SSI program superseded state programs for the elderly,
blind, and disabled. A mandatory federal minimum annual
benefit of $2,628 for elderly couples, 80 percent of their
poverty line, was established. The SSI resulted in large
income gains for poor elderly families in previously low-
benefit welfare states. When coupled with food stamp and
medicaid benefits, which SSI beneficiaries are almost universally eligible for, most elderly couples who participate
in the program escape poverty. Of course, transportation
problems again reduce program participation for nonmetro
families, but for those who do participate, welfare benefits
have increased significantly. In addition, states were
subsidized to increase benefits above the federal minimum.
But for elderly SSI recipients living alone, none of the
thirteen states in Table 10.10 has supplemented SSI above
the federal minimum.

In summary, it appears that despite their reliance on
transfers as a source of income, poor nonmetro people benefit far less from the current welfare system than do metro
residents. Overall, one in three metro poor benefit from
cash public assistance as compared to only one in five nonmetro poor. Despite the fact that 40 percent of the poor
lived in nonmetro areas in 1975, the nonmetro poor received
35 percent of federal SSI funds, 31 percent of food stamp
benefits, and only 18 percent of federal AFDC and AFDC-UP
funds (National Rural Center, 1978: 65). Further, despite
their severe poverty problems, none of the thirteen states
in Table 10.10 spent more than 17.2 percent of the state
budget for public welfare programs, although the national
average was 19.3 percent. Clearly the welfare effort in
nonmetro America is below par according to all of the
barometers listed in Table 10.10.

THE NONMETROPOLITAN NEGATIVE INCOME TAX EXPERIMENT

A nonmetro negative income tax (NIT) experiment was carried
out in North Carolina and Iowa under the directorship of
Lee Bawden between 1968 and 1973. The primary purpose was
to measure the effect of income maintenance programs on the

work effort of low-income rural families, particularly
those who work and have family responsibilities. In addition to work behavior, the effect of the experiment on
educational attainment, nutrition, occupational mobility,
and asset position was studied (U.S. Department of Health,
Education and Welfare 1976; Palmer and Pechman 1978). The
experiment resulted in a modest decline in hours worked for
wives and other family members, but no significant decline
for husbands (Bawden 1979). Blacks in North Carolina and
whites in Iowa responded in almost exactly the same way.
Farmers increased their hours worked on the farm, but
decreased off-farm hours worked by a slightly larger
amount.[22]

The most important findings were, however, the effects
of the experiment on human capital attainment in recipient
families (Schuh 1978). The decline in the labor supply of
wives and teenagers provided the opportunity to increase
home care of children and to improve educational attainment.
There was a significant improvement in nutrition in North
Carolina, an improvement in the health status of children,
and a sizable increase in the quality of school performance.
In the long run, the cumulative effect of better health,
nutrition, and school performance should produce a net
increase in labor supply.

For adults in both states, job search and occupational
mobility increased as well. Because benefits were made
available to the working poor, the program acted as a wage
subsidy for those who enjoyed their current jobs, and as a
job-search subsidy for those who quit their former job and
used the guaranteed income to support the family while they
searched for a better one. This "search subsidy" effect was
particularly important for younger family heads. Finally,
experiment families increased their purchase of automobiles,
which directly increased access to jobs in nearby urban
areas.

The experiment also indicated that a full-scale, permanent, guaranteed minimum income would have the effect of
increasing local wage rates as the labor supply of wives
and teenagers decreased. By providing an alternative to
low-wage jobs, a guaranteed income would force employers to
raise wage levels, thus narrowing the local and national
wage spread. However, as Schuh (1978: 233) has pointed out:
"These general equilibrium effects in the labor market may
give rise to political consequences different from those
considered in the experiment. A private sector faced both
with higher taxes to support an income transfer program,

and higher wage rates as a consequence of the program, may
become politically active against it."

WELFARE REFORM PROPOSALS

For at least a decade, the U.S. government has been considering overhaul of the federal welfare system. The Nixon
Family Assistance Plan, examined by Congress from 1969 to
1972 and finally rejected, would have provided a national
minimum income of $1,600 for a family of four persons. If
the plan had passed, about one-half of all FAP benefits
would have accrued to nonmetro residents, leading to an
average 35 percent increase in disposable income for poor
nonmetro families (Briggs et al. 1977). FAP would have
reduced poverty, but because benefit levels were not high
enough, it would not have eliminated it.

In 1977, President Carter proposed the Program for
Better Jobs and Income (PBJI) that was similar to FAP in
that it would have consolidated AFDC, SSI, and food stamps
into a single program with a national guaranteed minimum
income of about two-thirds of the poverty line. Under the
Carter plan, all individuals--including younger single
persons and childless couples--would have been eligible for
benefits. Unlike FAP, however, PBJI would have created 1.4
million public-service jobs for those persons (able-bodied,
two-parent family heads) who would be required to work in
order to receive benefits and who could not find a suitable
private sector job. All families with the head working full
time, full year (whether in private or public sector jobs)
would have received enough in wages and other benefits to
escape poverty. Although public sector employment has been
criticized by many, particularly with respect to its ability
to add to human capital or to lead to stable private sector
jobs, it does provide full-year, full-time work for residents of job-scarce nonmetro areas and lifts all families
with full-time workers from poverty. It has been estimated
that between 41.7 percent (Pryor 1979) and 51.7 percent
(Danziger et al. 1979a) of the net increase in personal
income from program expenditures, that is, up to $2.1 bil-
lion, would have accrued to the South. Moreover, PBJI would
have generated an additional net increase of up to $3.6
billion in output in the South due to estimated regional
multiplier impacts (Danziger et al. 1979a). Because of the
high incidence of nonmetro poverty in the South, PBJI would
have reduced nonmetro poverty both directly (via providing

higher welfare benefits and stable jobs) and indirectly
(via job creation due to the regional multiplier impacts of
the net increase in transfers to the South). For nonmetro
areas on the whole, PBJI would have increased transfers and
reduced poverty by a greater amount than in metro areas as
compared to the current welfare system (Pryor 1979). However, PBJI would have led to net increases in welfare expenditures for southern states (because their mandated 10
percent share of PBJI benefits would have exceeded current
AFDC expenditures) and also would have generated upward
pressure on wage levels in that area. PBJI died in committee
in 1978, due in part to lack of support from southern legislators.

In May 1979, the Carter administration introduced yet
another welfare reform proposal, somewhat similar to PBJI,
but not nearly as comprehensive. The reform would come in
two parts: the Social Welfare Reform Amendments of 1979
(SWRA) and the Work and Training Opportunities Act of 1979
(WTOA). Unlike PBJI, single persons and childless couples
would be excluded from both programs although food stamps
would be retained. The net increase in welfare costs under
both programs would be $5.7 billion in 1982.[23] Under SWRA,
a national combined guarantee of cash and food stamps of
$4,654 or 65 percent of the poverty line would be legislated
and AFDC-UP would be mandated for all states. In addition,
under WTOA the federal government would step up its efforts
to find jobs for unemployed poor family heads newly eligible
for SWRA benefits and provide 260,000 additional public
service employment jobs for family heads who could not find
private sector jobs. In order to enlist the support of
southern politicians, the plan would "hold harmless" southern states, guaranteeing that, unlike PBJI, they would
incur no increased welfare costs under SWRA for seven years.
In order to satisfy legislators from New York and California
who voted against PBJI, the new Carter bill contains fiscal
relief for state and local general assistance welfare programs as well as for all state AFDC programs, thus benefiting New York City and Los Angeles. However, in this period
of fiscal belt tightening the chances for passage of any
proposal that increases the federal deficit are slim. These
programs would again lead to significant increases in welfare benefits for nonmetro areas and for southern states.
Chernik and Holmer (1979) have estimated that 47.5 percent
of the net increase in direct SWRA benefits, and 43.5 percent of all new public jobs under WTOA, would accrue to
rural areas. The nonmetro South would alone receive 28.0

percent of the net increase in assistance spending under
SWRA and 20.6 percent of new WTOA jobs.

THE POLITICAL ECONOMY OF WELFARE REFORM

Whatever the fate of President Carter's new welfare reform
proposal, there will probably be little support from southern legislators. Senator Russell Long (D-La.), powerful
chairman of the Senate Finance Committee, has long been
opposed to the idea of a national minimum welfare floor. In
addition, legislators from other areas of the country are
acutely aware of the pro-South (and hence, prononmetro)
nature of the aggregate distribution of program benefits.
    If welfare reform would be so beneficial to nonmetro
areas in general and the nonmetro South in particular, it
seems fair to ask, why don't nonmetro and southern congress-
men support welfare reform? Radical economists (Persky
1977; Bould Van-Til 1977) have long argued that the large
pool of unemployed and underemployed workers in nonmetro
areas provide cheap labor for producers. In this way, poverty serves an important functional role for capitalists
in general and nonmetro entrepreneurs in particular. Yet,
although it is clear that all of the welfare reform proposals currently under review would increase wage costs and
provide alternatives to low-wage factory jobs in the nonmetro South, it is also quite likely that most southern
voters are in principle against any sort of minimum guaranteed annual income for able-bodied, working-age males[24]
(Davis and Jackson 1974; Moynihan 1973).

CONCLUSIONS AND FUTURE DIRECTIONS

This chapter has reviewed the nature and causes of nonmetro
poverty and also discussed potentially effective remedies
for these problems, such as more effective manpower training, labor mobility programs, and welfare reform. Although
the rate of poverty has declined significantly in nonmetro
America over the past twenty years, it still exceeds the
poverty rate in metro America--by more than 40 percent once
in-kind transfers are counted as income. To the extent that
nonmetro poverty has declined, and continues to decline due
to the out-migration of younger, more productive people,

the remaining nonmetro poverty will prove increasingly difficult to remedy.

Recently, Lynn Daft (1979) has summarized the nonmetro poverty situation as well as anyone:

> Ten years after the publication of the report of the Rural Poverty Commission, millions of Americans are still left behind. In the intervening years, significant improvements in programs and policies have been made. People's lives have been made more productive and more meaningful as a result. Still, the thrust has not been sufficient to overcome all the problems of rural poverty. Despite the many significant gains we have witnessed over the past decade, rural poverty therefore remains a problem of major dimensions. Unfortunately, it is not a current-day glamour issue and therefore tends to receive less attention than it merits. I remain convinced that poverty will not be overcome without extensive reform of welfare programs, a coordinated program of human resource development, and substantial additions to the capacity of local governments and other public institutions to deliver essential services and to better adapt to structural change. These are the major components of the unfinished agenda.

Little more need be said about directions for future research in this area.

NOTES

1. There are at least two caveats to this statement. First, the situation is somewhat changed once the census poverty estimates are adjusted for their obvious deficiencies (see the next section). Second, the farm poverty problem in the United States has, over the past twenty years, all but disappeared. Despite the fact that Table 10.1 shows a 17.1 percent poverty rate among persons living on farms, the farm poor total only 1.3 million--5.4 percent of all poor persons. There is recent evidence (Beale 1976) that the farm population is stabilizing, and becoming younger. Smaller farm operators (those with annual farm sales of $20,000 a year or less) receive the great majority of their income from nonfarm sources. Average nonfarm income for all

farmers rose from 42 percent in 1973 to over 52 percent in
1976 (USDA, 1975: 14; USDA 1977). Less than 10 percent of
all poor nonmetro workers listed agriculture as their major
occupation in 1975 (Hoppe 1979: USDA Sept. 1979). In sum,
the move off the farm and the farm poverty problem seem to
be practically over in the United States. Only in the rural
South will excess underemployed farm labor continue to
exert an influence on rural poverty, and even there the
influence will be small. It follows that the farm-nonfarm
dichotomy is of little use in this chapter. Policies designed to help raise the incomes (earnings) of the rural
poor in general will also aid the incomes (earnings) of
those who live on farms.

2. See next chapter, "Poverty: A Regional Political
Economy Perspective" by Candace Howes and Ann R. Markusen,
that reviews the literature on rural industrial development.

3. The interested reader should consult U.S. Bureau of
the Census, 1978, 1979, and 1975 for such analyses.

4. It is important to review the definitions of "rural"
and "nonmetro" that are most frequently used in this
context. As others (National Rural Center 1978; Zuiches in
Chapter 2; Beale 1979; Davis 1977) have argued, these definitions may be less than adequate depending on one's purposes. The U.S. Bureau of the Census, in Current Population
Reports, series P-20, defines metro residents as all people
living in counties with a city of 50,000 or more (an SMSA),
plus persons living in contiguous counties (with smaller
cities and rural areas) that are linked to metro areas by
daily commuting patterns. The nonmetro population is the
residual. By this definition the nonmetro population increased from 62.8 million in 1970 to 71.1 million in 1977
(U.S. Bureau of the Census, 1978). In contrast to this
definition, the 1970 Census defined "rural" as those persons living in places of 2,500 or less, both outside and
within metro areas. Hence 16 million rural people--about 26
percent of the 1976 rural population (61.5 million)--live
within metro areas (Beale 1979). This rural population is
the residual of the census "urban" population definition.
The problems with these definitions are mainly conceptual:
does "rural" mean open places or outside cities, no communities or small communities, or are we interested in access
to large cities (i.e., potential places of employment) or
the size of place per se? Depending on the typological
aspect of interest, different definitions of rural may need
to be employed. However, by using the term "rural" to refer
only to places of 2,500 or less, the official census defi-

nition is too narrow. People living in places of from 2,500
to 50,000 are classified as urban by this definition despite
the fact that many of the people in such places have rural
life-styles. Thus, in general, both our definitions of
nonmetro and rural coincide with the official census definition of nonmetro given above. "Farm" and "nonfarm" are
similarly difficult terms. For instance, in 1977, 382,000
or 17.6 percent of all farm families were located in metro
areas. Hence, farms are not necessarily located in rural
areas. The rural nonfarm population cannot be derived by
subtracting the farm population from the nonmetro (rural)
population.

5. Unless otherwise stated, all poverty data are computed on the basis of the official Census Bureau poverty
lines that vary by family size, composition, and farm-
nonfarm residence. In 1974, the census poverty line was
roughly $5,000 for a nonfarm family of four persons. The
farm poverty line is 85 percent of the nonfarm poverty
line, the difference reflecting the lower cost of living
that presumably favors farm families. No other cost-of-
living adjustments are included in the poverty line for two
reasons: first, because cost-of-living differences between
urban and rural areas and among regions of the country are
very slight at poverty-line income levels; and second, the
cost-of-living difference between urban and rural areas
within any region or state may be as large as the differences among regions or states. Hence, it is almost impossible to adjust poverty lines for regional cost-of-living
differences with any reasonable degree of accuracy (Smeeding
1974).

6. Several studies of rural poverty in specific low-
income areas can be recommended. One of the best and most
recent deals with four extremely poor southern rural counties located in Georgia, Louisiana, Texas, and Mississippi
(Rungeling et al. 1977). Other studies include: Kentucky
(Larson and Youmans 1978); Louisiana (Roy and Bordelon
1974); Mississippi Delta, Ozarks, Southeast Coastal Plain
(McCoy 1970); and the North Central area (Iowa Agriculture
and Home Economics Experiment Station 1974).

7. Holding constant the 20 percent cutoff for defining
rural poverty areas, the 1980 Census should produce a smaller and hence more useful and exact count of rural poverty
areas. However, such data will probably not be available
until 1983 at the earliest.

8. It is easy to confuse rates of population growth
and actual net increases in population. For instance, be-

tween 1970 and 1976, Orange County, California grew by
334,000 people, but only by 17.0 percent. In contrast,
Summit County, Colorado more than doubled its population,
but only grew by 3,000 people. Because nonmetro areas hold
fewer people than metro areas, greater rates of growth
often mean smaller actual increases in population. This is
particularly true of isolated rural counties whose largest
population center is less than 2,500 people to begin with
(Engels and Healy, 1979: 18).

9. The ten fastest-growing states in the U.S. from
1969 to 1975 and their percentage change in population are:
Ariz. (24.6), Fla. (21.9), Nev. (20.8), Alaska (20.5),
Colo. (15.0), Idaho (14.1), Utah (13.5), Wyo. (13.0),
Hawaii (12.8), and N. Mex. (12.5).

10. The one non-South exception is New Mexico.

11. One might legitimately question whether the extreme
levels of rural, southern poverty noted above are more
closely correlated with "rural" or "southern." Actually
both forces are at work. Poverty rates in the South generally exceed those found in other (metro and nonmetro) areas
of the country. However, the highest poverty rates are
found in the nonmetro South, particularly when in-kind
transfers have been taken into account (Table 10.4). In the
non-South, rural poverty levels are higher than urban poverty levels everywhere but in the Middle Atlantic states
(Table 10.4). Interestingly, these states (New York, New
Jersey, Pennsylvania) are just those states in which one
might most seriously question the metro-nonmetro (urban-
rural) dichotomy.

12. Postsecondary education includes college education
(contained in most national data) as well as vocational
education, manpower training programs, and other educational
"self-investments" that, unfortunately, are not contained
in most national data series.

13. Returns to education in general are comparatively
lower in nonmetro areas using mean earnings by education
level for adults as an approximate indicator of returns to
schooling. Mean earnings for metro residents were higher
than nonmetro residents in both 1970 and 1977 for each
level of education (less than eight years, eight years,
some high school, etc.); see U.S. Bureau of the Census
(1978). These figures are, however, averages and do not
account for variance within educational categories, or
cost-of-living differences between metro and nonmetro areas
that may be reflected by these wage (earnings) differentials.

14. Moreover, as previously mentioned, observers have argued that the basic problem of rural America, poverty, is no longer connected with farming (Booth 1969; Huffman 1977).

15. The Mountain-Plains Education and Economic Development program established in Glasgow, Montana in 1971 is a good example (Mountain-Plains 1976).

16. Briggs et al. (1977) and the National Rural Center (1978) are important exceptions.

17. This double ranking was chosen because both the absolute number of rural poor and the relative incidence of rural poverty are important for policy purposes (Hoppe 1979). The number of poor reflect the state with the largest concentrations of rural poverty, whereas the incidence of poverty (percentage of rural persons who are poor) indicates the states where poverty is most prevalent among the rural population.

18. Despite the fact that New Mexico has a poverty incidence figure of 24.4 percent, it ranks twenty-first in terms of the number of rural poor persons.

19. The recently enacted (1975) Earned Income Tax Credit (EITC) will probably provide some help for the working poor in current and future years. In 1979, all families earning less than $11,000 with children will be eligible for aid. Maximum benefits are, however, only $600 per year. Almost 35 percent of the benefits are expected to reach rural families (Carlin 1976). However, it should be remembered that the EITC does little more than refund the employer portion of OASDI payroll taxes for most of these families. For instance, in 1979, at the maximum EITC benefit earnings level of $600, the working-poor family receives a net transfer bonus of only $232.20 ($600 EITC minus $376.80 OASDI payroll taxes).

20. In 1979 the Food Stamp Program guarantees $2,400 of food vouchers to a family of four with no other income. In seven of the thirteen states in Table 10.10, the food stamp guarantee (maximum payment) exceeds the state maximum AFDC payment for the same size family.

21. Rungeling and Smith (1975) indicated that one reason for Food Stamp Program nonparticipation was the cost of the stamps. Prior to 1979, the recipient was required to pay a fee for food stamps that varied inversely with income. For instance, many financially strapped rural families could not afford the $100 purchase requirement necessary to purchase $175 worth of food stamps. However, the new 1979 Food Stamp Program has done away with the purchase requirement.

Hence, in the example above, the family would not pay anything for $75 worth of stamps. The effect of this rule change on program participation in rural areas remains to be seen.

22. Most researchers felt that this farm labor supply response was unfortunate in that these individuals were being subsidized to increase their work effort in a technologically inefficient farming enterprise. More importantly, administration of farm family (and other self-employed units) income and asset level eligibility tests and benefit determination proved to be an extremely difficult problem (Bawden 1979).

23. It was estimated that PBJI would have cost an additional $19 billion for cash assistance and job creation funds by the time it would have been fully implemented in 1982.

24. Nonmetro America contains 52.5 percent of all non-aged, employed, male-headed families with children versus only 32.3 percent of all families (Pryor 1979).

BIBLIOGRAPHY

Bawden, Lee. "Future Poverty Programs: Political Prospects and Implications for the Rural Poor." In Rural Poverty and the Policy Crisis, edited by R. O. Coppedge and C. G. Davis, pp. 186-93. Ames, Iowa: Iowa State University Press, 1977.
_____. "The Rural Income Maintenance Experiment." In Rural Development Perspectives, U.S. Department of Agriculture, RDP no. 2. September 1979.
_____. "Welfare Analysis of Poverty Programs." American Journal of Agricultural Economics 54 (1972).
_____. "Work Behavior of Low Income Rural Nonfarm Wage Workers." American Journal of Agricultural Economics 56 (1974).
Beale, Calvin L. "Demographic Typological Aspects of Nonmetro Areas." Mimeographed. 1979.
_____. "A Further Look at Nonmetropolitan Population Growth Since 1970." American Journal of Agricultural Economics 58 (1976): 953-58.
_____. "The Recent Shift of United States Population to Non-Metropolitan Areas." International Regional Science Review 2 (1977): 113-22.
_____. The Revival of Population Growth in Nonmetro-

politan America. U.S. Department of Agriculture.
ERS-605. June 1975.

Berry, Brian L. "Labor Market Participation and Regional
Potential." Growth and Change 1 (1970): 3-10.

Bickel, G., and MacDonald, M. "Participation Rates in the
Food Stamp Program: Estimated Levels for 1974." Legal
Action Support Project Papers on Poverty and Law.
Washington, D.C.: Bureau of Social Science Research,
Inc., 1975.

Blaug, Mark. "The Empirical Status of Human Capital Theory:
A Slightly Jaundiced Survey." Journal of Economic
Literature 14 (1976): 827-55.

Booth, E. J. R. "The Economic Dimensions of Rural Poverty."
American Journal of Agricultural Economics 51 (1969):
428-43.

Bould Van-Til, S. "The Social Cost of Poverty." In Rural
Poverty and the Policy Crisis, edited by R. O. Coppedge
and C. G. Davis, pp. 71-80. Ames, Iowa: Iowa State
University Press, 1977.

Briggs, V.; Rungeling, B.; and Smith, L. "The Significance
of Welfare Reform for the Rural South." In Proceedings
of the Thirtieth Annual Winter Meeting, pp. 226-34.
Industrial Relations Research Association, 1977.

Brown, D. "Racial Disparity and Urbanization, 1960 and
1970." Rural Sociology 43 (1978): 403-25.

Carlin, T. A. "The Impact of Earned Income Tax Credit."
Agricultural Economic Report no. 336. Economic Research
Service, U.S. Department of Agriculture, June 1976.

Chernik, H., and Holmer, M. "The Urban and Regional Impact
of the Carter Administration's 1979 Welfare Reform
Proposal." Mimeographed. June 1979.

Clawson, M. "Economic Implication of the Recent Population
Shift Toward Rural Areas." American Journal of Agricultural Economics 58 (1976): 963-66.

Coltrane, Robert; King, Chris T.; and Barnow, Burt. "Funding
Formulas." In CETA: An Analysis of the Issues, pp.
127-84. National Commission for Manpower Policy.
Washington, D.C.: U.S. Government Printing Office,
1978.

Congressional Budget Office. Poverty Status of Families
Under Alternative Definitions of Income. Background
Paper no. 17 (Revised). Washington, D.C.: U.S. Govern-
ment Printing Office, June 1977.

Daft, L. "The Rural Poverty Commission--Ten Years Later."
In Rural Development Perspectives. U.S. Department of
Agriculture RDP no. 20, September 1979.

Danziger, Sheldon; Haveman, R.; and Plotnick, R. "Income
    Transfer Programs in the United States: An Analysis of
    Their Structure and Impacts." Prepared for the Joint
    Economic Committee of the United States. Madison, Wis.:
    University of Wisconsin, 1979.
Danziger, Sheldon; Haveman, R.; Smolensky, E.; and Taeuber,
    K. "The Urban Impacts of the Program for Better Jobs
    and Income." Institute for Research on Poverty, Dis-
    cussion Paper 538-79. Madison, Wis.: University of
    Wisconsin, 1979a.
Davis, C. G. "Poverty and Rural Underdevelopment in the
    United States: Where Do We Stand?" In Rural Poverty and
    the Policy Crisis, edited by R. O. Coppedge and C. G.
    Davis, pp. 11-34. Ames, Iowa: Iowa State University
    Press, 1977.
Davis, K., and Schoen, C. Health Care and the War on
    Poverty. Washington, D.C.: Brookings Institution, 1978.
Davis, O., and Jackson, J. "Representative Assemblies and
    Demands for Redistribution: The Case of Senate Voting
    on the Family Assistance Plan." In Redistribution
    Through Public Choice, edited by H. Hochman and G.
    Peterson, pp. 261-88. New York: Columbia University
    Press, 1974.
Deavers, L. "Public Policy Issues in Rural Development."
    National Public Policy Conference, September 1978.
Engels, R. A., and Healy, M. K. "Rural Renaissance Recon-
    sidered." American Demographics May (1979): 16-19.
Fishelson, Gideon. "Returns to Human & Research Capital in
    the Non-South Agricultural Sector of the United States,
    1949-1964." American Journal of Agricultural Economics
    53 (1971): 129-31.
Fuchs, Victor. "Comments on Measuring the Low Income Popula-
    tion." In Six Papers on the Size Distribution of Wealth
    and Income, edited by S. Soltow. New York: National
    Bureau of Economic Research, 1969.
Greenwood, Michael J. "Research on Internal Migration in
    the United States: A Survey." Journal of Economic
    Literature 13 (1975): 397-434.
Hansen, Niles. The Future of Nonmetropolitan America. Lexing-
    ton, Mass.: Lexington Books, 1973.
_____. Improving Access to Economic Opportunity:
    Nonmetropolitan Labor Markets in an Urban Society.
    Cambridge, Mass.: Ballinger, 1976.
_____. Rural Poverty and the Urban Crisis. Bloom-
    ington, Ind.: Indiana University Press, 1970.
Hines, F., and Reid, J. N. "Using Federal Outlay Data to

Measure Program Equity--Opportunities and Limitations."
USDA Economic Research Service, Working Paper no.
7711. Washington, D.C.: U.S. Department of Agriculture, 1977.

Hoppe, B. "Poor People of Rural America." In Rural Development Perspectives. U.S. Department of Agriculture RDP
no. 20, September 1979.

Huffman, W. E. "Interactions Between Farm and Nonfarm Labor
Markets." Paper presented to the American Agricultural
Economics Association, July 1977.

Iowa Agriculture and Home Economics Experiment Station.
Patterns of Living Related to Income Poverty in Dis-
advantaged Families. North Central Regional Research
Publication no. 217, Special Report 74. Ames, Iowa:
Iowa State University, 1974.

Klein, D. P. "Gathering Data on Residents of Poverty Areas."
Monthly Labor Review Feb. (1975): 38-44.

Kotz, N. Hunger in America: The Federal Response. New York:
Field Foundation, 1979.

Larson, D., and Youmans, E. Problems of Rural Elderly
Households in Powell County, Kentucky. U.S. Department
of Agriculture, Economics, Statistics and Cooperative
Service, ERS 665. Washington, D.C., 1978.

Lieberson, S. "A Reconsideration of the Income Differences
Found Between Migrants and Northern-born Blacks."
American Journal of Sociology 83 (1978): 940-66.

Long, L. "Interregional Migration of the Poor: Some Recent
Changes." Current Population Reports, series P-23, no.
73. Washington, D.C.: U.S. Government Printing Office,
1978.

Lyday, J. M. "Political and Social Implications for Rural
Areas of a Nationalized System of Welfare." American
Journal of Agricultural Economics 53 (1971): 750-53.

McCoy, J. "Rural Poverty in Three Southern Regions." U.S.
Department of Agriculture, Economic Research Service
Report no. 176. Washington, D.C.: U.S. Government
Printing Office, 1970.

MacDonald, M. Food Stamps and Income Maintenance. New York:
Academic Press, 1978.

Marshall, Ray. Rural Workers in Rural Labor Markets. Salt
Lake City, Utah: Olympus Publishing, 1974.

Martin, P. "Rural Labor Markets and Rural Manpower Policy."
In Proceedings of the 30th Annual Winter Meeting, pp.
217-25. Industrial Relations Research Association,
1977.

_____, and Lane, S. "Distributional Equity of the

Food Stamp Program." American Journal of Agricultural
Economics 59 (1977): 1006-12.
Morrison, P. "The Shifting Regional Balance." American
Demographics May (1979): 9-15.
_____ et al. Review of Federal Programs to Alleviate
Rural Deprivation. Paper R-1651-CF. Santa Monica,
Calif.: Rand Corporation, 1974.
Mountain-Plains, Inc. Proposal FY75-FY76 Career Education
Model IV. Vol. 1. Glasgow, Mont., 1976.
Moynihan, D. P. The Politics of a Guaranteed Annual Income.
New York: Random House, 1973.
National Rural Center. The Rural State in Public Assistance.
Vol. 10. Washington, D.C.: National Rural Center, Dec.
1978.
Owens, E. W. "Income Maintenance Programs in the 1960s: A
Survey." American Journal of Agricultural Economics 54
(1972): 342-55.
_____. "Survey of Poverty Issues and Programs: Can We
Improve the Performance?" In Rural Poverty and the
Policy Crisis, edited by R. O. Coppedge and C. G.
Davis, pp. 163-80. Ames, Iowa: Iowa State University
Press, 1977.
Palmer, J., and Pechman, J., eds. Welfare in Rural Areas.
Washington, D.C.: Brookings Institution, 1978.
Parham, J. T. "Statement to House Agricultural Subcommittee
on Family Farms, Rural Development and Special Studies,"
pp. 547-70. 19 April 1978, Human Development Services,
Department of Health, Education and Welfare. Washington,
D.C.
Persky, J. "Radical Political Economics, Poverty, and Income
Distribution." In Rural Poverty and the Policy Crisis,
edited by R. O. Coppedge and C. G. Davis, pp. 114-24.
Ames, Iowa: Iowa State University Press, 1977.
Piven, F., and Cloward, R. Regulating the Poor: The Function
of Public Welfare. New York: Basic Books, 1971.
President of the United States. "Rural Development." 95th
Congress, First Session, House Document no. 95-51.
Washington, D.C.: U.S. Government Printing Office,
1977.
President's National Advisory Commission on Rural Poverty.
The People Left Behind. Washington, D.C.: U.S. Govern-
ment Printing Office, 1967.
Pryor, S. "Regional and Residential Impacts of the Proposed
Better Jobs and Income Program." Mimeographed. Economic
Development Division, ESCS, U.S. Department of Agricul-
ture. Washington, D.C., 1979.

Roy, E., and Bordelon, F. Economic Aspects of the Low Income-Limited Resource Problem in Louisiana. Report no. 467. Louisiana State University, 1974.

Rungeling, B., and Smith, L. "Factors Affecting Food Stamp Nonparticipation in the Rural South." Center for Manpower Studies. University, Miss.: University of Mississippi, 1975.

_____; Briggs, V.; and Adams, J. Employment, Income, and Welfare in the Rural South. New York: Praeger, 1977.

Schuh, E. "Policy and Research Implications." In Welfare in Rural Areas, edited by J. Palmer and J. Pechman, pp. 211-36. Washington, D.C.: Brookings Institution, 1978.

Schultz, Theodore W. "The Value of the Ability to Deal with Disequilibria." Journal of Economic Literature 13 (1975): 827-46.

Seninger, S., and Stevenson, W. "The Economic Impact of Family Based Rural Education and Training." Social Science Journal 16 (1979).

Smeeding, T. "The Antipoverty Effectiveness of In-Kind Transfers." Journal of Human Resources 12 (1977): 360-78.

_____. "Cost of Living Differentials at Low Income Levels." Institute for Research on Poverty Discussion Paper no. 190-74. Madison, Wis.: University of Wisconsin, 1974.

Thomas, G. "Regional Migration Patterns and Poverty Among the Aged in the Rural South." Journal of Human Resources 8 (1973): 73-84.

Tweeten, Luther. "Rural Employment and Unemployment Statistics." Background paper no. 4. National Commission on Employment and Unemployment Statistics. Washington, D.C.: U.S. Government Printing Office, 1978.

_____, and Brinkman, George L. Micropolitan Development: Theory and Practice of Greater Rural Economic Development. Ames, Iowa: Iowa State University Press, 1976.

U.S. Bureau of the Census. "Characteristics of the Population Below the Poverty Level, 1977." Current Population Reports, series P-60, nos. 115 and 119. Washington, D.C.: U.S. Government Printing Office, 1979.

_____. "Demographic, Economic, and Social Profile of States: Spring 1976." Current Population Reports, series P-20, no. 134. Washington, D.C.: U.S. Government Printing Office, 1975.

_____. "Social and Economic Characteristics of the

Metropolitan and Nonmetropolitan Population: 1977 and 1970." Current Population Reports, series P-23, no. 75. Washington, D.C.: U.S. Government Printing Office, 1978.

U.S. Congress, Joint Economic Committee. "Handbook of Public Income Transfer Programs: 1975." Studies in Public Welfare Paper no. 20. Washington, D.C.: U.S. Government Printing Office, 1974.

U.S. Department of Agriculture. Annual Food Stamp Program Evaluation, Fiscal Year 1978. Prepared for U.S. House of Representatives Committee on Agriculture, Nutrition, and Forestry. Washington, D.C., September 1979.

_____. "The Economic and Social Condition of Non-metropolitan America in the 1970s." Committee on Agriculture and Forestry, U.S. Senate, 94th Congress. Washington, D.C.: U.S. Government Printing Office, 1975.

_____. "Farm Income Statistics." Statistical Bulletin no. 576. Washington, D.C.: Economic Research Service, U.S. Department of Agriculture, 1977.

_____. "Rural Policy Background Paper." Prepared by the Economic Development Division of the Economics, Statistics, and Cooperatives Service. Mimeographed. U.S. Department of Agriculture, June 1979.

U.S. Department of Health, Education and Welfare. Aid to Families With Dependent Children Statement for Basic Needs, July 1975. Social and Rehabilitation Service. NCSS Report D-2, July 1975. Washington, D.C.: U.S. Government Printing Office, 1976.

_____. "Summary Report: Rural Income Maintenance Experiment." Washington, D.C.: U.S. Government Printing Office, 1976.

Zuiches, J., and Brown, D. "The Changing Character of the Nonmetropolitan Population 1950-1975." In Rural U.S.A.: Persistence and Change, edited by T. R. Ford, pp. 55-72. Ames, Iowa: Iowa State University Press, 1978.

Candace Howes
Ann R. Markusen

11

Poverty: A Regional Political Economy Perspective

INTRODUCTION

Poverty can be defined as the inability of a household to enjoy a basic livelihood. Livelihood should be thought of in physical rather than monetary terms, and can be secured through several institutions: the workplace, the household, the public sector, and the commodity marketplace. In this chapter, the focus is on the workplace and the household as settings for the generation of nonmetro poverty.

In most discussions of nonmetro poverty, lack of income has been equated with poverty status. Theoretical treatments of the origins of nonmetro poverty have therefore concentrated on the imperfections in the income generation process that result in lack of gainful employment for the poor. Unemployment is analyzed either as a function of deficiencies in worker's skills or of insufficient investment inducements to employers. These correspond to the supply and demand sides of the labor market. Health, education, and manpower training programs are aimed at enhancing the quality of labor supplied, and stimulants to invest, such as industrial parks, tax incentives, and financial subsidies, are supposed to expand the demand for labor. Although the stimulation of labor demand appears to be the more powerful approach, existing policies that seek to induce investment do not necessarily reach the poverty population, because they are based on an inadequate understanding of the way in which investment decisions affect the quality and quantity of jobs offered.

An alternate view is proposed here, that nonmetro poverty is a product of the dynamics of the accumulation process under capitalist evolution, rather than a result of characteristics of the rural poor or of insufficient investment demand. Three aspects of this evolution stand out: the breakdown of household and other nonwage labor production in certain nonmetro areas, the deliberate creation and maintenance of a reserve army of labor, and the changing

profitability and production features of particular capitalist sectors that have been or are currently concentrated in
nonmetro areas. The explanation of nonmetro poverty of
southern blacks and native Americans, in particular, but to
some extent nonmetro whites, lies in the previous modes of
production that characterized their livelihoods and the
erosion of these livelihoods as capitalist production has
supplanted them. The poverty of many whites can be traced
to the changing productivity and internal characteristics
of certain very disaggregated industrial sectors, each of
which produces a distinctive poverty problem.

In the second section a conceptual definition of poverty
is developed that both critiques traditional definitions and
lays the basis for the subsequent analysis of poverty. In
the next section, the problems of traditional approaches to
the alleviation of poverty based on employment creation are
discussed, followed by the presentation of a theory of poverty generation based on the three aspects outlined above. A
methodology and illustrative case study for studying these
sources of poverty based on disaggregated regional and industry studies is discussed in the next two sections, and finally, new directions for poverty research that follow from
this regional political economy perspective are suggested.

A CONCEPTUAL DEFINITION OF
POVERTY AND ITS INSTITUTIONAL SOURCES

Poverty can be defined conceptually as the household's inability to secure a livelihood, that is, to feed, clothe,
and shelter itself at a basic standard of living. The household, rather than the family, is the preferred subject,
because it encompasses every living arrangement from a
single individual to a group of unrelated individuals with
dependency or shared-consumption relationships. The basic
standard of living is politically defined and refers to
that level of well-being considered minimally acceptable by
the society. Several such levels have been developed for
operational purposes in the United States, though they are
subject to the deficiencies raised in the discussion below.
Perhaps the distinguishing characteristic of this definition
is its reference to the physical quality of life rather than
monetary or income criteria.

The sources of livelihood can be located in four different institutions: the household, the firm, the market-

place with its exchange relationships, and the government. The household produces and processes a large portion of the food, clothing, and shelter that it consumes. As the recent literature on women's productive role in the household shows (Markusen 1980), substantial labor time is spent in household production of commodities or services for direct use or barter, rather than exchange. If household members, particularly women, were not so employed, such goods and services would have to be purchased on the market (child care, restaurant meals, nursing services, etc.). Although the proportion of labor time and total standard of living accounted for by such work appears to be highest among households with inferior income-earning opportunities, substantial amounts of such labor time are expended in all but the highest-income households (where servants are paid wages to produce such services). In open country areas in particular, the production of homegrown foodstuffs, hunting and fishing, self-built shelter, and bartered goods and services may constitute important contributions to the standard of living of a household.

Wage labor is the second source contributing to a standard of living. Workers sell their labor power for a wage that is determined by the level of unemployment in the local labor market, by the level of worker organization and militancy, by the productivity of labor in a particular production process, and by any monopoly or monopsony advantages the employer may have in the product and labor markets. Effective annual income from wage labor is also affected by seasonal and cyclical unemployment or underemployment, and by any extraordinary costs borne by the worker in order to keep the job. Self-employment for market sale is a special case of wage labor.

The exchange process of the marketplace, where commodities produced by wage labor in capitalist firms are sold, is the third source shaping the household's standard of living. Workers who earn a wage must translate it into consumable commodities and services by purchases on this market. Depending on several factors, the prices that they confront may raise or lower the purchasing power of their wages. First, the relative wage depends on the rate at which prices are rising relative to wages. Second, the relative wage depends on the transportation costs of commodities produced elsewhere, because local markets may not be large enough to sustain local production at a cost below the cost of commodities transported from other areas. Third, the local market may be subject to spatial monopoly at the retail level or through control of the transportation system, resulting in higher prices. Finally, the structure of commodities that must be imported to a region may contain high concentrations of commodities produced by monopoly sectors, so that locally competitive wage rates confront higher relative prices than the wages in areas where the commodities originate. This phenomenon can also result from simple price discrimination.

The government is a final, significant source of live-lihood. Obviously, direct income transfers and income-in-kind such as welfare and food stamps enhance a household's ability to feed, clothe, and shelter itself. But taxation is also an important redistributor of income, both directly through income taxes and indirectly through business, sales, and property taxes. Furthermore, many of the services pro-vided by government (health care, recreational facilities, infrastructure such as dams, streets, highways, water, and sewer facilities, and municipal utilities) constitute in-kind contributions to the standard of living. More indirect-ly, subsidies to certain groups through tax rebates, con-trols on prices or trade that enhance incomes, price and income effects of regulatory policies and cheap government land-leasing rates, affect relative standards of living of various groups. Although what is generally labeled "welfare" is received largely by poorer households, this more exten-sive set of government services and advantages may favor higher income groups. In this chapter, the analysis is confined to the first two of the spheres determining live-lihoods: households and firms.

This definitional discussion suggests directions for improvement in the official conception of poverty as used in policy analysis. Official definitions of poverty gen-erally use low income as a proxy for poverty (see, for example, Chapter 10). Attempts have been made to include welfare receipts, narrowly defined, and federal income tax and social security subtractions, but not other forms of taxation and public sector service subsidies or income-earning advantages. The census definition includes a 15 percent reduction for farm families (formerly 30 percent) attributable to home food production, but no other form of nonmarket production (McCoy, 1970: 6; Seninger and Smeeding, in this volume). Regional price differentials are rarely accounted for; no such indices exist on a comprehen-sive disaggregated basis, although efforts along these lines are now in progress. Differentiated price structures,

from monopolization in either industrial or spatial forms,
have not been studied.

It is impossible to itemize comprehensively the change
a revised definition would have on the interpretation of
rural poverty, although a few examples might demonstrate
the significance of such a revision. For instance, subsidies
to nonmetro highways would enrich livelihoods whereas the
high cost of monopolized gasoline, given the required long
commute to work and dependence of farming on fuel, would
lower them. Price structures confronted by nonmetro people
are undoubtedly highly monopolistic (autos, oil, health,
processed foods) compared to the competitive locations of
sectors in which they work (agriculture, manufacturing).
The net incidence of all taxes--state, local and federal--
is believed to be highly regressive at the lowest income
levels, thus worsening the position of poverty households,
although the local tax burden is apt to be less in absolute
magnitude in nonmetro than in metro areas. On the other
hand urban poor households probably enjoy higher levels of
public services than do their rural counterparts. Greater
opportunities for household nonmarket production in rural
areas, if captured by the poverty definition, might modify
our evaluation of rural livelihoods substantially.

The income-based definition implies that poverty alleviation is synonymous with improvements in the conditions
of wage labor, via intervention in the labor supply (manpower) or in labor demand (economic development) fronts.
The livelihood-based definition suggests that poverty might
be alleviated by intervening on other fronts. For instance,
the elimination of monopoly in pricing, either spatial or
sectoral, might significantly improve the livelihoods of
the poor. The encouragement and elimination of barriers to
household production and barter is another route. Nonmetro
residents frequently complain of regulations such as meat
inspection that prevent them from selling slaughtered meat
to neighbors, building codes that unduly complicate self-
built structures, professional licensing, which discourages
bartering, and fish and game management policies that favor
urban sportsmen. Government-sponsored day care and similar
cooperatively organized activities, both consumption and
production-oriented, could lower income requirements substantially. The biggest resource of the nonmetro poor is
their labor time; wage labor may not always be the most
fruitful use of that time.

Changes in government regulation, tax policy, and service provision and distribution provide other routes to alleviating nonmetro poverty; food stamps and rural elec-trification are two existing programs that do so. But the possibilities are much broader. For instance, the federal government might convert farm subsidies for large absentee landowners to subsidies for poor farm workers. A national health care system, along the lines of the proposed Dellums Bill, for instance, could well provide much better care for the nonmetro poor than a national health insurance plan relying on private sector health production. Each such change poses its costs and political opposition, of course. Nevertheless, most such factors influencing rural poverty are never debated as contributors to it or as potential routes for alleviation.

THEORIES OF INADEQUATE EMPLOYMENT

Although the neglect of nonwage contributions to livelihood in the literature is emphasized in this chapter, it is agreed that conditions of wage labor are a major cause of nonmetro poverty. Current development policy appears to have dichotomized the causes of employment inadequacy in nonmetro areas. On the one hand, an extensive literature addresses problems on the labor supply side, and, on the other hand, an entire array of economic development pro-grams attempts to operate on the labor demand side. Each approach exhibits an implicit theory.

The labor supply research emphasizes the characteristics of individual workers and, sometimes, the characteristics of the entire supply in labor market areas. Workers are identified by age, race, sex, educational level, and oc-casionally by occupation or industry of previous (or pre-ferred) employment, but generally at the one-digit level, which is too aggregated to be revealing. The implicit theory behind the supply focus is that socioeconomic characteris-tics of workers are associated with low marginal productiv-ity. Therefore, by upgrading workers' skills, education, or other aspects, unemployment will be alleviated because such workers will be more attractive to employers.

The empirical work associating unemployment with worker characteristics yields a useful descriptive profile, but it generally does not link workers' handicaps or poverty status to the characteristics of industries that have employed them in the past or to the dynamics of economic development.

The divorcing of labor supply characteristics from labor demand results in the implicit suggestion that workers' characteristics cause their unemployment. But such characteristics may merely reflect the distribution of unemployment, whereas the existence (and persistence) of unemployment arises from problems of profitability in a dynamic economic system. It is argued here that the unemployment and poverty status of groups with certain characteristics are primarily a product of the erosion of prior sources of livelihood, of decline in industrial sectors that previously shaped employment patterns, and of specific features of contemporary employing sectors.

On the other side of the labor market, employers demand workers when they can employ them in profitable production, and growth theories have generally treated investment as the engine of employment expansion. Insufficient investment opportunities, these theories hold, can be overcome through subsidies that, on the margin, increase profitability and stimulate capital investment (Siebert 1969). The subsidies might take the form of tax incentives, financial subsidies to lower borrowing costs (e.g., loan guarantees), or provision of infrastructure that directly or indirectly augments the capital stock (highways, industrial parks, etc.). The problem with such policies, and with the theory underpinning them, is that increased investment is not necessarily linked to the expansion of employment prospects for the rural poor. Investment tax credits, for instance, although clearly saving corporations money, have not been proven to influence the level of investment, though they may affect its timing, nor have they significantly affected the location of investment (Harrison and Kanter 1978). The inadequacy of the investment subsidy approach can be traced to its unwillingness to examine empirically and in detail the employment demand generation process; that is, how a decision to invest is linked to job creation in several affected sectors and locations, what kinds of jobs it creates, and the potential consequences of the substitution of capital for labor. What is needed, therefore, is a disaggregated study of industrial sectors and the job creation process in each.

AN ALTERNATIVE THEORY OF THE CREATION
AND MAINTENANCE OF NONMETROPOLITAN POVERTY

The major weakness in analyses of poverty to date lies in their disembodying the phenomenon from the processes that historically generate it and presently continue it. Those processes are best analyzed as aspects of the growth dynamic within capitalist economies. Firms and industries are constantly evolving, frequently in response to crises or conflicts inherent in the nature of growth. For instance, the generation of livelihoods in contemporary American agriculture reflects the conflict between an evolving corporate system, which organizes production in large-scale units, and the traditional family farm, which has mobilized politically to protect its institutional form through extensive government intervention. Much nonmetro poverty in the current period can be traced to three aspects of the growth process: (1) the breakdown of household or other nonwage labor production in certain areas; (2) the deliberate attempt to create and maintain a reserve army of labor; and (3) the changing profitability and production features of particular capitalist sectors located in rural areas. These aspects of the growth process are related to the supply of and demand for labor.

Growth is defined as the accumulation of capital on a firm, industry, or regional basis. Accumulation of capital involves the pursuit of profits in order to reinvest in further profit-producing enterprise, and, although such capital is quite mobile, it nevertheless exists in concrete and fixed forms within industries and places. Growth is shaped by competition among firms, where the growth of output and investment in one firm or place may result in or be contingent upon the decline of another. Growth of an industry implies the net growth of output or invested capital of firms within the industry. A region can be said to experience economic growth if there is net growth in operations of firms within the region.

But growth does not necessarily imply net increases in livelihoods or diminution of poverty in the places that host it. Expansion of capitalist production systems supplants previous modes of production and with it the livelihoods derived from them (e.g., the history of native Americans). Furthermore, due to the legacy of deterioration of certain precapitalist economies, and/or because of spatial monopoly over the labor force, entering enterprises frequently find they can employ labor at poverty-level wages. And, in certain areas, employers have made concerted efforts to create and maintain a reserve army of labor through immigration and welfare policies. As capitalist production intensifies, the specialization, competition for resources, and constant innovation required by its structure result in spasmodic sectoral growth and shrinkages in spatial relocations that may leave poverty in their wake. A theory is required that will explain why growth in a capitalist system does not necessarily take place ubiquitously and why it does not necessarily alleviate poverty, but may sustain, redistribute or exacerbate the difficulties of securing a livelihood even in areas of growth. Several bodies of work in regional political economy contribute to the construction of such a theory: (1) the debate on the transition from precapitalist to capitalist modes of production in developing countries; (2) work on the reserve army of labor; and (3) the detailed empirical work in Britain, France, and the United States on the changing industrial structure of regional economies and the determinants of industrial relocation.

POVERTY AS A FUNCTION OF NONCAPITALIST PRODUCTION SYSTEMS

The transition debate, a companion to the debate on dependency theory, is perhaps best summarized and arbitrated by Brenner (1977). The Brenner formulation is particularly useful because it hypothesizes the causes of nonaccumulation that may be responsible for conditions of nonmetro poverty in advanced industrial as well as developing countries. Brenner argues that the conditions of capital accumulation presuppose the following: that the means of production (capital equipment, buildings, land), the means of subsistence (food, clothing, shelter), and labor power (the capacity of workers to perform) should be for sale in the marketplace. Under these circumstances, workers must sell their labor power in the marketplace in order to acquire the means of subsistence. Thus a labor force will be available for employment by capitalists. If direct producers have, on the other hand, retained possession of means of production and subsistence (e.g., a garden plot) that consistently provide them with enough to survive, they have no absolute necessity to sell their labor power in the marketplace and can withdraw from the market if the conditions are unacceptable.

The capitalist entrepreneur in this situation operates

under a different imperative. If wage labor in a region is unavailable, the capitalist enterprise will not only lack a supply of direct labor but also a local market for commodities produced. Under conditions where direct producers are not constrained to purchase their means of subsistence in the market, there is no incentive for them to purchase consumer goods in the market, hence there is no market for consumer goods. Thus the maintenance of precapitalist sources of livelihood impedes capitalist growth in a dual manner—by restricting available wage labor and by circumscribing the market for capitalist-produced commodities. Historically, in many countries, taxation schemes, land seizures, conscription, and immigration propaganda, as well as gentler forms of inducement, have been used to hasten the creation of a wage labor force.

It remains to be explained why this process of proletarianization has proceeded more or less rapidly in different areas in the United States. Three cases come to mind that provide some insight: black rural poverty, Native American poverty, and poverty associated with the foreclosure of opportunities to engage in household, nonmarket production.

The case of black poverty in the nonmetro South gives an historically specific insight. According to Genovese (1965), the process of proletarianization was inhibited by the existence of the slave-based plantation economy. This mode of production depleted the land, was land intensive, inefficient, and incapable of innovating to increase productivity, and thwarted the development of manufacturing and wage labor. Its expansionary efforts took the form of territorial growth, as eastern planters on depleted land turned to breeding slaves and looked for westward markets, and as others sought richer western land.

Economic systems that rely upon feudal or slave forms of labor frequently ossify, driving a region into underdevelopment in the face of capitalist advances elsewhere. Much black poverty in the nonmetro South today can be traced to slavery and its legacy. The relatively less efficient slave mode of production put the South at a disadvantage in future development vis-à-vis the North, a gap that has not yet been closed for nonmetro areas. The North had a head start on the development of manufacturing that created a monopoly situation in the exchange of manufactured commodities for agricultural commodities. When the South did begin to develop a capitalist mode of production, it was competing with a more fully developed and, hence, more efficient North. In addition, the failure of any land reform to accompany emancipation following the Civil War resulted in a sharecropping system that replicated many of the inefficient and nondynamic practices of the slavery system in southern agriculture (Mandle 1978).

The displacement of one mode of production by another may also produce a group or class of people whose loss of livelihood may be very difficult to counter with incorporation into capitalist economic relations, and thus who may remain for decades in poverty. Native Americans form the largest such group in the United States. Whereas different tribes had very different economies prior to European entry into North America, all were dispossessed of their productive land, their principal source of livelihood. Their resistance to incorporation into capitalist cultures and economies, plus their victimization by land-hungry whites, resulted in their impoundment on reservations, where almost universally they were less able to secure a livelihood. The land to which they were sent has generally remained so remote and unattractive to employers that intense poverty persists despite a century of cultural assimilation. Recent renewed activity around energy development and mineral extraction on reservations may bring growth, though perhaps not jobs (Jorgensen et al. 1978).

A significant amount of labor is still performed outside the wage-labor sector. A developing literature documents the extent and nature of production for immediate consumption that takes place in households, primarily by women (Hartmann in press). The performance of this nonwage labor is diminishing as more women are incorporated into the labor force and tasks are performed outside the household (childcare services, restaurant meals, prepared foods, commercial launderies, etc.). Although this shift may represent efficiencies and gains in livelihood for some, it may also entail the erosion of circumstances that engendered household production, such as the tightly knit community that previously shared care of children and the aged, thus diminishing possibilities for supplementing livelihoods.

Similarly, social standards and government intervention that are required by a complex industrial society may hasten the erosion of favorable conditions for household-produced or bartered services. For instance, building codes and zoning in nonmetro areas have constrained self-built shelter, and professionalization and regulation of health care and social service systems may raise monetary costs to households while foreclosing older options (for example,

midwifery). The alternative technology and self-help housing movements, which are strong in nonmetro areas, may
counter these developments.

The above arguments all bear on the manner in which
capitalist growth is both impeded by nonwage-labor forms of
production and at the same time undermines them. It is not
suggested here that a majority of people in the United
States fared better under precapitalist economic systems,
but rather that some groups have suffered inordinately from
the transition. Some experience poverty because a precapitalist mode destroyed their means of livelihood (native
Americans), some because a previous mode retarded capitalist
development in a particular region (southern rural blacks),
and some because their location in the transition eroded
their independent means of livelihood without immediately
replacing them with sufficient income-earning possibilities
(rural whites). Because a fair share of poverty can be
attributed to these origins, any policy to alleviate it
must consider the particular circumstances that have shaped
each group's experience.

POVERTY AS A FUNCTION OF THE RESERVE ARMY OF LABOR

An argument frequently made by political economists regarding unemployment and poverty is that such conditions are
necessarily produced and required by a capitalist system.
The existence of a reserve army of labor enables capitalists
to keep wages below the value of marginal product thereby
ensuring profitability. Although it is clear that an excess
supply of labor may enhance profitability, the observation
of this functional role does not prove that such a requirement necessarily causes unemployment in a specific place or
case (Clark 1980). To make an argument that a reserve army
is deliberately created or maintained, one must identify
the behavior and mechanisms that constitute the formation
of a reserve army. A complete analysis would require theories of population growth, migration, and labor force participation, a task beyond the present scope. Instead, specific cases of reserve army formation should suffice to
suggest the importance of this source of poverty in the
United States.

In United States history, successive waves of immigration were frequently solicited by employers to provide
cheap labor for industrial expansion. For instance, in the
1880s, chamber of commerce propaganda urged Danes to immi-

grate to Minneapolis, where they frequently remained unemployed for several years and helped to keep wages down and
unions out. The most dramatic example of such recruitment
in rural America involves the successive waves of Asian,
Okie, and Mexican labor to work in West Coast agriculture
(McWilliams 1971). The poverty today among working Chicanos
in California and other western states can be traced to
this deliberate formation of a low-wage work force, solicited by western growers and supported through state and
federal immigration practices.

A reserve army of labor is frequently maintained by
legal and public sector service arrangements. In the Chicano case, agricultural wages have been kept low by government cooperation in maintaining the flow of workers across
the border (e.g., the old Bracero Program; laxness and
postharvest timing of deportations), by the exclusion of
agricultural labor from the National Labor Relations Act
and similar legislation covering workers' rights, by the
denial of basic civil rights to undocumented workers, and
by the liberal use of deportation (in many cases deported
workers are not paid for their labor).

Many groups that serve as a reserve army have also had
livelihoods denied them elsewhere, explaining in part their
migration or willingness to participate in the reserve army
(e.g., Puerto Ricans in New York and Okies fleeing the
1930s dust bowl). The reserve army argument must be used
with caution, and the particular mechanisms that maintain
it identified, if poverty associated with it is to be alleviated. These mechanisms are most likely to be discovered
through study of specific sectors such as fruit and vegetable production.

POVERTY AS A FUNCTION OF INDUSTRY STRUCTURE AND DYNAMICS

Not all poverty can be traced to the interaction between
wage-labor production and precapitalist sources of livelihood or to concerted efforts to build and maintain a reserve
army. Economic growth, conceived of as either the accumulation of capital or more conventionally as the growth in
gross national product, can occur simultaneously with the
maintenance of or increase in poverty in certain areas.
This is particularly true if we look at growth disaggregated
to a regional or local level. Hansen (1973) has shown that
in the United States counties experience tremendously divergent economic growth rates, many losing jobs in absolute

numbers—losses that can be traced to the sectors in which jobs are generated. To the extent nonmetro poverty is attributable to wage-labor conditions, it can be traced to the particular features of particular sectors.

Several attempts to summarize changes in locational patterns of employment across all industries as a function of fundamental changes in the organization of the modern corporation should be acknowledged. Following Hymer's (1972) effort to distinguish among three hierarchical levels of decision making in the multinational corporation, Cohen (1977) and Lasuen (1974) have attempted to draw the spatial consequences, arguing that control functions are increasingly located in "headquarters" cities while production becomes more decentralized. Others have argued that multinational and conglomerate firms have motivations different from the older industrial corporations. For instance, Bluestone and Harrison (1979) argue that conglomerates are much more apt than are corporations to use plants for all they can get, depreciating their assets rapidly. Pred (1977) has generalized from the existing spatial patterns of production to propose a hierarchical system of cities with particular production links and diffusion of innovation patterns. Although the observation of general spatial reordering with the emergence of the multinational, conglomerate firm is interesting, substantial evidence (e.g., Bluestone and Harrison 1979; Massey and Meegan 1978) underscores the variation of experience across sectors and cautions against overgeneralization.

The inherent drive toward profits produces continual technical innovation, product creation, reorganization of management and the work process, and reconfiguration of competitive structure and markets. Structural unemployment in a rural region may result from decline or technological innovation in a particular industry. Similarly, cyclical unemployment, a contributor to rural poverty, results from volatile production patterns in certain industries. Seasonal unemployment also results from specific industrial production patterns. High work-related costs that contribute to rural poverty, especially high health costs (such as in coal mining) and commuting costs, are attributable to specific production features. Working poverty may result from the monopoly of an industry on a local labor market or from an industry's attraction to a rural labor force that has some subsistence support in the nonmarket household sector, enabling it to pay lower wages. No real understanding of poverty, or its alleviation, can occur without a sector-by-sector analysis of major employers, past and present.

Several recent research efforts provide models for this type of analysis. The inaugural work on British industrial location by Massey and Meegan (1978) shows that disaggregated electronics and electrical machinery sectors have exhibited divergent locational patterns during the last ten years, a period of what they call "restructuring" due to the competitive pressures introduced by the British recession and growing international competition. Whereas the hard-hit electrical machinery sector moved to rural low-wage areas because its greatest need was reduction of labor costs, the more robust electronics sector moved to more prosperous areas where professional and skilled labor was abundant. Bluestone and Harrison's work (1979) on the New England economy broken down into three-digit Standard Industrial Classification codes indicates wide variation across industries and has identified particular features of industrial organization, such as conglomeration and new forms of competition, as sources of industrial out-migration and poverty-inducing unemployment. Simon's work (1980) on the underground coal industry in Appalachia shows, in a historical case, how virulent competition in the coal industry combined with vulnerability of the local labor force to produce a pattern of extraordinary exploitation of workers that retarded innovation and productivity increases in the industry and discouraged other industries from entering the region.

Nor does nonmetro poverty result only from stagnation, decline or out-migration of particular sectors. LeVeen and McLeod (1979) show that the most important new source of poverty in America can be attributed to low wages in manufacturing industries that are locating in the South. Similarly, Watkins and Perry (1978) have argued that the apparent prosperity of the Sunbelt is misleading, because although unemployment levels are low, the numbers of working poor are large relative to other regions. Malizia (1978) argues that the manufacturing sectors moving to the South are generally those in the slow-growth category, desperately in need of cheap labor. Exploratory work on fossil fuel and mineral extraction and power plant construction in the intermountain West and on Indian reservations (Sullam et al. 1978; Markusen 1978; Jorgenson 1978) suggests that certain forms of energy development may increase short- and long-run local unemployment and fail to improve substantially the lot of significant numbers of indigenous people.

These examples underscore the importance of doing disaggregated sectoral analysis of industries in particular
areas. Industrial location studies have generally operated
with one-digit industrial breakdowns, with the result that
their conclusions about inducements to location are frequently erroneous for certain areas and particular sectors.
Nor has the industrial location literature focused much on
the cause of out-migration of industry or on the disappearance of industries from an economic base. The proper direction for further research appears to be the identification
of different rural areas by the type of three- or four-digit
industries that predominate, with a subsequent study of the
production features and dynamics in those industries that
seem to be most strongly associated with poverty. As the
examples and studies cited suggest, the source of that
poverty may arise from: the competitive conditions within
the industry; a dramatic change in technology; the emergence
of a challenging substitute; labor cost-saving quests of
management; changes in resource availability or land-use
regulation; or unusual temporal production patterns in the
industry. Furthermore, conditions dating from the decline
of precapitalist economic structure may interact with the
nature of a particular sector to produce a situation in
which low wages and working poverty may accompany growth in
a nonmetro area. In the next section, the necessary components of an industry study are outlined.

METHODOLOGY: DISAGGREGATED INDUSTRY AND AREAL STUDIES

The critical link between specific industries and nonmetro
poverty lies in the employment practices of the firms located in nonmetro areas. Employment practices are here
construed to mean the type of jobs, number of jobs, regu-
larity of employment, segment of the population from which
workers are drawn, and the wage structure.

The demand for labor is a function of the growth of an
industry, the basic determinant of growth is capital investment, and the characteristics of growth are shaped by the
nature of capital investment. Of particular importance
are the relative capital intensity of an industry, its
occupational structure, and the segment of the labor force
from which that industry draws its employees. These characteristics of capital investment help determine the
distribution of income.

Capital investment is important to income distribution in both a static and dynamic sense. The structure of past capital investment determines the present distribution of income. The dynamics of capital investment also induce changes in income distribution. The dynamic path of capital investment in any region is a function of competitive forces in the economy, both nationally and locally. Whether the market structure of an industry is competitive, oligopolistic, or monopolistic, each firm in that industry is subject to competitive forces that lead it continually to seek out profitable investment opportunities.

The basic unit of analysis in any attempt to analyze income generation and distribution must be the firm, as the unit responsible for making investment decisions. In order to study the firm, however, it is necessary to study the industry. An industry study must include an analysis of not only the structure of the industry but also the competitive dynamic that changes that structure.

The structure of an industry includes those features that affect the competitive position of firms within it and the comparative profitability of that industry among other sectors. The competitive position of a firm is contingent on that firm's ability to maintain continually or reduce the unit cost of production comparable to other firms in the industry. The competitive position of the industry is contingent on its ability to generate high rates of profit compared to other sectors. Five main categories should initially be considered: the market or structure of demand, the structure of competition, the technology and organization of production, the type of control of labor, and the level of government involvement in the industry.

(1) The structure of demand considers the spatial and product dimensions of the market. For example, a firm may be participating in a market that is strictly circumscribed by the boundaries of a region, a nation, or an international market. A firm will also be competing in a market for specific products. Within these structural dimensions, a firm may try to reduce its unit cost of production by expanding its share of the market. Its ability to generate income depends upon changes in market characteristics over which it may have no control.

(2) The structure of competition considers whether the industry has a competitive, oligopolistic, or monopolistic structure, both in the sale of products and the purchase of inputs. This category is important for delimiting the type of competition that will occur in an industry. A competitive

industry will tend to compete on all fronts whereas an oligopolistic industry will establish certain ground rules for competition that limit the uncertainty of survival characterizing more competitive structures. Within the limitations established by the market structure each firm will try to reduce its unit cost of production. Oligopoly in the output market may permit relatively high wages to be won by unions; however, monopoly of a local labor force may depress incomes.

(3) An investigation of technology and organization of production probes the actual organization of the production process on several levels of spatial organization and the specific technology used in that process. So, for example, in a manufacturing industry, important distinctions might include whether the technology calls for batch production, assembly-line or continuous-flow production, and to what extent it is automated or computerized. This category would also consider whether production is specialized spatially on a regional, national, or international scale. Various features of the production process affect rural incomes; for instance, seasonal employment in agriculture and the rotating shifts in steel (Chinitz 1960) have been hypothesized to depress local incomes through underemployment. And technology frequently determines occupation and therefore income.

(4) The category of labor control is not fully separable from the organization of production but the study has been set up in this way in order to include broader dimensions of capital/labor relations. This category considers whether labor control is based on direct, technological, or bureaucratic control (Edwards 1979), and what role unions or other forms of labor organizations play in the relations between capital and labor. The form of labor control used is highly determinant in the occupational structure of the industry, and therefore affects incomes generated. Innovations in labor control may also induce unemployment and extend poverty.

(5) The role of the state is also not strictly separable from these other categories for it is instrumental in promoting, permitting, or suppressing various forms of competition, the size of the market, technology, and labor relations. This intervention occurs through taxation, regulation, tariff or import policy, subsidies, complementary infrastructure provision, research and development, land-use controls, land-leasing policies, resource development, and contracting.

Frequently, strong interrelationships among various of these features characterize certain industries or firms within them. For instance, the type of competitive structure has been found by Edwards (1979) to be correlated with the type of labor control that, in turn, is correlated with the type of jobs and distribution of the labor force among categories of jobs.

In addition to industry structure, the dynamics of each industry are central to an understanding of rural job generation. The composition of the industrial base and the structure of individual industries within it are highly determinant in the employment structure of any particular rural area. Competition within the industry and changes in the form of competition (especially those that affect the structure of the industry) are, accordingly, important in analyzing changes in the employment opportunities for any region in which that industry is operating. Referring to our five categories, an industry study should identify the contemporary competitive conditions particular to the industry and the changes that are occurring in its structure. An innovation in technology that significantly increases the minimum efficient scale of production may mean that the relevant market for the industry will be larger. For example, an industry that previously found production on a regional scale to be the most profitable may find upon adoption of such an innovation that the relevant market now exceeds regional boundaries. Thus it may expand production at an existing location while closing down older facilities or build an entirely new plant that supercedes all existing production units.

Changing industrial structure is linked to employment via the responses of particular firms to the competitive pressure of the new market situation. As the dimensions of the market, the technological base of the industry, labor control practices, or government involvement change, competitive shakedown will eliminate the now less efficient firms until a homogeneity of production conditions across firms is approximated. In evaluating the effect of changing structure on rural employment in specific places one has to look at the manner in which local firms respond to the new competitive pressure, that is, how they reduce costs.

The following points provide general guidelines for analyzing the forces and form of competition. Is competition occurring through: (1) new entry, or growth of existing firms; (2) expansions of present facilities, or investment in new plants; (3) expansion in the same region, or new regions; (4) expanded production of current products, or introduction of new products; (5) use of the same production technology, or new technology; and (6) use of the same type and proportions of labor, or through a new use of labor. All these forms of competition will result in immediately identifiable change in the distribution of employment and income.

It should be clear by now that such studies can only be carried out on a disaggregated level. The conditions in the various subsectors of manufacturing alone vary dramatically across the features enumerated. Food processing, textile manufacture, and steel making have very different market structures, concentration ratios, production processes, labor control features, and interrelationships with government. Even within food processing, brewing has a very different set of features from fruit and vegetable canning. Variation within the service sector is perhaps even greater. Furthermore, the same industry in different regions may exhibit different industrial structure characteristics. The following discussion of coal production demonstrates the necessity for regional and sectoral disaggregation, as well as the links between industry features and rural poverty.

CASE STUDY: THE COAL INDUSTRY AND POVERTY IN NONMETROPOLITAN APPALACHIA AND THE WEST

Mining industries are typically nonmetro in location and have long been associated with depressed areas. But the poverty and unemployment associated with different types of mining vary tremendously, so that no generalization can be made. This section examines just one type of mining-- coal--and its relationship to poverty in two different rural regions, Appalachia and the West (including North Dakota, Wyoming, Montana, Colorado, Utah, New Mexico, and Arizona).

The market demand for coal has historically been somewhat volatile, due to energy substitutes such as oil, environmental regulations that discourage the use of coal, and to changing patterns of industrial production and location, particularly in manufacturing (e.g., steel, aluminum) and transportation (railroads to trucking), that shift the market spatially. Until the most recent revival in the 1970s, these factors have been in part responsible for a long-run decline in coal production in Appalachia and a shift toward midwestern and western coal production. The shift has contributed to unemployment in Appalachia, a significant cause of nonmetro poverty there.

The nature of competition among coal companies is also a major factor in conditions of coal production. In Appalachia, production is still dominated by small producers operating under severely competitive circumstances. Simon (1980) argues that this competition resulted historically in employment and labor force management practices that impeded technological innovation in coal mining, principally by pursuing profitability through keeping wages extraordinarily low. The long-run damage to productivity in the industry is still a cause of low wages and rural poverty in the region. In the West, almost all of the coal is produced by either large companies like Peabody or by multinational energy corporations such as the oil companies. There, the monopolistic structure and degree of vertical integration obviate the need to keep wages low as a source of profitability.

Furthermore, the technology employed in the two regions differs strikingly. The bulk of Appalachian coal is mined underground, whereas the bulk of western coal is strip-mined. The former is still a highly labor intensive process, with relatively low labor productivity. The latter is highly capital intensive with few workers operating massive amounts of machinery. Labor costs are thus a low proportion of total costs. The necessity to keep wages low is much greater in the Appalachian case.

Landownership patterns and corresponding forms of rent are also significantly different. Much Appalachian land is privately owned and landowners attempt to extract profits from coal production in the form of rent. A significant portion of western land is publicly owned and has been leased at extremely low rates (Council on Economic Priorities 1974). In the latter case, de facto subsidized land costs permit larger returns that can be used to pay higher wages as well as to raise profits.

Occupational structures differ across the two regions because of differences in capital intensiveness. Machine operators in strip mining are frequently skilled workers from outside the community, who are drawn from construction trades or farm households where members have experience driving farm machinery. Deep mining requires less skill and more frequently workers are drawn from the local population. Wages in western strip mining are unusually high, due to the small proportion of production costs accounted for by

labor and the efforts by producers to keep out the United
Mine Workers (UMW), whose contracts have included a type of
severance tax, which goes to fund union benefits, on every
ton of coal produced. Unionization is quite high among
underground miners in both regions, and relatively high in
Appalachia among strip miners, but almost nonexistent among
strip miners in the West. Fortune magazine, immediately
following the 1978 coal strike, predicted that within two
years the growth of western coal would destroy the ability
of the UMW to hurt coal-dependent utilities through a strike
(Faltermeyer 1978). Unionization has clearly been a factor
that improves the poverty status of those Appalachian coal
miners who continue to find employment while also encouraging coal production elsewhere. At the same time, the historic bargain struck between the competitive Appalachian
coal companies and John L. Lewis included the union's
agreement to widespread mechanization, which has significantly decreased the labor requirements of Appalachian
underground coal mining, contributing to high levels of
local unemployment.

The dependence of the coal industry on the public sector
has been substantial, chiefly through subsidization of infrastructure and cheap public land. These have subsidized
the expansion of western coal, with its lower labor demand
component, at the expense of Appalachian production. Recent
national energy policy has favored western capital-intensive
energy development and thus may contribute to nonmetro poverty in both regions.

The coal industry in Appalachia dominates the local
labor market because operators act in concert through
associations that represent them in collective bargaining,
constituting a monopsony in the local labor market (Walls
et al. 1979). Historically, they have used this advantage
to pursue hiring practices that result in underemployment
(Simon 1980), to recapture profits by controlling some aspects of consumption costs of workers (the company store),
and to prevent effective union monopoly of the labor supply
by threat of unemployment.

Because coal is a nonrenewable resource-using industry,
its production patterns are necessarily of the boom-bust
type, with the speed of the depletion process being accelerated in strip-mining operations. After an area is mined out,
significant unemployment may ensue, imposing extraordinary
costs of relocation on workers in that sector. Wage levels
in strip mining may be set higher to cover such costs, but
in underground mining they are not.

The introduction of coal mining into a local community may also affect jobs in other sectors and regions. Coal consumes land, especially in strip mines, and affects the water table (coal is an aquifer). Both may therefore hurt agricultural employment in the region. Coal-related production of electricity, frequently at the mine mouth, pollutes the environment, may damage crops, and discourages tourism, which is at times an alternative source of employment and livelihood for the community. Coal-related in-migration of skilled workers may completely change the commercial sector of the local economy, displacing local businesses and service industries with entry of franchise retail outlets. These events are characteristic of western energy boom towns, where significant redistribution of poverty occurs even if employment opportunities increase. A preliminary look at employment growth in southeastern Montana indicates that coal-related development in the 1970s resulted in high employment levels, but greater numbers of unemployed people and a higher rate of unemployment, because in-migration of workers seeking jobs outdistanced the creation of jobs (Sullam et al. 1978). Furthermore, boom-town growth frequently results in extraordinary rates of local inflation, particularly for housing but for other commodities and in local tax rates as well, eroding boom sector incomes and pushing other residents into poverty.

The obvious association of poverty with coal production in Appalachia is not simply due to decline in labor intensiveness and production levels. What has been shown here is how industry features can affect wage levels, costs of employment, alternative forms of employment, and price levels shaping the poverty of the population. Ironically, the entire Appalachian regional development effort of the 1960s explicitly ignored these links (Simon 1980).

The fear that coal production will not alleviate current poverty but may in fact worsen economic conditions has resulted in: (1) opposition to mining by the Peabody Company on the Navajo reservation, which is deep mined and employs relatively small numbers of Navajos who are in the UMW (Robbins 1978); (2) the Cheyenne's recent decision to stop further leasing of their lands in Montana and their continued opposition to the construction of units three and four of the Colstrip generating facility (Owens 1978); and (3) the coalitions of ranchers and environmentalists in Wyoming, Montana, and North Dakota to control, if not stop, strip-mining in those states (Markusen 1978).

This review of the coal industry suggests multiple

relationships between local poverty levels and industry characteristics. Although the emphasis has been suggestive rather than deterministic, hopefully the case has been made with this and the previous example, that a detailed empirical look at industries in nonmetro areas is required to understand the nature of nonmetro poverty and the possibilities for its redress.

RESEARCH RECOMMENDATIONS

This discussion has identified the persistence, stagnation or decline of nonwage forms of production, the attempts to form a reserve army of labor, and the evolving features of certain industrial sectors employing wage labor as major determinants of rural poverty. This analysis suggests that the alleviation of poverty in nonmetro areas requires: (1) improving the conditions for the production of nonwage subsistence by strengthening nonwage production; (2) improving conditions of employment in the wage sector through the provision of higher-paying, more stable jobs, improving the organizational strength of labor, and elimination of monopoly in local markets and discrimination on the basis of race and gender; and (3) improving service and welfare provision. In addition to the research priorities and nonwage livelihood issues raised above, research is needed on sectorial-spatial planning approaches to dealing with nonmetro poverty. Such a conclusion is suggested by the identification of individual industrial sectors as primary determinants in specific cases of nonmetro poverty. It has been argued that economic planning currently takes place in large corporations, where the alleviation of unemployment and poverty are not goals of the locational and production decision-making processes. Corporate planning needs to be complemented by research and planning that attends to these social goals. An understanding of the poverty-inducing consequences of private production decisions is required as a prerequisite to the commitment of public sector resources (tax incentives, capital subsidies, manpower planning expenditures, etc.) to aid private sector development.

Important research on the development of schemes to introduce worker and community control over investment decisions integrated with national planning goals is now being done by the National Center for Economic Alternatives in Washington, D.C. When Lykes Corporation closed down the

Campbell works of its Youngstown Sheet and Tube Subsidiary
in September 1977, local religious leaders formed an Ecumenical Coalition of the Mahoning Valley that included
leaders from the city's political, labor, and business
communities. With the financial assistance of the U.S.
Department of Housing and Urban Development, the Ecumenical
Coalition commissioned a study of the feasibility of re-
opening the Campbell works as a community- and worker-owned
enterprise. This feasibility study was done under the direction of the National Center for Economic Alternatives
(Smith and McGuigan 1979). Such an initiative is representative of a growing movement on both a local and national
level for greater popular control over investment decisions
(Alperovitz and Faux 1975). This is the most promising
approach to researching the problems of rural as well as
urban poverty and unemployment.

BIBLIOGRAPHY

Aaron, Henry. Shelter and Subsidies: Who Benefits from
    Federal Housing Policies? Washington, D.C.: Brookings
    Institution, 1972.
Alperovitz, Gar, and Faux, Jeff. "An Economic Program for
    the Coming Decade." Washington, D.C.: Exploratory
    Project for Economic Alternatives, 1975.
Bluestone, Barry, and Harrison, Bennett. "Capital Mobility
    and Economic Dislocation." Paper presented at the
    Regional Science Association Meetings, Ithaca, N.Y.,
    November 1979.
Brenner, Robert. "The Origins of Capitalist Development:
    A Critique of Neo-Smithian Marxism." New Left Review
    104 (1977): 25-92.
Chinitz, Benjamin. "Contrasts in Agglomeration: New York
    and Pittsburgh." American Economic Review (1960):
    279-89.
Clark, C. Conditions of Economic Progress. Spanish version
    by J. Vergara and M. Paredes. Madrid: Alianza Editorial,
    1967.
Clark, Gordon. "Capitalism and Regional Inequality." Annals
    of American Association of Geographers 70 (1980): 521-32.
Cohen, Robert B. "Multinational Corporations, International
    Finance, and the Sunbelt." In The Rise of the Sunbelt
    Cities, by David C. Perry and Alfred J. Watkins, pp.
    211-26. Beverly Hills, Calif.: Sage Publications, 1977.

Council on Economic Priorities. "Leased and Lost: A Study
    of Public and Indian Coal Leasing in the West." Economic
    Priorities Report 5 (1974).
Edwards, Richard C. Contested Terrain: The Transformation of
    the Workplace in America. New York: Basic Books, 1979.
Faltermayer, E. "What the Coal Strike Has Obscured." Fortune
    97 (1978) pp. 30-31.
Genovese, Eugene D. The Political Economy of Slavery:
    Studies in the Economy and Society of the Slave South.
    New York: Pantheon Books, 1965.
Hansen, Niles M. The Future of Non-Metropolitan America:
    Studies in the Reversal of Small Town and Rural Popula-
    tion Decline. Lexington, Mass.: Lexington Books, 1973.
Harrison, Bennett, and Kanter, Sandra. "The Political Econ-
    omy of 'States Job-Creation and Business Incentives.'"
    Journal of American Institute of Planners 44 (1978).
Hartman, Heidi. "Class, Gender, and the State: The House-
    hold as the Focus of Conflict." Signs: A Journal of
    Women in Culture and Society, in press.
Hymer, S. H. "The Multinational Corporation and the Law of
    Uneven Development." In Economics and the World Order,
    edited by J. W. Bhagwati, pp. 113-40. New York: Mac-
    millan, 1972.
Jorgensen, Joseph et al. Native Americans and Energy Devel-
    opment. Cambridge, Mass.: Anthropology Resource Center,
    1978.
Kelly, Kevin D. "The Independent Mode of Production." Review
    of Radical Political Economics 11 (1979): 38-48.
Lasuen, J. R. "Spain's Regional Growth." In Public Policy
    and Regional Economic Development: The Experience of
    Nine Western Countries, edited by Niles M. Hansen, pp.
    235-47. Cambridge, Mass.: Ballinger Publishers, 1974.
LeVeen, Phillip, and McLeod, Daryl. "American Agricultural
    Policy in an Inflationary Era." Unpublished paper for
    the Agricultural Policy Project, Department of Agricul-
    tural Economics, University of California, Berkeley,
    1979.
McCoy, John. Rural Poverty in Three Southern Regions. Wash-
    ington, D.C.: U.S. Department of Agriculture, Economic
    Research Service, 1970.
McWilliams, Carey. Factories in the Field. Santa Barbara,
    Calif.: Peregrine Publishing Co., 1971.
Malizia, Emil. "Organizing to Overcome Uneven Development:
    The Case of the U.S. South." Review of Radical Political
    Economics 10 (1978): 87-94.
Mandle, Jay. The Roots of Black Poverty: The Southern

Plantation Economy after the Civil War. Durham, N.C.: Duke University Press, 1978.

Markusen, Ann. "City Spatial Structure, Women's Household Work and National Urban Policy." _Signs: A Journal of Women in Culture and Society_ 5 (1980 supp.): S23–44.

_____. "Class, Rent and the State: Uneven Development in Western U.S. Boomtowns." _Review of Radical Political Economics_ 10 (1978): 117–29.

_____. "Regionalism and the Capitalist State: The Case of the United States." _Kapitalistate_ 7 (1979): 39–62.

Massey, Doreen, and Meegan, Richard. "Industrial Restructuring Versus the Cities." _Urban Studies_ 15 (1978): 273–88.

Owens, Nancy. "Can Tribes Control Energy Development?" In _Native Americans and Energy Development_, by Joseph Jorgensen et al., pp. 49–62. Cambridge, Mass.: Anthropology Resource Center, 1978.

Pred, Allan Richard. _City Systems in Advanced Economies: Past Growth, Present Processes, and Future Development Options_. New York: Wiley, 1977.

Robbins, Lynn. "Energy Developments and the Navajo Nation." In _Native Americans and Energy Development_, by Jorgensen, Joseph et al. Cambridge, Mass.: Anthropology Resource Center, 1978.

Siebert, Herst. _Regional Economic Growth: Theory and Poverty_. Scranton, Penn.: International Textbook Co., 1969.

Simon, Richard. "The Labor Process and Uneven Development in the Appalachian Coalfields." _International Journal of Urban and Regional Research_ 4 (1980).

Smith, David, and McGuigan, Patrick. _Towards a Public Balance Sheet_. Washington, D.C.: National Center for Economic Alternatives, 1979.

Sullam, Carolla et al. _Montana: A Territorial Planning Strategy_. Working paper no. 294. Institute for Urban and Regional Development, University of California, Berkeley, 1978.

Walls, David et al. "A Baseline Assessment of Coal Industry Structure in the Ohio River Basin Energy Study Region." University of Kentucky, Appalachian Center, 1979.

Watkins, Alfred, and Perry, David. _The Rise of the Sunbelt Cities_. Beverly Hills, Calif.: Sage Publications, 1978.

John Moland, Jr.

12
The Black Population

INTRODUCTION

The migration patterns and demographic composition of the
black population in the United States have varied according
to changes in race relations and economic conditions at
local, state, and national levels. Consequently, population
structures of black communities differ by county, state,
and region. Such variations pose different community needs
and problems, from leadership to physical facilities, and
necessitate broad, flexible social policies in effecting
solutions to social and economic problems. Because of the
high concentration of poverty, unemployment, and underemployment among nonmetro blacks, especially in the South,
special attention should be given certain key areas in the
formation of social policy. Several of these areas, especially those linked to population composition and distribution, are mentioned here but will be discussed in greater
detail later in this chapter. They are leadership programs,
employment opportunities (including on-the-job training
programs especially geared to youth), and the identification and consideration of community needs and problems as
perceived by the people indigenous to the community, county,
state, and region. This chapter addresses these and other
issues first by examining the sociodemographic characteristics of rural and nonmetro blacks by region, with special
attention given to the South, and then by a discussion of
findings concerning perceived community needs and problems,
and factors relating to social well-being as reflected in
social indicators.

BACKGROUND

In 1790 the black population numbered about 757,000 or 19.3
percent of the total population of the United States. Until
1910, over 90 percent of all blacks were in the South, with

a majority (78 percent) concentrated in rural areas. Rural
blacks outside the South numbered 190,572 or less than 2
percent of the total (Myrdal, 1944: 183; U.S. Bureau of
the Census 1978b). The great migration, beginning about the
time of World War I, brought continuous shifts in the distribution of the black population, such that the proportion
of all blacks living outside the South rose to 24 percent
in 1940.

From 1910 to 1940, the southern rural black population
declined from 78 percent of the total southern black population to 63 percent. On the other hand, the number of
rural blacks outside the South increased from 190,572 to
269,760, and of this number, 218,963 were rural nonfarm and
50,797 were rural farm residents (Myrdal: 183). By 1940
only about one-half of all blacks in the United States (51
percent) lived in rural areas with only 35 percent residing
on the farms (see Table 12.1).

Thirty years later, in 1970, the percentage of all
blacks residing in nonmetro areas had dropped to 19, with
only 2 percent living on farms. Within a period of fifty
years, the black population had shifted from four-fifths
nonmetro to four-fifths metro. This massive movement of
blacks from the South carried them to all regions of the
nation, to the North, East, and West, with the greatest
exodus occurring between 1940 and 1960 (see Table 12.2).

The social forces underlying this great movement were
as much push factors as pull factors. A major traditional
push factor was the desire to escape a biracial caste system of inequality built on the "Plantation Syndrome," which
was viewed by blacks "as menial, cruel, status degrading,
and oppressive" (Durant and Knowlton 1978). Allied with the
desire for social improvement through relief from the subordination and restrictions forced upon them in the rural
South, blacks were pulled from the nonmetro areas by the
greater abundance of employment opportunities in metro
places and other regions of the nation. Consequently, the
migration of blacks from the rural South may be viewed as
an adaptive response to the inequality of minority status.

Throughout the years, the propelling forces pushing
blacks from the nonmetro South have been seeded in limited
economic opportunities and related tactics employed in the
system to prevent blacks from achieving access to equal
economic opportunities. The strategy has been one of maintaining the status quo by denying free and equal access
to the means, technical, vocational, and on the job, of
preparing for employment opportunities and denying equal

Table 12.1. Distribution of the Black Population
by Residence for Selected Years, 1890 to 1970

Year	Total Population	Urban Areas	Rural Areas Total	Farm
	(000s)	%	%	%
1890	7,489	20	80	na
1910	9,828	27	73	na
1940	12,866	49	51	35
1950	15,045	62	38	21
1960	18,849	73	27	8
1970	22,539	81	19	2

Source: U.S. Bureau of the Census, "The Social and
Economic Status of the Black Population in the United
States: A Historical Review, 1790-1978," p. 14.

na=Not available.

opportunity for employment considerations once prepared
(Marshall 1978). These points will be discussed in greater
detail in subsequent sections of this chapter.

SOME SOCIODEMOGRAPHIC CHARACTERISTICS OF RURAL BLACKS

Rapid massive out-migration such as has occurred among
blacks has its impact on community social structure, and a
fundamental aspect of any community, as related to institutional development and social policy, is a knowledge of the
size, distribution, and composition of its population. The
age and sex composition of the population is of utmost
importance, because it has a direct bearing on marital
status, reproduction rate, employment status and needs, as
well as the character of other social institutions and
indicators of social well-being (Smith 1941; Moland 1953).

RURAL BLACK POPULATION DISTRIBUTION BY REGION

Given the past decades of mass migration of blacks from the
nonmetro South, it is of interest to examine the current

Table 12.2. Distribution of the Black Population by Region
for Selected Years, 1790 to 1975

Area	1790	1870	1910	1940	1960	1970	1975
	%	%	%	%	%	%	%
South	91	91	89	77	60	53	52
North	9	9	10	22	34	39	39
Northeast	9	4	5	11	16	19	18
North Central	*	6	6	11	18	20	10
West	*	*	1	1	6	8	9
Total	100	100	100	100	100	100	100
Percentage of total population							
United States	19	13	11	10	11	11	11
South	35	36	30	24	21	19	19
North	3	2	2	4	7	8	9
Northeast	3	1	2	4	7	9	9
North Central	*	2	2	4	7	8	9
West	*	1	1	1	4	5	6

Source: U.S. Bureau of the Census, "The Social and Economic
Status of the Black Population in the United States: A
Historical Review, 1790-1978."

Note: Black population figures for years indicated above are
as follows: 1790, 1 million; 1870, 5 million; 1910, 10 million; 1940, 13 million; 1960, 19 million; 1970, 23 million;
1975, 24 million.

*Represents or rounds to zero.

nonmetro black population structure by region with regard
to size, sex, and age. Tables 12.3 and 12.4 reveal that
although blacks are found in nonmetro areas in all regions
and subregions of the nation, they constitute a relatively
small number in all regions except the South. The South has
a majority of all nonmetro nonfarm and farm blacks in the
nation, 92 and 93 percent, respectively. In addition the
South has the largest percentage of blacks with rural farm
residence, 11 percent, whereas other regions have smaller
percentages, as little as 2 percent with farm residence.

Table 12.3. Distribution of Rural Blacks by Region
and Residence, 1970

Region	Total		Farm		Nonfarm	
	(000s)	%	(000s)	%	(000s)	%
All regions	4,211	100.0	447	11	3,764	89
Northeast	129	100.0	2	2	126	98
North Central	124	100.0	8	6	116	94
South	3,907	100.0	435	11	3,472	89
West	52	100.0	2	4	50	96

Source: U.S. Bureau of the Census, U.S. Census of
Population: 1970, Subject Reports: Negro Population,
Table 1, p. 1.

According to Simmons and Lee (1974), the abandonment
of nonmetro areas by young blacks is evident not only in
the South but also throughout the nation. The authors provide evidence to support the notion that a large part of
the rural black population outside the South is attracted
to nonmetro areas by adventitious circumstances that do not
lead to permanent residence. It is a population with an
extraordinary number living in group quarters and institutional situations, as well as one in which the sexes are
out of balance and which depends upon migration for growth.

As shown on Table 12.4, black males outnumber black
females in nonmetro farm and nonfarm areas in all regions
except the South. The largest sex difference is found in
the West, with a sex ratio of 174 males to 100 females,
nearly twice as many males as females. Considerable variation is also found in the number of males and females
within regions by subregion and nonfarm residence as well
as between regions by subregion. For example, in the nonmetro nonfarm mountain subregion of the West, males outnumber females by 28 percent, but in the nonmetro farm
areas of this subregion the difference is only 2 percent.
In the South, however, women are as numerous as men in the
nonmetro areas, with slightly more women than men in the
nonfarm areas.

Table 12.4. Nonmetropolitan Black Population by Sex and Residence, 1970

Region	Nonfarm				Farm			
	Total	Male	Female	Ratio[a]	Total	Male	Female	Ratio[a]
Northeast	126,281	69,721	56,560	123	2,431	1,312	1,119	117
New England	15,387	9,014	6,373	141	269	166	103	161
Middle Atlantic	110,894	60,707	50,187	121	2,162	1,146	1,016	113
North Central	116,077	66,618	49,459	135	7,651	3,873	3,778	103
East North Central	88,196	51,852	36,344	143	3,705	1,829	1,876	97
West North Central	27,881	14,766	13,115	113	3,946	2,044	1,902	108
South	3,471,906	1,697,042	1,774,864	97	435,124	216,954	218,170	99
South Atlantic	1,930,208	945,422	984,786	96	215,158	107,412	107,746	100
East South Central	843,574	407,616	435,958	94	151,893	75,868	76,025	100
West South Central	698,124	344,004	354,120	97	68,073	33,674	34,399	98
West	50,021	31,745	18,276	174	1,903	1,102	801	138
Mountain	9,070	5,788	3,282	176	428	219	209	105
Pacific	40,951	25,957	14,994	173	1,475	883	592	149
Total	3,764,285	1,865,126	1,899,159	98	447,109	223,241	223,868	100

Source: U.S. Bureau of the Census, U.S. Census of Population: 1970, Subject Reports: Negro Population, Table 1, p.l.

aRatio of males per 100 females.

AGE DISTRIBUTION

A median age of 20 is found for nonmetro nonfarm blacks in
the United States (see Table 12.5); however, the median age
is strikingly greater than 20 years in each region other
than the South, where it is less than 20 for the nonmetro
nonfarm population. In the farm population, the median age
for blacks is 19.8 years. Here again it is found that for
the Northeast, North Central, and West regions, the median
age for farm populations (29.1, 28.7, and 35.2, respectively) is significantly greater than both the national average
and that of the nonmetro farm South (19.7). Although the
difference by region in the median age of nonfarm males and
females is only about two years, there is a significant
difference by sex in the nonmetro farm populations of the
West and the Northeast, where the male median age exceeds
that for females by ten years and six years, respectively.
In the South, however, the difference between males and
females is less than 1 percent.

Of considerable importance is the distribution of the
nonmetro population by the proportion in the dependency age
categories: less than eighteen, and sixty-two years of age
and more. Forty-six percent of the blacks in rural areas of
the United States are less than eighteen years of age (see
Table 12.5). There is, however, a smaller percentage of
blacks less than eighteen years of age in the nonmetro
nonfarm regions of the Northeast, North Central, and the
West (38, 37, and 35, respectively). Blacks younger than
eighteen constitute only 34 percent of the black farm population in the West. On the other hand, the percentage
of nonmetro blacks in both nonfarm and farm populations
under eighteen in the South is slightly greater than 46
percent.

Although little difference in sex ratios is found among
those less than eighteen years old in the South, considerably more females than males are younger than eighteen in
the West--13 percent more in the nonmetro nonfarm population
and 10 percent more in the farm population.

In each region a larger percentage of the nonmetro farm
population than the nonmetro nonfarm population is sixty-two
years of age and more. The North Central region has the
largest percentage of nonfarm residents in this group,
followed by the South, Northeast, and West, respectively.

The migration of rural blacks has effected significant
compositional changes and variations in the nonmetro population, not only among regions but also within regions

(Lee and Bowles 1974; Simmons and Lee 1974; Tucker 1974;
Beale 1973, 1979). Whereas rural blacks continue to be an
important component of the South's overall population and
socioeconomic structure, significant changes have occurred
in the composition of this population, many of which have
major social implications for nonmetro areas. A closer look
at the age composition of this group is provided in the
next section.

NONMETROPOLITAN BLACKS IN THE SOUTH:
TRENDS IN AGE STRUCTURE

In spite of great differences among populations and groups
with respect to extreme ages in the dependency categories,
the proportions of the adult population in the "prime working ages" of 20 to 44 are similar from society to society
(Bogue 1969). A characteristic feature of almost all populations is that "about 35 percent fall in the interval
between 20 and 44 years, irrespective of their detailed age
composition" (Bogue: 149). The patterns of change in the
prime-working-age category for blacks and whites in nonmetro
areas of the South between 1950 and 1970 are presented in
Table 12.6. Here it is revealed that in 1950, 34 percent of
the white population in the nonmetro South was in the prime-
working-ages category whereas 30 percent of the nonwhite
population was in this age group. In 1970, nearly 7 percent
more whites (30.8) than blacks (24.2) were in the prime
working ages.
    Further examination of the 20 to 44 age group of the
nonmetro farm and nonfarm population indicates important
percentage differences by race and residence. In 1950, 37.3
percent of the nonmetro nonfarm whites and 30.7 percent of
the farm whites were in the prime-working-age interval as
compared to 34 percent and 27.2 percent of the nonwhites,
respectively. As of 1970, the extent of departure from a
prime-working-age population of 35 percent was of considerable magnitude for nonmetro blacks, especially among farmers. Although only 24.2 percent of southern nonmetro blacks
as compared to 30.8 percent of the nonmetro whites were in
the 20 to 44 age category in 1970, a mere 19.8 percent of
the black farm population fell in this age range. These
figures present a picture of an amazing decline in the
number of rural blacks, especially farm blacks, in the
prime working ages. The number of black farmers constitutes
only about one-half of the percentage that has been suggest-

Table 12.5. Age of the Nonmetropolitan Black Population by
Sex and Region, 1970

Region and Age in Years	Nonfarm					
	Total		Male		Female	
	N	%	N	%	N	%
Northeast						
All ages	126,281		69,721		56,560	
Less than 18	47,818	38	25,558	37	22,260	39
18 and more	78,463	62	44,163	63	34,300	61
62 and more	11,770	9	6,140	9	5,630	10
65 and more	9,409	7	4,903	7	4,506	8
Median age	23.9		23.9		24.0	
North Central						
All ages	116,077		66,618		49,459	
Less than 18	42,630	37	23,701	36	18,929	38
18 and more	73,447	63	42,917	64	30,530	62
62 and more	14,648	13	7,370	11	7,278	15
65 and more	12,147	10	6,153	9	5,994	12
Median age	24.1		23.7		25.2	
South						
All ages	3,471,906		1,697,042		1,774,864	
Less than 18	1,618,916	47	818,297	48	800,619	45
18 and more	1,852,990	53	878,745	52	974,245	55
62 and more	374,752	11	172,183	10	202,569	11
65 and more	302,917	9	138,576	8	164,341	9
Median age	19.6		18.7		20.6	
West						
All ages	50,021		31,745		18,276	
Less than 18	17,440	35	9,595	30	7,845	43
18 and more	32,581	65	22,150	70	10,431	57
62 and more	3,938	8	2,226	7	1,712	9
65 and more	3,048	6	1,735	5	1,313	7
Median age	22.7		22.9		21.9	
United States						
All ages	3,764,285		1,865,126		1,899,159	
Less than 18	1,726,804	46	877,151	47	849,653	45
18 and more	2,037,481	54	987,975	53	1,049,506	55
62 and more	405,108	11	187,919	10	217,189	11
65 and more	327,521	9	151,367	8	176,154	9
Median age	20.0		19.3		20.8	

Table 12.5. (continued)

Region and Age in Years	Farm					
	Total		Male		Female	
	N	%	N	%	N	%
Northeast						
All ages	2,431		1,312		1,119	
Less than 18	944	39	489	37	455	41
18 and more	1,487	61	823	63	664	59
62 and more	317	13	197	15	120	11
65 and more	247	10	157	12	90	8
Median age	29.1		31.8		25.6	
North Central						
All ages	7,651		3,873		3,778	
Less than 18	3,066	40	1,598	41	1,468	39
18 and more	4,585	60	2,275	59	2,310	61
62 and more	1,271	17	724	19	547	14
65 and more	1,026	13	574	15	452	12
Median age	28.7		27.6		29.8	
South						
All ages	435,124		216,954		218,170	
Less than 18	201,155	46	101,771	47	99,384	46
18 and more	233,969	54	115,183	53	118,786	54
62 and more	53,691	12	28,159	13	25,532	12
65 and more	41,852	10	21,941	10	19,911	9
Median age	19.7		19.3		20.1	
West						
All ages	1,903		1,102		801	
Less than 18	655	34	335	30	320	40
18 and more	1,248	66	767	70	481	60
62 and more	200	11	119	11	81	10
65 and more	157	8	89	8	68	8
Median age	35.2		37.5		25.7	
United States						
All ages	447,109		223,241		223,868	
Less than 18	205,820	46	104,193	47	101,627	45
18 and more	241,289	54	119,048	53	122,241	55
62 and more	55,479	12	29,199	13	26,280	12
65 and more	43,282	10	22,761	10	20,521	9
Median age	19.8		19.4		20.2	

Source: U.S. Bureau of the Census, U.S. Census of Population: 1970, Subject Reports: Negro Population, Table 2, pp. 2-5.

Table 12.6. Distribution of Southern Nonmetropolitan
Blacks and Whites Aged Twenty to Forty-four Years,
by Residence, for 1950 and 1970

Residence	1950		1970	
	White	Nonwhite[a]	White	Black
	%	%	%	%
Nonmetro Population	34.2	30.0	30.8	24.2
Nonfarm	37.3	34.0	*	24.7
Farm	30.7	27.2	-	19.8

Source: U.S. Bureau of the Census, U.S. Census of
Population: 1950, vol. 1., Table 61, pp. 110-11;
U.S. Bureau of the Census, U.S. Census of Population:
1970, vol. 1., p. 288; U.S. Bureau of the Census,
U.S. Census of Population: 1970, Subject Reports:
Negro Population, Table 2, p. 4.

[a]Reported only by nonwhite, inclusive of blacks.

*Breakdown by residence for whites was not given
in report.

ed as a near universal norm for this age category. Certainly
a population structure with the absence of a large percentage of persons in the highly productive, breadwinning age
category, has negative implications for the structure and
function of the family, as well as for the lives of the
people in the community. For it is not only the quality of
life, in terms of income and level of living, that is affected but also leadership, role models, attitudes, and values as they related to initiative and direction for change.

The picture presented above highlights the impact of
selective migration on the nonmetro black population structure. Migrants from black communities tend to be young
adults in the prime working ages, with more education and
more favorable social backgrounds than nonmigrants (Blevins
1971; Hansen, 1970: 58). By and large, this movement of a
significant number of the active, aggressive persons as
potential leaders from the nonmetro black community makes
it highly probable that the mantle of leadership falls to
the less capable or that it may not be worn at all. Thus,
out-migration altered the population composition and pro-

duced functional role changes that have not been altogether beneficial to blacks in many communities (Lee and Bowles 1974).

DEPENDENCY AGE GROUPS

One of the less beneficial effects of migration patterns is the dependency load the productive population must bear. The dependent segment of the population is determined as the ratio of the population less than twenty and sixty-five years and more to the population twenty to sixty-four. For this analysis, however, only the percentage of the total population in these age groups will be examined (see Table 12.7).

In 1950, 41.5 percent of the nonmetro white population and 49.5 percent of the nonwhite population (largely black) were less than twenty years of age--a difference of 8 percent. By 1970, 37.6 percent of nonmetro whites and 50.7 percent of blacks were under twenty--a difference of 13.1 percent. Thus, it appears that although the nonmetro white population in this age interval has declined, the nonmetro black population has increased slightly or remained about the same. About 1 to 2 percent more whites than blacks are found in the age category of 65 years and more (see Table 12.7). When the two dependency age categories are combined, the percentage of dependents in 1970 was 47.9 for whites and 59.5 percent for blacks.

For nonmetro nonfarm and rural farm blacks the dependency percentages were about the same in 1970--59.4 and 60.2, respectively. This figure is especially significant for farm blacks, given the small percentage of this population in the prime working ages as shown in Table 12.6. The importance of this point cannot be overstated in view of the disappearing black farmer and the declining need for farm labor (Wadley and Lee 1974; McGee and Boone 1979). Given the decline in farm activities and employment among blacks, the potential for work participation on the part of some persons in the dependency ages is greatly lessened. This is especially significant for young blacks between the ages of fifteen and nineteen, who have an exceedingly high unemployment rate, as well as for older blacks, who because of their age lack the necessary skills for new types of employment and are less likely to acquire them.

Based on the above statistics, what appears to be the result of a high rate of reproduction among blacks is not

Table 12.7. Distribution of Southern Nonmetropolitan
Blacks and Whites Less than Twenty Years Old and
Sixty-five Years and More, by Residence for 1950
and 1970

Residence	1950		1970	
	White	Nonwhite[a]	White	Black
	%	%	%	%
Less than 20 Years Old				
Nonmetro population	41.5	49.5	37.6	50.7
Nonfarm	40.3	44.5	–	50.7
Farm	42.9	53.5	–	50.6
65 Years and More				
Nonmetro population	7.2	6.4	10.3	8.8
Nonfarm	6.8	7.3	*	8.7
Farm	7.5	5.8	–	9.6

Source: U.S. Bureau of the Census, U.S. Census of
Population: 1950, vol. 1., Table 61, pp. 110-11;
U.S. Bureau of the Census, U.S. Census of Population:
1970, vol. 1., p. 288; U.S. Bureau of the Census, U.S.
Census of Population: 1970, Subject Reports: Negro
Population, Table 2, p. 4.

[a]Reported only by nonwhite, inclusive of blacks.

*Breakdown by residence for whites was not given
in report.

the case. In fact, the black farm population is diminishing
(see Table 12.1), and what appears as a high reproduction
rate is the result of the relative absence of young adults
because of migration and the presence of children in the
rural black household who are not members of the nuclear
family. On this point Wadley and Lee (1974: 283) report:
"As of 1970, 17 percent of all the children under the age
of 18 in such households were grandchildren of the head,
and an additional 4 percent were also not children of the
head. The proportions were higher for the youngest children;
no less than 30 percent of the children under five were
grandchildren of the head and only 65 percent were children

of the head. Thus, a high proportion of the black children
in rural farm areas are the children of people who are
dead, who are living elsewhere, or are the children of
parents who are not heads of the household in which they
are living." This is further evidence of the need to recognize and be sensitive to functional role changes that
bring about changes in demands for various services, for
example, child care, health, and recreation.

Since the 1920s the nonmetro black population has continued to decline through displacement from agriculture and
out-migration. The rate of decline was accelerated after
World War II. Black agricultural workers dropped from
767,000 in 1950 to 349,000 in 1960 and 159,000 in 1969, a
decline of 608,000 or 79 percent within twenty years
(Christian and Pepelasis 1978). The corresponding figures
for whites were 2,741,000 in 1950; 2,173,000 in 1960; and
1,192,000 in 1969, a decline of 1,549,000 or 56 percent
within twenty years. For a variety of reasons, the rate of
displacement for black farm labor has been faster than that
of whites. These reasons include: concentration on small
farms; difficulty in adapting to technological change; inability to convert to capital-intensive methods of production; unavailability of credit; poor vocational training;
unfavorable land tenure arrangements; lack of diversification; and unequal treatment by government programs (Christian and Pepelasis: 28). Future displacements on a smaller
scale are anticipated with the growth of mechanization and
decline in the number of small farms. Davis (1978) reports
a statistically significant inverse correlation of nonmetro
poverty with farm size in Louisiana due to the fact that
large farms are capital intensive and use smaller amounts
of labor output.

Declining farm employment has increased the percentage
of nonmetro nonfarm blacks making a living from nonfarm
work so that farm residents are now a minority in the nonmetro South. Yet the average socioeconomic level of the
nonmetro black population remains low in spite of the shift
to nonfarm occupations. As part of the group labeled "the
people left behind," they constitute the poor whose problems
include: unemployment, underemployment, inadequate housing,
isolation from community services, and lack of access to
resources and leadership to meet these and other needs.

THE VANISHING BLACK FARMER

Nonmetro blacks have been characterized as a vanishing population with the black farmer becoming extinct (Jones and Lee 1974; Wadley and Lee 1974). Black farm operators numbered 926,000 in 1920 and comprised one-seventh of all farmers in the nation, but by 1969, there were only 87,000 --a drop of 90 percent since 1920 and 85 percent since 1950 (Beale, 1976: 290). There were only 44,800 black-operated farms remaining in 1974, many of which lacked sufficient income-earning capacity, and were operated by aging owners whose children will not succeed them (Beale 1977).

With few exceptions, black farm communities outside the South are also disappearing. Although 9,400 black-operated farms were located in the North and West in 1900, by 1969 this number had dropped to only 2,100 (Beale, 1976: 292).

Rapid growth in the mechanization of farming after World War II increased the need for large landholdings while making it more difficult for small nonmechanized operations to compete. Along with the out-migration of blacks from the rural South, there occurred a sharp decrease in the number of farms and a pronounced increase in farm size. Black operators began the period of technological advancement on much smaller farms than whites and experienced serious disadvantages with respect to obtaining credit and converting to capital-intensive methods of production. These and other factors have contributed to the decline in the number of black farmers (Christian and Erwin 1978).

It has been estimated that in 1910 black landownership in the United States amounted to fifteen million acres. Browne (1973) and Salamon (1974) reported that by 1969 the number of acres owned in full or in part by blacks had declined to less than six million. Although it is widely accepted that factors related to black migration from the South and nonmetro areas generally have contributed to the great decline in black landownership, it is also noted that "the less than altruistic behavior patterns of land officials contributed most to the loss of rural land by blacks" (McGee and Boone, 1979, p. xx).

EMPLOYMENT PATTERNS: DISCRIMINATION AND INEQUALITY

Because most southern blacks had been employed in agriculture, the declining labor requirements brought about by mechanization forced them to seek nonagricultural jobs.

Employment discrimination throughout the years, however,
has restricted blacks to certain menial and low-wage occupations. Although blacks made some economic progress
during the 1960s, it was uneven, especially as related to
nonmetro areas and the South. In addition, the economic
gains of the 1960s have been slowed down and even reversed
in some cases during the 1970s (Levitan et al., 1972: 389).
Thus, the historically wide economic gaps between blacks
and whites persist with little change, and racial employment patterns throughout the nation contribute to maintaining these gaps--particularly in the nonmetro South. In this
respect, underemployment and unemployment rates are considerably higher for blacks than for whites (see Chapter 9).

Table 12.8 reveals that blacks are overrepresented in
menial service jobs. Nearly one-half of all the private
household workers (45 percent) in nonmetro nonfarm areas
are black, while about one-fourth of all farm laborers are
black. On the other hand, blacks are sharply underrepresented in professional, technical, managerial, clerical,
and sales occupations. In addition, within these categories
blacks are more likely to hold low-paying, low-status positions. Black employment in low-paying service positions is
more pronounced in the nonmetro South. For example, of all
private household workers in nonmetro nonfarm areas in
Mississippi, 90 percent are black; in South Carolina, Louisiana, and North Carolina, the percentages are 92, 83, and
78, respectively. Blacks comprise 43 percent of all service
workers in nonmetro nonfarm areas of Mississippi, 44 percent
in South Carolina, 30 percent in Louisiana, and 29 percent
in North Carolina. On the other hand, blacks are grossly
underrepresented in higher-status, higher-paying occupations. With respect to employment discrimination, Marshall
(1978: vi) writes: "It is an area which calls for further
policy-oriented research. We need better understanding of
the dynamics of employment discrimination, how to remedy
it, and how to prevent it. Such research is not likely to
spring from the narrow perspectives of any one academic
discipline. Nor is it likely to come from concentration on
any one group, such as employers. Rather, it will develop
from a systematic overview of all the actors and environmental factors involved in employment discrimination."

Table 12.8. Occupation by Nonmetropolitan Residence Status
for Persons Sixteen Years Old and More, 1970

Occupation	All Employees	Black	
	Nonfarm Residence		
			%
Professional	1,784,180	52,610	3.0
Engineers	171,698	763	.4
Physicians	67,541	501	.7
Health	188,524	5,222	2.8
Teachers	518,007	28,804	5.6
Technicians	176,422	2,056	1.2
Other	661,988	15,264	2.3
Managers	1,224,956	15,698	1.3
Salaried			
Manufacturing	155,533	756	.5
Retail trade	212,877	2,427	1.1
Other industries	517,865	6,868	1.3
Self-employed			
Retail trade	192,569	3,105	1.6
Other industries	146,112	2,542	1.7
Salesworker	843,245	10,143	1.2
Manufacturing	154,747	1,281	.8
Retail trade	523,519	7,323	1.4
Other industries	164,979	1,539	.9
Clerical and kindred	1,977,136	41,371	2.1
Bookkeepers	272,891	1,557	.6
Secretaries	503,221	7,364	1.5
Other clerical	1,201,024	32,450	2.7
Craftsman, foreman	2,714,854	92,702	3.4
Automobile mechanics	261,163	10,674	4.1
Mechanics	394,765	9,982	2.5
Machinists	88,731	1,795	2.0
Metal craftsman	163,441	2,966	1.8
Carpenters	301,470	12,675	4.2
Construction	543,972	28,066	5.2
Other craftsmen	961,312	26,544	2.8
Operatives, except			
transportation	2,855,446	217,344	7.6
Durable	1,104,560	67,171	6.1
Nondurable	1,104,624	105,406	9.5
Nonmanufacturing	646,262	44,767	6.9

Table 12.8. (continued)

Occupation	All Employees	Black	
	Nonfarm Residence		
			%
Transport	768,802	61,264	8.0
Truck drivers	430,133	34,873	8.1
Other transport	338,669	26,391	7.8
Laborers, except farm	905,138	138,195	15.3
Construction	186,723	29,998	16.1
Freight	282,246	35,809	12.7
Other laborers	436,169	72,338	16.6
Farmers and farm managers	224,440	12,586	5.6
Farm laborers	444,874	103,968	23.4
Service workers[a]	1,648,141	153,704	9.3
Cleaning	377,518	64,254	17.0
Food	563,321	45,078	8.0
Health	235,436	20,167	8.6
Personal	210,884	9,250	4.4
Protective	145,386	3,505	2.4
Private household	265,805	120,654	45.4
Total	15,657,017	1,020,230	6.5
	Farm Residence		
Professional	193,308	5,388	2.8
Engineers	8,579	31	.4
Physicians	4,892	31	.6
Health	23,941	436	1.8
Teachers	82,002	3,540	4.3
Technicians	14,222	100	.7
Other	58,672	1,250	2.1
Managers	111,591	1,382	1.2
Salaried			
Manufacturing	10,128	111	1.1
Retail trade	15,726	138	.9
Other industries	51,566	526	1.0
Self-employed			
Retail trade	17,676	400	2.3
Other industries	16,495	207	1.3

Table 12.8. (continued)

Occupation	All Employees	Black	
	Farm Residence		
			%
Salesworker	89,672	781	.9
Manufacturing	11,768	78	.7
Retail trade	62,325	554	.9
Other industries	15,579	149	1.0
Clerical and kindred	239,539	3,226	1.3
Bookkeepers	40,494	164	.4
Secretaries	60,861	610	1.0
Other clerical	138,184	2,452	1.8
Craftsman, foreman	267,542	6,628	2.5
Automobile mechanics	21,269	703	3.3
Mechanics	37,946	761	2.0
Machinists	8,547	211	2.5
Metal craftsman	15,606	162	1.0
Carpenters	42,370	1,369	3.2
Construction	53,911	1,801	3.3
Other craftsmen	87,893	1,621	1.8
Operatives, except transportation	328,757	18,060	5.5
Durable	129,658	5,649	4.4
Nondurable	132,094	9,551	7.2
Nonmanufacturing	67,005	2,860	4.3
Transport	99,523	5,244	5.3
Truck drivers	51,324	2,373	4.6
Other transport	48,199	2,871	6.0
Laborers, except farm	104,236	9,770	9.4
Construction	24,852	2,575	10.4
Freight	31,203	2,450	7.9
Other laborers	48,181	4,745	9.9
Farmers and farm managers	1,093,204	20,289	1.9
Farm laborers	274,248	25,178	9.2

Table 12.8. (continued)

Occupation	All Employees	Black	
		Farm Residence	
			%
Service workers[a]	189,057	11,466	6.1
Cleaning	39,965	4,745	11.9
Food	65,502	3,355	5.1
Health	34,904	1,358	3.9
Personal	22,120	655	3.0
Protective	13,245	338	2.6
Private household	32,054	9,193	28.7
Total	3,022,731	116,605	3.9

Source: U.S Bureau of the Census, U.S. Census of Population: 1970, vol. 1., Table 91, p. 393.

[a]Includes allocated cases, not shown separately.

UNEMPLOYMENT AND THE DISCOURAGED WORKER

Blacks have experienced persistently higher unemployment rates than whites--in a ratio of about 2 to 1, on average. There are, however, locations and age categories in which differences are much greater. Whereas, in 1975 the national average unemployment rates were 13.9 percent for blacks, and 7.8 percent for whites, in the same year 17.1 percent of the southern black nonmetro labor force was unemployed (Beale 1977). Blacks are relegated to jobs in which unemployment tends to be high such as nonfarm labor, operative or service work, and seasonal farm labor. Because of this restriction on employment opportunity, there exists high underemployment as well as unemployment.

Both unemployment and underemployment are especially acute among young blacks. Nationwide in 1974, for white males sixteen to nineteen years of age, the unemployment rate was 13.6 percent, and for black males of the same age it was 31.6 percent. In 1970, the nonmetro farm unemployment rate in Mississippi for white males fourteen and fifteen was 6.1, but for black males of the same age it was 25.1,

or more than four times that of white youths (U.S. Bureau
of the Census, U.S. Census of Population: 1970, Mississippi,
PC(1)-C26, Table 53). States vary with respect to the unemployment rate for this age group in rural areas.

These statistics are saying that young blacks are denied
an opportunity at an early age to have the necessary work
experiences that are so crucial to the formation and maintenance of a stable family life. In the absence of work
opportunities, they are denied the chance to form habits of
punctuality, dependability, and consistency while acquiring
skills and knowledge of the world of work. Because nonmetro
blacks subscribe to the same dominant social values as
whites with respect to the formation and achievement of
life goals (Larson and Brown 1978), parents and older adults
encourage black youth to leave these areas in search of job
opportunities. Larson and Brown (p. 18) report from a comparative study of dominant values in a statewide survey
conducted in North Carolina, that "within rural and small
town areas there are black-white differences in the intensity with which some of the personal values are held, blacks
for instance, giving more weight to achievement." Thus,
black parents having a strong concern for the success and
achievement of their children encourage them to leave the
nonmetro community. In findings from studies of such communities in ten parishes in Louisiana, Moland (1978) observed
that from one-third to more than three-fifths of the respondents in each parish said they "encouraged their children to leave this community." Three-fifths to over nine-
tenths of the respondents in each parish agreed with the
statement: "Many people around here feel that their children can make a better living if they leave this community."
From the study of adolescent career attitudes and achievements, Thomas and Falk (1978) observed that black youth
reported occupational expectations considerably lower than
their aspirations. More than 65 percent of the black male
youth expected occupations equal to or less than a socioeconomic index score of 45. According to Thomas and Falk,
"this low level may indicate the debilitating effects of
discrimination and a generally poor prognostication for
the future--in short, the antithesis of 'great expectations,' a resignation to accept one's lot in life" (p. 87).
Thus, the lack of employment opportunities may lead to the
lowering of expectations and produce the discouraged
worker.

Unemployment rates are imperfect indicators of black
labor market disadvantages because they reflect only those

who are able to work and are actively seeking employment.
Not included are those underemployed, those working part
time who would like full-time jobs, those working but not
earning enough to raise themselves above the poverty level,
or those who have become discouraged and stopped looking
for jobs altogether (Levitan et al., 1972: 392). Discouraged workers, persons who want to work but are not looking
for work because they think they cannot obtain a job, are
not counted as unemployed (U.S. Bureau of the Census, Social
Indicators, 1977). The U.S. Department of Labor reports that
a majority of these persons gave as a reason for their discouragement: "I could not find a job," followed by such
reasons as "think no job available," "employers think person
too young or too old," and "lacks education or training"
(U.S. Bureau of the Census, Social Indicators, p. 383).
Among those who responded "I could not find a job," the
white percentage has increased from 18.9 in 1967 to 35.8
in 1976, and among blacks the increase for the same period
has been from 31.0 to 63.6 percent (U.S. Bureau of the
Census, Social Indicators, p. 383).

INCOME INEQUALITY: THE WIDENING GAP

Unemployment and underemployment contribute to the fact
that the median family income of blacks in the United States
($8,006) was 60 percent of that of whites ($13,408) in 1974;
62 percent in 1975 and 59 percent in 1976, a decline of one
percentage point as compared with 1974 (U.S. Bureau of the
Census, Social and Economic Characteristics of the Metropolitan and Nonmetropolitan Population: 1977 and 1970, p. 194).
The median black family income in 1974 was $5,402 lower
than the median white income. By 1976, the gap had grown to
$6,295. The median family income of blacks in nonmetro areas
($6,132) was only 54 percent of that of white ($11,446) in
1974; 56 percent in 1975; and 56 percent in 1976, an increase of 2 percentage points. Whereas the median black
family income in nonmetro areas was $5,314 lower than the
median white income in 1974, by 1976 the gap had grown to
$5,883. These figures indicate that the relative socio-
economic condition of blacks is getting worse instead of
better.
     The dismal economic condition of nonmetro blacks is
further reflected in the percentages below the poverty
threshold for 1974, 1975, and 1976--36.1, 37.1, and 34.7,
respectively (U.S. Bureau of the Census, Social and Eco-

nomic Characteristics of the Metropolitan and Nonmetropolitan Population: 1977 and 1970, p. 205). On the other
hand, the percentages of white families below the same
level were 9.0, 10.1, and 8.9 for the same years. Thus
nonmetro black families are still about four times as
likely as white families to be living on incomes below the
poverty threshold.

Certainly these findings indicate the need to increase
and equalize employment opportunities in nonmetro areas
and in the nation in general. The great differentials by
race and place tend to perpetuate the separation of the
"have's" and "have not's," and the fact of racial discrimination is evident, given the relative position of blacks
vis-à-vis whites on factors of occupational representation, unemployment, underemployment, income, and poverty
status. Built-in institutional discrimination in the form
of differential training opportunities, union requirements,
seniority systems, and unequal pay for equal work, maintains
the socioeconomic gap between blacks and whites (Levitan et
al. 1972).

STRUCTURAL INEQUALITY, ALIENATION, AND COMMUNITY NEEDS

EDUCATION AND INCOME INEQUALITY

Expenditure per pupil is a widely used index of the quality
of education one receives. That is, higher expenditures per
pupil indicate higher quality of education and lower expenditures indicate lower quality of education. This expenditure in nonmetro areas is only about 75 percent of the
figure in urban areas (Tamblyn 1973). Because of funding
difficulties, rural/nonmetro school systems have relatively
fewer personnel supporting their instructional function
(Fratoe 1978). Consequently, people living in nonmetro
areas, including a relatively high proportion of blacks,
receive a lower quantity and quality of education than that
provided in the metro areas.

Table 12.9 shows that in 1970 for persons twenty-five
years and older slightly more than three-fifths of the
nonmetro blacks and one-third of the whites had less than a
ninth grade education as compared to less than two-fifths
of the metro blacks and only about one-fifth of the metro
whites. These data reveal a substantial gap between the
educational attainment of nonmetro blacks as compared to
nonmetro whites and metro blacks and whites. Almost 60

Table 12.9. Years of School Completed by Persons Twenty-five Years Old and More by Race and Residence for 1970 and 1977

Years of School Completed	Nonmetropolitan				Metropolitan			
	Black		White		Black		White	
1970	(000s)	%	(000s)	%	(000s)	%	(000s)	%
Elementary or less	1,533	62	9,926	32	2,872	38	15,306	22
1-4 years high school	785	32	15,389	50	3,812	50	33,963	52
Some college or more	155	6	5,488	18	887	12	16,325	25
Total	2,473	100	30,803	100	7,581	100	65,594	99
Percentage high school graduates	18.4		48.8		35.6		57.9	
1977								
Elementary or less	1,408	47	8,460	24	2,323	27	11,434	16
1-4 years high school	1,287	43	19,022	53	4,686	54	36,157	51
Some college or more	300	10	8,316	23	1,693	19	23,829	33
Total	2,995	100	35,795	100	8,702	100	71,420	100
Percentage high school graduates	31.1		60.7		50.4		70.2	

Source: U.S. Bureau of the Census, Social and Economic Characteristics of the Metropolitan and Nonmetropolitan Population: 1977 and 1970.

percent more metro than nonmetro blacks had completed high school whereas a significantly larger percentage of whites than blacks in both locations had graduated from high school. Although some improvement is shown by 1977 in the educational attainment of nonmetro blacks, substantial differences are still found when compared with the educational attainment of whites and metro blacks (see Table 12.9).

Differences in educational attainment between nonmetro blacks and whites are brought into sharper focus when examined by size of the largest place within the county. As shown in Table 12.10 the smaller the size of the largest place within the county the greater the percentage of persons with an elementary school education or less, while the larger the size of the place within the county the greater the percentage of persons with one to four years of high school or more. Slightly more than two-thirds of the blacks in counties with no place of 2,500 or more, 64 percent in counties with a place of 2,500-24,999, and 52 percent in counties of 25,000 or more have only an elementary school education or less as compared to 41, 33, and 26 percent of the whites, respectively.

It is of interest here to examine the relationship between school years completed and income by race for nonmetro residents. The mean earnings of nonmetro residents twenty-five years and older in 1973 are presented in Table 12.11 by education, sex, and race, and it is noteworthy that differences between the mean earnings of blacks and whites by sex and completed education are much less striking than the differences found between the incomes of black and white males by educational attainment. The mean earnings of nonmetro black males as a percentage of the earnings of white males range from a low of 54 percent to a high of 67 percent. The greatest monetary difference ($3,580) is found between black and white high-school graduates. In fact the mean earnings of black males with a high-school education are less than the earnings of white males with only eight years of education.

When these data in Table 12.11 are examined in terms of sex differences (based on averages across rows, regardless of race), the mean earnings of females as a percentage of the earnings of males range from a low of 39 percent to a high of only 42 percent. A monetary difference of $3,456 is found between nonmetro females and males with eight years of completed schooling and a difference of $4,999 is found between females and males with one to three years of high school. The disadvantaged earnings position borne by blacks and white women is evident from these data.

ALIENATION AND RURAL BLACKS

Studies of the aspirations of nonmetro black youth, their perceptions of available education opportunities, and their

Table 12.10. Years of School Completed by Nonmetropolitan
Residents Twenty-five Years Old and More by Race and
Residence, 1970

Years of School Completed	Counties with No Place of 2,500 or More (000s)	%	Counties with a Place of 2,500-24,999 (000s)	%	Counties with a Place of 25,000 or more (000s)	%
Black						
Elementary or less	227	68	1,044	64	262	52
1-4 years high school	93	28	499	30	193	39
Some college or more	15	4	96	6	44	9
Total	335	100	1,639	100	499	100
Percentage high school graduates	13.7		17.1		26.1	
White						
Elementary or less	1,473	41	6,457	33	1,996	26
1-4 years high school	1,599	45	9,764	50	4,026	52
Some college or more	499	14	3,268	17	1,722	22
Total	3,571	100	19,489	100	7,744	100
Percentage high school graduates	40.8		47.5		55.6	

Source: U.S. Bureau of the Census, Social and Economic
Characteristics of the Metropolitan and Nonmetropolitan
Population: 1977 and 1970, p.55.

Table 12.11. Mean Earnings of Nonmetropolitan Residents
Twenty-five Years Old and More, by Years of School
Completed, Sex, and Race, 1973

Years of School Completed	Male			Female		
	Black	White	Difference	Black	White	Difference
	$	$	$	$	$	$
Elementary						
< 8	3,463	5,791	-2,328	1,256	2,489	-1,233
8	3,966	7,381	-3,415	1,710	2,724	-1,014
High school						
1-3	5,727	8,506	-2,779	2,666	2,990	- 324
4	6,789	10,369	-3,580	3,346	3,814	- 468

Source: Frank A. Fratoe, "Rural Education and Rural Labor
Force in the Seventies," Table 21, p. 21.

reported occupational expectations, suggest that the debilitating effects of discrimination lead to acquiescence and
the acceptance of one's "lot in life." (See for example:
Thomas and Falk 1978; Picou and Howard 1978; Cosby and Falk
1977; and Kuvlesky et al. 1977.) It is reported that structural elements are perceived as blocking social mobility
and goal accomplishment to a much greater extent than personal inadequacies. When repeatedly confronted with structural interference one may come to view the situation as
hopeless and unmanageable and therefore give in to feelings
of alienation and resignation. Such is the plight of the
discouraged worker who lacks success in finding a job.

In their study of alienation and poverty among nonmetro
Georgia blacks, Walker and Beauford (1978) found that perceived control of opportunities (influenced by race, sex,
and education) is related to the ability to advance and
break the poverty cycle. Perceived lack of control, resulting from restrictions in educational, employment, and
income opportunities, is experienced by blacks regardless
of age and socioeconomic status. Consequently, in Louisiana,
Moland (1978) found perceived anomie to be higher among
rural blacks than whites. In addition the recognized control
variables (age, sex, education, and income) either failed

to differentiate among blacks with respect to feelings of
high and low anomie or provided relationships counter to
those found among whites. However, a significant inverse
relationship between anomie and income was found for rural
blacks living in three parishes adjoining a large metro
center (Moland 1975).

In a southern regional study of anomie in traditionally
low-income nonmetro counties, Steelman and McCann (1978: 68)
found that education and social organization participation
were not related to anomie among blacks, and that income
was more closely related to anomie among blacks than whites.
These findings suggest that discrimination produces feelings
of powerlessness among nonmetro blacks that overrides and
restricts the effects of education and occupation for status
attainment. Income is important, however, in that it provides more direct and immediate advantages over education
and occupation. A black person and a white person with
money can purchase identical items, while with similar
educational and occupational attainment they do not receive equal pay or have equal access to participation in
society.

The positive association between occupation and income
and between education and income as found in the larger
society are not consistently evident to blacks, particularly nonmetro blacks. The inconsistency is seen in the case
of a black high-school graduate who cannot find a job; or
can find only a low-paying dead-end position under the
supervision of a white high-school dropout who receives
higher wages for less work. The interracial status inconsistency tends to disparage education as an avenue to success in occupational and income attainment. Consequently,
blacks with more as well as less education perceive discriminatory interference with socioeconomic goal achievement as emanating from institutional structures and situations over which they have no control. Moreover, it is
generally concluded that lower achievement value orientations among nonmetro black adolescents appear to reflect
the perceived and actual restricted opportunities for
mobility (Turner 1972).

Generally speaking, the vocational-technical education
available to nonmetro blacks is usually of a traditional
and menial nature, which reinforces their perception of
discriminatory interference through restricting their preparation for a wider range of job opportunities. In addition, lack of program offerings, restricted admission, lack
of knowledge of available jobs, and limited job opportuni-

ties were reasons given by principals, directors, and other
adults for the underrepresentation of blacks in vocational-
technical schools (Louisiana State Advisory Council for
Vocational-Technical Education 1977). The updating of nonmetro vocational-technical school programs and their educators is long overdue in view of the industrial development
and potential for change taking place in these areas,
especially in the South (Wheelock et al. 1978).

Lack of awareness of and involvement in program development in the larger community reflects the widespread perception of powerlessness among nonmetro blacks. In a study of
nonmetro community problems, Jacob and Lilley (1978: 7-8)
write: "local officials are often reluctant to increase and
expand opportunities for citizen participation beyond what
is minimally required by law, if such participation could
ultimately represent a threat to the local officials' own
power or relative status in the community." This point is
especially relevant for nonmetro blacks, as they are either
denied the opportunity to participate or made to feel that
their input is not welcomed and if given will not contribute
to the solution of the community's needs and problems. Ideally, program planning and strategies geared to nonmetro
populations should reflect an understanding and knowledge
of the needs and problems as perceived by blacks.

LEADERSHIP IN THE BLACK COMMUNITY

The exodus of young adult blacks from nonmetro southern
communities and the population shifts within nonmetro areas
have resulted in the decline and weakening of traditional
and established black institutions including the church,
school, and voluntary associations (Moland 1953; Moland and
Haynes 1972). These changes have resulted in the loss of
the established and potentially most capable leadership in
these communities as well as the institutional mechanisms
through which much needed new leadership would ordinarily
emerge (Lee and Bowles 1974). Thus, many nonmetro southern
blacks, particularly in farm communities, are without know-
ledgeable and capable leadership so necessary for vocalizing
and communicating problem issues and needs, acquiring and
giving information, and providing motivation for the
achievement and fulfillment of needs and goals.

In a study of social services and their utilization in
South Carolina, Howie and Hanna (1978) report that many
nonmetro blacks fail to receive services for which they are

eligible because they do not know about them or they do not
have transportation to the location of the services. Consequently, programs developed to address the needs of these
people should be planned and implemented in a manner that
takes into account such limitations of the population as
age and education level, the probable lack of capable community leaders, and the lack of transportation.

PERCEIVED NEEDS AND PROBLEMS

As previously indicated, it is important in program planning
and implementation to know and understand community needs
and problems as perceived by area residents. Studies of
major needs and problems of nonmetro blacks in seven parishes of Louisiana report twelve problem areas (Means 1973;
McManus 1973; Moland 1977). The eight most frequently mentioned included: better jobs and the elimination of unemployment, utility services (private and public), better
housing, recreational facilities, better schools, transportation, civil rights, and interpersonal relations (including
leadership, communication, and cooperation). Significant
dissimilarities in the rank order of importance given these
problems were found among the parishes and between leaders
and nonleaders. However, better jobs, schools, housing, and
recreational facilities occupied prominent rank positions
in all parishes.
    Perceptions of the need for better schools and recre-
ational facilities coupled with the need to eliminate unemployment as major problems facing nonmetro residents,
suggest the presence and importance of a significant segment of the nonmetro population--those less than twenty
years of age. The previous examination of the rural black
population revealed that in 1970, 93 percent of all nonmetro
blacks (3,907,030) lived in the South with over 50 percent
of that number less than twenty years old. The identified
needs and problems, education, recreation, and employment
are of particular relevance to this age group in the 1970s
and 1980s. Bowles (1976) reports that the potential for
labor force increase in the 1970-80 decade is proportionately greater among blacks than among whites in both metro and
nonmetro areas. About 15 percent of the new nonmetro jobs
will be needed by blacks and other minority races (p. 268).
According to Bowles (p. 269): "Potential labor force changes
between 1970 and 1980 clearly indicate the extent to which
employment opportunities must be generated in the United

States if all the people who will reach working age and
enter the labor force are to be accommodated. . . . To
reverse the traditional patterns of rural-to-urban migration, proportionately more jobs must be generated in nonmetropolitan areas between 1970 and 1980 than in previous
decades as the metropolitan areas no longer need to rely on
migrants from rural areas to supply part of their needs."
The presence of the high rate of unemployment among nonmetro blacks, youth in particular, and the large percentage
below the poverty level indicate that the challenge to create more jobs in nonmetro areas has not been met. Although
it is clear that educational programs and training for
nonfarm employment are needed, little has been done to
develop and promote such programs in nonmetro areas. There
is the need to develop and expand vocational-technical
training opportunities. Vocational educators need to retool
more rapidly and the educational programs should involve
more experiences with industry and business (including
on-the-job training experiences) so as to provide nonmetro
blacks with the opportunity to become acquainted with and
pursue the necessary skills for high-level employment in
business and industry.

The number of youths in the nonmetro black population
underscores the need for recreational facilities with super-
vised programs, and greater use should be made of schools
and abandoned school buildings for programmed after-school
recreation. Churches in nonmetro areas should become more
involved in providing recreational activities, and federal,
as well as state, funds should be identified and made
available for the employment of community recreational
personnel.

Problems of substandard housing, inadequate health care,
and malnutrition are relatively widespread among southern
nonmetro blacks--conditions that are closely associated
with poverty and vary according to socioeconomic circumstances. Although a core of human services has been mandated
through federal and state legislation (for example, Public
Health and Agriculture Extension Service), Sampson (1979:
166-67) reports that in Tennessee, "The number and range of
services available differ by county, with a greater number
and range in counties with larger populations and a higher
economic base." Although these services are centrally located in all counties, distance seriously affected availability for a large number of rural respondents, and the
use of these services varied with education, income, and
age. Major gaps in services provided rural areas included:

the need for medical services, public transportation, improved housing, day-care services, improved roads, social services, and employment services.

IMPLICATIONS AND CONCLUSION

The nonmetro black population is caught in a vicious circle of inequality of economic and educational opportunities and inadequate community services that perpetuate the out-migration of young adults seeking to improve their life chances. Consequently, an imbalance in the population structure by age and/or sex has occurred in all regions of the nation.

In the nonmetro South, particularly in farm areas, there is an imbalanced age structure that is characterized by having a relatively small proportion of the population in the prime working ages and a large percentage in the dependency age categories. The discriminatory practices of unequal access to employment, income, education, and other services have produced over the years a nonmetro population with a high dependency load. The migration of young black adults from the nonmetro south, as an adaptive response to minority status and inequality of opportunity, has produced an older farm population, which is less likely to actively seek to bring about the needed social changes. Nevertheless, those left behind in these communities have identified and expressed their needs and problems as follows: better jobs and the elimination of unemployment, better leaders, schools, housing, transportation, utilities, recreational facilities, and others.

The resolution of these needs and problems, many of which are imbedded in institutional racism and discrimination, necessitates active and informed leadership. This is the challenge to those who design and implement development programs for nonmetro areas.

BIBLIOGRAPHY

Beale, Calvin L. "The Black American in Agriculture." In The Black American Reference Book, edited by Mabel M. Smythe, pp. 284-315. Englewood Cliffs, N.J.: Prentice-Hall, Inc. 1976.

John Moland, Jr. : 496

_____. "Demographic Typological Aspects of Nonmetro
    Areas." Mimeographed. 1979.
_____. "Migration Patterns of Minorities in the
    United States." American Journal of Agricultural
    Economics 55 (1973): 938-46.
_____. "Recent Rural Population Trends of Signif-
    icance to the Professional Agriculture Workers Confer-
    ence." Paper delivered at the Professional Agriculture
    Workers Conference, Tuskegee Institute, Ala., 5 December
    1977.
Blevins, Audie L., Jr. "Socioeconomic Differences Between
    Migrants and Nonmigrants." Rural Sociology 36 (1971):
    509-19.
Bogue, Donald J. Principles of Demography. New York: Wiley,
    1969.
Bowles, Gladys K. "Potential Change in Labor Force in the
    1970-1980 Decade for Metropolitan and Nonmetropolitan
    Counties in the United States." Phylon 37 (1976):
    263-69.
Browne, Robert S. Only Six Million Acres: A Decline of Black
    Owned Land in the Rural South. New York: The Black
    Economic Research Center, 1973.
Christian, Virgil L., Jr., and Erwin, Carl C. "Agriculture."
    In Employment of Blacks in the South: A Perspective on
    the 1960s, edited by Ray Marshall and Virgil L. Chris-
    tian, Jr., pp. 39-77. Austin, Tex.: University of Texas
    Press, 1978.
Christian, Virgil L., Jr., and Pepelasis, Admantois. "Rural
    Problems." In Employment of Blacks in the South: A
    Perspective on the 1960s, edited by Ray Marshall and
    Virgil L. Christian, Jr., pp. 19-37. Austin, Tex.:
    University of Texas Press, 1978.
Cosby, Arthur G., and Falk, William W. "The Dynamics of
    Occupational Projections: Observations on the Changing
    Orientations of Nonmetropolitan Black Youth in the
    South." In Black Youth in the Rural South: Educational
    Abilities and Ambitions, edited by William P. Kuvlesky
    and William C. Boykin, Sr., pp. 59-65. Austin, Tex.:
    National Educational Laboratory Publishers, Inc.,
    1977.
Davis, Leroy. "The Relationship of Farm Size and Rural
    Poverty." Journal of Social and Behavioral Sciences 24
    (1978): 6-16.
Durant, Thomas J., and Knowlton, Clark S. "Rural Ethnic
    Minorities: Adaptive Responses to Inequality." In Rural
    U.S.A.: Persistence and Change, edited by Thomas R.

Ford, pp. 145-67. Ames, Iowa: Iowa State University
Press, 1978.

Fratoe, Frank A. "Rural Education and Rural Labor Force in
the Seventies." Rural Development Research Report no.
5, U.S. Department of Agriculture, Economics, Statistics, and Cooperatives Service, Washington, D.C., 1978.

Hansen, Niles M. Rural Poverty and the Urban Crisis. Bloomington, Ind.: Indiana University Press, 1970.

Howie, Marguerite R., and Hanna, Kathleen. "How the Rural
Poor Choose Agency Services: Communication and Transpor-
tation as Factors in the Decision Making Process."
Paper delivered at the meeting of the Southern Assoc-
iation of Agricultural Scientists, Rural Sociology
Section, Houston, Tex., February 1978.

_____. "What People Say They Do and What They Do:
Explorations in the Sociology of the Rural, Limited-
Resources Community." Journal of Social and Behavioral
Sciences 24 (1978): 31-43.

Jacob, Nelson L., and Lilley, Stephen C. "Perception of
Community Problems by Rural Residents and County
Leaders: Implications for Citizen Participation." Paper
delivered at the meeting of the Southern Association of
Agricultural Scientists, Rural Sociology Section,
Houston, Tex., February 1978.

Jones, Lewis W., and Lee, Everett S. "Rural Blacks--A
Vanishing Population." Paper delivered at W. E. B.
DuBois Institute for the Study of the American Black,
Atlanta University, Atlanta, Ga., 1974.

Kuvlesky, William P. "Overview and Discussion." In Black
Youth in the Rural South: Educational Abilities and
Ambitions, edited by William P. Kuvlesky and William C.
Boykin, Sr., pp. 79-88. Austin, Tex.: National Educa-
tional Laboratory Publishers, Inc., 1977.

_____ et al. "Historical Change in Educational
Aspirations and Expectations." In Black Youth in the
Rural South: Educational Abilities and Ambitions,
edited by William P. Kuvlesky and William C. Boykins,
Sr., pp. 66-78. Austin, Tex.: National Educational
Laboratory Publishers, Inc., 1977.

Larson, Olaf F., and Brown, Minnie M. "The Rural Black
Comparative Perspective: Dominant Values, Community
Problems, and Government Spending." Paper delivered at
the Rural Sociological Society Annual Meeting, San
Francisco, Calif., August-September 1978.

Lee, Anne S., and Bowles, Gladys K. "Policy Implications of
the Movement of Blacks Out of the Rural South." Phylon

35 (1974): 332-39.

Levitan, Sar A. et al. Human Resources and Labor Markets. 2nd ed. New York: Harper & Row, 1972.

Louisiana State Advisory Council for Vocational-Technical Education. "The Availability of Vocational-Technical Education to Blacks, Other Minorities and Women." Unpublished study prepared by investigators at Southern University and Grambling State University, Baton Rouge and Grambling, La., 1977.

McGee, Leo, and Boone, Robert. "A Study of Rural Landowner-ship, Control Problems, and Attitudes of Blacks Toward Rural Land." In The Black Rural Landowner--Endangered Species, edited by Leo McGee and Robert Boone, pp. 55-65. Westport, Conn.: Greenwood Press, Inc., 1979.

_____, eds. The Black Rural Landowner--Endangered Species. Westport, Conn.: Greenwood Press, Inc., 1979.

McManus, Delilah A. "Rural Community Needs and Problems as Perceived by Indigenous Leaders and Non-Leaders in West Feliciana and East Baton Rouge." Masters thesis, Southern University, Baton Rouge, La., 1973.

Marshall, Ray. "The Old South and the New." In Employment of Blacks in the South: A Perspective on the 1960s, edited by Ray Marshall and Virgil L. Christian, Jr., pp. 3-17. Austin, Tex.: University of Texas Press, 1978.

_____ et al. Employment Discrimination: The Impact of Legal and Administrative Remedies. New York: Praeger, 1978.

Means, Emma J. "Rural Community Needs and Problems as Perceived by Indigenous Leaders and Non-Leaders in East and West Baton Rouge Parishes." Masters thesis, Southern University, Baton Rouge, La., 1973.

Moland, John, Jr. "Addor, North Carolina: The Social Structure of a Declining Rural Community." Master thesis, Fisk University, 1953.

_____. "Community Needs and Problems as Perceived by Rural Leaders and Non-Leaders of Three Parishes in Louisiana (Acadia, Avoyelles, and East Carroll Parishes)." Annual report for CSRS, USDA, project 216-1519, Southern University, Baton Rouge, La., 1977.

_____. "Differences in Perceptions of Anomie Among Rural Blacks and Whites in Louisiana." Journal of Social and Behavioral Sciences 24 (1978): 71-84.

_____. "Rural Community Needs and Problems, Alienation, and Social Structure." Mimeograph tables prepared from CSRS, USDA research project 8-1567, Southern

University, Baton Rouge, La., 1978.

_____. "Some Social Structural Correlates of Anomie Among Rural Blacks of Louisiana." Paper delivered at the meeting of the Southern Association of Agricultural Scientists, Rural Sociology Section, New Orleans, La., February 1975.

_____ and Haynes, L. L., Jr. "The ABC's of Getting Things Done for Our Communities." Unpublished manual of social services, Southern University and A & M College, Baton Rouge, La., 1972.

Myrdal, Gunner. An American Dilemma. New York: Harper and Brothers, 1944.

Picou, J. Steven, and Howard, William G. "Determinants of Career Orientations and Early Educational Attainments: Evaluation of a Causal Model." In Education and Work in Rural America: The Social Context of Early Career Decision and Achievement, edited by Arthur G. Cosby and Ivan Charner, pp. 139–86. College Station, Tex.: Texas A & M University, 1978.

Salamon, Lester M. Black Owned Land: Profile of Disappearing Equity Base. Washington, D.C.: Office of Minority Business Enterprise, U.S. Department of Commerce, 1974.

Sampson, Joylean P. "Inequity of Human Services: The Rural Tennessee Dilemma." Tennessee State University, Nashville, Tenn., 1979.

Simmons, Jane T., and Lee, Everett S. "The Extraordinary Composition of Rural Black Population Outside the South." Phylon 35 (1974): 313–22.

Smith, Lynn T. "Some Aspects of Village Demography." Social Forces 20 (1941): 15–25.

Steelman, Virginia Purtle, and McCann, Glenn C. "Black-White Differences in Predictor Variables of Anomie in Traditionally Low-Income Rural Southern Counties." Journal of Social and Behavioral Sciences 24 (1978): 58–70.

Tamblyn, Lewis R. Inequality: A Portrait of Rural America. Washington, D.C.: Rural Evaluation Association, 1973.

Thomas, John K., and Falk, William W. "Career Attitudes and Achievements." In Education and Work in Rural America: The Social Context of Early Career Decision and Achievement, edited by Arthur G. Cosby and Ivan Charner, pp. 75–111. College Station, Tex.: Texas A & M University, 1978.

Tucker, Charles Jackson. "Changes in Age Composition of the Rural Black Population of the South 1950 to 1970."

Phylon 35 (1974): 268–75.

Turner, Jonathan H. "Structural Conditions of Achievement Among Whites and Blacks in the Rural South." *Social Problems* 19 (1972): 496–508.

U.S. Bureau of the Census. *U.S. Census of Population: 1950.* Vol. 1, General Characteristics of the Population, United States Summary. Washington, D.C.: U.S. Government Printing Office, 1952.

_____. *U.S. Census of Population: 1960.* Vol. 1, Characteristics of the Population, United States Summary, pt. 1. Washington, D.C.: U.S. Government Printing Office, 1962.

_____. *U.S. Census of Population: 1970.* Vol. 1, Characteristics of the Population, United States Summary, pt. 1, General Social and Economic Characteristics. Washington, D.C.: U.S. Government Printing Office, 1973.

_____. *U.S. Census of Population: 1970.* General Social and Economic Characteristics: Louisiana, PC(1)-C20. Washington, D.C.: U.S. Government Printing Office, February 1972.

_____. *U.S. Census of Population: 1970.* General Social and Economic Characteristics: Mississippi, PC(1)-C26. Washington, D.C.: U.S. Government Printing Office, February 1972.

_____. *U.S. Census of Population: 1970.* General Social and Economic Characteristics: North Carolina, PC(1)-C35. Washington, D.C.: U.S. Government Printing Office, April 1972.

_____. *U.S. Census of Population: 1970.* General Social and Economic Characteristics: South Carolina, PC(1)-C46. Washington, D.C.: U.S. Government Printing Office, March 1972.

_____. *U.S. Census of Population: 1970.* Subject Reports: Negro Population, PC(2)-1B. Washington, D.C.: U.S. Government Printing Office, May 1973.

_____. *Social and Economic Characteristics of the Metropolitan and Nonmetropolitan Population: 1977 and 1970.* Special Studies P-23, no. 75. Washington, D.C.: U.S. Government Printing Office, November 1978a.

_____. "The Social and Economic Status of the Black Population in the United States: A Historical View, 1790-1978." *Current Population Reports*, series P-23, no. 80. Washington, D.C.: U.S. Government Printing Office, November, 1978b.

_____. *Social Indicators, 1976.* Washington, D.C.:

U.S. Government Printing Office, December 1977.
Wadley, Janet K., and Lee, Everett S. "The Disappearance
of the Black Farmer." Phylon 35 (1974): 276-83.
Walker, M. E., Jr., and Beauford, E. Y. "Alienation and
Poverty: A Case Study." Journal of Social and Behavioral
Sciences 24 (1978): 47-57.
Wheelock, Gerald C. et al. "Countering Macro-Structure in
the Location of Area Vocational Training Centers:
Implications for Emerging Rural Communities." Paper
delivered at the meeting of the Southern Association of
Agricultural Scientists, Rural Sociology Section,
Houston, Tex., February 1978.

Marta Tienda

13

The Mexican-American Population

INTRODUCTION

The Chicano population is more heterogeneous in social and
economic composition than any other immigrant minority
group in the United States (Grebler et al. 1970; Moore
1976; Peñalosa 1970a). Delineating this heterogeneity and
explaining its sources are the keys to understanding the
present and future status of population of Mexican ancestry.
In the following pages the Chicano population will be characterized in demographic and socioeconomic terms, and the
sociopolitical and institutional factors will be identified
that produced the changes within this population. The basic
concern of this chapter is the rural and nonmetro population
of Mexican origin or descent, but due attention is given to
the urban and metro Chicano population, as appropriate, to
clarify the significance of the current residential and
socioeconomic configuration of this population.

Although about four-fifths of the Mexican-American[1]
population resided in metro areas in 1978 (U.S. Bureau of
the Census, Current Population Reports, hereafter CPR,
series P-20, no. 328), studying the nonmetro population is
justified for two important reasons. First, relatively
little is known about nonmetro ethnic minorities, especially those experiencing rapid social changes. Chicanos are
one of the fastest growing minorities due in part to high
fertility rates and to the continued flow of legal and
illegal Mexican immigrants (Durant and Knowlton 1978).

This research was supported in part by funds granted to the
Center for Demography and Ecology (HD-05876) and by the
College of Agricultural and Life Sciences, the University
of Wisconsin. I wish to thank Ms. Mary Miron for technical
assistance and Mr. Steve Garcia for computational assistance. Thanks are also due to Peter Morrison for valuable
comments and suggestions, and to Linda Clark for patience
in typing several drafts.

Moreover, they are becoming a national rather than a regional minority because of the patterns of internal migration. Chicanos are only one of several Hispanic groups in the United States,[2] but they are and have traditionally been the least urban. The generational and locational transition has left a legacy of disadvantage. Second, solutions to the problems of Chicanos residing in depressed nonmetro areas continue to be difficult (Briggs 1973; Hansen and Gruben 1971; Miller and Maril 1978; Miller 1976). Future attempts to address social policy to the pressing needs of Chicanos in nonmetro areas must be grounded in a solid understanding of their current circumstances.

Until Grebler and his associates published the benchmark study entitled The Mexican American People, knowledge of Chicanos was sparse and largely based on a number of small community studies such as those conducted by Peñalosa and McDonagh (1968), Peñalosa (1969), Heller (1969), Knowlton (1961), Francis (1956), Watson and Samora (1954), McDonagh (1948-49, 1955), and Loomis (1941, 1943). Despite its many merits, the seminal work of Grebler et al. in 1970 (see Alvarez 1971) did not begin to fill the void because the study was based on surveys from two large metro centers in the Southwest--San Antonio and Los Angeles. Thus, their generalizations should be restricted to metro populations in the Southwest. This leaves out many important subgroups, including all nonmetro residents, midwestern Chicanos, and even the Spanish-American population (often referred to as "Hispanos") of northern New Mexico and southern Colorado.

This chapter will begin to address this problem of a lack of information by using recent published and unpublished national data. An attempt will be made to summarize the state of knowledge about the socioeconomic and demographic circumstances of Chicanos residing in rural and nonmetro areas, in order to bring into focus issues that might require policy attention. The discussion begins with a sociohistorical overview in which the forces leading to the creation and the diversification of the Chicano population are outlined. Then a demographic and socioeconomic profile is developed using current published and unpublished census materials, and, because of its salience in current discussions about the income and employment status of Chicanos, the matter of immigration from Mexico is given special attention.

SIGNIFICANCE OF THE CHICANO POPULATION

Over the last two decades the Mexican-American segment
of the total population in the United States has increased
steadily, but reliable estimates are possible only for the
five southwestern states because comparable data are not
available for the entire nation. Conservative estimates
based on decennial censuses indicate that the proportion of
Chicanos residing in the Southwest increased from 10.8
percent in 1950 to 12.9 percent in 1970. Although regional
concentration in the Southwest is a distinctive feature of
the population of Mexican ancestry, it is important to
differentiate this concentration in terms of geographic
space and population density. This concentration is illustrated in Figure 1.3 (see Chapter 1). Thus, in spite of the
fact that Texas and California contain the largest absolute
numbers of Mexican-Americans, historically the relative
share of Chicanos in New Mexico has been considerably higher. Nearly one-third of all New Mexico residents in 1970
were classified as persons of Spanish surname. Mexican-
Americans comprise the lowest proportion of the population
in Colorado, where they represent less than 10 percent of
the total. The relative share of Chicanos in Arizona and
New Mexico has been decreasing over the last two decades
whereas the proportion of Chicanos in Texas, Colorado, and
California has increased or remained stable.

The pattern of geographic concentration in the Southwest
coupled with more limited geographic dispersal in a direction extending toward the Northeast began early (Broadbent
1941; Hernández 1966). In 1910, the majority of the Mexican-
American population was evenly distributed throughout the
agricultural areas of the Southwest, but also included
urbanized areas scattered throughout these areas.[3] The
year 1920 marked the onset of a long-term process of internal redistribution as Mexican-Americans began to cluster
near larger urban places and in the center of major agricultural areas (Broadbent 1941). This transition from scattered to concentrated rurality continued throughout the
1920s and was particularly evident in the specialized crop
areas that required large volumes of cheap labor during
peak seasons. The contemporary significance of a pronounced
concentration in nonmetro areas of the Southwest is that
Chicanos were hampered in their prospects for long-term
social and economic mobility (Taeuber 1966).

Until 1950 close to 90 percent of all people of Mexican
parentage resided in the Southwest, but since then the

proportion residing outside the Southwest has increased
slightly as many families moved north in pursuit of better
employment opportunities. In addition, there was an important internal redistribution of the Chicano population beginning in 1930, as the members of both native and foreign-
born generations became involved in an extensive process of
urbanization. Proportionately more native-born people migrated to metro places and their migration coincided with
the development of the second generation in metro areas
(Hernández 1966). Because the concurrent processes of
immigration and urbanization played a major role in the
differentiation of the Chicano population, it is appropriate to highlight briefly the key elements molding the
experience of successive generations.[4]

GENERATIONAL SUCCESSION AND THE
DIVERSIFICATION OF THE CHICANO POPULATION

In comparison with other national and immigrant minorities,
Chicanos are distinguished by their entry into the United
States through conquest and subordination (Murguia 1975;
Amaguer 1974; McLemore 1973) and by their concentration in
the Southwest (Hansen 1970; Moore 1976). These factors and
others, including distance from the Mexican border, technological change in agriculture, fluctuating labor demands
and immigration policies, and the resurgence of Mexican
ethnicity that accompanied the Chicano movement, were de-
cisive in molding the psychohistorical and socioeconomic
circumstances of Chicanos in the United States (Alvarez
1971, 1973). A brief overview of four generations[5] reflecting different phases of the Chicano experience best
illustrates the inherent heterogeneity of the current
population, providing important information for an understanding of the future prospects of nonmetro Chicanos.
    The Mexican-Americans were created as a people with
the signing of the Treaty of Guadalupe Hidalgo in 1848,
hence the term "creation generation" refers to the resident
population at the time of the territorial annexation of the
Southwest. The experience of Mexican-Americans differs
significantly from that of all other ethnic populations
that migrated willingly to this country during the nineteenth and twentieth centuries, because the rapid and clear
break with the parent country and the socioeconomic and
cultural subjugation took place on the land that the indigenous population considered its own (Alvarez 1973).

The migrant generation represents those individuals
who, during a time of expansion in the demand for labor in
the United States (particularly in agriculture, mining, and
the railroad industries) and political upheaval in Mexico,
moved north in search of employment opportunities and political asylum. This generation differs from the first
because a voluntary choice was made to live in the United
States. There are three especially significant aspects of
the experiences of the migrant generation that have implications for later generations: (1) the contribution to the
expansion of the Mexican-descent population of the Southwest; (2) the unnegotiable relegation to low status in the
American social hierarchy; and (3) the incorporation of
this population into the nonmetro economy as a largely
mobile, seasonal, and docile agricultural work force
(Alvarez 1973).

The Mexican-American generation approximating the period
of the mid-1940s to mid-1960s is distinguished by its development of a sense of cultural loyalty to the United
States. This receptivity to cultural assimilation was advanced by a number of factors, including the transition
from an agricultural, nonmetro and foreign-born population
to a blue-collar, metro and native-born group (Taeuber
1966). Noticeable advances in education, income, and political efficacy engendered a false sense of social acceptance
and psychic security because most of the members of this
generation were blind to the fact that members of the dominant group were experiencing relatively greater social
gains (Dworkin 1965). Nevertheless the socioeconomic and
political achievements of the Mexican-American generation
improved the life chances of the following generation.

The Chicano population emerged during the late 1960s
when social movements to restore civil rights to minorities
made more manifest the pain of social rejection and accumulated disadvantages. At this time the Mexican-descent population was predominantly metro and, in spite of absolute
gains in educational attainment and income levels, Chicanos
were clearly disproportionately represented among the ranks
of the working underclass (Alvarez 1973). The critical
absence of older role models with certified middle-class
status bolstered the development of a new consciousness
that led to the succession of social activities known as
the Chicano movement.[6] Among the more militant, nothing
short of national separation and decolonization would suffice, whereas among the liberals, the resurgence of Mexican
ethnicity was manifested in demands for self-determination,

equality, and a cultural self-redefinition as Chicanos
rather than Mexican-Americans (Loomis 1974). The former
term eulogizes the Mestizo (Spanish and Indian) heritage
and a legacy of exploitation (Miller 1976; Peñalosa 1970b).

Agricultural workers were definitely a minority by the
late 1960s, although they received a considerable amount of
attention as the solidarity of metro militants made evident
the social injustices endured by earlier generations of
Mexican and Mexican-American farm workers. Independently
the voices of Chavez in California, Tijerina in New Mexico,
and Corky Gonzalez in Colorado joined in a social chorus to
broadcast the plight of the Mexican-American people. A
decade and many volumes of social science writing later,
the imprint of social inequality persists. The generational
transitions help clarify the extent of diversity among
Chicanos, but because these transitions were themselves
shaped by the peculiarities of the Southwest, the forces
of change were at times synonymous with the forces of persistence. This point will be elaborated in the following
section.

DIMENSIONS OF DIVERSITY: PERSISTENCE AND CHANGE

In many parts of the Southwest, people of Mexican ancestry
are clearly in the majority. Their language and culture
serve as a reminder to the nation that the regional distinctiveness is attributable to the original settlers, and
in particular, the comingling of indigenous peoples with
the Spanish conquerors (Forbes 1970). Yet despite their
common origins, it is difficult, if not impossible, to
provide a straightforward operational definition of Chicanos (Peñalosa 1970a). The most general view is that Chicanos are individuals of Mexican origin or descent who
reside in the United States, but there is no consensus
about when a Mexican-born individual stops being a Mexicano
and becomes a Chicano. Theoretically, this is related to
the internalization of Anglo culture, but the nature of
this process has never been clarified. Perhaps it should
not be. The continuing influx of new immigrants from Mexico
feeds the existing diversity and makes the drawing of clear
distinctions between Chicanos and Mexicanos, on the one
hand, and Chicanos and Anglos--that is, non-Hispanic, non-
black persons--on the other hand, even more problematic.
Nevertheless, using a definition of Chicanos to include

those who identified themselves as being of Mexican ancestry, it is possible to characterize the population in
socioeconomic and demographic terms. Other important
aspects of heterogeneity among Chicanos, which must be
considered in statistical profiles, are racial characteristics, nativity status, degree of adherence to ethnic ties,
socioeconomic differentiation, metro-nonmetro residence,
and regional contexts (Peñalosa 1970a).

DATA LIMITATIONS

During the course of several decades the U.S. Census Bureau
has modified the identification of Mexican-Americans,[7]
thus posing serious problems of comparability over time
(Bradshaw and Bean 1973). In addition, census materials are
subject to undercounts that may be particularly serious for
the accurate enumeration of Mexican-Americans. Three significant sources of undercount are: (1) the failure to
include mobile illegal aliens, (2) the exclusion of young,
mobile families, and (3) the exclusion of families of migrant laborers who frequently reside in metro places but
work in nonmetro areas. Of special interest for the following analysis is the suspicion that all three of these influences may have affected the nonmetro-metro distribution
of the Chicano population, but this cannot be established
with certainty.
    Nevertheless, census materials constitute the primary
source of data for characterizing the status of Chicanos in
nonmetro areas. Besides information available in published
form from the 1950, 1960, and 1970 decennial censuses of
population and selected intercensal Current Population
Reports, special tabulations from the 1960 and 1970 Public
Use Samples and the 1976 Survey of Income and Education are
available. Both the Spanish-surname and Mexican-origin
ethnic identifiers are used in special tabulations from the
1970 census materials to compensate for the noncomparability
of data between 1960 and 1976. It is, however, understood
that census counts based on the previous three decennial
censuses may exclude between 20 and 35 percent of the eligible population, depending on the unit of analysis (i.e.,
region, state, or nation) and the ethnic identifier (i.e.,
the term used to identify Hispanic groups).[8] Because
Chicanos are the largest of the Hispanic groups, in some
instances inferences drawn from aggregate data about the
total Spanish-origin population may delineate the Chicano

population. Whenever more accurate estimates are available they are used.

FORCES OF PERSISTENCE AND CHANGE

The Chicano experience differed notably among the south-western states. Chicanos in Texas experienced a much more exclusive and repressive cultural structure compared to those in California or New Mexico (Alvarez 1971). Moreover, the pronounced regional poverty in south Texas is the con-sequence of a long legacy of discrimination and conflict with the dominant Anglo system. Moore's three models of colonialism that evolved in New Mexico (classic colonial-ism), Texas (conflict colonialism), and California (economic colonialism) are illustrative in this regard. Although the colonial model of Mexican-American subordination is no longer accepted, Moore's informed account demonstrates how the process of Anglo domination was itself a diversifying experience, not only because it signaled the introduction of still another cultural strand to be woven with the Mes-tizo heritage, but also because of the uneven economic development and urbanization experiences that were forth-coming in each of the southwest states.

It is beyond the scope of this chapter to discuss at length all the factors that account for the persistence of cultural, socioeconomic, and demographic diversity among Chicanos, but a brief summary highlighting those elements that continue to feed the existing heterogeneity is appro-priate. Among these, the mechanization of southwestern agri-culture (Galarza 1968; Briggs 1973) and the breakdown of the village communities through land transfers (Knowlton 1961, 1969; Leonard and Hannon 1977) were important in the pronounced out-migration from nonmetro to metro areas. Geographic redistribution and the generational transitions implied by the upward mobility of older residents (Peñalosa and McDonagh 1968), coupled with the continued entry of new immigrants at the lower end of the status hierarchy (Galarza 1968; Bogardus 1928-29, 1965), make the aggregate process of cultural and socioeconomic assimilation appear to improve slowly or not at all.

What little is known about the process of cultural as-similation among Chicanos is reflected in patterns of lan-guage usage (Patella and Kuvlesky 1973; Lopez 1976, 1977; Skrabanek 1970), patterns of intermarriage (Mittlebach and Moore 1970; Murguia and Frisbie 1977), and rates of social

mobility (Peñalosa 1969). For the most part, conclusions
about the role of culture conflict in precluding high-status
attainments among Chicanos are based on untested assertions[9]
and questionable analyses (Neal 1972). If subsequent generations of native-born Chicanos hold the key to transform-
ing the cultural value system, then studies that show cultural orientations favoring early marriage and large families among Chicano youth are not encouraging (Edington
and Hays 1978; Marshall and Miller 1977).

Explanations for the persistence of ethnic distinctiveness among Chicanos include geographic, cultural, and institutional factors. Clearly, the regional concentration
of Chicanos in the Southwest not only vitalizes their Mexican heritage by keeping alive the use of Spanish as well as
the maintenance of selected cultural traits and traditions,
but it also facilitates the continued supply of new generations of immigrants. In the cultural sphere, however, the
importance of distinctive value orientations as a basis for
the failure of many Chicanos to assimilate with the dominant
population has been exaggerated. Examples derived from this
reasoning range from family size preferences (Edington and
Hays 1978; Marshall and Miller 1977) to achievement orientations (Henggeler and Tavormina 1978; Anderson and Evans
1976) and authoritarian family norms (Montiel 1970; Mirandé
1977; Bean et al. 1977; Hawkes and Taylor 1975). In fact,
there is very little empirical basis for inferring that
culturally rooted value orientations are what ultimately
account for the lower achievements of Chicanos. Instead,
signs of lower aspirations and attainments are more a
reflection of realistic assessments of the prospects for
actualizing aspirations (Lamare 1977; Anderson and Evans
1976; Henggeler and Tavormina 1978) than a unique attribute
of the socialization experiences of Mexican-heritage youth.

Although there is little dispute that the Chicano family
is a source of stability (Eberstein and Frisbie 1976),
which also shelters its members from dominant social institutions (Mirandé 1977), the relationship between social
mobility and family orientation has not been explored well
(Tienda 1980). It is unlikely that family orientation plays
a critical role in keeping Chicanos in the lower echelons
of the social structure. Rather, the legacy of unequal
treatment in school and limited opportunities for securing
well-paying, high-prestige jobs are more appropriately
identified as the key institutional barriers to mobility.
Nevertheless, it would be erroneous to leave the impression
that no improvements in the socioeconomic well-being of

Chicanos have occurred over the past two decades or so. The remainder of this chapter will identify what gains have been made in the 1960s and early 1970s and whether nonmetro populations have benefited from social gains to the same extent as metro residents.

DEMOGRAPHIC PROFILE

Based on current population reports, the Bureau of the Census estimated that 7.2 million people of Mexican ancestry[10] resided in the United States in 1978. This figure represented a 60 percent increase over the 4.5 million people enumerated in 1970. Although there is no doubt that one of the distinguishing characteristics of the Chicano population is its rate of growth (Briggs 1973; Bradshaw and Bean 1972, 1973), it is probable that part of the increase registered between 1970 and 1978 resulted from the alleged undercount in the earlier census. This interpretation is supported by the intercensal results disclosed by the 1973 Current Population Reports, which showed an implausible increase of nearly 40 percent within only three years. Critics concerned with the problems of underenumeration of Hispanics agree that although recent estimates are more in line with reality, undercounts persist because some individuals refuse to identify with the categories provided by the Census Bureau and because the survey procedure failed to identify an unknown number of illegal aliens (Durant and Knowlton 1978). A reasonable estimate for 1979 is closer to 8 million or more people of Hispanic descent, but this figure awaits confirmation by the 1980 Census results.

In spite of the many imperfections of the census enumerations of Chicanos, it is appropriate to highlight the more important patterns of population change over the last decade or so. The two most salient aspects are the pronounced redistribution of population and the rate of growth, both of which are discussed below.

POPULATION DISTRIBUTION:
PATTERNS OF DISPERSAL AND CONCENTRATION

In 1970, 87 percent of people of Mexican ancestry in the United States resided in the Southwest (U.S. Bureau of the Census, U.S. Census of Population: 1970, PC(2)-1C, Table

1), but more recent estimates are slightly lower, ranging
from 82 to 85 percent (U.S. Bureau of the Census, CPR,
series P-20, no. 290 and no. 329, Table 1). Furthermore,
Mexican-Americans are not uniformly distributed within the
Southwest, and about three-fourths lived in two states--
Texas and California--in 1970. This figure represents nearly 84 percent of all those residing in the Southwest region.
Although the three remaining southwest states of Arizona,
Colorado, and New Mexico combined held only 10 percent of
the total Mexican-origin population (representing 16 percent of those residing in the Southwest), Mexican-Americans
still represent the most numerically significant minority
by a considerable margin over blacks, Native Americans, and
Asian Americans (Moore 1976).

The second distinctive characteristic of the Chicano
population is its concentration in metro areas. In all
areas, the shift from nonmetro to metro areas has been a
highly significant trend (Peñalosa, 1970a). Even though
the Spanish-surname population in the Southwest was less
metro than the non-Spanish-surname group in 1950 (Beegle,
Goldsmith, and Loomis 1960), only about one-third of the
Mexican-American population lived in nonmetro areas, with
the majority of those residing in nonfarm places. The shift
out of nonmetro areas continued through the 1960s, and by
1970 it was estimated that more than 85 percent of the
Chicano population resided in metro places (see Table 13.1).

The extent of metro concentration among Chicanos is
not uniform across states, which is not surprising because
the current configuration is rooted in a diverse urbanization process begun decades ago. By 1950 more than three-
fourths of the Spanish-surname population residing in California reported metro residence compared to only 50 and
41 percent respectively in Colorado and New Mexico. California's Spanish-surname population was almost completely
urbanized by 1970 with more than 90 percent registered as
metro residents compared to only 65 percent in New Mexico.
Virtually none of the nonmetro residents in any of the
southwest states lived on farms. Perhaps the scarcity of
farm ownership can partly explain the limited incentives
for Chicanos to remain in rural areas (Moore 1976; Knowlton
1961; Galarza 1968).

Intercensal demographic surveys provide evidence that
the metro concentration of Chicanos has continued during
the 1970s. Information from the Current Population Reports
indicates that the Mexican-origin population has gradually
become more metro since the last census. As shown in Table

Table 13.1. Distribution of the White Spanish-
Surname Population by Residence and Year for the
Southwest, 1950-1970

Residence	Year		
	1950	1960	1970
	%	%	%
Urban	66.4	79.1	85.4
Rural nonfarm	21.5	15.6	12.9
Rural farm	12.1	5.3	1.6
Total	100.0	100.0	99.9
Number	2,289,550	3,464,999	4,511,031

Source: U.S. Bureau of the Census, U.S. Census of
Population: 1950, Table 2; U.S. Census of Popula-
tion: 1960, PC(2) - 1B, Table 2; U.S. Census of
Population: 1970, PC(2)-1D, Table 1.

13.2, the proportion of Spanish-origin persons who resided
in nonmetro areas declined gradually during the 1970s. This
process was due largely to the slight declines in counties
with less than 25,000 residents, because between 1970 and
1977, the proportion of Spanish-origin individuals residing
in nonmetro counties of 25,000 or more increased slightly.
For the total population, by contrast, nonmetro counties of
all size classes experienced relative population gains.
Apparently the Spanish-origin population has not participated in the population turnaround as much--if at all--
compared to the total population. More specifically, the
proportion of Mexican-origin families residing in nonmetro
areas decreased from 24 to 19 percent between 1972 and 1978
(U.S. Bureau of the Census, CPR, series P-20, no. 280,
Table 7; and no. 328, Table 4).
   The current metro-nonmetro configuration of the Chicano
population is the product of a complex set of cultural,
economic, and social forces, among which the employment
patterns of adult males played a particularly important
role. The use of Mexican laborers as strikebreakers, reserve
workers during times of labor shortages, and as a pool of
seasonal, migratory agricultural workers was almost single-

Table 13.2. Distribution of the Total and Spanish-Origin
Population by Residence, 1970 and 1977

Residence	Spanish-Origin		Total	
	1970	1977	1970	1977
	%	%	%	%
Metro areas of				
1,000,000 or more:	52.8	55.1	39.8	38.7
In central cities	32.8	31.2	17.2	15.0
Outside central cities	20.0	23.9	22.6	23.7
Metro areas less than				
1,000,000:	29.7	29.0	28.8	28.7
In central cities	18.8	18.2	14.3	13.3
Outside central cities	10.9	10.8	14.5	15.4
Nonmetro areas:	17.5	15.9	31.4	32.6
In counties with no place of 2,500 or more	1.4	1.2	3.6	4.0
In counties with a place of 2,500 to 24,999	11.6	10.0	19.8	20.4
In counties with a place of more than 25,000	4.5	4.7	8.0	8.2
Total	100.0	100.0	100.0	100.0
Number[a]	8,988	11,269	199,819	212,566

Source: U.S. Bureau of the Census, Current Population
Reports, Special Studies, P-23, no. 75, Table 1.

[a]In thousands, excluding inmates of institutions and armed
forces in barracks.

handedly responsible for the geographic dispersal that
began around 1930 and gained greater momentum after World
War II (Durant and Knowlton 1978). Because Mexican-American
metro concentration grew largely through migration from
nonmetro areas, the matter of successful (or unsuccessful)
adjustment to metro life would seem to be an issue of considerable importance (Peñalosa 1970a), particularly in
terms of projecting future prospects. Although studies of

the urban adjustment experiences of Chicano migrants have
not been accorded much serious investigation in the social
science literature, a selected number of studies based on
specific localities have provided a few useful insights.

Samora and Larson (1961) identified three factors that
increased the likelihood that nonmetro Chicano migrants
would adjust successfully to their new metro environment.
These are: (1) the size of the migrant group, (2) the possibility of a slow chain migration process,[11] and (3) a
nonghetto residential settlement pattern in metro destinations. Whereas these authors emphasized the ability of
Chicanos to adjust well in urban settings, Choldin and
Trout (1969) arrived at a singularly unusual conclusion
that a comprehensive resocialization process was necessary
to facilitate the transition from nonmetro to metro life
because most of the Mexican-descent migrants to Michigan
were reared in relatively small Texas towns in the Rio
Grande valley. Exactly what such a program might consist of
or how it might be implemented is not immediately obvious,
however.

Economic conditions are usually the primary force that
motivates individuals to leave nonmetro areas, and it is
not surprising that most migrants are financially better
off in metro areas than their nonmigrant counterparts. This
holds for Chicano as well as black and Anglo migrants (Price
1970; Blevins 1971). Although the comparative benefits from
migration are not uniform among all groups, Chicano migrants
differ from Anglo and black migrants in two significant
respects. These are the differences in social background
and movement as a family unit. Apparently, migration does
not disrupt family ties of Chicanos because, like Anglos
but unlike blacks, Chicanos usually migrate as whole families. Also, even though Mexican-Americans tend to move
longer distances than either blacks or Anglos, they maintain
much closer ties to their areas of origin. This has implications for the design of relocation programs (Hansen and
Gruben 1971) to involve broader kin groups (Loomis 1941).
Interestingly, 60 percent of the Mexican-American migrants
residing in Chicago indicated a willingness to return to
south Texas if economic conditions improved, whereas only
42 percent of those who migrated to San Antonio were willing to return under these circumstances. These findings
shed light upon the potential for future flows to nonmetro
areas, but they also illustrate how migration is an adaptive
response to limited opportunities for social and economic
betterment (Durant and Knowlton 1978).

POPULATION GROWTH

The Spanish-surname population almost doubled between 1950
and 1970, thus rendering Chicanos the fastest-growing segment of the southwestern population. More specifically,
the Spanish-surname population increased from 2.3 to 3.5
million between 1950 and 1960, and an additional 1.0 million during the 1960s.[12] By contrast, between 1950 and
1970 Anglos and blacks residing in the Southwest increased
only 67 and 61 percent respectively (Moore 1976). In the
latter decade alone, the Spanish-surname population increased 30.2 percent whereas the respective gains for Anglos
and blacks were 25 and 7 percent. The rapid growth of the
Chicano population is the consequence of two demographic
forces: (1) inordinately high fertility rates that averaged
between 40 and 80 percent higher than those of Anglos
(Bradshaw and Bean 1973) and (2) continued immigration from
Mexico that was largely unrestricted until 1968 (Briggs
1973, 1975).

Fertility Trends
      Chicano women have higher fertility than any other
Spanish-origin group as well as the black population (Bradshaw and Bean 1972). The historical antecedents for high
fertility date back as far as 1850 when Mexican women averaged one-third more children than other whites in the Southwest. Apparently, very little convergence in fertility differentials occurred through 1950. Since then, the reproduc-
tive behavior of Mexican-Americans has paralleled that of
Anglos in the Southwest, but at a consistently higher level.
That is, fertility of women in both groups was higher in
1960 than in 1950, but by 1970 the average age-adjusted
number of children ever born to Mexican-American women
under thirty-five had declined somewhat (Bradshaw and Bean
1973). However, because comparable declines were experienced
in Anglo fertility, the differential between the two populations remained close to its 1960 level, rendering little
evidence of any convergence between 1950 and 1970. Notable
variation in age-specific fertility rates persists, as does
variation by metro-nonmetro residence. The 1978 Current
Population Reports showed the metro Spanish-origin women
who have completed their childbearing have an average of
3.2 children, compared to 3.9 for their nonmetro counterparts (U.S. Bureau of the Census, CPR, series P-20, no.
341, Table 9).
      A number of factors have contributed to the persistence

of high fertility among Mexican-American women. Among the
most commonly noted are differences in socioeconomic status,
younger marriage, closer birth spacing intervals, minority
status, and offspring gender (Bradshaw and Bean 1972; Marcum and Bean 1976; Wood and Bean 1977), but these factors
are insufficient to account completely for observed differentials. An additional factor thought to have produced
high fertility is family-size norms (Edington and Hays
1978; Marshall and Miller 1977). It is curious that in
spite of the fact that the metro-nonmetro fertility differentials have been acknowledged, no attempt has been made
to investigate whether previous farm worker status has
served as a disincentive for couples to scale down family-
size goals. That is, if children have in the past been
valued as productive agents, this fact may have exerted an
independent effect on fertility, one whose effect will
diminish only gradually.

Several consequences of sustained high fertility are a
relatively young population with a large share of individuals in dependent ages and large families. The median age
of Chicanos is low: 20.3 years for both sexes in 1976 compared to 28.9 for the total population. Males are slightly
younger, with a median age of 19.8 years compared to 20.9
for females (U.S. Bureau of the Census, CPR, series P-20,
no. 310, Table 2). These ages contrast with medians of
27.8 for all males and 29.9 years for all females. In 1976
children under 18 years of age comprised 45 percent of
the Mexican-American population. By contrast, less than
one-third of the total United States population was under
18 years of age. Finally, in comparison to the average
family size of 3.6 in 1970, Chicano families are large,
averaging 4.5 persons. By 1976, the average family size
dropped slightly to 4.3 persons, but in families with incomes below poverty the size was slightly larger, with an
average of 4.6 persons (U.S. Bureau of the Census, CPR,
series P-20, no. 310, Table 30).

Immigration

Mexican immigration to the United States began with
the colonization of the American Southwest, but the number
of border crossings was not significant until after 1910,
when the Mexican Revolution propelled thousands to seek
refuge in the United States. Fortuitously, employment
conditions in the host society were conducive to the absorption of unskilled workers because of the labor shortages associated with World War I (Briggs 1975). As shown

in Table 13.3, the pool of Mexican immigrants continued to
increase during the 1920s, a period when the foreign-born
played a prominent role in the development of agricultural,
railroad, and extractive industries. By 1929, when the
Depression curtailed immigration from Mexico (rather than
legislation), Mexicans were firmly established in both the
metro and nonmetro communities of the Southwest and, to a
much lesser extent, the Midwest. The migration to the metro
areas of the Midwest, particularly to the large cities in
Illinois, Michigan, and Indiana was well underway (Hernández
1966; Romo 1975). Thus, although the recruitment of labor
for agriculture was a major factor during the early stages
of immigration, its influence seems to have subsided for a
period, only to be resumed during the 1940s with the
legislation establishing the contract labor system known as
the Bracero Program.[13]

As shown in Table 13.3, the phenomenon of illegal immigration emerged about the time that legal immigration was
restricted. The Depression renewed interest in preventing
illegal entries and the Deportation Act of 1929 further
legitimated efforts to search for and expel aliens. This
activity subsided somewhat when economic conditions improved. From 1940 through the late 1960s, legal immigration
continued unrestricted until Congress imposed a quota maximum of 120,000 persons a year from the Western Hemisphere
beginning in 1969. Official constraints on legal immigration
coincided with an increase in illegal entrants from Mexico
to the United States. The figures in Table 13.3 must be
interpreted with caution because no adjustment for double
counting is made and because the number of deportations in
any period partly reflect the selective enforcement of
immigration laws (Samora 1971; Stoddard 1976), as well as
the need to provide a visible scapegoat for domestic
unemployment problems (Bustamente 1976; Stoddard 1976).

The significance of Mexican immigration since the turn
of the century (illustrated in Table 13.4) transcends
demographic bounds. Although there is no doubt that the
majority of Mexican-Americans are native born, the fact
that they also represent the largest foreign-born ethnic
group currently living in the United States is itself
highly significant. Moreover, in spite of the fact that
Chicanos are currently a metro minority, the foreign born
remain quite visible in nonmetro and rural areas. More
specifically, in 1970, about 13 percent of all Spanish-
surname people residing in rural areas of the Southwest
were foreign born compared to roughly 17 percent in urban

Table 13.3. Mexican Immigration to the
United States, 1900-1973: Legal and Illegal
Entrants by Five-Year Intervals

Year of Entry	Legal Entrants	Illegal Entrants[a]
1900-1904	2,830	--
1905-1909	28,358	--
1910-1914	82,588	--
1915-1919	91,075	--
1920-1924	249,248	--
1925-1929	238,527	25,570
1930-1934	19,200	58,629
1935-1939	8,737	46,268
1940-1944	16,548	80,339
1945-1949	37,742	949,875
1950-1954	78,723	3,386,086
1955-1959	214,746	357,514
1960-1964	217,827	213,629
1965-1969	213,689	578,418
1970-1973	228,753	1,620,753

Source: 1900-1973 data adapted from Vernon
M. Briggs, 1975, Tables 1 and 2.

[a]Refers to individuals apprehended. These
figures do not include those who are never
detected but they are upwardly biased by
multiple counts of repeat offenders.

areas. These proportions have not changed greatly since
1950.

For the United States as a whole, it was estimated
that about 18 percent of the Mexican-origin population was
foreign born in 1970 (U.S. Bureau of the Census, U.S.
Census of Population: 1970, PC(2)-1C, Table 5). Published
data for nonmetro and metro areas are not available. However, special tabulations from the Survey of Income and
Education disclosed that foreign-born Mexican-Americans may
have increased slightly to 21.5 percent by 1976. In light
of the current patterns of legal and illegal immigration,
it is unlikely that this share will decrease in the fore-

Table 13.4. Proportion of Foreign-born
Persons of Spanish Surname by Residence
in Five Southwestern States, 1950-1970

Residence	Year		
	1950	1960	1970
	%	%	%
Rural	16.5	14.3	12.6
Urban	17.6	15.7	16.5
Total	17.2	15.4	16.0

Source: U.S. Bureau of the Census,
Census of Population, 1970, PC(2)-1D,
Table 2; Census of Population: 1960, PC
(2)-1B, Table 2; Census of Population:
1950, Table 5.

seeable future. More importantly, the settlement patterns
will surely have a significant impact on the socioeconomic
composition of the Chicano population for some time to come
(see Downes 1977).

The Chicano-Mexicano interface has been discussed in
terms ranging from civil liberties (Gandara 1977), to welfare utilization (Bustamente 1976), and job competition
(Briggs 1973, 1975). Numerous stereotypes exist about Mexican immigrants as a rural, semiilliterate peasantry, but
these images are not borne out by empirical data. Recent
research findings indicate that Mexican immigrants are
somewhat more urban than the Mexican source population
and that the overwhelming share seek residence in metro
areas (Portes 1978). This does not mean, of course, that
nonmetro areas are unaffected by the flow of legal immigrants; neither does it address the issue of whether undocumented aliens are more likely to settle and work in
nonmetro areas than their legal counterparts.

Although the educational and occupational status of
legal Mexican immigrants, including those who previously
had been in the United States illegally, is higher than
that of the Mexican population as a whole, recent immigrants
are essentially a segment of the working class with some
formal schooling (Portes 1978). Very few are represented in
the professional and technical fields, but neither is farm

work the usual occupation.[14] Rather, the bulk of Mexican
immigrants are nonfarm laborers working in unskilled and
semiskilled urban jobs as well as in low-skill service
occupations (Portes 1978). There is no doubt that the
continued flow of low-skill wage laborers has influenced
the current socioeconomic circumstances of Chicanos.[15]

THE CURRENT SOCIAL AND ECONOMIC STATUS
OF CHICANOS IN NONMETROPOLITAN AMERICA

In spite of the dramatic improvements in opportunities for
minorities over the last decade, social and economic difficulties continue to be widespread among the Chicano population. This is in part due to the pattern of regional
concentration in economically depressed areas, especially
poverty areas such as the Rio Grande valley of south Texas
(Hansen and Gruben 1971; Miller and Maril 1978; Miller
1976), and in part to the influx of low-skill workers.
Out-migration to metro areas has offered limited social
mobility (Price 1970; Blevins 1971), but socioeconomic
parity with the dominant white population is a long way
off. Low educational attainment is a partial cause, but
racism and institutional discrimination also play important roles.

   In 1960 the median educational attainment level for
the adult Spanish-surname population in the Southwest was
slightly over 8 years, but this average concealed wide
disparities between the native and foreign-born segments of
the population. Mexican immigrants had completed an average
of 4.5 years of school compared to 8.6 for the native-born
groups (U.S. Bureau of the Census, U.S. Census of Population: 1960, PC(2)-1B). By 1970 the median schooling levels
had risen to 8.6 years for the total southwestern adult
population of Mexican ancestry. Again, the native born
fared slightly better with a median education of 9.9 years
compared to 5.4 years for the foreign born. State comparisons show that school completion levels were higher in
California with a median of 9.7 years and lowest in Texas
with 6.7 years on the average (U.S. Bureau of the Census,
U.S. Census of Population: 1970, PC(2)-1D). Anglos residing
in the Southwest compared favorably with an average completion of 12 years of school in 1970. However useful for
outlining the broad differences between Chicanos and Anglos,
these census statistics cannot begin to address the very

fundamental question of quality which is so crucial for
the transition between rural schools and urban jobs.

In spite of low levels of schooling, Chicano income
and employment records are consistently more favorable than
those recorded for blacks (Briggs 1973; Price 1970). Although blacks have on the average three additional years
of schooling, they generally reap lower occupational and
income rewards than Chicanos. Nevertheless, there is no
question that the low levels of education continue to handicap the achievements of Chicanos. Even though education
will never provide a total solution to the problems of
social mobility, it is at least a prerequisite for better
jobs and salaries. The recent employment and earning experiences of Chicanos illustrate some of the consequences
of poor schooling.

ASPECTS OF LABOR FORCE PARTICIPATION

The socioeconomic circumstances of Chicanos are linked with
their labor market experiences as reflected by patterns of
labor force participation and occupational income attainments. Both employment and unemployment rates are sensitive
to variations in the age, sex, and residential composition
of labor force participants. These factors have proven
particularly important for the experiences of Hispanic
workers. As shown in Table 13.5, the aggregate labor force
participation rate for Spanish-surname males declined between 1960 and 1970 whereas the female rate increased.
These changes mirror a similar pattern in the general population. However, declines in the male rate of labor force
participation were more pronounced in nonmetro areas, where
between 1960 and 1970 an 8.5 percent decrease was registered
compared to a 5.7 percent point decline in urban areas. Female labor force participation rates increased approximately
5.5 percentage points and this was, in contrast to men, due
to relatively greater increases in the rates for rural
women.

More recent estimates of changes in labor force participation among persons of Spanish origin are available from
the Current Population Reports,[16] but frequently these
are not disaggregated by national origin groups. Nevertheless, the recorded patterns of change among all Hispanics
are instructive about the recent experiences of Chicanos.
It was estimated that by 1977 Hispanic men participated in
the labor force at a rate of 84.8 percent compared to 79.7

Table 13.5. Labor Force Participation Rates for
Persons of Spanish Surname in the Southwest by
Sex and Residence, 1960 and 1970

Sex	Residence					
	1960			1970		
	Urban	Rural	Total	Urban	Rural	Total
	%	%	%	%	%	%
Male	76.7	72.8	75.8	71.0	64.3	70.0
Female	30.8	19.9	28.7	35.5	25.6	34.2

Source: U.S. Bureau of the Census, U.S. Census of
Population: 1960, PC(2)-1B, Table 6; U.S. Census
of Population: 1970, PC(2)-1C, Table 9.

Note: Civilian labor force aged fourteen years and
more.

percent for the total population (Newman 1978). Dissimilar
age distributions largely explain the higher labor force
participation rates of Hispanic males because of the
greater proportion of non-Hispanic white males aged twenty
to twenty-four who are enrolled in school (McKay 1974).
Hispanic females, on the other hand, have lower overall and
age-specific participation rates compared to their white
and black counterparts (Newman 1978).

Hispanic workers are disproportionately represented
among the ranks of the unemployed.[17] Nearly 105,000 persons
of Mexican ancestry were jobless in 1970, of which more
than one-half (58 percent) were males. Official unemployment
rates were 6.3 and 9.0 percent for males and females respectively. Rates of joblessness in metro areas were virtually identical to the overall rates for both sexes because
of the disproportionate concentration of Chicanos in metro
areas, but nonmetro rates were slightly higher at 7.3 percent for males and 9.8 percent for females (U.S. Bureau of
the Census, U.S. Census of Population: 1970, PC(2)-1C,
Table 7). Between 1972 and 1977, the rate of joblessness
among Chicano males increased from 7.9 to 9.5 percent,
after reaching a peak of 12.2 percent during the 1975 recession. Changes in female unemployment followed suit except
that registered increases were from 9.1 percent in 1972 to

a high of 13.3 in 1977. Thus, in 1977 Chicano unemployment
rates were 2 percent higher than those of Anglo males,
whereas Chicanas experienced unemployment rates nearly 5
percent higher than Anglo women (U.S. Bureau of the Census,
CPR, series P-20, no. 230, Table 6; no. 290, Table 10; and
no. 329, Table 10).

Variations in jobless rates and the duration of unemployment stem from differences in human capital and demographic characteristics of workers as well as the regional,
seasonal, and cyclical variations in the demand for labor.
Unemployed Mexican workers had the shortest unemployment in
1977, averaging 5.1 weeks overall (Newman 1978). Although
this compares favorably with the mean duration of 7 weeks
for all workers and 6.2 for all Hispanic workers, it suggests that the reasons for unemployment between Hispanic
and non-Hispanic workers may differ somewhat. It is possible, for example, that the shorter average unemployment
recorded for Chicanos conceals a greater number of more
frequent periods, as might be expected among individuals
concentrated in industries where the demand for labor is
largely governed by seasonal factors. Available data do not
permit a direct examination of this premise, although it
can be addressed indirectly by examining the employment and
income patterns of nonmetro and metro Chicano workers. This
information is also pertinent for addressing additional
issues concerning the current social and economic circumstances of Chicanos in nonmetro areas.

Industry Distribution of Chicano Workers

According to Briggs "agriculture . . . has been the
mainstay of the rural economy for Chicanos" (1973: 21). In
1970, when more than one-fourth of all Chicano workers were
engaged in agricultural activities, the agricultural industry maintained its unrivaled first place as the source of
employment for nonmetro Chicanos. This situation changed
by 1976 when fewer than one in eight Chicanos were employed
in agriculture. Approximately 40 percent of the nonmetro
Spanish-surname labor force in the Southwest was engaged in
agricultural activities in 1960, but during the next decade,
agricultural employment decreased 16 percentage points for
this group.[18]

As illustrated in Table 13.6, agricultural employment
in the nonmetro Southwest declined by two-fifths between
1960 and 1970, a change more significant than that experienced in nonmetro areas defined by conventional census
criteria. However, the reduction in agricultural employment

by over one-half between 1970 and 1976 is even more impressive. Other nonmetro industry employment sectors in which the relative shares of Chicanos have declined are wholesale trade and personal services, but these changes are quite small. Overall change in the industry allocation of labor can be summarized by noting that approximately one in five workers shifted industry of employment in the nonmetro Southwest between 1960 and 1970. For the total United States, a similar share (18 percent) of the nonmetro Chicano work force changed industry employment sectors between 1970 and 1976.[19]

Shifts out of agriculture, wholesale trade, and personal services have resulted in an increased representation of nonmetro Chicanos in almost all other industries, most notably manufacturing and professional and related services,[20] but to a slightly lesser extent retail trade and construction. The expansion of employment in retail trade at the national level was foreshadowed by the 1960 to 1970 employment shifts in the Southwest, but the increase in manufacturing was not. It is noteworthy that the 1970 to 1976 employment shift into manufacturing industries—especially nondurable goods production—was slightly higher in the nonmetro Southwest than in the nation, having increased 6.3 and 4.5 percent, respectively, from 1970 to 1976. Employment of Chicanos in durable goods production increased slightly between 1960 and 1970 at the expense of nondurable goods production. Thereafter, growth in durable manufacturing employment stabilized in the Southwest and even declined slightly at the national level.

By 1976, nondurable manufacturing industries accounted for more than twice as many Chicano workers as durable goods production in the nonmetro United States. In the nonmetro Southwest, this ratio was almost 3 to 1. These are important findings that should be heeded by labor force analysts and, particularly, advocates of nonmetro industrialization or formulators of manpower policy. Results of the 1980 Census will determine whether manufacturing employment in the nonmetro Southwest has continued to expand through the 1970s, and, if so, whether the durable and nondurable components are becoming more or less similar to the nonmetro United States. Further research should consider the significance of the transformation of the industry employment structure for earnings patterns of Chicanos.

Table 13.6. Industry Distribution of the Nonmetropolitan
Spanish-Surname and Mexican-Origin Population for Five
Southwestern States and Total United States, 1960-1976

| Industry | Five Southwestern States | | | | Total U.S. | |
| | Spanish-Surname | | Mexican-Origin | | Mexican-Origin | |
	1960	1970	1970	1976	1970	1976
	%	%	%	%	%	%
Agriculture, forestry, and fisheries	40.5	23.0	27.5	12.0	27.8	11.9
Mining	1.1	2.4	2.3	4.4	2.1	4.1
Construction	6.8	7.7	7.5	8.9	6.6	8.5
Manufacturing:						
Durable	3.3	4.3	4.4	4.7	6.6	6.1
Nondurable	7.7	6.6	7.2	13.2	8.3	13.3
Transportation	2.6	2.1	2.0	3.1	2.2	3.0
Communication	.4	.5	.3	.9	.3	.8
Utilities and sanitary services	.9	1.7	1.8	1.2	1.5	1.1
Trade:						
Wholesale	5.1	2.7	3.3	2.6	3.1	2.7
Retail	14.5	17.8	16.4	19.7	15.4	19.5
Finance, insurance, and real estate	.9	1.6	1.6	1.9	1.4	1.8
Business and repair services	1.5	1.8	1.7	1.0	1.6	1.0
Personal services	8.1	8.4	8.0	7.3	7.6	6.9
Entertainment and recreation services	.9	.5	.5	.4	.6	.6
Professional and related services	3.8	14.3	11.8	13.7	11.4	13.8
Public administration	2.0	4.6	3.6	5.1	3.5	4.8
Total	100.0	100.0	99.9	100.1	100.0	99.9

Source: 1960 and 1970 Public Use Samples of Basic Records
from the 1970 Census: Description and Technical Documentation,
Washington, D.C.; Survey of Income and Education, Washington,
D.C.: Bureau of Labor Statistics, 1976.

Occupational Distribution of Chicano Workers

Overall, the pattern of occupational change in the
nonmetro Southwest parallels what has more recently trans-
pired in nonmetro areas in the nation as a whole, with one
noteworthy difference. This is the dramatic decline in the
farm labor category and corresponding increase, rather than
decrease, in the proportion of nonmetro Chicano workers
employed as operatives and nonfarm laborers. The latter
difference may reflect the greater attractiveness of nonmetro areas outside the Southwest to prospective industrialists as suggested by Miller (1976).

Given the persistent concentration of Chicano workers
in industries with low capital-labor ratios, it is not
surprising that disproportionately large numbers are employed in low-paying, low-prestige occupations (Durant and
Knowlton 1978). As illustrated in Table 13.7, the proportion
of Spanish-surname workers in the nonmetro Southwest who
held professional-technical and managerial-administrative
occupations doubled between 1960 and 1970, but this only
represents an increase of 3 percentage points. Members of
the metro labor force fared no better, as less than 10
percent of the Spanish-surname workers in the metro Southwest labor force were engaged in better paying, more prestigious occupations in 1970. Changes in the occupational
allocation of Chicanos between 1970 and 1976 were almost
identical for the total United States and the nonmetro
Southwest, but in neither case are the circumstances laudable because only 10 percent of the nonmetro Chicano work
force occupied upper white-collar jobs as recently as 1976.
Between 1970 and 1976, the increase in professional employment among Chicano workers in the nonmetro Southwest was
only 1 percent, a meager change that was also paralleled at
the national level.

At the opposite end of the spectrum, it is evident that
metro and nonmetro workers alike are disproportionately
represented in blue-collar jobs, a pattern that has changed
remarkably little since the early 1960s (Bullock 1964;
Moore 1976). In accordance with the observed changes in the
industry allocation of labor, there was an appreciable
decrease in the number of agricultural occupations in the
nonmetro Southwest. The proportionate share of Spanish-
surname farm workers declined from about one-third to one-
fifth of the total labor force. Slight reductions in the
proportions of nonfarm laborers and transportation operatives accompanied the shift out of agricultural occupations,
but these decreases were offset by increases in the propor-

Table 13.7. Occupation Distribution of the Nonmetropolitan
Spanish-Surname and Mexican-Origin Population for Five
Southwestern States and Total United States, 1960-1976

| Occupation | Five Southwestern States | | | | Total U.S. | |
| | Spanish-Surname | | Mexican-Origin | | Mexican-Origin | |
	1960	1970	1970	1976	1970	1976
	%	%	%	%	%	%
Professional, technical and kindred	2.0	4.9	3.3	4.4	3.4	4.7
Managers, administrators, except farm	2.3	3.2	2.5	4.9	2.6	4.5
Sales workers	4.6	4.7	4.1	2.8	3.9	2.8
Clerical and kindred workers	5.2	9.1	7.5	10.4	7.5	10.3
Craftsmen and kindred workers	6.9	10.6	10.0	12.0	9.6	11.8
Operatives, excluding transportation	14.1	14.8	15.2	18.5	16.0	19.3
Transportation operatives	4.8	3.3	3.4	4.7	3.1	5.1
Laborers, except farm	9.7	8.0	9.0	10.3	9.3	10.2
Farmers and farm managers	4.3	1.2	1.1	1.0	1.0	.9
Farm laborers and farm foremen	33.6	19.6	24.2	10.0	24.6	9.7
Service workers excluding private household	7.9	16.6	15.6	17.8	3.4	2.9
Private household workers	4.6	4.1	4.1	3.1	15.5	17.9
Total	100.0	100.1	100.0	99.9	99.9	100.0

Source: 1960 and 1970 Public Use Samples of Basic Records
from the 1970 Census: Description and Technical Documentation,
Washington, D.C.; Survey of Income and Education, Washington,
D.C.: Bureau of Labor Statistics, 1976.

tion of workers engaged in almost all other occupations.
Of these, expansion in the clerical, craft, and service
categories was among the most pronounced.

INCOME AND POVERTY STATUS OF CHICANOS

Income directly reflects the occupational patterns of a
group as well as the wage differentials characteristic of
geographic regions. Between 1960 and 1970, increasing earnings disparities between Anglos and Mexican-American male
workers were documented by Poston et al. (1976). Optimists
hoping that this phenomenon was more a cyclical aberration
than a long-term trend may be largely disappointed to learn
about the remarkably small improvement during the 1970s.
Although absolute income thresholds have continued to rise
for all groups, the absolute income differentials increased
rather than decreased between 1971 and 1977. However, as
shown in Table 13.8, the ratio of the Chicano median family
income to that of the total population remained remarkably
stable.[21]
    Failure of the aggregate Chicano family income levels
to improve relative to the levels characteristic of the
total population is not inconsistent with economic betterment at the individual level, but neither is there any
assurance that this is in fact occurring. One reason is
that per capita income levels depend on the proportion of
the total population actively engaged in the labor force.
Two additional considerations are pertinent; the number of
earners per family and the wage rates corresponding to
individual workers. Regarding the first point, distress-
ingly few data are available for the population as a whole,
although it is well known that migrant labor family incomes
are frequently below poverty thresholds in spite of the
fact that several members contribute to the income resources
(Smith 1976; Burawoy 1976). Analyses of earnings for nonagricultural Chicano workers are not promising because
results also show low economic rewards relative to Anglos
(Carliner 1976; Poston et al. 1976; Romero 1979).
    Work income is a product of individual differences in
ability, human capital, and pay scales set by employers.
Wage levels are also circumscribed in significant ways by
geographic and regional factors where labor supply and
demand are out of balance. Although there is no doubt that
low levels of formal education and vocational training play
an important role in relegating Chicanos to low-paying jobs

Table 13.8. Median Family Income for Total and
Mexican-Origin Population in the United States,
1971-1978

Year	Total	Mexican-Origin	Mexican-Origin as Percentage of Total
	$	$	%
1971	10,285	7,486	73
1973	12,051	8,434	70
1975	13,719	9,546	70
1977	16,009	11,742	73

Source: U.S. Bureau of the Census, Current Population Reports, series P-20, No. 238, Table 9; No.
267, Table 9; No. 302, Table 9; No. 328, Table 9,
1978.

with limited occupational mobility (Chiswick 1977; Smith
1976; Moore 1976), this begs the question about why different rates of return to education should correspond to
racial and ethnic groups. The continuing out-migration of
Chicanos from nonmetro areas to metro areas can basically
be explained in terms of the desire to improve monetary
rewards (Price 1970). Because of a more diversified range
of high wage possibilities, even in the blue-collar occupational categories, Chicano incomes are notably higher in
metro areas, irrespective of region. As shown in Figure
13.1, metro residence afforded Chicanos a $2,500 family
income advantage over nonmetro residence (U.S. Bureau of
the Census, CPR, series P-20, no. 280, Table 15). By 1976
the absolute dollar advantage of metro family income had
decreased by almost $600, but on the average, it remained
almost $2,000 higher than nonmetro family income (U.S.
Bureau of the Census, CPR, series P-20, no. 329, Table 28).
Moreover, in nonmetro areas, nonfarm incomes are consistently higher than farm incomes.
    Still another dimension of income differentials among
Chicanos is the regional factor. As noted above, since the
early 1930s there has been a movement to the Midwest, which
was largely motivated by a desire for better work and pay
conditions, yet the majority of all Chicanos reside in the
Southwest. Because of the different opportunities in the

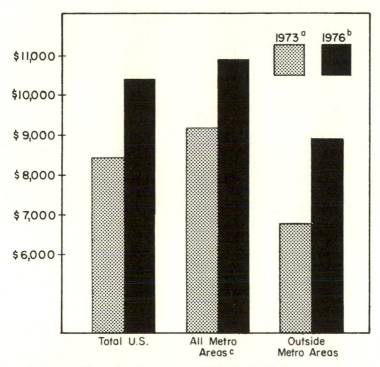

^a Current Population Report, no. 280, Table 15.
^b Current Population Report, no. 329, Table 28.
^c All Metro Areas, 1976 -- Aggregate for all central cities is
$10,322 and for noncentral cities is $11,411.

Figure 13.1 Median Income of Mexican-Origin Families by
Metropolitan/Nonmetropolitan Residence, 1973 and 1976

Midwest and Southwest, significant regional discrepancies
in income thresholds persist. Specifically, the 1975 median
family income of Chicanos residing in the Midwest was approximately $3,000 higher than that of families in the
Southwest, but the income advantage of midwestern Chicano
families is reduced by one-half when compared to regions
other than the Southwest.[22]

Solutions to regional economic inequities have been the
subject of considerable academic dialogue, but consensus
about viable and realistic solutions has not been reached.
The contradictions of an economic system that permits Hidalgo County in south Texas to lead the state in total

farm income while rendering its residents the lowest per
capita income (Miller 1976) require more imaginative and
constructive policy solutions than restrictive border policies, relocation assistance programs, or improvements of
social welfare benefits. Anything short of an alteration
of the ownership of land and capital and a strengthening of
the industrial base is likely to do relatively little to
change income possibilities of rural Chicanos. Otherwise,
poverty and social deprivation will persist.

Although the existence of widespread poverty among
nonmetro Chicanos has been known for some time, before 1973
there existed no single major work devoted to the study of
Chicano poverty. In spite of the fact that the poverty
literature expanded rapidly in the 1960s, very few of the
major writings even mentioned Chicanos. Moreover, the few
exceptions did so in a very minor way (see Rochin 1973).
Relatively little attention has been devoted to the study
of farm workers until the mid-1960s, and then, only in a
sporadic fashion (for a review of this literature, see
Miller 1975). Yet, although Chicanos comprised about 5
percent of the population in 1970, they represented 31
percent of all the poor in the Southwest. Stated in different terms, whereas the incidence of poverty among white
persons in the Southwest was 5.6 percent in 1970, comparable
rates were 26.6 and 21.1 percent for blacks and Chicanos
respectively (Rochin, 1973: Table 3). Rates of poverty
among Chicanos are considerably higher in nonmetro areas.
In 1970, the incidence of Chicano poverty in the urban
Southwest was 21 percent compared to 32 and 28 percent for
nonmetro nonfarm and farm areas respectively (Rochin, 1973:
Table 6).

As shown in Table 13.9, during the 1970s there was a
fairly modest decline in the incidence of poverty among
Chicano families. Specifically, from 1969 to 1975 the proportion of metro families with below poverty incomes improved only marginally, but the circumstances in nonmetro
areas were more promising. Whereas 40 percent of all nonmetro Chicano families had incomes below the official poverty threshold in 1969, only 28 percent did so in 1975.
The proportion of near-poor families (i.e., with incomes
less than 125 percent of the poverty threshold) decreased
only slightly during this period. On an encouraging note,
the proportion of nonmetro families with income at least
one and one-half times greater than the poverty threshold
increased 33 percent. This represented a percentage point
change of 12, having risen from 36 to 48 percent. More

Table 13.9. Ratio of Family Income to Poverty Level by
Residence for Mexican-Origin Families, 1969 and 1975

Poverty Cut-Offs	Metro	Nonmetro	Southwest	Midwest[a]	Rest of Nation
	%	%	%	%	%
1969					
Below poverty	22.1	39.5	26.6	20.5	11.1
100 to 124% above	9.2	13.2	10.3	8.9	6.2
125 to 149% above	8.5	10.9	8.9	9.1	9.5
150% or more	60.2	36.5	54.2	61.5	73.3
Total	100.0	100.1	100.0	100.0	100.1
1975					
Below poverty	21.4	28.3	23.1	12.0	20.6
100 to 124% above	9.6	10.9	10.0	6.9	8.0
125 to 149% above	8.0	12.7	9.5	7.7	7.3
150% or more	61.0	48.1	57.5	73.4	64.1
Total	100.0	100.0	100.1	100.0	100.0

Source: 1960 and 1970 Public Use Samples of Basic Records
from the 1970 Census: Description and Technical Documentation, Washington, D.C.; Survey of Income and Education,
Washington, D.C.: Bureau of Labor Statistics, 1976.

[a]Includes Michigan, Illinois, Indiana, and Ohio.

recent data reinforce the results shown in Table 13.9. For
the nation as a whole, the incidence of poverty among Chicanos was 21 percent in 1977 whereas the comparable shares
for metro and nonmetro areas were 20 and 25 percent respectively (U.S. Bureau of the Census, CPR, series P-60,
no. 119, Table 42). The incidence of poverty was twice as
high for individuals living in female headed households.
    Changes in the number of poor families among the broad
geographic regions indicate, as expected, that much greater

improvements in the economic welfare of Chicano families
were made in the midwestern states as compared to the southwestern states where the majority of Chicanos reside. In
the Southwest the incidence of poverty among Chicano families decreased from 27 to 23 percent during the early 1970s,
but in the Midwest the decline in the incidence of poverty
was much more dramatic, dropping from 20 to 12 percent in a
six-year period. This is not surprising given the greater
diversity of better-paying blue-collar jobs in the large
industrial midwestern cities. On the other hand, the probability of being poor for Chicano families residing outside
of these two areas almost doubled between 1969 and 1975.
There is no obvious explanation for these results except,
unfortunately, for the possible chance variation due to the
sampling design of the Survey of Income and Education.
Nevertheless, it is imperative to monitor more closely
regional discrepancies in the incidence of poverty, particularly the pattern of convergence between the Midwest
and Southwest regions, to determine with more precision the
underlying sources of variation and their sustaining
circumstances.

CONCLUSIONS

Currently, a very popular explanation for the relatively
disadvantaged status of Chicanos vis-à-vis Anglos is that
much of the population is foreign born and also from low-
status backgrounds. From this perspective, Galarza's (1971)
"escalator" metaphor appropriately characterizes the significance of Mexican immigration for the persistent generational and socioeconomic diversity of the Chicano population. Presumably, the foreign born represent the newest
generations that enter at the bottom of the socioeconomic
structure whereas the second and later generations are
better represented at higher levels of the socioeconomic
escalator.

      If this view is approximately correct, there are many
qualifications that must be noted because, as has been
demonstrated elsewhere (Peñalosa 1968 and Briggs et al.
1977), the incomes of third-generation Chicanos are not
much better than those of the second generation. This fact
is partly attributed to the older Hispano settlements that
have been traditionally concentrated in isolated rural
enclaves (Briggs et al. 1977), but as these groups become a

smaller share of the total, this explanation is weakened.
Obviously, the escalator metaphor only represents a tip of
the iceberg. Thus, one priority item on future research
agendas should be the task of spelling out more explicitly
the social, economic, and demographic dimensions of the
impact of Mexican immigration on the Chicano population.
Once these impacts are identified, the sensible approaches
for dealing with them will be more apparent.

The future impact of the continued influx of low-skill
workers from Mexico is an especially pertinent consideration
for further labor market analysis. Unfortunately, the significance of a substantial flow of legal and illegal immigrants from Mexico on future employment conditions in
nonmetro areas will remain an unknown until more precise
estimates of the volume and settlement patterns of foreign-
born workers are provided (Rochin 1978). Fogel (1974) maintains that the direction of the impact of sustained immigration from Mexico is clear in that wages will be lower
than they would ordinarily be in the absence of a steady
pool of cheap, foreign labor, but he acknowledges that the
magnitudes will depend on the extent of concentration or
dispersal of immigrant laborers. Presently this area of
impact assessment is a fertile ground for speculation. Both
Briggs (1973, 1975) and Fogel (1974) subscribe to the thesis that the major burden of the influx of Mexican labor
to the United States has been borne by Chicanos. The basic
problem is that this assertion has not been empirically
demonstrated in any compelling manner, but rather arrived
at tautologically from an analysis of the depressed circumstances of the Chicanos. Such reductionist conclusions reflect the significant changes in the aspirations and rising
expectations of the Chicano population as the bases of
social comparison changed and the accumulated disadvantages
of a legacy of unequal treatment surfaced (Alvarez 1973).

Besides the increasing proportion of low-skill foreign-
born workers from Mexico, three additional factors have
been identified to explain the comparatively low earnings
of Chicano workers. These are: (1) low levels of educational
attainment and technical skills; (2) geographic concentration along the United States-Mexican border, where incomes
are characteristically low; and (3) various forms of labor
market discrimination (Briggs et al. 1977). Providing Chicanos with more schooling and technical skills that can
facilitate their entry into higher-status positions is
needed, but will not by itself bring about occupational
parity with the Anglo population. In addition, individual

employers, including those paying relatively high wages, must be willing to make promotional decisions that do not discriminate against Chicanos. This clearly calls for a better enforcement of affirmative action and equal opportunity legislation. However, in the absence of solid enforcement policies, it is unlikely that existing legislation will contribute to bringing about these changes. Moreover, once Chicano workers gain entry into higher-status occupations, employment in low-wage establishments can still hurt their earnings considerably (Briggs et al. 1977). In this connection, it is important to emphasize that moves away from blue-collar industrial jobs do not always result in higher incomes because white-collar jobs sometimes pay less than average wages. The continued pattern of relative concentration in nondurable goods production and the recent shift to the professional and related service industry categories speak to this issue.

Agricultural activites continue to provide employment for nonmetro Chicanos. Despite the continuing decreases in the proportion of Chicanos employed in agriculture, including the migratory hired hands (Choldin and Trout 1969; Smith 1976), Chicanos continue to be disproportionately represented among the ranks of the farm workers (Rochin 1973). This means that many are subjected to low standards of living with their attendant implications for limited mobility (Galarza 1968; Hawkes et al. 1973; Gecas 1973; McDonagh 1948-49) and social acceptance (McDonagh 1955; Perry and Snyder 1971; and Snyder and Perry 1970).

Looking to the future, a major consideration that deserves attention is the significance of continued rapid population growth--both through high fertility and continued immigration--for the employment conditions likely to be experienced over the next decade or so. Bradshaw's (1976) analysis of potential labor force supply in the Texas-Mexico border region does not suggest that employment problems in the Southwest will diminish. Similarly, Miller (1976) and Hansen and Gruben's (1971) assessments of the possibilities for expanding employment opportunities in economically depressed areas such as in the lower Rio Grande valley of south Texas are not very encouraging.

To summarize, improvements in the general economic well-being of Chicanos in nonmetro America depend largely upon increased entry to higher-paying jobs. This does not necessarily imply industrial jobs in metro areas because, as noted above, many Chicano migrants would willingly return to their places of origin provided that economic op-

portunities improved. In many senses, therefore, the potential for return migration to nonmetro areas among Chicanos depends on the success of nonmetro development efforts. The development of manpower programs to provide
education and skill levels required for other types of
employment can only be a partial solution to increasing
nonfarm employment opportunities. Program development and
implementation efforts should consider also the characteristics of Chicano workers, which may indicate special manpower training needs. Specifically, their high degree of
migrancy, strong agricultural backgrounds, and educational
disabilities need to be considered in program formulation
(Smith 1976). It bears repeating that education is only a
partial remedy and must be recognized as a necessary, but
clearly insufficient solution. It is associated with changes
in the supply and not the demand for workers. Concomitant
changes in the structure of employment must also occur for
supply and demand to coincide.

NOTES

1. The terms "Mexican-American" and "Chicano" are used
interchangeably throughout this paper to refer to the population of Mexican origin and descent, irrespective of
generational status. However, the terms differ in sociopolitical connotation, as discussed in Miller (1976) and
Peñalosa (1970b). The term "Chicano" rather than "Mexican-
American" appears to be more closely associated with the
rising level of ethnic consciousness and the movement for
equitable treatment (Briggs et al. 1977).

2. Hispanic group categories conventionally used by
the U.S. Bureau of Census include: Mexican-American (Chicano), Puerto Rican, Cuban, Central and South American, and
Other Spanish (presumably from Spain or other Spanish-
speaking island groups).

3. According to Broadbent (1941), only four cities
(San Antonio, Laredo, El Paso, and Los Angeles) had Mexican-
descent populations greater than 5,000 each and only in El
Paso did the number of Mexicans exceed 10,000.

4. The term "generation" is used to reflect broad periods of time during which the socioeconomic and demographic
experience of the Chicano population was similar.

5. The following generational categories were adapted
from Alvarez (1971 and 1973).

6. Members of the previous generation, particularly those who had attained middle-class status, had mixed reactions to the movement, particularly the more militant aspects, which rejected outright the Anglo culture. From their perspective, the definitive test had to be the demonstration that upward social mobility does not require a complete shedding of ethnicity and total assimilation, but the convincing proof is yet to come.

7. For example, in the 1930 Census "race" (Mexican) was used whereas "Spanish mother tongue" was used in 1940 to identify persons of Mexican origin or descent (Estrada et al. 1977). Some improvement came in both 1950 and 1960 with the introduction of "Spanish surname" to identify Mexican-Americans, but this term was restricted to the population residing in the five southwestern states. Moreover, because the surname criterion was applied to only 15 percent of the population, estimates for small areas are subject to considerable sampling error. The Spanish-surname criterion was used again in 1970, but a sample item about Spanish origin which differentiated the Hispanic national origin groups was also included. In 1980, this item will be used as a 100 percent item and hopefully will permit an accurate estimate of the Mexican-origin population in the United States for the first time.

8. The simple fact that estimates of the Chicano population for the Southwest based on the Spanish-surname criterion and for the entire nation based on the presumably more accurate Spanish (Mexican) origin item both rendered a count of 4.5 million in 1970 illustrates this point well.

9. Bullock stated, for example, that cultural values of Chicanos "have been strongly influenced by a folk or rural culture in which organized and continuous striving for future monetary gains plays little part" (1964: 149).

10. For the sake of precision all statistics will be associated with their corresponding population according to census designations rather than with the generic terms Chicano or Mexican-American. Mexican ancestry refers to those of Mexican origin or descent.

11. This refers to movement in which prospective migrants learn of opportunities and/or are provided with transportation, initial accommodation, and employment through primary social relationships with previous migrants.

12. Of course, the population of Spanish surname is not coterminous with the Mexican-origin population but, surprisingly, an almost identical number of persons of Mexican ancestry were enumerated for the U.S. as a whole.

13. Because of the difficulties of separating permanent entrants from the total gross flow, it is not possible to arrive at a quantitatively precise estimate of temporary and permanent immigrants from Mexico. Briggs (1973) and his associates (Briggs et al. 1977) have illustrated how various types of visas available to Mexicans further complicate the task of assessing the population impact of immigration from Mexico. More recent analysts (Heer 1979; North 1978) have addressed themselves to the problem of illegal immigration and have attempted to quantify the magnitude of undocumented immigration and, in particular, to arrive at "reasonable" estimates of the permanent and temporary illegal aliens, but the size of the undocumented alien population is not known.

14. The proportion of farm laborers for the 1974 cohort of Mexican immigrants is 4 percent--essentially the same as for the total cohort of immigrants during that fiscal year.

15. Although there is no conclusive evidence to demonstrate that Mexicans make poor Chicanos poorer as Briggs (1973) maintains, there is no doubt that the presence of low-skill immigrant workers is reflected in the aggregate socioeconomic composition of the population.

16. Until recently, employment statistics were not tabulated separately for persons of Spanish origin except for once a year. Since 1973, labor force statistics have been tabulated separately as part of the monthly survey of the U.S. labor force. However, in most monthly surveys, the sample sizes are too small to permit detailed tabulations by specific Hispanic subpopulations because the high degree of sampling variability subjects the estimates to a high degree of error (McKay 1974).

17. The 1973 unemployment rate of 7.5 percent of all Hispanics was more than halfway between the rate of 4.3 percent recorded for white workers and 9.3 percent for black workers. Thus, while workers of Spanish origin accounted for over 6 percent of total unemployment, they represented only 4 percent of the labor force (McKay 1974).

18. Workers of Mexican ancestry were slightly more likely to be employed in agriculture (about 5 percentage points) than the Spanish-surname population of the Southwest. Except for agricultural activities in which Chicanos are disproportionately represented, the industry distribution of the Spanish-surname and Mexican-origin populations are quite similar. More specifically, the Index of Dissimi-

larity between columns (2) and (3) is .72 percent and
between columns (3) and (5) is .5 percent.

19. The Index of Dissimilarity indicates the number
of shifts required for two distributions to be equal. Indexes of 21 and 18 percent were produced by comparing the
1960-70 nonmetro Southwest and the 1970-76 nonmetro U.S.
industry distribution of Chicano workers.

20. This includes activities that may represent para-
professional and menial occupations, such as medical and
health services; hospitals; legal services; educational
services; welfare and religious services; nonprofit membership organizations, etc.

21. It is unclear to what extent the apparent failure
of family income of the Mexican-origin population to improve relative to that of the total population may result
from differential coverage of low-income and foreign-born
workers in the various survey years because the CPR estimates are subject to large standard errors. However, it is
certain that greater demands are placed on the economic
resources of Chicano families because of their relatively
larger family sizes.

22. These results are based on special tabulations of
the Survey of Income and Education and may not be directly
comparable to those based on Current Population Surveys.
Because there are no comparable published statistics
available, these figures should be regarded as tentative.

BIBLIOGRAPHY

Alvarez, Rodolfo. "The Psycho-historical and Socioeconomic
    Development of the Chicano Community in the United
    States." Social Science Quarterly 54 (1973): 920-42.
    _____. "The Psycho-historical Experience of the
    Mexican-American People." Social Science Quarterly 52
    (1971): 15-29.
Amaguer, Tomas. "Historical Notes on Chicano Oppression:
    The Dialectics of Racial and Class Domination in North
    America." Aztlan 5 (1974).
Anderson, James G., and Evans, Frances B. "Family Social-
    ization and Educational Achievement in Two Cultures:
    Mexican American and Anglo American." Sociometry 39
    (1976): 209-22.
Bean, Frank D. et al. "Familism and Marital Satisfaction
    Among Mexican Americans: The Effects of Family Size,

Wife's Labor Force Participation, and Conjugal Power."
Journal of Marriage and the Family 39 (1977): 759-66.
Beegle, Allan J.; Goldsmith, Harold F.; and Loomis, Charles
P. "Demographic Characteristics of the United States-
Mexican Border." _Rural Sociology_ 25 (1960): 107-62.
Blevins, Audie L., Jr. "Socioeconomic Differences Between
Migrants and Nonmigrants." _Rural Sociology_ 36 (1971):
509-20.
Bogardus, Emory Stephen. "The Mexican Immigrant and Segre-
gation." _American Journal of Sociology_ 36 (1965): 74-80.
_____. "Second Generation Mexicans." _Sociology and
Social Research_ 13 (1928-29): 276-83.
Bradshaw, B. S. "Potential Labor-Force Supply, Replacement,
and Migration of Mexican-American and Other Males in
Texas-Mexico Border Region." _International Migration
Review_ 10 (1976): 29-45.
_____, and Bean, Frank D. "Some Aspects of Fertility
of Mexican Americans." In _Demographic and Social
Aspects_, vol. 1, edited by Charles F. Westoff and
Robert Parke, Jr., pp. 141-64. Commission on Population
Growth and the American Future, Research Reports, 1972.
_____. "Trends in the Fertility of Mexican Americans:
1950-1970." _Social Science Quarterly_ 53 (1973): 668-96.
Briggs, Vernon M. _Chicanos and Rural Poverty_. Baltimore,
Md.: Johns Hopkins University Press, 1973.
_____. "Mexican Workers in the U.S. Labor Market."
International Labor Review 112 (1975): 351-68.
Briggs, Vernon M., Jr.; Fogel, Walter; and Schmidt, Fred H.
The Chicano Worker. Austin, Tex.: University of Texas
Press, 1977.
Broadbent, Elizabeth. "Mexican Population in Southwestern
United States." _Texas Geographic Magazine_ 5 (1941).
Bullock, Paul. "Employment Problems of the Mexican Ameri-
can." _Industrial Relations_ 3 (1964): 35-50.
Burawoy, Michael. "The Functions and Reproduction of Migrant
Labor: Comparative Material from Southern Africa and the
U.S." _American Journal of Sociology_ 81 (1976): 1050-87.
Bustamente, Jorge. "Structural and Ideological Conditions
of the Mexican Undocumented Immigration to the United
States." _American Behavioral Scientist_ 19 (1976):
364-76.
Carliner, Geoffrey. "Returns to Education for Blacks, Anglos
and Five Spanish Groups." _Journal of Human Resources_ 11
(1976): 172-84.
Chiswick, Barry R. "An Analysis of Earnings Among Mexican
Origin Men." _Proceedings of the Business and Statistics_

Section of the American Statistical Association, 1977.
Choldin, Harvey M., and Trout, Grafton D. "Mexican Americans
    in Transition: Migration and Employment in Michigan
    Cities." Final Report to U.S. Department of Labor.
    Department of Sociology, Rural Manpower Center and
    Agricultural Experiment Station, Michigan State Univer-
    sity, East Lansing, Mich., 1969.
Downes, Richard. "The Future Consequences of Illegal Immi-
    gration." The Futurist 11 (1977): 125-27.
Durant, Thomas J., and Knowlton, Clark S. "Rural Ethnic
    Minorities: Adaptive Responses to Inequality." In Rural
    U.S.A.: Persistence and Change, edited by Thomas R.
    Ford, pp. 145-67. Ames, Iowa: Iowa State University
    Press, 1978.
Dworkin, Anthony G. "Stereotypes and Self-images Held by
    Native-born and Foreign-born Mexican-Americans."
    Sociology and Social Research 49 (1965): 214-24.
Eberstein, Isaac, and Parker, W. Frisbie. "Differences in
    Marital Instability Among Mexican-Americans, Blacks and
    Anglos: 1960 and 1970." Social Problems 23 (1976):
    609-21.
Edington, E., and Hays, L. "Difference in Family Size and
    Marriage Age Expectation and Aspirations of Anglo,
    Mexican Americans and Native American Rural Youth."
    Adolescence 13 (1978): 393-400.
Estrada, Leo F.; Hernández, Jose; and Alvirez, David.
    "Using Census Data to Study Spanish Heritage Population
    of the United States." In Cuantos Somos: A Demographic
    Study of the Mexican American Population, edited by
    Charles H. Teller, Leo F. Estrada, Jose Hernández, and
    David Alvirez, pp. 13-59. Austin, Tex.: The University
    of Texas, Center for Mexican American Studies, 1977.
Fogel, Walter. "Mexican Labor in U.S. Labor Markets." In
    Industrial Relations Research Association Series,
    Proceedings of 27th Annual Winter Meeting, edited by J.
    L. Stern and B. D. Dennis, pp. 343-49. 1974.
Forbes, Jack D. "The Mexican Heritage of the U.S.: An His-
    torical Summary." In Educating the Mexican American,
    edited by Henry Sious Johnson and William G. Hernandez.
    Valley Forge, Pa.: Judson Press, 1970.
Francis, E. K. "Multiple Intergroup Relations in the Upper
    Rio Grande Region." American Sociological Review 21
    (1956): 84-87.
Galarza, Ernesto. "The Mexican-American Migrant Worker--
    Culture and Powerlessness." Integrated Education 9
    (1971): 17-21.

_____. "Rural Community Development." El Grito 1 (1968): 22-27.

Gandara, Arturo. "The Chicano/Illegal-Alien Civil Liberties Interface." Paper presented at joint national meetings of LASA and African Studies Association, Houston, Tex., 1977.

Gecas, Viktor. "Self-Conception of Migrant and Settled Mexican Americans." Social Science Quarterly 54 (1973): 579-95.

Grebler, Leo; Moore, Joan W.; and Guzman, Ralph C. The Mexican-American People: The Nation's Second Largest Minority. New York: The Free Press, 1970.

Hansen, Niles M. "The Mexican Americans." In Rural Poverty and the Urban Crisis, pp. 193-221. Bloomington, Ind.: Indiana University Press, 1970.

_____, and Gruben, William C. "The Influence of Relative Wages and Assisted Migration on Locational Preferences: Mexican-Americans in South Texas." Social Science Quarterly 52 (1971): 103-14.

Hawkes, Glenn; and Taylor, Minna. "Power Structure in Mexican and Mexican-American Farm Labor Families." Journal of Marriage and the Family 37 (1975): 807-11.

_____; and Bastian, Beverly E. "Patterns of Living in California's Migrant Labor Families." Research Monograph no. 12, Department of Applied Behavioral Sciences, University of California-Davis, 1973.

Heer, David M. "What is the Annual Net Flow of Undocumented Mexican Immigrants to the U.S.?" Demography 16 (1979): 417-23.

Heller, Celia. "Class as an Explanation of Ethnic Differences in Upward Mobility--The Case of Mexican Americans." In Structured Social Equality, edited by Celia Heller, pp. 396-402. 1969.

Henggeler, Scott W., and Tavormina, Joseph B. "The Children of Mexican-American Migrant Workers: A Population at Risk." Journal of Abnormal Child Psychology 6 (1978): 97-106.

Hernández, Jose. "A Demographic Profile of the Mexican Immigration to the United States, 1910-1950." Journal of Inter-American Studies 8 (1966): 471-96.

Knowlton, Clark. "Changing Spanish American Villages of Northern New Mexico." Sociology and Social Research 53 (1969): 455-74.

_____. "The Spanish Americans in New Mexico." Sociology and Social Research 45 (1961): 448-55.

Lamare, James W. "The Political World of the Rural Chicano

Child." <u>American Politics Quarterly</u> 5 (1977): 83-108.

Leonard, Olen E., and Hannon, John H. "Those Left Behind: Recent Social Changes in a Heavy Emigration Area of North Central New Mexico." <u>Human Organization</u> 36 (1977): 384-94.

Loomis, Charles P. "A Backward Glance at Self-identification of Blacks and Chicanos." <u>Rural Sociology</u> 39 (1974): 96.

_____. "Ethnic Cleavages in the Southwest." <u>Sociometry</u> 6 (1943): 7-26.

_____. "Informal Groupings in a Spanish American Village." <u>Sociometry</u> 4 (1941): 36-55.

Lopez, David E. "Chicano Language Loyalty in an Urban Setting." <u>Sociology and Social Research</u> 62 (1977): 267-78.

_____. "The Social Consequences of Chicano Home/School Bilingualism." <u>Social Problems</u> 24 (1976): 234-46.

McDonagh, Edward C. "Attitudes Towards Ethnic Farm Workers in Coachella Valley." <u>Sociology and Social Research</u> 40 (1955): 10-18.

_____. "Status Levels of Mexicans." <u>Sociology and Social Research</u> 33 (1948-49): 449-59.

McKay, Roberta. "Employment and Unemployment Among Americans of Spanish Origin." <u>Monthly Labor Review</u> 97 (1974): 12-16.

McLemore, Dale S. "The Origins of Mexican-American Subordination in Texas." <u>Social Science Quarterly</u> 53 (1973): 656-70.

Marcum, John P., and Bean, Frank. "Minority Group Status as a Factor in the Relationship Between Mobility and Fertility: The Mexican-American Case." <u>Social Forces</u> 55 (1976): 135-48.

Marshall, Kimbal P., and Miller, Michael V. "Status and Familial Orientations of Rural Mexican-American Youth: Integration and Conflict Within Aspirational Frames of References." <u>Journal of Vocational Behavior</u> 11 (1977): 347-62.

Miller, Michael V. "Mexican-American and Mexican National Farm Workers: A Literature Review." Paper presented at Annual Meeting of Rural Sociological Society, San Francisco, Calif., August 1975.

_____. "Mexican-Americans, Chicanos and Others: Ethnic Self-identification and Selected Social Attributes of Rural Texas Youth." <u>Rural Sociology</u> 41 (1976): 234-37.

_____. "Poverty and Problems of Development in the Lower Rio Grande Valley of Texas." Cooperative State Research Service (Department of Administration), Washington, D.C., February 1976.

_____, and Maril, Robert Lee. "Poverty in the Lower
   Rio Grande Valley of Texas: Historical and Contemporary
   Dimensions." College Station, Tex.: Texas A&M Univer-
   sity, 1978.
Mirandé, Alfredo. "The Chicano Family: A Reanalysis of
   Conflicting Views." Journal of Marriage and the Family
   39 (1977): 747-56.
Mittelbach, Frank G., and Moore, Joan W. "Ethnic Endogamy--
   The Case of Mexican Americans." In Mexican-Americans in
   the United States, edited by John H. Burma. Cambridge,
   Mass.: Schenkman Publishing Company, Inc., 1970.
Montiel, Miguel. "The Social Science Myth of the Mexican
   American Family." El Grito 3 (1970): 56-63.
Moore, Joan W. "Colonialism: The Case of the Mexican Ameri-
   can." Social Problems 17 (1970): 463-72.
   _____. Mexican-Americans. 2nd ed. Englewood Cliffs,
   N.J.: Prentice-Hall, Inc. 1976.
Murguia, Edward. Assimilation, Colonialism and the Mexican
   American People. Austin, Tex.: University of Texas,
   Center for Mexican American Studies, 1975.
   _____, and Frisbie, W. Parker. "Trends in Mexican
   American Intermarriage: Recent Findings in Perspective."
   Social Science Quarterly 58 (1977): 374-89.
Neal, Justin. "Mexican-American Achievement Hindered by
   Culture Conflict." Sociology and Social Research 56
   (1972): 471-79.
Newman, Morris J. "A Profile of Hispanics in the U.S. Work
   Force." Monthly Labor Review 101 (1978): 3-14.
North, David S. Seven Years Later: The Experiences of the
   1970 Cohort of Immigrants in the U.S. Labor Market.
   Washington, D.C.: Linton and Co., Inc., 1978.
Patella, Victoria, and Kuvlesky, William P. "Situational
   Variation in Language Patterns of Mexican-American Boys
   and Girls." Social Science Quarterly 53 (1973): 855-64.
Peñalosa, Fernando. "Education-Income Discrepancies Between
   Second and Later Generation Mexican-Americans in the
   Southwest." Sociology and Social Research 53 (1969):
   448-54.
   _____. "Recent Changes Among the Chicanos." Sociology
   and Social Research 55 (1970b): 47-52.
   _____. "A Socio-economic Class Typology of Mexican-
   Americans." Sociological Inquiry 36 (1966): 19-30.
   _____. "Toward an Operational Definition of the
   Mexican-American." Aztlan 1 (1970a): 1-12.
   _____, and McDonagh, Edward C. "Education, Economic
   Status and Social Class Awareness of Mexican Americans."

Phylon 29 (1968): 119-26.

Perry, Joseph B., and Snyder, Eldon E. "Opinions of Farm Employers Toward Welfare Assistance for Mexican-American Migrant Workers." _Sociology and Social Research_ 55 (1971): 161-69.

Portes, Alejandro. "Immigration and the International System, Some Characteristics of Recent Mexican Immigrants to the U.S." Paper presented at meetings of the Society for the Study of Social Problems, San Francisco, Calif., September 1978.

Poston, Dudley L.; Alvirez, David; and Tienda, Marta. "Earnings Differences Between Anglo and Mexican-American Male Workers in 1960 and 1970: Changes in the 'Cost' of Being Mexican American." _Social Science Quarterly_ 57 (1976): 618-31.

Price, Daniel O. "Rural to Urban Migration of Mexican-Americans, Negroes and Anglos." _International Migration Review_ 5 (1970): 281-91

Rochin, Refugio I. "Economic Deprivation of Chicanos: Continuing Neglect in the Seventies." _Aztlan_ 4 (1973): 85-99.

_____. "Illegal Aliens in Agriculture: Some Theoretical Considerations." _Labor Law Journal_ (March 1978): 149-67.

Romero, Fred E. _Chicano Workers: Their Utilization and Development_. Monograph no. 8, Chicano Studies Center Publications. Los Angeles: University of California, 1979.

Romo, Ricardo. "Responses to Mexican Immigration, 1919-1930." _Aztlan_ 6 (1975): 173-94.

Samora, Julian. _Los Majados: The Wetback Story_. Notre Dame, Ind.: University of Notre Dame Press, 1971.

_____, and Larson, Richard F. "Rural Families in an Urban Setting: A Study in Persistence and Change." _Journal of Human Relations_ 9 (1961): 494-503.

Skrabanek, R. L. "Language Maintenance Among Mexican-Americans." _International Journal of Comparative Sociology_ 11 (1970): 272-82.

Smith, Leslie Whitener. "Social and Economic Characteristics of Spanish-Origin Hired Farm Workers in 1973." Economic Development Division, Economic Research Service, Agricultural Economic Report no. 349. Washington, D.C.: U.S. Department of Agriculture, 1976.

Snyder, Eldon E., and Joseph B. Perry. "Farm Employer Attitudes Toward Mexican-American Migrant Workers." _Rural Sociology_ 35 (1970): 244-52.

Stoddard, Ellwyn R. "A Conceptual Analysis of the 'Alien Invasion': Institutionalized Support of Illegal Mexican Aliens in the U.S." International Migration Review 10 (1976): 156-90.

Taeuber, Irene B. "Migration and Transformation: Spanish Surname Populations." Population Index 32 (1966): 3-34.

Tienda, Marta. "Familism and Structural Assimilation of Mexican Immigrants in the U.S." International Migration Review 14 (1980): 383-408.

U.S. Bureau of the Census. Current Population Reports, series P-20, no. 230, "Characteristics of New Voters: 1972." Washington, D.C.: U.S. Government Printing Office, 1972.

_____. Current Population Reports, series P-20, no. 238. "Selected Characteristics of Persons and Families of Mexican, Puerto Rican and Other Spanish Origin: March, 1972." Washington, D.C.: U.S. Government Printing Office, 1972.

_____. Current Population Reports, series P-20, no. 267. "Persons of Spanish Origin in the United States, 1973." Washington, D.C.: U.S. Government Printing Office, 1974.

_____. Current Population Reports, series P-20, no. 280. "Persons of Spanish Origin in the U.S.: March 1974." Washington, D.C.: U.S. Government Printing Office, 1975.

_____. Current Population Reports, series P-20, no. 290. "Persons of Spanish Origin in the U.S.: March 1975." Washington, D.C.: U.S. Government Printing Office, 1976.

_____. Current Population Reports, series P-20, no. 302. "Persons of Spanish Origin in the U.S.: March 1976." Washington, D.C.: U.S. Government Printing Office, 1976.

_____. Current Population Reports, series P-20, no. 310. "Persons of Spanish Origin in the U.S.: March 1976." Washington, D.C.: U.S. Government Printing Office, 1977.

_____. Current Population Reports, series P-20, no. 328. "Persons of Spanish Origin in the U.S.: March 1978." Washington, D.C.: U.S. Government Printing Office, 1978.

_____. Current Population Reports, series P-20, no. 329. "Persons of Spanish Origin in the U.S.: March 1977." Washington, D.C.: U.S. Government Printing Office, 1978.

_____. Current Population Reports, series P-20, no. 341. "Fertility of American Women: June, 1978." Washington, D.C.: U.S. Government Printing Office, 1979.

_____. Current Population Reports, special series P-23, no. 75. "Social and Economic Characteristics of the Metropolitan and Nonmetropolitan Population: 1977 and 1970." Washington, D.C.: U.S. Government Printing Office, 1978.

_____. Current Population Reports, series P-60, no. 119. "Characteristics of the Population Below the Poverty Level: 1977." Washington, D.C.: U.S. Government Printing Office, 1979.

_____. U.S. Census of Population: 1950. Vol. 4, pt. 3, chap. C. Washington, D.C.: U.S. Government Printing Office, 1953.

_____. U.S. Census of Population: 1960. Subject Reports. Persons of Spanish Surname. Final Report PC(2)-1B. Washington, D.C.: U.S. Government Printing Office, 1963.

_____. U.S. Census of Population: 1970. Subject Reports. Persons of Spanish Origin. Final Report PC(2)-1C. Washington, D.C.: U.S. Government Printing Office, 1973.

_____. U.S. Census of Population: 1970. Subject Reports. Persons of Spanish Surname. Final Report PC(2)-1D. Washington, D.C.: U.S. Government Printing Office, 1973.

Watson, James B., and Samora, Julian. "Subordinate Leadership in a Bicultural Community: An Analysis." American Sociological Review 19 (1954): 413-21.

Wood, Charles H., and Bean, Frank. "Offspring Gender and Family Size: Implications from a Comparison of Mexican-Americans and Anglo-Americans." Journal of Marriage and the Family 39 (1977): 129-39.

IV.

The Distribution
of Amenities

Wilbur R. Thompson
James J. Mikesell

14

Housing Supply and Demand

Most would agree that, lacking a direct measure of wealth,
income is the single best indicator of material well-being;
but for most households housing "condition" would be the
next best measure. Housing in rural areas is generally
perceived to be inferior, in large part because incomes are
lower there. But one of the main purposes of this chapter
is to look beyond income as it limits access to housing,
into the comparative price of housing (corrected for quantity and quality differences) in places large and small, to
see if rural households are twice burdened by both income
and cost.

Because we add only about 2 percent to our housing stock
each year, most of us live in housing that was built a few
or many years ago. Because many of us are second, third, or
later users of our residence, the nature of house "filtering" is examined in some detail. Filtering theory deserves
review not only because of its inherent importance but also
because it was conceived in a big city context and has not
been reconsidered and modified to fit smaller places.

Finally, our attention turns to the impact of growth
on local housing markets, both because rapid growth and
decline leave in their wake housing shortages and surpluses
and because smaller local economies would seem likely to
experience greater variations in rate of growth in employment, population, and households.

The opening section begins by reviewing, in a matter-
of-fact way, the housing picture in metro and nonmetro
America, describing some of the differences in housing

The authors wish to acknowledge the ideas and general feel
for this topic which were gained from Ronald Bird's talk,
"Status of Housing in Nonmetropolitan Areas," presented at
the National Agricultural Outlook Conference in Washington,
D.C., 14 November 1978; and from a background paper, "Rural
Housing," written in 1979 by Earl W. Morris and Mary Winter
of Iowa State University.

units, the people who live in those homes, and financial aspects of home purchase. Thus, the stage is set for the primary focus on how local rural housing markets operate, with emphasis placed on the influences of density and scale, and more generally those factors that differ by general degree of rurality/urbanity.

NONMETROPOLITAN AND METROPOLITAN
HOUSING DIFFERENCES: A DESCRIPTION

Basic characteristics of the national housing stock change slowly. Although housing construction is subject to cyclical fluctuation new units total about 2 to 3 percent of the housing stock each year. Therefore, data in this study, generally descriptive of the housing situation near the end of 1977 (as taken from the 1977 Annual Housing Survey) are sufficiently current for most uses.[1] Also comparing 1970 to 1977--a period of rapid household formation and economic change--can improve our understanding of filtering and the dynamics of housing markets. In nearly every year of the 1970s more homes (both mobile and built on the site) were completed in nonmetro America than were completed in any prior year, leading to the recent historical peak level.

Although there is significant governmental involvement in housing markets--particularly in the areas of finance and special assistance for low-income households--the construction, purchasing, and renting of housing remain mainly private-sector activities. No attempt is made in this work to differentiate the role of the government from that of the private sector.

For most people a home is their largest purchase, indebtedness, asset, and the largest single continuing expenditure item--thus constituting the single most important material dimension of their lives.

NONMETROPOLITAN HOUSEHOLDS

The demand for housing--in quantity, quality, and characteristics--is largely determined through the marketplace, by the wants and needs of actual and potential residents. Therefore the differences between metro and nonmetro households have an important influence on the respective housing markets. Nationally, even as households are increasingly

inclined toward smaller size and unmarried status, owning
one's home is on the increase. Surely tenure--whether owner
or renter--is one of the most important characteristics
linking a household with a home; and a higher proportion of
nonmetro than metro households own their home (Table 14.1).
Although the ownership share is growing in both housing
markets it is increasing at a faster rate in nonmetro areas.
This is closely tied to the greater proportion of married
couples among nonmetro households. Such households are a
substantial proportion of the total and are increasing
their rate of homeownership more rapidly than are other
household types. The ownership share has grown, largely
from the married couple influence, despite the fact that in
both metro and nonmetro areas they show one of the slowest
rates of increase of any household type.

Nonmetro households are more often headed by an older
person or a white person. The heads of 23 percent of nonmetro households are sixty-five or older, compared to 18
percent for metro households. This proportion has remained
fairly constant in nonmetro areas, while climbing slowly in
metro areas. The nonmetro-metro difference in the proportion
of households headed by a black or other nonwhite person
has also widened so that the already higher metro level is
increasing, whereas nonmetro areas show little change.
Although growing faster, and thus having more opportunity
for change, nonmetro America is not generally part of the
national trend toward greater racial and ethnic diversity.

As discussed elsewhere in this volume, nonmetro areas
generally grew faster during the 1970s, with the South and
West together growing faster than the North Central region
and the Northeast. However, there was little nonmetro-metro
difference in growth rates in either the South or the West.
Moreover, in the Northeast, nonmetro areas grew at triple
the metro rate, although more nonmetro housholds are in the
South and fewer in the Northeast or West.

NONMETROPOLITAN HOMES

The housing stock of nonmetro areas reflects a typically
lower density of settlement. In 1977, 86 percent of nonmetro homes were detached single-unit structures, either
site-built or mobile homes (Table 14.2), compared to only
60 percent of all metro homes. Furthermore, the use of
mobile homes is rising rapidly in both areas, up over 80
percent in nonmetro areas between 1970 and 1977 and repre-

Table 14.1. Characteristics of Metropolitan and Nonmetropolitan Households in 1977 and the Change Since 1970

Characteristic	Number of Housing Units in 1977		Percentage of Housing Units in 1977		Percentage Change in Number of Housing Units from 1970 to 1977	
	Metro	Nonmetro	Metro	Nonmetro	Metro	Nonmetro
	(000s)	(000s)	%	%	%	%
All occupied housing units:						
Northeast	13,146	3,492	25.6	14.6	5.1	17.3
North Central	13,026	6,830	25.4	28.5	12.1	15.4
South	13,727	10,652	26.8	44.4	26.4	26.8
West	11,414	2,993	22.2	12.5	28.5	30.7
Total	51,314	23,966	100.0	100.0	17.0	22.4
Tenure:						
Owner occupied	31,286	17,479	61.0	72.9	19.9	26.7
Renter occupied	20,028	6,487	39.0	27.1	12.7	12.0
Number of persons:						
1	11,210	4,587	21.8	19.1	41.3	42.6
2	15,616	7,626	30.4	31.8	22.7	25.9
3	8,895	4,059	17.3	16.9	17.3	22.1
4	8,037	3,900	15.7	16.3	17.0	33.2
5 or more	7,556	3,702	14.7	15.8	13.6	1.6

Married couple	30,894	16,129	60.2	67.3	5.2	16.4
Other male head						
2 or more persons	2,742	976	5.3	4.1	40.5	16.6
1 person	4,416	1,620	8.6	6.8	53.9	52.4
Other female head						
2 or more persons	6,469	2,274	12.6	9.5	40.1	35.8
1 person	6,794	2,967	13.2	12.4	34.1	37.7
Head of household: 65 or older:						
Yes	9,444	5,591	18.4	23.3	20.9	22.8
No	41,870	18,375	81.6	76.7	16.2	22.2
Race:						
White	44,077	22,035	85.9	91.9	14.1	22.5
Black	6,177	1,779	12.0	7.4	30.4	24.0
Other	1,060	152	2.1	0.6	109.5	− 5.0

Source: Derived from U.S. Bureau of the Census, Annual Housing Survey: 1977, Part A.

Note: Because of rounding some totals vary slightly from the sum of their parts.

senting 8 percent of all homes there in 1977. Additionally, the use of mobile homes is substantially greater in the more rural parts of both nonmetro and metro areas.

In comparison to site-built metro homes, nonmetro units are more often either very new or very old; and including mobile homes increases the nonmetro advantage in new homes. In part the larger percentage of new homes in nonmetro areas reflects the greater population growth since 1970; and the substantial number of nonmetro homes built prior to 1940 is the legacy of past decades when an even greater proportion of people lived in rural areas.

Since 1970, nonmetro units that began the decade at ten to thirty years of age have left the housing stock at a much slower rate than their metro counterparts, reflecting a possible net upgrading of older metro homes. Although nonmetro areas lost significant numbers of homes built prior to 1940, the number of such homes in metro areas remained essentially unchanged during the 1970s.

Nonmetro areas have a higher proportion of the newest houses as well as more of the substandard units. Therefore, on the basis of commonly used indicators of inadequate housing--either a lack of complete plumbing facilities or crowding (more persons than rooms)--nonmetro housing units are of poorer quality than metro units. And whereas both metro and nonmetro housing have improved markedly since 1970, they both have improved at similar rates leaving the gap in quality substantially unchanged. But perhaps this diminishing deficiency should begin to be weighed less heavily in our evaluations of "housing condition."

These inadequately housed persons are disproportionately members of low-income, black, older-person, and single-person households. Because low income is the most critical of these characteristics, and is a more pervasive problem among nonmetro households (Mikesell, 1977: 14), the central issue then becomes whether there is a housing problem or strictly one of income--a matter to which we turn next.

HOUSING FINANCES

For the most part access to housing is determined by financial considerations, and the amount of income that can be made available to purchase housing may not be directly proportional to total income. It can be generally assumed that lower-income households can spend a smaller proportion of their income on housing, because of the need to purchase

nonhousing necessities. Other things being equal, this
would suggest that nonmetro households, with their lower
incomes, should typically be spending a smaller proportion
of their income for housing than are metro households.

But, although both incomes and housing values are lower
in nonmetro areas the median value to income ratio is the
same for metro and nonmetro owner occupants (Table 14.3).
This does not mean that at any given income equivalent
housing is equally affordable in nonmetro and metro America.
In addition to the argument that lower-income households
should spend less of that income for housing, recent increases in home values have outpaced increases in incomes
by a wider margin in nonmetro areas. Additionally, the
homes reflected in these price comparisons are not equivalent, as nonmetro homes are typically smaller and more
often of poor quality.

Measured solely by the median percentage of income
spent on rent, nonmetro residents appear to enjoy a slight
advantage; however, this may not be the case, because the
previous comparisons for nonmetro and metro owner occupants
also hold for renters. Nonmetro renters have lower incomes
and their rental units are of poorer quality; but in contrast to the situation for owners, median rent and renter
income have risen much more slowly than have home prices
and homeowner income. This seems to reflect a general lowering of the position of renters within the income distribution and of rental units within a quality distribution.
Many of those who in the past would have been renters,
although they could afford to purchase a home, are now
opting for homeownership. As discussed in the next section,
the shift to homeownership is increasingly prompted by
investment motives, especially as a hedge against inflation. In addition, a growing proportion of rental units are
likely to be smaller and more basic because of the size of
new units and the conversion of many larger, more expensive
rental properties to owner occupancy. Such conversion is
particularly easy in nonmetro areas, where most units are
detached single-unit homes.

During the last decade, high levels of construction
have combined with an increasing rate of owner occupancy.
Because this has fostered a substantial increase in the use
of long-term amortized mortgage financing, the housing
sector is particularly sensitive to a "credit crunch," when
loans become both scarce and expensive. There is also evidence that some rural areas have a chronic shortage of
mortgage credit, due in significant part to a relative

Table 14.2. Structural Characteristics of Metropolitan and Nonmetropolitan Housing Units in 1977 and the Change Since 1970

Characteristic	Number of Housing Units in 1977		Percentage of Housing Units in 1977		Percentage Change in Number of Housing Units from 1970 to 1977	
	Metro	Nonmetro	Metro	Nonmetro	Metro	Nonmetro
	(000s)	(000s)	%	%	%	%
All year-round housing units						
Structure type:						
1 unit detached	30,853	20,375	56.6	77.9	13.4	15.9
1 unit attached	2,700	405	4.9	1.5	48.8	130.1
2 to 4 units	8,291	2,127	15.2	8.1	15.4	16.7
5 or more units	11,096	1,174	20.3	4.5	24.2	31.2
Mobile homes	1,611	2,082	3.0	8.0	72.7	82.6
Total	54,552	26,164	100.0	100.0	18.4	21.0
Year structure built:						
After April 1970	9,475	5,084	17.4	19.4		
1965 to March 1970	6,280	3,064	11.5	11.7	3.9	8.2
1960 to 1964	5,886	2,221	10.8	8.5	1.4	− 2.4
1950 to 1959	10,016	3,751	18.4	14.3	− 6.5	− 1.1
1940 to 1949	5,460	2,533	10.0	9.7	−11.2	− 4.0
1939 or earlier	17,434	9,511	32.0	36.4	0.3	− 5.6

Lacking complete
plumbing

Lacking complete plumbing	916	1,625	1.7	6.2	-38.7	-44.0
Occupied housing units						
Lacking complete plumbing:						
Owner-occupied	167	518	0.5	3.0	-64.3	-56.6
Renter-occupied	480	640	2.4	9.9	-40.1	-38.9
Total	647	1,158	1.3	4.8	-49.0	-48.3
Crowded:						
Owner-occupied	949	685	3.0	3.9	-40.1	-30.5
Renter-occupied	1,150	495	5.7	7.6	-33.1	-36.2
Total	2,099	1,180	4.2	4.9	-36.4	-33.0
Lacking complete plumbing or crowded:						
Owner-occupied	1,102	1,127	3.5	6.5	-44.4	-42.6
Renter-occupied	1,587	1,011	7.9	15.6	-33.8	-33.9
Total	2,689	2,138	5.3	8.9	-38.6	-38.8

Source: Derived from U.S. Bureau of the Census, Annual Housing Survey: 1977, Part A.

Note: Because of rounding some totals vary slightly from the sum of their parts.

Table 14.3. Financial Characteristics of Metropolitan and Nonmetropolitan Households and Housing Units in 1977 and the Change Since 1970

Characteristic	1977		Change from 1970 to 1977	
	Metro	Nonmetro	Metro	Nonmetro
	Owner Occupants			
	$	$	%	%
Median income	17,800	12,900	61.8	72.0
Median value of home	39,900	30,400	110.0	149.2
	Ratio			
Median value/ income ratio[a]	2.3	2.4	27.8	35.3
	Renter Occupants			
	$	$	%	%
Median income	9,200	7,700	37.3	45.3
Median gross annual rent	2,316	1,788	69.3	77.4
	Percentage			
Rent as percentage of median income	25	23	19.0	21.1

Source: Derived from U.S. Bureau of the Census, Annual Housing Survey: 1977, Part A.

[a]These are median values of individual ratios and not ratios of the medians shown above.

scarcity in many rural areas of the nation's major mortgage lenders--savings and loan institutions (S&Ls). The shortage of S&L lenders is moreover most acute in the less dense, more remote rural areas (Spurlock, 1978: 7). This relatively short supply of mortgage credit may burden home buyers with higher down payment requirements, shorter repayment terms, more stringent tests of credit worthiness, or higher interest rates.

SIZE OF PLACE AND HOUSING DEMAND

Both cost and quantity of housing are determined by the
interaction of supply and demand. Even if new housing cost
is set from the supply side--as when supply is nearly perfectly elastic--the quantity of homes produced is still
determined by demand. In the existing home market, however,
the supply is highly inelastic (some units can be converted
from seasonal to year-round homes and from nonresidential
to residential use) and price is set by demand. There are
several ways in which housing demand in a particular market
might be influenced by the size of that market, and there
are also some basic changes that seem to have generally
influenced housing demand in the United States.

The expanded housing construction and increasing rate
of owner occupancy of the 1970s were accompanied by a rise
in housing prices that outstripped income growth and a
decline in the proportion of husband/wife households, traditionally the principal homeowners. This seems clear indication that the demand for owned housing has increased.
And, judging by the greater amount by which nonmetro housing prices have exceeded income growth, that shift has
perhaps been greater for nonmetro areas.

Overall, increased owner occupancy is probably reflected in what some view as an abnormally low propensity to
save on the part of American households. Methods of measuring savings typically view outlays on housing as consumption
expenditures, and correctly so from a macroeconomic viewpoint; however, for most home purchases the motivation of
home buyers is as much personal savings and investment as
consumption. From 1970 to 1977 the median value of nonmetro
homes rose at an average rate of 13 percent. This is faster
than the rate of increase in metro home values and encourages the perception of nonmetro homes as a good investment.

There are several factors, developed later, that may
favor rural housing as an investment and generally increase
the demand for rural via-à-vis urban homes. Urban neighborhoods, with less diversity and more competition from
alternative housing, may be more prone to accelerated deterioration. Net urban out-migration has added to housing
demand in smaller communities; and higher income enables a
number of these new rural families to purchase a home, particularly at the lower rural prices. The lack of acceptable
rental units in smaller places also adds to the incentive
for home purchase.

But homes in large communities also have their at-

tractive points as investments, casting doubt on the net
nonmetro-metro balance. The greater number of exchanges in
urban markets should improve the ease and speed with which
properties are sold and decrease the likelihood of sudden
large price declines. Furthermore, as transportation costs
rise urban houses should become more attractive to persons
who live in surrounding smaller places and commute to work
in a larger town.

It may also be that the life-style of rural communities
places a greater value on owning a home and generally has a
substantial influence on the demand for housing. Of course,
for most persons the choice of housing is not, at the margin, the selection of a necessity. Indeed most persons
are consuming much more than the minimum acceptable level
of housing, as defined by any reasonable set of societal
norms. Perhaps nonmetro households have a greater personal
preference for housing; therefore, at a given income level
they choose to spend more on housing than do their metro
counterparts. However, there is no evidence that this is
the case. In conclusion it is unclear whether there is a
nonmetro-metro difference in the demand for housing.

SIZE OF PLACE AND COST OF HOUSING:
A CONCEPTUAL FRAMEWORK

The problem of access to adequate housing is primarily an
income problem, and rural incomes are particularly low. But
some may argue that there is no rural housing problem because rural housing is correspondingly less costly. Others
may counter that, although prices of rural houses are indeed lower, they are actually more costly than urban houses
when corrections are made for quality differences. But
either position is hard to establish and defend because
of the complexity of the question, the many crosscurrents
of cost and price between rural and urban areas, and the
paucity of relevant data.

The "cost of housing" is a supply concept--the total
cost of producing a unit of housing. That "unit of housing"
has time, quantity, and quality of living dimensions; for
example, illustrating the time dimension: when two homes
are by all appearances identical, but one is expected to
have a longer average life, that home also has more units
of housing.

Housing costs range across such diverse components as:

(1) land costs, (2) construction costs, (3) maintenance
costs and building life, (4) mortgage financing costs (often affected by differential credit availability), and
(5) operating costs, including utilities and taxes. One
cannot leap to a quick and easy intuitive judgment, or good
guess, about the net result of these many and diverse factors because the position of advantage (disadvantage) of
rural and urban areas shifts so often and sizably among
these five broad components and their many subcomponents. A
first impression of the maze of comparative rural and urban
housing costs can be gained by tracing through the many
lines of relationship between the size of a "place" (local
housing market) and the cost of housing sketched in considerable (but very incomplete) detail in Figure 14.1.

LAND PRICE VERSUS SITE COST

Beginning at the top of Figure 14.1 with the land market
and land cost, we can follow the logic of growing population
size through horizontal expansion of towns into cities and
suburbs, with rising tansportation cost from the urban
(housing) fringe to downtown. Classic location theory argues that transportation costs incurred by locating farther
away from the center of things can be reduced only by competing for the relatively (and increasingly) scarce sites
nearer the center. As a first approximation, the transportation cost reduction in being closer is about equal to
(and causes) the premium land rent that must be paid for
that choice site. But some caution is in order here because
standard rent theory assumes that going to town is most
important, and does not weigh at all any benefits derived
from getting out of town and close to open space, an assumption that sets uneasily with rural analysis. Additionally,
the center city is an increasingly weak economic magnet,
particularly for employment. Nor should we confuse land
price per acre with site costs because of the normal inverse relationship between price and quantity consumed.
If, for example, the price elasticity of demand for land is
close to unity, site costs will vary little at different
land prices, with only lot size varying inversely with
price.
    One might of course argue that, because space is an
amenity, the larger house sites characteristic of rural and
small-town living are a quality difference--a consumer
preference reflected as more units of housing--and need not

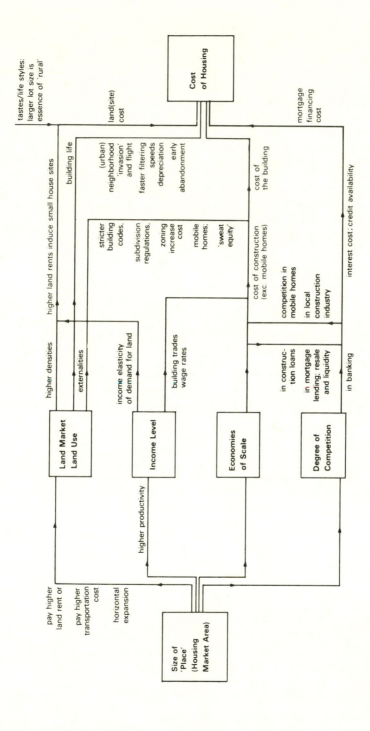

Figure 14.1 Interacting Elements That Determine Housing Cost

be introduced into a cost-price comparison. Rural or small-town households could choose to live at higher density, still having a small community, and while having little choice, urban dwellers may actually prefer small lots. If so, no adjustment is necessary in the amount of housing (measured in "units of housing") to reflect differences in lot size. Larger rural and small-town lots may be viewed simply as a difference in style of living and not a housing quality difference at all. Would a town of 5,000, where most people lived at the density typical in a city of 500,000, have "rural living?" Land prices may therefore be lower (per acre) for rural construction but rural living will change site costs in a lesser amount. Clearly, the definition of "rural" is at issue: Is it small population or low density or both? (And all of this is further complicated by land speculation, such as that in farm real estate, developed in Chapter 17.)

CONSTRUCTION COSTS: SCALE AND COMPETITION

Whatever housing cost advantages smaller settlements may enjoy in the land market may be offset by economies of scale in construction in larger places. Typically, land cost is about one-fourth the total of housing price, with labor and materials adding about one-half of the total price. Other things being equal, mass production, greater competition in the building materials sector (including economies of large-scale purchasing), and a much finer specialization of labor could more than offset the higher land costs in larger places. But other things may not be equal. Land use and construction regulations that bring compliance costs, a differential ability of home purchasers to provide some of their own construction labor, and differences in building trades wage rates and/or labor productivity favor smaller places. Besides, the residential construction industry is not noted for technologically advanced, capital-intensive processes, characteristics favoring large scale. Economies of scale may well be most notable in the mobile home industry and these are equally available to smaller places—more available to the extent that mobile homes are more welcome there. All in all, any building cost advantage to either smaller or larger places seems, deductively, to be indeterminate and likely quite small if there is any consistent relationship of housing cost to size of community.

Sheer population size offers another potential advantage in housing cost: a greater degree of competition among builders. But here again a general position favoring larger places must be modified to admit the distinctive nature of the mobile home industry. Because competition in this segment of the local housing market extends to a reasonable shipping distance, say, two hundred miles, small places that are not extremely isolated do enjoy the benefit of competition from this kind of housing, provided that mobile-home sites are readily available. Competitive prices for these units tend, moreover, to keep the prices of conventional housing more in line, to the extent that they are regarded as good substitutes for the latter. Again, the building cost disadvantage of smaller places seems, deductively, to be modest at most.

FINANCING COSTS: SCALE AND COMPETITION

Larger places seem to be favored by less expensive mortgage financing arising out of access to an adequate supply of mortgage funds and those same economies of scale and greater degree of competition that favored them in building cost. Scale economies in mortgage lending offer potential economies in home financing and the lower cost of construction loans should surface in the form of lower housing costs. The greater competition among lending institutions and among builders should ensure that much, if not most, of this reduction in lending costs would be passed on to the home buyers. The cost-price advantages of larger places could, of course, be disguised by legal or customary rigidities in interest rates and/or lending practices and take the form of differential credit availability; loans might carry about the same interest rate in large and small places but a larger down payment, shorter term or superior credit standing might be demanded in smaller places. Another possible advantage--that of mortgage interest rate differences-- might favor either rural or urban borrowers depending on the national credit situation. Interest rates of small-town lenders tend to fluctuate less than those of urban lenders and thus would tend to favor urban lenders when credit is ample, and rural areas when credit is tight.

Larger population size, that is, a larger local housing market, may merit mortgage loans with lower total cost because the collateral is more liquid. The larger the local housing market and more frequent the sales, the more liquid

and safer the loan--not unlike the "close, quick market"
that characterizes frequently traded common stocks. Beyond
simple liquidity of the collateral, residential property in
smaller places would seem to pose more risk to the extent
that such places, dependent on thinner economic bases, are
more susceptible to long-term stagnation and the threat of
almost unmarketable housing in the face of declining population. However, this risk may be partly offset by the
greater diversity of small-town neighborhoods, which are
less subject to self-accelerating decline.

CONCLUSION

This very brief review and conceptualization of some of the
major lines of linkage between the population size of a
place (local housing market) and the cost of housing does
not lead to easy, broad generalizations, and at most suggests data needs and promising lines of inquiry. Positions
of advantage and disadvantage shift back and forth between
large and small places so often that the most we might
reasonably expect is to be able to draw limited conclusions
about comparative costs of different size places for different types of housing, and by implication for different
types of households. (It is perhaps worth noting here that
because the Annual Housing Surveys are not much concerned
with cost information they are not especially useful in
this work.) Prospects for policy refinements based on housing cost analyses are promising but probably only with
considerable commitment and effort and, as always, more and
better data.
     All in all one cannot at this time argue easily, com-
fortably, or convincingly that housing cost differences
between larger and smaller places tend either to offset or
to reinforce the clear disadvantage of lower rural incomes,
on the way to explaining the easily observable fact that
rural housing is poorer than urban.

THE HOUSE FILTERING PROCESS IN SMALLER PLACES

The cost analysis of the preceding section was oriented
largely toward the cost of delivering a new housing unit to
its owner, including not only the cost of construction but
also land and financing costs. But most of us live in, buy,

and sell houses that were built years ago at very different
land and building costs than those that now prevail.
Analyses of the cost of housing are therefore complicated
by the fact that houses are the most expensive and most
durable of all consumer goods and are traded many times
long after they are built. New and used housing are of
course close substitutes for each other and the price of
used housing will therefore tend to reflect the cost of
production of new houses. Even so, one must inquire into
the special characteristics of the used housing market
where the older and cheaper housing finds it value, especially in light of the present concern about the housing
well-being of the lower-income households who live in these
houses and trade in these markets. The importance of re-
considering the process by which housing "filters down"
from higher- to middle- to lower-income households over the
course of its long life is highlighted when we recall that
the concept of filtering is borrowed from city housing
markets.

Although the filtering process is regarded as a general
theory of housing market operation, surely those who first
identified this process and those who have amended and
applied the theory over the years have had in mind housing
in cities rather than in rural areas and towns. A brief
survey of this intellectual legacy, to adapt it, if need
be, to small scale and low density, seems fundamental to an
inquiry into nonmetro housing affairs.

THE FACT OF FILTERING

Even casual observation supports the thesis that houses
do in general filter down from higher-income first users to
middle-income subsequent users and finally to lower-income
terminal users. That is to say, in large measure, disproportionately high numbers of higher-income households live
in newer housing and lower-income households disproportionately occupy older housing. But casual observation also
provides many exceptions to this general rule, enough in
fact to create considerable uneasiness with this broad
generalization. There are many almost ageless fine old
houses with high values occupied by very-high-income households. This, coupled with subsidized, very basic, low-
income new housing acts to weaken the correlation between
house age, value, and household income.

Still, cross-classified data from the Annual Housing

Survey, matching the year structures were built with their
value and the income of households occupying them, show a
clear and strong tendency for both median house value and
median household income to fall with house age, for both
metro and nonmetro areas in all four national regions, as
shown in Figure 14.2. There are only minor exceptions to
the inverse association between house age and value, but we
do find that the single major exception to the strong general inverse association between house age and household
income falls in the subgroup of special interest here—
nonmetro areas. The noticeably weaker correlation between
house age and household income in nonmetro areas reinforces
the note of caution raised above that one must take care in
transferring big-city filtering theory to smaller places.

FAMILY SIZE AND FILTERING

The house filtering process would be seriously disrupted if
upper middle-income households were on the average significantly smaller than middle and lower income ones. If that
were so, those who buy new houses and determine thereby the
physical characteristics of the housing stock would tend to
substitute quality for quantity—elegance for more rooms,
especially bedrooms—and cause thereby significant mismatch-
ing between the physical characteristics of the houses and
the demographic characteristics of households farther down
the housing ladder.
    More and larger rooms are an amenity for which even
small households often have a strong preference, and
higher-income households are more able to afford the
luxury of a guest room, den, or office that can later become another bedroom, and larger bedrooms that can more
easily serve more than one child. Also, smaller high-income
households could anticipate that units with three or more
bedrooms would be easier to resell than those with one or
two bedrooms and, with this in mind, select house sizes in
excess of their own needs. Still, one would feel more comfortable that the house filtering process is reasonably
efficient if it does not have to contend with the larger
family size of successive users.
    Current data on number of children by income class,
derived from the 1977 Annual Housing Survey, do indeed
suggest that family size is probably not a major impediment
to orderly filtering. Examining the most demanding case in
Figure 14.3, households with three or more children under

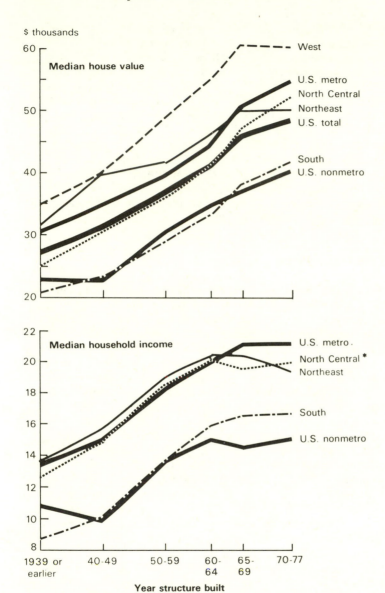

$ thousands

Median house value

West
U.S. metro
North Central
Northeast
U.S. total
South
U.S. nonmetro

Median household income

U.S. metro.
North Central *
Northeast
South
U.S. nonmetro

1939 or earlier   40-49   50-59   60-64   65-69   70-77

Year structure built

* almost coincident with West

Source: Current Housing Reports, Annual Housing Survey: 1977, Part C,
Tables A through E.

Figure 14.2 Association Between House Age and Value and Household
Income for Metropolitan and Nonmetropolitan Areas by Region, 1977

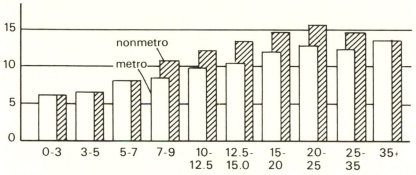

% of households with 3 or more children

Income of families and primary individuals, 1976 ($ thousands)

Source: Current Housing Reports, Annual Housing Survey: 1977, Part C,
Table A-1, pp. 6, 9, 21, 24.

Figure 14.3 Relationship Between Household Income and Household
Size in Metropolitan and Nonmetropolitan Areas, 1976

eighteen years of age and living at home, we see that
larger households are even more common among potential new
house buyers, for example, those earning $15,000 per year
or more, than among those households that must passively
inherit whatever the more affluent choose to buy. And this
is even more characteristic of nonmetro areas. However,
care must be taken in interpreting these static, cross-
section data linking family size and income because house
filtering takes place over long periods of time. By way of
illustration, if the trend were toward larger families,
houses built for upper middle-income households in 1970
could prove too small for lower middle-income households in
1990, even if both income classes exhibited the same
preferred family size in any given time period. But the
trend is more toward smaller families, and this should
further assure us that household and house size are not
likely to be serious sources of mismatch in the filtering
process, in either metro or nonmetro areas.

OWNING VERSUS RENTING

On first impression one might conclude that larger places
would ordinarily exhibit a wider variety of house types,
sizes, designs, and locations, and thereby smooth the
filtering process by providing something for everyone. But
it is not variety that is so much at issue as the stability
of preferences from the top of the filtering chain to the
bottom. If values and tastes are similar in smaller places,
regardless of income, there will be fewer qualitative bottlenecks in the filtering process. (Quantitative bottlenecks
could of course still occur under, for example, conditions
of very rapid growth.) Perhaps small towns come closest to
approximating the implicit assumption of filtering theory
that households have the same needs and preferences for
housing, differing only in income and therefore mostly in
the age of the house they can afford. This is supported by
the greater concentration of nonmetro households in specific
categories shown in Table 14.1. For instance, nonmetro
households are more homogeneously white, married couples,
and owner occupants.

A greater uniformity of housing preference across income
classes in nonmetro areas is suggested by data on the split
between owner occupancy and rental tenure. Table 14.4 reveals a steady decline with lower household income in the
percentage of owner-occupied housing, but the decline from
91 to 56 percent in nonmetro areas is substantially less
than the 89 to 34 percent drop in the metro areas.

ALTERNATIVES TO FILTERING UNDER LOW DENSITY

When one places house filtering in a strong spatial context,
intuition and deduction lead to mixed results. The basic
concept of filtering--moving from lesser to better housing
while continuing to work in the same place--would seem
alien to many rural situations. While former farm housing
within reasonable commuting distance to jobs in nearby
towns may be passed from hand to hand, maintenance of farm
houses still occupied by farmers working adjoining fields
would seem to depend on the fortunes of the farm family
that continues to live in that same place. Farm families
that choose to live in town and commute to their fields
could however fit into a house filtering process. But even
here, small-town housing, built at much lower densities,
offers the opportunity for substantial improvement and,

Table 14.4. Owner-Occupied Housing Units as Percentage of All
Units, by Household Income, for Nonmetropolitan and Metropolitan
Areas, 1977

Area	1977 Household Income in $000s									
	<3	3-5	5-7	7-10	10-12.5	12.5-15.0	15-20	20-25	25-35	>35
Metro	34.1	38.7	44.4	46.0	51.7	60.5	67.7	78.5	85.5	89.1
Nonmetro	56.3	60.9	62.7	66.1	70.6	78.7	82.7	86.3	89.6	91.4

Source: U.S. Bureau of the Census, Annual Housing Survey: 1977.

more distinctively, easy enlargement. Households in small
towns, more easily than in large cities, can move up without moving out. Moreover, if the small-town dweller is
more often a jack-of-all trades than the urbanite, do-
it-yourself housing expansions seem most probable.

Any move within a smaller town leaves the person within
the same community, resulting in less of a change than
would be the case in a larger town. Even moving to the best
block in town changes only the house and the immediate
neighbors--shops, schools, and public services are probably
the same. But, some of the same factors that discourage
moving by people hoping to achieve an overall upgrading of
life-style, also make moving from lesser to better houses
easier in small towns than in big cities for those seeking
mainly a change in their housing unit. The moving distances
are so short that children do not need to change schools,
old neighborhood friendships are retained more easily, and
commuting distance to work is less affected.

HOUSE AND NEIGHBORHOOD AND SIZE OF PLACE

When one places housing in a broader social context, the
propensity to move, a critical element in the filtering
process, seems likely to increase with size of place. Small-
town residents are typically under less pressure to move to
retain or attain the social status of living in a better
neighborhood because an address is a less critical measure
of one's social standing than in the anonymity of the city.
Without arguing that class structure is more rigid in small-

er places, one might argue that an individual's occupation and standing are better known by role and deed, and living near persons of lower social standing is not as demeaning as in cities. Nor can one gain higher standing by simply acquiring a prestigious new address.

As distinct from the desire to move, the pressure to move to a newer house and better neighborhood seems, impressionistically, to increase markedly with population size. Because in a large city a whole square mile may have been built within the span of a few years, embracing a full grade-school district, the houses age in lockstep and virtually the whole neighborhood can pass over from middle- to lower-middle income hands in a few years. Wholesale changes in neighborhood population can destabilize community life, discourage home maintenance, and threaten panic selling--"tipping points," and "invasion and succession."

One might in fact argue that large concentrations of the poor amplify negative externalities and thereby accelerate depreciation and premature abandonment--exaggerating filtering into almost cancer-like growth and change. Smaller places, more because the pockets of poverty are small, than due to any superior social or land-use policy, may indeed follow a more normal or at least economically efficient and socially beneficial form of filtering.

Residential neighborhoods in larger cities are more likely to feel the impact of market pressures of alternative land use. Economic pressure from higher density residential or commercial use raises lot values, thus encouraging earlier abandonment of the affected houses and discouraging any improvement and all but the most basic maintenance. Once transition is underway, social externalities from both the transition activities and final higher density use are likely to reinforce economic pressures and further hasten the decline of original residences.

Such pressure for accelerated change is unlikely to occur in smaller towns, where land quite similar to that on which houses are already built is likely to be in abundant supply, and it is less likely that the volume of economic forces necessary to force neighborhood transition would be as focused in a small town.

Viewing housing as separate from neighborhood, the housing position of the big-city poor would seem to be favored over the poor of towns and rural areas by the likelihood that large ghetto formation, middle-class flight, and faster filtering will transfer good, used housing from middle- to lower-income hands sooner than would otherwise occur. Faster

filtering tends, other things being equal, to redistribute
income toward greater equality. Whether or not this is a
social gain may be debatable, but apparently this forced
residential succession is characteristically a big-city
rather than a small-town or rural phenomenon, one that is
associated in a complex way with large numbers and high
density (externalities).

But the other face of neighborhood flight and accelerated house filtering is that housing maintenance in
threatened areas tends to be deferred, and faster population
turnover in changing neighborhoods makes even more difficult
the building of those strong community organizations that
are needed to enhance personal safety (e.g., "crime watch")
and to bargain with city hall for better public services.
In fact one might reverse this argument and say that declining neighborhoods lower prices and increase filtering.
In either case, although the flight of middle-income households may bring good, used houses into low-income hands
sooner, so too these same forces could promote premature
abandonment of these same houses, keeping the low-income
housing market tight and prices high.

One derives the firm hypothesis, even tentative judgment, that house filtering tends to proceed more rapidly in
larger places, and acts thereby to place not-so-old houses
in lower-income hands sooner than in smaller places. But
receiving houses at a younger age does not necessarily mean
that the structures will be in better physical condition or
usable for a longer time to come. Larger places tend to
generate more negative externalities--adverse spillovers--
that cause whole neighborhoods to filter down at excessive
rates of change. It is a fine line indeed that separates
rapid filtering of neighborhoods from rampant blight and
deterioration.

Smaller places are more likely to constrain filtering
to the house alone, and not speed downgrading of the whole
neighborhood, partly because of the diverse age mixture of
dwellings at close proximity, easily within grade-school
districts and often within the same block, and partly because one cannot flee easily by taking relatively short
steps across school district or municipal boundaries. Is
it better then for low-income households to: (1) receive
houses that are only thirty years old but see them last
only thirty years more (the big city syndrome), or (2) to
have to wait until those houses are forty years old but
find them livable for forty more years?

Surely, from the perspective of the conservation of

capital and energy, the slower filtering rate of the smaller
place tends to be more beneficial for society. But the price
of this is a longer wait for new supplies of housing along
the lower rungs of the housing ladder, a significant sacrifice during periods of rapid growth and general housing
shortages. But here again, the greater use of mobile homes
in smaller places can ease the pressure by adding to the
supply of middle- and low-income housing.

THE DISTRIBUTION OF INCOME

Perhaps the principal reason that house filtering is more
characteristic of cities than of towns or rural areas is
that metro areas generate substantially higher incomes and
are thereby able to feed proportionately more new houses
into the top of the filtering process. The superior position
of metro areas (cities and suburbs) over rural places in
nonmetro areas, in households of $20,000 annual income and
over, is evident in Table 14.5, and it is these upper
middle-income households that supply the grist for the
filtering mills.
     Housing studies have all, quite properly, emphasized
the level of household income as the prime determinant of
housing well-being, but much more attention should have
been paid to the distribution of income. Average incomes
could rise in a way that intensifies rather than relieves
local housing pressures, as when lower middle-income households rise to full middle-income status--due to a new manufacturing plant that raises local wages from five to six
dollars per hour--but this income rise falls short of shifting demand from the used to the new house submarkets. Compare that with the same increase in average income achieved
by the in-migration of a smaller number of households with
$20,000 annual income that build new houses rather than
compete for the limited supply of existing used houses. And
when these affluent households build another new house a
decade later they will release these now ten-year-old
houses, increasing the supply of good used housing.
     The complex relationship between the distribution of
income and the operation of the filtering process is a
serious (but apparently not so conspicuous) gap in the
theory and literature on filtering. What, for example, is
the nature of income distribution in rapidly growing
smaller places, and how has it affected their local housing
problem?

Table 14.5. Distribution of Household Income by Area, 1977

Area	Income in $000s					
	<15	15-20	20-25	25-35	>35	Total
	%	%	%	%	%	%
Urban within metro	55.0	14.7	11.1	11.3	7.9	100.0
Rural and open country within nonmetro	65.0	14.3	9.2	7.1	4.4	100.0

Source: U.S. Bureau of the Census, Annual Housing Survey: 1977.

CONCLUSION

Even the most preliminary reflections on the distinctive nature of house filtering in smaller places serve to impress one with the unexplored nature of the terrain, the importance of the subject matter, and the considerable potential for a more sophisticated housing policy. It is clear that smaller places with larger lot sizes offer residents better alternatives to "moving out to move up" and low-cost new housing (mobile homes) is more readily available as a substitute for filtering. But careful study may also show that, if filtering is less pervasive and slower in smaller places, it is probably also more orderly and socially efficient than in larger cities where the more rapid rate of filtering leads to the accelerated aging and premature abandonment of housing stock.

The value of serious study of the filtering process is also persuasively suggested by the steadily decreasing proportion of households that buy new homes, as new house prices rise faster than incomes. Apparently, the recent resurgence of smaller places portends tighter housing markets, higher house prices, longer house life, and other economic pressures favoring increased filtering in the future. Moreover, as smaller places grow rapidly they become bigger and more subject to a more pervasive and apparently less benign form of house filtering. In sum, the operation of the filtering process in rapidly growing smaller places would seem to deserve a high priority on any nonmetro area housing research agenda.

LOCAL GROWTH INSTABILITY AND
IMBALANCE IN THE HOUSING MARKET

The relationship between household income and housing well-being is clear, direct, and immediate: poor people live in poor houses. But too little noted is the clear and complex relationship between the pattern of local growth and the general state of the local housing market. Obviously, in addition to the level of household income and housing costs, the demand for local housing is a function of the current rate of local growth in population and household formation. Much more subtle, the local supply of used housing--the overwhelming portion of the total supply--is a function of previous rates of local growth, that is, the historic growth pattern of the community.

The 1980 supply of fifty-year-old housing is precisely the number of houses built in that local housing market in 1930, minus the number destroyed over the ensuing period. And the level of residential construction in 1930 was determined largely by the economic and demographic events in that place at that time--job formation, marriage and birthrates--in relation to the then existing stock of housing. In general, the present supplies of used housing are a function of past demands for new housing, as expressed in past rates of residential construction.

Almost wholly unrelated to the determinants of their supply, the current demand for fifty-year-old houses in a given locality is determined by the number of households now earning an income normally associated with houses of that age and price (plus some who choose not to move out and up) plus those owners whose incomes have fallen but who are under no pressure to move out. The 1980 income pattern is closely tied to the current structure and performance of local industry, which are very different from 1930. With the 1930 supply of and 1980 demand for houses derived from local industry growth rates and wage rates separated by five decades, extraordinarily strong equilibrating forces may be needed in the used housing market to bring demand and supply together: either very sharp price and rent adjustments or public subsidies that permit below-cost prices.

This fresh perspective on local housing markets points up the riskiness of relying on the filtering-down of housing to accommodate low-income or even middle-income families. Serious mismatches can easily develop in the demand for and supply of various subsets of older housing. The classic example of this is the fifteen-year moratorium on residen-

tial construction that extended from the Great Depression
through World War II; we are still struggling with the
housing market distortions caused by this gap in the age
distribution of housing. Each decade, the successive lower-
income class--roughly pentile--must in turn face a very
small supply of that subset of houses that it would normally occupy. Because of a deep national depression and a hard
war, all localities find the stairway to better housing has
a couple of steps missing.

Less dramatic but more common and frequent are sharp
shifts in rates of local growth. A period of slow growth
leaves a hollow in the age profile of housing whose effects
can become especially severe. If local growth subsequently
accelerates, heavy net in-migration will increase the size
of all income classes, including the middle- and low-income
classes that must, each in turn, try to fit into an age-
class of housing that is much too small.

EFFECTS OF RAPID LOCAL GROWTH

As a working hypothesis, suppose that, under rapid local
growth and heavy net in-migration, the newcomers are a
cross section of all income classes. If so, the local housing shortage will be most severe and persist longest in
the low-income housing submarket. Because this is much less
obvious than the complementary observation that housing
expansion is easiest in the upper-income new housing market,
somewhat more detailed argumentation seems indicated.

The supply of high-income (new) housing can be appre-
ciably increased in a single building period, therefore
making modest and short-lived any local inflation of new
house prices due to rapid growth. But low-income families
live primarily in old houses that have filtered down from
former owners, and at any given time the supply of old
houses is virtually fixed in supply. How indeed can a
community increase the supply of fifty-year-old houses? The
very poor can, of course, make small, painful sacrifices by
cutting back other spending to bid away a few forty-year-
old dwellings from the near poor, who will release them
only if they can, in turn, bid away an even greater number
of thirty-year-old units from the middle class. One must
remember that, if all income classes are growing rapidly in
number, the near poor also need more dwelling units, even
before releasing some to the very poor.

Under rapid local growth, every time a given income

class passes down a few extra dwelling units above the
normal rate of filtering, this transfer greatly intensifies
the shortfall of its own normal supply. In short, house
filtering under growth pressure can be accelerated only
slightly and then only at very sharply increasing supply
prices for each class (age) of housing. Deductive logic
would lead to the hypothesis that shortages and price rises
should be: (1) least in the high-income, new housing
market, where supply is highly elastic; (2) greater in the
middle-income used housing market, where supply is fixed,
but where modest additions to supply can be attracted away
from the highly elastic, high-income market, and where the
lowest price new homes are an alternative; and (3) greatest
in the low-income, old-used housing market, where supply is
also fixed, but where additions to supply must be attracted
away from a quickly tightening middle-income housing
market.

Just as rising prices can ease shortages in the supply
of used housing, and thereby impart some elasticity to the
filtering process, so too there are offsetting behavioral
and institutional frictions at work. Low-income households
with modestly rising incomes may find their way to newer
housing blocked by middle-income households that do not
want to move. Those who can afford a newer, more expensive
house, but who decide not to move because they like the
local school or church or work nearby can impede the whole
process. Not only can a wide variety of sociological events
upset the economics of filtering but also these disruptions
may well be hailed as progress toward some social goal,
such as neighborhood stability.

THE IMPORTANCE OF TREND SHIFTS AND THEIR DURATION

The link between variations in the rate of local growth and
the state of the local housing market becomes even more
subtle and complex when we introduce more precise consideration of the timing involved. A surge in the rate of local
growth following a relatively short period of local stagnation of about a decade, would be more easily accommodated
if accompanied by a high local vacancy rate. The cushion of
surplus housing would absorb the early stages of the growth
shock, and increases in house prices and rents would be
moderated by the previous period of decline. But two or
more decades of local stagnation would seem to be long
enough to adjust the local housing stock to the diminishing

demand and to eliminate the price-moderating housing surplus
that eases short period growth swings.

However, two or more decades of local stagnation act
not only to reduce the housing stock but also to age and
depreciate it qualitatively. The relatively short supply of
houses less than thirty years old would force middle-income
households to retain ownership of the forty- and fifty-year-
old houses, blocking the path of the poor to the better,
older houses. In short, one reaches the tentative conclusion
that population trend reversal could be easier or harder to
accommodate in a local housing market than sustained growth,
depending on the timing of contraction and expansion. Even
if most of the mathematical possibilities are unlikely to
occur, the local growth scenarios that one would reasonably
expect to find are still so varied that a major quantitative
effort would be required to carry this line of inquiry to
the point of comprehensive taxonomy of the important lines
of linkage between local growth patterns and housing well-
being.

THE INDUSTRIAL BASE OF LOCAL GROWTH AND HOUSING PATTERNS

Weaving together the demand and supply sides of the local
housing market, we can describe in broad terms that combination of local industrial-occupational mix and pattern of
growth rates, past and present, that either promises a
looser housing market and better accommodations or threatens a tighter market and deprivation. First, a high-wage
local economy makes it possible for a relatively large
proportion of households to buy new houses frequently and
thereby release relatively large supplies of good used
houses. Or, an industry mix that pays only average wage
rates but generates a complete array of jobs that balances
the attributes of the labor supply, increases labor force
participation, and increases household income. Among younger
couples, new house buyers are predominantly two-income families, and in about one-half of all families buying new
houses the wife works outside of the home. Obviously, a
combination of high wage rates and a diverse skill mixture
produces the highest family incomes and the largest demand
for new (and supply of used) houses.

Concerning growth patterns, the combination that most
eases local housing shortages is a low current rate of
growth linked with higher previous rates. Slow current
growth reduces net in-migration and thereby the demand for

both new and used housing, whereas higher earlier growth
rates leave a legacy of large supplies of used housing.
Note that high incomes and slow current growth are additive
and that when they occur together, as they do now throughout
most of the manufacturing Midwest, they create the loosest
(best) housing market of all. Durable goods centers that
boomed in the 1950s have today huge supplies of twenty- to
thirty-year-old housing to match against a near zero rate
of household formation. And their suburbs have the higher
incomes to keep new residential construction going forward
at the replacement rate, thus keeping the local housing
market soft.[2]

The worst combination of industries and growth patterns,
in terms of impact on the local housing market would be a
set of low-wage industries, employing largely males (e.g.,
heavy or dirty work) or females (e.g., apparel)--located in
a place that has languished for years--ones that have sud-
denly expanded their operations or are joined by similar
industries in a quantum leap forward. Rapidly growing places
in the Carolina Piedmont have, in point of fact, suffered
severe housing shortages, so much so in many cases as to
slow their industrial growth. In general, the migration of
low-skill manufacturing to smaller places, often in the
South, draws along in its train a housing problem to mix
this blessing.

The worst of all worlds for the low-income residents
of a rapidly growing place is the in-migration of households
whose incomes exceed those of the residents, but which are
still too low to position them in the new house market,
thereby forcing direct competition for the fixed supply of
older homes. This is of course especially difficult for
renters who must not only pay higher rents in a tightening
housing market, but who also find homeownership increasingly
inaccessible. Young adults in the process of accumulating
the down payment needed to become first-time homeowners may
find themselves running on a treadmill as rising house
prices and down payments remain discouragingly ahead of
their slowly growing savings.

Homeowners, however, will be relatively insulated from
the influx of newcomers and will in fact enjoy capital
gains, which can of course be realized only by selling or
refinancing (with little gain in the latter case if interest
rates have been rising). Unrealized capital gains may
moreover be small comfort if property values are reassessed
upward, increasing property taxes. Still, although rural
areas and towns may experience sharper spurts of growth,

they would seem to be less vulnerable to the inflation in
used housing prices because of their higher proportion of
owner-occupied units.

There are too many intermediate combinations of industry
and occupation and current and past growth rates to discuss
all of them in detail. There is, moreover, a touch of un-
reality about the two extreme cases outlined above. Rapid
growth tends to tighten local labor markets and thereby not
only reduce unemployment but also increase labor force
participation rates by adding second earners. Rapid growth
therefore operates to moderate the effect of an unbalanced
occupation mixture and reduces the impact of the worst
scenario discussed above. Similarly, slow current growth
may reduce the demand for used houses in a helpful way but,
to the degree that it idles secondary workers, slow current
growth acts to depress the demand for new houses and thereby
the supply of used ones.

Finally, and perhaps most important, housing has been
treated as a consumer good only, ignoring it as an investment. Not only have houses proven in recent years to be a
good hedge against general inflation, as discussed earlier; but also houses in fast-growing localities become
an even better speculation against future prices. A comprehensive theory of local growth and housing would therefore
include the investment motive in housing demand. Clearly,
we are a long way from having any finely spun theory that
traces the impact of the local economy through growth and
income patterns and on into the local housing market.

LOCAL GROWTH STABILITY AND SIZE OF PLACE

A priori, a strong case can be made for the generalization
that smaller places have, of arithmetic necessity, more
specialized industry mixes than larger ones and would
therefore tend to be more subject to growth instability--
sharp breaks and reversals in trend. If so, local housing
markets with smaller populations should experience more
frequent and severe housing shortages or surpluses. But
this hypothesis proves surprisingly difficult to formulate
in a testable way and even harder to prove.

The very notion of "growth stability," in contrast
to cyclical stability, has received almost no attention by
regional analysts, and careful conceptualization is of
course a clear prerequisite to sophisticated and sensitive

measurement (Thompson, 1965: 160-64). In a very preliminary and tentative attempt to determine whether smaller places do indeed surge and sag and leave behind an uneven (distorted?) age-distribution of housing, a simple index of growth instability was prepared for this chapter by averaging the three percentage point differences between each pair of four successive postwar decennial growth rates: 1940 to 1950, 1950 to 1960, 1960 to 1970, and 1970 to 1980 (as approximated by raising the 1970 to 1977 population change by 10/7s).[3] This index was computed for all of the nonmetro counties of Arkansas and for twenty surrounding metro areas, as shown in Table 14.6.

The least populous counties of Arkansas, those reporting less than 10,000 population in 1960, did exhibit the greatest growth instability, with an average change of 22.6 percentage points between successive decennial growth rates. Whereas these smallest counties did show about twice as much growth-rate-shift as medium and large places, increases in size beyond 10,000 population were accompanied by only modest and somewhat irregular reductions in growth instability. In essence, this preliminary and very limited empirical inquiry into size and stability is moderately supportive but far from convincing. Part of the explanation could lie in the likelihood that the index used is biased toward showing greater growth instability in rapidly growing places, that is, percentage point changes tend to be larger if the base percentages (growth rates) from which they are derived are larger. And, on average, metro areas of that region grew much faster than nonmetro counties through the postwar period.

Even if a carefully designed and broadly based empirical effort were to establish that small places are more likely to experience growth instability, the radical shifts in demand for local housing that would then characterize smaller places may not necessarily cause greater transitional shortages and gluts of housing. Smaller places may also exhibit an offsetting greater elasticity of supply because they tend to be more accommodating to mobile homes, but by virtue of either more tolerant or little local zoning. The greater availability of building sites and simpler and speedier building regulatory processes all add to the easier expansibility of nonmetro residential construction. Housing supplies in smaller places may also be more responsive, in relative magnitude, because of the very high mobility of the construction industry. A small town could therefore much more easily double or triple its rate of

Table 14.6. Relationship Between Size of a
Local Economy and the Stability of Local Growth

1960 Population of Nonmetro County or or Metro Area[a]	Number of Areas	Index of Growth Stability[b]
000s		
0-10	18	22.6
10-20	24	12.8
20-40	19	11.0
40-80	7	9.9
80-160	6	11.3
160-320	4	10.2
320-640	2	8.0
640-1,280	4	8.9
1,280 or more	2	8.4

Source: Derived from the U.S. Decennial Census
of Population, 1940-70, Arkansas Volumes, and
U.S. Bureau of the Census, Current Population
Reports, series P-26.

[a]Includes all Arkansas counties and 18 surrounding metropolitan areas.

[b]Average percentage point difference between
decennial rates of change in population, 1940-
1977.

home building in a short period than could a metro area.
The local elasticity of supply of new construction would
tend to be greatest in smaller local economies located
within approximately fifty miles of a metro area—an acceptable commute for itinerant construction workers.

The way in which larger shifts in housing demand can
be offset by greater elasticity of housing supply in smaller places can be most simply and convincingly demonstrated
through use of the (almost) traditional demand and supply
analysis, as shown in Figure 14.4. (Note that the horizontal
axis in Figure 14.4 is calibrated in relative change—
percentage change in number of new housing units.) As drawn,
a greater shift in demand for housing in smaller places
(D_{small} to D'_{small}) along a very elastic housing supply

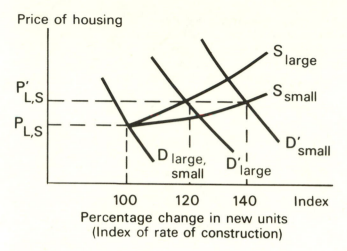

Figure 14.4 Housing Market Equilibriums in Small and Large Communities

curve (S_{small}) produces the same increase in local housing prices (P to P') as that experienced by larger places in which a lesser relative increase in demand for housing (D_{large} to D'_{large}) presses against a less elastic housing supply curve (S_{large}).

Even so, one might argue, these attributes of smaller places only act to increase the elasticity of supply of new housing--a small part of the total supply--and at that, available only to higher-income households. But mobile homes are also in highly elastic supply and are especially welcome in nonmetro areas, where they now account for about one-quarter of new homes (compared to one-twelfth in metro areas) and they serve the middle- and low-income housing submarkets as substitutes for used conventional housing.

The supplies of used housing are made more elastic in smaller places located in well populated agricultural areas by long-distance commuting from farmhouses and dwellings in quiet hamlets. Rapid local growth and improving conditions act to extend the commuting radius of all places, large and small, but the percentage increase in houses encompassed would tend to be especially large in smaller trade centers in well-populated agricultural areas.

CONCLUSION

The impact of the rate of local population growth on the local housing market is so powerful and complex in nature that it opens up an area of unsurpassed potential return on investment in research, both conceptual and empirical. Clearly, the level and distribution of income is the single most important set of determinants of housing well-being. How could it be otherwise when housing services command close to one-quarter of household income? But the impact of current and past rates of local growth (including their projection into expected rates of future growth and the speculation in land) would seem to merit considerable attention. Moreover, given the very large oscillations in metro and nonmetro population growth rates throughout the postwar period, and the high likelihood that there is much more potential change, any serious research agenda on housing--be it city, town, or rural setting--is critically incomplete without a carefully conceived local growth component.

But incisive inquiry into the complexities of local growth and housing will call for data well beyond those available in the Annual Housing Survey. National aggregates, or data for such large regions as the Northeast, North Central, South, and West are of little use in measuring the tightness or looseness of local housing markets, and they are not much enhanced in value by disaggregation into metro and nonmetro and urban and rural within that dichotomy--not while they still encompass and average-out the critical variation within a dozen-state region. Although the 1980 Census will bring the spatial disaggregation that is so important, growth and housing analyses will still suffer the lack of time series (annual) data with which to track this phenomenon.

NOTES

1. Although adequate from the standpoint of timeliness in describing the national and regional situation (and that of some selected SMSAs), the Annual Housing Survey is of little use for the analysis of local housing markets.

2. For the nation as a whole, where net (internal) migration is zero, the best combination is a low birth rate twenty-five years ago, linked with higher previous rates,

and a high and rising income that feeds in new units and
induces everyone down the filtering line to trade-up frequently into newer housing. We might even add to this sharp
taste and technological changes that breed discontent with
present housing and further accelerate buying and filtering
(e.g., planned unit developments, with swimming pools,
tennis courts, and exterior maintenance), especially
with a shift to small families.

3. For example, Arkansas County, the most stable of
all, registered decennial growth rates of -3.2, -1.3, 0.0,
and 1.3 (1970-1977), raised to 1.9 percent as an estimate
for 1970-1980. Successive percentage point differences of
1.9, 1.3, and 1.9 sum to 5.1, which divided by 3 yields an
average percentage point shift in decennial growth rate of
1.7. In sharp contrast, Baxter County, one of the most
unstable by our measure, exhibited successive population
growth rates of 13.6, -14.9, 54.1, and 89.0 for the decades
1940-1950, 1950-1960, 1960-1970, and 1970-1980, respectively. The three differences sum to 132.4 for an average of
44.1 percentage point shift per decade. Clearly, the variable chosen does at least have the attribute of varying
substantially.

BIBLIOGRAPHY

Mikesell, James J. Population Change and Metro-Nonmetro
    Housing Quality Differences. Agricultural Economic
    Report no. 388. Washington, D.C.: Economic Research
    Service, U.S. Department of Agriculture, 1977.
Spurlock, Hughes H., and Bird, Ronald. Housing Credit:
    A Rural-Urban Comparison. Rural Development Research
    Report no. 6. Washington, D.C.: Economics, Statistics,
    and Cooperatives Service, U.S. Department of Agricul-
    ture, 1978.
Thompson, Wilbur R. A Preface to Urban Economics. Baltimore,
    Md.: The Johns Hopkins Press, 1965.
U.S. Bureau of the Census. Current Housing Reports, series
    H-150-77. Annual Housing Survey: 1977, pt. A-E. Wash-
    ington, D.C.: U.S. Government Printing Office, 1979.
    _____. Current Population Reports, series P-26,
    Arkansas issue. Washington, D.C.: U.S. Government
    Printing Office, 1977.

Stephen P. Coelen
William F. Fox

15

The Provision of
Community Services

INTRODUCTION

The provision of public services in nonmetro America is
complicated by the dispersed population and low incomes,
which often occur in these areas, as well as by shifting
populations that have been oriented first away and now
toward nonmetro areas. These factors coupled with the lack
of municipal governments in many open-space places have led
to either nonexistent or insufficient and inefficient provision of services. These are often the root causes of
the failure of nonmetro areas to achieve the economies of
scale inherent in public goods, to obtain sufficient funding that is necessary to offset expenditures, and to plan
optimally for the long-run provision of services.

   This chapter will show that these theoretical tenets
are integral to new nonmetro development policies promulgated by state and federal agencies.[1] The theoretical issues
have achieved such prominence because it has been soundly
demonstrated that public services are critical in attracting, holding, or losing the human resources necessary for
development in nonmetro areas. The national emphasis on
balanced growth precludes a laissez-faire approach. First,
this chapter will define the diversity of the available
services. The next section contains a theoretical evaluation
of the basic premises on dispersed populations, low incomes,
and population dynamics. The final section summarizes the
rural dilemma, showing the impact that these services may
have on rural quality of life.

SERVICES AND THEIR CLASSIFICATIONS

The public services included in the nonmetro public sector
are the same as those found in the metro sector: health,
education, recreation, transportation, safety, justice,

water, wastewater, solid waste, energy, telecommunications, and fire safety.[2] These, of course, differ widely and include everything from purely public goods (Musgrave 1959) to what Breton (1956, 1966) and Weldon (1966) have called local nonprivate goods. There are capital-intensive and labor-intensive services and services that vary in the amount of the nonmetro family's budget they absorb.[3] Some services are provided by private firms that substitute for the public sector, and some are services regulated by some suprastate or federal agency (Bailey 1973).

Each of these distinctions among the services has been a major source of dichotomization and theory relevant to nonmetro as well as metro areas, and this chapter proposes another classification scheme, which keys upon the service delivery system. Of the twelve services mentioned above, some are delivered and consumed in (or on) the capital facility used in producing the service, and others are delivered where public and private facilities meet. In this case the production takes place in the public or community domain, but consumption takes place in the private domain (within the household establishment). These two general kinds of delivery are designated as service oriented and production oriented:

Service-Oriented	Production-Oriented
Health	Water
Education	Wastewater
Recreation	Solid waste
Transportation	Energy
Safety	Telecommunications
Justice	Fire safety

Consumption on or in the public facility capital structure is common for the service-oriented goods. It is obvious that health services are consumed and produced in hospitals and clinics as well as in private physicians' offices. On the other hand, water is "produced" in a community well field or from a surface source of water and it is treated at a treatment plant. Consumption is separate, occurring through the pipes of an individual home or business establishment. Wastewater, in reverse, is the service of taking spent water and effluent from individual private facilities and treating it in public facilities. Solid waste is conceptually equivalent to wastewater. Energy and telecommunications are delivered to private homes and establishments. Fire safety requires the inspection of private buildings by

public inspectors and the delivery of fire fighters to
private facilities to extinguish fires and administer emergency services.

There are exceptions to this classification. Notably,
police safety often is extended into investigations, chases,
and arrests on private property but search warrants and
the requirement to show probable cause often provide an
entrance barrier before the transgression onto private
property occurs. In fire safety, the fire department trans-
ports part of its productive capital onto private property
in order to perform its service. Conversely, the citizen
takes part of his capital, his automobile, onto the highway's public domain in order to consume services. By and
large, however, the analysis holds up.

The most useful feature of this classification is that
it subsumes so much. Yet the strength of the analysis is
also its most notable paradox. In service-oriented services
that, with the exception of transportation, are labor intensive, there is more interest in production facilities
than there is for the production-oriented services, which
are generally capital intensive. Conversely almost to the
exclusion of production facilities, there is more singular
concern with the outputs for the production-oriented goods
than with the production facilities. The reason for this
paradox is that in the view of consumers the production
facilities become one component of output for service-
oriented services.

We are more interested in the quality of water supply
at its point of use than the quality of the construction of
the treatment facility that produces the supply. On the
other hand, we are interested in both the quality of health
care services and the quality and condition of health care
delivery buildings. The interest in fire safety, asbestos
removal, lighting capacity, and access for the handicapped
that is inherent in school construction, the emphasis on
withholding accreditation from multistory wood-frame nursing homes, and recent state and federal programs replacing
bridge decking are the result of this concern about the
condition of facilities.

Production-oriented services, although placing emphasis
on control of the output and deemphasizing capital inputs,
are generally more capital intensive than service-oriented
facilities.[4] Service-oriented goods are produced more
rarely by private market substitutes for public supplies
than production-oriented goods. Production-oriented goods
are frequently heavy users of natural resources and hence

are subject to the economics of scarcity. These are also
goods that are more heavily regulated in terms of cost and
pricing. Their outputs are more readily measured than the
outputs, for example, of health, education, recreation, and
the others that contain large psychic components of "consumers' surplus" and immeasurable impacts on human physical
productivity.

THEORY OF NONMETROPOLITAN PUBLIC SERVICE DELIVERY

It has been noted above that the three major constraints in
nonmetro areas are dispersed populations, low incomes, and
shifting populations. Each of these can be shown to have
specific influences on the delivery of services. In this
section these constraints are explored theoretically.

DISPERSED POPULATION

"Dispersed population" is a term that defines an area with a
low population density level. The term is most often also coincident with areas having low absolute levels of population
although the latter is often corrected in nonmetro areas by
defining the overall government in such a way as to include
more land area, thus providing a catchment for a greater
population size but maintaining a low average density.

This desire to increase the population served is one
cause of the other problem mentioned earlier--the lack of
municipal governments. Nonmetro areas have tended to retain
county governments to provide many public services rather
than incorporating a smaller municipal government, thereby
obtaining sufficient population size to capitalize on whatever size economies exist. Special service districts and
voluntary associations are overlaid on this network of
county governments in the open-space places wherever necessary in order to deal with those services that cannot
be provided at the broader county scale.

Hirsch (1968) has reviewed the early statistical literature that shows that the general forms of average costs of
public services are U and L shaped over both density and
population. Average costs are found to be U shaped, for
example, in secondary education and L shaped in wastewater
service. Of the two determinants, density and population,
density is by far the more critical. The fiscal decentral-

ization theories of Tiebout (1961) also support this conclusion. A recent review by Fox (1980) has updated this
work, again consistently showing many studies that report U
shaped average cost curves with respect to both population
and density. The U shape of average cost has led many authors such as Tiebout (1961), Ostrom et al. (1961), and
Hirsch (1964) to suggest metropolitanization or areawide
service provision as a means of obtaining optimal scale for
small governments in urban areas. In most nonmetro areas,
however, the diseconomies of low population density offset
any economies from large-scale production. For example,
there are economies in providing more water to the same
customers but the costs of distributing the water to new
customers in nonmetro areas will override the production
economies. The literature on economies of size in producing
community services has generally received more attention
than the production relationships between input and output
factors (Fox et al. 1979)--though this research frequently
mixes production and cost analysis.

Hirsch (1968) has categorized local government services
as horizontally integrated, vertically integrated, and
circularly integrated in order to predict the likelihood of
size economies. Horizontally integrated services are those
services that use a number of separate production plants to
produce the same type of service. Police and fire protection
are examples. Hirsch notes that 80 to 85 percent of government expenditures are spent on these services. Vertical
integration characterizes the production of services that
involve several different stages of production. Generally
these are the production-oriented goods like water and
electricity, which account for 8 to 10 percent of expenditures. Goods and services that complement one another are
circularly integrated; central administration is the example
given by Hirsch. These services represent 3 to 6 percent of
government expenditures.

Hirsch notes that size economies are unlikely to occur
in horizontally integrated government services. These services are generally produced in small plants near the consumers so that few economies would result from large plants.
Labor is the only input that is generally purchased in large
amounts. Unionization of public employees, however, can
actually increase wage rates for places with many employees,
leading to diseconomies of large size. Further, legal restrictions on salary levels and political patronage can preclude the hiring of the best qualified management. In spite
of these factors, which are critical in horizontally inte-

grated services, Hirsch argues that size economies could be expected over a substantial range of production for vertically integrated services and within a smaller range for circularly integrated services. There is generally a greater ability for these services to be produced in large plants.

Hirsch's conclusion that economies are unlikely for horizontally integrated services is based on consideration of metropolitan communities with populations exceeding 50,000. Full twenty-four-hour service delivery is already provided and few economies are available because labor can be purchased in relatively continuous units and facilities have achieved the best, though small, size. However, size economies can be expected for many nonmetro community services as they move towards continuous, full provision of services.

It is this conceptual work on size economies, based on metro locales, that has misled planning for nonmetro places by suggesting that bigger is better. This work shows why average unit costs are higher in nonmetro places than metro places, and prescribes expansion of the scale of operations to obtain greater efficiency. This was for many years the prevailing philosophy of service delivery, particularly for production-oriented services. Yet the research on size economies is frequently inapplicable to nonmetro areas because it considers a given production technology and because the diseconomies of low population density may eliminate potential cost savings.[5] Diseconomies of density were noted above and problems of production technologies are discussed below.

In analyzing any change in policy, cost functions must be considered as part of a technology. In water supply, for example, cost functions may represent a conventional draw upon local surface water, a reservoir or river tied to a piped distribution system. Alternatively, the costs might represent a conventional draw upon a local well field and (again) a distribution system.[6] For solid waste, the technology may be a municipal or private collector with rear-loading compacting trucks, a transfer station, and a sanitary landfill. In the service-oriented services, in health, for example, it may be a municipal hospital providing primary care through an outpatient department as well as secondary care through a range of self-contained departments.

Associated cost functions have been well developed in the technological engineering-economic literature. But the major shortcoming is that the research concentrates on large-scale technology for metro areas where sizable population concentrations exist (see United States Department of Agriculture 1977 and Foster 1974). Seldom has there been

much work with small-scale technology.[7] An excellent design
manual, but one reflecting planning without considering
technology for different size places, is available from
the Arizona Department of Health Services (1978). It concentrates on large-scale technologies and misses technologies that are efficient at small scale.

Cluster-well water systems are a prime example of a
small-scale technology which has not received the institutional support of the federal government. These systems
were first adapted to rural water supply by the National
Demonstration Water Project affiliates in Jasper County,
South Carolina (by the Levy-Limehouse/Bellinger Hill Project) and in Franklin County, Virginia (by the National
Demonstration Water Project). These systems are based on a
technology of drilling multiple, but physically separate,
wells in low-capacity sources. Each source is centrally
located for different user groups. Although the sources are
not interconnected, the system is then centrally managed
and maintained. Hughes and Israelson (1976) provide a complete description of cluster-well technology. The institutional resistance of federal and state agencies is documented by Cobb and Morgan (1978).

Graphically, a typical, average cost function for a
conventional water system may look like line AA' in Figure
15.1, which is adapted from the classic work of Hirshleifer
et al. (1960, p. 56). This conventional cost curve, AA',
reflects costs for many levels of output. Inherent in it is
a variation in the fixed capital in the water facility. Any
given level of fixed capital produces a short-run cost
function, several of which are shown as smaller U-shaped
curves for which AA' is the "envelope" curve. Consistent
with Hirsch's comments (1968) on vertically integrated
production, the conventional technology's cost curve shows
scale economies. Up to a water output of Q' an increase in
the capital facility results in a decline in the cost per
unit of water if one is using conventional technology.

A representation of the long-run cost curve of cluster-
well technology is superimposed in Figure 15.1 by line BB'.
Because it represents many production plants integrated by
a single management, it lacks scale economies as do most of
Hirsch's horizontally integrated production processes. Like
AA', the cost function, BB', is a long-run envelope of its
short-run functions which in turn depict costs, holding
capital facilities constant.

The important lesson here is that for any communities
that demand less than Q units of water output, there are two

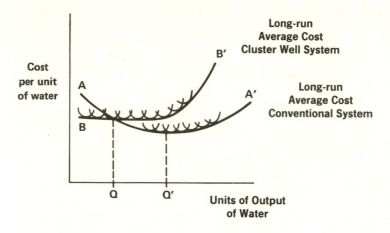

Source: Hirshleifer et al., p. 56.

Figure 15.1 Conventional and Alternative Water Technology
Cost Functions

ways in which to reduce costs. The first way--which Foster
has said is typical of water management--establishes the
conventional technology and pushes output unnecessarily toward high levels, Q', where per unit costs will be minimized
but where total cost would be greater. The second way is to
accept the small scale and to adapt to it, utilizing the appropriate technology--in this case, cluster wells. Little
literature exists concerning the adoption of alternative
technologies. In part the decision depends upon the anticipated growth for the community in question, and additional
technical research is needed to define the cost functions
and relevant tradeoffs. New research should follow the style
of analysis established by Higgins and Okun (1972) in analyzing the extent to which conventional systems can penetrate
from large urban centers into less densely settled fringes.

LOW INCOMES

Among the services under consideration some are absolute,
life-supporting necessities such as health and water, and
others are "merit goods" (Musgrave 1959) like recreation
and education. Still others are associated with the produc-

tion of positive externalities or the reduction or elimination of negative externalities--safety, solid waste. For each, society benefits from their production. Therefore the governmental objective should be to provide for the optimal level of services when it is infeasible for private producers to do so. In the case of nonmetro areas, however, low incomes may hamper this production and increase the need for state or federal intervention either in the form of regulation or subsidy.

Generally, most community services are provided by governmental units because of significant positive externalities in consumption (for example, education) or to offset negative externalities from other actions (wastewater, for example). The negative externalities are usually directly related to population density. So demand (and need) for many services is likely to be greater in more densely settled metro areas. In addition, higher metro incomes result in higher community service demands in metro relative to nonmetro areas. Therefore, though nonmetro unit costs may be greater, metro expenditures are greater (Stocker 1977).

There is a need for a general method to determine levels of output for the public sector. The techniques used have been reviewed by Hitzhusen and Napier (1978): (1) individual preference, (2) voter behavior, (3) benefit-cost analysis, and (4) professional standards. The approach used for setting service levels depends substantially on the characteristics of the particular service. Individual preferences serve as the mechanism for determining the consumption of private market goods including some community services such as private schools and nursery schools. Similarly, preferences can be used to set output levels (consumption) for public sector services that are essentially private in consumption, such as school lunches. In other words, individual preferences are a useful means to determine the correct output in the public sector when price can be used to separate people by the strength of their preferences for goods. The community sets user charges and then provides the output or service level chosen by consumers through their consumption. User charges are frequently set to cover costs (public utilities) or to ration consumption (public tennis courts). Reliance on individual preferences is desirable because it can result in many private market advantages including efficiency in consumption, and, from a local government's perspective, it permits simultaneous decisions on service levels and budgets. Services where individual preferences set consumption levels include water, wastewater, solid waste, health services, state liquor sales, school lunches, and higher education.

Current charges for these goods were reported in the 1972 Census of Governments to amount to 18.3 percent of non-metro government own-source revenues in fiscal year 1972, whereas governments in metro areas raised only 13.8 percent of their revenues from current charges. Greater use of user charges has occurred and will likely continue as a result of legislation similar to Proposition 13, so individual preferences can be expected to play an ever increasing role in setting service levels (see Chapter 20 in this volume).

Though the individual preferences approach has many advantages for determining optimal service levels, it may not work well for some services in nonmetro areas because relatively low incomes may result in insufficient demand. Nonetheless, it may be desirable for the good to be provided with a subsidy from general revenues used to cover the loss.

A simple, albeit extreme, example drawn from small-scale water supply suffices to show this need for subsidies. Consider a situation in which the demand for an output of public service such as water is given in Figure 15.2 by line DD'. Average costs are given by the function AC. We assume that this is the most appropriate function and that there are no externalities associated with the output.

It is a well known result of welfare economics, see for example Bator (1957), that the socially optimal output level is determined when price (P) for the next unit of output and marginal cost (MC) are equal. In the case of Figure 15.2, output should be set at Q, but doing so results in a loss because at Q, average cost (AC) exceeds average revenue (AR).

For the case in Figure 15.2, it is indeed beneficial to subsidize the service because total costs are less than total benefits. This follows from observing that a measure of benefits is the full area under the demand curve. The costs equal the area of the rectangle, OECQ. We can observe in Figure 15.2 that area ABC of total costs is smaller than area EDA of total benefits;[8] hence the result follows. Without charging a different price for each unit sold (perfect price discrimination) or a two-tier pricing structure such as is used for telephone service, there is no way that the service provider can obtain sufficient revenue from his customers, without subsidy, to cover operating expenses.

This result, showing a need for subsidy,[9] holds even when demand is more expansive; for example, cutting the average cost curve from above where the condition that price and marginal cost are equal simultaneously implies that

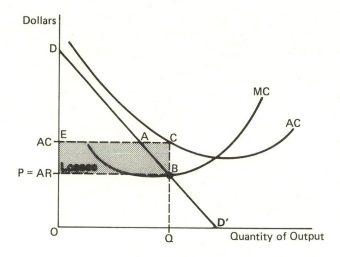

Figure 15.2 Demand and Costs of a Public Service

average costs are greater than average revenues. The only difference between these two situations is that several outputs exist in the latter case for which profits could be made. A subsidy is necessary only to induce the producer to provide output such that the social optimum is reached. By contrast, in the former case shown in Figure 15.2, the subsidy is needed to tempt the producer into the market in the first place. Although operating subsidies could help both, a capital subsidy to get production started is likely to be necessary for the first case.

This kind of consideration is the focus of both the Environmental Protection Agency (EPA) income policy on sewer grants and the Farmers Home Administration (FmHA) "hardship" definition for water and wastewater grants and loans. The EPA rule is that user-charge costs to handle normal operations and maintenance should not exceed 1 percent of annual average per capita income and debt retirement costs plus user charges should not be greater than 2 percent of per capita income (Train 1976). These policies are attempts either to insure efficient provision of the service or to redistribute income through subsidized provision of the services.

These percentages are statements about the maximum average cost that can be withstood by the users. No doubt it is expressible in terms of AC depicted in Figure 15.2 in which AC exceeds AR. Whenever the condition is violated, as a rule of thumb, either alternative technology or grants rather than loans (in the FmHA case) would be required.

Relying on individual preferences to determine community service levels has many advantages. It cannot be relied upon in cases such as those described above when low incomes prevent successful operation of the market. Unfortunately, individual preferences also cannot be relied on for services with substantial public good characteristics--where exclusion is very expensive--or for merit goods. In these services a voter preference approach is frequently applied. Examples include police protection, primary and secondary education, and some transportation functions. The voter preference approach is also used to set service levels when the individual preference approach could be utilized.

The voter preference approach can be viewed as a weak extension of the individual preference approach and permits some consumer control over service levels. Voters express their preferences on issues, tax levels, expenditures, or candidates that they presume will lead to their desired service level. Voters may not obtain the desired service levels through this process because voting decisions and production decisions by officials are widely separated and the voting choices are generally discrete, making it difficult for voters to make marginal decisions that can lead to optimal service levels. Thus, desired and actual service levels are likely to differ. Diversity in income, tastes, and socioeconomic characteristics within the community can exacerbate unhappiness with service levels because each consumer cannot choose his optimal service package. Residents can "vote with their feet"--choose a residential location on the basis of its community services characteristics--to achieve more desirable service levels (Tiebout 1956). To significantly improve well-being, this works only if many local government options exist within the narrow geographic area of residential locations. In metro areas like Cuyahoga County, Ohio, with more than thirty school districts and nearly fifty cities, towns, and villages, relatively continuous options are available to residents. Nonmetro residents, however, are likely to have greatly reduced options, so "voting with the feet" is unlikely to substantially increase well-being.

Another alternative to inadequate service levels is the purchase of private market supplements. Smoke alarms and sprinkler systems add to fire protection, locks and burglar alarms upgrade police protection, and wells and ponds increase water services. Many of the private market supplements are equally available in nonmetro areas, though low incomes and dispersed populations may make some, like private schools, less available.

Goods for which voter preference determines output are not rationed by price and are generally not pure public goods, so a distributive scheme is necessary. This results in limits, for example land-use zoning, which determine potential residents' access to water, sewer, and other services. Little is known about the way in which services are distributed. There have been some court cases, and a small body of literature about discrimination in service provision exists (Michelson et al. 1970). Local leaders often seek to please a subset of influential citizens by providing service levels that vary with community characteristics. Hirsch (1970) discusses three distribution schemes based on economic efficiency and equity grounds. The first is the efficiency approach that would achieve maximum total output from a given amount of inputs. The second is the equity approach that would provide each recipient with equal outputs. But this may not result in optimal output because the cost of serving residents is not uniform. Application of either of the above two approaches is very difficult given the output measurement problems. A compromise is to seek equal inputs per consumer, though the results of this procedure can vary greatly because the output effects will depend on resource quality and service conditions where production takes place.

The third approach, benefit-cost analysis, gives decision makers and consumers information for evaluating demand. This has been used to examine such diverse projects as water resources and industrial subsidy programs (Sazama 1970). Though it provides useful information, benefit-cost analysis fails to adequately account for distribution of benefits and costs and is likely to include substantial subjective influences. Evaluation standards promulgated by the Water Resource Council (1973) attempt to remedy this by requiring distributional accounts for regions and social well-being.

Professional standards are the last criteria used to set service minimums or maximums in areas where substantial externalities are present. For example, professional standards are used in certain licensing and certification procedures to establish desirable facility and labor characteristics. In a sense, local leaders may also use standards when they set service levels through emulation of other communities. Measuring the relative importance of this approach to setting service levels is difficult, but it is an important service demand proxy continually used in actual practice.

SHIFTING POPULATIONS

The metro-turnaround of the early 1970s has been well documented and analyzed. Recently Fuguitt (1979) concluded that:
(1) for perhaps the first time in American history, nonmetro
areas are growing faster than metro areas; (2) the most rapid growth in the countryside is in the most rural counties
with the smallest (or no) urban places; (3) open-space areas
are growing faster in rural counties than the towns and cities in these same counties; and (4) nonmetro growth occurs
uniformly in all of the United States census regions. Detailed analysis of this phenomenon is provided in other
chapters in this book by Zuiches and by Brown and Beale. Although there is some evidence presented by Engels and Healy
(1979) that rural growth may be selective and the Urban Land
Institute argues that it may be short-lived, the phenomenon
can have dramatic impacts on the provision of services in
nonmetro areas. This is intensified in these areas by the
relative size of the effect of migration on the original
population. As Engels and Healy point out, the move of 3,000
people during 1970-1976 into Summit County, Colorado represents a 100 percent growth in the original Summit County
population. The records of Orange County, California (the
fastest-growing metropolitan area between 1970-1976) showed,
on the other hand, that population increased on average by
3,000 people every twenty-nine days during the same period
(334,000 people). Yet, growth in population in Orange County
occurred at a rate of only 17 percent. In terms of both
relative requirements for new services and relative impacts
on per capita costs of those services, it is reasonable that
the impact of Summit County growth was greater than Orange
County growth. Empirical investigation of this assertion
would be a useful addition to the literature.

There are many ways in which shifting nonmetro populations and the provision of services in these areas interact.
Three will be considered here: the way population dynamics
affect service provision, the way service provision affects
population dynamics, and the simultaneous interaction
between the two.

An important fact is that public services are a focal
point, in part causing population redistribution. This is
consistent with the recent theories of residential preferences as well as the older Tiebout hypothesis of "voting
with one's feet" (Tiebout 1956). Certainly Liu (1975) has
shown that environmental and other quality-of-life variables
including public services are growing in importance relative

to economic variables in determining migration to and from
metropolitan areas. The early work of Oates (1969) and
later work of Polinsky and Shavell (1976) and others have
shown that intraurban differences in service provision
influence population distribution. Few, if any, of these
studies, however, have shown that services are as effective
in influencing nonmetro area development.

It was stated above that there are fewer contiguous
nonmetro governments and fewer private substitutes for
public providers in nonmetro areas to choose among in
making intralabor market choice of residence as meaningful
a process as it is in metro areas. Nevertheless, the Urban
Land Institute finding that there is a selective bias within
counties to nonmunicipal places is one source of scant
evidence that decision making within nonmetro areas may be
influenced by relative levels of public services and their
associated tax costs. A dissertation by Bunjun (1978),
extending the Liu methodology into nonmetro Pennsylvania
counties, supports this assertion.

The Influence of Population on Services

Thompson (1972) and Riew (1973) have shown that the average cost of typical public services is U shaped as depicted
in Figure 15.3. Further they argue that population does
equilibrate at points such as B and C, representing nonmetro
and metro places, respectively. These points are drawn in
Figure 15.3, wherein the quantity of service delivered per
capita is held constant. The 1960s migration from nonmetro
to metro areas considered by Riew shows a loss in typical
rural populations of B-A and a gain in urban population of
D-C. This flow is shown in Figure 15.3 by the arrows on the
line labeled "nonmetro to metro." For such a migration flow
at least one public sector impact of migration has been uniformly bad, raising average prices of public services in
both metro and nonmetro places. When the reverse flow of
migration occurred in the 1970s (shown in Figure 15.3 by the
arrows labeled "metro to nonmetro"), sending migrants back
to nonmetro areas from the metro places, the reverse effect
on average service costs occurred, uniformly lowering costs
in both metro and nonmetro places.

Beyond this impact on service cost, migration has secondary effects involving a short-run loss in the value of
wealth for out-migration areas and the possibility of short-
run inefficiency in production in both areas. The latter is
certainly true in out-migration areas and is likely to occur
as well for short periods of time in areas of in-migration.

The efficiency problems follow because of the lengthy planning periods associated with capital facilities in public
services. In some services, water for example, the length of
the planning period (determined by interest rates, population size and dynamics, capital durability, and other factors) is over twenty years (Binkley et al. 1975). This
causes communities to operate at least for the duration of
the planning period on a suboptimal short-run cost curve,
whereas it would be preferable for them to operate on the
long-run average cost curve. There is some presumption that
it is easier to adjust from the short-run curve to the long-
run curve during periods of community growth when new capital can simply be added than during periods of decline when
it may be hard to withdraw incremental parts of the capital
facility from production. Even if one can withdraw part of
the capital facility from production, the community continues to suffer from the continuing payments for the capitalized costs of the parts that are withdrawn.

Losses in the value of services produced with a given
capital facility are actually a reflection of these short-
run changes where areas of in-migration have in-sufficient
capital relative to labor and areas of out-migration have a
surplus of capital relative to labor. This forces the price
of the capital either up or down. Revaluation of capital
assets alters the value of the existing community wealth.
In practical terms, areas of out-migration have underutilized facilities such as roads, hospitals, and schools, and
areas of in-migration find facilities becoming crowded--a
factor forcing change by the addition of new facilities.

The Influence of Service on Population

It has been well demonstrated that some services, particularly water and wastewater, are catalysts of development
(Lewis et al. 1973). Others, such as education and health,
are amenities that influence the final residential choice of
the mobile population. The provision of services can thus
influence growth, affecting inter- and intraarea land prices
as well as business[10] and residential location decisions.

The literature is clear about water and sewerage effects
on growth. The funding policies of FmHA have recently been
criticized (Jacobson 1978; Urban Systems Research 1974) for
abetting sprawl in nonmetro areas. Also, EPA intercepter
sewer programs show case studies where communities were primarily interested in grant money as a source of more general
development capital. These communities planned expansively
for hundreds of years of future growth and obtained unwanted

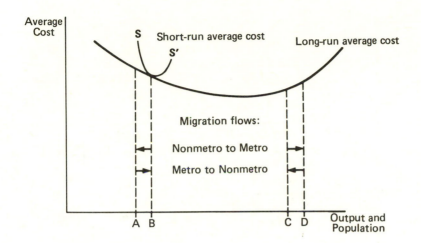

Figure 15.3 Public Service Average Cost Curve

and unconstrained sprawl at the less densely settled fringe. Aron and Coelen (1977) show some evidence that these investment programs fail to control for the distribution of benefits. In a case study of suburban and rural fringes of Philadelphia, it was determined that developers captured more than 75 percent of the benefits of water and sewer investments not paid for by user charges. The New Jersey Department of Community Affairs (1975) has developed a proposal that would absorb these benefits in taxes that could be spent on orderly green spaces, thus eliminating the private market incentives encouraging sprawl. A page-one article in the New York Times has documented the general dilemma (1975).

Generally, the distribution of population and business within small geographic areas will be affected by differentials in service levels provided and taxes imposed. Services such as education and health care affect the location of people and business within a commuting range of employment opportunities. Water, sewerage, and utilities can be viewed as prerequisites to location, and areas without these services may not be viable choices so that locational effects may be important over a wider geographic area.

The Interaction of Services and Population

The sections above have stated that population affects services and that services affect population. It is also

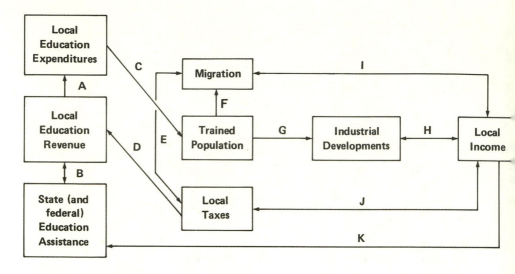

Linkage	Rationale
A	Schools operate balanced budgets and expenditures are limited by revenue.
B	The local tax effort affects state assistance payments.
C	Education expenditures presumably influence the quality of output.
D	Higher local revenues for education require higher local tax receipts and vice versa.
E	Taxes influence at least intraregional location decisions of labor. Also migration affects the size of the tax base.
F	A more highly trained populace is more mobile.
G	A trained populace is attractive to industrial developers.
H	Industrial development influences the level of local income. Also higher local income is attractive to some industry, particularly commercial establishments.
I	Migration can add to or subtract from the flow of local income. Also the level of local income has some effect on the amount or type of migration.
J	Local income influences the ability to pay local taxes. Also taxes are subtracted from personal income to obtain disposable income.
K	The income of a community along with tax collections determines effort, a basic determinant of state aid to education formulas.

Figure 15.4 One Sector of a Nonmetropolitan Development Model

reasonable to inquire about the synergistic effects of the
two. To do this, it would be necessary to develop a full-
scale model of nonmetro growth, but none exist at the appropriate level of detail. The core of a dissertation by Stout
(1978) provides one attempt at a model focusing on the influence of education, but concentration on other issues
prohibits the necessary broad detail of a general model.

The substance of an appropriate model focusing on educational services can be summarized in Figure 15.4. The
linkages of this model are based upon some existing research
and can be explained by the rationale for the figure.

Although there is no doubt that local leaders do not con-
ceptualize their education expenditure decision making as
part of such an elaborate system, surely they perceive some
of the implications of the model in Figure 15.4. The amount
of their spending is determined by population and yet also
influences population, and the amount should not be great
enough in poverty-stricken nonmetro places to strap the resource base and hasten the out-migration of their most valuable human resources. But certainly sufficient amounts must
be spent to attract industry to provide growth. Is there a
solution? Is it stable? Is it optimal? The answers to these
questions depend significantly on the lag structure of some
of the linkages in the model. However, these questions can
be answered only with empirical research and there is an urgency to this research. For example, the findings of Holland
and Tweeten (1973) indicated significant outflow of human
resources from local education districts in Oklahoma. Because of this they recommended that education expenditures
should be more heavily subsidized at higher fiscal levels of
government. Similar questions abound in other service areas
and these, too, require investigation.

CONCLUSIONS

This chapter has outlined the simple proposition that dispersed population, low incomes, and migration have prevented
optimal delivery of public services in nonmetro areas. The
case was made for governmental intervention in these areas,
providing the planning of the level of services to be delivered, determining the appropriate technology to be applied,
and producing the actual service delivery. Delivery of services was shown to depend on an appropriate small technology
and further that services should be provided or controlled

by an appropriate level of government. Given American federalism, this should be the lowest level of government for
which there are no spillovers into a larger jurisdiction. It
may be at a lower level of government only when spillovers
are compensated by subsidies or taxes. Services such as elementary and secondary education, primary health care, water
supply, wastewater treatment, solid waste disposal, and recreation can generally be handled best at the local level of
government. Regulation of service delivery (involving, for
example, externalities among water region subareas and river
basins, migratory patterns of the young and educated, peak-
load sharing among power producers and coordination of
transportation scheduling), often requires the higher level
intervention of states or the federal government.

Much of the effort to establish a proper level of output
or to foster an appropriate technology requires financial
assistance. When it does, the assistance is inevitably
intended for worthy purposes. These government policies are
designed best when they overcome market inefficiencies, with
interjurisdictional neutrality, but practically it is difficult for them ever to be neutral with respect to economic
behavior. Warford (1969) has shown that such investments can
be harmful because of the resulting undesired side effects.
In an evaluation of water supply in England (conducted as a
prelude to the massive regionalization and the subsequent
supply of public water to nearly every English resident),
Warford considered the general equilibrium effects of water
subsidies. He computed the "extra costs" of providing mail
service, transportation, telecommunications, and other services in more expensive, remote areas whose growth would be
initially spurred by the subsidized water supply. Because
most of these services did not discriminate by place of residence, the average user charge for these other services implicitly includes additional subsidies for rural areas. One
subsidy (water) tempts people to locate in remote areas;
and the others result from the need to provide additional
necessary services. The real cost of the first subsidy
should include the others, and the real benefits should also
include the net benefits associated with the other services.

This argument implies for the general services considered in this chapter that investments in any service should
be contingent upon the extent to which they promote in-
migration, growth, and development that in turn will require
subsidization and provision of other services. In sum, decisions on facility and output levels for community services
must be made in a broad context that considers the inter-

action of community services as well as their direct and peripheral effects.

NOTES

1. Many public services have become the focus of White House initiatives. Task forces exist for rural initiatives in water and waste-water, health, transportation, and energy. State policies, summarized by Bivens (1977), have concentrated on these as well as on land use, housing, and education.

2. These twelve service areas are the focus of a current major study by Abt Associates, Inc. (1979) for Farmers Home Administration. Called the National Rural Community Facilities Assessment Study, it is a survey of 2,346 rural communities, open spaces, and incorporated municipalities to provide an objective assessment of current capital facilities.

3. The per capita costs of these services in counties of 10,000 and less, as reported by Hitzhusen and Napier (1978), range from $1.06 for corrections through $1.54 for solid waste, $1.70 for recreation, $1.78 for fire protection, $2.89 for wastewater, $8.86 for water supply, $10.06 for police, $27.17 for health, and $55.71 for transportation to $222.37 for education. This leaves out spending for public goods produced by a private firm and not a governmental agency. Thus, neither energy nor telecommunications of the Abt study are in the Hitzhusen and Napier list.

4. Here transportation and fire safety, the latter considering heavy voluntary inputs of labor, are exceptions.

5. The size economies research may also be inappropriate for the quality of outputs may decline with larger service-providing units. Though the evidence is not yet clear, Sher and Tompkins (1977) argue this point for local education.

6. Little work exists on integrating these alternative technologies. Aron et al. (1974) have provided one of the few insights into integration from an engineering viewpoint.

7. The most notable examples of recent work are studies of energy-biomass, solar power, and wind; cluster wells; health clinic hospital substitutes, the use of nurse practitioners, and small area telecommunication hookups to tertiary hospitals, etc.

8. Area OQBAE is common to both of the areas that represent total costs and total benefits.

9. In work on micropolitan development, Tweeten and Brinkman (1976) argue that a subsidy from the appropriate

level of government (federal, state, or local) is also useful in cases of externality and income redistribution.

    10. Business decisions seem to be more finely tuned. Due
(1961) and Stinson (1968) report that taxes are more likely
to be effective in intra- than in interregional decisions.

BIBLIOGRAPHY

Abt Associates, Inc. Interim Report, Phase I, National Com-
    munity Facilities Assessment Study. Report submitted to
    Farmers Home Administration, U.S. Department of
    Agriculture. Mimeographed, January 1979.

Arizona Department of Health Services. Minimum Requirements
    for Design: Submission of Plans and Specifications of
    Sewage Works. Bulletin no. 11, July 1978.

Aron, Gert, and Coelen, Stephen P. Economic and Technical
    Considerations of Regional Water Supply. Report submitt-
    ed to the U.S. Army Engineer Institute for Water
    Resources, IWR Contract Report 77-7. Fort Belvoir, Va.,
    July 1977.

Aron, Gert et al. A Method for Integrating Surface and
    Ground Water Use in Humid Regions. Institute for
    Research on Land and Water Resources, no. 76. Pennsyl-
    vania State University, February 1974.

Bailey, Elizabeth E. Economic Theory of Regulatory Con-
    straint. Lexington, Mass.: D. C. Heath and Co., 1973.

Bator, Francis M. "Analytics of Welfare Maximization."
    American Economic Review (Mar. 1957): 22-59.

Binkley, Clark et al. Interceptor Sewers and Urban Sprawl.
    Lexington, Mass.: D. C. Heath and Co., 1975.

Bivens, William E., III. State Development Strategies for
    Rural Communities. Report prepared for the Council of
    State Planning Agencies. Washington, D.C., 1977.

Breton, Albert. "Public Goods (and Federalism): A Reply."
    Canadian Journal of Economics and Political Science 32
    (1966): 238-42.

_____. "A Theory of Government Grants." Canadian
    Journal of Political Economy (Oct. 1956): 416-24.

Bunjun, Seewoonundun. "Quality of Life Indices and Their
    Role in Explaining Migration." Ph.D. dissertation,
    Pennsylvania State University, 1978.

Cobb, Edwin L., and Morgan, Mary E. Drinking Water Supplies
    in Rural America. National Demonstration Water Project,
    1978.

Commonwealth of Massachusetts, Division of Water Pollution
    Control. Notice of Public Hearing to Hear Comments on
    the Construction Grants Project Priority List for
    Fiscal Year 1979.
Due, J. F. "Studies of State-Local Tax Influences on Loca-
    tion of Industry." National Tax Journal 14 (1961):
    163-73.
Engels, Richard, and Healy, Mary Kay. "Rural Renaissance
    Reconsidered." American Demographics 2 (1979): 16-19.
Foster, John E. "City Water: Rural Water System Design."
    Water Well Journal (Feb. 1974): 26-27, 53-55.
Fox, William F. "A Review of Size Economics in Local Govern-
    ment Services." Mimeographed, 1980.
_____ et al. Economics of Size in Local Government:
    An Annotated Bibliography. Rural Development Research
    Report, no. 9. Washington, D.C.: U.S. Department of
    Agriculture, Economic Development Division, 1979.
Fuguitt, Glenn Victor. Growth and Change in Rural America.
    Washington, D.C.: Urban Land Institute, 1979.
Higgins, John M., and Okun, Daniel A. Regional Development
    of Public Water Supply Needs. Water Resources Research
    Institute of the University of North Carolina. Chapel
    Hill, N.C., 1972.
Hirsch, Werner Z. The Economics of State and Local Govern-
    ment. New York: McGraw-Hill Book Co., 1970.
_____. "Local Versus Areawide Urban Government Ser-
    vices." National Tax Journal 17 (1964): 331-39.
_____. "The Supply of Urban Public Services." In
    Issues in Urban Economics, edited by Harvey S. Perloff
    and Lowdon Wingo, Jr. Baltimore, Md.: Johns Hopkins
    University Press, 1968.
Hirshleifer, Jack et al. Water Supply: Economics, Tech-
    nology, and Policy. Chicago, Ill.: University of
    Chicago Press, 1960.
Hitzhusen, Fred, and Napier, Ted. "A Rural Public Services
    Policy Framework and Some Alternatives." In Rural
    Policy Research Alternatives, edited by David L. Rogers
    and Larry R. Whiting. Ames, Iowa.: Iowa State University
    Press, 1978.
Holland, David W., and Tweeten, Luther. "Human Capital
    Migration: Implications for Common School Finance."
    Land Economics 49 (1973): 278-84.
Hughes, Trevor C., and Israelson, Earl. "Rural Water Systems
    Design." In Rural Water Views. Washington, D.C.:
    National Demonstration Water Project, 1976.
Jacobson, Tom. "How Farmers Home Encourages Urban Sprawl."

Planning (Oct. 1978): 21-33.

Lewis, W. Cris et al. _Regional Growth and Water Resource Investment_. Lexington, Mass.: D. C. Heath and Co., 1973.

Liu, Ben-Chieh. _Quality of Life Indicators in U.S. Metropolitan Areas_. Washington, D.C.: U.S. Environmental Protection Agency, 1975.

Michelson, Stephan et al. _A Research Report for the Plaintiffs: Hobson v. Hansen_. Report submitted to U.S. District Court for the District of Columbia as an appendix to plaintiffs' reply memorandum, 8 December 1970. Cambridge, Mass.: Center for Educational Research, Harvard University, 1970.

Musgrave, Richard A. _The Theory of Public Finance_. New York: McGraw-Hill Book Co., 1959.

New Jersey Department of Community Affairs and Division of State and Regional Planning. "Secondary Impact of Regional Sewage Systems." June 1975.

New York Times. "Thirsty Metropolis." 18 Mar. 1975.

Oates, W. "The Effects of Property Taxes and Local Public Spending on Property Values: An Empirical Study of Tax Capitalization and the Tiebout Hypothesis." _Journal of Political Economy_ 77 (1969): 957-71.

Ostrom, Vincent et al. "The Organization of Government in Metropolitan Areas: A Theoretical Inquiry." _The American Political Science Review_ 55 (1961): 831-42.

Plews, Gary D. "The Adequacy and Uniformity of Regulations for On-Site Wastewater Disposal--A State Viewpoint." _Less Costly Wastewater Treatment Systems for Small Communities_. Reston, Va.: U.S. Environmental Protection Agency, 1977.

Polinsky, A. Mitchell, and Shavell, Steven. "Amenities and Property Values in a Model of an Urban Area." _Journal of Political Economics_ 5 (1976): 119-29.

Riew, J. "Migration and Public Policy." _Journal of Regional Science_ 13 (1973): 65-76.

Sazama, Gerald W. "A Benefit-Cost Analysis of a Regional Development Incentive: State Loans." _Journal of Regional Science_ 10 (1970): 385-96.

Sher, Jonathan P., and Tompkins, Rachel B. "Economy, Efficiency and Equality: The Myths of Rural School and District Consolidation." In _Education in Rural America: A Reassessment of Conventional Wisdom_, edited by Jonathan P. Sher. Boulder, Colo.: Westview Press, 1977.

Stinson, Thomas F. _The Effects of Taxes and Public Financing Programs on Local Industrial Development--A Survey of the Literature_. Agricultural Economics Report, no. 133.

Washington, D.C.: U.S. Department of Agriculture, Economic Research Service, 1968.

Stocker, Frederick D. "Fiscal Needs and Resources of Non-metropolitan Communities." In National Conference on Nonmetropolitan Community Services Research. Prepared for the Committee on Agriculture, Nutrition, and Forestry, United States Senate, 12 July 1977. Washington, D.C.: U.S. Government Printing Office, 1977.

Stout, Robert. "An Economic Analysis of the Relationship of Educational Expenditures and Migration in Penn County: 1960-1970." Ph.D. dissertation, Pennsylvania State University, 1978.

Thompson, Wilbur R. "The National System of Cities as an Object of Public Policy." Urban Studies 9 (1972): 99-116.

Tiebout, Charles M. "An Economic Theory of Fiscal Decentralization." In NBER, Public Finances: Needs, Sources, and Utilization. New York: National Bureau of Economic Research, 1961.

_____. "A Pure-Theory of Local Expenditures." Journal of Political Economy 64 (1956): 416-24.

Train, Russell E. "Encouraging Less Costly Wastewater Facilities for Small Communities." Washington, D.C.: U.S. Environmental Protection Agency, 1976.

Tweeten, Luther, and Brinkman, George. Micropolitan Development: Theory and Practice of Greater-Rural Economic Development. Ames, Iowa.: Iowa State University Press, 1976.

Urban Systems Research, Inc. Interceptor Sewers and Urban Sprawl: The Impact of Construction Grants on Residential Land Use. Vol. I and II. Prepared for the Council on Environmental Quality. Springfield, Va.: National Technical Information Service, 1974.

U.S. Bureau of the Census. Census of Governments, 1972. Vol. 5, Local Government in Metropolitan Areas. Washington, D.C.: U.S. Government Printing Office, 1974.

U.S. Department of Agriculture. Rural America: Poverty and Progress. December 1977.

Warford, J. J. The South Atcham Scheme: An Economic Appraisal. London: Her Majesty's Stationery Office, 1969.

Water Resource Council. "Water and Related Land Resources: Establishments of Principles and Standards for Planning." Federal Register, vol. 38, no. 174. Washington, D.C.: National Archives of the United States, 10 Sept. 1973.

Weldon, J. C. "Public Goods (and Federalism)." Canadian Journal of Economics and Political Science 32 (1966): 230-38.

Roger A. Rosenblatt

16
Health and
Health Services

INTRODUCTION

Health care services are an essential component of a healthy
community. Every individual must confront the problems of
illness and death, and in every society collective mechanisms evolve to assist the individual in his attempts to
mitigate the impact of illness. In rural America, the health
care system is a fundamental social service whose symbolic
and emotional impact goes beyond the boundaries of a technological response to disease. A stable, functional, and
culturally relevant health care system is a basic underpinning of rural society.

Rural society is characterized by low density of settlement; this sparseness of population is paralleled by a
relative paucity of social services. In a culture marked by
pluralism and abundance, even a wealthy community usually
has only one system of health care. This lack of diversity
or redundancy makes the rural dweller vulnerable to sudden
unpredictable interruption of basic health services; very
often the entire spectrum of health services is dependent
on an aging physician or obsolescent hospital.

Rural communities are keenly sensitive to these potential disruptions. All members of local communities can
mobilize themselves around the loss of health services;
often they are more effective in establishing a new practice
than maintaining it once it is in place. As Kane has observed (1977: 146), "health care seems to play a somewhat
unusual role. . . . Although strongly demanded when absent,
its effect on the community when present is hard to assess."

Rurality plays a role in American life that exceeds
the relative proportion of the population living there. The
comparative isolation of rural America from the artificial
environments created by dense aggregations of people serves
as a respite for the urban dweller, and a persistent internal frontier for the jaded or discouraged. The demographic
resurgence of nonmetro areas is the final common pathway

for the yearnings of diverse groups within our society, and for the first time in a century nonmetro areas are sought after actively by those with choices. Yet health services have continued to be relatively deficient in these areas, an impediment to the creation of the stable social networks needed to sustain nonmetro populations. Our national commitment to cultural and population diversity implies a commitment to the provision of adequate social services in all segments of the country.

The emphasis on creating stable rural health care systems must be understood in terms of the functional role they play in maintaining viable social systems. The relationship between health service and health status is elusive, particularly in a society marked by racial and socioeconomic heterogeneity, distinct regional characteristics, and high mobility. Although, as discussed below, nonmetro dwellers have fewer health resources and more illness and impairment than their metro counterparts, it is impossible to demonstrate a causal relationship between those two conditions. Yet the presence of a doctor and hospital in a rural community has a psychological impact on the community beyond the physical services they provide; and their absence undermines the integrity of the social fabric upon which the community's health depends.

HEALTH STATISTICS AND NONMETROPOLITAN AMERICA

Relative health status is difficult to measure in the United States. Health is a subjective state, a reflection of the individual's balance within his environment. Mortality rates are most often used as surrogates for health status, and are crude instruments for assessing the relative well-being of different groups within the population.

The impact of health services on health status is difficult to demonstrate in industrialized countries. Studies of health service utilization in the United States reveal there is no predictable relationship between the degree of health service utilization and an individual's subjective assessment of health (Anderson et al., 1975: 264). To further complicate the issue, health status statistics are often not collected in a way that makes it possible to compare the rates for nonmetro populations.

In examining health status in nonmetro areas, it is useful to understand the distinctions and interrelationships among health status, health care resources, and utilization of those resources. The major determinants of health status are intrinsic, stemming from the interaction between the individual's biological potential and the environment. Thus, demographic characterizations of a given population group are very powerful predictors of the health status of the group. Nonmetro populations contain higher percentages of elderly and higher proportions of poor than do metro populations (Martin 1975); because age and poverty both predispose to and interact with illness, nonmetro populations can be expected to have poorer overall health status whether or not rurality per se conveys its own health hazards.

The available data, though meager and at times contradictory, support this prediction. The data are flawed by the definitional imprecision that constitutes rurality; it is difficult to transform a continuous variable like rurality into quantifiably distinct chunks. The health field is further complicated by the fact that medical trade areas-- the patterns that people follow in their health-seeking behavior--rarely coincide with traditional geopolitical boundaries, and often run counter to the trade patterns that evolve for other goods and services. Thus, the jurisdictional categories in which data are presented often obscure the impact of, at times, profound variations in health status and health services. The difficulty of interpretation is further exacerbated by the long intervals between censuses in a volatile field in which technology and manpower change rapidly.

Table 16.1 compares infant and maternal mortality rates for metro and nonmetro areas. These rates are used internationally as an indicator of health status, and are very sensitive to changes in the health status of populations and organized interventions into health care services. The data are particularly interesting in that they demonstrate persistently higher mortality rates in the nonmetro population. Of equal interest is the fact that race--which is closely associated with socioeconomic status--is a much more powerful determinant of relative health status. However, the relative disadvantage of nonmetro populations is evident despite the effect of race. The more recent infant mortality data reveal that although the overall infant mortality rate has fallen, the metro-nonmetro gap is unchanged.

Corroborative evidence comes from two sources: the National Center for Health Statistics studies, presented in

Table 16.1. Infant and Maternal Mortality Rates by
Residence, 1968 and 1969-1973

Mortality Rate	Metro		Nonmetro	
	1968	1969-1973	1968	1969-1973
	Deaths per 1,000 live births			
Infant	21.1	18.8	23.0	20.7
White	18.6		20.2	
Nonwhite	32.5		39.3	
	Deaths per 100,000 live births			
Maternal	23.6		26.4	

Source: Adapted from Matthews, Table 14, p. 17 and
Ahearn, Table 10, p. 23.

Table 16.2; and a nationwide survey of elderly performed
under the aegis of the Social Security Administration,
presented in Table 16.3. In Table 16.2, the major chronic
health conditions are listed in order of decreasing prevalence; in every category except one these conditions are
markedly more prevalent among the nonmetro population. The
data from the elderly population echo this. The elderly--
whether recipients of federal old-age assistance or not--
are more likely to rate their health as poor, have a greater
number of health disorders, and are more likely to experience physical disability as a result of their afflictions.
Again, we see that low socioeconomic status--as indicated
by the necessity for federal assistance--is of itself a
more powerful determinant of ill-health than rurality alone.
However, these differences persist despite statistical
corrections for age and socioeconomic status. The authors
conclude: "the study demonstrates that the prevalence of
many chronic disorders and impairments is significantly
greater among the rural aged than for their cohorts in more
urban areas. These differences persist after controls for
age, sex and race are introduced" (McCoy and Brown, 1978:
14).

The information presented in the second half of Table
16.2 appears to demonstrate that nonmetro dwellers are less
disabled by acute conditions than their metro counterparts,
in contrast to their greater burden of chronic disabling

Table 16.2. Comparison of Rural and Urban Health Statistics
for Selected Health Conditions

Health Condition	Urban	Rural
	Prevalence per 1,000 persons	
Chronic conditions		
Hypertension	58.7	62.6
Chronic bronchitis	33.0	33.0
Coronary heart disease	16.2	16.6
Ulcer of stomach and duodenum	15.9	18.9
Hernia	15.3	17.6
Hypertensive heart disease	9.6	12.0
Gallbladder disease	9.0	12.5
Emphysema	5.4	8.8
	Days of bed disability per 100 persons per year	
Acute conditions		
All acute conditions	415.2	376.3
Respiratory conditions	317.5	259.0
Influenza	110.8	102.4
Injuries	66.1	65.8
Infective and parasitic diseases	47.3	38.1
Digestive system conditions	21.3	19.5

Source: Adapted from Kane, Table 2, p. 137.

disorders. The evidence in this area is confusing, however.
Other sources (Matthews, pp. 19, 20) exhibit data showing
higher injury rates for the nonmetro nonfarm population,
and greater disability and lost work among the nonmetro
blue-collar workers. The evidence, considered as a whole,
suggests that the nonmetro areas contain a sizable reservoir of the disabled elderly. Although some evidence suggests a higher injury rate among the accident-prone occupations of nonmetro areas, it does not appear that the
younger nonmetro population experiences significantly different health status than that in metro areas.

Table 16.3. Self-evaluation of Health Status by Elderly
Rural and Urban Dwellers

Evaluation	Farm or Open Country	Small Towns	Small City	Large City
	Recipients of old-age assistance			
	%	%	%	%
Self-rating of health as poor	59.9	51.3	43.4	43.1
Five or more health disorders	50.7	49.9	43.0	40.2
Severe physical activity limitation	46.4	50.0	48.1	41.5
Total number (000s)	378	554	225	475
Mean number of health disorders	5.27	5.20	4.81	4.59
	Nonrecipients of old-age assistance			
	%	%	%	%
Self-rating of health as poor	29.0	20.4	19.0	21.2
Five or more health disorders	30.1	24.9	34.3	22.3
Severe physical activity limitation	29.7	22.7	25.3	21.0
Total number (000s)	2,561	4,478	2,422	4,136
Mean number of health disorders	3.94	3.55	3.58	3.27

Source: Adapted from McCoy and Brown, Table 4, p. 20.

The relative deficiency of health resources in nonmetro
areas is dramatic, pervasive, and unequivocal. In a scholarly volume attempting to ferret out inequity in health service delivery, the authors conclude: "By the criteria used
here, the group most consistently experiencing inequity in
entering the system is the rural farm population. They are

less likely than the rest of the population to be admitted
to a hospital or to see a doctor or a dentist. Access
problems for inner city residents appear in contrast less
serious" (Anderson et al., 1975: 31).

The resource disparity is depicted graphically in Tables
16.4, 16.5, and Figure 16.1. The period since World War II
has shown a rapid escalation in the geographic maldistribu-
tion of physicians in the United States. The peculiar syner-
gism of the health industry, in which physician availability
is the base of the pyramid upon which all other services
depend, makes this particularly pernicious in its broad
impact on all available rural health services. In the 1960s
governmental attention at the federal and state levels
focused sharply on the doctor shortage, and it was naively
thought that increasing the aggregate supply of doctors
could improve the supply of physicians in underserved rural
areas. As Table 16.4 shows, the increase in the total physician supply resulting from those interventions between
1972 and 1976 has increased the number of physicians per
population in nonmetro areas; but the relative nonmetro
disadvantage has, in fact, increased for the nation as a
whole and for each of its four major regions. Figure 16.1
demonstrates an almost pristine linear relationship between
population size and physician supply; physicians cluster
where they are most numerous suggesting that the free market
alone will not insure an equitable distribution of health
providers.

The same pattern is repeated in attenuated form for
dentists and nurses, with the additional burden of the
southern United States being reflected in these two categories, part of the regional pattern that also applies to
the health status data for the elderly (McCoy and Brown,
1978: 25). Hospital beds, paradoxically, are distributed
much more equally with respect to population, largely as a
result of massive federal investment in nonmetro community
hospitals through the Hill-Burton program (Ahearn, 1979:
37). These hospitals, however, are considerably smaller,
offer fewer services, and are less financially stable than
their metro counterparts, a fact reflected in the figures
of Table 16.6. It is ironic that the most expensive component of the health care system, and that under most sustained attack from those seeking to contain costs, is the most
equitably if not logically distributed in the population at
large.

An important resource in a medical care system that
accounts for almost one-tenth of the gross national product

Table 16.4. Active Nonfederal Physicians (M.D.s) per 10,000
Resident Population by Region and Location, 1972 and 1976

Region	Within SMSA		Outside SMSA		United States	
	1972	1976	1972	1976	1972	1976
All regions	17.2	19.3	7.3	8.0	14.5	16.2
Northeast	20.2	22.2	10.0	10.9	18.8	20.6
North Central	15.0	17.3	6.9	7.5	12.5	14.2
South	15.3	17.6	6.4	7.2	12.0	13.8
West	18.4	20.2	8.6	9.5	16.4	17.9

Source: Adapted from U.S. Department of Health, Education
and Welfare, Health--United States 1978, Table 127, p. 342.

is the wherewithal to pay for medical services. The medical
marketplace is dominated by third-party payment, a combination of insurance, prepayment, and employee and governmental benefits, that insulates most people from the full
impact of medical bills. Nonmetro populations, because of
their low density and businesses employing few people, are
less likely to be covered by private health insurance (Department of Health, Education and Welfare 1978). Federal
and state programs such as medicare and medicaid take up
some of the slack. However, as Davis and Marshall have
demonstrated, the lower service density in nonmetro areas
also distorts the federal insurance programs so that fewer
monies flow into those areas (1977). This anomaly creates a
vicious cycle in which need cannot be translated into
effective demand because of inadequate fiscal resources;
without a mechanism to pay for services, poorer nonmetro
dwellers cannot provide the financial base for physicians
and hospitals seeking to locate in these areas.

The level of utilization of services by rural inhabitants is more a function of the level of resources available than the underlying need. Nonmetro dwellers have longer
waits to see their physicians and see them less frequently.
This is mirrored in the higher work loads and longer hours
of nonmetro physicians (American Medical Association 1974).
Closer analysis of the data reveals that the nonmetro dwellers are more likely to use family practitioners and general
practitioners than specialists, and that it is the decrement
in the specialist category that accounts for the fewer number of visits. On one hand, this is a reflection of the

Table 16.5. Physicians, Dentists, and Registered Nurses per 10,000 Resident Population by Profession, Region, and Location for Selected Years

Profession	Within SMSA	Outside SMSA	Overall
Active nonfederal physicians, 1976			
United States	19.3	8.0	16.2
Northeast	22.2	10.9	20.6
North Central	17.3	7.5	14.2
South	17.6	7.2	13.8
West	20.2	9.5	17.9
Licensed dentists, 1974			
United States	6.0	3.7	5.4
Northeast	7.2	4.8	6.9
North Central	5.6	4.2	5.2
South	4.8	2.8	4.1
West	6.9	4.8	6.5
Registered nurses employed in nursing, 1972			
United States	38.0	27.0	38.2
Northeast	46.7	47.7	51.4
North Central	36.7	29.6	38.4
South	32.2	18.7	28.8
West	35.3	28.8	36.5

Source: Adapted from U.S. Department of Health, Education and Welfare, Health--United States 1978, Table 129, pp. 344-46.

fact that almost no specialists locate in nonmetro areas, and, on the other hand, it may also indicate that the health care system itself is poorly integrated, with impediments to consultation and referral existing in nonmetro areas. The reduced number of visits to specialists per se does not indicate anything about the quality of care rendered. However, because generalists are often overworked and spend less time with individual patients, it may reflect a sit-

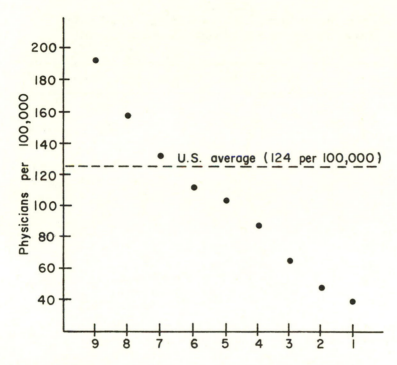

Source: Coleman, p. 3.

Figure 16.1 Nonfederal Physicians per 100,000 Population by County, from Most Urban (9) to Most Rural (1), 1970

uation where the rural dweller is shortchanged in his quest for adequate medical services.

Although the relationship of medical care to health status may not be totally clear-cut, the conclusion that emerges from this review of the statistics is that the nonmetro population, because of its demographic composition and the intrinsic characteristics of rurality, has a greater relative need for medical care services. Paradoxically, medical care services are distributed along gradients other than need, and the resulting disparity is particularly acute in nonmetro areas. During a period in which nonmetro areas are gaining population, a significant proportion of whom are elderly retired, the need for services is increasing. As the Papers on the National Health Guidelines point out: "Most medically underserved areas are 'underserved' in

Table 16.6. Community Hospitals, According to Selected
Characteristics, Geographic Regions, and Location of
Hospital, 1976

Characteristic	Within SMSA	Outside SMSA	Overall
Beds per 1,000 resi- dent population			
United States	4.6	4.3	4.5
Northeast	4.5	4.3	4.5
North Central	5.1	4.9	5.0
South	4.8	4.2	4.6
West	3.8	3.7	3.8
Average number of beds per hospital			
United States	237	84	161
Northeast	275	129	238
North Central	282	86	166
South	217	83	141
West	179	61	128
Occupancy rates (in percent)			
United States	76.3	67.4	73.9
Northeast	81.8	75.8	81.0
North Central	78.1	66.4	74.5
South	74.1	67.9	72.0
West	67.9	59.8	66.3

Source: Adapted from U.S. Department of Health, Education
and Welfare, Health--United States 1978, Table 139, pp.
368-69.

other important respects. Human resource development and
community development are likely to be deficient as well.
If appropriately designed, solutions to the health under-
service problem may have important spillover benefits for
human resource and community development" (Davis and Marshall, 1977: 3).

The health care system is a critical part of the integrity of the nonmetro community. The current system is inadequate to the task of guaranteeing this important human
service.

FACTORS CONTRIBUTING TO THE
PROBLEMS OF RURAL MEDICAL CARE

The preceding analysis of the available vital statistics
describing the status of health and health services in
nonmetro America discloses an apparent paradox; despite a
greater need for health services, nonmetro Americans have
fewer health care resources and are less a part of the
health care system. This situation is largely the by-product
of the profound changes in the context and delivery of
medical care since World War II, and of a general focus of
the medical care profession on the pathophysiology of disease rather than on the human beings in whom disease occurs.
Rural areas are marked by diversity: demographic, economic, dynamic, regional, and cultural. The medical care
system has become increasingly monolithic, with uniform
standards and expectations. In the pre-Flexnerian era, small
towns and country doctors went together so naturally that
they became part of the national tradition. The country
doctor emerged from and remained a part of his community,
and his passing has left a void unfilled by modern medicine.
The current mode of training and practice estranges
physicians from their roots. The technological imperative
has permeated medicine, and patients are approached as
mechanistic androids in which the goal is to understand the
biochemical interactions between cells and organ systems
rather than the less quantifiable interactions among human
beings. This approach has catalyzed a rapid advance in our
ability to intervene in catastrophic disease, a modest
ability in our skill at ameliorating everyday ills, and a
marginal increase in longevity or the quality of life. This
estrangement of medicine from life has led some critics to
argue that the medical profession has become a malevolent
force in our culture (Illich 1976).
Whatever the impact on society at large, the move towards the specialized application of exotic medical technologies has led to the depletion of nonmetro health care
resources. Complex systems administered by specialists
require large capital investments, sophisticated management
structures, and large populations to render them fiscally
viable. The lengthening course of medical training has
tended to socialize physicians--no matter what their back-
ground--into a mold that encourages them to practice in
larger medical centers; there is an explicit prejudice
against the rural generalist who is often perceived as an
inept bumbler whose mistakes filter into the teaching cen-

ters. In addition, the reward system has been structured--
largely by the medical profession and third-party payers--
so that the metro specialist earns considerably more than
the nonmetro generalist for much shorter work weeks (Thorndike 1977).

The result of these forces has been an apparent failure
of the market mechanism through which health care is distributed to provide adequate services in nonmetro areas.
Given the current structure of medicine, the more sparsely
populated and remote an area is, the more difficulty it
experiences in maintaining a functional medical care system. Although the pattern of physician distribution provides
the most dramatic example, virtually all other health and
related social services have similar distribution patterns.
The provision of hospital inpatient services is an increasingly acute problem in low-density areas, with few communities able to rationally partition needed inpatient services
between local hospitals and cooperating metro institutions
(Rosenblatt 1979). Despite widespread agreement that regionalization and health planning should determine the
distribution of health services, the nonmetro experience
has been one of watching helplessly as local resources are
depleted and the local health system becomes more fragile.
Regionalization is perceived as a means by which nonmetro
communities are absorbed into metro centers that can then
justify their further expansion by virtue of their services
to the now dependent nonmetro minions. The technological
transformation of medical care, if extrapolated to its
logical extremes, will lead to the virtual elimination of
all but satellite operations in nonmetro areas.

STRUCTURED INTERVENTIONS OF THE PAST DECADE

Although the above analysis deliberately describes the
situation as bleak, this deterioration has not gone un-
noticed. Beginning in the late 1960s, it became apparent
that American medicine was in crisis, a crisis made acute
by the unconsummated expectations generated by the great
technological optimism of the new specialty era. From many
segments of society, both within and outside the profession,
came a call for changes that would bring the focus of medicine back to the public it purportedly served (Millis 1966).
Many of the interventions that were shaped as a result of
the debate that ensued had direct or indirect effect on

rural areas. Many of the programs thus initiated have been
operational for almost a decade, and from the potpourri are
beginning to emerge those combinations of approaches that
have promise. The following discussion briefly touches on
these interventions, in preparation for showing which per-
mutations appear to offer the basis for further research
and intervention. Although almost every modification of
federal health policy or innovation in health professions
schools has a rural ramification, only those programs with
major nonmetro effects--intended and realized--are reviewed.

THE RENAISSANCE OF FAMILY MEDICINE AND PRIMARY CARE

The revival of the general practitioner grew out of a simultaneous realization by a variety of groups both within
and outside organized medicine that the near demise of the
general practitioner had deprived many Americans of their
personal physicians. The new family practitioner that emerged has the mantle of the generalist tied to rigorous post-
doctoral training linked to the creation of a new specialty.
Although at first grudgingly accepted by the traditional
medical education structure, enthusiastic responses by
federal and state government prompted the majority of
state-supported medical schools to incorporate the new
specialty into their curricula. Although still a discipline
struggling for academic recognition, family medicine has
gained a foothold, and it appears that the progressive
decline in the number of practitioners has halted and will
begin to reverse directions (American Association of Family
Physicians 1979).
    This broad-based trend offers considerable hope for
a solution to the rural health dilemma and has some advantages over the more narrowly targeted categorical approaches
described below. General practitioners provide the majority
of medical care in rural America, and, as Figure 16.2 shows,
the new specialty is stimulating a redistribution of new
graduates. Young family physicians are finding it alluring
to set up practices in nonmetro areas, reversing a long-
standing trend.
    At the same time, Figure 16.2 illustrates that the
attempt of the traditional specialties--internal medicine
and pediatrics for the most part--to create primary care
tracks is unlikely to have much impact on nonmetro physician
distribution. These graduates tend to locate in cities because they do not have the versatility or breadth of skills

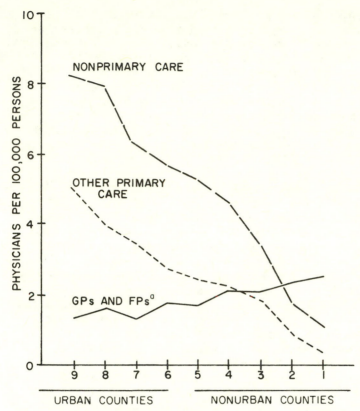

Figure 16.2 Geographic Distribution of 22,925 U.S. Medical School Graduates and Foreign Medical Graduates Licensed Between 1967 and 1971, by Specialty Groups

to practice without drawing on an at least partially referred population from more densely populated areas. In
addition, physicians trained as general internists and
pediatricians frequently go on to become subspecialists
later in their careers (Bovey 1978). For this reason, the
simple expansion of medical school classes in itself has as
yet had little demonstrable effect on the supply of physicians to nonmetro areas.

NEW HEALTH PRACTITIONERS (NHPs)

The creation of physicians' assistants and nurse practitioners as a means to extend the productivity of nonmetro
physicians also occurred in the late 1960s. Although new
health practitioners do tend to settle more frequently than
physicians as a whole in low density areas (Schaeffler
1977), these personnel have not yet found a stable and
predictable place in the American health care delivery
system. The educational tracks are extremely variable,
there is often destructive competition among physicians'
assistants, nurse practitioners, and physicians, and the
quality of the programs is variable. There is good evidence
that under supervision new health practitioners can provide
medical care that is both of adequate quality and acceptable
to patients (Lewis 1973). However, it does not appear that
this group will become a major independent force in American
medicine.

One possible use for NHPs is to staff clinics in rural
communities too small to support physician practices and
the hospitals that physicians for the most part demand.
There is good evidence from several areas of the country
that these clinics can be medically viable, although they
are financially unstable (Moscovice and Rosenblatt 1979;
Bernstein et al. 1979). One impediment to their financial
stability has been their inability to collect third-party
payment. In an attempt to remedy that situation the government passed the Rural Health Clinics Law (95-210) in 1977,
extending medicare and medicaid to NHPs in shortage areas
(Silver 1978). However, the process of certifying a clinic
is so cumbersome that only a fraction of eligible clinics
have sought to join the program, and a portion of those
that have joined find the administrative costs in excess of
the added revenue collected through that reimbursement
conduit. The bill stands as an example of how insensitive
some federal efforts are to the limited administrative
resources available in small communities.

THE FOUNDATIONS

Foundations, at their best, act in a catalytic fashion to
spur innovation and develop new modes of operation. In the
field of rural health, foundations have concentrated their
efforts both on delivery of health services and the education of providers.

The Sears and Roebuck Foundation initiated the first comprehensive effort to attract physicians to nonmetro areas by building clinics in a wide variety of communities (Kane et al. 1975). Although the effort mobilized coordinated community efforts in many cases, it did not succeed in keeping physicians in rural communities; however, many of the facilities have been passed down to later generations of physicians or new health practitioners. The lesson of the Sears intervention was that facilities were a necessary but not sufficient condition for the long-term viability of a rural clinic.

The Robert Wood Johnson Foundation embarked in the early 1970s on the Rural Practice Project, an initially ambitious attempt to create a model of community-responsive medical practice that wedded the complementary skills of a physician and an administrator in creating a new kind of practice (Madison 1975). Although the project began well, the RWJ Foundation withdrew support when the federal government began to create similar community-based programs through their granting mechanism. In many ways the termination of the project was premature, because it never gathered sufficient momentum to test the underlying hypotheses, nor could the thirteen programs formed under the program's aegis have a significant impact on rural health services delivery.

Almost paradoxically, the efforts of the Commonwealth Fund in supporting the regionalized medical education program in the Northwest called WAMI, and the Kellogg Foundation in creating community-based decentralized networks for the education of family medicine residents, probably have had more impact that the direct delivery programs. By intertwining medical education with community service and educating medical students and residents in culturally relevant settings, much has been done to combat the deculturalization of the normal medical education process. The Area Health Education Center (AHEC) Program is a direct outgrowth of a Carnegie Commission report, and has taken much of its shape from the previously mentioned efforts in regionalized medical education (Zwick et al. 1977). The thesis underlying all these efforts is that education and training occur most appropriately in the community of need; and that professional support networks are an integral part of a functioning health care system that must persist after cessation of formal training.

FEDERAL INITIATIVES

The range of federal interventions is broad, and at times
confusing. Among federal programs with substantial rural
impact is the Indian Health Service that provides direct
health care to reservation Indians, most of whom live in
rural areas. A second program aimed at a group living pre-
ponderantly in rural areas is the Migrant Health Program,
which provides health care to those in the migrant work
force. The two largest programs with such an emphasis and a
major rural effect are the National Health Service Corps
and the Rural Health Initiative Program.

The National Health Service Corps (NHSC) is the federal
program with the greatest chance of improving the distribution of health care providers in rural areas. After a halt-
ing beginning in 1970, the NHSC has become the most rapidly
growing and most flexible program in the federal repertoire
(Rosenblatt and Moscovice 1978a). Through the direct place-
ment of health care providers, the majority of whom are
physicians, the NHSC introduces a direct federal presence
in underserved areas. Early administrators of the NHSC,
charged with the goal of improving access to care in federally designed "critical health manpower shortage areas,"
targeted the program explicitly toward rural America. They
found the need great, the public sector cooperative, and
the problems amenable to solution.

Since its initiation, the NHSC has grown in size and
complexity. In 1972 and in 1976, major scholarship programs
were started that supported medical students during medical
school in return for obligated service in the NHSC. The
size of the scholarship program has, in fact, grown more
rapidly than the service element. Although there are approximately 1,300 health professionals in the field, there
are more than 8,000 scholarship recipients in the educational pipeline. And although the NHSC is slowly shifting
its focus towards the urban inner cities, the rapid growth
in the number of obligated personnel will insure an adequate
harvest of recent graduates with a legal commitment to serve
in underserviced rural areas.

The program is not without its weaknesses. The rapid
growth of the NHSC has made it a visible target for oppor-
tunistic legislators and administrators seeking flexible
resources to attain a variety of ends. As a result, the
relative simplicity of the NHSC has been tarnished with the
addition of cumbersome additional service mandates, most of
them laudable, but not all of them practical. The reliance

on the scholarship program for future recruitment has provided an assured stream of manpower, but the program has
been unwisely divided between the Health Resources Administration, which is responsible for awarding scholarships,
and the Health Services Administration, which places the
assignees and monitors site operations. This institutional
schizophrenia has led to a functional discontinuity in the
program, and future NHSC physicians still in training are
inadequately prepared for their future service. A reluctant
and embittered physician in a rural community is a boon
neither to himself or the community he serves; program
unity and support from the first day of the scholarship
award will be needed to insure a cohort of committed and
capable physicians in rural areas (Madison and Shenkin
1978).

Despite these internal inconsistencies, the NHSC remains
an excellent resource for rural communities. Research is
beginning to identify those settings that are likely to
support stable practices that can enter the mainstream of
the private sector, and those that will require external
subsidy and administrative support indefinitely (Rosenblatt
and Moscovice 1978a).

The Rural Health Initiative (RHI) represents a unique
federal attempt to administratively combine categorically
distinct programs to approach the problem of health care.
Deriving its financial base from the Community Health Centers Program, the National Health Service Corps, the Health
Underserved Rural Areas Program, the Migrant Health Program,
and the Appalachian Health Program, the RHI targets grants
to designated medically underserved areas in an attempt to
increase primary care capacity in underserved rural areas.
Although fraught with the minutiae of the federal granting
process, the program has enabled small communities to go
beyond the mere recuitment of manpower to more comprehensive
interventions in the total health services arena. With very
substantial granting authorities upon which to draw, the
program has often supplemented frail or narrow efforts, and
shored up programs in the areas where assistance was most
needed. The major criticisms of the program are that, at
times, the particular needs of a given area may be distorted
by some national enthusiasm or initiative of questionable
relevance to the nonmetro setting. Simplicity is a virtue
in administration as in art, and the creation of stable
health care systems where none previously existed is a
sufficient end in itself.

CONJOINT ACTIVITIES OF AGRICULTURE AND HEALTH

A new collaborative effort between the Farmers Home Administration (FmHA) and the Department of Health, Education and
Welfare (HEW) uses FmHA's guaranteed loan program to build
needed health facilities in areas receiving HEW funds.
Although still in its infancy, the program is of note
because it represents a rare example of cooperation in an
area too often marred by territorial squabbles. The Department of Agriculture has a long history of work in nonmetro
America, and through its extension service has become a
part of the infrastructure that is nonmetro America. The
use of agriculture funds and agricultural agents in the
service of improved health care delivery is an example of
the type of multifaceted approach that is required (Green
1979).

FINANCING

National Health Insurance (NHI) has been on the horizon for
the past decade, withdrawing tantalizingly out of reach of
each successive administration. Certainly, NHI--if ever
enacted--will assist in removing residual inequities attributable to poverty. Yet, if NHI follows the lead in
medicare and medicaid, the impact on nonmetro areas will be
minimal. Until reimbursement practices that discriminate in
favor of high-cost, technologically sophisticated interventions at the expense of primary care are changed, third-
party payment will continue to distort the health care
delivery system. And, until the payment discrepancies shift
in favor of the nonmetro provider, instead of the current
bias towards the metro setting with its higher prevailing
fee schedules, a skewed reward system will remain a barrier
to improved nonmetro health service.
    The Health Maintenance Organization (HMO) program,
although directed to set aside a portion of its support for
nonmetro areas, in reality is not feasible in sparsely
populated areas. One prepaid scheme that has great promise
has been recently marketed by the Safeco Insurance Company
under the name of United Healthcare (Moore 1979). The major
characteristic of this plan is that the primary care physician serves as the patient's entry into the health care
system, and shares in the financial risks and rewards of
managing his patient's care. The patient has the right to
choose a provider, but once he has chosen must go through

that physician for hospitalization and referral. In return, the patient pays a monthly premium, and receives comprehensive coverage identical to that offered through an HMO. The great advantage of the plan for rural areas is that expensive capital facilities and elaborate organizational structures are unneeded. Theoretically, any small community could enter into the plan if sufficient numbers of individuals signed up, and if the local physicians were willing to participate. Because the plan recognizes the central position of the primary care physician, and financially rewards efficient patient management, it might be expected that physicians would be attracted to the plan if there were sufficient patient demand. Although Safeco, the parent company, has not energetically marketed the plan in nonmetro areas, it would seem reasonable that Safeco would respond to inquiries from interested communities or employers.

PATTERNS OF SUCCESS AND MODELS FOR THE FUTURE

The current rural health situation is the result not of malevolent exploiters seeking to deprive residents of their basic rights, but an unanticipated side effect of fundamental changes in values of the medical-care establishment and the structure of the medical marketplace. There are specific instances of market failure that impede the flow of services to nonmetro areas. Physicians have an ability to set the price for their services and to create demand for the product they provide, thus insulating themselves from some of the competitive rigors of the free marketplace. Numerous barriers to entry into the profession, both at the training and the practice level, also tend to prevent the unrestrained forces of the market from influencing the diffusion of medical services to nonmetro areas. But the major problem is that the way in which medical care is produced has changed radically without a commensurate change in the organizational structure through which that care is distributed.

The challenge in the next decade is to develop methods of providing medical care that can be meshed with the spectrum of demographic diversity that characterizes nonmetro America. The problem of providing medical care to sparsely populated areas is analogous to the problem of providing water or school systems discussed by other authors in this volume. The conventional technology is very sensitive to

issues of scale, and highly sophisticated medical care
systems tend to be centralized in metro locations. Yet the
bulk of medical services can be adequately provided using
alternative approaches and less costly infrastructures. We
must determine the minimum efficient sizes for various
service configurations and then assist small communities in
establishing the system appropriate to its resources and
needs. This will not only insure health services to nonmetro
areas, but also increase local involvement in both the
initiation and management of health care establishments.
The growing national skepticism about medical care in general and the renewed emphasis on personal responsibility
for health maintenance through holistic medicine and self-
care will help fuel this process. As people in general
feel less awed and mystified by medicine, nonmetro areas
will have the opportunity to regain a measure of the self-
sufficiency they lost when they became dependent on distant
areas.

Analysis of successful and unsuccessful health care
practices in diverse rural areas suggests that there are
population equilibrium points that determine which set of
medical services will be viable in the current economic
environment. Although these equilibrium points vary from
region to region and could be significantly modified by
future technological changes, they do offer some insight
into which configuration might work best in communities of
various sizes. The notion underlying this particular approach is that health services should be available to most
people within a certain distance from their homes; the
transportation isochron adopted by the federal government
in the recent health planning standards is thirty minutes
travel time. This standard defines the relevant medical
catchment area, and the relative complexity of the local
medical care system then becomes a function of the population density within that area.

Three quite distinct patterns emerge from this review.
Larger rural communities--those with medical catchment
areas of more than 10,000 people--tend to develop fairly
stable medical care systems capable of providing basic
inpatient and outpatient services. These communities can
generally support five or more physicians and a local hospital. Although, in general, the quality and the range of
the service available is dependent on the size and wealth
of the community, historical antecedents, and relationships
with adjoining nonmetro and metro areas, this type of nonmetro area has the resilience to maintain an ongoing medical

care system. Some of these communities have become superlative centers and provide medical care to surrounding towns.

Communities with between 4,000 and 10,000 people in the medical catchment area are those where the health problems are most acute. These communities, many of which acquired hospitals as beneficiaries of the Hill-Burton program, have for the most part witnessed the erosion of their local medical care system. They have had difficulty recruiting physicians to replace those lost through death and retirement, and their hospitals have experienced falling occupancies and marginal finances. These are communities in which--because of their relatively small size--the medical care system is intrinsically unstable, and it is often difficult to maintain financial equilibrium without ongoing external subsidy. In these settings--and they are common--mechanisms need to be developed whereby physicians can be recruited and partially supported as part of a larger multicentric but decentralized system. It is in such areas that the National Health Service Corps and the Rural Health Initiative Programs have been popular, and from the many ongoing, simultaneous practical experiments some successful solutions should emerge.

Communities with less than 4,000 people within the medical trade area seem to be most satisfactorily served through one or two new health practitioners who have a collaborative relationship with a physician in the next largest town. Although research shows that these practices can approach economic self-sufficiency, the burden of professional isolation is such that as in the previous example, these practices will most likely need ongoing external support for long-term stability. Communities with less than 1,500 to 2,000 people cannot generate enough effective demand to fully utilize a full-time provider. In these cases, other solutions such as health aides or community health workers, with links to emergency medical systems and a means to gain access to the medical care system, appear most appropriate (Rosenblatt and Huard 1979).

All these solutions require explicit interconnections among the various levels of the regionalized delivery apparatus, with the full scope of potential services--from obstetrics to heart surgery--partitioned among the various alternative locations. No medical care system is entirely freestanding, and only through fashioning predetermined linkages can patients be assured that they will receive the appropriate services in a timely fashion. An excellent example is obstetric services. The opportunity to deliver

children in a natural setting close to home is a highly
cherished element of most communities. At the same time,
sophisticated techniques have evolved that decrease morbid-
ity and mortality for children and mothers alike. A good
rural system will insure that most patients receive their
obstetric care from a family doctor in their own community,
but will guarantee early detection of high-risk pregnancies,
and expeditious transfer to more sophisticated centers
should the need arise (Hein 1978). This pattern runs contrary to the totally insensitive initial federal planning
guidelines that would have centralized all obstetric care
in larger metro institutions, undermining both the nonmetro
medical delivery system and eroding the quality of local
life.

Thus, regionalization and stratification of services
are logical and necessary but must be governed by the central philosophical tenet that the best medical care is
that given closest to the patient with the least intervention. The perfect health care system is one that has rendered itself obsolete, and the closer we can come to fostering self-sufficiency and culturally consonant health
care, the less disruptive will be the impact of illness in
our society.

A second lesson that emerges from this review is that
the most effective interventions are synergistic, building
on a multifaceted approach from different vantage points.
Two examples are the regionalized networks established in
the Pacific Northwest by WAMI and by the Office of Rural
Health Services in North Carolina. In the WAMI example, a
central medical school in Seattle expanded its campus,
physically and psychologically, to include the states of
Alaska, Montana, and Idaho. At the same time the school
created a decentralized family medicine education program
that enrolled one-half of the student body and provided
residency training in nine affiliated sites in the same
geographic area. The National Health Service Corps and RHI
programs worked in tandem with the far-flung medical school
effort, serving as a conduit through which recent graduates
of the program could establish rural practices that required
initial subsidy. In North Carolina, the medical schools coordinated their activities through an Office of Rural Health
Services and an active AHEC system. Again, the coordination
of the educational resource with the delivery system itself
was extremely successful in a rapid improvement in the distribution of nonmetro health services. The similarity of
both these efforts was the work toward a common goal.

Several issues remain unresolved. In many ways, health care remains a hostage of the major national debate swirling around graduate medical education. Unless there is a substantial and ongoing commitment to the training of generalists for whom the well-being of patients transcends the elegance of pathophysiology, all the rhetoric about primary care will be submerged in the further growth of a system that has lost sight of the human aspects of medicine. Rural policymakers must not be dazzled by the prospect of creating tertiary care centers in each rural town. The opportunity exists to create nonmetro systems of care that will serve as examples with which to transform the larger health care system.

The continued technological transformation of medicine may also serve to revitalize nonmetro medicine rather than continue to undermine it. The wired society being created by rapid advances in communications technology should soon allow every health care provider to have instant access to the latest and most complex knowledge about current diagnosis and treatment. By substituting communications for transportation and expanding the capability of the primary care provider by giving him access to a larger network of knowledge, there will be less need to transfer patients to metro centers. And as systems of care crystallize, it will become more common for specialists to travel periodically to low-density areas, providing patient care, clinical support, and the stimulation of fresh ideas for their colleagues. As transportation becomes more expensive, the economic constraints will accelerate these trends.

The federal emphasis on cost containment collides head-on with attempts to increase access to care, particularly with regard to hospital-based services. Hospital services do consume the bulk of medical care expenditures, often for services of questionable value. However, the symbiotic relationship between the nonmetro physician and the local hospital is deep-seated, and it is shortsighted to jettison the entire local delivery system in search of marginal savings. The efforts should go into redefining nonmetro hospitals as part of larger cooperating networks and insulating them from the current financial penalties. Just as the Hill-Burton program created the needed bricks and mortar in the nonmetro areas, its successor program should support the creation of a new configuration for nonmetro hospitals such that their future is assured.

Currently the reimbursement system--private and government--discriminates against nonmetro medical care through

lower fee schedules and spotty coverage. Physician wages
reward most those who contribute least; the itinerant
radiologist earns more in his ten-second daytime review of
an x-ray than the physician who spends two hours in the
middle of the night caring for the patient for whom the
x-ray was taken. This anomaly is the result of federal and
state regulations mandating the unnecessary review and
third-party carriers who support irrational fee schedules.
National Health Insurance, unless it grapples with these
issues, will merely enshrine these disruptive patterns.

There are other problems with more limited impact.
The malpractice crisis of recent years forced some nonmetro
physicians to give up surgical and obstetric components of
their practices; local residents were then forced to travel
to obtain these services. "Credentialing," the process by
which every trained person in the health care system becomes part of a guild that limits entry and sets standards,
tends to increase costs and decrease the managerial flexibility of small-scale systems.

Yet despite these problems, the future holds promise
for rapid and meaningful improvement in rural health care
services. The basic cause for optimism lies in the same
stimuli that have sparked the rural demographic renaissance;
a change of values. To the extent that nonmetro areas become
attractive for a heterogenous group of people seeking the
amenities they offer, they will become increasingly capable
of providing their own needed social services. The spectrum
of governmental and educational programs also has acknowledged the current deficiencies in rural health care services, and has made some fundamental changes to remedy the
situation. The opportunity exists for nonmetro health care
to lead the nation in recapturing the medical field in the
service of the people.

BIBLIOGRAPHY

Ahearn, Mary C. "Health Care in Rural America." Agricultural
    Information Bulletin no. 428, U.S. Department of
    Agriculture, 1979.
American Association of Family Physicians. "Future Health
    Manpower Needs Projected in GMENAC Report." Reporter
    6 (1979): 1-26.
American Medical Association. Profile of Medical Practice.
    Chicago, Ill.: Center for Health Services Research and

Development, 1974.

Anderson, R. et al. Equity in Health Services: Empirical Analysis in Social Policy. Cambridge, Mass.: Ballinger Publishing Co., 1975.

Bernstein, James D. et al. Rural Health Centers in the United States. Cambridge, Mass.: Ballinger Publishing Co., 1979.

_____. "Rural Health Services--Studies of Workable Models." Paper presented at the American Public Health Association Annual Meeting, November 1977.

Bovey, J. D. "A Follow-up Study of Residents in Internal Medicine, Pediatrics, and Obstetrics-Gynecology Training Programs in Massachusetts." New England Journal of Medicine 298 (1978): 15-21.

Coleman, Sinclair. Physician Distribution and Rural Access to Medical Services. Paper Series R-1887-HEW. Santa Monica, Calif.: Rand Corporation, 1976.

Davis, K., and Marshall, R. "Primary Health Care Services for Medically Underserved Populations." In Papers on the National Health Guidelines: The Priorities of Section 1502, pp. 1-31. U.S. Department of Health, Education and Welfare publication (HRA) 77-641, January 1977.

General Accounting Office. "Progess and Problems in Improving the Availability of Primary Care Providers in Underserved Areas. Publication no. HRD-77-135, 1978.

Green, Bernal L. "Rural Health Delivery Sytems of the 1980s." Family and Community Health 2 (1979): 95-108.

Hein, Herman A. "The Quality of Perinatal Care in Small Rural Hospitals." Journal of the American Medical Association 240 (1978): 2070-72.

Illich, I. Medical Nemesis: The Expropriation of Health. New York: Random House, 1976.

Kane, Robert L. "Problems in Rural Health Care." In Health Services; The Local Perspective, by R. L. Kane. New York: Praeger, 1977.

_____ et al. "Mail-order Medicine: An Analysis of the Sears Roebuck Foundation's Community Medical Assistance Program." Journal of the American Medical Association 232 (1975): 1023-27.

Lewis, Charles E. "Evaluating the Performance of Intermediate Health Workers." In Intermediate Health Practitioners, edited by Vernon W. Kippard and Elizabeth F. Purcell, pp. 89-103. New York: Josiah Macy, Jr., Foundation, 1973.

McCoy, J. L., and Brown, D. L. "Survey of Low-Income Aged

and Disabled." Social Security Bulletin 41 (1978): 14-26

Madison, Donald. "The Robert Wood Johnson Foundation: The Rural Practice Project." Chapel Hill, N.C., 1975.

_____, and Shenkin, Bud. "Leadership for Community-Responsive Practice: Preparing Physicians to Serve the Underserved." Washington, D.C.: Department of Health, Education and Welfare, Bureau of Health Manpower, 1978.

Martin, Edward. "The Federal Initiative in Rural Health." Public Health Reports 90 (1975): 291-97.

Matthews, Tresa H. "Health Services in Rural America." Agricultural Information Bulletin no. 362, U.S. Department of Agriculture, 1974.

Millis, J. S. The Graduate Education of the Physician. Report of the Citizen's Commission on Graduate Medical Education. Chicago, Ill.: American Medical Association, 1966.

Moore, Stephen. "Cost Containment Through Risk-Sharing by Primary Care Physicians." New England Journal of Medicine 300 (1979): 1359-62.

Moscovice, Ira, and Rosenblatt, Roger A. "The Viability of Mid-Level Practitioners in Isolated Rural Communities." American Journal of Public Health 69 (1979): 503-5.

Rosenblatt, Roger A. "Planning Ensures Local and Referral Care for Remote Rural Area." Hospitals 53 (1979): 83-88.

_____. "The Scope and Role of the Small Rural Hospital." Hospitals, in press.

_____, and Huard, Bernadette. "The Nurse Practitioner as Physician-Substitute in a Rural Community." Public Health Reports 94 (1979): 571-75.

Rosenblatt, Roger A., and Moscovice, Ira. "Establishing New Rural Family Practices: Some Lessons from a Federal Experience." Journal of Family Practice 7 (1978a): 755-63.

_____. "The Growth and Evolution of Rural Primary Care Practice." Medical Care 16 (1978b): 819-27.

Schaeffler, R. M. "The Supply and Demand for New Health Professionals: Physicians Assistants and Medex." Final report submitted to U.S. Department of Health, Education and Welfare, contract 1-44184, November 1977.

Silver, Henry, and McAtee, P. "The Rural Health Clinic Services Act of 1977." Nurse Practitioner Sept.-Oct. (1978): 30.

Thorndike, N. "1975 Net Incomes and Work Patterns of Physicians in Five Medical Specialties." Research and Statistics Note 13, U.S. Department of Health, Education and Welfare, 21 July 1977.

U.S. Department of Health, Education and Welfare. Health--
    United States 1978. Publication (PHS) 78-1232, December
    1978.
Zwick, Daniel I. et al. "A Report on the National AHEC
    Program." Public Health Reports 92 (1977): 108-20.

V.

Growth, Environmental Impact, and Planning

Marion Clawson

17
Land-Use Trends

INTRODUCTION

The total land area of the fifty states is 2,263 million
acres, or almost exactly ten acres per person (Bureau of
Land Management, hereafter BLM, 1976). If the vast but
remote area of Alaska and the small but remote area of
Hawaii are excluded, as not relevant to the land-use problems and solutions for most Americans, there are still
about 1,900 million acres of land--approximately eight
acres per person (Clawson 1972). For comparison, the playing area of a football field includes about 1.1 acres.

When one considers the use of this land area, irrespective of its ownership which is considered later, there
are three big land users: cropland, at 467 million acres;
grazing and rangeland, at 598 million acres; and commercial
forest, at 718 million acres (in each case, omitting overlapping uses) (Frey 1977). These three major land uses
thus include about 79 percent of the total land area.
Though these are the largest land users, in many respects
they are less important than the much smaller area of more
valuable lands used for urban purposes, for transportation,
for parks and recreation, for reservoir sites, and for a
miscellany of other purposes. Although these account for
only 8 percent of the land area, their total value greatly
exceeds that of the three largest land users. Moreover, it
is among these smaller but highly important land uses that
the largest changes have been made in recent years.

If one looks only at the national statistics, a remarkably steady picture of land use in the United States seems
to emerge. That is, the totals by broad categories of use
have changed comparatively little since about 1920. At
various times we have expanded or contracted cultivated
cropland area somewhat, depending more upon economic conditions and the demand for agricultural commodities, including export demand, than upon any other factor; but
the variation has been in the range of 380 to 410 million

acres (Frey 1977). Some of the expansion of crop area has
come out of pasture and rangeland, and some of the abandoned crop area has gone into this use; but much of the grazing area, particularly the range, is wholly unsuitable for
cropping. Although some forested area has been cleared
for purposes such as farming, suburban development, highways and power line rights of way, reservoirs, and other
use, this has been offset in large measure by growing trees
on former croplands unsuited to continued cropping, and
thus the total forested area has been remarkably stable.

This apparent stability, as indicated by the national
figures on areas in each major use category, is somewhat
misleading. The available data measure only net shifts in
area; the gross shifts from one use to another are larger
(Frey 1973). Moreover, shifts in one county or state may be
offset by compensating shifts in another state or county.
These national statistics on the three major land uses
conceal changes that have taken place in the other uses
listed--changes that, while involving only a small proportion of the total land area, are large compared with the
area once used for these miscellaneous important purposes.
Various estimates, usually ranging around one-half million
acres, are made of the land annually taken out of cropping,
and put into suburban, transportation, or other miscellaneous uses (Brown 1979). Some of this, of course, has
been offset by the clearing of forest, the plowing up of
pasture or rangeland, or by irrigation of land not previously cropped, but this almost always involves shifting from
highly productive to less productive croplands.

The ownership of American land, irrespective of the
land use, is approximately as follows: (1) of the 894 million acres that are publicly owned, 760 million are federal
(national forests, national parks, grazing districts, wildlife refuges, military reservations, reservoirs, and other
miscellaneous categories) (BLM 1976), and 134 million acres
are state and local, much of which is in forests or parks
(U.S. Bureau of the Census, 1974: 199); (2) of the 1,016
million acres in farms, 359 million are owned by farmers
who farm only land that they own; 535 million are in farms,
some of which the farmer owns and some of which he rents
on some basis, and 122 million are in farms that are entirely rented; of all this farmland, some is forested and
some is range (U.S. Bureau of the Census 1977); (3) 234
million acres of privately owned forest, 68 million of
which are owned by forest firms, which have their own processing facilities (sawmills, paper mills, etc.), and 166

million of which are owned by private owners who have no
processing facilities (Forest Service 1978); and (4), some
119 million acres of land, the ownership of which does
not fall in any one of these categories.[1] This includes
most of the metro land not publicly owned, but it also
includes a great deal of nonmetro land.

In intensive studies of the suburbanization process,
it was found that in the megalopolis area from Washington
to Boston 44 percent of the total area was not in urban
uses, not in public ownerships, and not in farms, but owned
by individuals (or corporations), lying outside of built-up
areas (Clawson 1971). This percentage is higher than for
the nation as a whole, as well as most other regions. It
includes land owned by individuals for recreation uses,
forestry, land speculation, and various miscellaneous purposes.

Comparatively little is known about several of these
classes of landownership. Some of the land rented by farmers
is owned by other farmers or by the heirs of former farmers
or by retired former farmers; but much is owned by nonfarmers, often city people, corporations, or foreigners. Some
of the land listed as owned by farmers belongs to persons
or corporations, not resident on the land and possibly not
even citizens, who operate the farm with a hired farm
manager. The nonindustrial nonfarm private forest owners
are a very mixed group (Clawson 1979), and the substantial
areas not included in any of these categories represent a
truly mixed and largely unknown group of owners. We shall
return to this matter of changing landownership in nonmetro
areas.

PRESSURES ON NONMETROPOLITAN LAND USES

There are increasing pressures on rural land use in the
United States today, none of which alone has truly major
consequences but all of which, taken together, have a
substantial impact (Raup 1975).

First of all, there is movement of people from central
cities of metro areas to smaller cities, towns, and open
countryside, as earlier chapters have described in detail.
These residents new to small towns and countryside require
land on which to live--indeed, land often being cheaper and
more readily available than in the larger cities, they
often occupy much larger areas per family. One of the at-

tractions of the small town and countryside is privacy,
which often means distance from others, and another attraction is openness of landscape. Each of these requires
more land per dwelling unit. Some of the new residents may
indeed occupy houses and tracts of land that had previously
been occupied, but even this occupancy is an added demand
for land in that locality. But a great many of the newer
arrivals to open country areas and small towns will want a
tract of land that had not formerly been used as a dwelling
site.

Exceeding this demand for land in nonmetro areas for
permanent residences is a large, perhaps much greater,
demand for land for vacation or other seasonal residential
use. In many nonmetro areas, a good deal of subdivision,
much of it highly speculative, has been for recreation or
retirement homes. Forested areas have been subject to much
of this speculative subdivision, in part because buyers are
attracted to trees and wooded areas (Healy 1977). But some
of this subdivision has been in desert areas, where the
general openness of the landscape and the presumed clarity
of the air have been attractions.

Suburban expansion continues in many metro areas and
around many larger cities, even when total population is
growing very slowly or not at all. Regardless of city size,
the flight from the inner city continues; but to this is
added some flight from older suburbs or fringe areas--many
people are simply moving out, to the suburban fringes. In
the United States the problem of rebuilding older urban
areas still tends to be solved by running away from them.
When a family moves to a new suburban location, its former
residence will be taken over by someone else, and his former
place by someone else, and so on down the line; but some-
where the trickle-down process stops and the vacated dwelling unit remains idle--derelict. Moreover, more distant
lots will, on the average, be larger than closer ones, so
that some net land withdrawal takes place even though population numbers and dwelling unit numbers remain more or
less fixed (American Society of Planning Officials 1976).

From the viewpoint of other nonmetro land uses, a dominant fact about these spreading suburbs, vacation homes,
and new residences is the amount of land they remove from
other uses even when they do not use it themselves. That
is, a new subdivision a mile or so beyond the next closest
subdivision is likely to idle most of all of the inter-
stitial land; or a few new vacation homes scattered over a
large speculatively promoted subdivision will render the

interspersed vacant lots nearly useless for any other purpose (Clawson et al. 1960). It is not only the direct land
use of these new nonmetro projects that consumes land, but
also the land that is effectively withdrawn from agriculture, forestry, or even park use that is so significant.

In addition to residential use, some nonmetro land
is being taken by transportation and utilities. One of the
more obvious is the highway (especially the new multilane
interstate highway), but new airports are being built
around some cities, and electric power lines are becoming
more extensive, as demand rises and generating plants are
typically built some distance away from metro consuming
centers. These additional land uses may be essential to our
modern metro society and may be highly productive in an
economic sense, but they do take land, both directly for
their use and indirectly as they often render nearby land
less attractive for other uses. For example, it is undesirable to live adjacent to a major interstate highway or high
voltage power line.

Development of coal and other minerals also continues
to remove rural land from other uses, either temporarily or
permanently, because the demand for energy and its related
fuels and minerals is rising. The past mining of richer
deposits requires present development to be increasingly of
larger and often lower-grade deposits, frequently by surface mining methods that totally preclude other land uses
until the fuel or mineral has been extracted--permanently
so unless the land surface is effectively restored. The
data on the land areas involved are poor and the acreages
are in dispute; although small compared with the national
land area, they are often large for a region, state, or
county.

OUTDOOR RECREATION AS A SPECIAL FORM OF LAND USE

One nonmetro land use that merits special mention is outdoor recreation (Clawson and Knetsch 1966). The years since
World War II have seen a veritable explosion in outdoor
recreation in the United States. The total annual increase
of such activity in the United States has been about 10
percent, or a doubling each eight years. A number of factors combined to create such rapid expansion. In the first
place, the total population increased; and, more importantly, for many years the number of young people in the most

active recreation ages rose even more rapidly. Real per
capita income also rose, so that a large proportion of the
population had far more discretionary income to spend on
outdoor recreation. There was also a great improvement in
transportation, particularly in highways, so that people
could travel faster and farther in their leisure time. The
effect of any one of these factors would be to increase
outdoor recreation activity; their combined effect was very
great indeed.

To these changes in the general demographic, economic,
and transportation situations has been added a revolution
in the technology of outdoor recreation itself. A host of
ways of enjoying oneself in the outdoors exist today that
were virtually unknown before World War II--dune buggies,
snowmobiles, water skis, snorkels, faster boats and more
powerful motors, trailer houses, and many more. Each of
these would have added to the volume of outdoor recreation
activity but, again, their combined effect was very great.

The area of publicly owned land available for outdoor
recreation rose at each level of government--federal, state,
and local (Nature Conservancy 1977). Federal water reservoirs provided the opportunity for water sports in regions
of the country lacking natural lakes (the Great Plains, for
instance), and these were the scene of some of the most
rapidly growing recreation activities. Federal funds have
been available to states and cities for development of
outdoor recreation opportunities, and states have passed
bond issues to expand their port systems. Many of the large
private landowners have made their lands available for
outdoor recreation, especially for hunting, fishing, berry
gathering, and other forms of outdoor recreation not involving heavy expenditures for capital investments.

Although the attendance figures suggest that the average
person spends several days a year at some publicly owned
outdoor recreation area, a substantial proportion of the
people actually do not use such areas at all and others use
them very much. The impact of recreation, especially where
use is intense on relatively limited areas, is often detrimental to the area--vegetation is trampled, soils are
compacted and eroded, and the original quiet character of
the area is lost. Sometimes these effects involve surrounding areas or roads and highways leading to the popular
spots--not only the development of service facilities, but
also the beer can beside the road that has become as common
a nonmetro phenomenon as the beer can beside the suburban
street.

SUMMARY OF IMPACTS ON NONMETROPOLITAN LAND USE

It can well be argued that the areas of nonmetro land involved for each of these miscellaneous uses are small. They
are indeed small, often on the order of a very few million
acres or a very small percentage of the total national land
area. As noted, it is not merely the direct land use that
is often critical, but rather the indirect effects of land
taken out of other uses that are more important. The latter
might multiply the impact of direct land use by a factor of
two, three, or more, but even this, it may be argued, does
not make the land area required for urban housing, parks
and outdoor recreation, mining, transmission lines, or
highways a very large proportion of the national land area.
Nevertheless, the impacts of these various land uses on
nonmetro areas are cumulative and additive, so that in
total they are significant even when singly they are much
less so. Both land use and life-style in nonmetro America
are becoming urbanized to a substantial degree. The "country
hick" and backwoodsman are becoming rarities, as is the
bucolic land scene, untouched by modern technology and
modern life-styles.

Much of the recreational and residential subdivision and
related land use change in nonmetro areas in recent years
has been on land or sites inappropriate to the use (Rutgers
University 1978). Houses were built on flood plains or
slopes so steep that mudslides occurred shortly, and, all
too often, scant thought was given to the location of the
septic tank and virtually none to the location of the municipal landfill. In desert developments, the availability of
water for household purposes is always ignored by the devel-
oper and often overlooked by the buyer. And the provision of
social services, such as schools for the young and hospitals
for the elderly, is an often expensive afterthought.

All this is unfortunately the story of much nonmetro,
suburban, and exurban development of the past several generations. The price for environmentally inappropriate development has been paid many times over, but it may fairly
be argued that environmentally bad decisions have more
serious consequences today than in the past. Combined with
mounting pressure on the land, environmental pressures
are already severe enough in many areas that any increased
pressure is especially serious--streams have too little
oxygen content, too many pollutants, and too much soil
material is clogging waterways to tolerate any more unwise
nonmetro land developments.

USES OF PUBLICLY OWNED NONMETROPOLITAN LANDS

Many foreigners are amazed to discover that one-third of
all land is publicly owned in the United States. The explanation for the origin of this public landownership is
historical, but the explanation for its continuance and for
its widespread public acceptance is that the products and
services of the public land have been readily available
(with few exceptions) to private individuals. It is private
firms that harvest the timber from national forests, privately owned livestock that grazes on the public rangelands,
and private individuals who use the recreational opportunities on public lands.

The use of the public lands has increased greatly over
the past several decades, and because national forests have
been used for many purposes, the data on their use are some
of the best available. Comparing an average year around
1970 with an average year in the late 1920s, timber harvest
has increased eightfold, recreational use thirtyfold, wildlife numbers approximately threefold, and water use has
perhaps doubled (Clawson 1976). Only grazing of domestic
livestock has declined over those years. In particular
areas and times, increases in one of these uses have come
about only by virtue of declining outputs of other goods or
services, but for the national forest system during the
whole period, more of each use has been possible. Since
data were first available in 1910, total attendance in the
national park system has risen at an exponential annual
rate of between 8 and 10 percent. Recreation attendance at
all public lands, state and federal, declined during World
War II by as much as two-thirds at national parks, but
otherwise its increase has slowed noticeably only in the
more extreme depression years.

As the various uses have each increased, so has competition among them, requiring more intensive and more
sophisticated management if all major demands were to be
met. For instance, it has become necessary in several wilderness areas to limit either the number of parties, their
size, the length of their stay, the timing of their en-
trances to the area, or some of all these restraints, if
the character and quality of the wilderness experience was
to be maintained. Many parks have imposed limits on numbers
of campers allowed, with some establishing rather elaborate
systems of advance registration and reservation.

As use of public lands has increased, so has public
interest in their management. One measure of this increased

interest has been the passage of three truly major federal
land laws in much less than a decade: the Resources Planning Act of 1974, the National Forest Management Act of
1976, and the Federal Lands Policy and Management Act of
1976. These are in addition to important legislation such
as the Wilderness Act of 1964, the Wild Rivers Act of 1968,
and others. In each case, extensive hearings and debates in
the Congress and among the public accompanied the ultimate
passage of the legislation. In each case, substantial studies have been made by the agencies concerned, for application of the laws to the areas under their jurisdiction,
and in each case there has been substantial public involvement in the studies. The Roadless Area Review and Evaluation
of the Forest Service (RARE I and RARE II) were examples of
particularly active public participation in federal land
planning.

State land use, especially for outdoor recreation, has
also been increasing rapidly and steadily (Nature Conservancy
1977). Many states have been in the forefront of new management techniques, such as advance reservation systems,
and in financing some of the costs of management of their
lands by charges levied against the public users.

The very extensive public use of public parks, forests,
and other areas for outdoor recreation has often had serious
impact upon privately owned lands nearby or enroute because
many users have not distinguished between public and private areas. Trespass upon private land has been common and
often damaging. Thus the provision of needed services to
recreationists has provided local business activity and
employment, but it has had impact on local land use.

There is, of course, present uncertainty about the
future of outdoor recreation areas in nonmetro areas, particularly the more distant ones. Most users have to travel
considerable distances in order to enjoy such recreation
areas, and rising energy costs and limited energy availability may well cause use to fall in more distant areas
and possibly rise in the nearer ones. Although nothing like
the great decline of World War II is in prospect, it could
well be that attendance at more distant parks would either
fall or not increase in the future.

LAND PRICES

The increased local pressures for use of nonmetro land have
led to greatly increased bidding for such property, and in
typical land exchange transactions in the United States
willing sellers and willing buyers agree on a price. Some
land changes hands by inheritance, some by forced sale as a
result of defaults on mortgages or other indebtedness, and
small amounts by forced sale to units of government for
public use when negotiated sales fail. All land transactions take place within whatever laws, regulations, and
other social restrictions on land use, subdivisions, building codes, and the like exist, as well as within such general laws as those relating to contracts. Lenders play a
large, if indirect, role in these transactions, because
their willingness to lend money and their terms often are
critical to the land exchanges (Boxley 1977).

The bidding for farm real estate is most marked and
has been best studied in part because more and better data
on these prices and transactions exist than for any other
kind of nonmetro land. In recent years, between forty and
sixty farms out of each 1,000 change ownership each year,
about two-thirds of them by voluntary sales and most of the
rest by inheritance or by estate administrators' sales
(U.S. Department of Agriculture). In relatively prosperous
times, only a minute fraction of farm transactions are by
private foreclosure or because of delinquent taxes, but in
times of severe depression foreclosures have increased
greatly in the past. The prices at which farms change hands
include the value of any buldings, but most of the value is
attributable to the land. Although the actual number of
transactions involves only a small fraction of all farms
each year, the value of farm real estate for all farms
closely follows that of the prices of the farms actually
sold. This is, of course, a common phenomenon in stock
exchange and commodity markets--transactions at the margin
get translated into prices for the whole supply. It is this
aspect of land purchases by foreigners that may be the most
serious aspect of their operations, for their willingness
to bid up prices on the comparatively few farms they buy
may affect the price of all farms in the United States.

The price of farm real estate has been rising in the
United States almost continuously for about twenty-five
years (U.S. Department of Agriculture), but until 1973 the
rise had been well below an annual rate of 10 percent. With
the sharp increase in grain prices in that year, farm real

estate began a much more rapid climb, exceeding 20 percent in several recent years. For the years 1971 to 1977, net farm income for all farmers was $137 billion; in these same years, the value of farmland rose by $238 billion, or nearly twice as much (Healy 1979). The average farmer has made more money as a landowner and speculator than by tilling his land; of course, the gains in value of his land are realizable only by selling it or by borrowing on it as collateral, but unless prices should decline, which seems unlikely for the near future, these gains in capital assets are real.

The price of farm real estate is at a level where the average farmer has the greatest difficulty earning a going rate of interest on the sales value of his farm, in addition to earning a fair wage for himself. Some of the rise in farm real estate prices has been due to farmers buying land to enlarge their operations, but nonfarm people have often bought land as a hedge against inflation, among them, foreigners attracted by the favorable exchange rates and the general political stability of the United States.

The increase in farm real estate prices seems to have been matched or possibly exceeded by increases in the prices of forestland and of other recreation land (Healy 1977), but data on these other types of land are much less inclusive and detailed. Existing evidence suggests that all land prices have moved up significantly if not exactly proportionately. One would expect this to be true; urban investors buying land for personal use, as a hedge against inflation, or for capital gain, would tend to put their money where the prospects for increases in land price appeared the best and in the process would tend to raise land prices more or less proportionately.

The traditional economic approach to land prices has been to state that the present price of the land was equal to its annual net income divided by the appropriate interest rate. Thus, if the interest rate were 5 percent, the price of the land would be twenty times its annual net earnings. As with many economic formulations, this one raises as many questions as it answers. What is the appropriate interest rate, now and in the future, and how much do inflation, liquidity of investment, risk of decline in income, and other factors affect this appropriate interest rate? What changes in net income from the land are likely to occur in the future? The price of land is thus always inevitably somewhat speculative, and every landowner is to a degree a speculator in land, even when it is used for productive

purposes. Of course, some landowners are motivated primarily
by speculation or hopes of capital gains, whereas others
are primarily concerned with the use of their land.

The rapid upward movement of nonmetro land prices in
the past decade or so has been both a cause and an effect
of inflation. That is, a buyer expecting inflation to continue will pay more for land than he would if he expected
prices to remain stable. And when many thousands of metro
investors follow suit, the price of land gets bid up to the
point where the present expectation of future inflation is
fully incorporated into the present price. At that point,
land investment is no longer a protection against inflation
at the expected rate, but only protection against some much
greater rate of inflation. The land buyer has thus, perhaps
unconsciously, an interest in seeing inflation continue at
the past rate or at a future rate that exceeds it. Were
inflation to be fully arrested, these expectations of continually rising real estate prices would undergo serious
revision, and land prices would not only stop rising but
would probably fall. The land buyer is thus like the industry protected by tariffs and hence dependent on them.
As some economists have noted, Americans have a love-hate
relationship with inflation. We condemn it in general terms
as we avidly seek capital gains that are often inflation
based.

The rise in nonmetro land values closely parallels the
rise in prices of metro residential property--for the same
general reasons. There have always been those who argued
that high prices did not matter--if people paid them, these
were transactions between willing seller and willing buyer,
this was evidence that the property really was that valuable, and in any case the owners of such property gained
from further price rises. But others have pointed out that
high and rising property values have affected different
generations quite unequally.

Those having a great deal of property may benefit from
rising property prices unless capital gains taxes or the
cost of reinvesting offset profits from the sale. The transaction costs of selling and buying may also eat up much of
the apparent profit. When a child wants to acquire a home,
farm, vacation spot, or income-generating land, then the
high land prices extract another toll. If prices were always
proportional to the incomes of those who wanted to buy land,
then indeed it would not matter much, if at all, whether
dollar prices per acre were high or low. But it is precisely the disparity between land prices and incomes, whether

from land use or from wages and salaries, that creates the problem. In a great many nonmetro areas prices have been bid up to the point where landowners will strenuously oppose any land-use plan controls that they fear may limit their ability to get the highest possible price for their land.

DIFFERENCES AMONG REGIONS

The discussion thus far has been in general terms, applicable to the country as a whole. It should be obvious, however, that many of the situations and relationships described will differ according to where a particular local area falls in the classification outlined in Chapter 1. Counties that are growing rapidly will generally face more pressures on land and greater rises in land prices than counties that are growing slowly. But slow-growing counties that lie between two rapidly growing areas may face land pressures for transportation or power line purposes. The speculative promotion of forest or desert areas for retirement, recreation, or other subdivision purposes may strike at relatively quiescent counties. The bidding upward of land prices is likely to be greater, where pressures for land development and land-use change are greater, but because some investors are seeking overlooked or quiet areas, the pressures tend to be distributed. One may simply say that nonmetro land use is as complex and varied as the population changes noted in Chapter 1.

FEDERAL LAND-USE LEGISLATION

In recent years much federal legislation has dealt to some extent with nonmetro land use. There is a coastal zone management act that substantially limits the uses of land along the seacoasts and around the Great Lakes. A coal mining act controls or prohibits mining in nonmetro areas, and the clean water and clean air acts have affected some nonmetro land uses and have the potential for vastly greater effects. Flood insurance legislation requires local land-use regulation as a condition to the provision of flood insurance, and this in turn is required as a condition of loans in flood-prone areas. All of these laws are national in scope and origin, but their applicability varies considerably among localities depending upon the physical situation in each area. For example, flood insurance is meaningless for an area with no flood problem and coastal zone management does not apply where there are no coasts. Each of these acts deals with land use more or less incidentally to its main purpose.

But it is noteworthy that there is no general federal land-use planning legislation. Strenuous efforts have been made to pass such legislation several times in the past decade, but they have failed in one House or the other. At times they have seemed to have presidential support, only to see it withdrawn at other times. In efforts to win sufficient support to get an act passed, sponsors have successively weakened the original proposals, but in vain. Thus, the prospects for early general national land-use legislation are presently poor. Any such legislation would have to provide for a substantial degree of flexibility to meet local conditions, given the enormous variety of land-use situations, the great differences in land-use pressures, and the many different forms of local government in this country.

The various federal laws that do influence nonmetro land use may reasonably be described as creeping land-use legislation. That is, they do not deal with all uses of privately owned lands, particularly not in a coordinated and integrated way; but their total effect upon nonmetro land use is, or might become, considerable. It is, of course, possible that twenty years hence, our successors may look back and see the various present federal acts that affect or influence the use of some kinds of nonmetro private lands as having constituted an incremental approach to general land-use legislation. But this is by no means clear today.

IMPLEMENTATION OF LAND-USE PLANNING

Land-use planning may proceed independently of any efforts to translate the plans into action, or it may lead directly into actions of various kinds. Land-use plans without implementing mechanisms have limited value; the facts upon which they rest and the plans as one alternative form of future land use have informational value to landowners and others, but otherwise such plans may be simply intellectual exercises. A first step in implementation is to locate public works--sewers, highways and streets, schools, parks, and other public enterprises--according to the land-use plan. These public works exert a significant pressure on private land use. Moreover, urban land-use planning today typically proceeds into some form of control over private land use, by means of zoning, subdivision regulations, building codes, and similar regulations. Indeed, if land-use plans are to have any real significance they must limit private decisions. In the United States, as in nearly all economically developed countries in the world, we have rejected the purely private market for land as the sole allocator of private land use. We think some kinds of land uses should be kept out of residential areas, for instance; or we resist the building of high-rise apartments in typically single-family residential neighborhoods. Sometimes zoning and other land-use controls are imposed in the absence of a formal plan, but this practice is increasingly coming under adverse court and local political review. That is, if private land use is to be controlled, at least nominally in the public interest, then the landowner has a right to be aware of public plans and limitations on private land use.

STATE LAND-USE PLANNING

Although the legal right to plan for and control private land use by units of local government (counties, cities, and others) derived from the states, the latter, until rather recently, had not been involved very much in land-use planning and control. This has changed considerably in many states (Carter 1974; Little 1974; Myers 1974a, 1974b, 1976; Chapter 21, this volume). Some have passed laws specifying a little more precisely how cities and other units of local government may exercise their granted rights for land-use planning and control. The courts have taken a new interest in this matter and several state courts in a number of important cases have limited or directed the way in which local governments may apply their powers. The situation is complicated, especially for the nonlawyer, but much that has been done might be classed as insistence upon proper procedures and due process of law.

But some states have taken a more direct role in non-metro land-use planning and control. A substantial number have extended preferential tax treatment to certain types of land, especially farmland of higher productive capacity, if the land is left undeveloped (Atkinson 1977; Bryant and Conklin 1975; Council on Environmental Quality 1976; International Association of Assessing Officers 1975). This, however, is land-use inducement. By and large, it has been more tax relief for landowners than an effective means of controlling land use in part because eventual development of this land has generally met with few or weak penalties, in part because nonmetro landowners have tended to place under such laws only those lands for which the development pressures were not, in any case, very strong.

Other states have gone still further, sometimes for land in general and sometimes for land in special situations or of special characteristics (Miner 1975). For example, California has its own coastal zone act (Healy 1976), a notable feature of which is that it was passed by popular referendum and the general election process, not by the legislature. Florida, Vermont, Wisconsin, New York, and New Jersey, among others, have laws that are or may be considered general land-use planning and/or land-use control legislation, even when they may be applicable only to specific situations. In all these laws, the state as a unit of government has taken over land-use planning and land control functions that for a long time had been considered the domain of local government. A wider, broader, or more concerned outlook has superceded a more local, narrower, or more relaxed land-use planning and control process.

Some states, such as New Jersey, are experimenting with a special form of influencing private land use that is short of actual control but that conceivably may be politically more acceptable and at the same time effective. This is the idea of transferable development rights (Barrows and Prenguber 1975). Each landowner within a defined area is given some measure of development rights that are transferable and may be sold at private sale. In order to develop nonmetro land, the owner must have more development rights than he would have received for his land, hence he must buy some rights from other landowners. The hope is that this private bargaining process will achieve a degree of land-use control that is politically unacceptable when exercised by a unit of local government. Development will be limited to a fraction of the land area whose owners hope to benefit from development, and the limitation will be exercised through a private market rather than by application of government powers. There are clearly many difficult problems in applying this idea, for example, how large an area

to include in a trading zone, or how to define the development rights necessary for development of a particular tract.
The process probably cannot achieve as close a control of
precisely where development will take place as would the
older local government planning and zoning process. At this
point, experience with transferable development rights is
still too limited, both in time and in area, to reach any
firm conclusions as to the practicality of the approach.

LAND-USE PLANNING BY NONMETROPOLITAN COUNTIES

Some largely nonmetro counties have attempted to control
private land use, including the development of rural lands
for essentially urban purposes. The great variation among
counties in legal powers and political traditions has been
noted in earlier chapters; to these must be added the great
variations in natural land-use situations and development
pressures. A county is likely to undertake such controls of
private land use where there are politically powerful farm
or other landowner groups; where there is a strong local
sentiment to retain an established pattern of land use; and
where there is an imminent threat of land development, but
as yet not much pressure for such development as expressed
by rising land prices for development land (Ford Foundation
1974). In the absence of these factors, essentially nonmetro
counties are much less likely to undertake any form of
private land-use control.

Farmers, other nonmetro residents and/or landowners,
suburbanites, and exurbanites have always been ambivalent
about nonmetro land-use controls (Lyman et al. 1977). On
the one hand, they may wish to preserve a type of land use,
including aesthetic values of the pastoral scene, which
they value; or at the least to disturb these values as
little as possible by nonintrusive private developments
limited to purposes of which they approve (Whiting 1974;
Soil Conservation Society of America 1976). In support of
this position, they are likely to be vocal, often emotional,
even impassioned in their opposition to change. One who
proposes a change in nonmetro land use of which they do not
approve--even the tearing down of an old structure that has
or is alleged to have architectural or historic value--can
expect their initial strong opposition. These people, on
this basis, support land-use planning and strong public
controls over private land use.

On the other hand, those in these groups generally
want the opportunity to sell their land when they want, to
whomever they wish, at the best price they can get; and
this inevitably means, in practice, to someone who proposes
to develop the land for some purpose, to change its present
nonmetro character in some way. One can well sympathize
with these landowners on this point. For a considerable
proportion of them, the land is their major investment,
their major form of personal capital, and often virtually
their only savings. They are understandably loath to lose
any significant part of the value of that property, because
this may well have important consequences for their financial well-being. So, having previously opposed the development of some tract for a purpose deemed undesirable, a
landowner now defends his right to sell his land whenever
and for whatever he chooses--and, presumably, sees nothing
incongruous in these two positions.

Based on experiences to date, one cannot be very optimistic about the efficacy of nonmetro land-use controls,
especially by local governments. The variations in capacity
of such agencies to undertake any positive program are inherent in the variations in their character as described
in Chapter 19. Some states have counties where all governmental programs are very weak; in others, the counties are
small, with limited capacity. However, even in states with
large counties and strong governmental powers, the ambivalence of nonmetro landowners is a powerful deterrent to
effective land-use planning and control. Furthermore, strong
economic pressures for land development are accompanied by
developers, promoters, speculators, private lawyers, and
others eager to limit if not destroy local land-use controls. For example, in some areas of California, such as
Santa Clara County, strong efforts were made in the past to
limit, guide, and control development of open country land,
only to see such control efforts gradually eroded and
ultimately largely swept away by development pressures.

Many counties have gone through, or are going through,
an interesting political evolution as their essentially
nonmetro land use becomes essentially metro. When the
country was primarily agricultural, farmers, landowners,
and the local courthouse "gang" were in effective political
control. Initially, they were often opposed to change, but
also philosophically opposed to strong governmental controls over private land use, and thus ambivalent about the
whole issue. As economic pressures for land development
arose, perhaps creeping in as suburban development from

adjoining counties, the possibilities of making money from speculating or trading in land became apparent, and attitudes changed. Now the developers, larger landowners, land speculators, and a somewhat changed courthouse gang were in effective political control, willing to have land-use controls to insure that development followed what they considered to be sound lines, but much opposed to any limiting of the extent of such development. Still later, when the county had become largely suburban, at least in population, the new suburbanites were the dominant political force, more likely to favor stronger land-use controls, but still ambivalent as to the possibility that such controls might affect their freedom to realize gains in the value of their property. By this time, the pattern of land use in the county was largely set, and issues arose primarily over changes in its use; and here there would often be vocal conflict between the many supporters and opponents of change.

The more active role of some states in exercising direct controls over private land use arose in part from this limited political ability of local government to deal with the matter. It was thought, by raising local land-use control to a political level less controlled by local forces, that socially more sound decisions would be reached. This was not the only factor in increased state activity; concern for environmental effects outside the local area was a strong additional factor. It is true that state politics are often less dominated by local interests, as it is true that national politics are often not dominated by state interests, but it is equally true that raising the level of political decision does not automatically produce social wisdom or political morality. The ambivalence and sensitivity of legislative bodies to localized interests within their constituency may make the higher level of government no more capable of dealing with thorny issues of land-use planning and land-use control than were the lower levels of government, therefore, one cannot dismiss the long-term capabilities of states to deal with such planning and control.

IMPACTS OF CONTROLS OVER NONMETROPOLITAN LAND USE

Environmental controls over nonmetro land use have not really significantly affected such landowners. From an

environmental point of view, the equitable base for public
controls over private land use lies largely in the fact
that the landowner's activity affects people resident elsewhere, through stream pollution, degradation of air quality,
or in other ways. These are the matter of much current
concern. Since the earliest colonial days, erosion from
croplands has lowered water quality in streams and other
water bodies, and forest fires, burning of crop residues,
and other actions on essentially nonmetro lands have affected air quality in sometimes distant areas. But these
environmental impacts are more serious today, partly because physical degradation of rural lands is occasionally
greater, in part because chemical and other industrial
waste loads have been added to that nonmetro land use degradation, in part because larger populations have increased the damage effects, and in part because we as a people
no longer are as complacent about environmental damage as
we once were. Because of these adverse environmental effects, clean water and clean air legislation, federal as
well as state, might severely restrict rural land uses in
time. For example, proposals have been made that farmers be
forced to control soil loss to some defined tolerable level.

Attempts to control individual private land uses to
reduce adverse environmental effects to some acceptable
level would raise many difficult problems of administration,
regardless of which level of government undertook it as
well as the degree of popular support for the program in
general. Although there is legislation, much talk about
controlling adverse environmental effects upon other people,
and even some action, the overall effect of environmental
controls upon private nonmetro land use has been small.

NOTES

1. The data in this paragraph come from different
sources, apply to slightly different dates, and may not use
exactly the same definitions. Hence the residual figure,
although approximately correct, may not be exactly accurate.

BIBLIOGRAPHY

American Society of Planning Officials. "Subdividing Rural
    America." Report prepared for the Council on Environ-
    mental Quality, 1976.
Atkinson, Glen W. "The Effectiveness of Differential Assess-
    ment of Agricultural and Open Space Land." American
    Journal of Economics and Sociology (Apr. 1977).
Barrows, Richard L., and Prenguber, Bruce A. "Transfer of
    Development Rights: An Analysis of a New Land Use
    Policy Tool." American Journal of Agricultural Economics
    57 (1975).
Boxley, Robert F. "Landownership Issues in Rural America."
    U.S. Department of Agriculture, Economic Research
    Service, 1977.
Brown, David L. "Agricultural Land Use: A Population Dis-
    tribution Problem." In Farmland, Food, and the Future,
    edited by Max Schnepf. Ankeny, Iowa: Soil Conservation
    Society of America, 1979.
Bryant, William R., and Conklin, Howard E. "New Farmland
    Preservation Programs in New York." Journal of American
    Institute of Planners (Nov. 1975).
Bureau of Land Management. Public Land Statistics, 1976.
    Washington, D.C.: U.S. Government Printing Office, 1976.
Carter, Luther. The Florida Experience--Land and Water
    Policy in a Growth State. Baltimore, Md.: Johns Hopkins
    University Press for Resources for the Future, 1974.
Clawson, Marion. America's Land and Its Uses. Baltimore,
    Md.: Johns Hopkins University Press for Resources for
    the Future, 1972.
_____. The Economics of National Forest Management.
    Washington, D.C.: Resources for the Future, June 1976.
_____. The Economics of U.S. Nonindustrial Private
    Forests. Washington, D.C.: Resources for the Future,
    1979.
_____. Suburban Land Conversion in the United States:
    An Economic and Governmental Process. Baltimore, Md.:
    Johns Hopkins University Press for Resources for the
    Future, 1971.
_____, and Knetsch, Jack L. Economics of Outdoor
    Recreation. Baltimore, Md.: Johns Hopkins University
    Press for Resources for the Future, 1966.
Clawson, Marion et al. Land for the Future. Baltimore, Md.:
    Johns Hopkins University Press for Resources for the
    Future, 1960.
Council on Environmental Quality. Untaxing Open Space.

Washington, D.C.: U.S. Government Printing Office, 1976.

Ford Foundation. Ford Foundation Experiments in Regional Environmental Management. Naugatuck, Conn.: Ford Foundation, 1974.

Forest Service. Forest Statistics of the U.S., 1977. Review draft. U.S. Department of Agriculture, 1978.

Frey, H. Thomas. "Major Uses of Land in the United States, Preliminary Estimates for 1974." Working Paper no. 34. Washington, D.C.: U.S. Department of Agriculture, Economic Research Service, August 1977.

_____. Major Uses of Land in the United States: Summary for 1969. Agricultural Economic Report no. 247. Washington, D.C.: U.S. Department of Agriculture, Economic Research Service, 1973.

Healy, Robert G. "Land Market Issues." In Farmland, Food, and the Future, edited by Max Schneph. Ankeny, Iowa: Soil Conservation Society of America, 1979.

_____. Land Use and the States. Baltimore, Md.: Johns Hopkins University Press for Resources for the Future, 1976.

_____. "Rural Land: Private Choices, Public Interests." Conservation Foundation Letter, August 1977.

International Association of Assessing Officers. "Property Tax Incentives for Preservation: Use-Value Assessment and the Preservation of Farmland, Open Space, and Historic Sites." Proceedings. Chicago, Ill.: International Association of Assessing Officers, 1975.

Little, Charles E. The New Oregon Trail. Washington, D.C.: Conservation Foundation, 1974.

Lyman, Gregory A. et al. "Can Zoning Preserve Farmland? Yes, But It Requires Public Commitment, Appropriate Regulations, and a Valid Zoning Ordinance." Practicing Planner. Washington, D.C.: American Institute of Planners, September 1977.

Miner, Dallas D. "Agricultural Lands Preservation: A Growing Trend in Open Space Planning." In Management and Control of Growth, edited by Randall D. Scott. Vol. 3. Washington, D.C.: Urban Land Institute, 1975.

Myers, Phyllis. Slow Start in Paradise (Florida). Washington, D.C.: Conservation Foundation, 1974a.

_____. So Goes Vermont. Washington, D.C.: Conservation Foundation, 1974b.

_____. Zoning Hawaii: An Analysis of the Passage and Implementation of Hawaii's Land Classification Law. Washington, D.C.: Conservation Foundation, 1976.

The Nature Conservancy. Preserving Our Natural Heritage.
    Vol. 1, Federal Activities. Vol. 2, State Activities.
    In a report prepared for the National Park Service,
    U.S. Department of the Interior. Washington, D.C.: U.S.
    Government Printing Office, 1977.
Raup, Philip M. "Urban Threats to Rural Lands: Background
    and Beginnings." Journal of the American Institute of
    Planners (Nov. 1975).
Rutgers University. Environmental Management: Land and
    Water Resources Policy. New Brunswick, N.J.: Department
    of Environmental Resources, Rutgers, the State Univer-
    sity of New Jersey, 1978.
Soil Conservation Society of America. Journal of Soil and
    Water Conservation (Oct. 1976).
U.S. Bureau of the Census. Census of Agriculture, 1974.
    Washington, D.C.: U.S. Government Printing Office, 1977.
    _____. Statistical Abstract of the United States:
    1974. 95th ed. Washington, D.C.: U.S. Government Print-
    ing Office, 1974.
U.S. Department of Agriculture. Agricultural Statistics.
    Washington, D.C.: U.S. Government Printing Office.
    Various years.
Whiting, Larry R., ed. Communities Left Behind: Alternatives
    for Development. Ames, Iowa: Iowa State University
    Press, 1974.

Frederick H. Buttel

18
Environmental Quality and Protection

INTRODUCTION

The late 1960s and early 1970s were fertile years for the
coalescence of major social concerns into voluntary and
institutional[1] social movements. Two notable ones dating
largely from this era are the environmental and nonmetro
development movements. Neither environmental concern nor
nonmetro development was entirely new, of course. Large
nationwide conservation groups such as the Sierra Club and
Audubon Society had been actively promoting preservation of
the landscape during most of the twentieth century, while
nonmetro development was at least nominally present in
university and government organization charts for two decades. However, the departure of environmentalism from
the traditional conservation movement in the 1960s, and the
vigorous surge for nonmetro development from the previously
token character of this activity in the 1950s and early
1960s, are quite apparent.[2]

One interesting feature of the concurrent development
of these two movements is their potential conflict and
contradictory goals. This is not to suggest an ironclad
proposition that the development of nonmetro areas automatically implies environmental degradation. Indeed, one
might argue that the underdevelopment--decapitalization,
depopulation, and economic marginality--of nonmetro areas
had made their residents particularly vulnerable to destruction of their natural resources and natural environments.
Nevertheless, it is fair to say that the courses of growth
often envisioned by nonmetro development specialists (e.g.,
nonmetro industrialization) or dictated by enduring economic
changes in the larger economy (e.g., energy scarcity, which
compels more coal extraction in nonmetro areas) typically
involve major environmental problems. In the absence, then,
of broadly viable alternative trajectories of growth and
development, nonmetro development and environmental quality
to some extent become trade-offs that must consciously or

unconsciously be made. Development should not be viewed as
the major cause of environmental problems, unless the concept is made trivial by defining it as the sum total of
all of the social and economic changes that have occurred
in nonmetro America. But, as the resource problems of both
the metro and nonmetro sectors of the United States become
increasing complex, if not intractible, the trade-offs
between development as it is conventionally conceived and
environmental maintenance will become more pervasive.

This chapter begins by briefly discussing the range
of environmental problems that exist in nonmetro areas and
communities. Then attention is turned to an examination of
the causes of environmental problems, both in terms of
prevailing mythologies surrounding problems of the environment and the major social changes that have contributed to
these problems. The next portion of the chapter deals with
the distribution of environmental problems across communities with different characteristics. The final portions
focus on two central aspects of environmental issues relating to nonmetro areas--the socioeconomic distributional
impacts of environmental policy and the debate over local
versus centralized control of environmental decision making.

DIMENSIONS OF NONMETROPOLITAN ENVIRONMENTAL PROBLEMS

The ecological and social character of nonmetro America is
exceedingly diverse (see, for example, Hines et al. 1975),
and environmental problems accordingly are quite disparate.
This portion of the chapter will be devoted to exploring
these many and varied problems of the open country environment. In doing so, an admittedly arbitrary distinction
between agricultural and nonagricultural environmental
problems is used. The arbitrariness of this dichotomy is
manifest, for example, in the fact that an ostensibly nonagricultural environmental problem such as coal development
in the arid West can represent a significant loss of agricultural land, which equally clearly is an agricultural
environmental problem. Nevertheless, as will be pointed out
below, the environmental problems of agriculture can be
most conveniently traced to structural changes in the agricultural system itself, whereas problems of the nonagricultural environment have more varied causes (that typically
originate more directly from social changes in the larger
society and economy).

PROBLEMS OF THE AGRICULTURAL ENVIRONMENT

There is increasing consensus among observers from diverse
theoretical and disciplinary persuasions that soil erosion
and other forms of land degradation comprise the most
serious environmental affliction of agriculture (see, for
example, Perelman 1977; Carter 1977; Pimentel et al. 1976).
For example, Pimentel et al. (1976: 150) point out that:

> During the last 200 years, at least a third of the
> topsoil on the U.S. croplands has been lost. On the
> basis of erosion surveys and various soil surveys, it
> was estimated in 1935 that erosion had already ruined
> approximately 100 million acres for practical culti-
> vation. On nearly 100 million additional acres, "from
> one-half to all of the topsoil" had been lost. Thus
> about 200 million acres in the United States were ruined
> or seriously impoverished for crop cultivation by soil
> erosion before 1940; some of this land has since been
> put into forests. The nation's land, however, continues
> to be eroded.

Pimentel and his colleagues note that under normal conditions, about 1.5 tons of topsoil are formed per acre per
year, while average annual topsoil losses from erosion are
roughly 12 tons per acre. In certain portions of the country
soil erosion losses are staggering. For example, annual
soil losses on newly planted rangelands in the southern
portion of the Great Plains range from 15 up to 125 tons
per acre per year (Grant 1975). Perelman (1977: 53) calculates that annual soil erosion losses amount to almost 30
pounds of soil per pound of food produced and 20 tons of
soil erosion per capita. He notes that the average depth of
topsoil on American farmland has fallen from three feet to
six inches since this land underwent agricultural production. Pimentel et al. (1976) point out that the sediment
from eroded farmland costs the society about $500 million
annually, while losses in crop productivity from erosion
are even higher.
    Although sediment is a major component of water pol-
lution from agricultural runoff, large amounts of pesticide and fertilizer residues and manures find their way
into streams and lakes each year.[3] Although water pollution control efforts have demonstrated improvement in a
number of water quality dimensions, especially with respect
to reduction of toxic contaminants, nitrogen and phosphorus

contamination has shown little improvement or has even worsened. A study sponsored by the American Water Works Association (Task Group Report 1967) demonstrated the major contribution of agriculture to water impurity; the research group estimated that up to 60 percent of the nitrogen and 40 percent of the phosphorus in water supplies had their origin in agriculture.

Another water-related group of environmental problems concerns irrigation. Irrigation of agricultural land has intensified the struggle over scarce water resources in arid and semiarid regions of the country, and irrigation from well water is resulting in serious depletion of water tables in many areas. Perhaps the most ominous aspect of irrigation, however, is the destruction of agricultural land through salinization, waterlogging, or other problems. The emergence of severe salinization problems in the immensely productive San Joaquin and Imperial Valley areas of California has recently become a visible example of the fragility of semiarid agro-ecosystems, to the perturbation of modern agricultural practices (Small Farm Viability Project, 1977: 11).

Although not an environmental problem in the conventional use of the term, the high energy intensity of American agriculture can be viewed as a "sleeping crisis" that portends a future of vulnerability of agricultural production to scarcities of petroleum and natural gas. The agricultural production sector accounts for but 3.5 percent of total energy consumption in the United States, while the total food system, including processing, marketing, and home cooking and refrigeration, uses 16.5 percent of primary energy (Doering 1977). But roughly three calories of energy input are required to produce one calorie of food, and over ten calories of energy input are devoted to the production and flow of this calorie of food throughout the entire food system (Steinhart and Steinhart 1974a, 1974b). Further, the energy demands of agriculture are remarkably inelastic; even massive price increases would evoke little energy conservation in production agriculture because of the inflexibility of these needs (Dvoskin 1976; Buttel et al. 1979).[4] Thus substantial shortages of energy --particularly if agriculture is not given preferential allocations during times of scarcity--would find this agricultural sector quite vulnerable over the short to medium run.

A final potential environmental problem of agriculture that will be highlighted here is immediately related to the continually deteriorating energy situation discussed above. Although its extent is quite unclear, it is possible that the agricultural sector will be called upon to produce energy to meet the needs of the larger society. The use of agricultural residues for electrical energy production and the use of grains and crop residues for ethanol production have already begun on a small scale. Because the most difficult energy problem that the United States will face in coming decades is a shortage of liquid fuels, the conversion of biomass into ethanol will be the most likely arena for extending agriculture's role in energy production. Increased ethanol production will entail several distinct environmental problems, the most serious of which is likely to be increased soil erosion. The diversion of crop residues from fertilizer and fallow into an input for ethanol distillation would intensify erosion on existing land, while widespread ethanol production from grains would likely be accompanied by a significant return of marginal--usually quite erosion-prone--lands into production (Office of Technology Assessment 1979).[5]

PROBLEMS OF THE NONAGRICULTURAL ENVIRONMENT

It is often assumed that most American industry is concentrated in metro areas (especially the largest of cities), while nonmetro areas have relatively little manufacturing activity. However, the extent of industrialization of nonmetro areas is both substantial and increasing quite rapidly. Lonsdale (1979: 3) notes that the rate of increase in manufacturing employment in nonmetro areas has recently greatly exceeded the rate in metro counties, and since 1960, nonmetro areas have accounted for more than 50 percent of new manufacturing jobs, but less than 30 percent of the nation's population. Nonmetro and metro counties are virtually identical in their proportions employed in manufacturing (Lonsdale 1979; Hines et al. 1975). Thus, although industry is obviously less spatially concentrated than in metro areas, nonmetro regions face considerable environmental problems attributable to industrial production. Interestingly, the invocation of environmental legislation during the 1970s, especially the 1977 amendments to the Clean Air Act,[6] has likely increased the incentives to industry to move their plants, employment, and pollution to open country locales (Kale and Lonsdale, 1979: 52). Also, states with predominantly nonmetro populations (particu-

larly in the South) are less likely to have statewide environmental legislation with stricter standards than those
mandated by the federal government, making many nonmetro
areas even more attractive to prospective industry.

It should be kept in mind that the conventional image
of the process of growth in manufacturing employment--that
most new jobs are accounted for by large, established,
multinational corporations moving their plants from one
region of the country to another in search of cheap labor
or other benefits--is largely inaccurate. Birch (1979), for
example, demonstrates that nearly two-thirds of all new
jobs generated in the United States in the mid-1970s were
accounted for by small businesses (those with twenty or
fewer employees). Secondly, one-half of these new jobs were
due to "births" (new firms), and one-half were due to expansions of existing firms. Finally, the construction of
new branch plants was much more important than physical
migration of industrial plants from one region of the country to another in creating new manufacturing employment
in the mid-1970s. Birch's research thus suggests that it
would be inappropriate to view the flight of large-scale
industry from metro to nonmetro America as the single most
important source of nonmetro environmental problems resulting from industry. Indeed, one can anticipate that a substantial portion of new industry in nonmetro areas will
continue to be accounted for by new and existing small
business, even though the addition of branch plants to
existing large manufacturing firms will continue to be of
some importance.

Because of the rapid industrialization of nonmetro
areas, air and water pollution is becoming increasingly
troublesome. As indicated above, not all of this pollution
can be attributed to industrial production. However, the
localized effects of industry can be quite substantial as
is the case with large coal-fired power plants in the West
and paper mills in the upper Midwest and New England. At
this point it is instructive to note a linkage between the
environmental problems of industry and agriculture. It has
recently been noted that sulfur dioxide and nitrogen oxide
from air polluted in the border South, Ohio valley, and the
Northeast, when combined with water in the atmosphere,
yield sulfuric and nitric acids and rain in New England
with pH levels consistently as low as 4.2, with occasional
readings of 3.0 (Hill 1979). Because the range of effects
of acid rain is yet to be determined, consequences such as
decreased fresh water fish production, decreased agricul-

tural and forestry yields, depletion of nutrients from
soils and aquatic systems, disruption of the natural acid
or alkaline quality of soils, and inactivation of important
soil microorganisms seem likely. Nonmetro industry is a
modest but still consequential contributor to such a
phenomenon.

Industry is not the only contributor to inadequate
water quality in nonmetro areas. Nonmetro cities and towns
have been notorious in their violation of municipal water
pollution standards, often because of limited fiscal resources, and these areas increasingly contain the waste
disposal sites for metro industry and municipalities. Recent controversies surrounding leakage of toxic chemicals
from industrial waste disposal sites, the illegal dumping
of such chemicals along roadsides, and contamination of
streams and lakes by poly-chlorinated biphenyls (PCBs) have
given these problems more visiblity (National Rural Water
Association, 1977: 7-13). Other significant nonagricultural
sources of water pollution include thermal pollution from
electrical power plants, leeched acid and sediment from
surface mining, soil erosion from timber harvesting, and
seepage from poorly constructed septic tanks (Rosenbaum
1977; Wilkening and Klessig 1978). Disaggregated data providing general and local distributions of water quality
phenomena are virtually nonexistent, so that many of these
observations must remain qualitative and impressionistic.
However, ongoing research by the National Demonstration
Water Project, and the National Statistical Assessment of
Rural Water Conditions presently being conducted by the
Environmental Protection Agency and Cornell University will
soon close many of these data gaps.[7]

Because water impoundment projects for irrigation,
water supplies, flood control, and recreation were among
the first to come under the close scrutiny of the environmental impact assessment procedures deriving from the National Environmental Policy Act, the undesirable (as well
as some desirable) environmental impacts of water impound-
ments have become more widely recognized. Hagan and Roberts
(1975) have compiled a useful summary of the typical social
and environmental impacts of water projects, decomposing
these effects into four areas: (1) the area of the impoundment, (2) downstream from the impoundment or diversion, (3)
along conveyance routes for the water project, and (4)
areas of project water use (i.e., agricultural and urban
areas). A partial listing of the effects of water impound-
ments at only the area of impoundment includes disturbance

of the natural state of the area (e.g., erosion during construction and project operations), submersion of land areas (e.g., reduction of ecological diversity and stability), increased evaporation losses (e.g., reduction of downstream water supply), and increased "people pressure" (e.g., erosion caused by intensive recreation or housing construction). Although the environmental impacts of water projects are obviously quite variable, Hagan and Roberts suggest that recognition of these environmental impacts often makes the cost of projects surpass their possible benefits.

Solid and toxic waste disposal, as noted above, is increasingly threatening the quality of the nonmetro environment. In 1974, the Environmental Protection Agency (1974: 66) reported that there were over 17,000 waste dumps in the forty-six states they have inventoried. Blobaum (1978: 394) estimates that these dumps average thirty-four acres in size and occupy 476,000 acres of land, whereas approximately 500 new dumps are added per year in the United States at the present rate of filling. Waste disposal sites not only result in a significant loss of agricultural land, but also raise important threats of water pollution and deterioration of human health from toxic agents and carcinogens (see also Brown and Lebeck 1976; Environmental Policy Division, Congressional Research Service, 1974).

As Clawson notes in the previous chapter in this volume, the recent resurgence of nonmetro population growth through net migration has major implications for land use and related environmental problems. For example, new nonmetro housing construction involves rather extensive land use because a significant part of the motivation for metro-to-nonmetro migration is access to large tracts of residential land. In addition to the difficulty this generates in providing services, this extensive, dispersed type of land development results in significant loss of agricultural land and the threat of water contamination from septic tanks.

Surface mining has always been an important environmental problem. The proportion of coal that is surface mined has increased from 9.2 percent in 1940 to more than 40 percent at present, and this proportion is rapidly increasing with the opening up of new coal lands in the western states. Coal actually lags behind other materials in the proportion that is strip-mined; roughly 80 percent of all minerals mined in the United States are stripped from the earth's surface, yielding by 1970 more than 6,000

square miles of countryside that had been stripped--and
with relatively little reclaimed (Munn 1973; Rosenbaum
1977). A U.S. Department of Interior report (1967) lists a
veritable catalogue of environmental problems caused by
strip mining of coal and other minerals, including air and
water pollution, soil erosion, acid drainage, aesthetic
deterioration of the landscape, and the sacrifice of agricultural land. Reclamation legislation is quite recent,
and it is unclear how strictly it will be enforced by the
Department of Interior, especially in light of the government's high priority on expansion of coal production. Even
though reclamation is necessary to restore some semblance
of ecosystem integrity, it cannot always compensate for the
irreversible environmental deterioration that certain forms
of strip mining create. Strip mining of coal in the Appalachians, for example, may yield persistent ecological
destruction through the drainage of acid, while coal mining
in the arid and semiarid West presents extreme difficulties
in restoring the productive rangeland lost to the coal
shovel. It is widely accepted that the current deterioration of America's energy situation will result in rapid
expansion of coal mining in the West, particularly because
of the low sulfur content of western coal and its corresponding attractiveness in light of air pollution legislation.[8] The expansion of western coal production will
also aggravate chronic problems of water shortages and
create new water quality deterioration. Rosenbaum (1977:
232) describes a vivid example of "mine-mouth" coal/elec-
trical generation projects (where electrical generation is
done at the mining site):

> The Four Corners Project, located where the borders of
> Utah, Arizona, New Mexico, and Colorado meet, indicates
> the size to which mine-mouth projects can grow and
> graphically illustrates their environmental impact.
> Begun by a consortium of twenty-three power companies,
> the present two generating facilities are expected to
> grow to six large plants and several smaller ones gen-
> erating 40,000 megawatts of power. Today, the smoke
> emissions from the existing facilities have been seen
> as far as 215 miles west in Bryce Canyon and 150 miles
> south in Albuquerque. If all six large plants were
> operating at full capacity, their estimated daily
> emissions of fly ash, sulfur dioxide, and nitrogen
> oxides would exceed the load of these pollutants found
> daily in New York and Los Angeles combined. The largest

plant, yet to be constructed, will cool its generators
yearly with enough water to supply San Francisco's
requirements.

Two final problems of the nonagricultural environment
will be mentioned. First, timber harvesting has historically
contributed to degradation of the nonmetro environment
through aesthetic deterioration, erosion, and leeching from
clear-cutting, and fires fueled by slash left on timbering
harvesting sites (Hayes 1959). Although timber harvesting
practices have clearly improved over recent decades, expanded demand for timber will increase the rate of exploitation of America's forests and make improved harvesting
practices even more mandatory in order to control environmental deterioration. Massive clear-cutting of timber also
increases water runoff and the threat of more serious flooding (Bormann et al. 1968). Clawson's chapter also discusses
the rapidly escalating degradation of recreational environments caused by the explosive demand for outdoor recreation.
The parallel increases in demand for timber and outdoor
leisure sites promise that greater demands will be made on
forest resources, and growing environmental deterioration
will almost unavoidably ensue.

PREVAILING MYTHOLOGY

The theory, research, and literature concerning environmental problems in the United States infrequently make
distinctions between nonmetro and metro issues. In many
ways this neglect is reasonable and defensible (Buttel and
Flinn 1977); environmental degradation knows no political
boundaries, as demonstrated by the example of industrial
pollution causing acid rain and its many effects hundreds
of miles away in rural New England. But as will be pointed
out below, nonmetro environmental problems have some important physical and social characteristics that differentiate them from the environmental difficulties of metro
America. However, recognition of these unique characteristics or tendencies has been substantially limited by
prevailing myths about the nonmetro environment.

The first such myth or example of an overly simplistic
assumption is that the nonmetro environment, at least until
quite recently, has been largely pristine and free from
environmental degradation. A common corollary is that en-

vironmental problems tend to be confined to metro areas. Both portions of this aspect of environmental mythology have major shortcomings. First, it is important to recognize that the American nonmetro environment has long been subject to major perturbations. The more obvious of these perturbations are the Dust Bowl of the 1930s, wantonly destructive forestry practices in the few decades surrounding the turn of the century, and the more spatially limited but equally destructive surface mining practices that prevailed until the last decade (see, for example, Lockeretz 1978, 1979; Hays 1959; Wilkening and Klessig 1978). More subtle examples abound such as the progressive march of soil erosion discussed earlier. Nonmetro environmental problems are neither new nor uncommon.

A second myth is that existing environmental problems can be ascribed to the traditionalism and conservativism—usually associated with antienvironmentalism, resistance to planning, and preference for local control—among nonmetro people. The weight of empirical evidence, however, is decidedly to the contrary. First, nonmetro-metro differences in attitudes (e.g., in terms of political ideology and traditional-modern orientations) are now quite small and apparently continue to narrow (Glenn and Hill 1977). Second, differences in environmental attitudes have been found to be relatively modest and/or inconsistent in the eleven studies inventoried by Van Liere and Dunlap (1979). Dunlap's work (Tremblay and Dunlap 1978) has, however, indicated that nonmetro-metro differentials in general or in terms of national environmental problems, are virtually nonexistent, while these differences are somewhat larger for local (i.e., environmental problems in one's own community) ecological issues (see also Buttel and Flinn 1976). Finally, Geisler (1978, 1979) has found very little relation between conservative or traditional attitudes, on one hand, and preference for local control or resistance to planning, on the other. In sum, it would be quite erroneous to attribute environmental problems to the social and attitudinal composition of nonmetro people. In general, it seems much more reasonable to look toward the underdevelopment or dependent position of nonmetro areas as the principal source of their environmental difficulties. As will be explored in more depth below, market and other economic aspects of agriculture, for example, unstable prices, overproduction, and governmental policy, over which nonmetro people have had little control have been major contributors to deterioration of the agricultural environment. Likewise, extravagant resource consumption by the metro population and industry has led to an intensified search for raw materials in nonmetro areas, and urban malaise and fiscal crisis have caused metro residents and industry to invade nonmetro America. It is also appropriate to note that many past and present abuses of the nonmetro environment testify to the ability of metro populations to externalize the ecological costs of their modes of production and consumption to the detriment of nonmetro people, usually through the government policymaking process (Converse et al. 1978).

Although recognizing that environmental problems do not lend themselves to any unambiguous nonmetro/metro dichotomy, it is useful to state some of the special characteristics of environmental problems as they affect open country areas. The first unique characteristic of environmental problems is that many center around the undermining of renewable natural resource production. Loss and deterioration of agricultural and forest lands essentially amount to irreversible degradation that impairs the ability of the nation to achieve less dependence on nonrenewable resources (especially inanimate energy). Second, nonmetro environmental problems tend to be socially--if not physically--invisible. Major disturbances of the nonmetro environment often can and do occur with little recognition or notoriety; whereas, for example, incidents such as Love Canal, Three Mile Island, or the frequent smog alerts in Los Angeles are the daily staple of front-page or television news. The tragic pesticide poisonings of thousands of migrant workers each year remain virtually unknown,[9] whereas at this writing virtually all citizens are aware of the relatively more benign, in comparison with the human lives lost or impaired, contamination of beaches and loss of wildlife from the out-of-control Mexican offshore oil well. Nonmetro environmental problems thus are more likely to remain unrecognized than those that occur in metro America. This characteristic of environmental problems is intimately related to a third: many of those confronted by nonmetro environmental problems often have no readily organized or powerful constituency through which to seek redress. For example, solutions to soil erosion problems are dependent on the ebb and flow of concern within the U.S. Department of Agriculture (USDA). Farmers struggling under growing indebtedness and sharply rising costs must often maximize short-term profits, partially by ignoring erosion, merely

to stay in business, although the relatively invisible
nature of soil erosion implies that the problem is unlikely
to be recognized and acted upon by other groups.

SOCIOECONOMIC FORCES LEADING TO
NONMETROPOLITAN ENVIRONMENTAL DEGRADATION

The previous discussion of the diversity of environmental
problems alluded to some of their socioeconomic roots. This
section will discuss these factors in a more comprehensive
fashion, again utilizing the distinction between problems
of the agricultural and nonagricultural environment.

AGRICULTURAL ENVIRONMENT PROBLEMS

Degradation of the agricultural environment results principally from structural changes in the food production and
distribution systems. These major changes include the trends
toward: (1) large-scale, specialized farm production units,
(2) increased use of purchased biochemical inputs, and (3)
regional specialization of production. Each will be discussed in turn.

Large-scale, Specialized Farm Production Units
   Recent research has begun to examine how the well-
recognized trends toward increasing scale and specialization, which are themselves positively related, affect
resource use in agriculture (Perelman 1973). This research
has begun to establish that larger farms tend to require
more energy and off-farm inputs, especially fertilizers and
pesticides, per unit of production than do smaller farms
(Buttel and Larson 1979; Perelman 1977), corroborating the
simultaneous trends toward increased farm size and energy
intensity of agricultural production observed during this
century (see, for example, Steinhart and Steinhart 1974a).
Agricultural ecologists have also discovered that specialization of farm production units, which implies monoculture
and cessation of crop rotations, results in an increased
severity of pest infestations and greater needs for energy-
intensive--and potentially toxic or polluting--pesticides
(Pimentel et al. 1973). Specialized farms also have suboptimal manure management (Oelhaf 1978), and monoculture

generally results in higher rates of soil erosion than crop rotation practices (Pimentel et al. 1976).

Increased Use of Purchased Biochemical Inputs

As noted above, increased use of purchased biochemical inputs such as pesticides and fertilizers is partly a reflection of increased farm size. However, biochemical input use has certainly expanded beyond that dictated by changes in size alone. Fertilizers and pesticide residues are clearly major sources of water pollution, even though Public Law 93-523 (the Safe Drinking Water Act of 1974) has set maximum contaminant levels for six organic pesticides and ten inorganic chemicals, including three present in most fertilizers (National Rural Water Association, 1977: 7). Laws regulating nonpoint pollutants such as those from agricultural chemicals are very difficult to enforce. In addition to water pollution, one other potential environmental effect of agri-chemical use has been noted--the destruction of microbiotic life in soil that renders it at least temporarily unable to effectively recycle organic residues within the agro-ecosystem. This issue, however, still remains quite controversial within the agricultural science community (Allaby and Allen 1974).

Regional Specialization of Production

Although the degree of the farm and regional specialization are of course related, they are by no means coterminous. Theoretically the agriculture of a given region could be diverse whereas its individual farm units are highly specialized. Although this diversity of specialization phenomenon does indeed exist to some extent in the United States, in practice the specialization of farm firms and specialization of regional production systems go hand in hand. The most direct environmentally related effect of regional specialization is that it increases the use of energy in the food system in order to transport food commodities from the point of production to their points of processing and consumption (Steinhart and Steinhart 1974a; Belden and Forte 1976). Regional specialization has other important--albeit indirect--environmental impacts. Regional specialization intensifies the manure management problems noted above, because regional crop monocultures typically lack any animal manures to enhance soil fertility, and areas specialized in livestock production (especially huge cattle feedlots) view manure only as a waste disposal prob-

lem (which it surely is), rather than as a fertilizer resource. Regional specialization also tends to intensify the
effects of monocultural farm practices on pest infestation--
simplifying ecosystems so that pest eruptions are more
widespread and increased amounts of pesticides are necessary.
     At this point it is useful to comment further on the
more general social forces leading to increased farm size,
specialization, and use of inorganic biochemical inputs.
Each trend may be seen as a consequence of the endemic
overproduction, price instability, and economic insecurity
within American agriculture. Expanding the size of one's
farm, that is, land acquisition and mechanization, special-
izing in one or two major enterprises, and increased use of
biochemical inputs have clearly been economically rational
adjustments in the face of the cost/price squeeze (see, for
example, Pasour and Bullock 1977). Historic government
policies--especially price supports and tax policy--have
disproportionately benefited large farms and encouraged
increased farm sizes (Schultze 1971). Other aspects of
government policy such as agricultural research have tended
to benefit larger farms and emphasize mechanized, chemical-
intensive agricultural systems (Belden and Forte 1976).
Each has, therefore, contributed to degradation of the
agricultural environment.

NONAGRICULTURAL ENVIRONMENTAL PROBLEMS

The sources of problems of the nonagricultural environment
are obviously more diverse in light of the vast differentiation among production activities in nonmetro regions.
This section discusses the major causes of nonagricultural
environment degradation.

Economic Fragility and Vulnerability
of Nonmetropolitan Regions
     Nonmetro regions have historically had lower per capita
incomes than metro areas (Tweeten and Brinkman 1976). Industry quite obviously tends to move toward nonunionized
areas with low wage labor forces (Summers et al. 1976),
bringing pollution as well as employment. Small communities,
typically with meager tax bases, are ill-equipped to finance
pollution abatement facilities. Industries that locate in
nonmetro cities or towns typically transform these into
one-company towns along with the local powerlessness that
this implies; citizens or community officials are unlikely

to take local environmental actions that would cause their
principal employer to seek another location. The powerlessness of state and local officials in Appalachia in the face
of environmental destruction from strip mining has similar
roots (Caudill 1971).

Urban Malaise, Fiscal Crisis, and the Turnaround Migration
As noted by Zuiches elsewhere in this volume, the deterioration of large cities is connected to continued migration to nonmetro areas (see also Lonsdale, 1979: 5).[10]
This deterioration along with the protracted fiscal crises
of American cities, which present pressure to increase
property taxes on industry, and the attraction of cheap,
nonunionized labor have resulted in continued deconcentration of industry toward the nonmetro periphery (Haren
and Holling 1979).

Energy Scarcity
Emerging shortages of petroleum have already begun
to stimulate coal production, especially as a substitute
for petroleum in electrical power production, and mine-
mouth coal/electrical production installations exponentially
increase the level of environmental degradation (Rosenbaum
1977). Still on the horizon is a massive turn toward liquefaction of coal, almost certain to occur and clearly certain
to cause massive problems of air and water pollution and
land destruction. Also in the future is the distillation of
ethanol from agricultural biomass, a distinct possibility,
even though its energy production potential is modest and
comparative costs are unclear. The latter would be much
more environmentally benign than the former, however
(Office of Technology Assessment 1979).[11]

Increased Demand for Outdoor Recreation
Clawson points out in the preceding chapter that the
demand for outdoor recreation continues to grow greatly (at
the same time that many rural areas are increasingly dependent on income from tourism). This demand will come up
against an essentially constant supply of outdoor recreation
sites, further intensifying their deterioration.

Environmental Regulation in Metropolitan Areas
Environmental considerations are rarely the cause of
industry fleeing from metro locations or building new branch
plants outside the metropolis, but merely represent yet
another contributing factor. Nevertheless, under recent

amendments of the Clean Air Act that specify the classification of places into "attainment" or "nonattainment"
areas, metro areas are much more likely to fall into the
latter category than nonmetro ones. Because no new major
construction with significant air emissions is allowed in
nonattainment areas, nonmetro regions will increasingly be
attractive locations for these facilities. Regulation of
water supply quality is also more strict in metro areas
(National Rural Water Association 1977), providing further
incentives toward deconcentration of industry and pollution.

THE UNEVEN IMPACT OF
NONMETROPOLITAN ENVIRONMENTAL PROBLEMS

The problems of the nonmetro environment are obviously
unevenly distributed. Recognition of the pattern of this
distribution can, therefore, be of assistance to those
concerned with environmental policy who can then design
more effective programs and activities. This portion of the
chapter analyzes the uneven community impact of environmental problems according to five dimensions: population
change, structure of settlement patterns, degree of metro
influence, size of community, and regional context.

POPULATION CHANGE

Rapidly growing nonmetro communities tend to be more subject
to certain types of environmental problems than nonmetro
communities that are growing less rapidly. Many of these
difficulties center around the accelerated construction of
homes and the necessary services oriented toward this expanding population. Heaton and Fuguitt (1979), for example,
point out that nonmetro population growth through net in-
migration is much more strongly connected to increases in
services employment than to increases in manufacturing
employment. Counties experiencing growth in manufacturing
employment during the 1970s did not differ decidedly from
counties with little or no growth in industrial employment
in their rates of population growth through in-migration.
Although communities experiencing increases in industrial
or manufacturing employment will thus not usually face
abnormally large environmental impacts due to rapid population growth, some types of industrial location decisions

can have major environmental consequences through massive
in-migration. This is particularly the case with energy
development in the western states that typically generates
the haphazard development associated with boom-town conditions (Freudenburg 1976).

STRUCTURE OF SETTLEMENT PATTERNS

New rural housing tends to be spatially dispersed and to
occupy large parcels of land. Extensive, dispersed development, in fact, seems to be an emerging pattern of spatial
organization in nonmetro areas, and in many nonmetro areas
the conventional image of "open country" is disappearing as
roadsides are rapidly filling up with nonfarm housing.[12]
This settlement pattern has two major environmental consequences. First, dispersed housing cannot make use of
municipal sewer facilities, increasing the number of nonmetro open country residents using septic tank systems,
which are often poorly constructed, have limited effective
lifetimes, and can potentially threaten water quality for
both the homeowner and his/her neighbors.[13] Second, this
dispersed pattern of settlement may withdraw sizable amounts
of land from agriculture or forestry, increasingly contributing to a rapid loss of land for primary production and
intensifying the environment demands on the land that
remains (Blobaum 1978).[14]

DEGREE OF METROPOLITAN INFLUENCE

Small communities in close proximity to large cities or to
transportation routes leading to them will face more intense
environmental pressures than communities more isolated from
the metropolis. Proximate communities are most subject to
in-migration of industry and people. Fuguitt and Zuiches's
(1975) research on residential preferences indicates that
metro residents wishing to live in smaller communities tend
to prefer communities close to metro centers. Even where
people do not choose permanent residence in open-country
areas, second homes typically are located within driving
distance of large cities. Proximate communities are also
most likely to be sought out as sites for electric power
plants; solid, toxic, and nuclear waste disposal sites; and
"short-span" outdoor recreation.

SIZE OF COMMUNITY

Even though industry is rapidly deconcentrating toward
nonmetro communities, the largest of these communities will
be most attractive to industry because of their greater
availability of services, the "economies of agglomeration"
(Tweeten and Brinkman 1976). Larger nonmetro communities,
especially those of more than 5,000 residents, will likely
continue to attract the bulk of large-scale industry that
moves to nonmetro America, and these communities accordingly
will experience the greatest environmental problems resulting from industrial production and construction and related
impacts.[15] However, it should be noted that large communities typically have greater and more diversified tax
bases from which to garner the resources to handle the
environmental problems that new industries and construction
create (Tweeten and Brinkman 1976). In other words, the
disruptive social and environmental impacts of new industry
are more modest in relatively large places than they are in
small places where such perturbations create the disorga-
nizations of the boom town.

REGIONAL CONTEXT

A whole host of environmental problems, for example, increased danger of flooding due to deforestation, salinization of water from prolonged irrigation of semiarid farmland, and surface mining, are quite specific to particular
regions and are essentially based on the spatial distribution of climatic conditions and natural resources. Other
regional aspects of environmental degradation are more
clearly social and economic in origin. For example, the
Sunbelt is most dramatically affected by nonmetro industrialization because of its inexpensive and nonunionized
labor and, in some cases, its less stringent environmental
regulations (Lonsdale 1979; Kale and Lonsdale 1979). Insofar
as degree of metro influence can be considered a regional
characteristic, the factors discussed previously would also
apply here. For instance, nonmetro areas proximate to the
industrial Northeast are rapidly experiencing the many
problems associated with dispersed settlement patterns.

ENVIRONMENTAL QUALITY AND NONMETROPOLITAN DEVELOPMENT: IN WHOSE INTEREST? THE EQUITY PROBLEM

THE LIMITS OF ENVIRONMENTAL AND NONMETROPOLITAN DEVELOPMENT POLICIES

One of the cruelest ironies of America's environmental dilemma is the fact that while the poor suffer most from residential and workplace pollution (Burch 1976), they also tend to pay disproportionate costs of environmental reform (Schnaiberg 1975; Krieger 1970). The inegalitarian consequences of most environmental policies clearly are at least partially responsible for the attenuated momentum of environmental protection in the 1970s. Whereas it would be an oversimplification to argue that the poor are antienvironmental (see Buttel and Flinn 1978), the tendency for low-income, working-class persons to be lukewarm toward environmental protection policies--even though they tend to be the principal victims of environmental destruction--has resulted in a diminished constituency for efforts to enhance environmental quality.

Insofar as nonmetro residents are overrepresented among the nation's poor (Hines et al. 1975; Chadwich and Bahr 1978), the general thrust of environmental policy would tend to disadvantage nonmetro persons relative to metro residents. For example, serving pollution abatement orders on a small industry such as a paper mill may lead to a plant shutdown and the loss of hundreds of jobs, and the firm may merely relocate in another region of the country. Mandatory soil conservation legislation, were it to be enacted, would find larger farmers best able to comply, while the limited financial resources, and generally low quality, easily erodable land[16] of small farmers would probably lead to an even larger exodus of small farmers from agriculture. Small communities with modest tax bases find it difficult to comply with pollution abatement legislation that mandates investments in new plant and equipment.[17] It must be kept in mind that although national air quality legislation encourages industry to locate in nonmetro areas and bring badly needed employment (although this employment often bypasses the most needy residents because of their lack of skills; Summers et al. 1976), environmental policies do have a major potential for depressing small communities and their residents.

This leads to a number of thorny problems in the development of strategies to enhance the quality of the non-

metro environment and promote development. On one hand, it
is not in the long-run interest of either nonmetro people
or the nation as a whole to overlook environmental problems
in order to provide employment opportunities and increase
levels of living. For example, ignoring soil erosion to save
small farms has little long-term meaning if the quality of
the agricultural environment continues to be degraded at
the present rate. On the other hand, uniform enforcement of
national environmental regulations without regard to the
metro/nonmetro status of the community or the social characteristics of the parties involved will most dramatically
affect the nonmetro--especially the poor--portion of the
population.

At one level it is attractive to resolve this dilemma
by saying that policymakers should recognize the trade-offs
involved--a little bit of equity for a comparable increment
of environmental quality, according to the rules of cost-
benefit analysis and optimality. But this slightly misses
the point. To accept the fact that there inherently is an
ironclad trade-off between development and environmental
quality is to accept the notion that the present trajectory
of development--or "underdevelopment," if you will--of
nonmetro areas is a natural progression of economic change
to which there are no alternatives. One might, therefore,
pose the following question: does fostering continuation of
the present direction of development in nonmetro areas
really yield development, or do these strategies merely
rationalize nonmetro social organization so that it can
become a more effective adjunct to the metro economy?[18]
In other words, is what is being promoted really development, or is it a type of underdevelopment that increases
the vulnerability of local residents to the decisions of
absentee-owned enterprises and the policies of a federal
government more concerned with industrial and energy production than with the livelihood of nonmetro people?

The image that development conventionally conjures up
frequently has the net result of attracting more industrial
--and to a lesser extent, utility and mining--installations.
Despite evidence that industrialization may have limited
benefits for nonmetro people (Summers et al. 1976) and the
fact that there simply is not enough industry to go around
in order to meaningfully develop more than a handful of
communities (Nolan and Heffernan 1974), very few fresh ideas
have come to the fore other than striving to make sure that
nonmetro areas get their fair share of federal outlays.

It is also useful to briefly explore what amounts to

two nonsolutions to the problems of the environment. The first such strategy is to propose varying environmental standards for metro and nonmetro areas, with nonmetro areas enjoying the least restrictive regulations. This strategy would merely amount to a federal subsidy for polluting industries to relocate in nonmetro areas and postpone the need for the nation to grapple with the environmental consequences of its present course of development. The second nonsolution--striving to confine environmental problems to metro areas--has the same limitation. In addition, it would further marginalize many areas economically without accomplishing any significant reduction in environmental degradation.

NONMETROPOLITAN DEVELOPMENT/
ENVIRONMENTAL POLICIES ALTERNATIVES

The notion that much higher levels of environmental degradation must be tolerated to increase nonmetro development might as well have been included as a third myth concerning environmental problems. However, as indicated previously, this will remain a rather accurate reflection of reality unless far different strategies of development policy are adopted. In other words, it is possible to conceive of development initiatives that enhance environmental quality, or at least do little to aggravate environmental deterioration. There are two cornerstones of these alternative policies, one pertaining to the agricultural and the other to the nonagricultural sector of the nonmetro population.

It was noted earlier that many significant problems of the agricultural environment can be traced to economic insecurity among farmers and social policies that give large-scale farms an advantage over smaller ones. Not only do the adaptations of farmers to these factors lead to environmental problems, but also as has become more visible since the rediscovery of a now classic study by Goldschmidt (1947, 1978) of the consequences of large-scale agriculture in the Central Valley of California, increases in the scale of farm enterprises tend to result in a spiral of decline in local communities. Goldschmidt's research, which has been largely corroborated with more recent data (Fujimoto 1977; Sonka and Heady 1974; Sonka 1979), indicated that large-scale agriculture tends to result in a declining farm population, marginalization of small businesses that depend on purchases from farm people, and hence a decline in the

nonfarm population, and a whole host of secondary effects
that set in motion a downward multiplier of decline. Development policy, then, might at least partly become small-
or family-farm policy--that is, a policy to enhance the
viability of small- and moderate-scale family farms (Powers
et al. 1978). Efforts to control or reduce farm size could
include: (1) replacing price support payments geared to
level of production with income support payments administered with a progressive sliding scale of payments, in order
to redress the present biases of commodity programs against
the small farmer (see also Belden and Forte 1976); (2)
policies to curb land inflation such as revisions of tax
laws that encourage nonfarm or absentee investment in agriculture (Raup 1973); (3) expanded loan or new land banking
programs for new or existing small farmers (Powers et al.
1978); and (4) mandatory participation in soil conservation
programs (along with grants and loans to small farmers or
farmers with highly erodable land) as a condition for receiving government payments. Such efforts to enhance the
small or family farm would likely confer more benefits on
nonmetro communities through positive multiplier effects
than would industrial employment, while at the same time
attenuating the pressures for degradation of the agricultural environment.

A second focus for development and environmental policies might be encouragement of locally owned and controlled
commercial and industrial enterprises oriented toward meeting local needs. As energy--and hence transportation--costs
increase, it may be increasingly feasible for local enterprises to focus on import substitution, that is, substituting locally produced and processed goods for those formerly
imported from outside community or regional boundaries. One
obvious area for this substitution is food distribution and
marketing. Community development corporations or cooperatives focused on community canneries or other food processing activities, for example, could provide local employment
and reduce food costs to the local population (Britt et al.
1978).[19] Such production organizations could also make
use of local timber for manufacturing furniture, selling
firewood, or other resources. Another useful niche for
import substitution could be energy-related activities such
as the manufacture and installation of cellulose insulation,
production of ethanol from biomass, or construction of solar
energy converters. Community-owned firms might have several
generally unrecognized environmental and economic benefits.
First, a community-owned firm would be less likely to sub-

stitute capital and energy for labor, and hence reduce
unemployment, because such an action would amount to putting local community residents out of work. Second, one
can anticipate that a community-owned firm would be more
responsive in managing local natural resources for short-
term gain because this action would imperil the firm's--and
the community's--long-run survival. Third, community-owned
firms are unlikely to instigate the economic blackmail
discussed previously. For such a path of development to
proceed, the most obvious policy need is for governmental
financing of small businesses, particularly those that are
cooperatives or are community owned through the U.S. Department of Agriculture or the Small Business Administration.

ENVIRONMENTAL CONTROL AT WHAT LEVEL?

Regardless of the character of development programs or
continued trends of economic change, environmental controls
will be required. One major issue thus concerns the most
desirable level at which such controls are legislated,
implemented, and enforced. The prevailing wisdom of the
1970s is that effective environmental policy must be administered by centralized levels of government, either by
federal or regional planning agencies (see especially Bosselman and Callies 1971). Local communities--especially
those in nonmetro areas--are frequently viewed as being
excessively growth oriented, dominated by "special interests," and incapable of effective regulation of environmentally related decision making. The implication of such
arguments is that control over natural resource decisions
should be preempted by regional or national governments so
that environmental resources can be carefully planned and
allocated according to depoliticized management criteria.
But as noted above, the conservatism of nonmetro people has
likely been exaggerated (Buttel and Johnson 1977) and the
dependency of small communities on absentee-owned enterprises underplayed when examining the very real failures of
local control. The increasing resistance to power plant
sitings, electrical transmission lines, highway construction, pesticide applications on public lands, and other
issues belies this assumption of traditionalism and antienvironmentalism. The issue is thus not whether locals
possess the will to be environmentally progressive, but
rather whether there are systematic structural constraints

on local decision making (e.g., economic blackmail on the part of the employers and intercommunity competition for a relatively few industrial plant sitings) that make local control unresponsive.

The nature of certain environmental problems, especially their transcendance of political boundaries, may make centralized control desirable or imperative. A local community quite obviously can do little or nothing to address its problems of acid rain or soil erosion, for example. Control of air and water pollution will almost necessarily have to be confined to regional, state, and federal levels of decision making. However, several types of environmental decision making may be effectively retained by local levels of government, offering the possibility of more direct public involvement in policy. Many aspects of land use (e.g., building regulations, zoning, etc.) may be best kept in local hands, particularly if public participation can be expanded. This would be especially appropriate in communities where major economic enterprises are in the hands of local residents. Thus, while there is no obvious solution to the local/centralized control dilemma, it is not always clear whether substituting the typical metro bias of centralized (especially federal) levels of government for the parochialism of local control will always be in the interest of nonmetro people or the society as a whole. The most appropriate level of control will necessarily depend upon the nature of the environmental resources and the constraints on decision making that are involved.

DISCUSSION: IN ANTICIPATION OF HINDSIGHT

Environmental quality in the United States is becoming critical. A variety of circumstances--economic stagnation, energy scarcity, inflation--is threatening to dismantle both environmental constituencies and environmental programs. Energy scarcity, for example, is seemingly leading more toward a demand for increased energy production than it is toward a questioning of the desirability of the American course of development. Thus, although the nonmetro development alternatives discussed previously may indeed simultaneously address problems of development and environment, one cannot be sanguine about the possibilities for their implementation.

We might look toward two future scenarios for nonmetro

America that are based on two vastly different assumptions about the ability of the planet to provide the inanimate energy and other mineral resources that are increasingly demanded in the world economy. The first scenario would assume that these resources prove to be adequate over the next twenty to forty years, yielding little impetus to alter our conceptions about how development should proceed. Some 60 to 80 percent of industrial employment would be located in what are presently nonmetro counties, with large cities functioning principally as service and administrative centers. Metro to nonmetro migration would continue to predominate, although the composition of this movement would become more one of working-class persons in search of industrial employment. Metro areas would become considerably more pleasant in aesthetic and environmental respects due to the exodus of heavy industry, and their populations would be more uniformly middle class, although with strong remnants of underclass ghettos. Strip mining would proceed across the hills and hollows of Appalachia and the pastures and mountains of the West, and coal liquefaction plants in some areas would become more common than grain elevators. Many nonmetro communities that were so characteristically rural forty years ago would look like so many miniatures of Gary, Indiana. The rural would become what we now understand as urban, and the urban would become more rural.

Another scenario might begin with massive energy supply shortfalls that begin within ten years. They would develop so rapidly that all the tricks of modern technology--coal liquefaction, secondary extraction of petroleum, nuclear power--would be insignificant compared to the demands that would escalate in the 1980s. We would start to pick up the pieces again. Large-scale agriculture would become increasingly infeasible as scarce supplies of petroleum and natural gas cause skyrocketing prices for fertilizers, pesticides, and fuel for large machinery. Hundreds of thousands of people would return to agriculture in order to find employment and feed their families. Industries that had moved to nonmetro areas would find that transportation of raw materials into and finished goods out of remote locations is unprofitable. Their abandoned plants would be converted into facilities for production of goods from local resources to sell to local customers. Nonmetro areas would have some advantage in their access to energy, because their residents would find it economical and more dependable to rely on wood, agricultural biomass, or solar sources of power.

These two scenarios, although far fetched, indicate

the profound role that the capacity and bounty of the environment might play in the character of both nonmetro and
metro life. Neither is clearly optimistic nor pessimistic,
nor will the approximation of American life to these events
be determined solely by the capacity of societies to extract
nonrenewable energy resources. But each view provides a
glimpse that might be useful as Americans grope toward
decisions about the kind of economy and environment they
desire in the years to come.

NOTES

1. By "institutional," it is meant that governmental
agencies and personnel are an integral part of a social
movement. For example, the Environmental Protection Agency
is a major institutional social movement organization within
the larger environmental movement (see, for example, Morrison et al. 1972).

2. In particular, many of the social movement organizations formed during the late 1960s and early 1970s are
much more activist and innovative than their predecessors.
Examples from the environmental movement would include the
proliferation of "soft technology" groups at the local and
national levels, whereas Rural America, Inc. and the Conference on Alternative State and Local Public Policies
represent a considerable departure from the previous organizational milieus of rural development activity.

3. Pimentel et al. (1978) provide an especially useful
and thorough analysis of the social, economic, and environmental costs of pesticide use.

4. Dvoskin (1976), for example, estimates that a doubling of energy prices would result in only slightly more
than a 5 percent reduction in energy consumption in production agriculture, whereas even as little as a 10 percent
energy supply shortfall would entail massive adjustment
problems. Soil erosion interestingly has consequences for
energy consumption in agriculture. Pimentel et al. (1976)
estimate that soil erosion in the U.S. has diminished the
productive potential of the soil by about 10 to 15 percent,
and that between 5.0 and 7.5 percent of energy use in
agriculture merely compensates for fertility losses due to
soil erosion.

5. This discussion of agricultural environmental problems excludes the important issue of loss of agricultural

land that is covered in the chapter by Clawson in this
volume.

6. See Lonsdale's (1979: 52) discussion of the role
that enforcement procedures of the 1977 amendments to the
Clean Air Act might have in encouraging industries to move
toward nonmetro areas (see also below).

7. One of the heretofore neglected aspects of nonmetro
environmental conditions has been data on the quality of
water from individual well units. For example, preliminary
results from the National Statistical Assessment of Rural
Water Conditions under the direction of Joe D. Francis at
Cornell University suggest that only a very small minority
of these individual water systems has ever undergone a test
for mineral or bacteriological content. This underscores
the generally limited quantity and quality of data on rural
water conditions at the point of use or consumption.

8. Other spin-offs of U.S. energy problems for nonmetro
areas include the attractiveness of nonmetro locations for
coal-fired and nuclear power plant installations (especially
for the former because of air pollution legislation). The
report of the President's Commission on Three Mile Island
also recommended that future nuclear power plants be sited
in areas of low population density--in other words, nonmetro
areas. Whatever their type, nonmetro power plant locations
also entail environmental degradation during construction
and increased diversion of land for transmission lines.

9. Pimentel et al. (1978) report that an estimated
42,500 nonfatal pesticide poisonings occur annually across
the country, and roughly 2,800 were serious enough to require hospitalization. An estimated 217 persons die annually from pesticide poisoning. Dunbar and Kravitz (1976)
note that only one state, California, compiles comprehensive
statistics on pesticide poisonings. These available California data, however, show that roughly 50 percent of pesticide fatalities are farm workers, and slightly more than
one-half of these fatal poisonings occur among children
(Dunbar and Kravitz, 1976: 74).

10. This, of course, is not the only reason behind
metro to nonmetro migration. For example, the decentralization of industry (and the decentralization of population
that results) is closely connected to the quest for cheap
labor.

11. It is also interesting to note that the movement
of population toward nonmetro areas may have significant
energy consequences. For example, Brazzel and Hunter (1979)
demonstrate that rural farm and rural nonfarm households

tend to use more energy than urban households on both a per household and a per capita basis.

12. Seitz (1974), for example, reports data indicating that from 1960-1970, small places (2,500-30,000) in Illinois experienced declines in population density despite the fact that their population sizes tended to increase.

13. See, for example, Harkin et al. (1977). McClelland (1978) contains a useful compendium of research on individual on-site wastewater systems in rural and semirural contexts.

14. The extent to which urban development contributes to the loss of agricultural land remains a controversial matter. The Soil Conservation Service (SCS) of the U.S. Department of Agriculture (see Dideriksen and Sampson 1976) has estimated that annually from 1967 to 1975, there were losses of rural land totaling three million acres (two million of which were lost to urban use and another one million lost to water, e.g., lakes, ponds, reservoirs). In addition to these three million acres, SCS calculates that an additional two million acres are "leapfrogged" on an annual basis--that is, cut off from potential use by roads, etc., although not directly consumed for urban or water-based uses. Other studies, especially by the Economics, Cooperatives, and Statistics Service of USDA, report more conservative losses to urban and water uses (Brown 1979). Further, the SCS estimate of available farmland that could potentially be returned to production (roughly 111 million acres in the mid-1970s; Dideriksen and Sampson, 1976) is considerably lower than the estimate made by the Economic Research Service (1975), the agency that has eventually become consolidated into the Economics and Statistics Service.

15. This observation, however, does not imply that either: (1) the majority of new jobs for nonmetro Americans will come from large-scale manufacturing (see especially Birch 1979), or (2) nonmetro industrial expansion will lead to proportionately higher migration into large nonmetro places than into smaller nonmetro places. For example, research by Beale and Fuguitt (1978) has demonstrated that during 1970-1974, nonmetro counties with no place larger than 2,500 grew more rapidly than counties that had at least one place in excess of 2,500.

16. The tendency for smaller farms to have lower quality--and hence more highly erodable--lands was pointed out to me by William D. Heffernan, Department of Rural Sociology, University of Missouri-Columbia, in personal

communication. Heffernan suggests on the basis of research in progress that mandatory soil conservation programs without compensating mechanisms to assist small-scale farms would threaten their survival.

17. It is ironic to note that much federal government funding of rural sewer systems has been justified on the basis of these systems benefits to nonmetro communities in attracting manufacturing facilities (Rainey and Rainey, 1978: 139-40). As implied earlier, far more rural sewer systems have been funded than there are manufacturing branch plants available to locate in nonmetro areas.

18. This point, of course, leads to the decades-old controversy over what constitutes a useful definition of "development." The implicit definition of rural or nonmetro development that is used here is one that stresses that development must entail structural change that enables higher levels of living, economic security, and self-determination on the part of nonmetro people.

19. The suggestion that development focus more on smaller-scale, locally owned enterprises is likely to encounter the criticism that small firms are inefficient and would lead to reduced aggregate levels of efficiency in the nonmetro economic system. However, it is useful to bear in mind that small business remains the backbone of new employment in the U.S. economy, so that our suggestion is only a marked departure from ongoing trends in terms of ownership and function, not in terms of scale.

BIBLIOGRAPHY

Allaby, Michael, and Allen, Floyd. Robots Behind the Plow. Emmaus, Pa.: Rodale Press, 1974.

Beale, Calvin L., and Fuguitt, Glenn V. "The New Pattern of Nonmetropolitan Change." In Social Demography, edited by K. E. Taeuber, Larry L. Bumpass, and James A. Sweet. New York: Academic Press, 1978.

Belden, Joe, and Forte, Gregg. Toward a National Food Policy. Washington, D.C.: Exploratory Project for Economic Alternatives, 1976.

Birch, David L. "The Job Generation Process." Cambridge, Mass.: M.I.T. Program on Neighborhood and Regional Change, 1979.

Blobaum, Roger. "The Loss of Agricultural Land." In Change in Rural America, edited by R. D. Rodefeld et al. St.

Louis, Mo.: Mosby, 1978.

Bormann, F. H. et al. "Nutrient Loss Accelerated by Clear-Cutting of a Forest Ecosystem." Science 159 (1968): 882-84.

Bosselman, Fred, and Callies, David. The Quiet Revolution in Land Use Control. Washington, D.C.: Council on Environmental Quality, 1971.

Brazzel, John M., and Hunter, Leon J. "Distributional Patterns in Energy Expenditures Among Farm and Non-Farm Households." Unpublished paper, Science and Education Administration, U.S. Department of Agriculture, Washington, D.C., 1979.

Britt, Carolyn; Walker, Tom; and Schaaf, Michael. "Jobs and Energy in New England: Food Production and Marketing." Bath, Maine: Coastal Enterprises, Inc., 1978.

Brown, David L. "Agricultural Land Use: A Population Distribution Perspective." In Farmland, Food and the Future. Ankeny, Iowa: Soil Conservation Society of America, 1979.

Brown, F. Lee, and A. O. Lebeck. Cars, Cans, and Dumps: Solutions for Rural Residuals. Baltimore, Md.: Johns Hopkins University Press, 1976.

Burch, William R., Jr. "The Peregrine Falcon and the Urban Poor: Some Sociological Interrelations." In Human Ecology, edited by P. J. Richardson and J. McEvoy III. North Scituate, Mass.: Duxbury, 1976.

Buttel, Frederick H., and Flinn, William L. "Environmental Politics: The Structuring of Partisan and Ideological Cleavages in Mass Environmental Attitudes." Sociological Quarterly 17 (1976): 477-90.

_____. "The Interdependence of Rural and Urban Environmental Problems in Advanced Capitalist Societies: Models of Linkage." Sociologia Ruralis 17 (1977): 255-80.

_____. "Social Class and Mass Environmental Beliefs: A Reconsideration." Environment and Behavior 10 (1978): 433-50.

Buttel, Frederick H., and Johnson, Donald E. "Support for Liberal Development Policies among Community Elites and Non-Elites in a Rural Region of Wisconsin." Land Economics 53 (1977): 455-67.

Buttel, Frederick H., and Larson, Oscar W., III. "Farm Size, Structure, and Energy Intensity: An Ecological Analysis of U.S. Agriculture." Rural Sociology 44 (1979): 471-88.

Buttel, Frederick H. et al. "Energy and Small Farms: A Review of Existing Literature and Suggestions Concerning

Further Research." Report prepared for the National
Rural Center, Project on a Research Agenda for Small
Farms, Washington, D.C., 1979.

Carter, Luther J. "Soil Erosion: The Problem Persists
Despite the Billions Spent on It." Science 196 (1977):
409-11.

Caudill, Harry M. My Land Is Dying. New York: E. P. Dutton,
1971.

Chadwich, Bruce A., and Bahr, Howard M. "Rural Poverty."
In Rural U.S.A.: Persistence and Change, edited by T.
R. Ford. Ames, Iowa: Iowa State University Press,
1978.

Converse, Jim et al. "Alternative Responses to Changes in
Farm Technology, Structural Characteristics, and Rural
Communities." In Change in Rural America, edited by R.
D. Rodefeld et al. St. Louis, Mo.: Mosby, 1978.

Dideriksen, Raymond I., and Sampson, R. Neil. "Important
Farmlands: A National Viewpoint." Journal of Soil and
Water Conservation 31 (1976): 195-97.

Doering, Otto C., III. "Agriculture and Energy Use in the
Year 2000." American Journal of Agricultural Economics
59 (1977): 1066-70.

Dunbar, Tony, and Kravitz, Linda. Hard Traveling: Migrant
Farm Workers in America. Cambridge, Mass.: Ballinger,
1976.

Dvoskin, Daniel. "A National Model of Energy Use in Agricultural Production." Ph.D. dissertation, Iowa State
University, 1976.

Economic Research Service. Farmland: Will There Be Enough?
ERS-584. Washington, D.C.: U.S. Department of Agriculture, ERS, 1975.

Environmental Policy Division, Congressional Research Ser-
vice. A Legislative History of the Solid Waste Disposal
Act, As Amended. Washington, D.C.: U.S. Government
Printing Office, 1974.

Environmental Protection Agency. "Answers to Questions Sub-
mitted by Congressman James W. Symington." In A Legis-
lative History of the Solid Waste Disposal Act, As
Amended. Environmental Policy Division, Congressional
Research Service. Washington, D.C.: U.S. Government
Printing Office, 1974.

Freudenburg, William R. "The Social Impact of Energy Boom
Development on Rural Communities: A Review of Literature
and Some Predictions." Paper delivered at the seventy-
first annual meeting of the American Sociological
Association, New York, 31 August 1976.

Frederick H. Buttel : 700

Fuguitt, Glenn V., and Zuiches, James J. "Residential Pre-
ference and Population Distribution." Demography 12
(1975): 491-504.
Fujimoto, Isao. "The Communities of the San Joaquin Valley:
The Relation Between Scale of Farming, Water Use, and
Quality of Life." University of California-Davis,
Department of Applied Behavioral Sciences, 1977.
Geisler, Charles C. "Local Control: A Sociological Inter-
pretation of Land Use Planning in Advanced Capitalist
Society." Ph.D. dissertation, University of Wisconsin-
Madison, 1979.
_____. "The Radical Right and Land Use Planning:
A Political Ecology." Paper delivered at the seventy-
third annual meeting of the American Sociological
Association, San Francisco, 7 September 1978.
Glenn, Norval D., and Hill, Lester, Jr. "Rural-Urban Dif-
ferences in Attitudes and Behavior in the United
States." Annals of the American Academy of Political
and Social Science 429 (1977): 36-50.
Goldschmidt, Walter. As You Sow. Glencoe, Ill.: Free Press,
1947.
_____. As You Sow: Three Studies in the Social
Consequences of Agribusiness. Montclair, N.J.: Allan-
held, Osmun and Co., 1978.
Grant, Kenneth E. "Erosion in 1973-1974: The Record and
the Challenge." Journal of Soil and Water Conservation
30 (1975): 29-32.
Hagan, Robert M., and Roberts, Edwin B. "Environmental
Impacts of Water Projects." In Proceedings of Special
Session of Environmental Control for Irrigation Drainage
and Flood Control Projects, edited by International
Commission on Irrigation and Drainage. Delhi: S. P.
Dhawan, 1975.
Haren, Claude C., and Holling, Ronald W. "Industrial De-
velopment in Nonmetropolitan America: A Locational
Perspective." In Nonmetropolitan Industrialization,
edited by R. E. Lonsdale and H. L. Seyler. New York:
Wiley, 1979.
Harkin, John M.; Jawson, Michael D.; and Baker, Fred G.
"Causes and Remedy of Failure of Septic Tank Seepage
Systems." In Individual Onsite Wastewater Systems,
edited by Nina I. McClelland. Ann Arbor, Mich.: Ann
Arbor Science Publishers, 1977.
Hayes, Samuel P. Conservation and the Gospel of Efficiency.
Cambridge, Mass.: Harvard University Press, 1959.
Heaton, Tim, and Fuguitt, Glenn V. "Nonmetropolitan In-

dustrial Growth and Net Migration." In Nonmetropolitan
Industrialization, edited by R. E. Lonsdale and H. L.
Seyler. New York: Wiley, 1979.

Hill, Gladwin. "Acid Rain--No One Really Knows Yet How Bad
It Really Is." New York Times 12 August 1979.

Hines, Fred K. et al. Social and Economic Characteristics
of the Population in Metro and Nonmetro Counties, 1970.
Washington, D.C.: U.S. Department of Agriculture,
Economic Research Service, 1975.

Kale, Steven R., and Lonsdale, Richard E. "Factors Encour-
aging and Discouraging Plant Location in Nonmetropolitan
Areas." In Nonmetropolitan Industrialization, edited by
R. E. Lonsdale and H. L. Seyler. New York: Wiley, 1979.

Krieger, Martin H. "Six Propositions on the Poor and Pollution." Policy Sciences 1 (1970): 311-24.

Lockeretz, William. "The Dust Bowl: Its Relevance to Contemporary Environmental Problems." Paper delivered at
the Symposium on the Great Plains: Perspectives and
Prospects, Lincoln, Nebr., 2 March 1979.

_____. "The Lessons of the Dust Bowl." American
Scientist 66 (1978): 560-69.

Lonsdale, Richard E. "Background and Issues." In Nonmetropolitan Industrialization, edited by R. E. Lonsdale and
H. L. Seyler. New York: Wiley, 1979.

McClelland, Nina I., ed. Wastewater Treatment Alternatives
for Rural and Semirural Areas. Ann Arbor, Mich.: Ann
Arbor Science Publishers, 1978.

Morrison, Denton E. et al. "The Environmental Movement:
Some Preliminary Observations and Predictions." In
Social Behavior, Natural Resources, and Environment,
edited by W. R. Burch, Jr. et al. New York: Harper &
Row, 1972.

Munn, Robert F. Strip Mining. Morgantown, W.Va.: West
Virginia University Library, 1973.

National Rural Water Association. Rural Water and Sewer
Systems: Problems, Needs, Issues, Opportunities, and
Goals. Washington, D.C.: National Rural Water Associa-
tion, 1977.

Nolan, Michael F., and Heffernan, William D. "The Rural
Development Act of 1972: A Skeptical View." Rural
Sociology 39 (1974): 537-45.

Oelhaf, Robert C. Organic Agriculture. Montclair, N.J.:
Allanheld, Osmun and Co., 1978.

Office of Technology Assessment. Energy from Biological
Processes. Washington, D.C.: U.S. Congress, Office of
Technology Assessment, 1979.

Pasour, E. C., Jr., and Bullock, J. B. "Energy and Agriculture: Some Economic Issues." In Agriculture and Energy, edited by W. Lockeretz. New York: Academic Press, 1977.

Perelman, Michael. Farming for Profit in a Hungry World. Montclair, N.J.: Allanheld, Osmun and Co., 1977.

_____. "A Minority Report on the Economics of Spatial Heterogeneity in Agricultural Enterprises." In Monoculture in Agriculture. Washington, D.C.: U.S. Department of Agriculture, 1973.

Pimentel, David et al. "Environmental and Social Costs of Pesticide Use." Unpublished paper, College of Agriculture and Life Sciences, Cornell University, 1978.

_____. "Food Production and the Energy Crisis." Science 182 (1973): 443–49.

_____. "Land Degradation: Effects on Food and Energy Resources." Science 194 (1976): 149–55.

Powers, Sharon; Gilbert, Jess; and Buttel, Frederick H. "Small Farm and Rural Development Policy in the U.S.: Rationale and Prospects." In Rural Research in USDA. Hearings before the Subcommittee on Agricultural Research and General Legislation of the Committee on Agriculture, Nutrition and Forestry, U.S. Senate. Washington, D.C.: U.S. Government Printing Office, 1978.

Rainey, Kenneth D., and Rainey, Karen G. "Rural Government and Local Public Services." In Rural U.S.A.: Persistence and Change, edited by T. R. Ford. Ames, Iowa: Iowa State University Press, 1978.

Raup, Phillip M. "Corporate Farming in the United States." Journal of Economic History 33 (1973): 274–90.

Rosenbaum, Walter A. The Politics of Environmental Concern. New York: Praeger, 1977.

Schnaiberg, Allan. "Social Syntheses of the Societal-Environmental Dialectic: The Role of Distributional Impacts." Social Science Quarterly 56 (1975): 5–20.

Schultze, Charles L. The Distribution of Farm Subsidies. Washington, D.C.: Brookings Institution, 1971.

Seitz, Wesley D. "Conversion of Agricultural Land to Urban Uses." In Rural Community and Regional Development: Perspectives and Prospects. AE-4336. Urbana, Ill.: Department of Agricultural Economics, University of Illinois, 1974.

Small Farm Viability Project. "Natural Resources Task Force Final Report." In The Family Farm in California. Sacramento, Calif.: Small Farm Viability Project, 1977.

Sonka, Steven T. "Consequences of Farm Structural Change." Report prepared for the Project on a Research Agenda for Small Farms, National Rural Center, Washington, D.C., 1979.

_____, and Heady, Earl O. "Farm Size, Rural Community, and Consumer Welfare." American Journal of Agricultural Economics 56 (1974): 534-42.

Steinhart, John S., and Steinhart, Carol E. Energy. North Scituate, Mass.: Duxbury, 1974b.

_____. "Energy Use in the U.S. Food System." Science 184 (1974a): 307-15.

Summers, Gene F. et al. Industrial Invasion of Nonmetropolitan America. New York: Praeger, 1976.

Task Group Report. "Sources of Nitrogen and Phosphorous in Water Supplies." Journal of the American Water Works Association 59 (1967): 344-66.

Tremblay, Kenneth R., Jr., and Dunlap, Riley E. "Rural-Urban Residence and Concern with Environmental Quality: A Replication and Extension." Rural Sociology 43 (1978): 474-91.

Tweeten, Luther, and Brinkman, George L. Micropolitan Development. Ames, Iowa: Iowa State University Press, 1976.

U.S. Department of Interior. Surface Mining and Our Environment. Washington, D.C.: U.S. Government Printing Office, 1967.

Van Liere, Kent D., and Dunlap, Riley E. "Social Bases of Environmental Concern: A Review of Hypotheses, Explanations and Empirical Evidence." Paper delivered at the annual meeting of the Southern Sociological Society, Atlanta 1979.

Wilkening, Eugene A., and Klessig, Lowell. "The Rural Environment: Quality and Conflicts in Land Use." In Rural U.S.A.: Persistence and Change, edited by T. R. Ford. Ames, Iowa: Iowa State University Press, 1978.

Alvin D. Sokolow

19

Local Governments: Capacity and Will

INTRODUCTION

No other institutions are as central to the quality of life in small towns and rural areas as local governments. Alone among all community-based organizations, they have comprehensive legal powers and functions, revenue-raising abilities, and legitimacy. Although forms, resources, and competencies vary greatly, these three characteristics are common to local governments in all kinds of small communities--whether population centers or open-country areas, and with growing, stable, or declining populations.

The popular understanding of these governments today is that, because of the limitations of small size and isolation, they are not efficient and economic providers of public services. They lack adequate amounts of what is termed "capacity," the resources and expertise necessary to cope with increasingly complex problems. Much of the recent literature on local government in small communities is concerned with the capacity issue--how little of it there is, and how it can be improved.

Emphasizing the delivery of public services, this concern overlooks the other purposes of local government. For they also are devices of local democracy, agents through which citizens express, deliberate, and resolve community problems. The distinction is between capacity and political will, between the processes of management and those of rep-

This paper was prepared while the author was a visiting faculty member in 1978-79 at the Institute of Government and Public Affairs, University of Illinois, Urbana-Champaign. The generous support of the Institute is gratefully acknowledged. Several readers provided useful critiques of an earlier version of this paper. As well as members and staff of the Future of Rural America Advisory Committee, they included J. Norman Reid of the Economic Development Division, U.S. Department of Agriculture.

resentation and policymaking. Underlying and at times op-
posing values separate the two concepts. Efficiency and
economy are usually associated with improving capacity,
while the representational aspects of political will have a
built-in preference for accessibility and therefore simple
and small organizations. But the concepts are also very
much interrelated, because an improvement in local capacity
has limited effect without its acceptance and use by elected officials and others. The ability to act in this sense
is dependent on the desire to act.

 This chapter is a survey of the current status of local
government in nonmetro communities in the United States.
The focus is on the general purpose governments--primarily
municipalities and counties--the units with broad service,
regulatory, and policymaking responsibilities, as compared
to the more restricted school districts and special districts.

 In many parts of the nation these governments are confronted with new challenges because of recent population
increases after decades of decline or stability (see Chapter 1). New growth obviously presents small-town officials
with serious public service and regulatory problems. But it
also brings unprecedented opportunities for governmental
change, particularly as new issues and participants open up
the political process.

 A comment about terms and data concludes this introduction. "Nonmetro" and "small," rather than "rural," local
governments are the focus of this chapter. Although there
is considerable overlap among the three categories, virtually all of the available data on the number and characteristics of local units are arrayed according to metro-
nonmetro status or population size classifications. As
between capacity and will, the literature and data are
uneven. Data from the Census of Governments and various
surveys illuminate the relatively quantifiable issues of
capacity, whereas knowledge about political will relies on
more impressionistic and case-study forms of information.

THE LIMITS ON CAPACITY

Most definitions of capacity deal with rational management
and planning processes, the ongoing administration of public
services in the first case and the more long-range evaluation of alternative actions in the second (Executive Office

of the President, 1975: 22-23; Grosenick 1977). Improving
capacity usually requires the expansion of expertise and
the ability to acquire and use information. By whatever
standards are used, it is evident that the great majority
of local governments in nonmetro areas have limited capacity. Organizationally they are too small to afford or justify great amounts of expertise and information power.

NUMBERS AND SIZE

There are few differences in the basic forms and purposes
of local governments between metro and nonmetro areas of
the United States. The variations in size and number,
however, are striking.

As Table 19.1 indicates, communities outside of standard
metropolitan statistical areas (SMSAs) contain much more
than their share of local governments nationally. With a
little more than one-quarter of the population, nonmetro
areas have about two-thirds of the 80,000 units in the
country. Counties and townships, the units with primary
responsibility for unincorporated and rural localities, are
especially numerous in the nonmetro areas.

The typical nonmetro government thus serves a relatively
small population. Municipalities in metro areas on the
average are more than seven times as large as other cities
and villages (Table 19.2). The population ratio for county
governments is even wider with metro jurisdictions averaging
ten times the size of nonmetro counties.

The proposition that local governments in nonmetro
areas are too numerous and too small has long been accepted
by advocates of reorganization. Lacking the economies of
scale implicit in larger organizations, these small units
are unable to marshal the resources necessary to operate
efficiently and economically. These judgments, based on the
relationships of the per unit or per capita costs of services to size of organization, are complicated by issues
of demand, need, and quality (Bish 1977; Puryear 1977;
Tweeten and Brinkman 1976). Nevertheless, the calls for
reducing the number of local governments, and hence increasing their average size, have been persistent. Surveying the
scene in 1966, the Committee on Economic Development recommended an 80 percent reduction in the national number (Committee on Economic Development 1966). Most of these cuts
were to occur in nonmetro areas, including the consolidation
of 2,700 counties into not more than 500, elimination of

Table 19.1. Local Governments Inside and Outside SMSAs, 1977

Government Unit	United States	Inside SMSAs	Outside SMSAs	Outside SMSAs
				%
Counties	3,042	594	2,448	80.5
Municipalities	18,862	6,444	12,418	65.8
Townships[a]	16,822	4,031	12,791	76.0
Special districts	25,962	9,580	16,382	63.1
School districts	15,174	5,220	9,954	65.6
Total	79,862	25,869	53,993	67.6

Source: U.S. Bureau of the Census, 1977 Census of Governments, vol. 1, Governmental Organization.

[a]Includes New England towns.

most midwestern townships, consolidation of many small New England towns, disincorporation of most municipalities under 2,500 population, and the transfer of numerous special district functions to county governments. The "too many, too small" argument is also applied to metro situations, although the emphasis here is on the proliferation of overlapping and/or duplicative jurisdictions rather than on individual unit sizes.

The calls for reduction generally have not been heeded, as Table 19.3 points out. Although the total number of nonmetro governments decreased during the 1967-1977 period by about 6,500 (from 60,500 to 54,000), most of the reduction could be attributed to the designation of a number of areas as new SMSAs. Controlling for the effects of these reclassifications, in the right half of Table 19.3, the actual decrease through reorganization or abandonment in the number of nonmetro units for the ten-year period is only about 2,000--a net decrease of 2,974 from 1967-1972 and a net increase of 935 from 1972-1977.

The steady reduction in the number of school districts accounts for virtually all of the recent decrease in nonmetro totals (and in metro areas as well). Special district numbers, on the other hand, have risen sharply over the years. By contrast, changes in the numbers of other forms-- the general purpose governments--have been slight in non-

Table 19.2. Nonmetropolitan Municipal and County Governments by Population, 1977

Municipalities			Counties		
Population	N	%	Population	N	%
25 - 50,000	142[a]	1.1	100,000 or more	53	2.2
10 - 24,999	468	3.8	50 - 99,999	218	8.9
5 - 9,999	682	5.5	25 - 49,999	482	19.7
2.5 - 4,999	1,089	8.8	Less than 25,000	1,695	69.2
1 - 2,499	2,402	19.3			
Less than 1,000	7,635	61.5			
Total	12,418			2,448	
Average Population			Average Population[b]		
Nonmetro	2,214		Nonmetro	22,985	
Metro	16,956		Metro	224,617	

Source: U.S. Bureau of the Census, 1977 Census of Governments, vol. 1, Governmental Organization.

Note: Population estimates are as of 1975.

[a]Includes two cities with more than 50,000 population subsequently designated SMSAs.

[b]Estimates computed on the basis of population within counties.

metro areas. Although there has been a modest increase in municipalities through new incorporations, the numbers of county governments and townships have remained fairly constant in the past ten years. These are long-term trends in most respects, going back to the 1940s in the case of school district reductions and special district increases.

WHY NUMBERS CHANGE

What accounts for these patterns of change or lack of change among the different forms of local government? A believer in local determination would assume that govern-

Table 19.3. Change in Number of Nonmetropolitan Local Governments in 1967, 1972, and 1977

Government Unit	Number[a]			Change[b]			
	1967	1972	1977	1967–1972		1972–1977	
				N	%	N	%
Counties	2,645	2,600	2,448	– 2	– 0.7	– 2	–0.7
Municipalities	13,071	13,050	12,418	321	2.5	260	1.9
Townships[c]	13,850	13,529	12,791	– 91	– 0.6	–116	–0.8
Special districts	14,215	15,831	16,382	2,136	15.0	1,360	8.5
School districts	16,764	11,023	9,954	–5,338	–31.8	–567	–5.1
Total	60,545	56,033	53,993	–2,974	– 5.0	935	1.6

Source: U.S. Bureau of the Census, 1972 Census of Governments and 1977 Census of Governments, vol. 1, Governmental Organization.

[a]Units classified as outside SMSAs for the census years indicated.

[b]As controlled for decreases in units resulting from the designation of new Standard Metropolitan Statistical Areas during both periods. Nonmetropolitan classifications for both years of a time comparison are constant, and are based on the second or most recent year.

[c]Includes New England towns.

mental organizations are added and subtracted as communities grow or decline. This is only a partial explanation, applying uniquely to the rising numbers of special districts and municipalities both in and out of SMSAs. The formation of both types of governments is often a response to population increase, as residents of a growing community demand new and updated municipal services. Census of Governments data are not revealing as to the motivations for new formations, although one clue is that the types of nonmetro special districts recording the largest numerical increases in 1972-1977 were those that handled municipal services-- fire protection, sewerage, urban (domestic) water supply, and parks. The number of natural resource units, the most common type of district in nonmetro areas and traditionally associated with agricultural activity, remained relatively constant during this period.

There are fewer indications that population losses in nonmetro communities directly led to significant reductions in local agency numbers, either through merger into larger units or outright elimination through disorganization. Legal procedures for the consolidation of most types of units, and for the disincorporation of municipalities, are provided by most states. Yet considering the thousands of small villages in nonmetro areas, many if not most located in declining communities, the rate of decrease has been minimal. In the four years after 1970, fifty municipal governments nationwide were abolished through disincorporation (U.S. Bureau of the Census, 1974b) and from 1970 to 1976 another thirty-eight municipalities lost their separate identities through merger with other units (Forstall and Miller 1978). Most of these governments were very small units, serving less than 1,000 persons apiece, and were probably located in rural areas with declining populations.

By comparison, the record of decreasing numbers of school districts over the years is a remarkable one. Certainly this is the greatest success story in the history of local government reorganization. In the thirty-five-year period between 1942 and 1977, the total number of school districts nationwide dropped from 108,000 to just over 15,000, with most of the decrease occurring in nonmetro areas. Mergers reduced drastically the number of very small units, many operating one-room schools, primarily through the unification of rural elementary districts into larger K-12 jurisdictions centered in villages and cities. These accomplishments were not entirely the result of community desires. Although local referenda were often required and

some parents and educators saw combined districts and larger
facilities as the answer to better programs, other nonmetro
citizens strongly opposed the mergers and the loss of
schools as threatening the viability of their small communities. The crucial actions were at the state level.
Pushed by professional education groups and state departments of education, most state legislatures by the 1950s
had enacted programs that both encouraged and forced reorganizations, through a combination of financial incentives
and compulsory features (Sokolow 1977).

The trend to a smaller number of school districts seems
to have peaked; the decrease of 607 (567 in nonmetro areas)
from 1972 to 1977 is the smallest of any five-year period
in the past several decades. But the original aims of district reorganization have been largely realized. Few one-
room schools exist anymore on the nation's rural landscape,
and 91 percent of public school pupils in nonmetro areas
attend schools in districts that operate both elementary
and secondary programs (U.S. Bureau of the Census, 1978a:
Table 13).

State governments have not promoted the reorganization
of counties, municipalities, and townships as they have for
school districts. But the dominant factor in the retention
of small general purpose governments is that leaders and
residents of small-town and rural localities prefer their
small units. To argue that fewer and larger means a higher
quality of services delivered in a more efficient manner
does not persuade these folks, who place a higher value on
accessibility and who associate bigger government with
increased taxes.

A case in point is the persistence of the nonmetro
township in eleven midwestern states, despite predictions
twenty and more years ago that its demise was imminent
because of limited functions and the greater efficiency of
county governments (Snider, 1957: Ch. 9 and 538-40; Wager
1957; Wessel 1970). The number of such units was reduced by
only 108 from 1972 to 1977, out of a total of more than
10,000. No state has completely abolished townships since
the Census Bureau ceased counting them in Iowa as operational governments in the early 1950s, although many of
these units elsewhere were gradually reduced in importance
as some functions were transferred to counties. Midwestern
township government actually has undergone a minor revival
in recent years, with some units taking on new and expanded
services. A major reason was the General Revenue Sharing
program, which, beginning in 1972, granted virtually un-

restricted funds to township and other nonmetro units that
had not previously sought federal aid. Designated as general
purpose governments, the midwestern townships were given
the same automatic eligiblity as the more active counties
and municipalities for the quarterly checks from Washington.
The result in the eyes of some commentators was to prop up
these largely nonmetro units, stimulating an expansion in
their programs and reducing the incentive for consolidation
or elimination (Nathan et al. 1975: 290; 1977a: 141).

From the point of view of open-country and small-town
residents the reasons for reorganizing their local governments are not compelling and do not rank with taxes, crime,
land use, and health care as major problems. In fact people
in nonmetro areas may be less critical of their local government arrangements than residents either of core cities
or suburban communities (Luloff 1978). Some evidence for
this observation comes from a study of Montana's unique
experience with mandated voter review of local government.
As a result of a new constitutional provision, residents in
every city and county in the state from 1974 to 1976 formed
commissions to study their governmental organizations and
to recommend changes via local referenda. Commissioners in
smaller communities were more satisfied with existing arrangements than elsewhere and were less inclined to recommend major changes such as consolidation, new forms of
government, or adoption of the manager plan. As approved
by voters, major organizational changes fared better proportionately in larger than smaller communities (McKinsey
and Lopach 1979).

In general, reorganizations that involve the merger
of small into larger units are more acceptable in metro
than nonmetro areas (Rainey and Rainey 1978). City-county
consolidation, for example, is a widely discussed action
for reducing duplication and increasing economy. Seventeen
consolidations were approved and carried out between 1945
and 1977, all but four in SMSAs (Glendenning and Atkins
1977).

PROFESSIONAL STAFF AND OTHER RESOURCES

An obvious consequence of small size is limited resources.
In fiscal terms this means that small local governments
spend and raise smaller sums on a per capita basis than
larger units, and that they have proportionately smaller
revenue bases (Rainey and Rainey 1978; Stocker 1977).

Limited resources refer also to numbers of employees and administrative organization. Although local governments in smaller communities employ relatively large numbers of workers on a per capita basis (Stocker 1977), individually they are tiny bureaucracies. In 1977 the payrolls (full-time equivalents) of local governments for less than 10,000 population averaged fourteen employees for municipalities, one for midwestern townships, sixteen for New England and mid-Atlantic towns and townships, and seventy-four for counties (U.S. Bureau of the Census, 1979a: Tables 17, 18, 19). Organizationally these are simple structures, lacking elaborate hierarchies of supervision and staff specializations. Departmental organization is often missing and the few employees may report directly to the major, chairman, or elected governing board.

The most clear-cut measures of administrative capacity concern the extent to which governments employ professional and full-time chief executives, typically city managers in municipal governments and administrators or similarly named officials in county governments. Appointed by the elected legislative bodies, chief executives with professional training and experience bring considerable expertise and skill to their jobs. They serve as executors of policy, administrative coordinators, policy advisors, and information providers to their elected governing boards, and as federal and state grantsmen.

Small municipalities and counties employ proportionately fewer chief executives than large units, as Tables 19.4 and 19.5 indicate. Based on periodic surveys conducted by the International City Management Association (the major organization of professional executives in local government), these data do not report the metro-nonmetro distribution of city managers and county administrators. It is safe to say, however, that small cities in nonmetro areas are much less likely to have professional executives than the data in Tables 19.4 and 19.5 indicate for small units generally, because the council-manager form is most popular in suburban communities.

The International City Management Association (ICMA) defines the position of city manager or county administrator rather strictly according to its standards of professional management, and so the data in both Tables 19.4 and 19.5 do not include many positions in small and nonmetro governments that, in one way or another, involve central management or administration. In fact city councils and county boards throughout the nation use a variety of administrative ar-

Table 19.4. Cities with Council-Manager Government, 1978

Population	Total Cities	Cities With Council Manager	Percentage of Total
More than 250,000	58	20	34.4
100,000 - 249,999	105	57	54.3
50,000 - 99,999	257	144	56.0
25,000 - 49,999	586	324	55.3
10,000 - 24,999	1,471	621	42.2
5,000 - 9,999	1,659	561	33.8
2,500 - 4,999	2,210	425	19.2
Less than 2,500	329[a]	233	--

Source: Adapted from International City Management Association, The Municipal Year Book, 1978, Table 3, p. iii.

[a]Cities in this size category are limited to those recognized by the ICMA as "providing for the council-manager plan or providing for a position of overall management."

Table 19.5. Counties with Appointed Administrators, 1978

Population	Total Counties	Counties with Appointed Administrator	Percentage of Total
More than 250,000	137	94	68.6
100,000 - 249,999	206	99	48.1
50,000 - 99,999	336	115	34.2
25,000 - 49,999	595	128	21.5
10,000 - 24,999	981	146	14.9
5,000 - 9,999	496	51	10.3
2,500 - 4,999	193	5	2.6
Less than 2,500	96	4	4.2

Source: Adapted from National Association of Counties and International City Management Association, The County Year Book, 1978, Table 3, p. iv.

rangements. Numerous appointed and full-time executives
serve without the title of city manager or the full administrative autonomy and power usually associated with
that position. A recent study of six Iowa municipalities,
with populations between 1,600 and 3,500, showed that each
of the cities employed a person in a chief-of-staff position
to oversee city departments and provide information to the
council, although only one of these executives possessed
the training and experience of a professional manager
(Claxton 1976).

Regardless of title and formal powers, the chief executive in a small community usually has many and diverse
responsibilities. In a 1968 survey, managers in cities with
less than 5,000 population typically handled purchasing,
finance, personnel administration, zoning enforcement, and
some engineering and building inspection activities (Grigg
et al. 1968). With such multiple tasks, and as the only
administrators in their organizations, chief executives in
these settings are preoccupied with the daily routine of
supervision and paperwork. Rarely do they have time to
engage in long-range planning, research, capital programming, and comprehensive budget preparation (Booth 1968).

BRINGING CAPACITY TO THE COMMUNITY

With practically no progress over the years in establishing
fewer and larger units, small size continues to be the
dominant characteristic of general purpose governments in
nonmetro areas. But in many other ways the search for improved capacity has been an active and even inspired one.
The numbers of chief executives, planners, and other professional staff employed by small jurisdictions, for example, have steadily increased. In the case of small-county
executives, the recent trend has been almost spectacular.
Only 14 percent of all counties with less than 50,000 population employed professional administrators in 1978 (National Association of Counties, 1978: Table 3), but more
than 90 percent of these positions had been created since
1960. As one way of compensating for the diseconomies of
small size, numerous municipalities cooperate formally and
informally with other units in providing services and sharing facilities. In a 1973 survey of cities with more than
2,500 population, 51 percent of all nonmetro units--as
compared to 72 percent of metro governments--reported

service agreements with other units (Zimmerman 1973). One obstacle to greater use of these arrangements in many non-metro areas is the relatively small number of governments and wide distances separating them.

Most efforts to improve the capacity of small governments, however, originate from sources outside the community. Federal, state, regional, and private agencies contribute to an ever-expanding inventory of assistance programs for local governments. Especially for small units, these programs have proliferated greatly in the 1970s. They are not without limitations and problems. For example, it takes capacity to obtain capacity; with so many possible programs from which to choose, already overburdened elected officials without staff are often unable to assess whether the likely benefits of any one program can justify commitments of time and effort. A related limitation is that much assistance is specific to particular functions, and is not directed to elected policymakers or "generalists" in small governments (Executive Office of the President, 1975: 29).

CIRCUIT RIDERS AND OTHER FORMS OF ASSISTANCE

The list of assistance-providers includes most federal agencies that administer grant programs to local units. One estimate is that forty-one such agencies in fiscal 1974 budgeted $512 million in technical assistance to local governments, with the proportion going to small or nonmetro units not known (Executive Office of the President, 1975: 27). Additional sources of technical aid include departments for local affairs and other state government agencies, co-operative extension services, other extension and dissemi-nation programs operated by universities, regional planning agencies, municipal leagues and other local government associations at the state and national levels, and private consultants.

The topics and methods of dissemination are also di-verse. Officials from small towns can attend workshops on grantsmanship, request regional agency staff to prepare grant applications, commission planning and economic de-velopment studies from consultants, ask universities to conduct opinion surveys on community problems and goals, receive model personnel codes from their state associa-tions, and browse through manuals on financial management and budgeting published by the Municipal Finance Officers Association. There is no lack of information and material

on the techniques of running a small government; the limits
involve the ability of local officials to absorb and effectively use the knowledge and advice (Van Asselt 1978).

Perhaps the most imaginative and exciting of all assistance efforts is the "circuit rider" idea. In this type of
program, several small cities share the services of a professional administrator--usually a city manager, but sometimes a planner--who makes the rounds of four or five jurisdictions on a weekly or other regular schedule. Illustrative
of how this works is the program begun in 1975 by five
cities in southwestern Minnesota, each with a population of
between 250 and 750. Operating under a joint powers agreement, the cities obtained a federal grant (Intergovernmental
Personnel Act) for most of the funding for the first two
years and supplemented this with a $1,340 yearly cash and
services contribution from each jurisdiction. The circuit
rider spends a day a week in each city, working with the
clerk, mayor, council members, and others. This person
serves more as an expert adviser and project coordinator,
than as a typical small-town manager, because most of the
activities do not concern routine administration and supervision. Rather, the circuit rider deals with long-range
improvements, such as preparing grant applications, coordinating downtown improvements and other projects, and
helping the clerk and mayor to set up new budgetary and
other procedures.

For the combined populations of 2,500 in these five
cities the program seems to have been successful. Financial
savings were reached through a number of shared activities
(purchasing, legal services, etc.) and low grant administration costs. New management procedures were established,
and large amounts of federal grant money were acquired for
the communities. That the five cities agreed to continue
the circuit riding program beyond the initial two years of
grant support, apparently with full funding from city
sources, suggests its acceptance and effectiveness (Elam
1977; McCarty 1978).

Small towns in at least ten other states (Kentucky,
North Carolina, Maine, Missouri, California, Washington,
Pennsylvania, Texas, Colorado, and Iowa) have recently
experimented with circuit riders, but the overall extent
and impact of this type of program are not known. Like many
other forms of assistance to small jurisdictions, these
programs are instigated on a one- or two-year demonstration
basis, with federal or state support and with a combination
of high hopes and immeasurable uncertainties. What happens

when the grant money runs out; does the experiment become
an established activity? Only by looking at the management
and performance of local governments in the long run, can
one determine the effects of innovative efforts to build
capacity.

REGIONAL AGENCIES

Widely known as "substate multicounty districts," regional
agencies have an ambiguous relationship to local governments
in nonmetro areas. They are valued for providing technical
assistance to resource-poor local governments and for obtaining or clearing federal grants. Yet officials in many
small jurisdictions do not completely accept the existence
of the regional agencies. Despite their garb as voluntary
associations of local governments, they are perceived as
representing outside forces because they are really inven-
tions of state and federal governments. The regional agencies are seen as another layer of bureaucracy. The suspicion
is that they have the potential of becoming super governments, superceding and taking over certain functions from
conventional local units.
    As of now regional agencies are restricted to providing
advice and resources. Although they have statutory status
and spend public funds, they lack the powers of full-fledged
governments to deliver services directly to citizens and to
regulate private activities. Nevertheless they are a relatively new and important presence on the public scene in
metro and nonmetro areas alike. The Census Bureau began
counting regional organizations for the first time in 1977,
finding that 91 percent of the 1,500 units tabulated nationwide had been established since 1964. About 40 percent are
identified as "general purpose" organizations, which include
the Regional Planning Commissions (RPCs), Councils of Governments (COGs), and Economic Development Districts involved
in planning, development, and intergovernmental coordination
activities. The other 60 percent are more specialized organizations such as the Community Action Agencies and Criminal Justice Planning Agencies, which implement certain
federal programs.
    The 1977 census tabulation did not classify regional
organizations by metro-nonmetro status, although about
one-third of all general purpose agencies serve areas with
populations of less than 100,000, and slightly more than
another third are in areas of between 100,000 and 249,999

population (U.S. Bureau of the Census, 1978b: Table 1). A 1972 study identified a total of 356 regional councils (COGs and RPCs), of which about 160 were nonmetro or predominantly nonmetro (Advisory Commission on Intergovernmental Relations, 1973: Ch. 8).

It is the general-purpose organizations that are most critical for local governments, especially those involved in the A-95 review of federal grant applications. In nonmetro areas these agencies have staff resources and expertise not otherwise available. They assist small jurisdictions in grantsmanship, plan preparation, and information gathering. For example, during its first four years of operation, a six-county regional council in Illinois prepared studies and ordinances for individual communities dealing with zoning, mobile homes, capital development, solid waste disposal, and bike routes (Villanueva 1976).

Although appreciative of the services, officials in small jurisdictions are not eager to see regional agencies expand their activities. In nonmetro areas the agencies are not as involved in planning and coordinating public services as in metro areas, emphasizing more technical assistance to local units, grantsmanship, and industrial development (Advisory Commission on Intergovernmental Relations, 1973: Ch. 8).

FEDERAL AID IMPACTS

The impacts of federal aid have been especially profound for small governments in nonmetro areas. Most apparent are the fiscal effects--the increasing dependency of these units on revenues from both federal and state governments (Shannon and Ross 1977). Between 1971 and 1972 and 1976 and 1977, the proportion of the general revenues of city governments for less than 50,000 population that originated with the federal government increased from 5.8 to 12.3 percent, according to census data (U.S. Bureau of the Census, 1974a: Table 16; 1979, Table 16). The comparable increase for larger cities was a more modest one, from about 10 to 15 percent.

Before 1972 and the emergence of the Nixon Administration's "New Federalism," few such governments had had any experience at all with federal grants. Then came General Revenue Sharing (GRS)--the $6 billion a year program of automatic and virtually unrestricted transfers of funds to states and all general purpose local governments. Every county, municipality, and township--no matter how small or rural--began to receive the quarterly treasury checks according to the three-way entitlement formula of population-poverty-tax effort. Practically overnight the federal grants system had done an about-face, from a concentration on big cities and metro areas via categorical programs to an open-ended dispersal of funds to all communities throughout the nation.

In rapid succession there followed the CETA, Community Development Block Grant, and Antirecession programs--all somewhat more competitive and restricted than GRS, but with a considerably greater share of total funds set aside for small and nonmetro jurisdictions than had been the case for major grant programs before 1972. Add to the list the carrot-and-stick approach of cleaning up the nation's waters, in which thousands of very small and rural communities have been both mandated and given the federal/state funds to construct new sewerage systems or improve existing facilities, and the picture of nonmetro governments being brought into the federal grants system in the 1970s is complete.

Most analyses of the federal grant experiences of small jurisdictions concentrate on how these governments lack the capacity to compete adequately for and administer grants (Advisory Commission on Intergovernmental Relations, 1977: 51; Blakely and Zone 1976; U.S. Department of Housing and Urban Development, 1979: Ch. 6; Macaluso 1977; Rural America 1977; Stanfield 1978). Paperwork burdens are frequently mentioned. In addition there is the widespread belief that nonmetro areas are not allocated their fair share of funds, a difficult assertion to confirm or deny for federal spending overall as well as for grants distributed specifically to local governments (Reid et al. 1978). What the studies fail to acknowledge, however, is the fact that so many village and small urban governments in this decade have become new or more active participants in the federal grants system. As of yet there is no comprehensive assessment of what this means for local government and policymaking in small communities. Is it possible that the management of public affairs and the processes of problem solving are being changed as a result, in subtle, unanticipated, and long-term ways?

A qualified "yes" is suggested by a cursory review of small government experiences. These kinds of impacts have been noted in a few studies: (1) A breakdown of the traditional insularity of small-town politics in relation to the

federal system. As they seek additional grants and the
resultant community benefits, local officials become less
hostile to the programs and intrusions of Washington. It is
too much, however, to expect a radical alteration of the
essentially negative view of big and complex government
held by most officials in small communities. (2) Improvements in the management and fiscal skills of officials as
they deal with the complicated requirements and paperwork
of federal grant programs. Although gradual and unplanned,
these improvements in local capacity eventually may be as
significant as the effects of programs that deal more specifically with capacity building. (3) The emergence of
new actors and increased competition in local political
systems as federal funds raise the stakes of the public
sector. Much of this is due to the development of quasi-
public agencies, independent from mainline governments,
that are given federal funds and program responsibilities.
They include regional planning agencies and Community
Action Agencies, some of the latter with responsibilities
for manpower and other social service programs. (4) More
competition among small governments for those federal grant
programs that involve application procedures, including
the Community Development Block Grants. One possible consequence is to increase the economic and political disparities among small communities as the communities with
the greatest skills (capacity) and aggressiveness obtain
the lion's share of grants.

POLITICAL WILL: LIMITS AND OPPORTUNITIES

Political will refers to the extent to which a community,
ordinarily acting through its local governments, resolutely
deals with its problems. It implies a certain amount of
innovation and risk taking, particularly as population
growth, decline, or other types of socioeconomic change
call for unprecedented public actions. As such, it is a
more illusive concept than capacity, relating more to the
informal processes of representation, conflict, and policymaking than to the formal characteristics of organization,
professional expertise, and administration.

Particular instances of political will can involve
the actions either of public officials or private citizens
or both. For elected officials, political will suggests a
willingness to consider new policies and approaches to

government. Underlying specific actions there may be a
recognition of the pluralism of even small communities--
that local government has the responsibility to accommodate
varied intrests, and that political competition can bring
beneficial results. For citizens outside government, political will is expressed by actions as well as talk, especially the expenditure of time and energy to pursue specific
goals. Usually some degree of group organization is involved, whether the target is local government or a voluntary program.

THE LIMITS

Through legend and case study we know that political will
traditionally has been a scarce commodity in small and
especially rural communities (Crane 1956; Sokolow 1968;
Vidich and Bensman 1968). The general picture of local
government in these places is that of an inactive and conservative institution, slow to respond to conditions of
community change. At the heart of this inactivity are the
elected officials, primarily members of county, municipal,
and township governing boards, who effectively resist efforts to expand or otherwise change the scope of their
programs. The officials dislike having to deal with new
problems and to listen to demands for action, and are more
comfortable with the nonpolicy tasks of administering or
overseeing the routine delivery of existing services.
    Elected officials act or fail to act according to their
perceptions of dominant citizen desires. Two sets of community values are inherent in this government-citizen relationship. One is the desire to minimize the role of government, to keep the taxpayers' burden low, and to prevent
public interference in private activities. The second is
the desire for unanimity in community affairs, based on the
fear of generating serious conflicts and confusion by raising new issues for discussion. Many small and tight-knit
communities are unable to handle such open deliberations,
because disagreements over policy can easily become personal
and thus bitter animosities.
    With minimal expectations set out for local government,
there is little reason for seeking increased capacity. The
limits extend even further, to the underutilization of
existing capacity whether fiscal, legal, or managerial. It
is true that nonmetro local governments have relatively
small tax bases. Yet their tax efforts--the public revenues

raised in relation to personal income or other forms of
community wealth--are less than the efforts of larger and
more urban governments (U.S. Department of Housing and
Urban Development, 1979: 31-33). Small jurisdictions also
are reluctant to take full advantage of the legal powers
provided by state legislatures and constitutions. Proportionately few small counties operate regulatory programs
in the land use, planning, and building areas, for example
(National Association of Counties 1977). An Illinois study
notes that no county and only five cities in nonmetro parts
of the state adopted home-rule status as of 1978, an option
for expanding local powers that was granted to all small
communities by the 1970 constitution (Illinois Department
of Local Government Affairs 1979).

CASES OF POLITICAL WILL

Some of the traditional obstacles to local government
change in small communities were dissolving in the 1970s.
Certainly small community concerns and problems had become
much more visible in this decade than before, a trend marked by the recent proliferation of Washington-based organizations and national journals representing local governments
and other small community interests (Stanfield 1978). But
most of the action has been at the local level--in perhaps
thousands of nonmetro localities where a renewed interest
is seen in the uses of government to enhance the good life.
The shift from a view of local government as a necessary
evil to that as promoter and protector of positive values
is more fundamental to local political systems than the
mere acceptance of federal aid would suggest. It is impossible to document such developments on other than a case-
study basis, thus four summaries of recent incidents of
political will are presented here.

McLendon-Chisholm, Texas
    This ranching and residential town with a population
of 500 was beseiged by growth presures from a nearby metro
area. A small grant was obtained from the state humanities
commission to conduct a series of community forums, in which
residents openly discussed values and policy preferences.
From this emerged consensus for development controls. The
previously inactive city council was persuaded to establish
a planning board and enact a subdivision ordinance (Tate
1978).

Nevada City, California

In the 1960s this city of 2,300 in California's central Sierra foothills was split in two by a new state freeway. Shocked by the effect on the town's fragile hillside setting, businessmen, residents interested in historic preservation, and political leaders vowed to prevent further encroachments on the local environment. New development controls were imposed and most of the business district was placed into a historical zone, with strict regulations over signs and other building changes. The result was a recreation of the original "Mother Lode" architecture of the nineteenth century, an attraction for tourists, and a boon to local business (Hogan 1978).

Southern County

With a population of 5,300, Shiloh County (a pseudonym) had undergone extensive industrialization in the 1960s. Little of this wealth, however, was captured for the benefit of local public services because of the use of tax-exempt bonds in financing construction of the plants. After considerable discussion and pressure, the county board by a 3-2 vote passed an occupational license tax that tapped much of the industrial wealth. The key vote was cast reluctantly by a board member who faced a tough reelection battle. He lost to his challenger who, as the chairman of the board, spearheaded a program of improvements with the new revenues (Clinton 1978).

North Bonneville, Washington

This municipality of 500 on the Columbia River was doomed to extinction, as the Army Corps of Engineers planned to purchase the entire town for the site of a $300 million power plant. Instead of acquiescing in the sale of their individual residential and business properties at market value, most residents decided to stick together as a community. They fought for and won corps funding for a complete relocation of the town's buildings to a new site, including the construction of new public facilities. A further indication of the community's political sophistication was the retention of the old site within the relocated city's borders, so that the construction activity on the powerhouse could be taxed by the municipality (Myer 1977).

Some Generalizations

These and other cases of small community innovation suggest several generalizations about the sources and circumstances of political will. First, most instigations of governmental change seem to come from nongovernmental segments of the community--whether from new residents dissatisfied with existing services, businessmen concerned about downtown decay, or conservationists who want to protect the character of the community against hasty development. Second, the translation of an innovative idea into a specific public action--the development of political will--is often a slow and frustrating process. Consensus on a new public course of action is difficult to achieve and often hinges on electoral change in governmental office. Finally, external and internal circumstances are usually intermingled in the development of a community's political will. Outside forces may provide the problem in the first place, and some of the resources for dealing with it, but it takes local initiative and hard work to resolve the issue. The key skills of local leadership involve seeking out the optimal combination of the two.

COMMUNITY VARIATIONS: THE EFFECTS OF GROWTH OR DECLINE

Some community and governmental environments are more con-
ducive to political will than others. In small communities undergoing rapid or moderate growth, for example, political systems are relatively dynamic. At least two of the four case studies summarized above (McLendon-Chisholm and Nevada City) deal with communities beset by population increases. Because of the visible problems induced by growth and the increasing diversity of the population, debate, issues, and conflicts are relatively unrestrained in growing places. Much of the impetus for governmental change comes from new arrivals, particularly in the high-amenity communities that in the 1970s have attracted many former urbanites with education, organizational skills, and new ideas. Such newcomers are more inclined to jump into political and other civic affairs than migrants to small towns in the past, because of their desire to protect the rural or environ-
mental characteristics that brought them to these particular communities in the first place. They raise new issues and challenge existing policies and practices, either in coalition with like-minded old-timers or in conflict with other residents (Sokolow 1979).

By contrast, population decline in rural areas is often associated with a kind of political paralysis--an inability to gather the energy and desire to confront problems (Butwin

1968). To be sure there are important efforts to revitalize declining towns (Douglas and Scott 1977), but the obstacles to political will are greatest where population and economic losses cut into the supply of leaders and innovators.

Community size, population concentration, and governmental status are also important conditions. Perhaps the nonmetro environments most conducive to innovation are growing county seat municipalities of 10,000 or more population. Such communities contain more than their share of skilled and active citizens--including attorneys, other professionals, bankers, young businessmen, and educated and middle-class housewives with the time and interest to devote to community affairs. Small villages composed of retired farmers and persons who commute to jobs elsewhere are less politically resourceful.

Some obstacles to political will are implicit in the organization and representation of county government. A nonmetro county usually contains a mixture of subcommunities, some incorporated as municipalities but mostly unincorporated neighborhood areas. Considering the diversity of constituencies represented, and the lack of community identification and political focus more common to municipal governments, it is harder for county boards than for city councils to reach consensus on major questions. Rivalries and other differences among subcommunities prevent the easy formation of countywide interest groups. A further impediment to governmental change in small county government is the fragmentation of the governmental apparatus, with the election both of governing board members and a larger number of individual administrators (Hogan 1978; Marando and Thomas 1977).

VOLUNTARISM

Another possible source of political will is the voluntarism often found in the public life of small towns. As individuals and members of social and civic groups, citizens give their time and energy to meet community needs. The outstanding example of private contributions to a public good is the volunteer fire department, the prevalent form of fire protection in nonmetro areas. Most cities with less than 10,000 population rely completely on volunteer firemen and virtually all use volunteers in one capacity or another, according to a 1971 ICMA survey (International City Management Association 1971). Other kinds of voluntary activities

in public or quasi-public programs include reserve police
forces, ambulance services (Perlstadt 1975), recreation
programs and park improvements (Colfer 1978; Claxton 1976),
and the tendency of some elected and appointed officials to
work long hours without extra compensation or with no compensation at all.

Voluntarism is a decided asset for a community. It is
a way of extending limited public resources, thus keeping
down the costs of government (Hitzhusen 1977). It is also a
form of citizen involvement in civic affairs that the extensive literature on political participation scarcely
recognizes. However, voluntarism may not easily translate
into political will. Voluntary groups are best at building
public facilities and in delivering or helping to deliver
certain kinds of services. But it is another matter to add
to the consensus necessary for solving a major communitywide problem. The separate projects and concerns of different groups of volunteers, in fact, can fragment public
attention and resources in a community and detract from
efforts to examine issues in a comprehensive manner.

CONCLUSIONS: THE RELATIONSHIP
OF CAPACITY AND POLITICAL WILL

It has long been fashionable to criticize local governments
in small and especially rural communities as inefficient,
incompetent, and unresponsive. Roscoe Martin, a leading
student of public administration, used this strong language
two decades ago:

> What is required more than any other one thing for the
> administrative rehabilitation of rural government is a
> system that will command the confidence and respect of
> the citizen. A government which has no important ser-
> vices to perform, or which does not have resources
> adequate to its needs, or which is so inconsequential
> that it must content itself with part-time and amateur
> services, or which is satisfied to drift along an ad-
> ministrative channel marked out a century ago and not
> changed since, or which shares responsibilities with a
> dozen or a hundred other units and agencies--such a
> government will not enjoy because it will not have
> earned the confidence of the people. (Martin, 1957: 55.)

The "administrative rehabilitation" called for by Martin has not occurred, at least not in the substantial reorganization of the many small governments into fewer but larger units and the wholesale replacement of part-time and amateur officials by full-time professionals. Yet most small municipalities and county governments today hardly can be called "inconsequential." Among many there is a new vitality, stimulated by the challenges of new population growth, the benefits of federal and state grants, the interest and actions of citizens outside government, and the availability of various kinds of technical assistance. Local governments in nonmetro America have changed more in the past ten years than in the previous thirty or forty years combined, although these shifts cannot be detected alone by examining the quantitative data on numbers and sizes of units and the employment of professional executives.

Governmental capacity has been built in numerous ways, usually as the result of political will--the desire to act and change. Elected officials in small governments improve management and seek expertise and information because of conscious choices, and often only because they are pushed into these actions by the broader politics of the community. Even with improved capacity, political will remains an essential ingredient of local government because it takes a continuing devotion to innovation to make good use of expertise and information in long-range policymaking as well as in day-to-day management.

One compensation for limited governmental capacity in small communities is the interest and activity of their citizens. As demonstrated in widespread voluntarism, small-town people have considerable energy, ideas, and time to contribute to civic benefits. The difficulty is in directing this interest toward the overall problem-solving efforts of local government as well as to specific community projects and services. Except in crises and highly visible or immediate issues such as those related to rapid growth, citizens are inclined to leave their elected officials alone. Perhaps the close accessibility of officeholders in the small community lends an assurance that, when needed, governmental action can be obtained. If so, the indications of limited formal participation in elections and public hearings may not be accurate reflections of citizen interest in small local government.

CAPACITY FOR WHAT?

The concern for improving the capacity of small, general purpose local governments is well justified. Even the smallest jurisdictions need information, expertise, and professionalism to cope with tricky public issues. The source of the capacity is less important than its availability and utility. But some of this concern may be misplaced, particularly as it is focused on getting more federal grants for individual communities.

One reason is that improved grantsmanship increases the competition for federal funds without necessarily expanding the total pie set out by Washington for small or nonmetro local governments. There is some doubt that aggressive application preparation is a good or accurate measure of community need (Rainey and Rainey 1978), but the more serious objection is that it is a waste of scarce resources. As the House Subcommittee on the City pointed out, capacity is better spent on local problem solving, including the administrative and policymaking functions of local government (Subcommittee on the City 1978).

A related matter of local capacity has to do with the proliferation in recent years of quasi-public organizations independent of local government, including regional planning agencies and community action agencies. Largely produced by federal programs, the new agencies have been beneficial in aggregating resources and providing needed innovations in service areas long ignored by local governments. Lacking comprehensive authority and representative character however, they cannot be considered substitutes for municipal and county governments. Still their existence does emphasize the key question facing main-line government in small-town and rural America: How does one improve the capacity and responsiveness of local government, without losing the desirable qualities of representativeness and accessibility?

THE NEED FOR QUALITATIVE UNDERSTANDINGS

Quantitatively, we know a great deal about small and non-metro governments--about numbers, sizes, finances and functions, both nationwide and within individual states. The data about administrators and programs are relatively scarce for the smallest of jurisdictions (cities with less than 10,000 population in some cases, and less than 2,500 in others, for example), because they originate primarily

in the periodic mail questionnaires conducted by the
national associations of city and county officials. For
understandable reasons, officials in small governments
without professional administrators respond to these kinds
of surveys in less than statistically adequate numbers.

Even major improvements in the quantitative data, however, cannot give us more than a superficial examination of
the processes of policymaking, representation, and administration in small communities. The major need is for a
sorting out of important differences among the diverse
local governments in nonmetro areas, to distinguish between
politically resourceful and impoverished situations. Some
qualitative understandings are needed about how small governments and their broader political systems respond to
problems and opportunities. The design of federal programs
and policies intended to channel assistance to small communities could benefit from some systematic answers to these
kinds of questions: (1) Why do some communities, regardless
of governmental capacity and other resources, respond more
effectively and quickly to change than others? (2) What
types of capacity-building programs work, and what types do
not, in terms of lasting improvements in local problem-
solving processes? (3) What are the governmental and political effects of different kinds of federal aid strategies?
(4) What is the optimal mix of outside aid and internal
political will in the small community?

BIBLIOGRAPHY

Advisory Commission on Intergovernmental Relations. The
    Intergovernmental Grants System as Seen by Local,
    State, and Federal Officials. Washington, D.C.: Advisory
    Commission on Intergovernmental Relations, 1977.
    _____. Regional Decision Making: New Strategies
    for Substate Districts. Washington, D.C.: ACIR, 1973.
Bish, Robert L. "Public Choice Theory: Research Issues
    for Nonmetropolitan Areas." In National Conference on
    Nonmetropolitan Community Services Research, pp.
    125-40. Washington, D.C.: Committee on Agriculture,
    Nutrition, and Forestry, U.S. Senate, 1977.
Blakely, Edward J., and Zone, Martin. Small Cities and
    the Community Development Act of 1974. Davis, Calif.:
    Institute of Governmental Affairs, University of
    California, 1976.

Booth, David A. Council-Manager Government in Small Cities.
    Washington, D.C.: International City Managers Associ-
    ation, 1968.
Butwin, David. "Portrait of a Declining Town." Saturday
    Review 51 (1968) p. 17.
Claxton, Marcia L. Where Government Works: Six Small Cities.
    Iowa City, Iowa: Institute of Public Affairs, the
    University of Iowa, 1976.
Clinton, Charles A. "Shiloh: The Little County That Could—
    and Did." Rural Sociology 43 (1978): 191-203.
Colfer, Carol J. Pierce. "Inside Bushler Bay: Lifeways in
    Counterpoint." Rural Sociology 43 (1978): 204-19.
Committee on Economic Development. Modernizing Local Gov-
    ernment. New York: Committee on Economic Development,
    1966.
Crane, Wilder W. "Reflections of a County Board Member."
    The County Officer (Sept. 1956): 202-4.
Douglas, Louis H., and Shelley, Scott. Community Staying
    Power: A Small Rural Place and Its Role in Rural
    Development. Manhattan, Kans.: Agricultural Experiment
    Station, Kansas State University, 1977.
Elam, Jon. "Small City Administration: A New Twist in Rural
    Cooperation." Small Town 7 (1977): 11-13.
Executive Office of the President. Strengthening Public
    Management in the Intergovernmental System. Washington,
    D.C.: U.S. Government Printing Office, 1975.
Forstall, Richard L., and Miller, Joel C. "Annexations
    and Corporate Changes: 1970-76." In The Municipal Year
    Book, 1978, pp. 61-64. Washington, D.C.: International
    City Management Association, 1978.
Glendenning, Paris N., and Atkins, Patricia S. "The Politics
    of City-County Consolidation." In The County Year Book,
    1977, pp. 62-69. Washington, D.C.: National Association
    of Counties and International City Management Associa-
    tion, 1977.
Grigg, Charles M.; Bilbija, Zarko G.; and Long, Huey B.
    "A Survey of Cities Under 10,000 Outside Metropolitan
    Areas." In The Municipal Year Book, 1968, pp. 137-51.
    Washington, D.C.: International City Management Associa-
    tion, 1968.
Grosenick, Leigh E. "Grass Roots Capacity Building and
    the Intergovernmental System." In National Conference
    on Nonmetropolitan Community Services Research, pp.
    167-81. Washington, D.C.: Committee on Agriculture,
    Nutrition, and Forestry, U.S. Senate, 1977.
Hitzhusen, Fred J. "Non-Tax Financing and Support for

'Community Services.'" In National Conference on
Nonmetropolitan Community Services Research, pp. 43-53.
Washington, D.C.: Committee on Agriculture, Nutrition,
and Forestry, U.S. Senate, 1977.

Hogan, Joan. "Small Cities and Counties as Responsive Gov-
ernments." Paper presented to the annual meeting of the
American Society of Public Administration, Phoenix,
Ariz., April 1978.

Illinois Department of Local Government Affairs. Home Rule
for Small Municipalities in Illinois. Springfield,
Ill.: Department of Local Government, 1979.

International City Management Association. "Governmental
and Financial Data for Small Cities." In The Municipal
Year Book, 1971, pp. 269-75. Washington, D.C.: International City Management Association, 1971.

_____. The Municipal Year Book 1978. Washington,
D.C.: International City Management Association, 1978.

Luloff, A. E. "Identifying the Locus for Action: What Local
Residents Have to Say." Small Town 9 (1978): 11-14.

Macaluso, Ann C. "The Future of Small Communities." In
Small Cities in Transition: The Dynamics of Growth and
Decline, edited by Herrington J. Bryce, pp. 377-79.
Cambridge, Mass.: Ballinger, 1977.

McCarty, Daniel R. "Sharing a City Administrator." CURA
Reporter 8 (1978): 1-7. St. Paul, Minn.: Center for
Urban and Regional Affairs, University of Minnesota,
1978.

McKinsey, Lauren S., and Lopach, James L. A State Mandates
Local Government Review: The Montana Experience. Davis,
Calif.: Institute of Governmental Affairs, University
of California, 1979.

Marando, Vincent L., and Thomas, Robert D. The Forgotten
Governments: County Commissioners as Policy Makers.
Gainesville, Fla.: University Presses of Florida, 1977.

Martin, Roscoe. Grass Roots Politics. University, Ala.:
University of Alabama Press, 1957.

Mason, Bert; Sokolow, Alvin D.; and Foller, Varden. General
Revenue Sharing and the Small Community: A Study of
Five California Counties. Davis, Calif.: Institute of
Governmental Affairs, University of California, 1977.

Murphy, Michael J. "Governmental Data in Municipalities
25,000 and Under." Urban Data Service Reports 7 (1975).

Myer, Mary Lynne. "North Bonneville: A Small Community
Faces the Future." Small Town 8 (1977): 4-10.

Nathan, Richard P., and Adams, Charles F. Revenue Sharing:
The Second Round. Washington, D.C.: The Brookings

Institution, 1977a.

Nathan, Richard P.; Manuel, Allen D.; and Calkins, Susannah E. Monitoring Revenue Sharing. Washington, D.C.: The Brookings Institution, 1975.

Nathan, Richard P. et al. Block Grants for Community Development. Washington, D.C.: U.S. Department of Housing and Community Development, 1977b.

National Association of Counties and International City Management Association. "County Functions and Services." In The County Year Book, 1977, pp. 104-51. Washington, D.C.: National Association of Counties and International City Management Association, 1977.

_____. The County Year Book, 1978. Washington, D.C.: National Association of Counties and International City Management Association, 1978.

Perlstadt, Harry. "Voluntary Associations and the Community: The Case of Volunteer Ambulance Corps." Journal of Voluntary Action Research 4 (1975): 85-89.

Puryear, David. "The Relevance of City Size." In Small Cities in Transition: The Dynamics of Growth and Decline, edited by Herrington J. Bryce, pp. 155-66. Cambridge, Mass.: Ballinger, 1977.

Rainey, Kenneth D., and Rainey, Karen G. "Rural Government and Local Public Services." In Rural U.S.A.: Persistence and Change, edited by Thomas R. Ford, pp. 126-44. Ames, Iowa: Iowa State University Press, 1978.

Reid, J. Norman; Godsey, W. Maureen; and Hines, Fred K. Federal Outlays in Fiscal 1976. Washington, D.C.: Economic Development Division, Economics, Statistics, and Cooperatives Service, U.S. Department of Agriculture, 1978.

Rural America. Limited Access: A Report on the Community Block Grant Programs in Nonmetropolitan Areas. Washington, D.C.: Rural America, 1977.

Shannon, John, and Ross, John. "Cities: Their Increasing Dependence on State and Federal Aid." In Small Cities in Transition: The Dynamics of Growth and Decline, edited by Herrington J. Bryce, pp. 189-211. Cambridge, Mass.: Ballinger, 1977.

Snider, Clyde. Local Government in Rural America. New York: Appleton-Century-Crofts, 1957.

Sokolow, Alvin D. Governmental Response to Urbanization: Three Townships on the Rural-Urban Gradient. Washington, D.C.: Economic Research Service, U.S. Department of Agriculture, 1968.

_____. "The Politics of Small Town Growth: Newcomers,

Issues, and Local Government." Paper presented to the
Conference on Understanding Population Change, North
Central Regional Center for Rural Development, Cham-
paign, Ill., 12-14 March 1979.
_____. "Small Community Policy Making and the Revenue
Sharing Program." In Revenue Sharing: Methodological
Approaches and Problems, edited by David A. Caputo and
Richard L. Cole, pp. 3-19. Lexington, Mass.: Lexington
Books, 1976.
_____. "Too Many, Too Small? Local Governments in
Nonmetropolitan America." Paper presented to the
Western Political Science Association, Phoenix, Ariz.,
1 April 1977.
Solomon, Barbara W. Management Assistance to Small Local
Governments: Some Models. Urbana-Champaign, Ill.:
Cooperative Extension Service, University of Illinois,
1977.
Stanfield, Rochelle L. "Small Cities Are on the Prowl for
Help from Washington." National Journal 10 (1978):
1597-1601.
Stocker, Frederick D. "Fiscal Needs and Resources of Non-
metropolitan Communities." In National Conference on
Nonmetropolitan Community Services Research, pp. 25-41.
Washington, D.C.: Committee on Agriculture, Nutrition,
and Forestry, U.S. Senate, 1977.
Subcommittee on the City. Small Cities: How Can the Federal
and State Governments Respond to Their Diverse Needs?
Washington, D.C.: U.S. House, Committee on Banking,
Finance and Urban Affairs, 1978.
Sundquist, James L. Making Federalism Work: A Study of
Program Coordination at the Community Level. Washington,
D.C.: The Brookings Institution, 1969.
Tate, Gavin. "Small Town Values and the Problem of Growth."
Small Town 9 (1978): 4-10.
Thorwood, Thomas. "The Planning and Management Process in
City Government." In The Municipal Year Book, 1973, pp.
27-38. Washington, D.C.: The International City Manage-
ment Association, 1973.
Tweeten, Luther, and Brinkman, George L. Micropolitan De-
velopment: Theory and Practice of Greater Rural Economic
Development. Ames, Iowa: Iowa State University Press,
1976.
U.S. Bureau of the Census. 1972 Census of Governments.
Vol. 4, no. 4, Finances of Municipalities and Township
Governments. Washington, D.C.: U.S. Census, 1974a.
_____. 1973 Boundary and Annexation Survey. Washing-

ton, D.C.: U.S. Census, 1974b.

_____. 1977 Census of Governments. Vol. 1, Governmental Organization. Washington, D.C.: U.S. Census, 1978a.

_____. 1977 Census of Governments. Vol. 6, no. 6, Regional Organizations. Washington, D.C.: U.S. Census, 1978b.

_____. 1977 Census of Governments. Vol. 3, no. 2, Compendium of Public Employment. Washington, D.C.: U.S. Census, 1979a.

_____. 1977 Census of Governments. Vol. 4, no. 4, Finances of Municipalities and Township Governments. Washington, D.C.: U.S. Census, 1979b.

U.S. Department of Housing and Urban Development. Comprehensive Planning Assistance in the Small Community. Washington, D.C.: Housing and Urban Development, 1969.

_____. Developmental Needs of Small Cities. Washington, D.C.: Housing and Urban Development, 1979.

Van Asselt, Karl A. "Federal-Local Communications: Problems and Opportunities." Western City 53 (1978): 7-8, 33.

Vidich, Arthur J., and Bensman, Joseph. Small Town in Mass Society: Class, Power and Religion in a Rural Community. Princeton, N.J.: Princeton University Press, 1968.

Villanueva, A. B. "Western Illinois Regional Council: Supergovernment or Its Antidote?" Illinois Issues 3 (1976): 26-27.

Wager, Paul W. "Townships on Way Out." National Municipal Review 46 (1957): 456-60, 475.

Wessel, Robert I. "Structure, Change in Rural Government." In Contours of Change: The Yearbook of Agriculture, 1970, pp. 154-58. Washington, D.C.: U.S. Department of Agriculture, 1970.

Wilde, James A. "Intergovernmental Revenues: Current Theoretical and Policy Issues." In National Conference on Nonmetropolitan Community Services Research, pp. 77-93. Washington, D.C.: Committee on Agriculture, Nutrition, and Forestry, U.S. Senate, 1977.

Zimmerman, Joseph F. "Meeting Service Needs Through Intergovernmental Agreements." In Municipal Year Book, 1973, pp. 79-89. Washington, D.C.: International City Management Association, 1973.

Thomas F. Stinson

20
Fiscal Status of
Local Governments

INTRODUCTION

Local government services make a major contribution to the
quality of life in rural America. Citizens demand education,
health care, and public safety just as they demand food,
clothing, and housing; and the location of industries and
households is said to be influenced by both the quality and
the cost of local public services. Although the financial
problems of the large central cities and the metropolitan
areas have been well publicized and the subject of much
research, surprisingly little is known about the finances
of smaller local governments.

Research has been limited by problems of measuring
service quality, fiscal capacity, and tax effort, just as
it has in the urban areas. The lack of a consistent set of
annual data has been still another constraint. The Census
of Governments, conducted once every five years, is the
only source of detailed, consistent national data on the
finances of small cities, counties, and school districts.
This data limitation has resulted in a concentration and
perhaps overanalysis of the status of local government
finances during census years, with little attention paid
to long-term trends.

This chapter follows that same tradition. It offers no
answers to the question of whether rural local governments
faced more serious financial problems in 1977 than they did
in 1962 or 1972. Instead, it reviews and updates basic
information about the finances of smaller local governments.
An update seems particularly important now, because several
major changes have occurred since 1972 in the institutional

The author benefited from discussions with Andrea Lubov and
Norman Reid. The opportunity to read an unpublished manuscript by Norman Reid, Susan Brown, Maureen Godsey, and
Eleanor Whitehead was also of great value. Ronald Larson
provided statistical assistance.

structure within which local governments operate, changes
that may have had significant but as yet unrecognized
effects. Federal revenue sharing, rapid inflation, and the
reemergence of population growth in rural areas are among
those structural changes.

This chapter has three major sections. The first and
largest presents material from the 1977 Census of Governments describing local government finance outside the metro
areas. Current (1977) expenditures and revenues are also
compared with those in 1962 and 1972 to provide historical
perspective and a view of long-term trends. The second
section divides nonmetro counties into four groups based on
their population growth rates and identifies some special
problems that may affect them. The third section discusses
the effect of inflation on local government finances.

Throughout the chapter the focus is on county areas
rather than on cities, counties, and school districts. This
allows comparisons among states where the responsibility
for a particular service differs among types of government.
Data on finances of cities, school districts, and counties
are included, but only for illustrative purposes.

THE FINANCES OF NONMETROPOLITAN
LOCAL GOVERNMENTS IN 1977

In 1977 per capita expenditures by local governments in
SMSA counties were about one-third greater than those in
counties outside the SMSAs (Table 20.1). Expenditures in
the smallest counties (those with less than 10,000 residents) exceed those in counties with populations between
10,000 and 50,000, but were still 15 percent less than the
average for all counties. Residents of larger nonmetro
counties and of SMSAs simply spend more for public services
than do people in rural areas.

But this does not mean that services are on the average
one-third better in metro areas or that one-third more
services are available. Nor does it mean that nonmetro
counties are facing financial problems. Conclusions about
service levels and relative needs are impossible to draw
from data of that type. Dollars spent cannot be translated
directly into measures of either quality or quantity of
services.

This section presents a brief discussion of problems
and potential pitfalls in analyzing local government fi-

Table 20.1. Per Capita Expenditures by Local Government County Areas, 1977

Expenditure	All Counties	SMSA Counties	NonSMSA Counties	Population 10,000 to 50,000	Population Less than 10,000
	$	$	$	$	$
Current	699	751	559	516	583
Capital	103	108	89	85	93
Total	802	859	648	601	676

Source: U.S. Bureau of the Census, 1977 Census of Governments, vols. 4 and 5.

nancial data. It then turns to an examination of local finances based on the 1977 Census of Governments. Following that general discussion, local revenues, expenditures, debt, and employment are each examined in more detail in an attempt to determine the changes that have occurred since 1962.

PROBLEMS IN INTERPRETING LOCAL FINANCIAL DATA

Comparisons of per capita expenditures by local governments may be misleading if expenditures are interpreted to be measures of service production. The particular character-istics of the services produced and differences in produc-tion techniques and costs of production make meaningful comparisons impossible. Indeed, the problem is so compli-cated that it is not possible even to determine the direc-tion of any bias.

Focusing on expenditures, or the cost of inputs, ignores the fact that consumers demand results, not physical units of inputs. For example, the demand for police protection is not a demand for a fixed number of hours of police patrol near one's home. What taxpayers want, and are willing to pay for, is a reduction in the probability that members of their household will be affected by crime. Consumers are unconcerned about the number of man-hours of patrols re-quired to achieve the desired level of safety, and in theory

would be willing to pay the same amount whether it took one
patrol per week or one per hour to reach the target service
level. As a result, communities spending $5 per capita and
communities spending $50 per capita could be providing the
same level of protection.

Hirsch (1977) deals with this problem by including
service conditions as an argument in his local government
production function. In that framework, a community in
which there is a lower underlying risk of crime has different service conditions, allowing it to achieve a given
level of protection at a lower cost. For this chapter the
point is clear, if service conditions cannot be assumed to
be the same, dollar comparisons of expenditures cannot be
assumed to reflect differences in quantity or quality of
service.

There are, however, other reasons why expenditures
cannot be compared even if service conditions are similar.
Costs of inputs vary. Labor costs--the major input for all
local government services--depend on the cost of living in
an area, so differences in wages may not reflect differences in the productivity of the work force. Production
techniques also may not be comparable. Nonmetro areas, for
example, tend to rely on volunteer and part-time labor more
than their larger, metro counterparts. To the extent that
volunteer labor and donated inputs are used in place of
purchased inputs, costs of producing a given amount and
quality of service will be less (Stinson 1978).

Other reasons, such as economies of size (dealt with
in detail in Chapter 15 in this volume), the fact that
smaller local governments do not all necessarily provide a
full complement of goods and services, and the fact that
private contractors provide varying amounts of such services
as education, hospitals, and sanitation, only complicate
comparisons and make them even less meaningful.

Revenue comparisons can be more useful, but problems
remain. Ability to pay and tax effort are important considerations and without a good measure of local fiscal
capacity one cannot distinguish between communities or
groups of communities whose revenue production is low due
to a lack of taxable capacity and those whose revenue is
low by choice.

These problems do not, however, invalidate all comparisons of local financial data. They only restrict the
interpretation of the comparisons, limiting possibilities
to make statements about relative needs or quality. Census
data can be used to determine whether there have been

changes in the importance of certain types of revenues or
in expenditures for certain services as well as to trace
patterns in the growth of local government spending. The
remainder of this section concentrates on those and similar
issues.

LOCAL GOVERNMENT FINANCES IN 1977

Expenditures and revenues of local governments in 1977 are
summarized in Table 20.2. For all local governments, intergovernmental aids provide more than 43 percent of general
revenue. Property taxes account for about one-third of
revenue, while other taxes (8 percent) and charges and
miscellaneous revenue (15 percent) make up the remainder.
The pattern is similar in both metro and nonmetro counties,
although metro counties receive a somewhat larger portion
of their total revenue from property taxes and slightly
less from intergovernmental aid. Smaller counties raise
slightly more from the property tax--nearly 38 percent for
those with populations less than 10,000--and receive slightly less in both dollar and percentage terms in state aid.
Charges and miscellaneous revenues are more important outside the metro areas, whereas other tax revenues are relatively more important in SMSA counties.
      Education, including local postsecondary schools, was
the major expenditure item. Nearly 45 percent of all local
government expenditure, or more than $350 per capita, went
for this service. In small counties, education-related
expenditures were more than 50 percent of general expenditures, with nearly all funds going to elementary and secondary education.
      No other single item accounted for as much as 10 percent
of the total expenditure. Welfare, the next largest item,
accounted for only 7 percent, and 3 percent or less in
small and nonmetro counties. Hospitals and highways were
the only other two categories containing more than 5 percent of all expenditures, although for small counties highway expenditures exceeded 12 percent of the total, and
both highway and hospital expenditures increased in percentage share as county population declined. With those
exceptions, however, the mix of services provided in the
nonmetro counties appears to be quite similar to that
provided in the metro areas. The major difference is in the
magnitude of the expenditures.
      Per capita local government debt is much higher in SMSAs

Table 20.2. Per Capita Revenues, Expenditures, and Debt of
Local Government by County Area, 1977

Revenue, Expenditure, or Debt	All Counties	SMSA Counties	NonSMSA Counties	Population 10,000 to 50,000	Population Less than 10,000
	$	$	$	$	$
Total general revenue	840	908	657	606	694
Intergovern- mental revenue	361	380	308	293	291
Federal	78	88	50	42	49
State	283	292	258	250	242
Property tax	282	313	203	175	261
Other tax	68	84	29	26	21
Miscellaneous charges	128	133	116	113	121
Total expendi- tures	802	860	648	601	676
Capital	103	108	89	85	93
Current	699	752	559	516	583
Education	355	363	335	320	360
Welfare	56	68	23	18	12
Hospitals	42	40	44	45	52
Health	14	16	8	7	8
Highways	43	39	55	55	82
Capital	14	14	14	14	20
Police	42	49	23	21	22
Fire	21	25	10	8	5
Sewerage	32	36	20	17	8
Capital	21	24	14	11	4
Sanitation	11	13	7	5	4
Parks and recreation	18	22	8	7	5
Housing	15	18	7	4	2
Correction	8	9	4	3	2
Libraries	6	7	3	3	2
Financial ad- ministration	11	11	9	9	13
General control	21	23	17	15	22

Table 20.2. (continued)

Revenue, Expenditure, or Debt	All Counties	SMSA Counties	NonSMSA Counties	Population	
				10,000 to 50,000	Less than 10,000
	$	$	$	$	$
Buildings	9	9	7	6	6
Interest	29	34	17	16	16
Other	71	74	49	44	54
Total debt	795	894	531	375	421
Long term	749	838	512	361	413
Full faith and credit	439	510	248	na	na
Long-term school debt	159	166	140	146	142

Source: U.S. Bureau of the Census, 1977 Census of Governments, vols. 4 and 5.

na=Not available.

($894) than outside them ($531). Counties with populations between 10,000 and 50,000 had considerably less debt, $375 per capita, while counties with less than 10,000 residents had local government debt of $421 per capita. Nearly all local debt in 1977 was long term with only 6 percent of the debt in SMSA counties and 3 percent in nonSMSA counties in short-term notes. Nationally more than 55 percent of all local debt was backed by the full faith and credit of the issuing government. For nonmetro areas the nonguaranteed portion was much larger with nearly 52 percent of all long-term debt falling in this category. More detail about revenues, expenditures, and debt, including some historical comparisons, is provided below.

Revenues
    Per capita revenues for all local governments increased from $214 in 1962 to $513 in 1972 and to $840 in 1977. (See U.S. Bureau of the Census, Census of Governments, vol. 5, for 1962, 1972, and 1977.) The rate of increase was higher in the SMSA counties than in the nonSMSA counties, but even

in nonSMSA counties revenues in 1977 were nearly triple
those of 1962. Property tax revenues, although not increasing quite as rapidly, also nearly tripled going from $112
in 1962 to $313 in 1977 in the SMSA counties and from $76
to $203 in those outside the SMSA.

The most important structural change in revenues was
the increased dependency of local governments on aid from
higher levels of government. Federal revenue sharing, for
example, was just beginning in 1972, so the 1977 data provide the first opportunity to see its impact.

The percentage of general revenue obtained through
intergovernmental aid has increased dramatically since 1962
(Table 20.3). State and federal aid made up only 30 percent
of all local government revenues in 1962. In 1977 they accounted for more than 43 percent of local revenue. Governments outside SMSAs received a higher proportion of their
revenue in aid (47 percent), but their percentage increase
since 1962 was less because they also received more than
the national average at that time.

The sources of increased aid have been pretty well split
between federal and state governments for local governments
in the metro areas. Outside the SMSAs, however, most of the
increase can be attributed to increased federal aid. Revenue
sharing has had a distinct impact on all areas, but its
effect appears to be neutral between metro and nonmetro
areas. Census figures show that local governments in SMSAs
received $20.73 per capita from revenue sharing while those
outside the SMSA received $20.39 (U.S. Bureau of the Census,
1977 Census of Governments, vol. 5, p. 298).

Data on city revenues provide some additional insight
into the magnitude of the changes. In 1962 intergovernmental
aid was less than 20 percent of all city revenue; in 1972,
33 percent; and 1977, nearly 38 percent. Federal aid, which
was approximately 4 percent of total revenue in 1962, jumped
to 8 percent in 1972 and to nearly 15 percent in 1977. For
smaller cities (those with less than 10,000 population) the
change is even more dramatic with federal aid rising from
2.5 to 12.5 percent of total revenue between 1962 and 1977,
a fivefold increase.

Shannon and Ross (1978) note that in 1962, of all units
of local government cities were the least dependent on
outside aid. By 1975, only counties were more dependent.
They also note that if present trends continue, cities will
become a financial arm of the federal rather than the state
government because much of their growth has come through
federal aid.

Table 20.3. Local Government Revenues by Source as Percentage of Total Revenues for County Areas in 1962, 1972, and 1977

County Area	Total	Intergovernmental			Taxes		Charges and Other Revenue
		Federal	Revenue Sharing	State	Property	Other	
	%	%	%	%	%	%	%
All counties							
1962	30	2	*	28	48	7	15
1972	38	5	*	33	40	8	15
1977	43	9	2	33	33	8	15
SMSA counties							
1962	27	2	*	25	50	8	15
1972	36	5	*	32	40	9	14
1977	42	10	2	32	34	9	14
NonSMSA counties							
1962	38	2	*	37	44	3	15
1972	42	3	*	39	37	4	17
1977	47	8	3	39	31	4	18
Counties with population between 10,000 and 50,000							
1962	40	1	*	39	42	3	15
1972	44	3	*	41	34	4	19
1977	48	7	3	41	28	4	19
Counties with population less than 10,000							
1962	38	1	*	37	46	4	13
1972	39	2	*	37	43	3	16
1977	42	7	3	35	38	3	17

Source: U.S. Bureau of the Census, 1962 Census of Governments, 1972 Census of Governments, and 1977 Census of Governments, vol. 5.

Note: Revenue sharing is derived from the federal revenue figure.

*Program did not exist.

A second, somewhat related revenue change is the decline
in importance of the local property tax. For all local governments property taxes declined from 48 to 33 percent of
general revenue between 1962 and 1977. Declines were similar
in and out of the SMSA. In SMSA counties property taxes
went from 50 to 34 percent of local government revenues,
while in the nonmetro areas the decline was from 44 to 31
percent of revenue. Counties with less than 10,000 residents
showed the smallest change with property taxes decreasing
only from 46 percent to 38 percent of general revenues.

When particular types of local government are examined
separately the results are similar. For all municipalities
property taxes as a percentage of total revenue declined
from 44 percent in 1962 to 25 percent in 1977. For cities
with less than 10,000 residents the results were almost
identical. School districts followed the same pattern with
tax revenue as a percentage of general revenue declining
from more than 50 percent in 1962 to 35 percent in 1977.

It is important to keep these findings in perspective.
The results are from 1977, the year before Proposition 13
and the much-heralded tax revolt. Although there is only
anecdotal evidence, it appears that the 1978 furor over
property taxes has struck home with local officials, and
that attempts are being made to further reduce local property bills.

Finally, there has been concern that charges and fees
for services are increasing in importance, particularly
outside the urban area. The 1977 data indicate that trend
has continued but at a much slower rate. However, charges
may be much more important now than in 1977. Proposition 13
and other proposed tax-expenditure limitation measures have
stimulated increased interest in this revenue source and
many cities are reexamining their service fees and user
charges to insure that they charge at full cost for those
services that primarily benefit an individual or a firm.
Licensing and inspection fee structures are receiving special attention. Many other services--such as recreation,
libraries, sewers, and sanitation--are also receiving an
increasing percentage of their support from user charges.
In 1977, 48 percent of charges and fees revenue for local
governments outside the SMSAs came from hospital charges
while another 20 percent came from school-lunch charges and
other school-related fees including tuition at community
colleges. Sewer charges made up another 7 percent of the
total. (See U.S. Bureau of the Census, 1977 Census of
Governments, vol. 5.)

The census data indicate that, at least through 1977, fees were not an important source of revenue. Despite this, their increased use has important implications for local government. To the extent that the charges reflect the true cost of service, their use can produce a more efficient allocation of resources in the public sector. Further, to the extent that fees are charged for services that not everyone in the community uses, or for services that are a legitimate cost of doing business such as licenses and inspections, their increased use removes a subsidy that flowed from some residents to others.

There are, however, problems as well. Merit goods--goods with significant external benefits associated with their consumption--may be priced beyond reach of some consumers. Because by definition these goods are those whose consumption is in the best interest of the community, the use of fees to support them would appear to be counterproductive.

Also, because "relative tax effort" is a factor in the distribution formula for federal revenue sharing and some state aid programs, there is some concern that communities that rely more heavily on fees than on taxes will receive less aid (Hitzhusen 1977). The 1977 census data do not suggest that this is a problem. But, even if it were, the present dominance of user-charge revenue by hospital and school-lunch fees leaves one hesitant to advocate a change that will produce more aid to the community when hospital rates or school lunch prices increase.

The changes in the proportion of local expenditures financed through intergovernmental aid, property taxes, and user charges have enormous implications for the future of local government. The connection between the amount paid for services through the local tax system and the amount and quality of local services provided has always served as a check, albeit a rather indirect and clumsy one, on the efficiency of local government. Now, with more than half of all money spent coming from nontax sources, the connection between cost and service levels is greatly reduced. Political scientists, sociologists, and economists should all find this a fertile area for future research. The responsiveness of local government, changes in demand for services, and, perhaps most important, whether the current aid system is maintaining local governments that would either consolidate or fade away, are important topics for research that is of particular significance to nonmetro areas.

Expenditures

Spending by local government has also increased significantly since 1962. Total expenditures by local governments in SMSA counties rose from $234 in 1962 to $860 per capita in 1977 (see Table 20.2). In counties outside the SMSAs spending rose from $180 to $648 per capita. Per capita expenditures by cities were $116 in 1962; $271 in 1972; and $443 in 1977--an annual rate of increase of slightly more than 9 percent (See U.S. Bureau of the Census, Census of Governments, vol. 4.4, for 1962, 1972, and 1977.) School districts showed a similar increase going from $492 per pupil in 1962 to $1,640 in 1977 (U.S. Bureau of the Census, Census of Governments, vol. 4.1, for 1962 and 1977).

The rates of increase are deceiving, however, because prices for almost all goods and services have increased dramatically since 1962. Expenditures must be expressed in dollars of constant purchasing power if changes in the real purchasing power of local government are to be shown. By using constant dollars expenditure increases attributable to higher prices for inputs can be separated from those due to increased quality or quantity of service.

A number of price deflators and price indexes are published by the federal government, including one especially designed to take account of price changes affecting state and local governments (see U.S. Bureau of Economic Analysis). In 1962 this index--the state and local government price deflator--stood at 60.3; by 1977 it had climbed to 148.5, an incease of nearly 150 percent. In contrast, the Consumer Price Index, the most popular measure of prices of goods purchased by households, increased from 72.3 to 144.8, or approximately 100 percent during that period. What appears to have happened is that between 1962 and 1977 prices for state and local public services increased more rapidly than the prices of consumer goods.

Economic theory indicates that under normal circumstances when relative prices change between two goods, consumers will demand less of the good whose price increased and more of the good whose price decreased. Here, one would expect to see a decline in public sector activity and an increase in the private sector purchases, all other things equal. Problems of measuring both the quality of government services and the productivity of public activity prevent us from obtaining any direct evidence on the size and extent of the shift. But the increased public concern over taxes, evidenced by Proposition 13 and other tax-expenditure limitation measures, does lend support to the belief that

Table 20.4. Selected Real per Capita Expenditures by Local
Governments and County Areas in 1962, 1972, and 1977

County Area	Total	Current	Local Education	Welfare
	$	$	$	$
All counties				
1962	222	177	100	14
1972	316	268	144	26
1977	326	284	135	23
SMSA counties				
1962	234	183	95	16
1972	348	293	141	33
1977	349	305	137	28
NonSMSA counties				
1962	180	149	94	10
1972	240	207	128	11
1977	263	227	131	9
Counties with population between 10,000 and 50,000				
1962	167	140	90	8
1972	226	196	125	10
1977	244	210	130	7
Counties with population less than 10,000				
1962	188	161	100	10
1972	241	212	133	8
1977	274	237	146	5

Source: U.S. Bureau of the Census, 1962 Census of Governments, 1972 Census of Governments, and 1977 Census of
Governments, vol. 5.

Note: Dollar amounts are given in 1962 dollars.

*Includes expenditures for health.

**Excludes natural resources.

strong pressures exist for a decrease in local government
spending.
    Per capita local government expenditures by county area,
deflated to 1962 price levels, are presented in Table 20.4.

Hospitals	Highway	Protection	Sewer	Environment and Housing	Adminis- tration
$	$	$	$	$	$
12*	21	17	7	17	11
16	19	23	10	22	15
17	18	25	13	20	16
11	18	20	8	22	12
17	17	28	12	26	16
17	16	30	15	22**	17
8	23	8	4	7	10
14	23	10	5	9	11
18	22	13	8	9**	14
10*	23	7	3	6	9
15	22	9	4	8	10
17	22	12	7	9	12
9*	32	6	2	6	12
15	34	7	2	7	14
21	33	11	3	8	17

The pattern is similar in all types of counties, a rapid increase in spending between 1962 and 1972 followed by almost no increase between 1972 and 1977. Only in counties with less than 10,000 residents was there a relatively constant growth rate for real expenditures. In those counties expenditures in 1962 dollars rose from $188 per capita in 1962 to $241 in 1972 and $274 in 1977. Per capita expenditures in all counties grew from $222 to $316 in 1972, but to only $326 by 1977. In counties outside the SMSA expenditures were $180 per capita in 1962, $240 in 1972, and $263 in 1977.

City and county government expenditure patterns were

similar (see U.S. Bureau of the Census, Census of Governments, vol. 4.4, for 1962, 1972, and 1977). A large increase
from 1962 to 1972 was followed by little or no growth from
1972 to 1977. Real city expenditures, for example, went
from $116 per capita in 1962 to $164 in 1972, an increase
of over 40 percent. But, from 1972 to 1977 expenditures in
1962 dollars increased only 3 percent to $169. County ex-
penditures were similar, increasing more than 44 percent,
from $55 in 1962 to $81 in 1972, then increasing only 9
percent to $89 by 1977.

School districts were the only unit of local government
to continue their pattern of growth in real expenditures,
going from $492 to $602 per pupil between 1962 and 1972, a
22 percent increase, followed by an increase of 10 percent
in the five years between 1972 and 1977 to a total of $666
per pupil. Even there, however, major shifts occurred. Between 1962 and 1972 the salaries portion of the budget
increased by more than 30 percent while increases from 1972
to 1977 were concentrated in the "other cost" section of
the budget. (See U.S. Bureau of the Census, Census of Governments, vol. 4.1, for 1962 and 1977; also, U.S. Bureau
of Economic Analysis.)

Although expenditures by both small cities and counties
increased more rapidly than those of their larger counterparts during 1972 to 1977, their rate of increase still
does not match the growth that occurred during the 1960s.
This leveling off in real expenditures raises important
questions for those involved in local financial planning.
For example, is the leveling off due to traditional supply
and demand forces discussed earlier, or can it be explained
in other ways. Some states may have assumed increased responsibility for locally provided services, such as welfare,
thus transferring responsibility and expenditures to the
state level while maintaining the same service level. Or,
productivity may have increased, allowing services of the
same quality or better to be provided at lower cost. Economies of size might also be playing a more important role
than before. Finally, it is possible that, as population
growth slowed, the need for additional capacity at the
local level declined, allowing increases in quality to be
financed more easily.

Determining why real local spending remained relatively
constant between 1972 and 1977 is an important area for
research. A better understanding of what has occurred should
be of great value to those planning for future needs in
both nonmetro and metro areas. Although such a discussion

is beyond the scope of this chapter, some clues to the present situation may be found by looking at changes in relative patterns of expenditures.

Expenditures on selected services as a percentage of total county area expenditures are presented in Table 20.5. From 1962 to 1977 the most notable item is the consistency of expenditure patterns. In 1977 expenditures for education and highways had declined as a percentage of total expenditures, while expenditures for sewage disposal increased. All other major functions maintained their relative share of the local budget. These results held for counties both inside and outside the SMSA, although in counties with less than 50,000 residents hospitals consumed an increased percentage of the local budget as well. Looking at individual units of government, cities changed their expenditure pattern only slightly between 1972 and 1977 and counties changed less than other units of government.

Differences in expenditure by size of county between 1962 and 1977 are also given in Table 20.5. Education expenditures are a much larger percentage of total expenditure in nonmetro and smaller counties than they are for the United States as a whole. Per capita highway expenditures are also much greater in smaller counties, whereas expenditures for protection (police, fire, and correction) and welfare are noticeably smaller percentages of the budget. They are also, of course, much less on a dollar basis. When expenditures by smaller cities in 1972 and 1977 are compared, there is little change in the structure of the budget, other than a continuing decline in the importance of welfare and highway expenditures and an increase in hospital expenditures. It is particularly notable that increases in expenditures for sewerage do not appear. It appears that no particular type of program, except highways, has been singled out for cutbacks during this period of little real growth in expenditures, and that no services are receiving large increases in real resources.

EMPLOYMENT

The Census of Governments also contains information about local government employment. These data provide a view of changes in local government from a slightly different perspective. Local government employment in selected services for 1962, 1972, and 1977 is shown in Table 20.6. Employment is shown on a full-time equivalent per 10,000 residents

Table 20.5. Expenditures on Selected Functions as a
Percentage of Total Expenditures by Size and Type of County
in 1962, 1972, and 1977

County Area	Current	Local Education	Welfare	Hospitals
	%	%	%	%
All counties				
1962	80	45	6	5*
1972	85	46	8	5
1977	87	44	7	5
SMSA counties				
1962	78	42	7	5
1972	84	43	9	5
1977	87	39	8	5
NonSMSA counties				
1962	83	53	5	5
1972	87	55	5	6
1977	86	50	3	7
Counties with population between 10,000 and 50,000				
1962	84	54	5	6*
1972	87	55	4	7
1977	86	53	3	8
Counties with population less than 10,000				
1962	86	53	5	5*
1972	88	55	4	6
1977	86	53	2	8

Source: U.S. Bureau of the Census, 1962 Census of Governments, 1972 Census of Governments, and 1977 Census of
Governments.

*Includes expenditures for health.

**Excludes natural resources.

***Less than .5 percent.

(FTE/10,000) basis to standardize for differences in staff-
ing patterns and size of community.
    Two things are apparent. First, the relatively rapid

Highway	Protection	Sewer	Environment and Housing	Administration
%	%	%	%	%
9	8	3	8	5
6	8	4	7	5
6	8	4	6	5
8	10	4	9	5
5	9	3	8	5
5	10	4	6**	4
13	5	2	4	5
9	5	2	4	5
8	5	3	5**	5
14	4	2	4	5
10	4	2	4	4
9	4	3	4	5
17	3	1	3	5
14	3	***	3	6
12	4	1	3	6

increases in local government employment, which occurred during the 1960s, are over. Employment increased by only slightly more than 8 percent during the five years from 1972 to 1977, less than half the rate of increase from 1962 and 1972. Public education appears to be the major service affected. For all counties, educational employment increased from 183 to only 185 FTE/10,000. The decline in the number of school-age children has been a major force contributing to this change. But increases for other services have also been relatively small. Police and "other protection" increased only from 40 to 43 FTE/10,000 in metro areas and

Table 20.6. Full-time Equivalent Employment per 10,000
Residents for Selected Services by Size and Type of County
in 1962, 1972, and 1977

County Area	Total	Local Education	Highway	Welfare
All counties				
1962	250	131	15	na
1972	332	183	14	9
1977	361	185	14	9
SMSA counties				
1962	248	120	11	5
1972	340	179	11	10
1977	362	177	11	10
NonSMSA counties				
1962	229	137	19	3
1972	316	194	20	6
1977	357	206	20	7
Counties with population between 50,000 and 25,000				
1962	226	134	18	na
1972	307	190	18	5
1977	343	200	18	6
Counties with population between 25,000 and 10,000				
1962	233	144	23	na
1972	317	197	23	5
1977	353	209	22	5
Counties with population less than 10,000				
1962	264	161	30	na
1972	353	216	31	5
1977	396	230	31	5

Source: U.S. Bureau of the Census, 1962 Census of Governments, 1972 Census of Governments, and 1977 Census of
Governments.

*Includes expenditures for health.

na=Not available.

Hospitals	Police	Other Protection	Environment and Housing	Administration
19*	16	9	na	14
22	21	13	20	18
24	23	14	22	20
17	19	12	20	13
21	24	16	24	17
21	26	17	26	20
15	10	5	9	14
25	14	7	11	18
33	17	7	13	22
18*	9	4	na	13
26	13	7	11	16
32	16	9	14	19
16*	8	2	na	15
30	13	5	9	19
38	15	4	11	22
15*	8	1	na	25
30	14	4	7	29
39	18	2	9	35

from 21 to 24 FTE/10,000 in rural counties, in contrast to the 25 and 50 percent increases in those functions between 1962 and 1972. Employment has increased significantly only in the hospital classification in nonmetro and small counties. There increases of 30 percent were not uncommon even though the increases in SMSAs and the nation as a whole were 10 percent or less.

Table 20.7. Average Earnings per Full-time Equivalent
Employee by Selected Services for SMSA and NonSMSA Counties
in 1962, 1972, and 1977

County Area	Total	Local Education	Instructional Personnel	Hospitals
		1977 Dollars		
SMSA counties				
1962	482	529	589	333
1972	853	904	1,023	668
1977	1,150	1,192	1,327	914
NonSMSA counties				
1962	377	420	461	239
1972	641	705	785	452
1977	874	942	1,033	668
		1962 Dollars		
SMSA counties				
1962	482	529	589	333
1972	602	638	722	471
1977	572	594	661	455
NonSMSA counties				
1962	377	420	461	239
1972	452	497	553	318
1977	436	470	516	334

Source: U.S. Bureau of the Census, 1962 Census of Governments, 1972 Census of Governments, and 1977 Census of
Governments.

    Average wages of local employees are considerably
greater in the metro counties, reflecting increased costs
of living as well as the composition of skills, experience,
and training of the work force (Table 20.7). But, when
average October salary is compared in real terms, local
government employees in both metro and nonmetro counties
suffered a loss in real wages from 1972 to 1977. Teachers
appear to have been particularly hard hit, for at the same
time the composition of the teacher work force was shifting
so that it included a larger percentage of more experienced

olice	Fire	Welfare	Financial Administration	General Control
1977 Dollars				
496	509	391	424	475
962	977	678	737	812
,328	1,391	936	1,005	1,097
353	376	285	319	304
609	669	519	541	549
881	919	705	758	777
1962 Dollars				
496	509	391	424	475
678	689	478	520	572
662	693	466	501	547
353	376	285	319	304
430	472	366	382	388
440	482	352	378	388

and more educated (and thus more highly paid teachers), real salaries dropped by more than 10 percent. Only hospital employees and policemen in nonmetro areas, and firemen in nonmetro and metro counties were able to maintain their real wage at or above 1972 levels. By way of contrast, for all private, nonfarm workers in the United States real wages decreased by less than one-half percent between 1972 and 1977.

SUMMARY

This section has presented an overview of changes in local finances during the mid-1970s. The result in many instances was that there was no change. However, some major shifts did occur, especially in sources of revenue. Federal revenue sharing and increased state aid have greatly reduced that portion of the local budget that must come from local sources, in turn reducing pressure on the local property tax. This trend was well underway before Proposition 13 was approved in California, and is likely to continue. The result, among other things, has been a decline in the real level of property tax payments.

Changes of this sort have both positive and negative effects. By providing basic revenue with no strings attached, revenue sharing and state aid provide a framework within which more equal access to services and facilities can be provided. It is likely, for example, that small nonmetro communities may receive a greater impact from these general aid programs than do the larger metro counties, because small communities are guaranteed a share of the money without having to apply for it. At the same time, there is also the possibility of loss of local control and increased dependence on higher levels of government.

Two other changes in revenue were apparent. First, the use of local nonproperty tax revenues, such as local sales and income taxes, increased. During the 1960s, revenue from these sources was negligible (U.S. Bureau of the Census, 1962 Census of Governments). In 1977, however, they accounted for more than 8 percent of total revenues and probably significantly more in metro areas (U.S. Bureau of the Census, 1977 Census of Governments). The second development is an apparent increase in the use of user fees and charges to support local services. This process, which is only just now reflected in the 1977 statistics, will probably become much more important during the 1980s because it is one way local governments can maintain service levels while at the same time holding down taxes.

Another factor affecting local finances during the 1970s has been inflation. Its full impact on government services in nonmetro areas is difficult to determine without nonmetro cost-of-living indexes and better cost indexes for local services. Everywhere, however, real local government services appear to be growing either very slowly or not at all. It appears, although it is by no means certain, that real expenditure growth in smaller counties has exceed-

ed that in the metro areas between 1972 and 1977. Again,
though, better price indexes are necessary before services
in rural areas can be said to have improved in relation to
those in metro areas.

Inflation also has had an impact on local government
debt. Real local government debt in 1962 dollars actually
declined from $350 per capita to $323 per capita between
1972 and 1977 (U.S. Bureau of the Census, Census of Governments, vol. 4.4, for 1962, 1972, and 1977). Communities
that grew during the 1960s and that had high debt levels
now find inflation reducing the real burden of their debt
considerably. Suburban communities in metro areas building
infrastructure probably benefited most, although the real
value of the long-term portion of local government debt
outside the SMSAs declined from $267 to $209 per capita.
Communities with relatively static or declining populations
that did not borrow have received little help. Now, if they
need to borrow, future expectations of inflation could
saddle them with higher interest rates for the future.

The final factor affecting local government finances
has been the change in population structure across the
nation. This change is discussed in detail in earlier chapters in this volume. It is interesting to note the apparent
lack of impact that population change has had on patterns
of expenditure and revenue in rural counties. Although
there are no doubt individual cities, counties, and school
districts that have had severe impacts from growth, the
national figures do not reflect any noticeable changes.
Instead, it appears that the population growth overall is
being absorbed with relatively little strain on local
finances.

THE POPULATION GROWTH RATE AND LOCAL GOVERNMENT FINANCE

Local officials had little control over the changes in the
structure of local government finance that occurred during
the 1970s. Inflation, increased state and federal aid (especially revenue sharing), and state-assumed responsibility
for some local services were the major factors contributing
to the trends toward less dependence on the property tax,
increased dependence on federal aid, and a lack of growth
in real per capita expenditures.

Even those shifts due to the most easily foreseen demographic changes such as the decline in the birthrate, the

aging of the population, and the renewed migration to nonmetro areas, were beyond the direct control of local officials. There were few opportunities to initiate changes
at the local level. Instead, local officials were forced to
respond to changes dictated by federal and state programs
and the national economy.

During the next decade it is doubtful whether local
government will regain any of its lost autonomy. Indeed, if
local officials treat federal aid as a costless transfer of
income to the community, they have little incentive to try
to move in other, unsubsidized directions, and most important decisions affecting the structure of local government
finance will remain beyond their control.

Individual communities, however, will face problems in
coping with growth or decline. Their problems will not be
common to all governments but depend on the particular
characteristics of their community and the type of growth
that occurs. This section notes potential financial problems facing four types of communities--two types of rapid-
growth areas, a moderate-growth community, and a declining
area--providing some indication of the types of financial
pressures that may emerge. Rapid growth areas, the areas
with the potentially most serious financial problems, are
divided into two groups because the source of growth has a
significant impact on local government finances.

RAPID GROWTH FROM RESOURCE AND ENERGY DEVELOPMENT

Energy and resource development will be a major cause of
growth in nonmetro areas during the coming decade. Although
energy development through mining and drilling will be limited to a relatively small number of counties in the West
and Appalachia, power plant construction and synthetic fuel
plants may be located anywhere. Other resource development--
such as nonfuel minerals and timber--will also occur. In
broad areas of the country resource development appears to
be the major force producing rural development.

Resource-based development creates two problems for
local government. First is the problem of matching new revenues with service needs. New employment and local population are often greatest during the second or third year of
development and the operating work force is often far less
than that necessary during construction. The result is that
service requirements often peak before the mine or plant is
completed and on the tax rolls, creating a front-end cash

flow problem. This problem is further complicated by the
lags that exist between completion of a facility and its
assessment, and between assessment and the levying and collection of property taxes. For many resource-based projects
population will have declined from its construction levels
before the locality receives any increase in tax revenues.

The second, and more serious, long-term problem for
some governments is that they may never receive enough
additional revenue to meet the needs for new services.
Studies in the northern Great Plains indicate that counties
and school districts in which a new project is located are
not apt to face financial problems (Krutilla and Fisher
1978; Murdock and Leistritz 1979; and Stinson and Voelker
1978). Indeed, they may have an embarrassment of riches and
be able to reduce taxes. Cities and school districts not
containing the mine or power plant but receiving new population, however, may face long-term financial difficulty.
Impact aid programs, funded by severance taxes or energy
production and conversion taxes, are available in many
states to provide help for affected localities.

RETIREMENT AND VACATION COMMUNITIES

The increased popularity of nonmetro areas as sites for
vacation and retirement homes is a second major cause of
population growth. Much of this activity centers in the
warmer climates, but there is some spillover into the northern states as well. This form of growth creates a whole
different set of problems for the nonmetro community. In
fact, vacation areas with a seasonal trade face a different
set of problems than do retirement communities.

The financial problems of local government in retirement
areas are centered on the discrepancy between tax revenues
and expenditure needs. In most communities basic industry--
manufacturing, agriculture, or mining--pays more in taxes
than it requires in direct services, in effect subsidizing
the consumption of public services by local households.
But, when a large segment of the community is supported by
transfer payments, the nonresidential property-tax base may
be much less than it would be for a town of equivalent size
with a standard age distribution. The result is that even
though residents of a retirement community could be on
average wealthier and have higher incomes than residents of
the typical small town, total taxable property value in the
retirement community may be considerably less.

This problem has been eased somewhat by the increased availability of state and federal aid. But rapidly growing retirement areas can be expected to continue to face financial problems. Even though services required for retirees may be less expensive, there will be a smaller tax base supporting them. And, to the extent that new developments are allowed when the full cost of the extension of public services such as water, sewer, and roads are not included in the development costs, local taxes may increase considerably.

Vacation communities and summer home areas face similar problems. Again, there is no major source of tax revenue to the community aside from residential and commercial buildings. Revenue problems are reduced somewhat by increased commercial activity in the area. But expenditure requirements are greater because the permanent residents are apt to have a more traditional age distribution, thus requiring more for schools.

A second problem that many overlook is that services must be provided for part of the year for a population much larger than the full-time resident population. This involves investment in excess capacity in physical facilities--water, sewer, highways, and health care, for example--as well as developing some method of expanding and contracting the labor force necessary to provide services. Maintaining that excess capacity is expensive, so service costs are likely to be higher for a given level of service in a vacation community than in a traditional community. Again local taxes may be higher than those in a typical small town.

MODERATE GROWTH AREAS

Most smaller communities will not undergo rapid growth. Instead, population is likely to increase slowly and gradually and such an increase is unlikely to create major financial problems. But officials should not expect that local per capita expenditures will gradually decline due to economies of size. Production economies are much more complicated (see Chapter 15 in this volume). There are several problems. First, inputs are "lumpy"--it is, for example, difficult to hire one and one-half policemen. As a result, there is often excess capacity in the system, and at times service delivery can be expanded at little or no cost to the community. But, when that excess capacity is exhausted the incremental cost of bringing on the next production unit is considerable, producing a sizable increase in the local budget.

Other reasons why economies of scale may not be observed include the fact that service conditions may change (mentioned previously in this chapter), as well as the number of people using the service, thus canceling any expected savings. Also, because smaller local governments usually do not offer a full complement of services, the community may demand new services as well as an increase in existing service levels. Finally, volunteer labor is an important factor of production for some services. If population growth or any other factor produces a decrease in volunteers or a shift away from their use, their replacement with paid workers is likely to cause a significant change in the budget.

DECLINING AREAS

Declining areas face problems similar to those of retirement communities. Their tax base is limited due to the exit of industry and some commercial activity. In addition, residential property values will not increase as rapidly as in growing areas. Again, residents may be forced to carry nearly the entire cost of providing services on their tax bill with little assistance from business or industry. In nonmetro communities this situation is often further complicated by the fact that many residents derive their income from transfer payments or from agricultural enterprises located outside the taxing jurisdiction of the community. The result is a squeeze to pay for current operations and any upgrading of facilities required. However, increased state and federal payments to local governments help ameliorate their problems.

INFLATION AND LOCAL GOVERNMENT FINANCE

Inflation, if it continues to have significantly different effects on prices for public and private goods, is likely to be the single most important influence on local government during the next decade. Relative price changes will have no impact if all prices--including housing prices and assessed values--and consumer's incomes increase at the same rate. However, when the prices of public and private goods diverge rapidly, as has occurred during the past

fifteen years, local governments undergo enormous financial
pressure. The situation is only further complicated when
real incomes decline or when housing prices (and assessed
values and property taxes) increase more rapidly than real
incomes. The direction of the changes in local government
activity is predictable, given information about changes in
relative prices and income. The problem is anticipating
those changes. What might be expected under several alternatives is given below.

First, the gap between prices of public goods, measured
by the state and local government price deflator, and prices
of private goods, measured by the gross national product
deflator or the Consumer Price Index, could continue to
widen. This has been the pattern since 1962, and there is
no particular reason to expect a change. Most services
provided by local governments in both nonmetro and metro
areas are labor intensive, and there are relatively few
areas where the introduction of new capital equipment can
increase productivity.

This price situation, especially if accompanied by
constant or declining real income, creates the most stress
on local government finances because the public will desire
fewer publicly provided goods and there will be pressure
for a cut in real local expenditures. If housing prices
increase more rapidly than income, the problem worsens.
Demands for a tax cut will intensify because the tax system
has automatically taken more real income than it did before
even though taxpayers now want to spend less. This situation
is, of course, essentially what is observed today throughout
the country.

If, however, the same price situation holds, but real
incomes are assumed to increase, the problem is less serious. Increased real income, even coupled with increasing
relative prices for public sector goods, can--depending on
the relative income and price elasticities of demand--lead
to a situation where some increased demand for public services exists. Although the new level of demand is less
than it would have been given no relative price increase,
it still reduces public pressure for cuts in taxes and
expenditures.

The alternative situation, a more rapid increase in
the price of privately produced goods, would produce much
less stress on local government. Here, the demand for local
services would increase and there would (in theory at least)
be less resistance toward increased taxes to finance them.
Again, however, if housing prices and assessed valuations

increase more rapidly than income, local taxpayers could be caught in a situation where they are forced to pay for more public services than they desire, even though they desired an increase.

In each situation the problems facing nonmetro and metro areas, and those facing rapidly growing areas and declining areas, are similar. The major difference is in the relative rates of price increase and the rate of housing price increase. When the demand for public goods increases, either due to increased real income or a decrease in relative prices, the public sector can be easily expanded. Local officials' jobs are much easier, and there is margin for error in setting the budget and room for compromise. Both policymakers and pressure groups find that bargaining for portions of an increase in real resources is much more comfortable than trying to allocate cuts required because of retrenchment.

When there is no real growth to allocate resources among competing interests, or when retrenchment is necessary, it is a different situation. Then policymakers have less margin for error. It is at these times that pleas are most often heard for increased federal and state aid, or for state or federal takeover of particular services, and local officials are most receptive to trading some local autonomy for increased revenue. These are not metro or nonmetro problems. They are problems facing all local governments and are likely to continue during the 1980s.

BIBLIOGRAPHY

Hirsch, Werner Z. "Output and Costs of Local Government Services." In Proceedings of the National Conference on Nonmetropolitan Community Services Research, pp. 307-21. U.S. Senate Committee on Agriculture, Nutrition, and Forestry, 1977.

Hitzhusen, Fred J. "Non-tax Financing and Support for Community Services: Some Policy Implications for Nonmetropolitan Governments." In Proceedings of the National Conference on Nonmetropolitan Community Services Research, pp. 43-55. U.S. Senate Committee on Agriculture, Nutrition, and Forestry, 1977.

Krutilla, John V., and Fisher, Anthony C. Economic and Fiscal Impacts of Coal Development: Northern Great Plains. Baltimore, Md.: Johns Hopkins University Press,

1978.

Murdock, Steven H., and Leistritz, F. Larry. Energy Development in the Western United States: Impact on Rural Areas. New York: Praeger, 1979.

Perkinson, Leon B. "Local Government Employment Trends: Some Perspectives on Growth and Tax Revolts." EDD Working Paper no. 7908. U.S. Department of Agriculture, 1979.

Shannon, John, and Ross, John. "Cities: Their Increasing Dependence on State and Federal Aid." In Small Cities in Transition: The Dynamics of Growth and Decline, edited by Harrington Bryce. Cambridge, Mass.: Ballinger, 1978.

Stinson, Thomas F. "Household Allocation of Voluntary Labor in the Production of Fire Protection: Minnesota Evidence." American Journal of Agricultural Economics 60 (1978): 331-37.

_____, and Voelker, Stanley W. Coal Development in the Northern Great Plains: The Impact on Revenues of State and Local Governments. Agricultural Economic Report no. 394, U.S. Department of Agriculture, 1978.

Stocker, Frederick D. "Fiscal Needs and Resources of Nonmetropolitan Communities." In Proceedings of the National Conference on Nonmetropolitan Community Services Research, pp. 25-42. U.S. Senate Committee on Agriculture, Nutrition, and Forestry, 1977.

U.S. Bureau of the Census. 1962 Census of Governments. Vol. 3, Compendium of Public Employment. Vol. 4, Compendium of Government Finances. Vol. 4.1, Finances of School Districts. Vol. 4.4, Finances of Municipalities and Township Government. Vol. 5, Local Government in Metropolitan Areas. Washington, D.C.: U.S. Government Printing Office, 1964.

_____. 1972 Census of Governments. Vol. 3, Compendium of Public Employment. Vol. 4, Compendium of Government Finances. Vol. 4.4, Finances of Municipalities and Township Government. Vol. 5, Local Government in Metropolitan Areas. Washington, D.C.: U.S. Government Printing Office, 1974.

_____. 1977 Census of Governments. Vol. 3, Compendium of Public Employment. Vol. 4, Compendium of Government Finances. Vol. 4.1, Finances of School Districts. Vol. 4.4, Finances of Municipalities and Township Government. Vol. 5, Local Government in Metropolitan Areas. Washington, D.C.: U.S. Government Printing Office, 1980.

U.S. Bureau of Economic Analysis. Survey of Current Business. Washington, D.C.: U.S. Government Printing Office, 1965 and 1969.

Pat Choate

21

Public Institutions and the Planning Process

INTRODUCTION

Public planning is a fundamental nonmetro development function. During the past four decades, nonmetro public planning
has been expanded beyond traditional budgetary and land
planning roles into basic policy and coordinative and administrative functions. This reflects the expansion of
the scope, size, and directive influence of the public
interventions in the economy.

A diverse array of nonmetro planning institutions has
been created during the past forty years. These institutions
exist at the federal, multistate, state, substate, and
local levels. In large measure, the creation and operation
of these institutions represent the principal public sector
attempts to bring improved policy and administrative coher-
ence to the conduct of public business.

The conduct of nonmetro planning is increasingly influenced by a number of distinct institutional, political,
and technical considerations including: the changing objectives of the public intervention; incoherence in the
intergovernmental grant-in-aid system; institutional in-
capacities of nonmetro planning bodies; the expanding influence of state governments; the inadequacy of training
programs for nonmetro planners; issues of scale; growth
issues such as land planning; and the sharp historical/
development variations that exist among regions of the
nation.

This chapter will briefly describe the existing principal nonmetro planning institutions as well as a number of
contemporary nonmetro planning issues. The focus of the
chapter will be planning by public bodies, that is, by
government. The first section will delineate the principal
nonmetro planning institutions at the federal, multistate,
state, multijurisdictional, and local government levels.
Special attention will be given to multijurisdictional
planning institutions as they are a relatively new insti-

tutional form that has the flexibility and potential for addressing the fragmentation that hampers many nonmetro development practices. Special definitions of different types of planning can be found in the working notes.[1] The second section will describe a number of contemporary non-metro development issues. Although many of these issues are generic to all areas, the nonmetro characteristics and implications of these issues will be highlighted.

A diverse array of planning institutions has been created in this nation, reflecting varying development circumstances and the existence of almost 80,000 units of government--over 50,000 of which are nonmetro agencies. This section will briefly describe some of the more pertinent of these nonmetro planning institutions.

FEDERAL NONMETROPOLITAN PLANNING INSTITUTIONS

The federal government is involved in nonmetro planning in the following three fairly distinct ways: (1) National policies that guide the multiple tax, expenditure, monetary, trade, sectoral, and regulatory activities of the federal government are a major directive force on the level, nature, and location of development. Macro policies and programs focus on issues concerned with national levels of production, employment, and price stability. These policies and programs are not geographically neutral in their consequences. Yet, these geographic consequences are given only secondary consideration in the formulation and the conduct of federal macro policies. (2) Basic development programs that affect nonmetro areas. Among these are the Bureau of Land Management and the U.S. Corps of Engineers. The planning processes of these organizations involve nonmetro residents and units of government through a variety of public participation processes. However, the ultimate responsibility resides with the federal government. (3) Federal, state, and local grant-in-aid assistance programs that mandate and/or sponsor nonmetro planning activities. The growth of these programs and the directive nature of their planning requirements have been a major influence and source of federal involvement in nonmetro planning.

Historically, federal development activities have always involved some degree of public planning. In the early years of the Republic, this planning largely consisted of policy decisions associated with acquiring large tracts of continental territory, giving transportation subsidies, providing military protection, operating the postal service, establishing immigration policies, and creating land distribution procedures. Within this broad context, the private sector was given the balance of development responsibilities. These early development activities of the federal government were heavily financed by the sales or gifts of public lands. However, by the end of the nineteenth century, with the closing of the frontier, it became necessary to use other financing techniques. This change marks the beginning of the modern era of public planning.

New financing methods were introduced as early as 1887 with the passage of the Hatch Act (Advisory Commission on Intergovernmental Relations, hereafter ACIR, 1978: 15). This act made annual $15,000 cash grants available to states for the creation and operation of agricultural experiment stations. As the cash-grant approach was expanded into other activities, qualifications were imposed for the receipt and use of these federal funds. Many current federal planning and administrative requirements are direct outgrowths of similar requirements in these early federal nonmetro development assistance programs. For example, the Hatch Act of 1887 was amended in 1894 to permit federal audits of the agricultural experiment station grants by the secretary of agriculture. The Weeks Act of 1911, to promote state forestry, was the first federal program in which funds were allocated according to an administratively determined discretionary formula. This was also the first grant-in-aid program in which advance approval of state plans was required prior to the disbursement of federal funds. The Smith-Lever Act of 1914 established the Agricultural Extension Service, and the Smith-Hughes Act of 1917 created detailed planning and administrative requirements for the extension activities. These two acts and the Highway Act of 1916 mark the introduction of modern practices in which federal grant-in-aid assistance is coupled with federal planning and administrative requirements.

The Depression marks the beginning of an era of expanded public planning. Early in the first administration of Franklin Roosevelt, the National Resources Planning Board was created. This board was responsible for some of the nation's first strategic and comprehensive planning efforts--efforts that identified many of the basic public issues to be confronted during the following four decades. These issues included the need to coordinate federal programs, questions about the division of development authorities and responsibilities among the various levels of

government, the need for regional commissions, the role
of multicounty planning districts, and the substance of
comprehensive planning activities.

Since 1933, the federal government has created many
different federal institutions and programs to provide both
states and localities with developmental and remedial assistance. In the aggregate, these programs now dispense
almost $80 billion annually (Table 21.1). Some of these
institutions, such as the Environmental Protection Agency,
serve all population groups and all geographic areas. Others, such as the Farmers Home Administration, the Appalachian Regional Commission, and the Economic Development Administration, are limited to specific geographic areas and
specific populations. As these programs have been created,
corresponding federal administrative and planning requirements have been imposed on metro and nonmetro institutions.

The Advisory Commission on Intergovernmental Relations
(ACIR) has traced the expansion of the federal planning
requirements and planning assistance programs. This is
graphically represented in Table 21.2 for the fifteen-year
period of 1962-77. In 1978, ACIR analyzed the nature of
these federal planning assistance programs and found that:
there are forty federal planning assistance programs; planning activities are funded with federal dollars in community
and economic development, environmental protection, transportation, energy, social services, public safety, and
general policy development and management; the A-95 federal
aid review and comment process applies to about 200 federal
aid programs available to state and local governments;
planning requirements have been attached to approximately
150 federal aid programs; of the 150 federal programs that
require planning about 100 require state plans, 20 require
areawide or local plans, and 30 require both state and
local plans; and, approximately 70 of the 150 programs
requiring plans are concerned with physical development.

The ACIR concluded that "plans have very real locational
and territorial implications concerning the impact of federal aid (and in some cases, direct federal activities as
well). These effects, of course, are major components of
the federal influence on the nation's growth and development" (White House Conference, 1978b: 292).

At present the federal government has no policy or
administrative machinery that coordinates these individual
planning programs. Consequently, there is substantial policy and administrative confusion in the conduct of the
federally sponsored nonmetro planning efforts (see the last

Table 21.1. Federal Aid to State and Local Governments in 1965, 1970, 1975, and 1978

Type of Aid, Function, and Major Program	1965 (000,000s)	1970 (000,000s)	1975 (000,000s)	1978 (000,000s)
Total grant-in-aid shared revenue	$10,904	$24,018	$49,832	$77,889
National defense	33	37	74	60
International affairs and finance	4	5	**	**
Natural resources and environment	182	429	2,436	3,898
Energy	9	25	43	180
Agriculture	517	603	404	426
Transportation	4,100	4,539	5,864	8,837
Commerce and housing credit	*	6	8	13
Community and regional development	689	2,428	2,842	7,078
Education, employment, training, and social services	981	5,745	12,131	20,557
Health	624	3,850	8,810	12,725
Income security	3,530	5,813	9,389	13,782
Veterans benefits and services	8	18	32	76
Administration of justice	0	42	725	572
General government	13	49	101	164
General purpose fiscal assistance	214	430	6,971	9,523

Source: U.S. Bureau of the Census, Statistical Abstract of the United States: 1979, Table 481, p. 290.
*The amount was less than $500,000.
**Funds for this function are now provided to a private institution.

Table 21.2. Planning Assistance Programs in 1962, 1972, and 1977

1962	1972	1977
1. Urban Planning Assistance	1. Comprehensive Planning Assistance	1. Comprehensive Planning Assistance
2. Community Renewal Program	2. Neighborhood Development Program	2. Community Development Block Grant
3. Advances for Public Works Planning	3. Model Cities	3. Highways
4. Highways	4. Advances for Public Works Planning	4. Urban Mass Transportation
	5. Highways	5. Airport Systems
	6. Urban Mass Transportation	6. Area Economic Development
	7. Airport Systems	7. Appalachian Development
	8. Area Economic Development	8. Rural Development
	9. Appalachian Development	9. Multistate Economic Development
	10. Rural Development	10. Coastal Zone Management
	11. Air Quality	11. Air Quality
	12. Solid Waste	12. Solid Waste
	13. Water Quality	13. Water Quality
	14. Comprehensive Health	14. Health Systems
	15. Manpower	15. Aging
	16. Community Action	16. Social Services
	17. Law Enforcement	17. Manpower
		18. Community Action
		19. Law Enforcement

Source: Advisory Commission on Intergovernmental Relations, The Role of Federal Planning Assistance Programs and Requirements in National Growth and Development: A Background Paper for the White House Conference on Balanced Growth and Economic Development.

sections of this chapter). To a large extent, the federal
planning programs operate through other units of government.
The following sections describe the planning institutions
at the multistate, state, substate, and local levels of
government.

MULTISTATE PLANNING INSTITUTIONS

Many development challenges extend past the traditional
boundaries of individual states. Thus, to address these
issues effectively it has been necessary to create a number
of multistate development institutions and programs.

Some development situations absolutely require joint
planning and action by two or more states, and often the
federal government as well, if specific problems are to be
treated. An example of such a problem is flood control of a
river that flows through two or more states. Other development issues, such as poverty in areas like Appalachia, may
not absolutely require multistate planning and action,
although joint approaches are often desirable because many
issues can be addressed more economically and effectively
than would otherwise be possible.

The principal multistate institutions that have been
created to facilitate planning and action, often with the
federal government, include: the Tennessee Valley Authority
(TVA); the Appalachian Regional Commission (ARC); the ten
regional action commissions (Title Vs); the approximately
160 interstate compacts including the two special river
basin compacts (Delaware River Basin Compact and the Susquehanna River Basin Compact); the six Title II basic commissions; and the numerous multistate policy boards and
coalitions. These organizations are engaged primarily in
functional planning and limited purpose activities--although
some multistate organizations such as TVA and ARC have
responsibilities in several functional areas.

The Tennessee Valley Authority (TVA)

The TVA is a unique public planning and development
institution. It was created in the 1930s as a prototype
organization, but remains the only such organization in the
United States. Its geographic coverage includes parts of
seven southern states. The TVA was originally an experiment
in public planning and a public organization for flood
control, navigation, power generation, recreation, and
general development.

The TVA operates twenty-eight dams, a network of 650
miles of waterways recreation facilities, and 10 percent of
the installed electric generating capacity existing in the
United States. It is engaged primarily in functional planning for flood control, navigation, and power generation
(Academy for Contemporary Problems, 1979: 29). TVA has
created small-scale comprehensive plans for these three
areas.

TVA's success in both its public planning efforts and
its operations can be attributed generally to the following
characteristics. The organization has both strong political
support and a strong financial base. The electric generation
facilities of TVA are financed by private debt instruments;
thus, TVA is not in competition for publicly allocated
resources. The TVA Board sets rates without review by state
utility boards and, therefore, it can guarantee adequate
returns to bondholders. The area served is sufficiently
large to facilitate economies of scale, thus reducing costs
to consumers--which strengthens the political base. Because
TVA has sufficient funds to hire and maintain a competent
technical, planning, and managerial staff, the level of
service has been high, and its quality has been translated
into broad public support that in turn generates political
support. Also, the board that governs the organization is
relatively autonomous and is composed of three individuals
appointed by the president to nine-year terms.

In the functional fields in which TVA plans, duplication
has been limited. TVA, by its size and authority, has been
able to dominate and/or lead in related planning and operational activities in the area it serves.

The Appalachian Regional Commission (ARC)

The ARC is another innovative experiment in public
planning and intervention. It was created in 1965 to assist
in the development of parts of eleven and finally thirteen
states that are wholly or partially in the Appalachian
mountain range. This area of the nation is nonmetro in
character and has long been crippled by chronic poverty,
unemployment, poor housing, inadequate health facilities,
limited recreation facilities, an inadequate education
system, and a minimal transportation infrastructure.

The commission is governed by the thirteen governors
and a federal representative who reports to the president.
The approval of a majority of the governors and the federal
representative is needed for action to be taken. The basic
activities of the commission have focused on the improvement

of the planning and development capabilities of state and
local governments; reduction of environmental problems
peculiar to mining areas; provision of financing for the
Appalachian Highway System and provision of funds for selected activities such as child development, education,
health, public housing, and conservation activities.

The planning for the Appalachian highway network has
essentially involved the participant states in political
and technical processes of defining transportation goals
and objectives within the confines of limited resources and
the allocated monies received from the federal government.
Over time, planning for other functions has been attempted,
but it is essentially a political ritual for dividing limited federal monies among the participant states. Thus,
except for the highway programs, planning and program activities of ARC have served as a form of block grants and/
or revenue sharing for member states.

The Regional Action Commissions (Title Vs)

After the creation of the ARC, similar organizations
for other parts of the nation were authorized by Title V of
the Public Works and Economic Development Act of 1965.
Originally these institutions were confined to nonmetro
areas, but subsequently the federal government permitted
the boundaries to be expanded statewide. These organizations' peculiar, and perhaps even dysfunctional, geographic
coverage is outlined in Figure 21.1. The organizations
differ from the ARC in two significant respects: the federal representative of these organizations reports to the
secretary of commerce rather than to the president and
funding for the Title Vs has always been anemic.

In the mid-1960s many governors were initially attracted
to this institutional form because of federal assurances
that the Title Vs would serve as conduits for federal revenue sharing with the states. However, other approaches
such as block grants and direct revenue sharing were in-
stituted and proved to be less cumbersome and more popular.

The Title Vs were stunted in their development almost
from inception because of limited funding. At present, the
commissions, in the aggregate, dispense less than $70 mil-
lion annually. Approximately one-half of the funds are
supplemental to other federal categorical programs. The
balance of the funds is distributed as federal block grants
for state and local planning, research, and technical
assistance.

Instead of preparing strategic, comprehensive or even

Dates represent when Commissions were organized.

U.S. DEPARTMENT OF COMMERCE   5/28/80

Figure 21.1 Economic Development Regions

limited functional plans, these organizations are primarily
forums for discussions of developmental issues and used, to
a very limited degree, for the distribution of small amounts
of federal funds to state planning and program groups. Unlike the experiences of TVA in taming an uncontrollable
river or ARC with its regional transportation problem, the
member states of the Title V commission have addressed few
joint issues that could sustain a common focus for planning,
action or political support. Thus, these entities continue
to exist more for their future promise than for past
accomplishment.

The Compact Commissions

Compact commissions exemplify a versatile institutional
approach to multistate planning and development for specialized nonmetro challenges that transcend the boundaries
of two or more states. A compact is a formal, legal agreement among states providing a basis for intergovernmental
joint action on prescribed functions and activities. The
administration of these compacts may or may not include
permanent staff.

There are three types of compact commissions: (1) those
to which the federal government is a signatory part, (2)
those requiring the consent of Congress, but to which the
federal government is not a party, and (3) those that do
not require action by the federal government.

More than 160 compacts have been formed for a variety
of development purposes. There are interstate compacts on
bridges, ports, water allocations, flood control, pollution
abatement, education, taxation, regional planning, and
parks and law enforcement. Some examples of the interstate
compacts that currently exist include: the Great Lakes
Regional Commission, created to provide information and
advice for regional water resources management in the Great
Lakes basin; the Interstate Oil Compact Commission that
conserves physical waste of oil and gas reserves in producing states (previously, it played a major role in determining production levels among the oil and gas producing
states); the Interstate Pest Control Compact that estab-
lishes a multistate pest control insurance fund; the Interstate Sanitation Commission that controls and abates existing and future water pollution in the states of Connecticut,
New Jersey, and New York; the Multistate Tax Commission
that provides information and assistance to multistate
taxpayers; the New England Compact on Radiological Health
Protection that promotes the radiological health protection

of the public within the participating states in New England; the Southern Interstate Nuclear Board that assists southern states in the acquisition and utilization of nuclear energy resources; and the Tennessee-Tombigbee Waterway Development Authority that assists in the planning and development of a navigable interstate waterway connecting the Tombigbee and Tennessee rivers.

The federal government is not a signatory party to the overwhelming majority of the more than 160 existing interstate compacts. It is, however, a signatory party to two prominent river basin compact commissions--the Delaware River Basin and the Susquehanna River Basin compacts.

The Delaware River Basin Compact includes the federal government and the states of New York, Pennsylvania, New Jersey, and Delaware. This compact, created in 1961, is authorized within a set of prescribed limits to develop laws and policies for water conservation, control, and use and management.

The Susquehanna River Basin Compact of 1970 has as signatory parties the federal government and the states of New York, New Jersey, and Pennsylvania. The compact permits the Susquehanna River Basin Commission to perform the same services as provided by the Delaware Commission with the exception of floodplain management and related services.

Compacts are flexible, multistate public planning tools. Institutionally, within broad constitutional limits, compacts can be structured to meet the needs of all parties. Available powers and responsibilities are sufficiently broad to permit great latitude in program development. Compacts can be useful forums for integrating federal and state programs into coherent functional plans. The delegation of authority to such compacts by participants and the subsequent negotiation requirements help to create strategies and an interactive process between states and federal agencies that often does not exist otherwise.

Title II River Basin Commissions

The Water Resources Planning Act of 1965 created a national resources council to oversee federal water policy. River basin commissions were authorized in Title II of the act, and are generally known as "Title IIs" (see Figure 21.2). These commissions are major planning entities affecting water development in nonmetro areas. Six of these commissions have been formed and given the power to plan and set priorities. They coordinate activities of involved

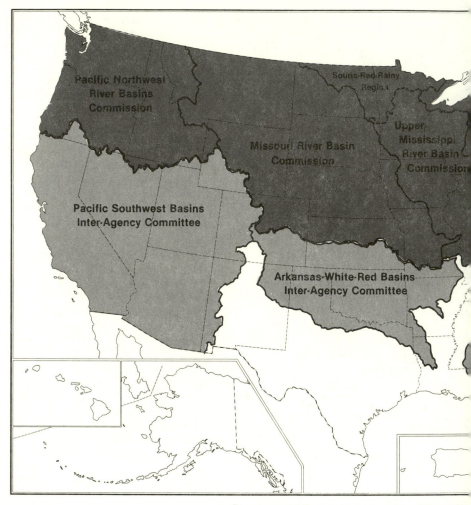

Regional Water Resources Plannin

Source: U. S. Water Resources Council

Figure 21.2 Regional Water Resources Planning Entities

reat Lakes Basin
Commission

New England
River Basins
Commission*

Ohio River Basin
Commission

Delaware River
Basin
Commission

Susquehanna
River Basin
Commission

Southeast Basins
Inter-Agency
Committee

*The New York State portion of the Lake
Champlain drainage area and the
Westchester County, N.Y., portion of the
Long Island Sound drainage area are
outside official NERBC boundaries, but
are included in NERBC plans.

Entities

water development agencies, but have no regulatory or operational functions.

Unlike the Delaware and Susquehanna River compacts that have one federal appointee, these Title II commissions have several federal representatives. Any agency with a substantive interest in water-related matters is eligible to be a member of a Title II commission. The chairmen of these commissions, who function as chief executive officers, are appointed by the president. These organizations serve primarily as forums for a planning process.

Multistate Policy Boards and Coalitions

The majority of the existing multistate organizations, compacts, and commissions have been created for very specific or limited functional purposes. Consequently, there is a need for multistate bodies through which the governors can identify and integrate multiple issues and programs into overall multistate development objectives, strategies, and policies. Within the past ten years, a number of such formal organizations have been created. They are forums for broad-based planning for multistate action. The principal ones are the Southern Growth Policies Board, the Council of Northeastern Governors, the Western Governors' Policy Office, and the High Plains Study Council. Because these are still relatively new organizations with limited experiences, it is too early to analyze their impact. However, their mere creation manifests state recognition of the need for regional action and a frustration with other multistate institutional approaches.

STATE NONMETROPOLITAN PLANNING

State governments exert influences on nonmetro planning in three basic ways. First, the conception, planning, and administration of overall state policies, as with federal macro policies, directly influence nonmetro areas. Presently thirty-six states have some form of state planning and almost all states have state-level policy-planning processes.

Second, state governments serve as a conduit for federal funds. In 1977 the value of these federal funds administered by state governments was almost $46 billion (U.S. Bureau of the Census, 1979: 300). These funds were used by state governments to support planning and to finance specific programs. For example: the HUD small cities 701 planning

assistance program is administered by the state governments;
states administer transportation funds from the U.S. Department of Transportation; and states manage the Comprehensive Training and Employment Act funds (CETA) for nonmetro areas. Thus, states exert important planning and
program influences on nonmetro development.

Finally, the state governments manage state programs
and regulatory activities that influence nonmetro development. The total value of these state-financed programs was
almost $150 billion in 1977 (U.S. Bureau of the Census,
1979: 300). Although many of these programs are directly
administered by state agencies, much of this funding is
transferred to local governments through state grant-in-aid
financing.

The ACIR in 1976 conducted a survey of state and local
officials to determine their perception of the influence of
the state grant-in-aid programs in local planning, program
priorities, and actual expenditures (ACIR, 1977: 63). The
ACIR concluded: local officials view local decision making
as greatly impacted by state grants; almost one-half of the
responding city officials and almost three-fourths of the
county officials indicated that they would use state aid
differently if they were at liberty to do so; almost 80
percent of the city and county officials indicated that
they would like to make moderate or substantial realloca-
tions of their state aid; more than 50 percent of the respondents thought that state grants were influencing the
spending of local funds—about 67 percent of the respondents thought that this influence was stimulative in nature
rather than substitutive; and, more than 50 percent of the
city officials thought that their cities would have used
their local matching funds for other purposes if state
grants were discontinued, while almost 67 percent of the
county officials expressed this view. States are thus ex-
erting a major influence on local budget priorities and
the planning of both state and local activities for both
metro and nonmetro areas.

Perhaps as important as any power is the state responsibility for determining the boundaries and the authorities
of subordinate units of government. This state role exerts
fundamental influence not only on planning institutions but
also on the resulting substance of planning and conduct of
programs.

SUBSTATE MULTIUNIT PLANNING INSTITUTIONS

As with multistate issues, many local issues and concerns
extend past the boundaries of individual communities or
counties. To address these issues it is often desirable or
even necessary for two or more units of government to
jointly plan and take action. Almost 4,400 such multiunit
institutions at the substate level now exist (U.S. Bureau
of the Census, 1978: 1). A majority of these institutions
include all or parts of nonmetro areas.

These multiunit institutions can be divided into two
reasonably distinct governmental forms (U.S. Bureau of the
Census, 1978: 1). The first one to be described is the
special service district, of which there are approximately
2,418, and the second is the areawide or multijurisdictional
institution that numbers approximately 1,900.

Special Service Districts

In 1972 the census identified 2,418 special service
districts that served two or more counties. These districts
are generally either quasi- or wholly public organizations
providing specific services for geographic areas usually
bounded within counties. These districts provide such fundamental services as water supply, fire protection, sewers,
housing and urban renewal, flood control, highways, health
services and hospital facilities, libraries, drainage,
irrigation/water control, parks and recreation, electric
power generation/distribution, natural gas supply, and
transit authorities.

These organizations have widely varying forms of restrictions placed on their powers and operation. Restrictions usually involve the purposes of the organizations,
the methods by which the institutions are created, and the
manner in which the governing boards are selected. The
states establish the procedure for the creation of and the
limits for operation of special service districts. Often,
limitations are narrowed further by the local governments
that actually create the majority of the special districts.
These organizations are often the only means to provide
such services due to state or local legal or financial
constraints and, as such, they are effective for provision
of needed services.

The local or state governmental units responsible for
the creation of special districts, generally, are responsible for either appointing those persons who will govern
and administer the districts or determining the method for

their selection. In 1967, approximately 50 percent of the
officers of special purpose districts were elected (U.S.
Bureau of the Census, 1978: 1).

Multijurisdictional Institutions ⚹

Within the past twenty years, a relatively new form of
organization has appeared at the multicounty level in both
the metro and nonmetro areas--the areawide or multijurisdictional organization. These organizations are sponsored
by local, state, and federal governments. They are engaged
in a variety of development and technical assistance efforts
including public planning, program coordination, and even
the operation of select programs such as manpower training,
criminal justice, water quality, economic development,
transportation, and human resource development. The U.S.
Bureau of the Census, in an August 1978 report, Regional
Organizations, defined individual organizations as multijurisdictional if they have the following three organizational attributes: (1) They possess governmental characteristics (e.g., creation by statute or other public act,
public funding, and performance of governmentlike activities) but are not currently classified by the Bureau of the
Census as a government or as part of a government. (2) They
are multijurisdictional--that is, composed of or serving
more than one local jurisdiction. (3) They are involved
primarily with planning rather than direct delivery of
public services. Some organizations, however, both plan
and deliver services.

There are approximately 1,900 multijurisdictional organizations in the United States. As a further distinction,
the Census Bureau differentiates between 675 general-purpose
and 1,257 special-purpose multijurisdictional organizations.

The term "general-purpose organization" as defined by
the Bureau of the Census, includes a number of independent
institutions such as the substate regional planning councils, the Councils of Governments, Economic Development
Districts (see Figure 21.3), Planning District Commissions,
and Regional Planning Commissions. General-purpose organizations are usually created under joint provisions of state
and federal legislation and are staffed by representatives
from local governments. Directors are local government
leaders or appointees. The organizations are often funded
by specific federal development programs either wholly or
in part.

An example of a general-purpose organization is the
Southern Oklahoma Development Association. This organization

Source: U.S. Department of Commerce.

Figure 21.3 Economic Development Districts

Wisconsin

nesota

Iowa

Illinois

Michigan

Indiana

Ohio

New York

Pennsylvania

New Jersey

Delaware

Maryland

N. H.
Vermont
Mass.
R.I.
Connecticut

Maine

Missouri

Kentucky

Tennessee

W.
Virginia

Virginia

N. Carolina

Arkansas Mississippi

Louisiana

Alabama

Georgia

S. Carolina

Florida

PUERTO
RICO

VIRGIN
ISLANDS

in southern Oklahoma is directed by a board composed of
municipal and county representatives from ten counties as
well as representatives from the private sector. This particular organization operates a diverse array of economic
development, community development, health planning, and
education- and training-related planning and service programs. Funding for the organization is provided from agencies such as the Economic Development Administration, the
state of Oklahoma, and contributions from local communities
and the ten counties.

The existing 675 general-purpose organizations such as
the Southern Oklahoma Development Association are engaged
primarily in multijurisdictional planning, program coordination, and policy review activities in fields such as employment, criminal justice, water quality, economic development, transportation, and human services. These general-
purpose, multijurisdictional organizations are often able
to transcend the geographic, institutional, financial, and
staff limitations of the numerous smaller units of government they serve, and thus facilitate intergovernmental
cooperation, problem identification, and area planning
otherwise not possible.

Special-purpose organizations are engaged primarily in
multijurisdictional planning, coordination, and, in some
cases, delivery of services in a single functional or problem area such as aging or health. The 1,257 special-purpose
organizations have been created generally in response to
either federal legislation or federal administrative requirements mandating the existence of such organizations
(U.S. Bureau of the Census, 1978: 1). Members of the governing boards are selected to represent specific populations being served or specific professions and are not
usually drawn from government service.

The major examples of special-purpose institutions are:
Health Systems Agencies (HSAs); Water Quality Management
Agencies that develop areawide wastewater treatment management plans; Area Agencies on the Aging (AAAs) that plan
and, in some cases, provide services for the aging programs
funded by the public sector; Community Action Agencies
(CAAs) used by the Federal Community Services Administration to involve clientele groups in the planning, operation,
and evaluation of antipoverty efforts; and Criminal Justice
Planning Agencies that develop, organize, implement, and
evaluate multijurisdictional criminal justice systems.

The Census Bureau survey reveals the following information about the 675 general-purpose and 1,257 special-

purpose planning organizations: (1) The overwhelming majority of these organizations are relatively recent cre-
ations. Approximately 91 percent were established after
1964--85 percent of the general-purpose and 95 percent of
the special-purpose organizations, respectively. (2) The
method of establishment varies. Of the 1,567 respondents to
the census questionnaire, 818 reported that they were established under private, nonprofit incorporation statutes.
Of these, 95 percent are special-purpose organizations.
Approximately 82 percent of the general-purpose organizations were created under specific state or local authori-
zation such as enabling legislation, executive order or
voluntary agreements. (3) The governing boards of general-
purpose and special-purpose organizations differ substantially, particularly with respect to local government
representation. Sixty-eight percent of the governing board
members of general-purpose organizations are elected or
appointed local government officials. Special-purpose
organizations are governed by boards of which 62 percent of
the members are drawn from target populations and other
nongovernment sources. The Census Bureau report notes that
this probably reflects special federal requirements. (4)
There are substantial differences in local funding of
general and special purpose districts. Approximately 73
percent of the general-purpose organizations receive continuing public funding; only 9 percent of the special-
purpose organizations have such continuing support.

General-purpose organizations are heavily engaged in
the provision of grantsman assistance and administrative
assistance to overburdened local government officials. Only
rarely are they involved in local strategic planning processes or in the preparation of comprehensive and/or functional plans. Because many of the activities of these organizations are oriented to the receipt and administration
of federal and state funds, their planning is often shaped
by federal and state funding programs.

A 1977 General Accounting Office evaluation, Federally
Assisted Areawide Planning: Need to Simplify Policies and
Practices, concluded (pp. 1-3) that the use of areawide
organizations to plan or coordinate planning has not been
entirely effective up to the present primarily because: (1)
Programs were initiated haphazardly over a period of years
to satisfy isolated needs or demands without regard for the
larger framework in which the program was operative. Each
program built its own constituency at the state, areawide
or local level, which made it difficult for state and local

governments to integrate the programs into a coordinated
planning effort. (2) Federal agencies often ignored the
state-designated planning agency and set up separate planning groups for different geographic areas. (3) States
sometimes disregarded their own planning subdivisions in
implementing federal programs. (4) Federal agencies have
conflicting requirements that create impediments to coordinated planning and make it difficult for one planning
organization to satisfy all federal requirements.

Not included in the General Accounting Office report is
a recognition that the federal agencies often provide little
assistance to the general-purpose organizations after they
have been created, other than provision of annual funding.
The demands made by the federal agency often have less to
do with planning and delivery of services than with attempts
to use these entities as agency advocates with the Congress,
administration, and the states. This lack of attention by
the sponsoring federal agencies to activities such as creation of improved planning techniques, ongoing training
of staff, provision of technical assistance support, and
rigorous periodic evaluations is not without cost to the
quality of these nonmetro planning programs.

RESOURCE CONSERVATION AND DEVELOPMENT DISTRICTS

The Resource Conservation and Development Districts are
influential nonmetro planning and development organizations.
The primary stated purpose of these districts is the improvement of local economies and the environment through
conservation, development, and improved use of local resources. This program, created in 1964, includes 178
institutions--almost all of which are multicounty (U.S.
Department of Agriculture, 1978: iii). Approximately 1,200
nonmetro counties are involved in this effort. These entities are directed through a district council membership
composed of principal public and private leaders from the
areas served. The council is a forum for discussion and
identification of long-term development objectives and the
definition of roles of the various participants in the
achievement of mutually determined goals. The council objectives are regularly submitted for approval to the governors of the involved states and used by state planning
agencies.

The planning and coordination activities and the involvement of local public and private leadership infuses

these organizations with an influence over a diverse set of
programs that is disproportionately greater than the negligible resources provided for their use through the Department of Agriculture.

THE LOCAL GOVERNMENT PLANNING EXPERIENCE

Local public planning has a long and often distinguished
history that predates many federal and state grant-in-aid
programs with their planning and administrative requirements. Today much of this planning is still focused on
local public administration needs--although a lot of attention is increasingly directed toward the grant-in-aid
requirements.

Herrington J. Bryce, in Planning in Small Cities,
analyzes the current state of planning in cities with a
population of 10,000 to 100,000--many of which are in the
nonmetro category. Based on a survey of 550 small cities
and on other available information, Bryce concludes (pp.
47-65): (1) Many small cities lack planning resources. (2)
Of those cities approximately 80 percent are engaged in
planning for capital improvements; zoning and subdivision;
recreation and open space; water and sewer; garbage disposal; streets, roads, and highways; and public safety. (3)
Planning is generally conducted by city planning departments
or specialized departments. Small city planning departments
are primarily responsible for land-use planning, zoning,
and subdivision planning. (4) Small cities infrequently
have primary planning responsibilities for mass transit,
education, manpower programs, health, welfare, and social
services. Of the cities surveyed by Bryce, only 35 percent
had such responsibilities. (5) Although cities with a declining economic base indicate that economic planning and
housing are their highest priorities, about one-half of
them do not have primary responsibility for these areas.
Consequently, Bryce concludes, "In this respect, they have
limited ability to plan their own future" (p. 66).

Communities with a population of less than 10,000 generally are unable to afford public planning staffs. In
recognition of this reality, the federal government has
made monies available for all small cities and towns to
support comprehensive and functional planning activities.
The primary sources of federal support for comprehensive
planning by the small local governments are the Department
of Housing and Urban Development (HUD) 701 program, the

Economic Development Administration (EDA) 302 program, and
the Farmers Home Administration Section 111 program. However, each of these has only limited funds to assist the
thousands of eligible local governments. The aggregate
value of the funds is less than $75 million annually. In
theory, small cities and towns can use revenue sharing
funds or community development block grants for comprehensive planning activities. In reality, the funds received by
many of the smaller communities from block grants and
revenue sharing can only be described as miniscule. Local
planning in nonmetro areas is limited by lack of funds and
is thus increasingly dependent on multijurisdictional units
for this basic function.

SELECTED NONMETROPOLITAN PLANNING ISSUES

The conduct of nonmetro planning is influenced by a number
of distinct institutional, political, and technical issues.
Some of the more pertinent of these will be briefly reviewed, including: the changing objectives of public intervention; incoherence in the intergovernmental grant-in-aid system; institutional capacities of nonmetro planning bodies;
the state government role; the training of nonmetro planners; issues of scale; growth issues; and regional variations.

THE CHANGING OBJECTIVES OF PUBLIC INTERVENTION

Over time the objectives of government interventions in the
economy have shifted their focus, and this has implications
for public planning. In the early years of the nation, the
focus of public interventions, particularly in nonmetro
areas, was economic efficiency--settle the lands, increase
production, and expand the nation's economic base. Beginning with the first administration of President Franklin
Roosevelt, government interventions increasingly emphasized
economic and social equity--the sharing of income, wealth,
and equal access to opportunities for individuals, groups,
and even geographic areas. This was of basic importance to
the nonmetro residents in regions such as the South. In the
past two decades, government interventions also have come
to stress quality-of-life considerations such as environmental protection, worker safety, and product reliability.

There is a close interdependence among these three objectives. The pursuit of one often requires trade-offs with
the other two. For example, to improve the environment by
totally stopping the use of coal may result in the closing
of factories, the loss of employment opportunities for
individuals, and also putting workers in nonmetro parts of
Appalachia out of work.

The resolution of conflicts among these three objectives
is a technically complex and politically sensitive task. It
is compounded by the existing policy and administrative
disorder found in the public programs, and further hampered
by the rise of single-issue advocate groups. However, the
creation and implementation of processes that can make such
reconciliations is now one of the most important functions
of public planning given the size, scope, and influence of
government interventions in the economy.

INCOHERENCE IN THE INTERGOVERNMENTAL GRANT-IN-AID SYSTEM

The intergovernmental grant-in-aid system is in structural
and administrative disarray. This disorder imposes planning
and administrative burdens on all levels of government,
particularly those in nonmetro areas where there are limited planning and administrative capabilities.

The structural and procedural disorder in the grant-
in-aid system is particularly acute at the federal and
state levels. Federal and state development assistance
programs are distinguished by their fragmentation, conflicting program procedures, divergent delivery systems,
and a lack of congruence between authorities and responsibilities.

The policy and administrative incoherence at the federal
and state program levels is transmitted to the local governments through the disordered regulations and grant-in-aid
requirements, and results in administrative confusion, excessive burdens, barriers to private sector involvement,
impeded abilities of local areas to pool resources from
multiple sources, and disorientation in local priority
setting processes.

The problems at the federal and state levels derive
from several sources. Most important is the fact that neither the federal nor state governments operate in the context of overall goals and objectives. This permits individual agencies to preside over management and control processes that often result in very different versions of

national, state, and local development objectives. Too
often, these agency perceptions become clouded and mis-
directed by parochial, political, bureaucratic, and ideological considerations that reflect agency needs rather
than client needs.

In a more narrow sense, at all levels of government,
the creation of functional plans--for specific areas such
as health, education, recreation, transportation, training
or provision of water and wastewater infrastructure--is
impeded by the extensive fragmentation and duplication in
the federal and state programs. For example, there are
seven separate federal water and sewage treatment programs,
each of which is operated independently. These separate
programs have different legislative and administrative
criteria, different planning requirements and funding
cycles, and they often use different local planning units.
To take joint funding under these circumstances is most
difficult and expensive for local governments.

Another example is the CETA program. Although federal
manpower programs were simplified in 1973 through the consolidation of several federally sponsored programs into
a block grant approach, the functional area of manpower
training is still plagued by fragmentation problems. In May
1979 the General Accounting Office (GAO) released a report
on federally assisted manpower programs that included a
case study of the manpower programs in Tidewater, Virginia
(General Accounting Office, hereafter GAO, 1979: i). The
GAO found that in fiscal year 1977 this area had forty-four
federally assisted employment and training programs dis-
pensing a total of $24.2 million. The programs involved
five federal departments, three independent federal agencies, one federal regional council, twenty-six national
organizations and state agencies, and more than fifty local
administering agencies. The local administering organizations received only approximately two-thirds of these
funds. The GAO concluded: "No federal, state or local
organization was responsible for coordinating all of the
(manpower) programs" (GAO, 1979: i).

As these two examples illustrate, the reconciliation
of multiple management and control planning processes is
a major obstacle to creation of functional plans. These
examples are paradigms for virtually every area in which
the public sector's grant-in-aid programs are operative.

Numerous techniques have been used to focus the individual agency management and control planning processes
into functional and even limited comprehensive plans.

The most notable of these federal efforts include: interagency task forces of technicians assigned to homogenize
planning and program requirements; interagency agreements;
Office of Management and Budget program simplification
efforts; creation and use of the A-95 intergovernment
review process; assignment of convening authorities by
Executive Order; assignment of coordinating responsibilities by legislation including the Public Works and Economic Development Act of 1965 as amended (Title V), the
Housing Act of 1970, and the Rural Development Act of 1972;
and, creation of an Under Secretaries' Working Group, later
succeeded by the Assistant Secretaries' Interagency Coordinating Committee.

One promising coordination reform is the Joint Funding
Simplification Act of 1974 (Public Law 93-510). The objective of this legislation is to allow state and local governments, as well as private, nonprofit organizations,
to use federal assistance more effectively by drawing on
resources from more than one federal program to achieve a
common purpose or a single goal.

Since the enactment of this legislation in 1974 until
1978, only ten projects were conducted under these authorities. An evaluation of the act by the Office of Management
and Budget (OMB) in 1979 concluded (pp. 1-2) that although
those few projects already conducted were successful, there
has been only limited use of these authorities because: (1)
The act is permissive and OMB did not provide adequate or
timely leadership, support, and supervision to assure aggressive compliance by federal agencies. (2) There is widespread ignorance of the act at both the federal and regional
levels. (3) The federal agencies were not committed to implementing joint findings and did not relate to their own
program objectives.

The OMB assessment also noted that although there were
statutory and administrative barriers to the implementation
of the act, these problems were correctable. If such approaches are to be effective not only is a more competent
federal government required, but also more competent state
and local governments.

The status of the planning and administration of federal
assistance programs is best summarized in the President's
Reorganization Project report, Reorganization Study of
Local Development Assistance Programs (OMB, 1979: 10): "At
the present time, federal development assistance programs
are organized in a way that impedes the implementation of a
coherent development approach. In fact, the present system

diverges <u>from</u> <u>what</u> <u>is</u> needed <u>in</u> almost <u>every</u> respect." Much
of the disorder in nonmetro planning is simply a reflection
of this structural, procedural, and administrative chaos
that pervades the intergovernmental grant-in-aid system. If
major improvements are to be made at the nonmetro level,
substantive reforms must be made at the federal and state
levels.

INSTITUTIONAL CAPACITIES OF NONMETROPOLITAN PLANNING BODIES

Nonmetro planning is largely defined as the capacity of
public sector institutions to identify strategic objectives,
marshal a public consensus, and identify, secure, and manage
the necessary resources in a prudent, effective, and efficient manner. Often nonmetro planning and development
institutions are inadequate to this task.

There are numerous sources of this weakness. The most
fundamental is the existence in nonmetro areas of a disproportionate share of the nation's 80,000 units of government.
Although the nonmetro areas have about one-third of the
nation's population, they have 85 percent of the 3,042
county governments; 70 percent of the 18,000 municipalities;
67 percent of the 16,000 townships and towns; 67 percent of
the 26,000 local special districts and authorities; and 45
percent of the almost 2,000 substate multijurisdictional
districts (areawide planning bodies, Economic Development
Districts, etc.).

The existence of such a large number of governmental
units creates planning obstacles. Specifically, planning
coordination is made increasingly difficult as the number
of involved units increases. The fragmentation of authority
and responsibilities among multiple units of government
generates expensive administrative and bureaucratic burdens.
Also the fiscal base of individual units of government is
weakened. This, in turn, hampers governmental efforts to
employ and retain administrative and planning staff.

One of the primary means being used by federal, state,
and local governments to address these weaknesses is the
creation of areawide planning bodies. At present some of
the principal sponsors of such organizations include the
Farmers Home Administration, the Economic Development Administration, the Department of Housing and Urban Development, the Appalachian Regional Commission, and the Title V
Commissions.

Institutionally, these multijurisdictional entities

are past the organizational stage. They have generally
secured local support and have established at least working
relationships with federal and state agencies. For the
future, a number of basic capacity issues now seem pertinent, including the relationship among local, areawide,
state, and federal development plans. At present, the planning processes among these areawide and many federal and
state programs are only tenuously linked. Recently, HUD
and EDA have attempted to strengthen these linkages through
creation of experimental, three-year planning processes,
and the Farmers Home Administration in 1978-79 altered
their delivery system to an areawide configuration. But
it is still too early to assess the success and/or failure
of these efforts. Also relevant is the linkage between areawide plans and federal/state project investments. At present, areawide plans are often simply used as justifications
for scheduled project fundings from the federal and state
development assistance agencies. The quality of areawide
planning is also important. There is substantial evidence
from internal reviews of existing areawide plans, such as
EDA's Overall Economic Development Programs (OEDPs), that
substantive deficiencies exist. If such plans are to exert
more than a justification function for preconceived investments, not only will qualitative improvements be necessary,
but also a redefinition of the federal and state responsibilities in provision of staff and technical assistance
funds, training, and ongoing evaluations.

THE STATE GOVERNMENT ROLE

The state governments have a major effect on the shape of
nonmetro development. Increasingly, the states have come to
recognize the directive influences of their taxing, expenditure, regulatory, development, and service policies and
practices. Accordingly, virtually every state in the nation
has created state planning offices or planning process and/
or community affairs departments. Also, nearly every state
has a department or at least staff assigned to address
intergovernmental relations.
     Even with this progress made by the states in recog-
nizing and focusing their nonmetro development activities,
there are a number of issues that continue to merit attention. The first of these is the exclusion of the state
governments from the conduct of numerous federal programs.
For example, the HUD Small Cities Program, the development

grant and loan programs from the Farmers Home Administration, and the programs of the Economic Development Administration are conducted with only limited linkages to state planning and development efforts. In turn this results in minimizing the potentials of both the federal and state investment.

Another issue concerns the implicit lack of recognition by the administration of numerous federal government programs that there are differences among states in the allocation of powers among the various executive, legislative, and judicial branches. In many states, substantive policy, budgetary, and administrative functions are often exercised by legislatures, independently elected officials or independent boards. The provision of federal planning and development assistance must be made with a recognition of these realities. For example, the planning of many development-oriented manpower functions is often conducted by independently elected state school heads. Thus the provision of the planning funds for this should properly go to those agencies rather than to a governor's office. Also, consideration should be given to extending planning assistance to state legislatures from programs such as EDA, HUD, and FmHA. This will complement planning grants made to governor's offices. State legislatures are often the only place where an overview of all nonmetro development activities sponsored by the state is possible, yet many state legislatures are underfunded and understaffed. Given their role and importance, the investment of federal planning funds with state legislatures would foster improved state decision processes.

THE TRAINING OF NONMETROPOLITAN PLANNERS

Effective nonmetro planning programs are very dependent on the quality of nonmetro planners. At present nonmetro planning is given only secondary consideration in most planning curricula, and only minor attention in the federal development assistance programs. For example, the federal government expends over $80 billion annually through the grant-in-aid system, spends several hundred million dollars annually on sponsored planning programs, but makes virtually no investments to train and improve the quality of the planning staff at the state and local government level.

The principal source of federal training funds is the Intergovernment Personnel Act program of the Office of

Personnel Management. In the aggregate, for all of its
functions, this program has only approximately $20 million
available annually. However, individual agencies make some
limited funds available for training.

There are a number of fundamental issues that merit
future attention, including: strengthening the nonmetro
dimensions of planning training in academic institutions;
strengthening and expanding the training of existing practitioners; and linking training and evaluation activities.
At present the federal planning sponsors engage in virtually no ongoing evaluation activities. Such evaluations would
not only assist in improving planning programs, but they
would also serve as a basic learning tool for practitioners.

ISSUES OF SCALE

Issues of scale are those issues concerned with low demands
and high costs in the provision of public and private goods
and services. These affect nonmetro planning in two basic
ways. First, issues of scale are often the basis for altering the traditional division of responsibilities between
business and government. For example, although many traditional private sector services such as the operation
of ethnic restaurants cannot be profitably provided by the
private sector and may not be generally regarded as crucial
to nonmetro life, other services such as provision of health
care, electricity, and telephone services are critically
important. In these and other instances when the private
sector is unable to perform its traditional role, nonmetro
governments and residents must determine whether public
action is required and how it will be taken--subsidies for
the private business or the assumption of some or total
public responsibility for the direct provision of goods and
services (see Chapter 15). Planning plays a crucial role in
these determinations, both in the political decision processes and in the technical decisions for implementation.

The second way that issues of scale influence planning
is the need for careful consideration of the uses for limited nonmetro resources. This involves identifying available choices and consequences, exercising classic public
administration approaches after choices are made, and,
increasingly, taking grantsmanship actions associated
with securing external public funds.

Scale considerations also influence both the substance
and method of delivery of traditional public programs in

nonmetro areas. Often, federal or state subsidies for services such as rural water systems are necessary if the
service is to be provided at all or at a price level that
can be borne by nonmetro residents. Also, it is often impossible for many federal programs to deliver services to
nonmetro areas that are qualitatively similar to the services that are provided in metro areas. For example, although HUD can effectively use intermediaries (savings
and loan companies and commercial banks) for the provision
of housing funds in metro areas, this is often not done in
nonmetro areas either because such institutional funding
conduits do not exist or their capacity is insufficient.

GROWTH ISSUES

There is substantial evidence that growth is occurring in
numerous nonmetro areas (see Chapter 1), producing a number
of fundamental planning concerns and challenges. The first
and most obvious is the need to accommodate this growth and
prevent future blight conditions. Nonmetro areas must determine which public services are to be provided and how
they will be financed and administered.

Second, growth creates demands for land planning (see
Chapters 17 and 18). Growth processes have the potential
for substantial abuse of land and community resources in
nonmetro areas that will be difficult if not impossible to
correct. Land planning in the future must be concerned with
issues such as preservation of farmland, open space, foreign ownership, and the appropriateness of land use. This
planning will be controversial because it confronts the
balance between needs and rights of individuals and those
of the community. The subject is further complicated because of the mischievous but serious attempts of some urban
development advocates to create highly restrictive federal
and state nonmetro land-use requirements as a means to
divert future growth into urban areas. Achieving a balance
among the best uses of the land, the needs of nonmetro
areas, and the needs and rights of landowners is one of the
basic planning functions to be performed in the future.

REGIONAL VARIATIONS

There are substantial economic, social, institutional,
and demographic differences among regions of the South,

industrial Midwest, Northeast, and West. These differences must be both recognized and accommodated in nonmetro planning.

Nonmetro planning in the South must proceed with a recognition of several basic considerations. First, the nature, extent, and antecedents of southern underdevelopment must be identified. These antecedents, such as Reconstruction and the discrimination against blacks in the past, often are the source of many contemporary planning and development problems.

In spite of its recent progress, the South still continues to have the largest concentration of poor people in the nation--43 percent of the total. It has almost 35 percent of its residents in nonmetro areas who equal over two-thirds of the nation's nonmetro poor (see Chapter 10). It is fair to characterize the nation's nonmetro underdevelopment as very much a southern problem.

The long-term economic underdevelopment of the South continues to limit the locally generated fiscal resources of nonmetro governments. This inadequacy of fiscal capacity, the low investment in the past in basic public infrastructure, and the necessity for such investments in the future make the region dependent on the intergovernmental grant-in-aid system and thus susceptible to its attendant administrative and policy problems. This places special responsibilities on nonmetro planning to address local needs and avoid imposed conflicts while accessing external funds.

The region has approximately one-half of the nation's black population (see Chapter 12) and, although much progress has been made in the past fifteen years in eliminating discriminatory practices and improving public services, there are still substantial numbers of black citizens suffering from past discriminatory practices and underdevelopment as measured in terms of low educational attainment, poor health, poor housing, inadequate training, and low income. The integration of these black citizens into the national economic and social framework cannot adequately proceed unless they have personal economic opportunities and are sufficiently educated to have access to them. Identifying and facilitating such processses for all nonmetro Southerners is a major responsibility and consideration for the future nonmetro planning of the region.

If the trends of the immediate past continue, many parts of the South will experience substantial increases in population. The preparation for this growth--particularly in nonmetro areas where there is only limited development

capacity--must be a basic concern to the public sector at
all levels.

The Northeast and industrial Midwest have substantial
numbers of residents living in nonmetro areas. Of the approximately 90 million persons living in the Census Bureau's
Northeast, Middle Atlantic, and East North Central regions,
almost 17.5 million persons in 1976 were classified as
nonmetro. Many of these residents, for example in the state
of Maine, experience economic distress that is often quite
acute.

Planning for these nonmetro areas must proceed with
the recognition of several unique characteristics. First,
these regions have metro areas that are severely distressed
and public resources from both the region and the federal
government are being focused on these urban problems--often
at the expense of nonmetro needs. This focus must be recognized and either accommodated or altered in the process of
planning for the region's nonmetro areas. Second, the continuing dispersal of metro populations and economic activity
into nonmetro areas increases the urgency for nonmetro land
planning. Third, this region as a whole is experiencing a
structural change that is slowing the region's growth and
is reflected in outflows of capital and people and reduced
start-ups of new firms. It appears that much of the growth
is taking place in nonmetro areas and its impact on the
development capacities of specific areas must be analyzed
so that the growth can be accommodated.

Yet, in spite of these changes, the region still retains
the highest per capita incomes in the nation, the nation's
largest concentrations of wealth, and is the country's
largest center of production and productivity. These unique
strengths can be a base for future development.

Nonmetro planning in the western parts of the nation
is also defined by several characteristics unique to that
area. Many of the states in the West have small populations
that produce a number of issues of scale. First, the western
states, unlike the rest of the nation, have large portions
of their land owned and managed by the federal government.
For example, almost 87 percent of the land in the state of
Nevada is owned by the federal government. Second, much of
the western land is in Indian reservations and is thus
subject to treaties and other agreements between the tribes
that must be accommodated. Third, the West is generally
arid and the availability of water determines much of the
nature and direction of the region's economic activity and
population movement. Areas such as the plains regions of

Texas, Oklahoma, Colorado, New Mexico, Kansas, and Nebraska
face severe disruptions of their agricultural production in
the next ten to twenty years because of the depletion of
their fossil water resources—resources used to irrigate
over ten million acres of land or 25 percent of the nation's
total irrigated production (U.S. Department of Commerce,
1978: 4). The shift back to dry-land practices will induce
fundamental structural changes in these areas. Other parts
of the West, such as Arizona, face similar water resource
challenges. Finally, and perhaps as important as the water
issues, are the questions surrounding the development of
the energy resources of the West. The region has significant
energy resources, both on federal and private lands, whose
development will heavily influence the future character of
the region's economy and life-style of the residents. The
planning of this development—or no development if that is
a choice—must be a basic concern of future nonmetro development planning (see Chapter 8).

SUMMARY

Planning has increasingly become a major nonmetro development tool. During the past five decades, a number of planning institutions have been created at the federal, multistate, state, substate, and local levels to conduct nonmetro
planning. One of the most promising of these new institutions is the multijurisdictional or areawide planning body.
These organizations have the potential to provide an institutional framework in which the more than 50,000 nonmetro
units of government can plan their long-term development.
These new institutional forms also provide planning staff
to areas that otherwise cannot afford such assistance.

Although substantial progress has been made in nonmetro
planning there are a number of fundamental issues that merit
special attention in the future. Among these are the changing objectives of public interventions, the disarray in the
intergovernmental grant-in-aid system, the variances in institutional capacities of the individual nonmetro planning
bodies, the lack of clear definition of the state role in
nonmetro planning, the inadequacy of present training programs for nonmetro planners, the effects of issues of scale,
the increasing importance of a number of growth issues such
as land planning, and the effects that regional variations
have on the substance and the conduct of nonmetro planning.

NOTES

1. For the purposes of this paper the following working definitions will be used:

Functional planning--planning concerned with such limited purposes as transportation, education or environmental protection.

Comprehensive planning--planning that combines several functional plans into a single planned approach in an effort to meet specific objectives.

Strategic planning--the process of determining overall objectives, changes in these objectives, the resources used to attain these objectives, and the policies that are to govern the acquisition, use, and disposition of these resources.

Management and control planning--the process by which managers assure that resources are obtained and used both effectively and efficiently in the accomplishment of the organization's objectives.

Operational planning--the process of assuring that specific tasks, services or projects are conducted effectively and efficiently.

Developmental planning--that planning and those processes directed toward altering the nature, level or location of future change or events.

Adaptive planning--those planning activities and processes designed to accommodate past, ongoing or predictable events, conditions or circumstances. This is generally remedial action.

BIBLIOGRAPHY

Academy for Contemporary Problems. Regional Economic Development in the United States. Washington, D.C.: U.S. Department of Commerce, 1979.

Advisory Commission on Intergovernmental Relations. Categorical Grants: Their Role and Design. Washington, D.C.: ACIR, 1978.
_____. The Intergovernmental Grant System as Seen by Local, State and Federal Officials. Washington, D.C.: ACIR, 1977.
_____. The Role of Federal Planning Assistance Programs and Requirements in National Growth and Development: A Background Paper for the White House Conference

on Balanced Growth and Economic Development. Washington, D.C.: U.S. Government Printing Office, 1978.

Bryce, Herrington J. Planning in Small Cities. Lexington, Mass.: Lexington Books, 1979.

General Accounting Office. Federally Assisted Areawide Planning: Need to Simplify Policies and Practices. Washington, D.C.: U.S. Government Printing Office, 1977.

_____. Federally Assisted Employment and Training: A Myriad of Programs Should be Simplified. Washington, D.C.: U.S. Government Printing Office, 1979.

Hartley, David. State Planning and Economic Development. Washington, D.C.: Council of State Planning Agencies, 1976.

Office of Management and Budget, Executive Office of the President. Reorganization Study of Local Development Assistance Programs. Washington, D.C.: Office of Management and Budget, 1979.

_____. Report to Congress, Implementation of the Joint Funding Simplification Act of 1974 (Public Law 93-510). Washington, D.C.: U.S. Government Printing Office, 1979.

Resources for the Future. New Deal Planning: The National Resources Planning Board. Washington, D.C.: 1979.

U.S. Bureau of the Census. Regional Organizations. Washington, D.C.: U.S. Government Printing Office, 1978.

_____. Statistical Abstract of the United States, 1979. 100th edition. Washington, D.C.: U.S. Government Printing Office, 1979.

U.S. Department of Agriculture. Report of the Task Force on USDA's Resource Conservation and Development Program. Washington, D.C.: U.S. Government Printing Office, 1978.

U.S. Department of Commerce, Economic Development Administration. A Description of The High Plains Project. Washington, D.C.: U.S. Government Printing Office, 1978.

White House Conference on Balanced National Growth and Economic Development. Nonmetropolitan Growth and Development. Washington, D.C.: U.S. Government Printing Office, 1978a.

_____. The Role of Federal Planning Assistance Programs and Requirements in National Growth and Development. Washington, D.C.: U.S. Government Printing Office, 1978b.

List of Contributors

MARK BALDASSARE is an assistant professor of sociology at Columbia University. He is the author of Residential Crowding in Urban America and The Growth Dilemma, which are both published by the University of California Press. Current research interests include the social impacts of population growth, the effects of residential crowding, and inner-city revitalization.

CALVIN L. BEALE is a demographer with the Economics and Statistics Service, U.S. Department of Agriculture, Washington, D.C. His research has focused on rural, regional, and ethnic population trends and composition. He is author or coauthor of "The Revival of Population Growth in Nonmetropolitan America," "The Black American in Agriculture," and Economic Areas of the United States.

VERNON M. BRIGGS, JR. is professor of labor economics and human resource studies in the New York State School of Labor and Industrial Relations at Cornell University. He is author of Chicanos and Rural Poverty and coauthor of Employment, Income, and Welfare in the Rural South. He has also written a number of articles and chapters on rural labor market problems and human resource policies.

DAVID L. BROWN is principal sociologist with the U.S. Department of Agriculture's Science and Education Administration—Cooperative Research. His research interests include urbanization and population redistribution, service delivery in low-density areas, and sociodemographic correlates of land use change. Dr. Brown recently completed two tours of duty in the White House—as senior demographer with the National Agricultural Lands Study and as sociologist with the Domes-

tic Policy Staff. The purpose of the latter appointment was
to provide a substantive basis for increased attention by
the White House to rural development.

FREDERICK H. BUTTEL is assistant professor of rural sociology at Cornell University. He received his Ph.D. in sociology at the University of Wisconsin and held faculty positions at Michigan State University and Ohio State University
before coming to Cornell in 1978. His research focuses on
environmental sociology, agricultural structure in the
United States and Latin America, rural development, and
political sociology. He is coeditior of The Rural Sociology
of the Advanced Societies: Critical Perspectives, and coauthor of the forthcoming book, Environment, Energy, and
Society.

PAT CHOATE ia a visiting federal fellow at the Academy for
Contemporary Problems. He has held policy and administrative
positions in the federal government and the state governments of Tennessee and Oklahoma. He holds the doctorate
from the University of Oklahoma.

MARION CLAWSON is an agricultural economist who received
his Ph.D. from Harvard University in 1943. He has served
seventeen years in the U.S. Department of Agriculture and
six years in the Department of Interior in public land
management, five years of which were as the director of
the Bureau of Land Management. He has been been with Resources for the Future for twenty-five years, including
serving as acting president and vice-president. He is the
author, editor, or coeditor of thirty books dealing with
various aspects of land use in this country and in other
parts of the world.

STEPHEN P. COELEN is associate professor of economics and
director of the Tennessee Econometric Model in the Center
for Business and Economic Research at the University of
Tennessee, Knoxville. Formerly, Dr. Coelen was the deputy
project director of the National Rural Community Facilities
Assessment Study, a study funded by the Farmers Home Administration, U.S. Department of Agriculture. His work

includes research on infrastructure development in small
communities as well as resource, regional, and demographic
economics.

WILLIAM F. FOX is assistant professor of finance and research in the Center for Business and Economic Research
at the University of Tennessee, Knoxville. He is the author
of research related to industrial location, taxes and expenditures of governmental units, government service costs,
and regional economic development. He is serving as a consultant for the U.S. Department of Agriculture on the
National Rural Community Facilities Assessment Study.

AMOS H. HAWLEY received his Ph.D. from the University of
Michigan in 1941. He is or has been: Kenan Professor Emer-
itus, University of North Carolina at Chapel Hill; fellow,
American Academy of Arts and Sciences; president, Population
Association of America, 1971; and president, American Soci-
ological Association, 1978. He is the author of: Human
Ecology: A Theory of Community Structure (Ronald 1950); The
Changing Shape of Metropolitan America (the Free Press
1955); The Metropolitan Community: Its People and Govern-
ment, with Basil Zimmer (Sage 1970); and Urban Society: An
Ecological Approach (Wiley 1980).

IRVING HOCH has a Ph.D. in economics from the University of
Chicago and is a senior fellow at Resources for the Future,
Inc., Washington, D.C. He is a natural resource economist
primarily concerned with the economics of population distribution. He is the author of four books, fourteen research
reports, and author or coauthor of forty journal articles
or contributions to edited volumes. His publications include
"City Size Effects, Trends, and Policies," Energy Use in
the United States by State and Region, and "Settlement
Size, Real Income, and the Rural Turnaround."

CANDACE HOWES is a Ph.D. candidate in economics at the
University of California, Berkeley. She received her undergraduate degree from Barnard College.

OLAF F. LARSON is professor emeritus of rural sociology

at Cornell University and was the first director of the
Northeast Regional Center for Rural Development. His research interests have included rural poverty and low-income
farmers, migrant farm workers, black farmers, small communities and rural trends. In addition to numerous journal
articles and bulletins he is author of Ten Years of Rural
Rehabilitation, and has constributed to more than twenty
books including: Rural U.S.A.: Persistence and Change;
Rural Development: Research Priorities; Rural Poverty in
the United States; and Goals and Values in Agricultural
Policy.

ANN R. MARKUSEN, a Ph.D. economist trained at Georgetown
and Michigan State universities, is currently assistant
professor of city and regional planning at the University
of California, Berkeley. She has written broadly on regional
growth theory, western energy boom town planning, local
public finance, women's regional planning issues, and
national urban and regional policy.

SARA MILLS MAZIE is a research associate at the Urban Institute. She previously worked as a policy analyst for
the Farmers Home Administration at the U.S. Department of
Agriculture, and served as executive director of the Future
of Rural America Advisory Group. She has an undergraduate
degree from Cornell University and a masters degree in
urban planning from Columbia University. As director of
research on population distribution at the Commission on
Population Growth and the American Future, she contributed
to and edited the commissioner's research volume no. 5,
Population Distribution and Policy.

MARK DAVID MENCHIK is a member of the senior research staff
of the Rand Corporation. He has conducted research on topics
in regional and urban economics, local public finance, and
migration. His writings include Hospital Use Under Medicaid
in New York City and Fiscal Containment of Local and State
Government. Currently he is investigating out-migration
from economically declining areas (both rural and urban)
and studying the effects of local fiscal restraints like
Proposition 13.

JAMES J. MIKESELL is an economist with the Economics and
Statistics Research Service of the U.S. Department of Agriculture. He received a Ph.D. in economics from Iowa State
University in 1969, and is a student of housing and credit
markets with particular emphasis on the rural perspective.
He is the author of numerous reports and articles on a
variety of housing topics including mobile homes, innovative financing, quality measures, and demographic trends.

JOHN MOLAND, JR., professor of sociology and director of
the Center of Social Research at Southern University, holds
the B.A. and M.A. from Fisk University and the Ph.D. in
sociology from the University of Chicago. His articles and
book reviews have appeared in a number of professional
journals. He has served as president of the Southwestern
Sociological Society and the Association of Social and
Behavioral Scientists. Currently he is actively involved in
rural development research and training programs in the
United States and Africa, including the countries of Kenya
and Tanzania.

LAWRENCE W. NEWLIN served as staff assistant to the president for intergovernmental affairs with principal responsibility for monitoring the implementation of the Carter
administration's Small Community and Rural Development
Policy. His previous rural development policy experience
includes economic development director of the National
Association of Towns and Townships and assistant director
for community programs of the National Rural Center. At the
National Rural Center he edited Rural Public Transportation
Newsletter and Resource Guide for Rural Development.

ROGER A. ROSENBLATT is associate professor and director of
the research division of the Department of Family Medicine
at the University of Washington School of Medicine, and
adjunct associate professor in the School of Public Health
and Community Medicine. Dr. Rosenblatt has been active in
the planning and implementation of new rural health care
delivery systems, and has worked as an administrator,
clinician, consultant, and researcher in the United States
and abroad. His publications include evaluations of many of
the recent innovations in rural health care, and he has
testified before Congress on this subject. His upcoming

book, <u>Rural Health Care</u>, is a comprehensive treatment of
the field, and will be published by John Wiley and Sons.

ARTHUR SALTZMAN is associate professor and director of the
Transportation Institute at North Carolina A&T State University. He received his B.S. in physics from Brooklyn
College, M.S. in management from M.I.T., and Ph.D. in the
social sciences from the University of California, Irvine.
Professor Saltzman is a pioneer in research on paratransit,
small-city and rural transit, and transportation for the
elderly, handicapped, and economically disadvantaged. He is
the author of "Paratransit: Taking the Mass Out of Mass
Transit," which appeared in <u>Technology Review</u>, "Coordination of Transportation by Human Service Agencies: An
Interorganizational Perspective," and articles on transit
history, demand responsive transportation, and transportation planning. He chairs the Transportation Research Board's
Committee on the Transportation Disadvantaged and has received the UMTA Administrator's Award for outstanding public
service.

STEPHEN F. SENINGER is associate professor of economics and
associate director of the Institute for Human Resource
Management. He is a student of labor economics and urban-
regional growth and development. He is author or coauthor
of a number of journal articles and of books and monographs
dealing with labor market problems and issues.

TIMOTHY M. SMEEDING is associate professor of economics at
the University of Utah, and American Statistical Association
Research Fellow at the U.S. Bureau of the Census for 1980-
81. He has written extensively on poverty, income distribution, and welfare reform in such journals as <u>Public
Policy</u>, <u>Journal of Human Resources</u>, and <u>Review of Income
and Wealth</u>. His current research interests center on broadening empirical measures of economic well-being to include
both government in-kind transfers and fringe benefits.

ALVIN D. SOKOLOW, born in Chicago, Illinois in 1934, is
associate professor of political science, and associate
director of the Institute of Governmental Affairs at the
University of California, Davis. His research and teaching

concern local government and politics, with an emphasis on
politics and policy in small and especially rural communities. This chapter was prepared when he was a visiting
faculty member at the Institute of Government and Public
Affairs at the University of Illinois, Urbana-Champaign.

THOMAS F. STINSON is an economist with the Economic Development Division, Economics and Statistics Service, U.S.
Department of Agriculture, and associate professor, Department of Agriculture and Applied Economics, University of
Minnesota. He holds a bachelor's degree in political science
from Washington State University and a Ph.D. in economics
from the University of Minnesota. He has published articles
and monographs on the provision of government services in
rural areas, the taxation of farmland, and financial incentives for industrial development in rural areas. During
the last four years he has written extensively about the
impacts of increased coal development on local governments
in the northern Great Plains.

WILBUR R. THOMPSON is professor of economics at Wayne State
University. He received a doctorate in economics from the
University of Michigan in 1953 and has specialized in regional and urban economics since that time. For the past
decade he has been engaged equally in both teaching and
research and free-lance consulting and lecturing. He is
the author of A Preface to Urban Economics and numerous
articles on regional and urban development.

MARTA TIENDA received a Ph.D. from the University of Texas
at Austin in 1976 and is associate professor of rural sociology at the University of Wisconsin, Madison. Her current
research interests are in population and economic development in Latin America and in the integration of Spanish-
origin groups in the United States. She is currently con-
ducting research on labor market experiences of Hispanics
in the United States and the influence of community characteristics on fertility differentials in Peru.

THOMAS E. TILL is currently director of economic development
programs for the National Rural Center in Atlanta, Ga. Possessing a masters in Latin American studies from Vanderbilt

and a doctorate in economics from the University of Texas
at Austin, he has been chairman of the Department of
Economics and Business Administration at Franklin College
and staff director for the Secretary's Committee on Rural
Development of the U.S. Department of Labor. His specialty
is rural manpower programs and rural economic development.

JAMES J. ZUICHES is program director of the sociology program at the National Science Foundation. He is also an
associate professor (on leave) in the Department of Sociology, Michigan State University. He received his Ph.D. in
1973 from the University of Wisconsin, Madison, and his
research areas are demography, urban and rural community
studies, and energy and society. His work in the area of
residential preferences and migration has been published by
the U.S. Commission on Population Growth and the American
Future, and the work on energy conservation in the home by
the National Academy of Sciences in its report, Sociopolitical Effects of Energy Use and Policy.

Index